HISTORY
of the U.S.
ECONOMY
since
WORLD
WAR II

HISTORY
of the **U.S.**
ECONOMY
since
WORLD
WAR II

HAROLD G. VATTER
and
JOHN F. WALKER
editors

M.E. Sharpe
Armonk, New York
London, England

Library of Congress Cataloging-in-Publication Data

History of the U.S. economy since World War II /
Harold G. Vatter and John F. Walker, editors.
p.   cm.
Includes index.
ISBN 1-56324-473-X (alk. paper.)
—ISBN 1-56324-474-8 (pbk.: alk. paper.)
1. United States—Economic conditions—1945–
2. United States—Economic policy.
I. Vatter, Harold G.
II. Walker, John F.
HC106.5.H516   1995
333.973′092—dc20
95-19965
CIP

Printed in the United States of America
The paper used in this publication meets the minimum
requirements of American National Standard for
Information Sciences—Permanence of Paper for
Printed Library Materials, ANSI Z 39.48-1984.

BM (c)   10   9   8   7   6   5   4   3   2   1
BM (p)   10   9   8   7   6   5   4   3   2   1

For
Pat Walker and Rita, Terry, and Marc Vatter

CONTENTS

LIST OF TABLES

PREFACE

The U.S. mixed economy of large government spending and participation in the market system has been firmly rooted for half a century, an era with distinct characteristics and its own economic history. Yet there is no single up-to-date work that portrays this era comprehensively and in a way that is accessible to teachers, students, and interested members of the general reading public. The present book is designed to remedy this surprising deficiency. It is intended to be an inclusive work, not supplementary to other sources.

Those persons familiar with both standard economic history texts and the actual postwar economic evolution will welcome, we trust, the selection of innovative topics to be found herein. All too frequently, and we think unfortunately, many of these subjects are bypassed.

There were two compelling reasons we chose to make this a written-and-edited work. The first was to expeditiously fill the aforementioned gap in overall treatment of the post–World War II era. An acute awareness of that deficiency emerged partly from personal teaching experience over the years. Existing economic histories do not, and as presently constituted cannot, even begin to do justice to this half century of rich and turbulent experience. One has to scrounge around distressingly to find and integrate masses of supplementary material, readings that swamp in sheer volume any basic work used as a fulcrum. A second reason was the abundant diversity of topics and interpretations that the written-and-edited format provides. The typical historian's criticism that contemporary history has unfolded too recently for "proper" interpretive digestion, however correct or misguided such a view may be, is thus basically allayed.

We are, therefore, comfortable with the inclusion in this volume, for example, of extracts from the *Economic Report of the President* that clearly reflect the bias of certain presidential Adviser's Councils. We are confident also that, once the illusion of objective historiography is cast off, exposure to a variety of constructions adds to the richness of reader experience.

Additionally, the inclusion of contributions by others allows us to draw upon well-informed, expert analysis that may be factually and in-terpretively rather better than what we have produced. Many of the se-lections are by people who are among the most eminent in the field. These selections were written over a period of almost fifty years. Conse-quently references to this year, last year, next year, currently, etc., are relative to the date the selection was first published.

Some may feel that a more extensive and unified treatment, reaching back at least to the quarter century before the crystallization of the mixed economy, is desirable. Obviously, that past significantly shaped the sub-sequent history of the social market economy. Such is particularly true of the Great Depression and the New Deal's transition from the laissez-faire 1920s to the distinctively new system that came out of the 1940s.

But an era is an era. Background works covering the 1920s and the decade of the Great Depression are readily available. For example, com-panion pieces to the present book are provided by Peter Fearon's *War, Prosperity, and Depression: The U.S. Economy 1917–45* and by the earlier work of Jim Potter, *The American Economy between the World Wars*. Either combination makes a quite adequate package for general survey pur-poses, covering the evolution of the economy since 1914, the heart of the twentieth century.

Most papers in this collection are by major scholars in their area. We have excerpted what we believe is the best of their work. We have also dropped all footnotes and references. We strongly urge readers who are interested in particular topics to go to the original sources, cited at the beginning of each paper, which in most cases are longer, more complete, and fully referenced. They should be available in any adequate university library.

We have tried to make sure that this volume provides an integrated economic history, not a collection of discrete topical treatments. We are aware that the moment one treats a subject, as in a chapter, the connec-tions of the subject with the total process are in danger of being severed. This has ever been the curse of the topical format. We have attempted to avoid this defect in part by deliberately overlapping the topical with the chronological. Furthermore, we have cross-referenced subjects by fre-quently treating the same subject in different contexts (chapters). Finally, integration of particular aspects is fostered by our reiteration of the cen-tral theme—economic growth and its determinants.

Selections from outside sources are organized as continuous discus-sion under headings usually taken from the titles and subheads of the selection.

ACKNOWLEDGMENTS

Because a primarily edited, comprehensive economic history requires a very great variety of source materials, it demands either the explicit or the tacit participation of a multitude of providers. We therefore embrace the opportunity to express here our profound thanks to all those authors and publishers who granted us permission to reprint copyrighted materials, and our gratitude to the numerous public agencies and writers of public documents, some of whom may to their surprise discover their compositions extracted in these structured pages.

The universally high quality of public research embodied in these extracts not only has been an encouragement to our effort, but also will be much appreciated, we believe, by the readers of this book. Such contributions, which make up the greater part of the work, are achievements of which the American public can well be proud.

The ongoing search for diverse, pertinent writings over the years was greatly expedited and eased by the ever ready assistance of the Multnomah County librarians, and in particular by the staff of the Portland State University economic and humanities library divisions—Daphne Allen, Anne McMahon, Joanne Morgan, Barbara Becker, Karen Nordgren, Gwen Newborg, Jerome DeGraaff, and Craig Wollner, among others. A plethora of source material on the African-American experience was also forthcoming from Darrell Millner, chair of the PSU Black Studies Department.

Our appreciation is due to several Portland State administrative personnel for providing a grant to help finance the considerable manuscript preparation and permissions costs. Particular consideration for the worthfulness of our project was extended in that connection by College of Liberal Arts and Sciences dean Marvin Kaiser and provost Michael Reardon.

The extensive permissions correspondence was greatly facilitated by Rita Spears, office coordinator of the Economics Department, and by Joy Spalding. Rita also worked extensively on manuscript preparation. The major contributors to preparation, however, were Bahar Jaberi and Connie Ledbetter. We owe them enormous, inestimable credit for their exceptional expertise and their untiring devotion to the project, much of the time under deadline stress. Special thanks are due to Kate Wittenberg, editor at Columbia University Press.

We also owe a large debt of thanks to Richard D. Bartel, Karen Byrnes, Aud Thiessen, and Christine Florie of M.E. Sharpe, Inc., for their lucid instructions, encouragement, cooperation in manuscript processing, and patience regarding deadlines not quite met.

HISTORY
of the U.S.
ECONOMY
since
WORLD
WAR II

CHAPTER I

The Economy at Midcentury

1. The War's Consequences
Harold G. Vatter

Excerpted and reprinted with permission from *The U.S. Economy in World War II* by Harold G. Vatter, copyright © 1985, Columbia University Press, pp. 145–77. Harold G. Vatter is professor emeritus of economics at Portland State University.

The study of the economy in World War II acquires a rich meaning for us only when its consequences are included in the inquiry. Those and some other consequences will be assembled here into a package in order to afford a more total view of the war's great impact on the economy. The totality of the war's economic effects is one of the chief reasons for choosing to explore the wartime experience.

The explosion of the veteran population can fruitfully be extracted from the welter of events and subjected to a careful exploration. Some effects of the war emerged only in connection with related actions taken after V-J Day, in certain cases a considerable time after. These actions and their connections with the war experience also demand treatment as a single package with the war, regardless of the time lapse between the war's ending and such lagged actions.

We may conveniently distinguish two sometimes overlapping kinds of war consequences: (1) changes occurring in the economy and economic behavior, and (2) changes in policy. Consideration of these two types will be given in order.

There were specific wartime developments that had long-run unique effects. An example of this set is the emergence of important, war-induced

3

new products, industries, and activities. The war economy greatly stimulated technological innovation. Perhaps the most prominent illustration is atomic power. The nuclear power industry was the offspring of the atom bomb. Radar and its industrial applications is another outstanding example of a wartime product with a significant industrial future. Many others could be listed, some of them products, some processes. Synthetic rubber production in large volume was both product and process innovation. It must be granted, however, that in the manufacturing sector the "production miracle" was accomplished largely on the basis of the preexisting system of industrial technology.

While technological advance was in some cases inhibited by wartime constraints, as with the new air-conditioning industry, in other cases it was stimulated, as with color television and numerous innovations in motorized material-handling equipment. Collier's *Year Book* for 1945 lists almost eight columns of war-connected innovations, or the activation and new application of older innovations, within the chemical industry alone, to say nothing of pharmaceutical. Outstanding examples were penicillin, synthetic quinine, atabrine, sulfa drugs, and the mass dissemination of DDT. Two studies by the Bureau of Labor Statistics of wartime technological developments for the Senate Military Affairs Committee listed 2,300 items of wartime (though not necessarily war-induced) technical advance, many with postwar applications. Particular mention was given television, railroad radio telephony, other communications media, jet-propulsion and gas-turbine engines, plastics, synthetic rubber, and metal fabricating machinery and methods.

Research activity by industry, as by government and the universities, was greatly enhanced under the high pressure of war needs. Large-scale research in electronics laid the basis for a postwar technological revolution. In the case of industry research, the prewar trend line was shifted dramatically upward. The National Research Council reported the existence of 2,450 industry research laboratories in 1947, employing 133,000 people, nearly twice the number of the employees so engaged in 1940. It was the war that instilled a new and heightened appreciation of scientific research. The link between science and technology was henceforth to become the hallmark of industrial progress in the postwar era.

There were additional changes wrought uniquely by the war that had lasting consequences. A second change unique to the war experience was the vast increase in the veteran population. In 1940 there were 4.3 million veterans in civil life; in 1950 there were 19 million. The effects of that tremendous increase were far reaching. For one thing, public outlays for veterans' education were almost nonexistent before World War II; but by 1947 over $2.25 billion were already being expended for that purpose. In this matter we are dealing with both a change in economic behavior and a war-induced policy development. The contribution of veterans' education to the training level of the U.S. labor force and to future technological advance was inestimable. We should also add here a reference to the improved quality of civil life enjoyed directly by those involved in the intellectually elevating process. The salutary spillover effects on the general population should also be acknowledged. Another repercussion, long delayed, however, was the explosive jump in veterans' health-care costs as the World War II contingent aged. It was that contingent (along with inflation), for example, that accounted for the rise in VA annual expenditures for medical, hospital, and domiciliary services from about $2 billion in 1970 to over $7 billion in 1981. Congressional budget analysts projected that VA's annual medical bill could well exceed $15 billion by 1990 (it was actually $11.6 billion).

A third change in the economy specifically produced by war conditions was a "pre-fisc" (i.e., before any impact of government taxing and spending) shift in the distribution of income toward slightly greater equality. It needs to be emphasized that the shift was apparently a one-time economic change that was irrevocable. A fourth change, uniquely created by war restraints on wage increases, was the development of the fringe benefit in labor-management contracts. The fringe benefit was by no means entirely new, but its widespread adoption during the war gives it a special, war-related character. It too turned out to be an irreversible and expanding change, one that among other things greatly influenced development in the postwar labor movement.

Mention should also be made in this summation of two specific wartime developments in the policy field that revealed achievement possibilities heretofore not appreciated or well understood. These were the success of the government's incomes policy (i.e., price control) and the effectiveness of volunteer community effort under conditions viewed by the public as critical. If kept alive in the collective consciousness, they are lessons that may prove useful at any appropriate social conjuncture.

Examination of the World War II economy reveals some abiding characteristics that were unaltered by the war except for the temporary, war-stimulated movement that they evinced. The first of such trends is population growth. The war eventuated in the baby boom, and the baby boom raised the total population rate substantially for a time. But only for a time: the long-run declining rate of American population growth was unaffected by that aberrant behavior pattern. A second similar war-connected deviation from trend was the jump in the economically significant women's labor force participation rate. Again, this proved to be episodic: It was an important but not a lasting consequence of the war. The third such event was government administrative direction of the economy. It did not turn out to be an abiding phenomenon, for that huge administrative apparatus was promptly dismantled. Economic planning was not to be the American way—at least not for a long time to come. All that did turn out to be enduring, as will be discussed below, was a residue of government guidance generically resembling in a watered-down way what the French call "indicative planning." All that remained was the "mixed economy."

Some economic trends or established characteristics of the system were accelerated as they passed through the wartime environment; and these particular changes were not, like the hump in the female participation rate trend, temporary. They were long lasting. It is tempting to mention the political example of the expansion in the executive power of the federal government, a speeding up of a trend instituted by the New Deal. But there are at least two more economic illustrations. One is clearly economic: the acceleration in black out-migration from agriculture and from the South, together with the very large black occupational shifts, men into industry, women out of domestic service and into both industry and commercial services. The wartime Fair Employment Practices Commission (FEPC) inaugurated a growing movement toward civil rights and fair employment practices.

A second example is provided by the wartime upsurge of business influence in government. During the war the Pentagon and the State Department were strongly infiltrated by Wall Street elements, a business stratum that to a substantial degree directed foreign policy into an anti-Soviet groove after the war. The central role of business during the war also terminated both the public disillusionment with business attendant upon the Great Depression experience, and the labor orientation of government under the New Deal. The enduring effectiveness of business influence is expressed in such postwar phenomena as the Taft-Hartley and Landrum-Griffin laws and the formation of what President Eisenhower termed the military-industrial complex. By the same token, reference to the two main pieces of postwar "labor" legislation is a reminder that the considerable participation of organized labor representatives in the wartime administrative machinery marked the completion of the process whereby business generally came to accept, subject to retraction should a shift in power relations occur, unionization and collective bargaining as permanent institutions in the market system. A third aspect of this legislation will be discussed below.

War, the Mixed Economy, and America's New Global Role

The war brought both accelerated change and the reshaping of domestic and foreign economic policy on the part of the federal government. These alterations in policy were at least as portentous as the whole collection of changes in the economy itself. On the domestic front, the war was a connecting rod between the New Deal's inauguration of the mixed economy and its quite unexpected crystallization during a span of a very few years following V-J Day. It is worth remembering that most Americans had probably believed the assumption of some measure of government responsibility for the economy's performance was only a cyclical, pump-priming episode.

On the foreign policy front, the war was responsible for (1) abrogating the temporary cooperation between the United States and the USSR that had reached a degree of closeness never achieved before or since, and (2) a vigorous presumption by the United States government that it must assume vast new responsibilities for world order, responsibilities that before the war were not dreamed of even in nonisolationist circles.

Domestic Policy

Unnoticed by almost everybody, a quietly growing domestic trend in the economy and in policy, a trend of lasting character, had been taking place since 1929. The proportion of personal consumption expenditures to GNP in current dollars had been 74.8 percent in 1929; in 1949 that proportion had fallen to 71.0 percent; and in 1946 it was down to 68.6 percent. The surprising concomitant was an offsetting rise in the ratio of all government purchases to GNP, together with a gross fixed business nonresidential investment ratio (domestic) that remained in the long run about constant at the 1929 level of some 10 percent. In the emerging U.S. mixed economy, private consumption was steadily yielding to collective (i.e., social, via government) consumption and *leaving the long-run private investment ratio unaffected* as compared with its laissez-faire antecedent. The irreversible march of big government, while no doubt but dimly anticipated by most, was clearly under way during the reconversion period.

The proportion of the labor force employed in the civilian public sector was rising along with the government budget. Meanwhile, it was expected that the Employment Act of 1946, proposed in embryo form as early as 1943 by the National Resources Planning Board, would guard against future recessionary episodes. And fortunately for the prescience shown on the public revenue side, the wartime addition of many millions of lower-income people to the federal taxpayer contingent had laid the foundation for big expenditures in the future. This same new tax (and expenditures) structure also created a "built-in," counter-cyclical stabilizer and slightly reshaped the distribution of income. The built-in stabilizers successfully passed their first test in the mild recession and revival of 1948–49. The 1946 government guarantee of maximum employment and purchasing power was an almost revolutionary commitment unprecedented in the history of government's relation to the economy. On the surface at least, the Congress was announcing that it would indefinitely underwrite high-level aggregate business sales, aggregate profits, the total wage bill, and economic growth in the context of a growing labor force.

The welfare state component of the budget in the now fixated era of big government was complemented in the U.S. case by the huge military outlays necessitated by what was to turn out to be a permanent Cold War, initiated shortly after the end of the war. The big Cold War and associated hot war military budgets made very large total budgets chronic and sullied the historic notion of a peacetime economy. Military appropriations soon acquired an almost sacrosanct status before a willing Congress, so that the persistent attacks on absolutely growing federal budgets in the decades following World War II were largely explicit or implicit assaults on the civilian component—which meant, for the most part, the welfare component.

Such assaults were directly rooted in the earliest controversial years of the infant mixed economy, when the New Deal's fledgling income security programs were held at bay by its laissez-faire adversaries. Had the U.S. mixed economy found it necessary to maintain high aggregate demand for employment through overwhelmingly civilian federal purchases of goods and services, as was notably more the case with the European mixed economies, the institutionalization of the new social consensus would probably have enjoyed the security of firmer foundations. The welfare state would have had to advance more rapidly—e.g., in the area of health insurance. Furthermore, Keynesian aggregate demand management (such as it was) would have been freer of the erratic influences on the federal budget emanating from the response of the military budget to the vicissitudes of cold and hot wars. After all, the size and the domestic economic impact of the military budget was not *supposed* to be an integral part of demand management.

Nevertheless, it was a most remarkable aspect of the history of the mixed-economy federal budgets that civilian plus military expenditures, when added to large and growing state and local expenditures, were sufficient to maintain a generally high level of employment and to avoid severe depressions.

The implied "inner logic" of the remarkable historical relationship involved in summing the military and civilian components of the all-government budgets has never been revealed, although it may be hypothesized that much controversy over welfare outlays was minimized or avoided by a heavy reliance on defense outlays. But the broad pattern can be observed. In the first half decade after World War II that pattern had barely emerged, but it did emerge.

It was of great historic significance that the war did not call into question the basics of the major legislative achievements identified with the New Deal. This was true, for example, of the minimum wage law, the Social Security Act, and the National Labor Relations Act. However, in two areas postwar actions were taken that properly warrant some treatment regarding how the pertinent New Deal policies fared as a result of the wartime experience and the immediately consequent crystallization of the mixed system. The two areas referred to are farm policy and government's role in labor-management relations.

The Great Reversal to Internationalism

Domestic interventionism in the now fixated mixed economy after the war was complemented by a transformation to an era of globalism in foreign policy. The changeover to internationalism was induced by the onset of the long-lived Cold War and the closely related U.S. concern with the direction to be taken by the flows of world trade and investment together with politicoeconomic evolution in the restive Third World countries.

The Cold War was a byproduct of World War II that enhanced an anti-Soviet tradition dating from the Russian Revolution. The post-World War II upsurge grew out of the weakening of the prewar European military power that had functioned as a capitalist buffer against the socialist Soviet giant. The spectre of a communist Europe coming out of a world war had terrified France and Britain before the war and had led them to favor peace at the price of almost any concession to the Nazis, such as the loss of Czechoslovakia that was negotiated at Munich in 1938. As the German ambassador to Paris reported in May of that fateful year, French Foreign Minister Georges Bonnet "considered any arrangement better than world war, in the event of which all Europe would perish, and both victor and vanquished would fall victims to world communism."

It had been widely believed before the war that the USSR was a paper tiger, but the demonstrated Soviet capability in the war changed all that. The similar war-enhanced U.S. economic and military capability, in the setting of a prostrated, devastated Europe open to a real or fancied threat in several places by a combination of indigenous and Soviet-supported communism, made the United States the apparent choice among the great capitalist powers to contain the socialist threat to the institution of private property and the capitalist order everywhere. This newly assumed responsibility determined the essential, although not the entire, character of postwar internationalism. As historian Paul Y. Hammond expressed it:

> The internationalists . . . by substituting anticommunism for the moral imperative of internationalism in the first postwar years . . . clinched their argument at

a time when foreign intervention could be quite clearly defined as helping European states under threat. . . .

Two conditions, then, prevented a thoughtful sifting of American interests and opportunities after World War II: the need to mobilize American political consent for an international role and the obtrusiveness of the Soviet Communist enemy. Furthermore, it became prudent for every presidential administration to adopt a cover-all-bets strategy toward the Communist world, which included support of anti-Communists all over the globe . . .

The U.S. policy, rejecting at that juncture a spheres-of-influence approach and favoring self-determination of the Eastern European countries bordering the USSR (American "universalism"), was seen by the Soviets as an effort to reopen those adjacent states to hostile capitalistic penetration. From then on the continued overt and covert wars involving the peculiar universalisms of the two superpowers all across the globe were fought taking those two perspectives as a starting point—i.e., to give self-determination, particularly for countries in the now largely decolonized third world, a character and direction desired by the respective contestants.

The major U.S. moves came in quick succession: enunciation of the Truman Doctrine in 1947, followed by its three chief instrumentalities, the Marshall Plan (1947) to reconstitute and stabilize Europe economically and politically, NATO (inaugurated 1949), and Point Four (1949) to stabilize and stimulate development in the third world economies. Some years later but in the same vein, President Kennedy inaugurated the Alliance for Progress for Latin America in response to Fidel Castro's Cuba. There were also two hot, overt wars: Korea and Vietnam. U.S. armed forces after the major World War II demobilization never again fell below about 1.5 million, and the military budget had already begun its long-run rise in 1948.

An Era Authenticated by War

There was thus much more to World War II than the war itself. For the United States, the integral parts of that great upheaval were not only the handful of vital changes occurring between 1941 and 1945; even more vital for the long run were the momentous policy developments during the few subsequent years of the war decade.

The leading contours of a whole postwar policy era were crystallized in that short span of years following the war's end. Those contours have been briefly indicated here: historically large public budgets with a huge military component at the federal level; the welfare state element; publicly underwritten employment, output, and growth; stabilization of the economic cycle; the intrusion of government as a third party in labor-management relationships; continued supply management in agriculture;

and vigorous U.S. participation in a new, higher level of international organizations (United Nations, International Monetary Fund, International Bank for Reconstruction and Development [World Bank], and General Agreement on Tariffs and Trade [GATT]), together with the unfolding Cold War.

These policies on the domestic plane became identified with the demand management phase of the evolving mixed economy—the phase whose transformation into a later stage was inaugurated by the crisis of stagflation (inflation with stagnant performance) and its attendant policy crisis threatening the Keynesian system of public management. When the stagflation crisis did develop in the seventies, the established interventionist arrangements, forged in the 1930s and 1940s, exhibited an irresistible capacity to survive in the face of exceptionally powerful and persistent attacks on them.

2. The Inheritance of the Preceding Decades
Harold G. Vatter

Excerpted and reprinted with permission from *The U.S. Economy in the 1950s* by Harold G. Vatter (New York: W.W. Norton, 1963), pp. 27–62. Harold G. Vatter is professor emeritus of economics at Portland State University.

The Institutional Setting

The Mature, Mixed Economy

By the end of World War II the American economy had long since been transformed into an advanced industrial system, with its agrarian component reduced to minor proportions. It was an economy rich in technological achievement, possessing a vast stock of durable capital and consumer goods. It was a mature economy of relative abundance. In the phrase of Professor W. W. Rostow, it was well into the age of "high mass consumption."

The private, nonfinancial sector of the business system that prevailed in the United States was a congeries of market types, with the small, unincorporated businesses numerically predominant and the corporate form economically predominant. For analytical purposes, the range of market structures may be classified into two main types: monopolistically competitive markets and oligopolistic markets. The first type embraced many small firms producing differentiated goods or services and was readily accessible to potential new entrants. Such firms, since each was small relative to the total market, could expect little or no reaction to their business decisions from their competitors. The second type of market—the "dominant-group" industry—was composed of a few large firms surrounded by a varying number of smaller concerns, the latter accounting for a minor proportion of total sales. Products were typically differentiated. Oligopolistic leaders had to be mindful of the reactions of other leading enterprises to their business decisions but could ignore the policies of individuals in the small-firm fringe. Entry into such markets was difficult in varying degree. It was relatively easy to enter the fringe but not easy to join the leading core.

The bipartisan decision in the Congress that legislated the Employment Act testified to the acceptance of economic reform, for an indefinite period, by American conservatism. However reluctant that acquiescence, it was to become one of the fundamental institutional conditions surrounding the economic system in the coming period. The conservative interventionist economics of Keynes was by 1950 fully incorporated into the legacy of public policy willed to the forthcoming decade. *For the next ten years, at least, the policy issue would be formulated chiefly in terms of a little more or a little less intervention.*

In acknowledging the possibility that trends in the private economy might interfere with national economic goals and in declaring war on economic fluctuations, the Employment Act officially called into question the performance of the private market mechanism. The operation of that mechanism had of course been continually brought under attack from one quarter or another ever since the agrarian revolt of the nineteenth century. There had been a long series of attempts to substitute conscious private group or social controls in place of what had been thought of as the automatically operating private market mechanism.

Soon after the farmers in the 1870s had mounted their attack, big business itself began to reject certain aspects of the private market mechanism, notably its tendency to generate price wars. Labor also intruded directly into the markets for its services and indirectly into the judicial and legislative superstructure surrounding industrial relations and the conditions of work. Small business also called for intervention to equate its bargaining power with that of large business. These groups interfered because of what they believed to be failures of the mechanism with respect to competition, use of natural resources, income distribution, industries and products "affected with a public interest," the speculative use of money and credit, and other spheres.

1

What Do Bosses Do?

The Origins and Functions of Hierarchy in Capitalist Production

Stephen A. Marglin

I. Introduction: Does Technology Shape Social and Economic Organization or Does Social and Economic Organization Shape Technology?

Is it possible for work to contribute positively to individual development in a complex industrial society, or is alienating work the price that must be paid for material prosperity? Discussions of the possibilities for meaningful revolution generally come down, sooner or later, to this question. If hierarchical authority is essential to high productivity, then self-expression in work must at best be a luxury reserved for the very few, regardless of social and economic organization. And even the satisfactions of society's elite must be perverted by their dependence, with rare exception, on the denial of self-expression to others. But is work organization determined by technology or by society? Is hierarchical authority really necessary to high levels of production or is material prosperity compatible with nonhierarchical organization of production?

Defenders of the capitalist faith are quite sure that hierarchy is inescapable. Indeed their ultimate line of defense is that the plurality of capitalist hierarchies is preferable to a single socialist hierarchy. To seal the argument the apologist may call on as unlikely a source of support as Friedrich Engels. Perhaps it was a momentary aberration, but at one point in his career at least Engels saw authority as technologically rather than socially determined:

Originally published in *Review of Radical Political Economics,* vol. 6, no. 2, Summer 1974, pp. 60–112. Reprinted with permission.

> If man, by dint of his knowledge and inventive genius, has subdued the forces of nature, the latter avenge themselves upon him by subjecting him, in so far as he employs them, to a veritable despotism, *independent of all social organization.* Wanting to abolish authority in large-scale industry is tantamount to wanting to abolish industry itself, to destroy the power loom in order to return to the spinning wheel.[1]

Going back to the spinning wheel is obviously absurd, and if the producer must typically take orders, it is difficult to see how work could in the main be anything but alienating.

Were the social sciences experimental, the methodology for deciding whether or not hierarchical work organization is inseparable from high material productivity would be obvious. One would design technologies appropriate to an egalitarian work organization, and test the designs in actual operation. Experience would tell whether or not egalitarian work organization is utopian. But social science is not experimental. None of us has the requisite knowledge of steel-making or cloth-making to design a new technology, much less to design one so radically different from the present norm as a serious attempt to change work organization would dictate. Besides in a society whose basic institutions—from schools to factories—are geared to hierarchy, the attempt to change one small component is probably doomed to failure. For all its shortcomings, neoclassical economics is undoubtedly right in emphasising *general* equilibrium over *partial* equilibrium.

Instead of seeking alternative designs, we must take a more round-about tack. In this paper it is asked why, in the course of capitalist development, the actual producer lost control of production. What circumstances gave rise to the boss-worker pyramid that characterizes capitalist production? And what social function does the capitalist hierarchy serve? If it turns out that the origin and function of capitalist hierarchy has relatively little to do with efficiency, then it becomes at least an open question whether or not hierarchical production is essential to a high material standard of living. And workers—manual, technical, and intellectual—may take the possibility of egalitarian work organization sufficiently seriously to examine their environment with a view to changing the economic, social, and political institutions that relegate all but a fortunate few to an existence in which work is the means to life, not part of life itself.

It is the contention of this paper that neither of the two decisive steps in depriving the workers of control of product and process—(1) the development of the minute division of labor that characterized the putting-out system and (2) the development of the centralized organization that characterizes the factory system—took place primarily for reasons of technical superiority. Rather than providing more output for the same inputs, these innovations in work organization were introduced so that the capitalist got himself a larger share of the pie at the expense of the worker, and it is only the *subsequent* growth in the size of the pie that has obscured the class interest which was at the root of these innovations. The social function of hierarchical work organization is not technical efficiency, but accumulation. By mediating between producer and consumer, the capitalist organization sets aside much more for expanding and improving plant and equipment than individuals would if they could control the pace of capital accumulation. These ideas, which are developed in the body of this paper, can be conveniently divided into four specific propositions.

I. The capitalist division of labor, typified by Adam Smith's famous example of pin manufacture, was the result of a search not for a technologically superior organization of work, but for an organization which guaranteed to the entrepreneur an essential role in the production process, as integrator of the separate efforts of his workers into a marketable product.

II. Likewise, the origin and success of the factory lay not in technological superiority, but in the substitution of the capitalist's for the worker's control of the work process and the quantity of output, in the change in the workman's choice from one of how much to work and produce, based on his relative preferences for leisure and goods, to one of whether or not to work at all, which of course is hardly much of a choice.

III. The social function of hierarchical control of production is to provide for the accumulation of capital. The individual, by and large and on the average, does not save by a conscious and deliberate choice. The pressures to spend are simply too great. Such individual (household) savings as do occur are the consequence of a lag in adjusting spending to a rise in income, for spending, like any other activity, must be learned, and learning takes time. Thus individual savings are the consequence of growth, and not an independent cause. Acquisitive societies—precapitalist, capitalist or socialist—develop institutions whereby collectivities determine the rate of accumulation. In modern capitalist society the pre-eminent collectivity for accumulation is the corporation. It is an essential social function of the corporation that its hierarchy mediate between the individual producer (and shareholder) and the market proceeds of the corporation's product, assigning a portion of these proceeds to enlarging the means of production. In the absence of hierarchical control of production, society would either have to fashion egalitarian institutions for accumulating capital or content itself with the level of capital already accumulated.

IV. The emphasis on accumulation accounts in large part for the failure of Soviet-style socialism to "overtake and surpass" the capitalist world in developing egalitarian forms of work organization. In according first priority to the accumulation of capital, the Soviet Union repeated the history of capitalism, at least as regards the relationship of men and women to their work. Theirs has not been the failure described by Santayana of those who, not knowing history, unwittingly repeat it. The Soviets consciously and deliberately embraced the capitalist mode of production. And defenders of the Soviet path to economic development would offer no apology: after all, they would probably argue, egalitarian institutions and an egalitarian (and community oriented) man could not have been created overnight, and the Soviet Union rightly felt itself too poor to contemplate an indefinite end to accumulation. Now, alas, the Soviets have the "catch-up-with-and-surpass-the-U.S.A." tiger by the tail, for it would probably take as much of a revolution to transform work organization in that society as in ours.

The following sections of this paper take these propositions one by one, in the hope of filling in sufficient detail to give them credibility.

II. Divide and Conquer

Hierarchy was of course not invented by capitalists. More to the point, neither was hierarchical production. In precapitalist societies, industrial production was organized according to a rigid master-journeyman-apprentice hierarchy, which survives today in anything like its pure form only in the graduate departments of our universities. What distinguished precapitalist from capitalist hierarchy was first that the man at the top was, like the man at the bottom, a producer. The master worked along with his apprentice rather than simply telling him what to do. Second, the hierarchy was linear rather than pyramidal. The apprentice would one day become a journeyman and likely a master. Under capitalism it is a rare worker who becomes even a foreman, not to mention independent entrepreneur or corporate president. Third, and perhaps most important, the guild workman had no intermediary between himself and the market. He generally sold a product, not his labor, and therefore controlled both product and work process.

Just as hierarchy did not originate with capitalism, neither did the division of labor. The *social* division of labor, the specialization of occupation and function, is a characteristic of all complex societies, rather than a peculiar feature of industrialized or economically advanced ones. Nothing, after all, could be more elaborate than the caste division of labor and its accompanying hierarchy in traditional Hindu society. Nor is the *technical* division of labor peculiar to capitalism or modern industry. Cloth production, for example, even under the guild system was divided into separate tasks, each controlled by specialists. But, as we have said, the guild workman controlled product and process. What we have to account for is why the guild division of labor evolved into the capitalist division of labor, in which the workman's task typically became so specialized and minute that he had no product to sell, or at least none for which there was a wide market, and had therefore to make use of the capitalist as intermediary to integrate his labor with the labor of others and transform the whole into a marketable product.

Adam Smith argues that the capitalist division of labor came about because of its technological superiority; in his view, the superiority of dividing work into ever more minutely specialized tasks was limited only by the size of the market.[2] To understand the limitations of this explanation requires clarity and precision on the meaning of "technological superiority," and the related ideas of technological efficiency and inefficiency; indeed, these ideas are central to the whole story told in this paper. We shall say, in accordance with accepted usage, that a method of production is technologically superior to another if it produces more output with the same inputs. It is not enough that a new method of production yield more output per day to be technologically superior. Even if labor is the only input, a new method of production might require more hours of labor, or more intensive effort, or more unpleasant working conditions, in which case it would be providing more output for more input, not for the same amount. It will be argued here that—contrary to neoclassical logic—a new method of production does not have to be technologically superior to be adopted; innovation depends as much on economic and social institutions—on who is in control of production and under what constraints control is exercised.

The terms "technological efficiency" and "technological inefficiency," as used by economists, have meanings that are slightly at variance with the ordinary, every-day ideas of better and worse that they evoke. A method of production is technologically efficient if no technologically superior alternative exists. It is inefficient if a superior alternative does exist. Thus more than one method of production may be—and generally is—technologically efficient if one looks only at a single product. Wheat, for example, can be efficiently produced with a lot of land and relatively little fertilizer, as in Kansas, or with a lot of fertilizer and relatively little land, as in Holland.

But if one views technological superiority and efficiency from the point of view of the whole economy, these concepts reduce, under certain circumstances, to *economic* superiority and efficiency. Under text-book assumptions of perfect and universal competition, the technologically efficient method of production is the one that costs least, and cost reduction is an index of technological superiority.[3] The relationship between minimum cost and technological efficiency is a purely logical one and does not depend at all on whether or not the world exhibits the assumptions of the model. On the other hand, the relevance of the identification of technological with economic efficiency depends absolutely on the applicability of the assumptions of the competitive model to the development of capitalism. In critical respects the development of capitalism necessarily required denial, not fulfillment, of the assumptions of perfect competition.

In a way it is surprising that the development of capitalist methods of work organization contradicts essential assumptions of perfect competition, since perfect competition has virtually nothing to say about the organization of production! Indeed, even the firm itself, a central economic institution under capitalism, plays no essential role in models of the competitive economy;[4] it is merely a convenient abstraction for the household in its role as producer and does nothing that households could not equally well do for themselves. Defenders of the faith from Wicksell to Samuelson have grandly proclaimed the perfect neutrality of perfect competition—as far as the model goes, workers could as well hire capital as capitalists workers![5] Alas, the failure of the competitive model to account for one of the most distinctive features of capitalism (and of socialism imitating capitalism)—the pyramidal work order—is for neoclassical economists a great virtue rather than a shortcoming; it is supposed to show the great generality of the theory. Generality indeed: neoclassical theory says only that hierarchy must be technologically efficient to persist, but denies the superiority of capitalist hierarchy (workers can just as well hire capital, remember!). This is to say very little, and that little, it will be argued, quite wrong.

To return to Adam Smith. *The Wealth of Nations* advances three arguments for the technological superiority of dividing labor as finely as the market will allow.

> (This) great increase of the quantity of work, which, in consequence of the division of labor, the same number of people are capable of performing, is owing to three different circumstances; first, to the increase of dexterity in every particular workman; secondly, to the saving of the time which is commonly lost in passing from one species of work to another; and lastly, to the invention of a great number of machines which facilitate labor and abridge labor, and enable one man to do the work of many.[6]

Of the three arguments, one—the saving of time—is undoubtedly important. But this argument has little or nothing to do with the minute specialization that characterizes the capitalist division of labor. A peasant, for example, will generally plow a whole field before harrowing it rather than alternating plow and harrow, furrow by furrow—in order to economize on the set-up time. But peasant agriculture is the antithesis of capitalist specialization; the individual peasant normally undertakes all the activities necessary to bring a crop from seed to marketable product. In respect of set-up time, there is nothing to differentiate agriculture from industry. To save "the time that is commonly lost in passing from one species of work to another" it is necessary only to continue in a single activity long enough that the set-up time becomes an insignificant proportion of total work time. The saving of time would require at most only that each worker continue in a single activity for days at a time, not for a whole lifetime. Saving of time implies *separation* of tasks and *duration* of activity, not *specialization*.

Smith's third argument—the propensity to invention—is not terribly persuasive. Indeed, the most devastating criticism was voiced by Smith himself in a later chapter of *The Wealth of Nations:*

> In the progress of the division of labor, the employment of the far greater part of those who live by labor, that is, of the great body of the people, comes to be confined to a few very simple operations, frequently to one or two. But the understandings of the greater part of men are formed by their ordinary employments. The man whose life is spent in performing a few simple operations, of which the effects too are, perhaps, always the same, or very nearly the same, has no occasion to exert his understanding, or to exercise his invention in finding out expedients for difficulties which never occur. He naturally loses, therefore, the habit of such exertion and generally becomes as stupid and ignorant as it is possible for a human creature to become . . .

It is otherwise in the barbarous societies, as they are commonly called, of hunters, of shepherds, and even of husbandmen in that crude state of husbandry which precedes the improvement of manufactures. In such societies the varied occupations of every man oblige every man to exert his capacity, and to invent expedients for removing difficulties which are continually occurring. Invention is kept alive, and the mind is not suffered to fall into that drowsy stupidity, which, in a civilized society, seems to benumb the understanding of almost all the inferior ranks of people.[7]

The choice does not, however, seem really to lie between stupidity and barbarity, but between the workman whose span of control is wide enough that he sees how each operation fits into the whole and the workman confined to a small number of repetitive tasks. It would be surprising indeed if the workman's propensity to invent has not been diminished by the extreme specialization that characterizes the capitalist division of labor.

This leaves "the increase of dexterity in every particular workman" as the basis of carrying specialization to the limits permitted by the size of the market. Now if Adam Smith were talking about musicians or dancers or surgeons, or even if he were speaking of the division of labor between pin-making and cloth-making, his argument would be difficult to counter. But he is speaking not of esoteric specializations, nor of the social division of labor, but of the minute division of ordinary, run-of-the-mill, industrial activities into separate skills. Take his favorite example of pin manufacture:

> . . . in the way in which this business is now carried on, not only the whole work is a peculiar trade, but it is divided into a number of branches, of which the greater part are likewise peculiar trades. One man draws out the wire, another straights it, a third cuts it, a fourth points it, a fifth grinds it at the top for receiving the head; to make the head requires two or three distinct operations; to put it on, is a peculiar business, to whiten the pins is another; it is even a trade by itself to put them into the paper; and the important business of making a pin is, in this manner, divided into about eighteen distinct operations, which in some manufactories, are all performed by distinct hands, though in others the same man will sometimes perform two or three of them. I have seen a small manufactory of this kind where ten men only were employed, and where some of them consequently performed two or three distinct operations. But though they were very poor, and therefore but indifferently accommodated with the necessary equipment, they could, when they exerted themselves, make among them about twelve pounds of pins in a day. There are in a pound upwards of four thousand pins of a middling size. Those ten persons, therefore could make among them upwards of forty-eight thousand pins in a day. Each person, therefore, making a tenth part of forty-eight thousand pins, might be considered as making four thousand eight hundred pins in a day. But if they had all wrought separately and independently, and without any of them having been educated to this peculiar business, they certainly could not each of them have made twenty, perhaps not one pin in a day . . . [8]

To the extent that the skills at issue are difficult to acquire, specialization is essential to the division of production into separate operations. But, judging from the earnings of the various specialists engaged in pin-making, these were no special skills. At least there were none that commanded premium wages. In a pin manufactory for which fairly detailed records survive from the early part of the nineteenth century, T.S. Ashton reported wages for adult males of approximately 20 shillings per week, irrespective of the particular branch in which they were engaged.[9] Women and children, as was customary, earned less, but again there appear to be no great discrepancies among the various branches of pin production. It would appear to be the case that the mysteries of pin-making were relatively quickly learned, and that the potential increase in dexterity afforded by minute division of tasks was quickly exhausted. Certainly it is hard to make a case for specialization of workmen to particular tasks on the basis of the pin industry.[10]

The dichotomy between specialization and the separate crafting of each individual pin seems to be a false one. It appears to have been technologically possible to obtain the economics of reducing set-up time *without* specialization. A workman, with his wife and children, could have proceeded from task to task, first drawing out enough wire for hundreds or thousands of pins, then straightening it, then cutting it, and so on with each successive operation, thus realizing the advantages of dividing the overall production process into separate tasks.

Why, then, did the division of labor under the putting-out system entail specialization as well as separation of tasks? In my view the reason lies in the fact that without specialization, the capitalist had no essential role to play in the production process. If each producer could himself integrate the component tasks of pin manufacture into a marketable product, he would soon discover that he had no need to deal with the market for pins through the intermediation of the putter-outer. He could sell directly and appropriate to himself the profit that the capitalist derived from mediating between the producer and the market. Separating the tasks assigned to each workman was the sole means by which the capitalist could, in the days preceding costly machinery, ensure that he would remain essential to the production process as integrator of these separate operations into a product for which a wide market existed; and specialization of men to tasks at the sub-product level was the hallmark of the putting-out system.

The capitalist division of labor, as developed under the putting-out system, embodied the same principle that "successful" imperial powers have utilized to rule their colonies: divide and conquer. Exploiting differences between Hindu and Muslim in India—if not actually creating them—the British could claim to be essential to the stability of the sub-continent. And they could, sometimes with ill-concealed satisfaction, point to the millions of deaths that followed Partition as proof of their necessity to stability. But this tragedy proved only that the British had *made* themselves essential as mediators, not that there was any inherent need for British mediation of communal differences.

Residential Construction

Also of high significance for the economic inheritance of the 1950s was the immediate postwar experience in the residential construction field. The American housing establishment was worth less in 1945 than it was sixteen years before—$6.6 billion, or about 7 percent less. In view of the fact that the number of households had risen by 7.9 million, or 26 percent, in the interim, there was the usual alleged "pent-up demand" or "backlog." Residential construction has been important not only from the standpoint of the people's level of living, but also because it has usually made up about one-fifth to one-fourth of aggregate gross private investment. The long cycle in highly volatile residential investment has often significantly influenced the amplitude and duration of the general business cycle. Residential construction powerfully influenced the upward course of total private investment during the upswing of 1946–48, contributed to and later cushioned the downswing of 1949, and sparked to an important extent the subsequent recovery.

But more important for present purposes are two strategic facts about housing in the contemporary economy: First, for various reasons the private housing market, if left strictly private, cannot build housing for the low-income groups, and it finds substandard urban rental housing too profitable to scrap; and second, largely because of the first fact plus its interest in stabilizing investment, the government has become heavily committed in the housing market.

The conversion of the private housing industry into a quasi-public activity—that is, a rather more public than private activity—began in a serious way under the New Deal. The New Deal had been anticipated by Republican President Hoover with the passage in 1932 of the Federal Home Loan Bank Act, the major purposes of which were to reduce foreclosures and stimulate residential construction by providing widely dispersed "banks" to extend long-term, low-interest loans payable in moderate installments.

Demoralization of the mortgage market was so serious during the Great Depression as to constitute one of the many "emergencies" that have since come to permeate the fabric of American life. The New Deal set up the Home Owner's Loan Corporation (HOLC) to take over mortgages in danger of default and the Federal Housing Administration (FHA) to insure the loans of private financial institutions. Then in 1937 the Congress passed the National Housing Act, setting up the United States Housing Authority (USHA), which was authorized to extend low-interest loans *with long amortization periods*—the crucial consideration—to local public agencies for slum clearance and low-cost housing projects and to grant subsidies for the purpose of maintaining low rentals in certain public housing projects. The USHA was active during World War II in the construction and operation of defense housing facilities. The Federal National Mortgage Association, which came to be known more popularly as "Fannie Mae," was set up under the Housing Act of 1938 to trade in FHA-insured mortgages on new residences. Fannie Mae was given authority in 1948 to trade in mortgages guaranteed by the Veterans Administration (VA). The purpose of Fannie Mae was to provide a second mortgage market within the nation's home financing system in which this quasi-federal agency (it was nominally "privatized" in 1954) would take over approved mortgages from lenders. In the late 1940s, given the Treasury-Federal Reserve low-interest rate policy, the federally underwritten mortgage loan was quite attractive. In effect, by the beginning of the 1950s the whole system of housing credit was substantially underwritten by the government. This was to be an important pillar in the underwritten economy of the coming decade.

Because of the vital part played by federal underwriting in the home-financing market, the high level of residential construction during 1946–49 must be adjudged a quasi-public performance. The same judgment must be made, in general, about the important role of residential construction throughout the 1950s, for the major emphasis of the federal programs in the residential financing field has historically been to encourage new construction. This has given the government a powerful weapon for contributing to stabilization or inducing economic growth. According to the midyear economic report of the Council of Economic Advisers for 1950, "Private residential construction accounted for about two-thirds of the increase of about 4 billion dollars in total private investment in new construction from 1946 to 1947. The credit policies and programs of Government played an indispensable part in the expansion of the market demand for homes. This expansion depended on low interest rates, small or nominal down payments, and long periods of amortization. Without public assurances, the policies of private investment institutions could not have been extended far enough to permit this type of financing." Statements of similar general import to this, made at the threshold of the 1950s, could have been, and often were, repeated in various years during the ensuing decade. The quasi-public nature of the important residential construction component of aggregate investment needs to be recognized and appraised by the acute observer of the private investment mechanism as it operates in our time. It is another aspect of that mechanism that must be incorporated into the previous discussion of the behavior of total private investment during the years 1946–49.

From the standpoint of intermediate and long-term performance of the quasi-private investment mechanism, the strategic components of capital formation that will have to be most carefully analyzed are nonfarm business structures and producers' durable equipment. Historically these, along with residential construction, have made up the essence of private capital formation and have in consequence sparked the growth process in the domestic private economy.

CHAPTER II

Highlights of Change in the Postwar Era

3. Some Deeper Currents in the Recent Past
Stuart Bruchey

Excerpted and reprinted with permission from *The Wealth of the Nation* by Stuart Bruchey (New York: Harper & Row, 1988), pp. 198–232. Stuart Bruchey is Allan Nevins professor emeritus of American economic history at Columbia University.

As the American people entered upon the closing years of the twentieth century, the vistas that opened before them were being shaped silently by two fundamental forces. One was demography, the other technology. As always, the two were closely connected. Technology in the form of medical research and improvements in health care was reducing mortality, lengthening the span of life, and increasing the proportion of the elderly in the population. Technology, especially in the form of lightning-quick flows of computerized information, was enriching the data bases on which investment and other strategic business decisions were being made. It was these private decisions, the many-tongued voice of the market, which were determining the pace at which the economy was growing. And the latter was deeply influencing family formation, birth rates, and immigration.

Between 1950 and the end of 1986 the population rose by nearly 77 million people. More than half the increase, some 42 million, came between 1950 and 1965. This "baby boom" caught demographers by surprise. They had confidently predicted a postwar continuation of the declining trends of the 1930s. Although a steep decline in births set in after the crest of the boom was reached in the late 1960s, it was clear to demographers that the baby boomers of the postwar years would confront American society with grave problems in the early decades of the twenty-first century.

The percentage of the population older than sixty-five was expected to climb moderately from 11.3 percent to 13.1 percent between 1980 and 2000, but by 2030 it would exceed 21 percent. In consequence there would be heavy pressures to spend more money on both hospital and long-term care for generations caught in the coils of degenerative illness. Chronic illness was one thing, acute illness another. Society was organized and financed to treat the latter—medical emergencies—but the sad truth was that chronic illnesses accounted for 80 percent of all deaths and 90 percent of all disabilities. A person suffering a heart attack might be sped to the nearest hospital. One with Alzheimer's disease was more likely to go broke gradually.

Baby boomers were not the only source of increase in the postwar population. Immigration from Asia and Latin America, especially from Mexico, was another. Its numbers may never be known, for much of it was illegal. Poverty and hopelessness at home sent tens of thousands of single men and families north of the farm fields of California and Texas, where they tried to melt into the native population. The influx reached its highest levels in the 1960s. In the seventies, legal and illegal immigration together accounted for perhaps one-third the nation's estimated 15 million. To discourage illegality, Congress enacted legislation in 1986 conferring resident alien status on illegal immigrants already in the country. Proprietors of farms and other businesses attractive to immigrants would presumably be reluctant in the future to hire immigrants lacking documentary proof of the new status.

While the problems of many elderly even today are very real, more people are surviving to old age than did so in 1950. And in general the population is healthier. In 1980 death rates for both sexes were lower at all ages and for all races than they were thirty years before, the decline greater for females than for males, and greater for nonwhites than for whites. The decrease in nonwhite death rates is the main explanation for the rise in the proportion of nonwhites in the population. Up to the mid-1950s, decline in mortality was owing in the main to the diffusion of a number of new antibiotic "wonder drugs." After leveling off, mortality rates once again began to fall in the late sixties, particularly for older men and women, reversing a historical tendency for improvement to have been most marked in younger age groups. Control of cardiovascular and cerebrovascular diseases, especially, and to some extent also infectious diseases, lay behind the drop in mortality at older ages, the decline in the former probably being due in part to new medical care developments permitting the identification as well as treatment of high-risk cases. Tragically, violent death—accidents, homicide, suicide—is the chief killer of young adults, especially males, and for this group mortality has failed to decline. The economic as well as human cost of this loss of years of productive activity hardly requires comment.

The population has not only become larger, healthier, and longer-lived; it has also redistributed itself in significant ways over the American landscape. Historically, the story has been one of the urban growth and rural depopulation in consequence of technological change in industry and agriculture. Since the mid-twentieth century, however, the United States has been on the brink of still another memorable epoch in geographic settlement—i.e., the repopulation of a number of previously rural areas. The first clue to this development appeared in the form of suburbanization in the earlier years of the century. Recently, however, population has been flowing to rural areas that do not border on major cities, and it has also been shifting to the Sunbelt. The latter is evident in net migration rates from the fifties through the seventies, with the South and West virtually tied as leaders in rates of population growth and net in-migration. In the eighties, however, both New England and the Midwest began to rebound, the former because of the movement of high-tech firms to an area abounding in educational resources. No less noteworthy was the fact that, in every region except the South, population growth in areas not bordering on major cities has been higher than in those areas which do.

What explains these shifts to the Sunbelt and to nonmetropolitan places? In part, the answer lies in the presence of such special factors as natural resource endowments or governmental decisions regarding the location of military, space, and educational activities. In the case of the South, for example, it appears that large military allocations and technological developments accompanying World War II provided the necessary external stimulus for the industrial and population growth long sought by the region's leaders. In the postwar decades, an increasing number of businessmen turned southward in response to lower operating costs, especially wages; promanagement state governments; and a growing regional market nurtured by increased federal expenditures. When the space industry boomed in the early 1960s, for example, Florida's population grew by nearly 3,000 persons a week. In the region as a whole, industrial development after the war first slowed population losses and then, between 1970 and 1976, spurred a net gain from in-migration of 2.9 million people.

But special circumstances do not explain longer-term developments. "Throughout the history of mankind residence decisions have been dominated by place of work." In long eras of the American past these decisions were governed by farming opportunities opened up by the vast extent of available land. Then with the advent of mechanized production in the nineteenth century, settlement patterns shifted in favor of urban locations. Unlike colonial shops, the new technology made possible important economies of scale; unlike shops, factories needed access to substantial markets for their products. Furthermore, the coal and iron ore required by industry were "much less ubiquitous than the agricultural and forest resources on which preindustrial technology was based." For this reason producers located at or near the sources of these new industrial inputs or at transport points that made them accessible at low cost.

In consequence, new business and job opportunities were opened up in urban centers, places which soon became key junctions in the railroad network. So-called agglomeration economies then accentuated the advantages of these centers as workers and consumers flocked to them. Rising per capita incomes then raised consumer demand for manufactured products, with the result that still more people were drawn to urban centers in search of job opportunities. The result was rural depopulation: In each of the two decades between 1940 and 1960, more than 3,100 American counties experienced absolute declines in their numbers of people.

Modern technology then proceeded to break the ties that bound the consumer's residence to his place of work. First the horse-drawn trolley and electric streetcar and then the automobile made it possible for many urban Americans to exercise their preference for rural or semirural living places, a preference made possible also by the shortened workday brought about by modern economic growth. In addition, the transmission of electricity supplied the power essential for the operation of households in nonurban residential communities. Nor can the open-air recreational facilities of rural areas—camping, picnicking, and water sports—be ignored.

Business firms as well as consumers have been affected by the relative advantages of rural locations. They are no longer, as in the nineteenth century, tied to narrow resource requirements. Technological progress has diversified industrial materials, permitting a shift, for example, from ferrous to nonferrous metals and plastics, from coal to petroleum, natural gas, and other sources. Trucks have altered the rigid rail transport network. Above all, information essential to all business decisions is now transmitted by the telephone and the computer. Furthermore, former economies of agglomeration have turned into diseconomies as urban pollution and congestion have increased. All in all, in this century the location of business firms is far less bound than it has been in the past to a limited urban network. It is more responsive than ever before to consumer preferences, not least those of workers for more attractive locations in which to work.

Rural repopulation, in sum, represents a personal and business response to ways of living and working made possible by technological advance. It does not bespeak an increased demand for agricultural labor. Indeed, the opposite is true. Between 1945 and 1981 the farm population fell from 17.5 percent of the total to merely 2.6 percent, with farm employment down from 10 million to about one-third of that. In 1947, more than one family in six lived on a farm, but by 1977 only one in twenty-six continued to do so. As late as 1929, payments for capital, labor, and natural resources by the agricultural, forestry, and fisheries sectors of the economy generated 10 percent of the national income, but by 1978 this percentage had fallen to 2.9 percent. Behind both of these developments in relation to agriculture lay major increases in productivity. The farm sector has shrunk by becoming more efficient. Crop output per hour quintupled between 1950 and 1979; output of livestock and livestock products rose sixfold. Meanwhile, hours of labor required on farms fell by more than two-thirds.

Capital has displaced much of this labor. An index of farm inputs shows labor falling from 217 in 1950 to 65 in 1980. In part, mechanical power and machinery took its place, the index rising from 84 to 128. More important, the index for agricultural chemicals, including fertilizers, lime, and pesticides, jumped from 29 to 174 during the period. Unfortunately, there is no index for another important input, viz., intangible capital in the form of better management and knowledge of improved production techniques. Large public and private investments in education, in schools, colleges, and research organizations, including those of the Department of Agriculture, have generated and spread this knowledge, stimulating new patterns of input use. Growing managerial efficiency and knowledge then, as well as technology, help explain one of the truly amazing facts of American history: In 1790, at the beginning of our existence as an independent nation, it required the labor of perhaps eighty-five out of every one hundred persons to provide for the agricultural needs for a population of 4 million, including needs that were met from the proceeds of modest exports. In 1981, in contrast, fewer than three people out of every one hundred were required to feed and clothe a population swollen to over 230 million, and to generate, besides, huge surpluses. Surely this is a miracle of agricultural science.

Agriculture has become industrialized. Most farms are now firms; some are factories. Around the time of World War II an agricultural revolution, comparable in many ways to the earlier Industrial Revolution, began to take place in the United States. One similarity between the two was the tendency for production to become concentrated in fewer, larger units. In 1980 the number of "farms" in the United States was only a third of their total in 1920, but their average size had grown from 147 to 453 acres. Small farms of less than 100 acres still continued to represent 43.5 percent of all farms in 1978, but they harvested only 5 percent of the country's total cropland. They were essentially noncommercial farms. Their annual sales averaged less than $2,500. In contrast, farms ranging in size from five hundred to more than two thousand acres harvested 60 percent of the cropland. These large units dominated American agriculture. Scarcely more than one farm in ten boasted annual sales of $100,000 or more, but these giants were responsible for 63 percent of the total sales. In many counties farm sales of leading commodities had become so concentrated on a few big farms by 1978 that the United States Department of Agriculture was prevented by disclosure laws from publishing the relevant figures in the agricultural census.

What brought about this result was not size alone but size together with heavy investments in capital, capital in the form of machinery and equipment, fertilizer, chemicals, and other inputs—in a word, mechanization. Widening mechanization, seeds with higher yields, improved breeds of livestock, and the use of herbicides, pesticides, and other products of agricultural chemistry are to be found today in all major agricultural regions of the United States except the Great Plains.

Despite the technological innovations which are at the heart of this agricultural revolution, the American farmer has by no means enjoyed a record of unparalleled financial success. Nor has his banker, his supplier, and those who service his equipment, processing, and transport needs—those, in short, who make up the complex of "agribusiness." "I've never seen a year like this," said Dean Jack, president of York State Bank in southeastern Nebraska in February 1985. "Half of our farmers are in good shape, about 25 percent are in trouble, and about 25 percent are already broke." He added: "We have good water for irrigation, we have land that is as good as anybody's, and we raise as good crops as ever, and half our farmers still can't pay their debts." More broadly, in early 1985 one-third of the nation's farms were encumbered by an average debt of $325,000. And when farms failed, they brought down the banks to which they were indebted. The year 1986 saw 138 bank failures, more than in any year since the establishment of the Federal Deposit Insurance Corporation in 1934. Most were located in farm and energy-producing states, with Texas, Oklahoma, Kansas, Iowa, and Missouri heading the list.

The fundamental explanation of the financial predicament in which so many American farmers found themselves in the mid 1980s is simple: They responded incautiously to the price signals of the marketplace. The explanation itself, however, has to be explained, and that is anything but simple. The chronic farm problem in the United States has long been that

of excess capacity, of an ability to produce more than domestic and foreign markets can absorb at remunerative prices, even with the aid of
goods taken off the market by government support programs. In other
words, in the aggregate, demand has been inelastic with respect to price.
Ever since the days of the New Deal, government has tried to cope with
this problem by mounting a host of programs—acreage allotments and
marketing quotas, purchase agreements, soil banks, and other—designed
to curtail supply by limiting production. And it has tried through commodity loans to farmers or to their cooperative marketing associations to
provide floors under market prices. In addition, numerous programs
have authorized payments to producers in the form of commodity price
supports, or in return for adopting soil conservation measures. Analysts
generally agree that average farm prices in the 1950s and 1960s would
have been considerably lower if these programs had not been in existence, perhaps from 10 to 25 percent lower.

In the later 1960s, prices, which with government support had held at
reasonably constant levels from 1953 to 1967, began to move upward.
And in 1973 they shot skyward to levels never before experienced except
during wartime. What had happened? The explanation is that foreign
demand rose massively in response to: (a) the Nixon administration's
approval of the sale of $750 million worth of wheat and feed grains to the
Soviet Union in the summer of 1972—a sale that sparked orders from
elsewhere in Europe and from Japan—and (b) the Nixon administration's
devaluation of the dollar in 1973, which cheapened American exports.

American farmers responded with enthusiasm to the prospect of up-
wardly spiraling demand, prices, and profits. Encouraged by their bankers to borrow, and by top officials in the Department of Agriculture to
plant "from fence to fence," they increased the area under crops by 54
million acres between 1969 and 1981—and adopted improved production
techniques besides to lower costs and raise output. Corn production, for
example, went up from 5.6 million bushels in 1972 to 8.4 million in
1982. In the meantime, however, agricultural production abroad also expanded, and American surpluses soared.

Enter the value of the dollar. In contrast with the sixties and seventies,
when the dollar was generally weak in relation to the currencies of Europe and Japan, the dollar of the earlier years of the 1980s developed
phenomenal strength. Exports of manufactured goods as well as farm
commodities were affected. Since they were priced in expensive dollars,
they fell. In contrast, imports rose. Indeed, in 1986 the excess of imports
over exports soared to a historically high deficit of $175 billion. The
strong dollar reduced foreign demand for American goods, and this lessened foreign demand, which, in turn, increased quantities available for
domestic sale. But although this lowered prices to consumers, it also

lowered incomes for farmers. Falling incomes, in turn, made it difficult for farmers to repay their investments in equipment and supplies, with obvious economic consequences for manufacturers and tradesmen. Thus, as always since the rise of industry, the fortunes of the agricultural and manufacturing sectors of the economy were closely entwined.

In some ways, manufacturers had an even harder row to hoe. In contrast with the remarkable record of productivity growth encountered in the postwar history of American agriculture, manufacturing, once the pacesetting embodiment of the American system, as it was known and envied abroad, could boast no similar accomplishment in recent years. Just the opposite: The rate of increase in productivity has been slowing down. From an annual average of 3.4 percent between 1948 and 1966, the rate of increase fell to 2.3 percent during 1966–73, to 1 percent during 1973–77, and to 0.4 percent between 1977 and 1978. Then in 1979 and 1980 growth stopped altogether, and productivity actually declined.

Naturally enough, this strange unhistoric phenomenon aroused concern, and economists have been pondering its causes since the late sixties. Among the numerous factors cited were an increase in the proportion of youths and women in the work force ("output per man-hour tends to be relatively low among women and among new entrants into the labor force"), relatively low rates of investment after 1973, a decrease in the proportion of the gross national product devoted to research and development in the late sixties and early seventies, and the shift of national output away from goods and toward services, where possibilities of productivity growth are more limited. The litany goes on and on. Some suggest that the solution to the puzzle might begin with the dismantling of government policies that have raised costs and discouraged savings. Others emphasize the importance of retaining workers displaced by computers, robots, and other technological innovations, and by the migration of production to low-wage centers overseas. In addition to new skills and knowledge, some suggest, workers also need greater motivation to excel not only as individuals but also as members of a team. Productivity in the era of human capital, writes a recent scholar, "will depend largely on collaboration, group learning, and teamwork."

Finally, one must consider the effects of decisions made by business managers themselves, especially those of the largest manufacturing corporations. According to one critic, professional managers, intent on a favorable reading of the bottom line, have gradually become "paper entrepreneurs" since the mid-1960s. Avoiding the costs and risks of investments in fundamentally new products or processes, their innovations have been neither technological nor institutional. "Rather, they have been based on accounting, tax avoidance, financial management, mergers, acquisitions and litigation. They have been innovations on paper." Instead of creating new wealth, they have merely rearranged industrial assets.

The conglomerate merger movement that began in the 1960s is a case in point. Before then, American business enterprises as a rule confined their expansion to lines of business related to their original products, entering markets appropriate to their managerial, technical, and marketing capabilities in search of competitive advantage. The conglomerate enterprises born after the mid-1960s—Gulf & Western, LTV, Textron, Litton, United Technologies, Northwest Industries, ITT, and Teledyne— were entirely different. Multibusiness giants, they have grown by acquiring existing enterprises, often in wholly unrelated fields. ITT, for example, owns Wonder Bread, Sheraton Hotels, Hartford Insurance, Bobbs-Merrill Publishing, and Burpee Lawn and Garden Products. Conglomerates rarely, if ever, bring managerial, technical, or marketing skills to the companies they acquire because they lack any direct knowledge of these unrelated businesses. Their expertise is in law and finance, and their relationship to their subsidiaries is that of an investor who diversifies to spread his risks.

Conglomeration has been taking place rapidly in recent years, with American companies increasing the amounts spent in acquiring other companies from $22 billion in 1977 to twice that sum two years later. Nineteen-eighty-one saw record-shattering expenditures of $82 billion for the purpose. Since conglomeration increases concentration ratios—that is, it increases the proportion of an industry's output accounted for by a few large firms—it follows that the movement must lessen the number of decisions affecting output and probably also the number of people making them. In sum, managerial emphasis has often in recent years shifted from cost-reducing and product-enhancing innovation through research and development to short-run profits from market manipulations of company assets. The consequence has surely been the placing of higher managerial premiums on expertise in law and finance than on engineering and other productivity-enhancing bodies of knowledge.

The causes of the decline in productivity are clearly complex. Just as surely, its consequences have been grave. Among them is an erosion of the average American standard of living. Real incomes began to slow their rate of growth in 1965, with real wages declining by one-fifth between 1968 and 1981. In addition, exports of American manufactured goods have fallen as a percentage of world manufactured exports ever since 1963, and this is partly attributable to a weak productivity performance. Ironically, the industries affected are those on which the industrial preeminence of the United States has long rested, a superiority due to its ability to produce with growing efficiency standardized goods in high volume. They are its basic steel, textile, automobile, electronics, rubber, and petrochemical industries, together with other high-volume industries dependent on them. Increasingly uncompetitive, the American proportion of world automobile sales fell by nearly one-third between 1963 and 1981. Sales of industrial machinery also declined by one-third, agricultural machinery by 40 percent, telecommunications machinery by 50 percent, and metalworking machinery by 55 percent. Nevertheless, the United States has remained a net exporter of capital goods and of chemicals ever since World War II, and the surpluses have grown rapidly since the late 1960s.

Historically, the United States has been a net importer of consumer goods. But this was not the case in the years immediately after World War II, when, in 1947, for example, exports of consumer goods yielded a net surplus of $1 billion. The explanation lies in the relative impact of the war upon the United States and other industrial nations. The United States escaped with its factories, mines, and transport net intact, capable, in 1950, of producing approximately 60 percent of world manufacturing output. In contrast, industrial capacity in almost every continental European country and in Japan had been destroyed and that of Great Britain crippled.

The distortion in the composition of trade was not destined to last. Public grants under the Marshall Plan of about $13 billion, by contributing significantly to European industrial and economic growth, paved the way to a return to traditional trading patterns. The European economies recovered and rebuilt capacity in the 1950s; in the next decade Japan entered competitive world markets in a major way; and in the 1970s several developing countries, aided by a gradual reduction of tariff levels after adoption of the General Agreement on Tariffs and Trade in 1947, and by relatively easy access to international capital through European, American, and Japanese banks (and also by a new postwar institution, the World Bank), began making important contributions to manufacturing output and trade. By 1979, the share of the United States in world industrial production had fallen from 60 percent to 35 percent, and its share in world exports of manufactured goods from 29 percent (in 1953) to 13 percent (in 1976). By 1980, the share of the developing nations in manufactured goods had soared to exact equivalence with that of the United States, while Japan's rose in the 1970s from 6 percent to 10.5 percent. From a transitory position of early postwar domination of the export trade, the United States thus moved to one of rough equivalence with other industrial countries, in the meantime resuming its historical posture as a net importer of consumer goods.

However, the growth of industrial capacity in other parts of the world, together with roughly comparable cost developments, does not wholly explain the declining share of American manufacturers in world exports. As with agricultural exports, the relative values of national currencies must also be taken into account. During the years of postwar decline, the American dollar was overvalued in relation to other currencies, and in consequence, foreign sales of American goods were impeded, imports stimulated, and American firms encouraged to invest abroad. Because, however, of the peculiar role which the dollar came to play under what was known as the Bretton Woods system, devaluation of the dollar was for a long time effectively ruled out. The result was that the United States trade balance, after reaching a peak surplus in the early 1960s, began to deteriorate. By July 1971 the balance-of-payments deficit was rising at the very high rate of $23 billion a year, and this generated increasing pressure to abandon the system.

But this could not lightly be done. Under that system adopted by a United Nations conference at Bretton Woods, New Hampshire, in 1944, the dollar had become the standard in terms of which all other currencies were measured. The Japanese yen and British pound, for example, were valued in terms of the dollar, with the dollar itself being valued in terms of gold. If a foreign central bank wished to exchange its dollars for gold, it was agreed that it could do so at the fixed price of $35 an ounce. The convertibility of dollars into gold was the system's theoretical anchor. Because of convertibility, other countries were willing to hold dollars in their monetary reserves instead of gold. Bretton Woods, in short, adopted what was technically known as the gold reserve standard.

Unfortunately, the ability of the system to function began to deteriorate in the late fifties, weakened by increasing surpluses of dollars in foreign hands. The dollar glut bespoke growing deficits in the balance of payments and led to loss of American gold reserves. (Ironically, it was the outflow of dollars made necessary by the deficits which enabled the dollar to function as the principal reserve currency and medium for payment of international transactions.) Deficits mounted for three principal reasons. Government loans, grants, and military expenditures placed large quantities of dollars in foreign hands. So too did a growing deficit in the balance of trade. Rising prices in the United States in the late sixties made American goods more expensive abroad while cheapening imports. Finally, American firms began in the late fifties to increase their direct investments abroad. They did so in part because of greater prosperity abroad than at home. Had the opposite been true, they would have been more likely in ordinary circumstances to keep their capital in the United States, to expand domestic production facilities. However, circumstances were not ordinary. What changed them was the organization of the European Common Market in 1958. Fearful that the member countries might try to exclude competing American goods by high tariffs, many American firms elected to build or acquire plant and machinery behind the protective walls of the Market. Direct investments were especially prominent in European and Canadian manufacturing, petroleum, and mining and smelting facilities. Those in manufacturing alone increased eightfold between 1950 and 1970, rising from $3.8 billion to $32.3 billion.

In sum, government expenditures, private direct investment, and the effects of inflation on the trade balance led to a dollar glut abroad. But while these developments made for growing deficits in the balance of payments, it is worth calling attention to the fact that it might have been possible to cover the deficits more largely by means other than the export of gold. Had the economic growth of the United States been stronger than it was, Europeans and others would have been attracted to the securities of American firms. Alas, it was not so. A massive gold drain began in 1958, the United States losing some $3.5 to $4 billion a year between then and the mid-sixties. The nation's ownership of $22.9 billion of gold in 1957 had represented nearly 60 percent of the free world's supply. By 1965 the amount had declined to $15 billion, the proportion to 35 percent.

Some losses fed the fires of doubt that the United States would continue to be able to keep its pledge to redeem its dollars at the agreed-upon rate of $35 for an ounce of gold. Speculators reasoned that the United States would be compelled to devalue the dollar, to raise the dollar price of gold. They were right. After a massive speculative run against the dollar, the Nixon administration decided in 1971 that devaluation was the only way out. It suspended indefinitely the official convertibility of the dollar into gold and in 1973 made the suspension permanent. Not only was the dollar devalued against gold, nearly all the major industrial currencies were revalued against the dollar—the Japanese yen, for example, by approximately 17 percent. The purpose of the devaluation, it should be made clear, was to produce a major improvement in the United States' balance of payments, including the trade balance, and to put an end to the disadvantage under which American export industries were operating, in the belief that this, together with a hoped-for reversal of capital flows, would improve the balance of payments. The Bretton Woods system of fixed parities was abandoned. Floating exchange rates replaced fixed exchange rates, with the price of dollars in terms of gold and other currencies henceforth being determined by the supply and demand for dollars.

Despite the devaluation of the early seventies, the dollar became strong once again in the eighties. What made it strong was the impact of large budgetary deficits on real interest rates. By 1987 the deficit, swollen by huge defense expenditures, coupled with unwillingness on the part of the Reagan administration to raise taxes, had reached a historic high of $173 billion. Because the government must compete with private borrowers for available savings, the huge sums borrowed by the government to finance the deficit kept interest rates high. These high rates, in turn, along with the perceived stability of the American economy, attracted foreign capital to the United States. Ironically, foreign investment made it possible to finance the gargantuan American budget without still higher interest rates. Capital-losing countries, on the other hand, complained because the export of capital reduced sums available for their own development needs. The reply of the Reagan administration was that a reduced rate of inflation was responsible for the dollar's strength, and it urged other industrialized countries around the world to follow the example of the United States!

If falling productivity and relative currency values go far to explain the decline in American manufactured exports as a proportion of world sales, they also throw light on the ability of foreign imports to win larger shares of the domestic market.

> By 1981 America was importing 26 percent of its cars, 25 percent of its steel, 60 percent of its televisions, radios, tape recorders and phonographs, 43 percent of its calculators, 27 percent of its metal-forming machine tools, 35 percent of its textile machinery, and 53 percent of its numerically controlled machine tools. Twenty years before, imports had accounted for less than 10 percent of the U.S. market for each of these products.

However, productivity and currency are not the only relevant considerations. Since the 1960s a major structural change has been taking place in the world economy. Access to capital, technological knowledge and innovations, and global channels of sales and marketing have permitted less-developed countries to participate in that economy far more actively than before. Their participation, in turn, and that of third world countries as well, has permitted an international rationalization of the location of production to take place. The globe is thus becoming a single marketplace, with goods being made wherever they can be made the cheapest. Real wages are lower in third world countries, and many of them also have a favored access to cheap materials. In addition, the availability of data processing machines, microprocessors, and satellite communications facilities has made it possible for manufacturers to divide the process of production into separate operations that can be performed at different sites and then integrated into a single product. Such developing countries as Korea, Hong Kong, Taiwan, Singapore, Brazil, and Spain have been ideally suited to manufacturing standardized parts that are assembled into end products elsewhere. Sometimes the process is reversed. Since 1970, for example, the United States has been increasing its export of auto parts and its import of complete cars, its export of industrial textiles and its import of consumer textiles. South Korea's textile exports rose by 436 percent between 1970 and 1975, while those of Taiwan and Hong Kong increased by 347 percent and 191 percent, respectively. Imports to the United States from developing nations rose nearly tenfold from 1970 to 1980, from $3.6 billion to $30 billion (in constant dollars).

One consequence has been an intensification of competition in the American marketplace, where by 1980, foreign-made goods were competing with more than 70 percent of goods produced in the United States. Another has been a progressive shift in competitive advantage in high-volume standardized production to the newly developed and developing countries. The upshot of these rapid changes was that a number of old-line American industries, including textiles, steel, automobiles, petro-chemicals, electrical machinery, and metal-forming machinery, found themselves in trouble in the early 1980s.

Many of them had become stable oligopolies of three or four major firms. Unaccustomed to price competition, adhering to a system of ad-ministered prices and guaranteed wage increases, management often re-fused to allow prices to respond to market conditions. Technologically backward and reluctant to innovate, steel makers clung to open-hearth and ingot-casting techniques while their Japanese counterparts were investing heavily in superior basic oxygen furnaces and continuous casting. American automakers also held back, toying with changes in style while the Japanese were adopting new stamping technologies and experimenting with more efficient engines and pollution-control devices. The competitive threat came not only from the Japanese but also from the West German machine tool companies, French radial tire manufacturers, Swedish makers of precision instruments, and textile manufacturers in developing countries. The list of American compa-nies experiencing sharply reduced profits in the early 1980s included ghostly giants of the past: United States Steel, General Motors, Interna-tional Harvester, and RCA.

American producers in steel, automobiles, consumer electronics, and other industries sought protection from imports by forming political co-alitions with organized labor, petitioning the executive branch, lobbying Congress, and seeking support through the federal courts. Various sorts of trade restrictions followed, one example being the marketing agree-ment negotiated with Japan by the United States government limiting imports of Japanese color televisions to approximately 1.6 million sets a year, and similar agreements subsequently negotiated with Taiwan and South Korea. Besides quotas, protection has also taken the form of increased duties and a wide assortment of government subsidies, spe-cial tax credits and depreciation allowances, and subsidized loans and loan guarantees. According to one computation, the total cost to the federal government of special tax provisions for the benefit of specific industries rose from $7.9 billion in 1950 to $62.4 billion in 1980. During the same interval, the cost of subsidized loans and loan guarantees, as measured by interest charges and loan defaults, increased from only $300 million to $3.6 billion. Altogether, government subsidies and tax expenditures increased from $77.1 billion in 1950 to $303.7 billion in 1980. In addition, government subsidies have taken the form of ad hoc bailouts for particular failing firms—for example, Lockheed and Chrysler.

Is this the way America should go? Should we look to government to protect the bottom line of firms and industries whose economic good health is judged to be in the national interest? Some think so. "Ultimately," says a recent writer, "America's capacity to respond to economic change will depend on the vitality of its political institutions." The United States must accept the fact that economic advantage in high-volume production of standardized products has moved to the developing countries. The challenge of the "new American frontier" is to promote the growth of "flexible system" production by technically advanced, skill-intensive industries, a highly integrated system that can respond quickly to new opportunities. The answer to economic decline, then, is to fashion "a new productive organization requiring a different, less rigidly delineated relationship between management and labor and a new relationship with government." What we need is an industrial policy.

Others disagree. Writing in 1983, Charles Schultze, chairman of the Council of Economic Advisers under President Carter, pointed out that the essential purpose of such a policy was the creation of an industrial structure different from what the market would have produced. In that case policy makers would necessarily face a twofold task, that of protecting the losers and that of picking the winners. Protecting losers meant supporting major declining industries by such means as trade barriers, subsidies, favorable regulatory treatment, tax breaks, and subsidized loans. Protectionism, inefficiencies, and higher prices for consumers would soon manifest themselves. As for picking winners or providing various forms of government aid to specific companies and industries— fast growers, big employers, or technological leaders—Schultze wanted to know how government bureaucrats could be expected to be better judges of the likelihood of success than private investors. He feared such a policy would turn into a vast boondoggle for every industry with political clout.

The policy question was a significant political issue of the 1980s, and only time would tell the outcome of the debate. The debate itself, however, in Congress and out, appeared in the late 1980s to be approaching consensus on the need for government to join with private business firms in stepped-up efforts to retain workers displaced by technological change and by the migration of production to cheaper areas overseas. Furthermore, even dedicated proponents of free market solutions also acknowl-edged the need for government to provide a safety net for low-income people, a net consisting of such income-assistance programs as unem-ployment compensation, food stamps, and Aid to Families with Depen-dent Children.

Such an idea would have found few supporters before the debut of the welfare state during the anguished years of the Great Depression. Most looked to a healthy economy to provide jobs and income and to private charity to help the victims of misfortune. The New Deal marks the tri-umph of a more compassionate philosophy, namely, that it is a legitimate responsibility of the federal government to aid the provision of the mini-mal needs of the disadvantaged. Evidence of the new viewpoint took the form of enlarged government expenditures for such Social Security pro-grams as those providing for old age, survivors', invalidism, and public health insurance; for workmen's compensation; unemployment insur-ance; family allowances; public assistance; and public employee pro-grams. The welfare state of the age of Roosevelt was extended by, not reshaped under, President Truman (who supported legislation making Social Security available to 10 million additional people, authorizing new public housing for the slum dweller, and expanding public power, rural electrification, soil conservation, and flood control projects) and found its richest expression in the twentieth century thus far in the Great Society programs of Lyndon Johnson.

Some of the legislation of the Johnson years, such as medical care for the aged, had been bottled up in Congress since the Truman administra-tion. Other programs bore Johnson's personal stamp, and of these proba-bly the most important was the War on Poverty. In 1962 Michael Harrington wrote movingly about the 40 million or so people (one-fifth of the American population) who had "dropped out of sight," who dwelt in a culture of poverty. They made up a more or less permanent underclass. They were the elderly, the nonwhites, the poorly educated, and the unproductive small farmers; they were the inhabitants of urban ghettos and of Appalachia. "Poverty" is not only an absolute but also a relative concept and one whose definition necessarily changes over time, but roughly half of all those groups were at or below the poverty line as defined by the Social Security Administration in 1964 (i.e., as having annual incomes of $3,000 or less to support a family of four).

Acting on the belief that poverty of this kind was impacted, that it was the result of social problems little affected by broad economic forces, and hence could not be eliminated by indirect methods which stimulated overall economic growth, Johnson put the weight of his presidential au-thority behind direct approaches to the problem. The Economic Opportunity Act of 1964, which established ten programs, including Head Start, the Job Corps, and VISTA, represented the first concerted attack on poverty since New Deal days. Other major programs followed: Medicare and Medicaid, federal aid for elementary and secondary education, federal scholarships for college students, a multimillion-dollar program for medical research, legislation providing rent subsidies, demonstration cities, a teachers' corps, regional medical centers, vest-pocket parks, a rescue operation for the economically depressed region of Appalachia, and an assortment of consumer protection laws, including those designed to increase auto and highway safety.

Standing as a halfway marker between the Roosevelt and Johnson administrations, the creation of the Cabinet-level Department of Health, Education, and Welfare in 1953 symbolized the continuing enlargement of the federal presence in the area of human melioration. From 1950 to 1964, federal expenditures for these purposes nearly tripled, rising, in constant dollars, from $35.1 billion to $108 billion. Unhappily, the War on Poverty fell victim to the war on Vietnam, the escalating funding requirements of which induced Johnson, as early as the beginning of 1966, to reduce or eliminate his budgetary requests for the maintenance of civilian programs he came to regard as of lower priority. Nevertheless, the evidence of the past half century of government interest in the preservation and improvement of human capital is unmistakable.

In this, the United States is not alone. While elements of welfare or Social Security programs vary from one country to another, reflecting differences in governmental structure, tradition, and historical development, the major industrial powers have devoted increasing portions of their gross national product to welfare objectives in recent decades. Despite differences in the nature of their political societies, all have responded to underlying social pressures engendered by an advanced state of industrialization. As Table 3.1 shows, however, government expenditures by the United States represented a smaller share than those of any other country except Japan. Even this proportion was subjected to deep budgetary cuts by the Reagan administration. The slicing of expenditures on education aid and loans, job training and retraining, and nutrition benefits for expectant mothers placed in serious jeopardy the nation's future stock of human capital.

In the early 1980s the question of poverty also became ensnarled in statistical and definitional controversy. The Census Bureau reported that 34.4 million Americans whose cash incomes in 1982 were less than $9,862 for a family of four fell below the official poverty level. The poverty rate that year was 15 percent of the American people, up from 14 percent in 1981, and the highest rate reported since the start of President Johnson's antipoverty campaign in 1965. The director of the Office of Management

Table 3.1

Government Expenditures for Social Security Programs as a Percentage of GNP, Selected Countries, 1957–77

Country	1957	1960	1963	1966	1971	1974	1977
Canada	6.5	8.7	9.4	9.0	14.8	13.7	14.6
France	14.3	13.7	15.4	16.6	n.a.	22.4	26.5
West Germany	16.6	16.2	16.9	18.4	18.8	22.5	26.5
Japan	4.3	4.7	5.1	5.6	5.6	6.4	8.7
Sweden	10.5	10.9	12.1	14.5	20.6	24.4	30.7
United Kingdom	10.0	11.0	11.1	12.3	13.5	14.1	17.1
United States	5.0	6.3	6.8	7.7	11.1	12.1	13.7

Source: David P. Calleo, *The Imperious Economy* (Cambridge: Harvard University Press, 1982), 96.

and Budget, David Stockman, disputed these figures, however. In testimony before the House Ways and Means Committee in November 1983, he rejected the definition of poverty used by the Census Bureau and other federal agencies since 1964. "The official poverty count based on money income," he said, "substantially overstates the rate of poverty because it ignores $107 billion in in-kind medical, housing, food, and other aid that tangibly raises the living standard of many low-income families." When noncash benefits were counted as income, he added, the poverty rate for 1982 was reduced from 15 percent to 9.6 percent, the number of poor people from 34.4 million to 22 million. The point was not a new one. Scholars had emphasized the relevance of in-kind aid nearly a decade before, if not earlier. The influence on policy was delayed and even now is uncertain, but in 1983 the Census Bureau at least planned to issue future reports simultaneously displaying the official poverty rate, using the usual definition, and the rate if noncash benefits were counted as income.

According to Stockman, poor people in 1982 fell into four categories. The elderly (sixty-five and older) formed 10.9 percent of the total; female-headed households, 32.8 percent; young singles between sixteen and twenty-four years of age, 3.9 percent; and other adults between twenty-five and sixty-four years of age, 52.3 percent. The rising tide of economic growth would lift many boats but not all. It would alleviate poverty for people in their prime working years but would be largely irrelevant to the elderly poor, many of whom had retired. Cash welfare programs, on the other hand, were of less value to young singles than to poor people in female-headed households, for whom government checks were of "critical and overwhelming significance." The conjunction of family instability, race and ethnicity, and poverty were painfully apparent. Only 56.1 percent of black families were husband-wife families in 1978, in contrast to 85.9 percent in the case of whites. In 1981, for female-headed families with children under eighteen, the percentages of families under the poverty line were about 68 percent for blacks, 67 percent for Hispanics, and 43 percent for whites. Unhappily, a task force appointed by President Reagan to investigate the question of hunger in the United States reported early in 1984 that "quantitative information about the extent of the problem is not available." In a final report characterized by the *New York Times* as one of "chilly, bloodless neutrality," the task force acknowledged "the sad truth" that "there is hunger in America," but concluded that "general claims of widespread hunger can neither be positively refuted nor definitely proved." Early in 1984 the nation awaited the course of action by a president who in November 1983 had said: "If there is one person in this country hungry, that is one too many, and we're going to see what we can do to alleviate the situation." The nation continued to wait in 1987.

As is evident from a comparison of the amounts of cash income demarcating the official poverty line for a family of four in 1964 ($3,000) and in 1982 ($9,862), something more than inflation has affected the definition of poverty. Undoubtedly, the most important additional ingredient has been the rising standard of living. Need today is defined at a higher level than in the past because of the very success of the American economic system in providing the material wants of the average family.

> In 1900 15 percent of U.S. families had flush toilets; today [1976] 86 percent of our poor families do. In 1900 3 percent had electricity; today 99 percent of our poor do; in 1900 1 percent had central heating; today 62 percent of the poor do. In 1900 18 percent of our families had refrigeration, ice refrigeration; today 99 percent of our poor have refrigerators, virtually all mechanical.

It is this "upward trend in the reference standard" that makes the end of poverty "an ever-retreating goal, and an unachievable one." In sum, government has done much and must do more to alleviate the absolute poverty of hunger. But in the relative sense the biblical admonition that "The poor ye have always with you" will continue to be true as long as American capitalism generates not only more and more goods and services but also the desire to have them. For in creating wealth it at the same time creates want.

Modern industrialization not only heightened consciousness of the need for increased public responsibility for the alleviation of absolute poverty, it also generated public response to its environmental consequences—pollution of the air by automobiles, factories, electric-power plants, and garbage incinerators, and of water by chemicals washed into the rivers by factories using it as a coolant, by the oil spills which kill marine life and damage property, and insecticides washed off numerous farms into the national water supply. The federal government first gave official recognition to the problem of air pollution in 1955, when the Congress enacted legislation authorizing research under federal auspices and technical assistance to the states. The Clean Air Act of 1963 then broadened the federal role by establishing a program of grants to the states to assist them in setting up or maintaining agencies for the control of pollution, by authorizing the promulgation of federal standards for the control of emissions from cars beginning with model year 1968. Legislation enacted in 1967 strengthened substantially the powers of local, state, and federal authorities and authorized the Secretary of Health, Education, and Welfare to enforce air quality standards in designated federally financed regions throughout the country.

Environmental alarms were sounding throughout the country in the 1960s in response to the warnings of biologists Rachel Carson and Barry Commoner, French oceanographer Jacques Cousteau, and others that the damage being done by industrial man might prove irreversible. Popular interest in ecology snapped into focus on April 22, 1970, with the celebration of Earth Day, a day marked by teach-ins, various clean-up projects, and adjournment by Congress to permit its members to address rallies across the nation. The next four years produced the broadest and most expensive environmental legislation in the nation's history. Congress at last established firm deadlines for the reduction of pollutants from automobiles, enacted a comprehensive water pollution control measure aimed at cleaning up the nation's waters by 1985, made petroleum companies liable for the costs of cleaning up oil spills, and acted on a host of other environmental issues, including the banning of hunting from aircraft, conservation of wildlife, reforestation of national forests, and the creation or expansion of national wilderness, historical, or recreational areas. It even shifted the priorities of President Nixon by appropriating more money for pollution control than he had asked for and less than he had proposed for defense!

It was the high point. At the same time that Congress was churning out environmental legislation in unprecedented volume, a new problem was emerging: shortage of energy. The issue became real for millions of Americans in the winter of 1972–73, when the United States suddenly seemed unable to muster enough fuel to heat its homes and power its factories. "Popeye is running out of cheap spinach," quipped former Commerce Secretary Peter G. Peterson. Then, between October 1973 and January 1974 the cost of imported "spinach" went up nearly 400 percent as a result of the embargo on oil shipments imposed by the Organization of Petroleum Exporting Countries (OPEC). More and more, it seemed that the solution to the nation's dwindling supply of power might be in conflict with the concerns of environmentalists.

As the first environmental decade came to a close, the race to clean up the country, begun in such earnest on Earth Day 1970, began to slow down. Economic concerns, as well as the problems of energy, were tempering the nation's commitment to a clean environment. Shrinking oil supplies, soaring inflation, slowing economic growth, and rising unemployment were forcing serious consideration of the questions How clean? How fast? At what cost? In the early 1980s the Reagan administration gave decisive evidence of its preference for renewed growth over environmental renewal; the Steel Compliance Act of 1981, for example, amended the Clean Air Act to allow steel companies to defer compliance for three years. Were rollbacks on environmental and workers' safety regulations, improved educational opportunity, and health, housing, and nutrition programs justifiable on grounds that these were too expensive "social luxuries"? Or did they rather represent foolhardy reductions in the nation's investment in human capital? That was one of the great political questions for Americans to confront in the late 1980s and beyond.

The answers given to those questions will go far toward determining the strength and resiliency of American capitalism in the twenty-first century. Healthy and well-educated working men and women are likely to become ever more important sources of the nation's economic well-being. That is because of the increasingly crucial role of scientific, technical, and managerial knowledge in economic growth. Even in the first half of the twentieth century, advances in knowledge contributed an estimated 40 percent of the total rise in income per person employed. In all likelihood, the contribution has risen since then and will continue to do so. For in the second half of the century, the American economy began to experience a Second Industrial Revolution, a revolution in the organization and processing of information and knowledge.

At the center of this revolution is the electronic digital computer. Unlike the calculator, the computer has a memory, a set of preprogrammed instructions or mathematical rules which it applies automatically to new data introduced at a later time. Like radar, jet aircraft, and other complicated high-technology developments incorporating state-of-the-art scientific knowledge, the electronic computer was a product of governmental need during World War II. The first large electronic digital computer (the ENIAC) was built to enable the army's Ballistic Research Laboratory to calculate trajectories for field artillery and bombing tables, a tedious task previously requiring large numbers of mathematicians using desk calculators. It was an enormous contraption, 100 feet long, 3 feet wide, and 10 feet high, and it contained about 18,000 vacuum tubes. Even though technical improvement was soon forthcoming, computers remained very costly after the war; they were difficult to program, and they were vulnerable to failure because of the dependence of their complex circuitry on vacuum tube technology. Many companies had both the knowledge and resources to build them, but great uncertainty over the size of the potential market made them reluctant to invest the substantial scientific, technical and financial resources required if they were to become commercial suppliers of computer systems.

Even the company that was subsequently to dominate the computer market, International Business Machines (IBM), held back at first. Under the leadership of Thomas J. Watson, Sr., IBM had grown from a small, struggling manufacturer of punch-card products and time-recording equipment in 1914, when it owned cash items amounting to $35,000 plus less than $200,000 in treasury bonds, which it used as collateral for short-term loans, to a firm whose American revenues in 1949 approximated

$180 million. Watson was certainly interested in electronics—between 1937 and 1944 IBM had sponsored research in the techniques of electro-mechanical computation, and by 1947 it had developed and built a par-tially electronic and partially electromechanical stored program digital computer. But, faced with internal opposition on the part of engineers and executives, with continuing uncertainty about whether there was really likely to be a demand for a computer, with technical problems, and with the fact that the traditional product line was very profitable, Watson hesitated. Perhaps his age—he was seventy-one in 1945—also had something to do with it. At any rate, it was his son, Thomas Jr., only thirty-six years old in 1950, who eventually authorized the devel-opment of a high-performing general-purpose computer (the 701). Shipments began in 1953 at the rate of one a month, a production record unmatched at the time by any other company. Manufactured on an assembly-line basis, the 701 was from ten to one hundred times faster than the ENIAC.

It was also much smaller and cheaper; indeed, it was the first general-purpose computer that did not have to be built in the customer's com-puter room. Subsequent machines, both those produced by IBM and by such early competitors as Remington Rand and Burroughs, and by such later ones as General Electric, RCA, and Control Data, became still smaller and cheaper and increasingly versatile as types of uses and users multiplied. Eventually, in the late 1970s Apple, Commo-dore, and Tandy emerged as leaders among firms manufacturing mi-crocomputers. The technology of the industry had changed dramatically. First transistors, then silicon chips replaced vacuum tubes. Chips no larger than the head of a thumbtack could hold the equivalent of 100,000 transistors, and work on a far larger integration of circuitry was proceeding apace.

It will be many years before the full impact of computers can be as-sessed: on business decision making, structure of the firm, labor unions and employment, the legal system, the home, the school, learning, lei-sure, and privacy. Yet it is already clear that their influence in some areas has become very great. The ability to link a personal computer with huge quantities of data stored in a central data base—by means of a modem, or modulation/demodulation device, enabling it to communicate over telephone lines—helped transform information processing into infor-mation communication. Not only the curricula of hundreds of high schools and colleges, but the operations of small businessmen and professionals, have been affected. The business office is in the process of being changed radically: by the use of "teleconferencing" to save the time and expense of bringing together people from distant places for face-to-face discussions; by the use of electronic mail, word processing, and even electronic filing; by calling upon the computer for such routine business functions as the assembly of financial data and preparation of quarterly financial and actuarial reports, statistical analyses, and payrolls. Above all, the computer improves managers' ability to evaluate alternative investment projects, financing plans, production scheduling, and inventory control. In sum, the computer has revolutionized the science of management. In manufacturing, it seems like the computer will more and more assist in product design and in the control of welding robots and assembly line equipment. Finally, the public at large encounters the effects of computers at the checkout counters of supermarkets and when they make flight reservations, rent an automobile, or buy an insurance policy.

It is sometimes said that the United States has been entering a postindustrial era since the end of World War II, that it is now best described as an information economy. If so, this would represent the most recent in a series of fundamental changes in the structure of the American economy. Change was slow at first, certainly relatively so, for agriculture dominated American economic life during the first three centuries. After the mid-1880s, the value of manufactured goods regularly exceeded that of agricultural products. From the point of view of national income generated by payments for labor, land, and natural resources, manufacturing continues to be the largest and most conspicuous sector. But its proportional size has declined somewhat in the years after World War II. In contrast, the service industries—trade, transportation and utilities, finance, insurance and real estate, and education, health, and government—have increased their share of national income. The provision of information alone, according to a recent calculation, accounted for 46 percent of the net income of the economy in 1967, and an even larger proportion, 53 percent, of all employee income.

There is one last consideration, by no means the least. While the public sector has played an important part in aiding the historical development of the American economy, the truth must remain that the overwhelming majority of decisions on what to produce, and how and where and when to produce it, have been made by private persons and businesses—that is to say, by the market. The powerful persistence of the nation's democracy is in part cause and in part effect of that truth. The high standards of living which most of its people have been able to achieve owe much to it, too. Which is another way of saying that the wealth of the nation has been created by its people because they have been free to work, save, invest, and innovate. But they have been free to do these things only because they have believed it important that they be free to do them. In the end, then, the nation's wealth has been the product of the nation's values, and of the people and institutions in which they are embodied.

4. A Brief Overview of Post–World War II Expansions

Stephen K. McNees

Excerpted from "The 1990–91 Recession in Historical Perspective," *New England Economic Review* (January/February 1992), pp. 13–20. Stephen K. McNees is president and economist at the Federal Reserve Bank of Boston.

In contrast to recessions, whose durations have been fairly uniform with a standard deviation of only 3.5 months, the duration of expansions have ranged from 12 months to 106 months, with a standard deviation of 33 months. It is not surprising, then, that the cumulative change in real GNP over the course of expansions has also varied widely—from a low of 3.3 percent in the 1980–81 expansion to an increase of more than 50 percent during the longest expansion in U.S. history, which took place throughout most of the 1960s.

Despite the variety of their overall dimensions, postwar expansions have been roughly similar in the pace of economic growth, especially in their early stages. The 1949:IV to 1953:II expansion, which included the Korean War, was by far the fastest expansion in the postwar period, even though it was fairly normal in duration and cumulative changes. Clearly the weakest was the one-year expansion between the 1980 and the 1981–82 recessions, the only postwar example of a double-dip recession or "W-shaped" business cycle. Excluding these extreme cases, whose abnormality is easy to understand, the average rate of growth over the first two years of the remaining six postwar expansions has been extremely uniform, ranging only from a low of 5.3 in 1954–57 to a high of 5.9 in 1961–69. Slow growth in the first year (such as in 1971) was followed by a pickup in the second year of the expansion; rapid first-year growth (such as occurred in the 1950s) has been followed by a tapering down in the second year. The 1949–53 and 1980–81 experiences clearly illustrate, however, that this uniform pattern is simply a regularity and not an inevitability. An extraordinary source of demand (such as was associated with the outbreak of the Korean War) or an extraordinarily restrictive policy (such as the successful attempt to combat double-digit inflation in 1980–81) can alter the "normal" tendency for economic expansions to proceed at a 5.5 to 6 percent annual rate during their first two years.

Do Recessions Contain the Seeds of Recoveries?

It has literally become a cliché to say that the recovery from the 1990–91 recession will be weak because the preceding recession itself was mild.

The history of postwar recessions and recoveries provides little support for that alleged relationship. Both the simple (numerical) and rank (ordering) correlations show little relationship between the severity of recessions and the strength of the first year, of the first two years, and of the total length of the following expansion.

The 1990–91 recession was clearly one of the mildest in the postwar era. Owing to slower growth in the working-age population and declines in the participation rate, the increase in the unemployment rate has been smaller than in any previous postwar recession. This relative mildness of the recession seems to run counter to fears that have been raised about the fragility of the financial system, the massive debt overhang, the wave of restructuring, and the record collapse in consumer confidence. These issues may yet emerge during the recovery or in the next recession.

One reason that the current state of the economy is perceived to be worse than it appears when compared to previous recessions may be that the 1990–91 recession was preceded by a long period of slow growth. The Center for International Business Cycle Research at Columbia University has designated February 1989 as the start of a period of "below-trend" increases in economic activity—the onset of a "growth recession." This designation is consistent with the fact that nonfarm business productivity peaked at the end of 1988. Thus, the mild recession was preceded by seventeen months of substandard growth, the longest of any postwar recession.

The first concerns about the longevity of the economic expansion that began in November 1982 arose after the 30 percent drop in stock prices on October 19, 1987. Such precipitous declines had often preceded periods of slower economic growth, if not actual recessions. Despite those concerns, most analysts correctly anticipated that economic growth would remain strong in 1988. (Real GNP did slow down from its rapid 5.4 percent rate in 1987, but the decline was in large part due to the serious drought in 1988, which was presumably unrelated to the collapse of equity prices.) During 1988, nonfarm production grew 3.3 percent, and the unemployment rate declined from 6 percent in October 1987 to 5.3 percent a year later. The economy was clearly running close to, if not beyond, its full productive capacity.

Slower real growth did materialize in 1989 along with fears that the slowdown would turn into a "hard landing" (that is, a recession). Despite an evident deceleration, real economic activity did increase fast enough to hold the unemployment rate below 5.5 percent until the cyclical peak in July 1990. This combination of small but positive real growth and steady unemployment was heralded as the achievement of a "soft landing."

The term "soft landing," however, had taken on the connotation not only of sustainable, positive growth but also of a deceleration of inflation. Unfortunately, starting in late 1989, the "core" rate of inflation started to accelerate: The twelve-month change rose fairly steadily from the 4 to 4 1/2 percent range, where it had stayed through much of the 1980s, to 5.1 percent in the year ending in July 1990, while the more volatile three-month rate rose sharply from 3.8 percent in September 1989 to 6.5 percent in March 1990.

Recent recessions have generally been preceded by a sharp acceleration of inflation and followed by a sharp deceleration. This pattern is not as universal as is commonly thought. The rate of inflation was clearly decelerating in the year before the 1948–49 and the 1953–54 recessions and fairly stable prior to the 1960–61 recession. The 1957–58 recession was the only early postwar recession immediately preceded by accelerating inflation. The 1990–91 recession falls roughly in the middle, relative to prior postwar experience: The acceleration of inflation prior to the cyclical peak was not nearly so pronounced as before the peaks in 1957, 1973, and 1980, though obviously much different from the decelerations in the year before the 1948 and the 1953 peaks. The experience mirrored the gradual yet distinct increases in the inflation rate that preceded the relatively mild recessions of 1960–61 and 1969–70.

In late July 1990, the other leg of the soft landing scenario was also called into question. Instead of expanding at a 2.2 percent annual rate, enough to hold the unemployment rate steady, revised data showed that real GNP had grown only 1 percent at an annual rate in the second quarter and had been growing at 1.5 percent or less for five consecutive quarters. These downward revisions cast the soft landing and its sustainability in an entirely new light. Instead of converging toward roughly the growth of productive capacity, the deceleration of economic growth had been sharper. Some new source of strength would have to emerge to break the deceleration momentum.

Rising inflation, weakening real growth, and the threat of war in the Persian Gulf combined to generate a precipitous drop in consumer sentiment—the University of Michigan's index dropped an unprecedented 32 percent from its April peak to its October low. This drop, along with sharp increases in gasoline prices, brought about sharp declines in auto production. From 1990:III to 1991:I, the production of autos and light trucks dropped 28 percent, or nearly $50 billion in 1982 dollars, nearly as much as the decline in real GNP over the entire 1990–91 recession.

Although the record drop in consumer sentiment did not portend a severe recession by postwar standards, it was associated with a disproportionate decline in personal consumption expenditures. The largest previous drop had been the 1.0 percent decline in 1980, which was also associated with a large deterioration in measures of consumer sentiment. Relative to the decline in real GNP during the 1990–91 recession, the 0.9 percent decline in total consumption expenditures was disproportionately large. This abnormally large decline in consumption was offset by stronger than normal performances in exports, federal purchases, and producers' durable equipment. The 1990–91 recession was milder than average, mainly because the inventory cycle was more muted than in most previous postwar recessions.

The period leading up to the 1990–91 recession was a clear exception to the previous postwar experience. Whereas the average lead time had been only one month and the longest prior lead time only four months (in 1960 and 1969), short-term interest rates peaked in the spring of 1989, sixteen months before the business cycle peak. Prior to the 1990–91 recession, analysts could have correctly reasoned that no postwar recession had ever occurred after an extended period of declining short-term interest rates. It would seem a mistake to attribute the 1990–91 recession to rising interest rates; the proximate cause seemed more likely to lie elsewhere. Even though a sharper decline in rates might have offset the unidentified "causal" factor, it is difficult to imagine that a much larger decline would have been feasible at the time, in the environment of low unemployment and rising inflation.

Although forecasters took longer to recognize that a recession had begun than in 1973 or 1981, and far longer than in 1980, they were much more accurate in gauging its severity and duration, if this recession did end in the spring of 1991, as has been assumed here. With the possible exception of the 1980 recession, forecasts made near the peak tend to underestimate its severity. The underestimation of the 1990–91 recession was trivial, however, especially when compared to forecasts of the severe recessions of 1973–75 and 1981–82.

It is still too soon to write the history of the 1990 recession, let alone of even the early stages of the subsequent expansion. If the recession ended in the spring of 1991, the early recovery has been far weaker than previous recoveries. In other recoveries, economic activity has started to increase rapidly at about the same time that the recession ended (except for the expansion that began in 1954, when the lag was only a few months). In contrast, most of the monthly measures of economic activity, such as payroll employment, have increased very little since their decline ended in the spring of 1991. The composite indexes of both leading and coincident indicators have increased far less at this stage of the cycle than in all earlier expansions. The most unusual feature of the 1990–91 recession may well be that it was both preceded and followed by periods of subpar growth, so that the "growth recession" that began in early 1989 has persisted for nearly three years.

5. Science and Technology
The National Science Foundation

Excerpted from *Science and Technology: Annual Report to the Congress*, August 1978, pp. 1–33.

Americans can be justly proud of their role in the advancement of science. For example, U.S. scientists author almost 40 percent of the world's scientific and technical publications. There has been some worry, though, that the continued preeminence of American science is threatened. In the late 1960s and early 1970s there was a decline in real dollars in the level of support for U.S. basic research. It was believed that this trend would lead to reduced scientific productivity in the future.

Although those involved in basic research pursue their work to better understand nature, scientific achievement, in many cases, becomes linked to technological innovation and economic development. In a simple model of economic change, the sequence proceeds from basic research to applied research and development, then to technological innovation, and finally to economic growth and the increase in social welfare. Of course, our actual system is much more complex and subtle than this model implies. Often applied research or even development will open new avenues of inquiry for basic science, and all basic research cannot be expected to lead directly to technological advance. Nonetheless, a positive relation exists between research and development and increased social and economic welfare. Numerous recent advances in technology derive from recent results in basic science:

(1) Advances continue to be made in the development of large-scale integrated circuits, the electronic "brains" of control devices and computers. As the density of electronic components in the silicon chips that constitute the circuits has grown, the speed of operations has increased and the costs have declined dramatically. The advent of low-cost computers that this advance allows may well bring about remarkable changes in our society.

(2) The prenatal diagnosis of genetic disorders represents a major recent technological breakthrough in clinical genetic counseling. Sampling of amniotic fluid, visualization of the fetus, fetal blood sampling, and screening of maternal blood provide new methods of diagnosis of disorders. Not only do these techniques promote informed decision making in genetic counseling, but they also add new knowledge on the nature of genetic disease.

(3) A new technology, integrated optics, promises to transform our

communications systems by allowing the high-speed transfer of vast amounts of information using a beam of light. This wide-band communications system will make possible, for example, entirely new systems in the home for communication, education, and entertainment.

As science and technology advance and we unravel more of nature's secrets, some people may ask: "Can science solve our major problems?" The experience of recent decades suggests that often too much has been expected of our scientific and technological breakthroughs. Consider the different expectations: antibiotics would wipe out disease; the atom would provide an endless source of energy; the green revolution would conquer world hunger. Failure of technology to meet our expectations is, in part, a reflection of the fact that each new advance serves not only to satisfy old needs, but also to create new needs almost simultaneously.

The most significant thing we have learned may be that technological solutions are unlikely to be permanent or complete solutions. Antibiotics have curbed disease. But as they have helped in making inroads on the historic scourges of mankind's health, other diseases—cancer, cardiovascular disease, diabetes—have moved to the forefront. The atom has provided a new and important source of energy but at the possible cost of saddling future generations with the surveillance and safeguarding of nuclear waste. Each advance seems to generate new problems as it solves old ones. And in many cases, the new problems involve thorny institutional, cultural, or political dimensions that are difficult to resolve satisfactorily.

We are coming to realize that science and technology by themselves are often inadequate to insure enhanced social welfare. As a result, we are now more cautious and more sophisticated in our assessment of technology. We now demand critical analyses of what an advance can and cannot be expected to do, in what time frame, and with what social and cultural implications. And we try to count costs as well as benefits. Indeed, our frame of reference has expanded so that we often try to assess the distant effects of a new technology—economic, environmental, and social—before the technology has even been shown to be workable. Moreover, while decisions to encourage a new technology may not be irreversible, they can involve such large commitments of resources—money, people, and facilities—that careful analysis and thorough examination of issues are required to insure that our use of those resources is wise and in the public interest.

As a leading nation in the global system, the United States has a particularly important role in nurturing scientific and technological advance. The success of our effort hinges in large part on the research and development programs of the federal government. These programs provide support for more than half of all the nation's research and development work, most of which is conducted by our industry and our universities.

Obviously, the size, shape, and thrust of these programs are crucial. It is appropriate that we take a new look at our federal research and development policy in the context of past research and development choices and our current national position.

Viewing research and development as an investment choice implies recognizing that continuity and long-range support are essential to the entire scientific and technological enterprise. Although research and development should neither be disengaged from the federal budget cycle nor be locked into inflexible plans, the design and emphasis of our research and development programs should not be rehashed and redirected in each budget cycle.

Research and Development and Economic Progress

Insufficient research and development and technological innovation have been cited as possible contributors to unsatisfactory U.S. economic progress. Somewhat paradoxically, while the level of research and development and innovation in the United States has been called insufficient, the level of investment is substantial and the performer base is diverse. In absolute terms, the United States supports more than 50 percent of the research and development performed in the world. The question is whether that investment is adequate from a social and economic point of view, and whether available evidence suggests a reconsideration of existing government policies bearing on science, technology, and innovation.

Recently, economists have attempted to assess the contribution of research, development, and technological innovation to output and productivity growth. Results provide general support for a strong positive contribution. Research advances scientific knowledge, which, in turn, enhances the intellectual skills individuals bring to their work and provides a source of ideas for innovative technologies. These technologies lead to new and improved products, services, and production processes. They in turn contribute to a more satisfactory lifestyle and enhance the working skills of individuals.

A noted investigation of long-term U.S. economic performance by Edward Denison has indicated that about 50 percent of measurable U.S. economic growth between 1948 and 1969 derived from advances in knowledge. Denison defines "advances" in knowledge as:

> what is usually defined as technological knowledge—knowledge concerning the physical properties of things, and of how to make, combine, or use them in a physical sense. It also includes "managerial knowledge"—knowledge of business organization and of management techniques construed in the broadest sense. Advances in knowledge comprise

> knowledge originating in this country and abroad, and knowledge obtained in any way: by organized research, by individual research workers and inventors, and by simple observation and experience.

This computation does not take into account improvements which are not measured by national income accounting techniques. Examples would include major qualitative changes in products (e.g., better antibiotics) or developments of new forms of business organization (e.g., self-service stores and supermarkets in retail trade).

A recent study of select U.S. industries shows a strong association between the ratios of their research and development spending to sales and their growth of labor productivity and output. In addition, other empirical research studies have demonstrated substantial increases in output associated with expenditures for research and development (netting out increased inputs of labor and capital). These studies show $30 to $50 increases in annual output associated with $100 investment in research and development. These findings come from studies of chemicals, petroleum refining, and agriculture.

Investment in research and development can result in greater productivity and output not only for the firms developing the new or improved technology but for the buyers as well. This diffusion of benefits has been noted especially for machinery (e.g., computers, electrical generating equipment) and for materials (e.g., plastics) or components (e.g., semiconductors). One recent estimate of these benefits by Nestor E. Terlecky for the National Planning Association suggests that for manufacturing during the 1960s, the average productivity returns to research and development conducted by firms in the producing industry amounted to about 30 percent per year; the benefits accruing to firms purchasing from the producers of technological innovations were about 50 percent. Another study by Edwin Mansfield et al. of seventeen modest technological innovations showed that more than half of the measurable economic returns from these innovations went to the buyers and users.

Thus, there is persuasive empirical evidence (although surrounded by significant limitations) that research and technological innovation have had a significant positive effect on economic growth and productivity increases in the United States.

Rationale for Federal Actions to Enhance Economic Growth through Research and Development and Innovation

When the federal government is not the sole or primary consumer of research and development results, the existence of market or institutional imperfections provides a primary reason for considering government action. These imperfections arise when private decision making does not include all the costs and benefits of an action. Private markets and institutions may be unable to assure effective private property rights in such areas as research and development and technological innovation. These rights are required for markets to work effectively. The cost of acquiring necessary information about the feasibility of technical innovation may be prohibitive to firms or industries. Uncertainty, risk, and the need for large-scale investments may lead private firms to invest less than the socially desirable amounts in research and development and technology. Economic and financial conditions may lead some institutions to skew their investments away from basic or longer-term research toward the more applied and shorter-term. Thus both the level and the mix of research and development and innovation may diverge from that which would yield higher economic returns to society. If this is the case, then government (or other collective) action in the science and technology domain may be appropriate and necessary to correct market imperfections or compensate for unintended effects on research and development of government or private policy in other domains.

Another topic of discussion has been whether existing fiscal programs of the federal government provide incentives or disincentives to invest in research and development and technological innovation. Most prominent in these discussions are federal policies affecting capital formation, such as investment tax credits and federal credit programs. Positions have been advanced that changes in federal tax policies and shortage of venture capital have diminished activities for the development and marketing of new technologies. Whether the venture capital problem is one of under-supply or of unintended effects of certain types of securities and tax regulations is presently unclear. Economists generally agree that there has not been enough study and research with respect to the influence of these policies.

6. Overview of U.S. Science and Technology

The National Science Board

Excerpted from *Science and Engineering Indicators—1989* (Washington, D.C.: U.S. Government Printing Office, 1989), pp. 2–14.

The decade-long (1975–85) uninterrupted expansion of support for U.S. science and technology (S&T) has leveled off in recent years (1985–89).

With some important exceptions, most indicators of U.S. S&T show significant slowdowns and downturns. For example:

(1) Growth rates have slowed in both research and development (R&D) funding and science and engineering (S/E) personnel.

(2) While the United States still spends more on R&D than the next four industrialized countries combined, some international competitors (e.g., Japan and West Germany) have drawn ahead of the U.S. in terms of R&D expenditures as a percentage of gross national product.

(3) In several areas, U.S. producers of high-tech goods have lost significant global market shares.

(4) National and international indicators of U.S. school mathematics and science performance show little improvement, despite continuing major reform efforts.

(5) U.S. university and college freshmen show a downward trend in their choice of undergraduate majors in some S/E fields. Although undergraduate S/E degrees awarded have remained at about 30 percent of all bachelor's degrees awarded for the past three years, the freshman shift away from S/E majors portends reduced S/E degrees in coming years.

(6) Increases in graduate S/E enrollments (in doctorate-granting universities) slowed from an average annual rate of 2 percent from 1980 to 1987 to 1 percent from 1987 to 1988.

(7) Foreign students continued to increase (and U.S. citizens to decrease) their share of graduate S/E enrollments and S/E Ph.D. degrees granted by U.S. universities in all broad S/E fields except psychology.

(8) One area of continuing growth (albeit at a slightly slower rate than that of the past decade) is support for basic research and R&D in universities and colleges. This support has no doubt assisted the United States in maintaining its share of world scientific and technical literature.

Support for U.S. R&D continues to grow in constant-dollar terms but at a much slower rate than has been the case for the previous decade and a half. Although total R&D expenditures grew at an annual rate of almost 6 percent from 1975 to 1985, the rate of growth for 1986 to 1989 is estimated at about 2 percent per annum.

The slower pace of U.S. R&D growth in recent years is also reflected in a U.S. lag of three consecutive years behind Japanese and West German R&D expenditures as a percentage of GNP.

The recent slowdown in funding growth is most dramatic for the de-

velopment and applied research components of R&D (1 percent estimated annual growth rate from 1986 to 1989); basic research expenditures slowed only slightly to an estimated annual growth rate of 3
percent (in constant dollars). These trends are largely due to two sets of
policy decisions. Federal S&T policy has moved toward reducing the rate
of increase in defense R&D spending and toward maintaining growth in
basic research and academic R&D.

While the United States continues to be the world's foremost supplier
for high-tech products, its lead is shrinking. The U.S. share of global
markets for high-tech goods, which declined during the 1970s and then
recovered in the first half of the 1980s, showed renewed weakness in the
latest period measured (1985–86). During this period, U.S. producers lost
both domestic and foreign market shares. However, the U.S. trade balance in high-tech goods showed a slight upturn back into a positive
balance in 1987; this followed a seven-year period of decline and a first-
ever deficit in 1986. In terms of innovation, U.S. patent applications and
awards—both indicators of a country's S&T innovation—have increased
in the recent period, but not as rapidly as foreign patenting in the United
States.

U.S. R&D Investments in a World Context

In the world context, the United States spends more on R&D than the
next four largest countries—Japan, West Germany, France, and the
United Kingdom—combined. Over the past decade, the United States has
more or less maintained its share of the combined R&D budgets of the
five countries: 56 percent in 1975 versus 54 percent in 1986. This share
was significantly reduced from the 68 percent share the United States
enjoyed in 1966.

Despite the differences in total expenditures, in 1987 the major non-
communist industrialized countries each invested approximately the
same percentage of their GNPs in R&D. Both Japan and West Germany
have now exceeded the United States on this indicator for 3 years (1985–
87).

The nature of R&D investments has an important bearing on their
economic contributions. If only nondefense R&D is considered, Japan
and West Germany have been ahead of the United States for nearly two
decades; in addition, their rate of civilian R&D investment as a percentage of GNP has been rising faster than that of the United States since
1981. U.S. investment in nondefense R&D as a percentage of GNP has
declined for at least two years.

The overall rate of increase of U.S. R&D expenditures has slowed considerably in recent years. While total national expenditures for R&D grew

at an annual rate of almost 6 percent from 1975 to 1985 (in constant dollars), the rate of growth for the most recent period (1986–89) is estimated at only about 2 percent annually. The rapid rate of increase of development funding in the early 1980s has shrunk to an estimated annual rate of less than 1 percent in 1989. On the other hand, funding for basic research has continued to grow at only slightly less than its 1975–85 rate.

The massive increase in defense development expenditures from 1980 to 1985 was reduced to a very small growth rate by 1989. In civilian R&D, basic research maintained a significant growth rate in both periods, while civilian applied research and development expenditures remained approximately constant from 1986 to 1989 after suffering large cuts between 1980 and 1985.

Human Resources

International Comparison

Recent years (1984–86) have seen a slowing in the rate of growth of U.S. scientists and engineers engaged in R&D per ten thousand workers in the labor force. After two decades of rapid growth, Japan has now caught up with—and, in fact, slightly exceeds—the United States on this indicator. Japan has sixty-seven researchers per ten thousand, compared with sixty-six for the United States. France and West Germany continue to increase at about the same rate as the United States, while in the United Kingdom, the growth of researchers in the labor force has remained flat since 1981.

Closely paralleling the international comparative data on R&D funding, the United States in 1986 awarded more first academic degrees in natural science and engineering (NS/E) than the next four largest non-communist countries combined—about 214,000 persons versus about 175,000, respectively. The five countries also vary considerably in the proportion of first academic degrees that are in NS/E fields, as well as in the relative proportions of natural science to engineering degrees. The United States and Japan have the smallest proportions of all first university degrees in NS/E fields (20 percent and 26 percent, respectively) while France and the United Kingdom have the highest proportions (47 percent and 40 percent, respectively). Among the NS/E fields in Japan and France, first engineering degrees outnumber natural science degrees—in Japan, by a factor of four to one. In 1986, Japan, which has half the population of the United States, generated about 73,000 engineers, a number almost equal to U.S. engineering degrees awarded in that year (77,000). In contrast, in both the United States and the United Kingdom, natural science degrees outnumber engineering degrees by nearly two to one.

Private Sector Employment of U.S. Scientists and Engineers

Between 1977 and 1988, S/E employment in the private sector expanded at more than twice the rate of total employment. This trend encompassed major changes in the occupational and industrial mix of S/E employment. For example, S/E employment in services-producing industries grew 103 percent over the period, compared to a 38 percent growth in total services employment. S/E employment growth in the goods-producing sector stemmed from an increased share of a declining total in manufacturing jobs.

The expansion of the services-producing industries has been a key factor in the extraordinarily rapid growth of computer specialists between 1980 and 1988.

Women in S/E

Women scientists and engineers represented about 13 percent of the S/E workforce in 1986, up from 11 percent in 1980. By field, women accounted for a much larger share of employment among scientists than among engineers—26 percent versus 4 percent. Between 1980 and 1986, women experienced small percentage losses in the mathematics and environmental sciences but achieved sizable gains in the physical and life sciences. Small percentage gains were made in all engineering subfields.

7. Technology and Natural Resource Use
John F. Walker and Harold G. Vatter

John F. Walker is professor of economics and Harold G. Vatter is professor emeritus of economics at Portland State University.

Can the advance of technology overcome costwise the depletion of natural resources that it, together with accelerating human consumption, perpetrates upon the planet? The so-called doomsday scenario predicts long-run exhaustion; the bulk of the economics profession maintains that technological progress has always found needed substitutes for, and lowered costs of, declining supplies, and probably will in the future. The economists deny the grim Malthusian postulate of diminishing returns (rising costs) of the natural resource exploitation that accompanies population growth.

Three decades ago this issue was tackled in a work by Harold Barnett and Chandler Morse for Resources for the Future. They concluded that the notion of an absolute limit to natural resources availability is untenable, and that for the United States the unit costs of total extractive product fell substantially over the long-run period 1807 to 1957.

The issue continues to be widely argued, and the conclusion seems to be much the same as that drawn by Barnett and Morse. For example, the *New York Times Magazine* (December 2, 1990) reports a wager made in 1980 that the price in 1990 of five metals would or would not rise. Behind the wager between the pessimistic ecologist Paul Ehrlich and the optimistic economist Julian Simon was the old Malthusian prediction of long-run rising costs for extraction of a fixed quantum of natural resources. The agreed upon resources in this wager were copper, chrome, nickel, tin, and tungsten. The agreed upon question was: Will their prices rise or fall over the decade of the 1980s? Simon won the bet: the prices of all fell, even when adjusted for changes in the general price index (i.e., prices in constant dollars). While a decade is not a very long run, the results seriously threatened again the belief that a combination of population rise and per capita natural resource increase would not be offset by technology's ability to lower unit costs. Related issues such as pollution and technology's capacity to develop substitutes were outside the scope of the wager's strict conditions, however.

8. In the Shadow of the Bomb
Dick Russell

Copyright Fall, 1990, *The Amicus Journal*, a quarterly publication of the Natural Resources Defense Council, 40 West 20th Street, New York, NY 10011. Excerpted and reprinted with permission. Dick Russell is a contributing editor of *The Amicus Journal*.

The Department of Energy (DOE) acknowledged that over 540,000 curies of iodine 131 were "inadvertently" released into the atmosphere from Hanford's (Washington state) nuclear reactors between 1944 and the mid-1950s. Compare that to the 1979 accident at Three Mile Island, during which about fifteen curies were emitted. Families living near Hanford in the path of prevailing southwest winds may have received radiation doses over the years ten times higher than did residents living near Chernobyl at the time it melted down.

Few in the shadow of the bomb would disagree that Hanford—as well as the sixteen other sites nationwide whose function is some aspect of nuclear weapons production—comprise "an incredible mess." The DOE's fiscal 1991 budget contains over $3 billion to address environmental problems of the nuclear weapons complex, "a small down payment," according to the congressional General Accounting Office (GAO). Already over 3,600 radioactive and toxic waste sites have been identified around the country, as well as nearly 400 contaminated buildings and structures. Many of these sites are located in or near major metropolitan areas, and in ten states groundwater polluted by weapons-production waste poses a threat to public health. Over the next generation, some experts estimate the total cleanup tab could exceed $150 billion. The DOE's latest budget estimate, which includes replacing and refurbishing the facilities necessary to keep its weapons mission alive, calls for roughly $244 billion between now and 2010.

Three of the more critical weapons-assembly installations—Hanford; Savannah River, South Carolina; and the Rocky Flats plant near Denver—have now been shut down for extended periods because of safety and environmental problems, virtually halting the production of new nuclear warheads.

A tour of Hanford, a 560-square-mile "reservation" of arid desert half the size of Rhode Island, offers a staggering picture of just what the DOE is up against. Founded in 1943 to make plutonium for the Nagasaki A-bomb, Hanford saw the last of its processing plants closed in December 1988 for safety reasons and a lack of plutonium. The legacy of these plants and nine now-mothballed nuclear reactors includes two-thirds of the high-level radioactive waste from weapons production in the entire United States, as well as cleanup costs that could eventually mount to over $50 billion. For many years, cost cutting led Hanford to routinely dump millions of gallons of radioactive and chemically hazardous wastes into unlined trenches; surface contamination is still spreading by twenty acres per year. But the most frightening scenario concerns the waste "tank farm," where incompatible chemicals were combined over the years to reduce waste volume and to alleviate the need for new storage capacity. The risk of an explosive reaction, similar to that which forced ten thousand people to evacuate hundreds of square miles in the Soviet Ural Mountains in 1957, is considered by DOE to "present a serious situation, if not an imminent hazard."

Since World War II, the United States has spent over $250 billion to produce some sixty thousand warheads. The Manhattan Project, the effort that culminated in the construction of the first atomic bomb, has evolved into a vast industry, employing over 100,000 workers at seventeen locations in thirteen states; Savannah River, for example, is the largest single-plant employer in South Carolina. During the Reagan era, DOE revved up production, ignoring safety and environmental problems at antiquated facilities. By 1988, when a series of articles in the *New York Times* helped bring the staggering catalogue of the complex's woes to national attention, the bill was rapidly coming due.

While media attention has focused on the imbroglio at the big sites like Hanford and Savannah River, these are really but the tip of the pollution iceberg. Indeed, many smaller DOE facilities—there are seventy-eight around the nation—are located close to major population centers and are leaking toxic chemicals into the environment. Ninety-seven hazardous waste sites have been identified at a plant in Paducah, Kentucky; domestic water wells that directly border operations at New York's Brookhaven National Laboratories on Long Island have shown contamination; and the DOE announced that cleaning up PCBs and asbestos at Kansas City's Allied Signal Plant over the next five years will cost about $168 million, 43 percent more than it estimated only six months earlier.

A 1988 study by a House appropriations subcommittee revealed that, on average, DOE's cost estimates for various major projects increased by an average of about 500 percent between the time of proposal and either completion or cancellation. With the environmental bill ever escalating, somebody stands to get rich off the government—namely, the DOE's site contractors. With orders for military hardware on the downswing, corporations like Lockheed are expressing interest in getting involved in weapons plant cleanup and modernization. Westinghouse, as its business declined on the commercial nuclear power front, moved in to become the DOE's lead contractor at Hanford, Savannah River, and Fernald.

Between the DOE and Westinghouse, there are signs of discord. They surfaced first at Hanford, where the DOE's Tiger Team faulted the company for withholding information about the potential for an explosion at the tank farm and for continuing to maintain that such a risk was unlikely.

The DOE's increasingly strained relationship with its contractors began with a debacle at Rocky Flats, where, in June 1989, the Federal Bureau of Investigation conducted a midnight raid after being tipped that plant operators and DOE officials were hiding evidence of widespread radioactive contamination. Six months later, the Rockwell International Corporation was fired by DOE during a continuing probe of the firm's suspended criminal environmental law violation. The *Denver Post* revealed in a copyrighted story that Rockwell had previously "reaped $49.2 million in bonuses . . . at the same time it risked a major natural gas explosion, misplaced plutonium, and exposed workers to unsafe levels of radioactivity." The article's tale of the DOE-Rockwell alliance through the eighties continued: "The Energy Department once awarded Rockwell a $3.3 million bonus at the same time the Environmental Protection Agency was fining the plant $111,000 for pollution violations."

Little wonder, then, that the states have begun pushing for a much greater role in oversight of their weapons plant activities. At places like Hanford, where the DOE, EPA, and Washington Department of Ecology have entered into a comprehensive cleanup and compliance agreement, a battleground is almost certain to develop over who will certify the point at which a cleanup is really complete.

Rocky Flats, whose main mission until its shutdown over safety concerns was making the plutonium "triggers" for nuclear warheads, is another world from the austerity of Hanford. Paved streets within the plant have names like Cottonwood and Central Avenue. Take Safety Home With You, says a sign. But safety problems at Rocky Flats are no less severe than at Hanford. Alongside the outdoor 903 Pad, airborne releases of about 1.7 ounces of plutonium have occurred over the plant's twenty-eight-year history. The plutonium escaped from leaking barrels into the high winds blowing toward suburban Denver. Another 1.5 ounces of plutonium entered the atmosphere from plant fires in 1957 and 1969.

The DOE acknowledges that some of the surrounding area, including parts of Denver, has been contaminated by plutonium particles but says the risk to residents is minimal. Dr. Edward Martell, a radiochemist at the National Center for Atmospheric Research in Boulder, believes otherwise. The emissions, estimates Martell, are ten to twenty times higher than the government has stated. "Plutonium-induced cancers in people may take twenty or thirty years to develop. In effect, everybody living within eight or ten miles east and southeast of Rocky Flats may be a guinea pig."

As citizen lawsuits mount and government agencies fight for hegemony and their contractors chart new territories, the debate over the future of the nuclear weapons complex goes on.

CHAPTER III

Changes in the Structure of the Economy

9. Changes in Industry Shares of National Output
Charles J. Haulk

Excerpted from *Economic Review* (Federal Reserve Bank of Atlanta, September/October 1978), pp. 95–98.

The composition of national output—that is, the shares of income originating in various industries—has important implications for overall labor productivity and real economic growth. Within the last seventy-three years, there have been some significant changes in the makeup of U.S. output, partly secular and partly cyclical. These shifts have been dictated by alterations of the mix of goods and services demanded by consumers and by the government. The following analysis of specific changes in the composition of demand and output and their relationship to productivity and income growth should broaden our understanding of the past, present, and prospective path of U.S. economic growth.

History

The most obvious changes in national output mix that have occurred since 1904 have been the dramatic decline in agriculture's share and the rise in government's share. Other less pronounced shifts have been increases in the manufacturing and service shares and decreases in the shares of the group which includes transportation, communication, and utilities and the group consisting of finance, insurance, and real estate. The wholesale and retail trade share has remained almost unchanged over the years, while the combined share of mining and contract construction has fallen slightly.

The Commerce Department's official national income statistics allow us to track changes in industry shares since 1929 in greater detail. Agriculture continues its decline but not until after World War II. From 1945–49 to 1965–69, agriculture's average share fell from 9.2 percent of national income to 3.3 percent, a 60 percent drop in just twenty years. The share of income originating in mining and construction stood at 6.4 percent in 1975–77, down only slightly from 6.9 percent in 1929.

Manufacturing provided 26.1 percent of national income in the three years 1975–77, compared to 25.4 percent in 1929. However, the story of manufacturing is more interesting than the slight change would suggest. After falling sharply to average 20.8 percent in the years 1920–34, the manufacturing share began to climb, recovering its 1929 share in the late 1930s, and grew rapidly during World War II. After the war, the manufacturing share slipped for two years and then began an uptrend that continued through the mid-fifties, bringing the sector's share to a high of 32 percent. For the next fifteen years, the share of manufacturing was fairly stable, fluctuating only slightly around 30 percent. Then, in the early seventies, the share dropped suddenly to 26.5 percent and, since 1975, has averaged 26.1 percent. The manufacturing sector, more than any other, has followed the swings in the business cycle. (Kuznets made the same observation in his study of industry shares in the period 1919–38.) Largely because of inventory adjustment problems, manufacturing has had a greater sensitivity to and a greater impact on total income variations than any other sector.

The wholesale and retail trade share rose in the late 1930s and in the years just after World War II but, for the most part, accounts for a consistent 15.0 to 16.0 percent of national income. Services' share has exhibited a long-run upward trend and seems to increase most rapidly during economic slowdowns. The finance, insurance, and real estate group declined sharply and has only partially recovered. Starting at 15.2 percent in 1929, this share held steady through most of the thirties and then dropped abruptly to 8.5 percent in the late thirties and early forties. The share was fairly constant during the late forties, rose to 11 percent in the mid-Fifties, and has retained that level since (see Table 9.1).

The share of government increased dramatically in the thirties and early forties due to the Depression and war, reaching 13.4 percent in the 1940–44 period. It declined through 1954 but then grew steadily to 16 percent until 1970. In 1977, it fell below 15 percent for the first time since 1968. Transfer payments are not included in government's share.

Table 9.1

Shares of National Income, 1929–77 (in percent)

					Five year averages for the years ending in:						
	1929	1934	1939	1944	1949	1954	1959	1964	1969	1974	1977
Agriculture	9.9	8.5	9.6	8.4	9.2	6.7	4.6	4.0	3.3	3.5	3.1
Mining and construction	6.9	4.8	5.3	5.4	6.0	7.2	7.0	6.5	6.4	6.6	6.4
Manufacturing	25.4	20.8	24.4	31.9	29.2	31.9	31.3	29.8	29.9	26.5	26.1
Transport, communication, and utilities	10.9	11.9	10.2	9.0	8.4	8.5	8.4	8.4	7.9	7.8	7.8
Trade	15.7	15.8	17.0	15.5	17.8	16.1	15.7	15.4	15.0	15.3	15.7
Service	10.1	12.0	10.3	7.9	8.8	8.8	10.0	11.2	12.0	12.8	13.6
Finance, insurance, and real estate	15.2	15.0	11.3	8.5	8.5	9.6	11.0	11.6	11.3	11.5	11.6
Government	5.9	10.8	11.4	13.4	12.2	11.2	12.0	13.3	14.3	15.9	15.4

Source: U. S. Department of Commerce.

Why the Changes in Industry Shares?

In the short run, industry share changes can result from supply variations and special economic conditions which lead to rapid or slow growth in a particular sector. A protracted strike in the auto industry, for example, could cause the manufacturing sector's share of national income to drop temporarily. Stockpiling of coal in anticipation of higher prices or shortages could cause a temporary run-up in the mining share; speculative commercial or residential construction can lead to a momentary increase in the share of construction and real estate. However, over the long run, the composition of the sources of national output is primarily dictated by the composition of final demand for the nation's output. To some degree, the quantities and kinds of resources available and technology impact the relative sizes of industry shares. International trade possibilities can, to some degree, offset national resource constraints and alter the distribution of demand.

Since domestic consumption accounts for the largest portion of total output and reflects long-run changes in tastes and incomes, which, in turn, determine the composition of output, changes in these consumption patterns are the principal determinants of the shifts in the various industry shares. Changes in government expenditures indirectly reflect changes in the consumption preferences of the electorate.

Since 1929, there have been several noteworthy changes in consumer expenditure patterns. Although the proportion spent on goods was nearly the same in 1977 (54.5 percent) as in 1929 (55.5 percent), durable goods claimed a larger share, and nondurables, a smaller portion. Throughout the Depression and the years following the war, nondurables took an increasing share of consumer outlays, while durables declined in importance. But durables consumption climbed sharply between 1945 and 1950 and then leveled off at the roughly 15 percent share they've held since, fluctuating downward in recessions (see Table 9.2).

Nondurables' stake in personal outlays has fallen steeply since 1950. Food and apparel, in particular, have consumed dwindling shares of consumer budgets. Increased importation of textiles and apparel has further dampened demand for domestic production of these goods, reducing their importance to national output. Surprisingly, the shares of both consumer spending and total production accounted for by petroleum and coal products were slightly lower last year than in 1950, even though consumption of petroleum products has been at historically high levels ever since the oil embargo and quadrupling of prices.

The share of consumer outlays marked for services has regained its 1929 level only in the past couple of years. The rise in the goods' share prior to 1950 came at the expense of services, whose claim dropped nearly thirteen percentage points. Since then, strong increases in the pro-

Table 9.2

Percentage Shares of Consumption Expenditures

	1950	1955	1960	1965	1970	1975	1976	1977
Durable goods	16.0	16.2	13.3	14.6	13.7	13.6	14.5	14.8
Nondurable goods	51.1	48.4	46.5	43.8	42.8	41.7	40.5	39.7
Services	32.8	36.3	40.2	41.5	43.5	44.7	45.0	45.5
Food, includes eating out	22.7	25.4	24.2	22.5	21.6	21.1	20.2	19.9
Clothing	10.2	9.2	8.1	7.8	7.5	7.2	7.0	6.8
Housing	11.3	13.5	14.8	15.2	15.2	15.4	15.3	15.3
Household operation	15.2	14.5	14.2	14.3	14.2	14.6	14.6	14.7
Medical care	4.7	5.2	6.2	7.0	8.1	8.9	9.7	9.8
Personal business	3.4	3.8	4.4	4.6	4.7	5.2	5.1	5.0
Transportation	13.2	13.6	13.0	13.5	12.6	13.0	13.7	14.3
Recreation	5.8	5.5	5.5	6.0	6.6	6.8	6.6	6.7
Private education	0.9	1.0	1.2	1.3	1.6	1.5	1.5	1.6
Religion and welfare	1.2	1.3	1.5	1.4	1.4	1.2	1.3	1.3
Foreign travel and other	0.3	0.6	0.7	0.7	0.8	0.5	0.4	0.4

Source: U.S. Department of Commerce.

portion of family budgets spent for education and health care and a moderate rise in the personal business and recreation components have contributed to the rebound of services' share. Outlays for housing gained share until 1965 and held virtually constant as a percentage of consumption through 1977. The phenomenon of service expenditures rising relative to spending for nondurable goods has continued unabated if not stronger than ever in the past five years, in contrast to declines in earlier periods of similarly show real income growth.

Economic Impact of Industry Share Changes

Industry share changes have important implications for future economic growth prospects. The principal impact is on labor productivity—if an industry which has strong productivity potential loses part of its share of national income to an industry with little or no productivity growth, the result will be slower overall growth in output per worker. This is in essence what has happened to the U.S. economy since 1950. Two major productivity-enhancing sectors—manufacturing and agriculture—have lost relative output shares to services and government.

For instance, from 1972 to 1977, real output per worker rose only 2.25 percent, less than 0.5 percent per year. At the same time, the manufacturing sector's average share of national output was the lowest of any five-year period since the Great Depression. The results of a statistical analysis (multiple regression) support the notion that declining manufacturing and agriculture shares, combined with rising service and government shares, have led to slower growth in both productivity and real output.

10. Taking In Each Other's Laundry—
The Service Economy
Lynne E. Browne

Excerpted from *New England Economic Review* (Federal Reserve Bank of Boston, July/August 1986), pp. 20–31. Lynne E. Browne is vice president and economist at the Federal Reserve Bank of Boston.

Since 1969 the share of U.S. employment represented by manufacturing industries has fallen—from 25 percent to 19 percent in 1985. Since 1979 the level of manufacturing employment has fallen as well. This decline follows a long period, roughly sixty years, in which manufacturing's share of employment, while fluctuating with the business cycle, was fairly constant and the level of manufacturing employment increased at the same rate as total employment.

The sectors of the economy that have increased their employment shares since 1969 are trade; finance, insurance, and real estate; and services. The increase in the share of employment in services has been particularly pronounced and is almost a mirror image of the decline in manufacturing's share. Services now account for a larger fraction of U.S. employment—about 24 percent—than any other major industry group.

Many view the growing share of employment in services and the decreasing share in manufacturing with alarm. To some extent, this unease reflects the fact that the decline in manufacturing's share since 1979 has also been a decline in the number of employed in manufacturing, resulting in considerable hardship for those displaced. However, many would be concerned over the shift to services even if it were not accompanied by cutbacks in manufacturing. Services are seen as providing low-wage jobs with little prospect for advancement. In addition, services are commonly thought to be dependent upon the growth of other sectors, especially manufacturing, rather than capable of generating growth. They live off the rest of the economy rather than contribute to it. These attitudes towards services are summed up in the popular description of services as "taking in each other's laundry."

Definition of Services

Services is one of the "service-producing" industries. The others are trade; finance, insurance, and real estate; transportation, communication and public utilities; and government. The output of all these industries is intangible services—financial services, transportation services, telephone services, medical services—rather than tangible goods. The goods-producing industries are manufacturing, mining, and construction. Agriculture, forestry, and fishing are occasionally considered goods-producing industries but more frequently are treated as a separate category.

Table 10.1 shows the shifting composition of U.S. employment among these sectors and Bureau of Labor Statistics (BLS) projections of future shifts. The share of employment in service-producing industries has been rising steadily. In the 1960s it was government that accounted for most of the increase, with the agricultural sector experiencing a large decrease in both its share of employment and the actual numbers employed. More recently, the shift has been from goods production to service production and, in particular, from manufacturing to services. As the table indicates, these shifts are expected to continue, although at a more moderate pace.

Table 10.1

Distribution of U.S. Employment, Past and Future (in percent)

Industry	1959	1969	1979	1984	Projected	
					1990	1995
Total (000)[a]	67,784	81,508	101,471	106,841	116,865	122,760
Agriculture[b]	8.2	4.4	3.3	3.1	2.7	2.5
Goods-producing	31.8	31.1	27.6	24.7	23.8	23.1
Mining	0.9	0.6	0.7	0.6	0.6	0.5
Construction	5.8	5.4	5.8	5.5	5.3	5.4
Manufacturing	25.1	25.1	21.1	18.5	17.9	17.2
Durable	14.1	14.8	12.8	11.0	11.0	10.8
Nondurable	11.0	10.3	8.3	7.5	6.9	6.4
Service-producing	60.0	64.5	69.1	72.3	73.5	74.4
Transportation, communication, and public utilities	6.3	5.7	5.3	5.1	5.1	5.1
Trade	19.9	20.5	22.0	22.7	23.2	23.0
Finance, insurance, and real estate	4.4	4.7	5.4	5.9	6.0	6.0
Services[c]	17.5	18.6	20.7	23.6	25.1	26.2
Government	11.9	15.0	15.7	15.0	14.2	14.0

Source: Valerie A. Personick, "A Second Look at Industry Output and Employment Trends Through 1995," *Monthly Labor Review*, November 1985, Table 1.

Note: The projections are the U.S. Bureau of Labor Statistics' moderate growth figures.

[a]Includes wage and salary jobs and self-employed.
[b]Includes forestry and fishery.
[c]Includes private household employment.

Wages in Services

Part of the unease over the growth of services stems from the fact that wage levels in a number of services industries are low, particularly in comparison with manufacturing. Benefits, specifically employer contributions to private pension and insurance funds, are also lower relative to salaries in services than in manufacturing—although fairly comparable to those in most nonmanufacturing industries. Part-time employment is more prevalent in services than in most industries. Since most people who work part-time do so by choice, the prevalence of part-time work is not undesirable in itself. However, those who work part-time are less likely to qualify for pensions and other benefits or to be considered for advancement. Widespread part-time employment may also establish norms for compensation and advancement that affect those who work full-time. For example, in an environment in which many work part-time and would not, in any industry, qualify for certain benefits, there may be little incentive to offer such benefits even to full-time workers. Self-employment is also more common in services than in other industries. Since many doctors and lawyers are self-employed, the self-employed in services form a high-wage group. Comparisons of earnings in services with those in other industries are quite sensitive to the treatment of part-time workers and the self-employed.

Average earnings in services are about 3 percent below those in all industries, 8 percent below those in manufacturing. As one might expect given the diversity of services industries, there is considerable variation. Average earnings in the personal services grouping (hotels, private household workers, as well as personal services) are more than 40 percent below those in manufacturing. Average earnings in professional services (health, legal, educational, and miscellaneous services) match those in manufacturing and exceed the overall average.

Some of the difference between wages in services and manufacturing is sex-related. Women earn less than men, whatever the industry, and women account for a much smaller fraction of those employed in manufacturing than in services. As can be seen from the table, the average earnings of women in services and manufacturing are similar. Women actually fare better in business and repair, entertainment, and professional services than they do in manufacturing.

Services and Prosperity

The concern over the shift from manufacturing to services goes beyond wages, however. Manufacturing has commonly been seen as the basis for economic development. In *The Stages of Economic Growth*, W.W. Rostow argued that a country's economic "takeoff" requires "the development of one or more substantial manufacturing sectors, with a high rate of growth." Services, or more generally, the service-producing industries are seen as dependent upon the growth in goods production, especially manufacturing, rather than capable of stimulating growth and thus of contributing to overall economic progress—"parasitic" rather than "productive."

Despite this negative view, it was observed almost fifty years ago that countries with higher incomes tended to have larger shares of employment in the service-producing industries. This relationship still exists. GNP per capita is positively correlated with the proportion of employment in service-producing industries. The correlation between per capita GNP and share of employment in goods production is also strong—but no stronger than that between GNP per capita and service production. (These seemingly contradictory relationships are reconciled by the existence of a very strong negative correlation between employment in agriculture and per capita GNP.)

In addition, for most countries, the proportion of employment in service-producing activities rises over time and, thus, rises with income. Most frequently the shift is from agriculture to both goods and services production. However, in countries in which the proportion of employment in agricultural activities is already small, employment has also shifted from goods-producing to service-producing industries. One sees this shift not only in the United States but also in Germany, Canada, the United Kingdom, and others (Table 10.2).

While the production of services may not be susceptible to large productivity gains, the dissemination of some services outputs clearly is. Advances in communications have brought entertainment, consulting, and other services that have a large information content to much larger audiences, in this sense resulting in more output for the same input. Telephones, radios, televisions, and now satellites and computers are all part of an information delivery and exchange network that to a large extent has as its object the dissemination of various services products. The services industries are not the locus of technological change, but technological change in other sectors has been driven by the demand for service products.

Conclusions

It is very difficult to generalize about the services industry. This is certainly true in the case of wages. The sector induces the highest- and lowest-wage occupations. It is also true of the character of the services industries—the customers served and the impact on other sectors of the economy. Perhaps the only common element is the importance of the

Table 10.2

Shifting Composition of the Labor Force in Selected Industrial Countries, 1960–80

	Agriculture		Industry[a]		Service[b]	
	1960	1980	1960	1980	1960	1980
United States	7	2	36	32	57	66
Germany	14	4	48	46	38	50
France	22	8	39	39	39	53
Canada	13	5	34	29	52	66
Australia	11	6	40	33	49	61
Netherlands	11	6	43	45	46	49
Japan	33	12	30	39	37	49
United Kingdom	4	2	48	42	48	56
Italy	31	11	40	45	29	44
Spain	42	14	31	40	27	46

Source: World Development Report 1984, published for the World Bank, Oxford University Press, 1984, p. 259.
[a]Includes electricity, water, and gas as well as mining, construction, and manufacturing.
[b]Service-producing industries except for some public utilities.

human input, whether largely physical, as in the case of domestic services; artistic, as in the case of entertainment services; or intellectual, as in the case of legal and consulting services.

The shift to services generates concern because it is thought to have undesirable distributional consequences. Wages are lower in services than in manufacturing, but some of the difference arises from the higher proportion of women employed in services. Women fare no worse, in terms of wages, in services than in manufacturing. Average earnings for men working full-time are actually higher in services than manufacturing. It is true, however, that average earnings in services are pulled up by the relatively large number of professional workers at the top of the earnings spectrum. Services do have more low-wage workers and more very-high-wage workers than manufacturing, and fewer in the middle.

The shift to services is also a source of unease because services are commonly seen as "taking in each other's laundry." However, the expansion of services supports and is supported by growth in other sectors. Whether the services industries will be as conducive to economic progress as manufacturing industries is not clear. It is also far from clear whether manufacturing will be as conducive to economic progress in the future as it has been in the past. Services do not seem as susceptible to gains in productivity as manufacturing. However, major technological advances in communications and manufacturing have been for the purpose of disseminating services output. Services can also create new "wants" through the development of new and superior products. In health services and in computer services these new services products often depend upon new manufactured products, but the growth of services in turn stimulates the growth of related manufacturing industries and inspires additional advances.

11. Metropolitan and Nonmetropolitan Area Populations
Bureau of the Census

Reprinted from *Population Profiles* (Washington, D.C.: Bureau of the Census, 1989), pp. 12–13.

The nation's 282 metropolitan statistical areas (MSAs) were home to 187.1 million people, or 76.9 percent of the total population in 1987. Nearly half (48.9 percent) of all Americans lived in the thirty-seven metropolitan areas with at least 1 million residents, and one in four resided in the seven largest metropolitan areas: New York, Philadelphia, Boston, Chicago, Detroit, Los Angeles, and San Francisco. All of these areas have at least 4 million residents. In the Northeast region, 88.0 percent of the population lived in metropolitan areas in 1987, followed by the West with 83.9 percent, the Midwest with 71.1, and the South with 70.1 percent.

While metropolitan areas contain the majority of Americans, they cover only 16.5 percent of the nation's land area. The remainder of the country, or nonmetropolitan areas, had 56.3 million residents in 1987.

The trend of the 1970s .reversed in the 1980s as metropolitan areas grew faster than nonmetropolitan areas. The metropolitan population growth rate of 8.5 percent between 1980 and 1987 was more than twice the 4.1 percent nonmetropolitan increase. The 1980–87 period saw an increase of 14.6 million residents in 282 MSAs, while nonmetropolitan areas increased by 2.2 million. A major factor in the resurgence of metropolitan growth in the 1980s has been lower out-migration from northern metropolitan areas. However, metropolitan populations in the North are growing much more slowly than those in the South and West.

The growth rates of the twenty-five largest MSAs show major regional differences in growth patterns. Of these MSAs, only four had fewer people in 1987 than in 1980, and they are all in the North: Pittsburgh, Detroit, Cleveland, and Milwaukee. Of the other eight large northern areas, only two increased more than 4 percent: Minneapolis–St. Paul (9.3 percent) and Kansas City (7.9 percent). All thirteen large MSAs in the South and West, except Baltimore, grew by at least 10 percent. Overall, the fastest growing were Phoenix (29.8 percent), Dallas–Ft. Worth (27.1 percent), and Atlanta (24.3 percent). The largest absolute increase, by far, was in metropolitan Los Angeles, which added nearly 2 million people between 1980 and 1987.

Between 1980 and 1987, the four metropolitan groups had rather similar growth rates, although somewhat lower in the largest and smallest areas than in the middle-sized ones. This is different from the growth rates of the 1970s, when the smaller MSAs grew considerably faster than the largest ones. These areas with over 5 million residents increased by only 0.33 percent per year in the 1970s, compared with 1.08 percent nationally. But during the 1980–87 period, the largest group grew at nearly the same rate as that for the nation, 0.97 and 0.99 percent, respectively. This recovery in the areas with over 5 million people is largely due to the renewed growth of the New York metropolitan complex, which had lost 650,000 population in the 1970s.

In the 1970s and the 1980–87 period, nonmetropolitan counties with the highest levels of commuting to metropolitan centers grew more rapidly than counties not within easy commuting distance. Although the growth rates since 1980 for all groups of nonmetropolitan counties have been substantially lower than those in the 1970s, the decline has been greatest in the most remote counties. In contrast, only the counties with the closest ties to metropolitan areas have been growing faster than the nation as a whole since 1980.

12. City and Suburban Populations
Bureau of the Census

Reprinted from *Population Profiles* (Washington, D.C.: Bureau of the Census, 1989), pp. 14–15.

The population of metropolitan central cities increased only 0.9 percent during the 1970–80 decade. But even though the population of these same cities had already increased by 4.7 percent in the first six years of the 1980s, their growth rate was barely half the rate for suburbs—8.9 percent. (Suburbs are portions of MSAs that are outside central cities.) Nevertheless, the suburban growth rate for 1980–86 was slower than the rate for the 1970s (average annual increases of 1.4 versus 1.7 percent).

Some of the recent population growth of central cities is due to net annexations of territory from suburban areas. Central cities added more than half a million population through annexation, or about 15 percent of their 1980–86 increase. Most of these annexations were made by cities in the South and West.

As a group, central cities in the Midwest and Northeast are losing population. During the 1980–86 period, midwestern cities lost 1.4 percent of their population, while northeastern cities essentially had no population change (a loss of 0.1 percent). Meanwhile, growth of western cities (11.8 percent) and southern cities (8.3 percent) exceeded not only the national rate for cities (4.7 percent), but also the total national population growth rate (6.4 percent). However, some individual northern cities still have growing populations, while a number of southern and western cities have declining populations.

Suburban populations grew in all regions in the 1980–86 period, but they grew considerably faster in the South (15.4 percent) and West (14.5 percent) than in the Midwest (3.2 percent) and Northeast (2.8 percent).

If the populations of the largest city in each of the nation's 25 largest MSAs were combined, they would account for 28 percent of the total population of the MSAs in 1986. However, these cities accounted for widely differing proportions of the total population in their individual MSAs. Individual cities that accounted for nearly half of the residents in their metropolitan areas in 1986 were Houston (47.6 percent), Phoenix (47.4 percent), and San Diego (46.1 percent). At the other extreme, San Francisco contained only 12.7 percent of its metropolitan population, followed by Miami with only 12.8 percent, Boston with 14.1 percent, and Tampa with 14.5 percent.

Central cities in the North tend to contain less of their MSAs' population than those in the South and West, but there are many exceptions. Some cities with a relatively large share of their area's population have made substantial annexations of territory in the past thirty years (for example, Houston, Phoenix, San Diego, and Milwaukee). Some cities whose share of their metropolitan area's total population is relatively small are part of an MSA that contains more than one major central city (San Francisco, Minneapolis, Tampa).

There are eight cities with 1 million or more people residing within their corporate limits; this is an increase of two since 1980. New York (7,263,000 in 1986) remains the nation's largest city, with more than twice the population of Los Angeles (3,259,000) or Chicago (3,010,000). The other cities in the top eight are Houston (1,729,000), Philadelphia (1,643,000), Detroit (1,086,000), and, new to the list since 1980, San Diego (1,015,000) and Dallas (1,004,000).

13. State Population Trends
Bureau of the Census

Reprinted from *Population Profiles* (Washington, D.C.: Bureau of the Census, 1989), pp. 8–9.

The nation's population growth during the 1980s continues to be heavily concentrated in the South and West. These two regions, with 52 percent of the population in 1980, claimed just over 15 million or 89.2 percent of the nation's 16.9 million increase from 1980 to 1987. Over half (8.8 million) of the growth occurred in just three states—California, Texas, and Florida. Nearly half of the combined growth in the South and West was due to net immigration (7.4 million), while the Northeast and Midwest experienced net out-migration of 25 million and only modest population growth.

Some energy-producing states in the South and West experienced another year of declining population in 1987. West Virginia and Wyoming have had four consecutive years of population losses, and Oklahoma has had three straight years of declines. Even Alaska, the fastest-growing state in the 1980s, actually lost population for the first time since the late 1970s, and Louisiana lost population for the first time since World War II. During the 1986–87 year, growth in Texas fell by about one-third, and although it has had the second-highest amount of net immigration since 1980, the state experienced net out-migration between 1986 and 1987.

Several states with agricultural-based economies have registered population declines this decade. Iowa experienced the greatest loss of any farm state, with a population decline of 80,000 in the 1980–87 period; it also had the highest 1980–87 rate of net out-migration of any farm state (6.7 percent). Nebraska and North Dakota have both lost population every year since 1984. Idaho and Montana dropped in population in each of the last two years; their losses are probably due to declines in both agriculture and energy industries.

The offspring of the baby boomers have helped swell the ranks of the under-five age group to its highest level since July 1967. Over two-thirds of the states shared in the 1.9 million national increase (11.6 percent) in this age group between 1980 and 1987. Alaska had the largest increase in the zero-to-four age group (53.5 percent), and it was the state with the highest proportion of its population under five years of age (11.4 percent) in 1987.

Virtually every state in the Northeast and Midwest followed the 1980–87 national pattern of decline in the five-to-seventeen and eighteen-to-twenty-four populations. In the South, Florida and Georgia countered the national trend with growth in both age groups, and in the West, the mountain states showed growth in the five-to-seventeen group.

The twenty-four-to-forty-four population grew most rapidly in the 1980–87 period (23.8 percent), with every state showing an increase. The sixty-five-and-over group was the next fastest growing (16.8 percent): every state grew, with ten states gaining over 25 percent so far this decade.

The median age of our nation's population in 1987 was 32.1 years, up from 30.0 in 1980. A dozen states experienced increases of 2.5 years or more between 1980 and 1987. Among the regions, the Northeast had the highest median age (33.7 years) in 1987, while Florida had the highest median among the states (36.3 years). Utah's high birth rate has contributed to its being the state with the lowest median age (25.5 years).

Women had a median age that was 2.3 years higher than that for men in 1987 (33.2 vs. 30.9). The difference was largest in Florida (medians of 37.9 vs. 34.6). Alaska is the only state where males have a higher median age than females (28.8 vs. 27.8).

Females constituted 51.3 percent of the U.S. population in 1987. Percentages ranged from 52.1 in the Northeast to 50.3 in the West. Alaska, Hawaii, Nevada, North Dakota, and Wyoming are the only states with a preponderance of males.

14. Geographical Mobility
Bureau of the Census

Reprinted from *Population Profiles* (Washington, D.C.: Bureau of the Census, 1989), pp. 18–19.

The annual rate of residential mobility leveled off in 1987 at 18.6 percent, a level not different from that in 1986. This follows declines during the

1970s and early 1980s and a sharp increase in the mid-1980s. Moving rates fell from an average of about 20 percent annually during the 1950s and 1960s to a low 16.6 in 1983. The rate then climbed to 20.2 percent in 1985 before falling again to the current figure.

Most people who move stay within the same county. They are generally making housing adjustments (the purchase of a new home or a change of apartments) or responding to a life-cycle change (marriage, divorce, birth of a child, or a young person establishing his or her own household).

People frequently make long-distance moves, or moves outside the county of current residence, for economic reasons, including corporate or military transfers, new jobs, or looking for work. Others move to attend schools, while some people move for a change of climate, proximity to recreational areas, or family reasons.

Between March 1986 and March 1987, 43.7 million people changed residences; of those, almost two-thirds (27.2 million) moved within the same county. Of the remainder more people moved between counties in the same state (8.8 million) than moved between states or from abroad (6.6 million and 1.1 million, respectively).

The rate of local and long-distance moves also did not change between the 1986 and 1987 March Current Population Surveys. At both dates 11.6 percent of the population moved within the same county, 3.7 percent moved between counties within the same state, and about 3 percent moved between states.

Young adults had the highest moving rates: 34.7 percent for those twenty to twenty-four years old in 1987 and 31.8 percent for twenty-five to twenty-nine-year-olds. But moving rates decline as age increases: 18.9 percent for people thirty to forty-four years old, 9 percent for those forty-five to sixty-four years old, and 5.3 percent for persons sixty-five years old and over.

The moving rates for children reflect the average age of their parents. For example, children one to four years old had a moving rate of 26.7 percent in 1987, presumably because they have younger parents. The rates were lower for older children.

Men were somewhat more likely to have moved in the previous year than women (18.4 versus 17.8 percent). Blacks had higher rates of moving than whites (19.6 versus 17.8 percent), and Hispanics had higher rates of moving than non-Hispanic whites or blacks (22.6 percent as compared with 17.4 percent and 19.6 percent, respectively).

Between March 1986 and March 1987 the Northeast had a net loss of 334,000 migrants to the other regions, while the South had a net gain of 279,000 and the West had a net gain of 166,000. The Midwest had nearly equal numbers of in-migrants and out-migrants; the apparent net gain of 111,000 persons was not statistically significant.

People living in the West had the highest overall movement with 22.4 percent of the population reporting that they lived in a different house in the United States one year earlier. Westerners also made the most local moves, at 14.5 percent. Southerners had the second highest moving rates: 20.3 percent moving within the United States.

Northeasterners and midwesterners were the least mobile, although those who left those areas for the South or the West were counted in the latter regions at the time of the survey. People still living in the Northeast in March 1987 moved at an overall rate of only 11.9 percent, while the overall rate for midwesterners was 16.7 percent.

Only the West had particularly high rates of movement from abroad— 1.0 percent of westerners lived outside the United States one year earlier as compared with 0.3–0.4 percent for each of the other regions.

15. Allocation of the National Output among Functions
Council of Economic Advisers

Excerpted from the *Economic Report of the President* (Washington, D.C.: U.S. Government Printing Office, 1971), pp. 99–103. The members of the council responsible for the report were Chairman Paul W. McCracken, Hendrik S. Houthakker, and Herbert Stein.

This section presents estimates of the allocation of the national output by certain broad functions and also the share that government expenditures represent in the total for each function. It should be noted that the estimates are crude in many respects, the existing national accounts statistics not having been developed for the uses made of them here. The following discussion is offered as much to illustrate a fruitful approach that deserves more work as to suggest substantive conclusions.

The share of government expenditures in a functional category is not an adequate measure of the amount of the total that is "due to" government, with the implication that the total would be correspondingly lower if the government's share were lower. Obviously, government cannot be adding to the share of all functions. The output would be divided among all the functions somehow even if there were no government. It cannot even be assumed that government always enlarges those functions when it spends more than the average. Government expenditures on occasion

Table 15.1

**Percentage Distribution of GNP in Current Prices, by Function,
1955, 1966, and 1969**

Function	Percent of total GNP, current prices		
	1955	1966	1969
Total GNP	100.0	100.0	100.0
Basic necessities	45.7	42.3	41.6
Education and manpower	3.7	5.7	6.3
Health	4.1	5.6	6.4
Transportation	10.6	9.9	10.0
General government	2.0	2.7	3.1
Defense	9.3	7.8	8.3
New housing	5.9	3.5	3.7
Business fixed investment	9.6	10.9	10.7
Net exports and inventory change	2.0	9.0	8.8
All other	7.1	9.0	8.8

Sources: Department of Commerce and Council of Economic Advisers.
Note: Detail will not necessarily add to totals because of rounding.

may displace private or state and local expenditures—or it may attract them. Nevertheless, the figures provide an initial basis for thinking about how the national output is used and how the federal government may be influencing the process.

The allocation of the national output over the past fifteen years is shown in Table 15.1. The years that were chosen for Table 15.1 are years when the economy was at or near full employment; the comparisons between these years are therefore not affected by substantial differences in the economy's operating rate.

Changes over the past fourteen years have been substantial but not unexpected. With the advance in per capita incomes, it is not surprising that spending for basic necessities, such as food, clothing, and rents (actual and imputed), has declined in relation to GNP. There has also been a general trend away from defense and housing investment.

The sectors where strong growth in demand has occurred are education, health, and general government. The general government category includes expenditures for fire and police departments and natural resource programs, including pollution abatement. Those sectors where expenditures are increasing are also the sectors where prices have risen very rapidly. If the GNP and its functional components were adjusted for these relative price increases, the distribution of the functional compo-

Table 15.2

Percentage Distribution of Total Federal Government Expenditures, by Function, 1955, 1966, and 1969

Function	1955	1966	1969
Total federal expenditures[1]	100.0	100.0	100.0
Basic necessities	23.2	27.2	29.5
Education and manpower	2.3	3.7	3.8
Health	1.7	4.3	8.0
Transportation	1.8	4.3	3.5
General government	3.4	3.8	3.6
Defense	60.0	45.9	44.2
New housing	−0.3	0.7	1.2
All other	7.8	10.0	6.2

Sources: Department of Commerce and Council of Economic Advisers.

Note: Detail will not necessarily add to totals because of rounding.

[1]Includes purchases of goods and services, grants-in-aid, and transfer payments; excludes net interest and subsidies less current surplus of Government enterprises.

nents would be different and shifts in the distribution probably would not be as marked.

The role of the federal government in this shift in the character of output has been important. It is simple to measure the direct federal and state and local purchases in each of the functional categories. But the direct share of national output that the federal government purchases does not fully represent its influence in determining the composition of national output. For example, the federal government influences the functional composition of GNP through its grants programs. Large grants have been made to state and local governments, and these grants, which are tied to particular uses, have accounted for an increasing portion of the federal budget. Also, transfer programs, such as Medicare, have been increasing rapidly in recent years. These transfers are often tied to particular end uses of GNP, and so they are also important determinants of the final composition of GNP. Table 15.2 lists the functional composition of the federal.budget.

The direct and indirect share of the national output for each function that can be traced back to total federal expenditures is shown in Table 15.3. The general trends toward education and health care are evident in this table because the federal contribution in these areas is made primarily through grants and transfers. It is assumed here that a transfer or a grant for a specific function is equivalent to a direct purchase by the federal government. This is a reasonable assumption because many of the grants and transfers for these purposes are directly tied to purchases by

Table 15.3

Total Direct and Indirect Federal Government Expenditures as Percent of Output used, by Function, 1955, 1966, and 1969

	Percent of output used[a]		
Function	1955	1966	1969
Total federal expenditures[b]	15.5	17.0	18.6
Basic necessities	7.9	11.0	13.2
Education and manpower	9.8	11.0	11.2
Health	6.4	13.2	23.4
Transportation	2.7	7.5	6.5
General government	25.5	24.3	21.2
Defense	99.9	99.9	99.8
New housing	−0.7	3.6	6.1
All other	17.1	18.9	13.2

Sources: Department of Commerce and Council of Economic Advisers.
[a] Federal expenditures for each function as percent of GNP for that function. See footnote b.
[b] Total federal expenditures as percent of total GNP. Expenditures include purchases of goods and services, grants-in-aid, and transfer payments; exclude net interest and subsidies less current surplus of government enterprises.

the private sector or by state and local government sectors.

Transfers and grants that are not tied to specific purchase in a sector are assigned to "basic necessities." For example, federal welfare payments and social security payments are rarely tied to specific purchases, but it may be assumed that they are used by and large for food, clothing, and rents. On this assumption, it is evident that the federal share in this sector has grown very rapidly in the past fifteen years.

Finally, the total public share of these functions—both direct and indirect—is shown in Table 15.4. This table is similar to Table 15.3 except that it emphasizes the important traditional role of state and local governments in such functions as general government and education.

What do these data suggest about the uses of the nation's output? While the estimates are tentative and involve more than the usual quota of government statistics, several conclusions are at least suggested.

First, it is clear that since the mid-1950s the nation has been increasing steadily the share of its economic resources devoted to education and manpower training, health, general government, and business investment. In effect, we made room for their rising shares by reducing the proportion of our economic resources devoted to national defense, residential construction, and basic necessities. Since prices rose more rapidly in those markets where productivity growth was low and demand was

Table 15.4

Total Direct and Indirect Federal and State and Local Government Expenditures as Percent of Output Used, by Function, 1955, 1966, and 1969

Function	Percent of Output Used[a]		
	1955	1966	1969
Total federal, state, and local government expenditure[b]	23.2	26.7	29.6
Basic necessities	9.9	13.2	15.8
Education and manpower	89.3	86.7	87.0
Health	23.4	28.8	39.9
Transportation	16.3	20.4	20.2
General government	100.0	100.0	100.0
Defense	100.0	100.0	100.0
New housing	0.1	4.7	6.3
All other	18.8	20.8	15.0

Sources: Department of Commerce and Council of Economic Advisers.

[a]Government expenditures for each function as percent of GNP for that function. See footnote b.

[b]Total federal, state, and local government expenditures as percent of total GNP. Expenditures include purchases of goods and services and transfer payments; exclude grants-in-aid, net interest, and subsidies less current surplus of government enterprises.

strong, changes in the pattern of output would be more moderate if output were expressed in constant prices throughout, but the same pattern would be evident. This is a judgment that cannot be verified for the economy as a whole with existing price deflators; it can be verified, however, and is true for the private sector of the economy. Since the decline in resources absorbed by the provision of basic necessities was small, and would be expected in an economy with rising incomes, the significant shift was from national defense and residential construction to education, health, business capital formation, and general government.

Second, the data provide some indication of the extent to which public budgets have led the way in changing national priorities. The question itself is, however, a difficult one. Growing government outlays for a function which is itself growing in importance would suggest that this government activity was resulting in the allocation of more total economic resources to that function. Indeed, an increment of public outlays may attract private resources to the same use. Government's influence on the allocation of resources might, however, work the other way, if the government assumes more direct responsibility for certain functions. Therefore, we cannot be certain that more resources are being used in those areas where government contributions have increased. Government inevitably provides all services for some functions such as general government or national defense through public budgets, and it therefore has direct control over the share of the national output devoted to those functions.

Nevertheless, in spite of the ambiguities in the interaction of public and private decisions, some things can be said about the impact of government fiscal activities on changes in the use of our economic resources. For one thing, public outlays, as indicated in Table 15.4, have been growing in importance relative to the size of the economy. They have risen from an amount equal to 23.2 percent of GNP in 1955 to 29.6 percent in 1969, the growth being about evenly divided between federal outlays and outlays of state and local government units. The most dramatic and clear-cut effect of public budgets on uses of outputs seems to have occurred in health-related outlays. The share of our total economic output used for health care rose from 4.1 percent of GNP in 1955 to 6.4 percent in 1969. And the share of those outlays that was financed by public expenditures rose dramatically from 23.4 percent in 1955 to 39.9 percent fourteen years later. Public outlays also increased as a share of the total economic resources devoted to basic necessities, housing, and transportation.

Within the public sector the federal government increased its share in financing most of the categories of uses of output, health expenditures being the most striking example, with housing expenditures next. State and local governments, however, are providing a larger share of total general government services than in 1955.

These data suggest that there are many different forces influencing the final composition of the national output. Most of these express themselves in the private sector of the economy, primarily because it is still the largest sector. There has been a marked shift in the composition of the federal budget, but that shift is only weakly translated into a similar shift in the composition of national output. However, it is important to recognize that some government programs are designed to change not the composition of final output but the distribution of income. For example, the growth in federal expenditures associated with basic necessities is related to the large increases in income maintenance payments between 1955 and 1969. This type of program is designed primarily to redistribute income and not to change the functional allocation of the GNP. Consequently, expansion of programs to redistribute income could very well have substantial, little, or no effect on the functional allocation of GNP. This means that neither the breakdown of GNP by purchasers given in Table 15.1 nor the functional breakdown of GNP given in Table 15.2 is a completely appropriate framework for the analysis of government policies designed to change income distribution.

16. Regional Perspectives
Howard L. Friedenberg and Rudolph E. DePass

Reprinted from *Survey of Current Business*, April 1989, pp. 35–36.

Per Capita Personal Income: Continued Widening of Regional Differences in 1988

In 1988, the gap in per capita personal income (as a percent of the U.S. average) between the highest-income region—New England—and the lowest-income region—Rocky Mountain—was wider than in any year since 1969. The widening of regional differences in per capita income continued the pattern of the current economic expansion. In each year since 1982, per capita income in the high-income regions of New England and the Mideast has increased faster than the U.S. average; in the low-income Rocky Mountain and Southwest regions, it has increased slower than the average. In contrast to this widening, in the three other expansions since 1969, regional differences in per capita income had narrowed.

By slipping into last place in 1988, the Rocky Mountain region became the first region to record a per capita income below that of the Southeast region, which had been in last place since 1929—the earliest year for which Bureau of Economic Analysis (BEA) estimates regional per capita income. Rocky Mountain per capita income, at $14,282 in 1988, was 13 percent below the U.S. average of $16,444, the region's lowest relative level since 1937. In the Southeast, per capita income was $14,331; in the Southwest, it was $14,365. In the Rocky Mountain and Southwest regions, the below-average growth in per capita income since 1982 reflects the continuing weakness in oil and gas exploration.

The above-average increase since 1982 in per capita income in the New England and Mideast regions reflects rapid growth in total personal income combined with below-average population growth. Per capita income in New England, at $20,013 in 1988, was 22 percent above the U.S. average, the region's highest relative level since 1942.

Per capita income in the Plains region was below U.S. per capita income in each year of the current expansion, and it increased more slowly than the U.S. average in most of these years. In the Far West, Great Lakes, and Southeast regions, per capita income relative to the U.S. average has changed little since 1982.

Growth in High-Income Regions, 1982–88

In the New England and Mideast regions, rapid growth in service and construction industry payrolls boosted the growth of both total and per capita personal income. Population growth was dampened by relatively high housing costs, which discouraged workers from migrating to those regions despite increased job opportunities. Population growth in both regions was closer to the U.S. average in 1988 than earlier in the expansion.

In the Far West region, rapid population growth more than offset rapid growth in total personal income, resulting in a gain in per capita income slightly below the U.S. average.

Growth in Low-Income Regions, 1982–88

In the Great Lakes region, a gain in per capita income equal to the U.S. average reflects offsetting growth in total personal income and in population.

In the Plains region, slow growth in total personal income led to a below-average gain in per capita income. Population also grew slowly, despite accelerations in 1987 and 1988. Weakness in the farm economy, particularly in the drought year of 1988, has held down personal income growth.

In the Southwest and Rocky Mountain regions, slow growth in total personal income contributed to below-average gains in per capita income. Weakness in oil and gas exploration and in related activities, such as construction and financial services, dampened personal income growth. From 1982 to 1986, population migration to the Southwest was substantial despite reduced job opportunities in energy-related industries; after 1986, migration slowed considerably. Population in the Rocky Mountain region grew slower than the U.S. average from 1984 to 1987 and declined in 1988, following above-average growth earlier in the expansion.

The Southeast was the only low-income region in which per capita income grew faster than the U.S. average. Above-average gains in per capita income in the states along the Atlantic Coast and in Tennessee more than offset below-average gains in the other Southeast states; the net result was a gain in regional per capita income slightly above the U.S. average. In each of the Atlantic Coast states, rapid growth in durables manufacturing, construction, and service industry payrolls accounted for above-average gains in per capita income, despite rapid growth in population. In the states with below-average gains in per capita income, slow growth in total personal income was the restraining factor; population also grew slowly.

Per Capita Income by State

A similar picture of a widening of differences in per capita income from 1982 to 1988 emerges when the focus is on states instead of on regions. In eight of the ten states with the highest per capita income in 1988, per capita income as a percent of the U.S. average was higher in 1988 than in 1982. Most of the high-income states are in the New England and Mideast regions. Similarly, in nine of the ten states with the lowest per capita income in 1988, per capita income as a percent of the U.S. average was lower in 1988 than in 1982. Most of the low-income states are in the Rocky Mountain and Southeast regions.

17. U.S. Agriculture: Hard Realities and New Opportunities
Marvin R. Duncan

Excerpted from *Economic Review* (Federal Reserve Bank of Kansas City, 1989), pp. 3–13. Marvin R. Duncan was acting chairman and chief executive officer of the Farm Credit Administration.

The U.S. rural environment has changed dramatically in recent years. Its agricultural sector has evolved from a relatively isolated and independent sphere of economic and cultural relationships to a sophisticated business sector that has been almost fully integrated into the national and world economies. Worldwide crop conditions, monetary exchange rates, world economic conditions, and interest rate differentials now influence the financial performance of the agricultural business in the United States.

The growing awareness of the extent to which agriculture touches the lives of both rural and urban people has led to a broadening of the interest groups that influence farm policy. Disappearing are the days when farm income support and soil conservation totally drove that policy. In the future, people concerned with food safety and the environment will make their voices effectively heard. Those concerns could result in marked changes in agricultural production and processing practices in the years ahead.

Public policy makers have an uneasy feeling that the long-term problems of farmers and the agricultural sector cannot be solved by traditional commodity programs alone. Moreover, it is increasingly apparent that rural America's problems are much broader than the farm or agriculture itself. A growing realization is that the more fundamental challenge is to broaden economic opportunity in rural America. In doing so, many of the problems facing farmers and rural people could be eased. Therefore, the focus of policy should perhaps become one of providing opportunity for people rather than simply relying on payments for pounds or bushels.

The billions of taxpayer dollars being spent on agriculture are destined to be evaluated against criteria that reflect a broad range of public and social concerns. Agricultural programs and policies, as well as agricultural practices, will no longer be determined solely by the traditional farm interest groups, which means that the traditionalists will be seeking new coalitions.

Economic, demographic, technological, and trade developments have all played a role in altering socioeconomic conditions on the farm and throughout rural America. They will continue to do so in the years ahead.

Agriculture's Role in the General Economy

Agriculture traditionalists have always emphasized the importance of farming to the national welfare. Typically, they assert that a strong rural economy will produce a strong national economy. However, as important as agriculture is economically and culturally, its role in the nation's economy has eroded rather steadily over the past half century.

The food and fiber system, from the farmer to the consumer, includes all economic activities supporting the production, processing, and distribution of agricultural goods and services. In 1975, this system employed 21.0 percent of the civilian labor force and accounted for 20.4 percent of gross national product. Ten years later, it employed 18.5 percent of the labor force and accounted for only 17.5 percent of GNP.

The farm production sector is a small, but important, part of the whole food and fiber system. It employed 2.5 million people in 1985, or 11.7 percent of total agricultural employment. This is only 2.1 percent of the total civilian labor force. From 1947 to 1985, increases in final demand for agricultural products were matched by increases in farm labor productivity, which helped to keep employment in the farm sector relatively stable over this period at about 3 million people.

The farm sector's contribution to GNP, while varying from year to year, is declining. It dropped from 2.7 percent of GNP in 1975 to 1.8 percent in 1985. The percentage of personal consumption expenditures going for agricultural products has also changed significantly over the past forty years. In 1947, for example, 44 percent of total personal consumption expenditures went for food and fiber products; 31 percent alone went to purchase food. By 1985, total personal consumption expenditures going to food and fiber products dropped to 25 percent.

Food expenditures account for about 15 percent of family spending today. Because the farmer's share of the consumer's dollar is relatively small, fluctuating farm prices have only a small effect in overall consumer prices.

The fact that agriculture's role in the general economy is decreasing will likely lead to a vastly different public perception about this sector in the future. Arguments that agriculture should be protected because it is unique will continue to fade as commercial farmers are recognized as businessmen. The American family farmer of the future will face the reality of a farm sector that will be expected to succeed on the basis of its business performance in increasingly complex national and world economies.

Demographic Trends in Rural America

Agriculture is no longer the economic balance wheel for the United States; it is also no longer the primary focus of rural living. During this century, rural America has undergone a dramatic transformation, moving from the center of American life to a smaller but still significant component of the U.S. economy.

According to the U.S. Bureau of the Census, the rural population in 1987 was 63.9 million people, or just over a fourth of our total population. However, only 2 percent of the nation's population—about 5 million people—had a farm residence in 1987. This figure contrasts sharply with 1920, when almost 32 million people, or 30 percent of the population, lived on farms.

The 2 percent figure for 1987 is destined to decline further as the U.S. population continues to grow. In fact, according to the Census Bureau, 75 percent of all U.S. residents now live in metropolitan areas. In 1963, it was 63 percent. For the record, a metropolitan area includes a central city of at least 50,000 and towns and cities economically tied to it. Nonmetropolitan areas are rural, beyond the suburbs.

The decline in farm numbers has been occurring almost at a steady pace for the past fifty years. Even the recent period of financial stress did not materially affect the exodus rate, which has averaged about 2 percent per year throughout the post–World War II period.

While farm numbers will continue to decline from today's figure of about 2.2 million, they could begin to stabilize by the year 2000, especially if off-farm income opportunities expand in rural areas and permit more small and mid-sized farms to stay in business.

Most U.S. farms appear too small to provide an adequate income to the families that reside on them. Indeed, the data indicate that farms of under $20,000 in annual sales typically lose money on farming operations. However, on average, the residents of these farms earn enough income off the farm to obtain family income approaching that of the average U.S. farmer but still less than the average nonfarm family income of almost $35,000.

The disparity in farm size will continue to widen in the future because the mid-sized farmer will be pressured either to expand to achieve scale economies and/or more income, to scale back farming operations and seek off-farm employment, or to leave farming altogether. Mid-sized farms with sales of $40,000 to $100,000 and average family incomes of $28,000 continue to shrink in numbers. These farms numbered 360,000 in 1981 and today number 290,000.

Currently, farms with annual sales greater than $500,000 account for almost a third of all sales, yet they represent just 2 percent of all farms. In the years ahead, this relatively small group of farmers will increase somewhat and will account for an even larger share of total production. Rural communities that are primarily geared to serve the disappearing middle group of farmers will face serious economic challenges.

What is equally profound in its policy implications is the increasingly nonagricultural character of rural America. In 1987 only 9 percent of the Americans living in nonmetropolitan America were closely identified with farming or agribusiness. Manufacturing and mining were far more important in providing employment opportunities. For example, 40 percent of new job formation in nonmetropolitan America is in these endeavors. As a result, more rural Americans are relatively untouched by current agricultural policies.

Rural Lifestyles

Many Americans have an out-of-date view of the lifestyle and aspirations of farmers—a view more consistent with the picture painted in John Steinbeck's *Grapes of Wrath* than with the current reality.

Breakthroughs in worldwide communication systems, advances in biotechnology, and better transportation systems have dramatically altered the aspirations and living standards of rural America. Not only can farmers enjoy a better quality of life, but many can match their balance sheets and income statements with those of people in similar-sized businesses. However, because public programs and large government payments have played an important role in bringing about the accumulation of wealth in agriculture, they will be scrutinized more closely by policy makers in the future.

In spite of the difficulties experienced during the past five to eight years, many commercial farm operators continue to earn an attractive living at farming. A close look at the data will reveal some interesting discrepancies between how the sector and the individual farmer are faring financially. For example, while real earnings of farmers have been stagnant to declining for over thirty years, farm numbers have been dropping steadily. Thus, the remaining farmers are getting a bigger and bigger piece of a relatively constant-sized pie over time. Real net cash income per farm grew at about a 2 percent rate annually from 1950 to 1970. If the trend line established during that period were extended (prior to the boom and bust of the 1970s and 1980s), average real net cash income for the past four years would be above trend. Real incomes in agriculture are, in fact, growing.

The average real wealth of farmers has also been trending higher. From 1950 to 1970, real equity per farm grew at a compound annual rate of 3.8 percent. Admittedly, the recent downward adjustment has brought average real equity below the trend level established during the 1950–70 period. Still, equity levels are now rising again, which will help to stabilize the finances of the sector.

In current dollars, average farm equity is more than $300,000. If only commercial-sized farms (sales above $100,000) are considered, average equity is almost $900,000.

It is widely believed that U.S. farm programs provide income support to allow the nation's farmers to remain in business to produce an abundant supply of low-cost food. Many claim that without these payments, a grand exodus from farming would occur and our food supply would be threatened. In 1986, 56 percent of direct government payments went to about 14 percent of farmers. These farmers generated 70 percent of the sector's gross farm income and had sales of $100,000 or more.

In 1986, farms with sales between $100,000 and $500,000 earned an average net cash income of $83,294. Farms in the U.S. Department of Agriculture's highest sales category had an average income of almost $700,000. Farms in these two categories received average payments from the government of $200,000 and $36,000, respectively. If those government payments were deducted from these farmers' incomes and appropriate adjustments due to resulting market prices, costs, and acreage were made, any reasonable needs test would indicate that they are indeed doing all right, and government payments are not what is keeping them on the farm.

Technology and Productivity in U.S. Agriculture

U.S. farm productivity—output levels generated per unit of input—has exhibited significant gains in the last forty years. With output levels increasing by nearly 100 percent and input levels declining slightly, farm productivity has grown by 130 percent. The gains in productivity have been distributed just about evenly between livestock and crops.

Technological advancements are largely responsible for the growth in productivity. The fact that significant output gains have been attained with only minor changes in input levels indicates that much of the productivity gains up to now can be credited to advances in technology, particularly in the areas of machinery, chemicals, and plant breeding. This has resulted in an increase in labor productivity of the U.S. agricultural sector that has exceeded that of any other industry. In 1986, farm productivity per hour of labor was more than seven times greater than in 1947. And the role of the farmer, as important as it still is, is now shared with the important roles played by the chemist, the geneticist, the cellular biologist, the engineer, and the banker.

In general, the leaders in technological adoption have been the larger farms, which, consequently, reaped much of the benefits associated with early adoption. The willingness and, more important, the ability to adopt new technologies as they emerge may be the key to the future survival for many farms, especially the mid-sized family farms, which have experienced a squeeze over the years. Although off-farm income sources have helped many small and part-time farmers overcome the effects of inefficient production, the pressures on mid-sized farms will intensify in the future.

Genetic engineering and information technologies are rapidly proliferating. Much of this new technology can be adopted with low capital investment. The skill of the human resources employed in a business will more often than not determine the effectiveness of these types of technological advances. Hence, productivity advances on a global basis will increase competition, forcing U.S. farmers to become even more cost effective to maintain and build market share.

This new reality is another that will be difficult for many U.S. producers to accept. It means, of course, that technological transfers will become more rapid and that the competitive playing field between U.S. farmers and their foreign counterparts will become more level. All this heightens the importance of building a cost-competitive U.S. agriculture and of providing assistance to spur the growth of countries that could prove rich market opportunities for U.S. agriculture.

Internationalization of U.S. Agriculture

The performance of U.S. agriculture has become a case study of world interdependence. Both the importance of the United States in the world market and the importance of world markets for U.S. agriculture increased considerably in the 1970s and 1980s. The prospects for U.S. agriculture in the 1990s and into the early part of the twenty-first century will depend on how efficiently it can produce and how effectively it can market relative to trading partners and competitors.

The slowdown in world trade in the 1980s and global excess production have created disputes and an emotionally charged trading environment. Solutions to this agricultural trade dilemma will require improvements in U.S. trade and domestic economic policies. They will also require worldwide negotiations to reduce trade barriers and open up markets to more fair, if not free, competition.

Developments, while meaningful, are of a short-term nature. The longer-term economic viability of U.S. agriculture is tied to the resolution of two public policy issues:

(1)   U.S. macroeconomic policies and their linkage to the international financial and commodity markets through interest rates and exchange rates, and

(2)   more liberal trade policies to capitalize on the comparative advantages enjoyed by the United States in a number of agricultural products.

Although the linkage between various macroeconomic policies and agriculture may seem obscure, there is no question that volatile interest rates and exchange rates had a profound effect on the farm sector in the 1980s. Indeed, these policies have largely overshadowed the income support objectives of U.S. farm policies.

The longer-run competitiveness of U.S. agriculture also depends on the resolution of two largely private-sector issues: improvements in productivity, and efficient marketing and distribution systems.

Technological advances will clearly enhance farm productivity in the future, but this phenomenon will exist in competitor countries as well. These developments present a daunting challenge to the United States if its role is not to be that of the residual supplier to the world market.

However, the United States retains clear superiority in the agribusiness infrastructure—that is to say, in the capacity of agricultural supply and marketing firms to efficiently meet the requirements of producers and to move large volumes of quality products into consumers' hands worldwide. Thus, this infrastructure is as important to the well-being of U.S. agriculture as its rich farmland and those who till its soil.

18. Changes in U.S. Industrial Structure: The Role of Global Forces, Secular Trends, and Transitory Cycles

Robert Z. Lawrence

Excerpted from *Industrial Change and Public Policy* (Federal Reserve Bank of Kansas City, August 1983), pp. 29–77. Robert Z. Lawrence is a senior fellow of the Brookings Institution.

The Myth of U.S. Deindustrialization

The contention that declining U.S. international competitiveness has induced the deindustrialization of America is wrong on two counts. First, in the most relevant sense, the United States has not been undergoing a process of deindustrialization; and second, over the period of 1973 to 1980, the net impact of international competition on the overall size of the U.S. manufacturing sector has been small and positive.

The term "deindustrialization" requires further elaboration for precise communication. First, what is industry? Does it, for example, include the construction and mining sectors or refer more narrowly, as we will interpret it here (partly for reasons of data availability), to the manufacturing sector alone? Second, does deindustrialization refer to a drop in the output of industry, or to the inputs (e.g., capital and/or labor) devoted to industry? And third, does deindustrialization refer to an absolute decline in the volume of outputs from (or inputs to) manufacturing, or simply a relative decline in the growth of manufacturing outputs or inputs as compared to outputs or inputs in the rest of the economy?

Summary and Conclusions

In the 1970s, the share of manufacturing employment in total U.S. employment continued its secular decline as a consequence of the revealed preference of U.S. consumers for services and the more rapid increase of productivity in the manufacturing sector. U.S. industrial growth has been sluggish, but it has been what would have been expected, given the slow growth in GNP. From 1973 to 1980 the share of manufacturing fell less than labor productivity growth in the rest of the economy. Nonetheless, the United States did not experience absolute deindustrialization in the 1970s. U.S. employment in manufacturing expanded, and, given the growth rate of output, investment and R&D spending in manufacturing were remarkably strong. In contrast to its decline from 1960 to 1973, the share of manufacturing in total U.S. fixed business capital increased from 1973 to 1980. The growth rate of the capital labor ratio in manufacturing actually accelerated.

The finding that capital formation and R&D spending in manufacturing have accelerated should give pause to those who believe that channeling additional capital toward manufacturing is an appropriate remedy for our industrial problems. There is no evidence that on average U.S. manufacturers have failed to invest. The evidence points rather to the important role of aggregate demand in constraining manufacturing growth. If growth is resumed, job creation and investment in manufacturing will be stimulated, and reindustrialization will occur automatically. In the absence of demand for particular products, however, policies should facilitate the movement of resources away from activities in which they are no longer needed.

The manufacturing slump is a worldwide phenomenon. The increase in U.S. manufacturing input since 1973 has been about the same as the average of all industrial countries. The capital stock manufacturing grew as rapidly in the United States as in Europe, and real R&D spending increased at similar rates here and abroad. Although employment in U.S. manufacturing grew modestly, in other major industrial countries it declined. In fact, in virtually every major industrial sector, employment in the United States grew faster than in Japan. Although U.S. labor productivity growth was not as rapid as productivity growth in other industrial countries, U.S. productivity levels in manufacturing overall remain the highest in the world, as does the U.S. share of R&D spending in value-added manufacturing.

The perception of an absolute decline in the U.S. industrial base and the belief that foreign competition has made a major contribution to that decline stem from the reinforcing effects of U.S. trade and domestic growth and the nature of adjustment difficulties associated with declines in industries adversely affected. The troubled industries are largely highly unionized, and the average plant size is large. Workers displaced from several of these industries face the prospect of considerably lower wages.

The U.S. comparative advantage in unskilled-labor and standardized capital-intensive products has been declining secularly. And, because of slow domestic economic growth, the home market for those products has not expanded rapidly. But our comparative advantage in high-technology products has strengthened, while the demand for high-technology products has grown relatively more rapidly in a climate of stagnation. In general, however, structural changes in the U.S. economy during this period arose mainly from domestic factors.

19. Historical Data on Public Transit
American Public Transit Association

Excerpted and reprinted with permission from *Transit Fact Book* (Washington, D.C.: American Public Transit Association, 1990, 1992), pp. 5, 36–39, 78–79, and 106–9.

Major Trends in Transit Ridership

Transit ridership has gone through six major cycles of growth and decline during the twentieth century, influenced by social and economic forces external to transit. From 1900 to 1920, transit ridership grew steadily; first, due to technical innovation and investment opportunities during the early development of street railways and then due to the economic boom of World War I and the postwar period (peaking at about 23.4 billion passengers per year). The Great Depression caused a steep decline in ridership between 1929 and 1939, as people made fewer work trips and often could not afford to take pleasure trips. A new federal law limiting utilities' ability to subsidize transit, as had been normal practice, led to a decline in transit capital facilities (by 1933 ridership was down to about 12 billion). World War II caused motor fuel rationing and an economic boom that led to a new rapid growth cycle in transit ridership (to about 24 billion). Ridership quickly declined from artificially high war levels as people fled to suburbs, spurred by cheap fuel and government policy favoring low-density suburban growth (to an all-time low of about 5.3 billion). In 1973 the ridership cycle reversed again, and transit began a modest growth based on a partnership of local, state, and federal government committed to improving America's transportation infrastructure (it was up to 8.5 billion by 1990).

History and Provisions of the Federal Transit Act

In 1964 the United States Congress found that "the welfare and vitality of urban areas, the satisfactory movement of people and goods within such areas, and the effectiveness of housing, urban renewal, highway, and other federally aided programs were being jeopardized by the deterioration or inadequate provision of urban transportation facilities and services. . . ." To remedy this situation, Congress enacted the Federal Transit Act, known as the Urban Mass Transportation Act of 1964 until 1991, which provided a program for transit systems to purchase capital equipment.

Continuing this commitment through a third decade, Congress enacted the Intermodal Surface Transportation Efficiency Act of 1991 (ISTEA). The ISTEA not only authorizes higher levels of funding for transit than any previous law, it also provides for flexible use of additional funds for either highway or transit purposes and requires greater coordination of highway and transit planning to provide for the most efficient surface transportation system to meet local needs.

The federal transit assistance program has evolved over the years due to changing transit needs and changing federal objectives. Landmarks in this evolution include:

• 1961: The Housing and Urban Development Act provided funding for transit demonstrations and loans for mass transportation projects.
• 1964: The Urban Mass Transportation Act established the Urban Mass Transportation Administration (UMTA, now named the Federal Transit Administration) within the Department of Housing and Urban Development to administer a program of capital grants to transit systems.
• 1966: The Urban Mass Transportation Act expanded funding for capital purchases and allowed funding for research, planning, and training.
• 1970: The Urban Mass Transportation Assistance Act provided increased levels of federal funding by authorizing a $3.1 billion program of capital grants.
• 1973: The Federal-Aid Highway Act increased the federally funded portion of transit capital projects from two-thirds to 80 percent and authorized expenditure of Federal-Aid Urban Systems highway funds and Interstate Highway Transfers for qualifying transit projects.
• 1974: The National Mass Transportation Assistance Act increased authorizations for discretionary capital funding and created a formula grant program to allocate funding directly to urbanized areas that could be used for either operations or capital projects.
• 1978: The Federal Public Transportation Act, Title III of the Surface Transportation Assistance Act of 1978, expanded the formula grant program and divided it into categorical programs that included additional operating grants for fixed guideway systems, capital grants for bus purchases, and operating grants for places outside of urbanized areas.
• 1982: The Federal Public Transportation Act, Title III of the Surface Transportation Assistance Act of 1982, provided that one cent of a five-cent increase in Highway Trust Fund tax on motor fuels would be placed in a Mass Transit Account for capital projects, increased the portion of all funding allocated through the formula grant program, and altered the formula grant program allocation formula to include transit service data as well as population data.
• 1987: The Federal Mass Transportation Act, Title III of the Surface Transportation and Uniform Relocation Assistance Act of 1987, author-

ized the federal transit program through fiscal year 1991 and provided that a portion of the Mass Transit Account of the Highway Trust Fund would be allocated for capital purposes on a formula basis.
• 1991: The Federal Transit Act Amendments, Title III of the Intermodal Surface Transportation Efficiency Act of 1991, extended the authorization of transit assistance through FY 1997 at levels higher than any previous authorizations, changed the name of the transit law to the Federal Transit Act, changed the name of the Urban Mass Transportation Administration to the Federal Transit Administration, and continued a shift in funding distribution to formulas by distributing the rail modernization portion of Section 3 major capital funds by formula for the first time.

Surface transportation, Title I of the Intermodal Surface Transportation Efficiency Act of 1991, provided that specific funds authorized through the Federal-Aid Highways program are intended for use for either transit or highway projects. Called flexible funds, these monies are to be used for the mode of transportation best suited to meeting the needs of individual areas and states.

Funds for federal transit assistance come from two sources. Money from general revenue of the Treasury is appropriated each year by Congress. During the appropriation process Congress will also set a limit on the amount of money from the Mass Transit Account of the Highway Trust Fund that can be used to fund transit projects during the next year.

20. The Road More Traveled

Mark O. Hatfield

Reprinted from the *Hatfield Backgrounder*, August 1989, pp. 1–3. Mark O. Hatfield is a Republican United States Senator representing Oregon. The *Backgrounder* is a newsletter for his constituents.

Last year, cars, buses, and trucks in the United States traveled more than 2 trillion miles. Since 1956, the year in which the interstate highway construction program was initiated, annual travel mileage has more than tripled. In the past decade alone, motor vehicle travel in this country has increased almost 30 percent.

Americans now own and operate at least 183 million cars, buses, and trucks—more than one in every three vehicles in the world and a 27 percent increase over the past decade.

This record number of cars, buses, and trucks places enormous pressure on existing roads and bridges. The sixty-four-mile Beltway surrounding Washington, D.C., for example, carries an estimated 735,000 vehicles every day, almost twice as many as it did in 1976, despite the completion of the multimillion dollar Metro subway system. The Nebraska Department of Roads reported recently that Interstate 80 in Omaha is operating at two and a half times its capacity and requires total replacement. The New York State Thruway will need $51.8 billion worth of expansion by 1996 just to keep pace with the increased traffic.

The dramatic increase in the number of passenger vehicles is not, however, entirely to blame. In 1965, the nation's highways transported 359 billion tons of freight. By 1985, this figure had jumped 70 percent to 610 billion tons.

Racing against Time

Failing to build new roads and highways to keep pace with increased use is not the only problem: Existing roads and bridges in the United States, including the 43,000 miles of the interstate highway system begun by President Eisenhower and scheduled for completion in 1993, are falling into disrepair faster than funds are being appropriated to fix them.

Despite the tremendous increase in traffic, 92 percent of the 3.87 million miles of roads crisscrossing the United States were built before 1960. Given that the average road has a design life of only twenty years, it is little wonder that 62 percent of the paved highways in the United States are now in need of repair and 90 percent of all interstate highways will require capital investments in the next decade in order to remain in service.

An estimated $95 billion will be required to reconstruct the 161,000 miles of roads now rated "poor" and "very poor" by the Federal Highway Administration, and an additional $148.8 billion will be required to resurface the 1.19 million miles of roads now rated "fair." Although these price tags seem overwhelming, particularly in light of current budget deficits, costs will only increase in the years ahead. A two-lane road in fair condition today can be resurfaced for $125,000 a mile, for example, while the cost can jump to $600,000 a mile if it is allowed to deteriorate further.

Bridges in this country, 30 percent of which are at least fifty years old, are in a similar state of disrepair. Of the more than 576,000 bridges over twenty feet long that are now in use, almost 42 percent have been classified as "substandard" by the Federal Highway Administration.

The cost of repairing or replacing these bridges, 5,186 of which have been closed to traffic in recent years, is estimated at $50.7 billion. Although that cost also seems staggering, it is minimal in comparison to the hundreds of lives that have been lost due to collapsed bridges.

What It All Means

One of the immediate and obvious results of the deterioration of the nation's infrastructure is traffic jams. Called "go slows" in Nigeria and "commuting hell" in Japan, they are known to virtually all Americans for the frustration and delay they cause.

According to the U.S. Department of Transportation, Americans were delayed in traffic for a total of 722 million hours in 1985. In Southern California, the average travel speed on expressways is 33 miles an hour and is expected to drop to 15 miles per hour within the next decade.

Although many of the drivers caught in these traffic jams are people commuting to and from work, fire fighters, police, and paramedics are often delayed as well. A study released almost a decade ago suggested that every minute of delay in responding to a structural fire costs $1,000. The tremendous human cost of ambulances caught in traffic cannot be so easily estimated.

In addition to wasting valuable time and adding to North America's growing pollution problems, these traffic delays wasted nearly 3 billion gallons of gasoline, about 4 percent of the nation's annual consumption. If no changes are made, the U.S. Department of Transportation estimates that traffic delays, and the gasoline they waste, will quadruple by 2005, costing the United States an estimated $50 billion a year in lost wages and wasted gas. Even now, each one of the 162 million licensed drivers in the United States spends almost $100 a year because of wasted gas and added wear and tear on motor vehicles.

Finally, traffic delays add enormously to the cost of moving people and products across the country. In 1987, the most recent year for which figures are available, this cost was $792 billion, almost 18 percent of the gross national product. As American business and industry attempt to remain competitive in the international marketplace, keeping this cost down is ever more critical but increasingly difficult.

How Did We Get Here?

The reasons behind the nation's looming transportation and infrastructure crisis are varied but generally reflect larger national trends.

In recent years, the federal government's commitment to long-term investment in all public works programs and projects has eroded substantially. Between 1950 and today, total government spending on public works fell from 19.1 percent of all spending to less than 6 percent. In the last fifteen years alone, funding for public works construction and maintenance fell 33 percent. A recent U.S. Senate report on the nation's infrastructure, including roads and bridges, predicted a $443 billion spending shortfall by 2000.

A little noticed but even more disturbing trend is the declining commitment to research—particularly in light of the savings that could result. A 10 percent improvement in the average life of asphalt pavement could save $1 billion annually, and a noncorrosive de-icing agent could save $6 billion annually. Yet federal government spending on highway research is less than half of what it was only twenty years ago.

Even if all the deteriorating roads and bridges in this country were repaired and an increased number of mass transportation systems were created, few people would be willing to forgo the tremendous freedom and mobility that comes with owning and driving a car. Over 80 percent of the miles traveled by car in the United States are driven commuting to work and shopping. In many cities in the United States, including Denver, Houston, and Los Angeles, 90 percent of the people get to work by car. In Europe, that number is only 40 percent, and in Tokyo only 15 percent of the people drive to work.

In addition to using four times as much gas as the average European and ten times as much as the average Asian, the average American puts far more stress and strain on the nation's highways and bridges. The average American also puts a great deal of strain on the nation's land: More than half of all the space in the urban areas of this country is used for roads, bridges, parking lots, and garages. In Los Angeles, the figure is two-thirds.

21. Is There a Shortfall in Public Capital Investment?
George E. Peterson

Excerpted from Alicia Munnell, ed., *Is Public Infrastructure Undersupplied?* (Federal Reserve Bank of Boston, June 1990), pp. 113–42. George E. Peterson is a senior fellow at the Urban Institute.

Over the past decade, infrastructure issues intermittently have moved toward the forefront of the domestic policy agenda. The coming year promises to intensify debate. By September 1991, Congress must reauthorize the federal highway program. Unlike past reauthorizations, this time Congress almost certainly will have to set new priorities and incorporate new principles of cost sharing for highways, since the original mission of the federal highway program will have been accomplished. Sometime in 1991–92, workers will complete the last segments of the interstate highway network, bringing to an end an era of road building that began with Dwight D. Eisenhower in 1956 and has dominated infrastructure spending since that time. Any consensus that Congress reaches regarding the definition of a new federal role in the highway program, or the appropriate use of price incentives in grant programs, is likely to spill over to the financing of other infrastructure functions.

Most of the studies claiming extreme erosion of infrastructure investment start their story with the 1960s, which turned out to be the peak period for infrastructure spending. A somewhat longer perspective better captures the wave pattern that has characterized infrastructure investment, but the impression of a secular decline in gross investment is weakened. In this perspective, the late 1970s and early 1980s stands out as a period when the net public capital stock (after depreciation) almost ceased to grow.

It is one thing to demonstrate that capital spending has declined; it is another to prove it is also too low. Is public capital undersupplied? Recent approaches to this question have emphasized the role of infrastructure as an intermediate good contributing to private production. In a series of studies, Aschauer has argued that public capital enters strongly into the private sector's production function, raising the productivity of both private capital and labor. His findings imply rates of return to infrastructure investment as high as 50 to 60 percent. Insofar as these returns vastly exceed those available to private investment, they imply that, yes, public infrastructure capital is undersupplied.

Infrastructure also yields final consumption services for households. In many states, households still vote directly on the bond issues used to finance capital projects, or on the tax and fee revenues raised to recover initial investment costs. As a result, direct evidence is often available regarding household demand for infrastructure spending. The evidence of undersupply, using consumer willingness to pay as expressed in bond referenda, is almost as strong as the evidence derived from production function studies. Over the past six years, 80 percent by value of all state and local infrastructure bond proposals have passed. The average margin of voter approval exceeded 66 percent, a substantially higher approval rate than found in any other kind of expenditure referendum. These results imply that, at least in recent years, taxpayer-consumers have been willing to buy more infrastructure capital than was actually provided by public authorities.

This paradox merits more attention than it has received. How can one account for the apparent undersupply of infrastructure? Aschauer's results imply that private producers can benefit more in terms of private output from a dollar of public investment than they can from a dollar of their own investment in private plant and equipment. Since the costs of public investment are shared with households, it would seem that, out of self-interest, business groups should be lobbying violently for tax hikes to finance an expanded public capital budget; and, if this fails, they should volunteer to pay the costs of additional public capital investment entirely on their own. Furthermore, the recent rates of voter approval of infrastructure projects at referendum imply that, with even modest leadership from the business community, it should be possible to stitch together a politically persuasive constituency for greater infrastructure spending. Either the empirical results are exaggerated, or the political system has failed to undertake high-payoff investments that also have broad political support.

Political leaders have overreacted to what might be called the fear of rejection of referendum. Since the taxpayer revolt in the 1970s, the very act of referendum voting—and the possibility it brings of public repudiation—appears to intimidate officials. Rather than designing capital proposals that satisfy the median voter, they seem to aim higher (or with more risk aversion) to win support from as large a majority of the electorate as possible in order to minimize the chance of rejection. This tendency has been exacerbated in some states by formal changes in the laws, which now require super-majority approval for capital financing issues. Infrastructure spending at the state and local levels has become misaligned with taxpayer-voter preferences, in part because officials are reluctant to put forward capital proposals that go as far as the majority of voters want.

Traditional decision-making mechanisms are badly equipped to handle joint consumer and producer demand for publicly provided goods. Referenda and other voting proxies incorporate the principle of one man, one vote. No device is available for weighting votes by willingness to pay or by economic stake in the outcome. Business, for its part, is accustomed to expressing its expenditure demands largely through lobbying. As a result, a good deal of political ingenuity in recent years has gone into inventing institutions that can legally invest in infrastructure without submitting to the referendum process. This strategy seems to be a mistake. The most striking cases of turnaround in state or local infrastructure spending have occurred precisely where new business-consumer alliances have taken their cases to the public and asked for voter support. Typically, these proposals have included a redesigned tax or fee package that has targeted a greater share of costs to business and users, thereby relieving the cost burden on the general taxpayer who must approve the new spending.

Trends in Public Capital Investment and Capital Stock

The first warnings of an impending infrastructure crisis were issued more than a decade ago by authors who called attention to the sharp decline in public capital investment. This decline has been measured in several ways. For example, the National Council on Public Works Improvement (1988) reported a drop in public works capital outlays by all levels of government from 2.5 percent of GNP in 1963 to about 1.2 percent of GNP in 1978 and 1.0 percent in 1984. Growth in the public capital stock, net of depreciation, fell to less than 1 percent per annum between the late 1970s and the mid-1980s.

It is true that maintenance and operations costs associated with infrastructure facilities rose substantially over the same period. This makes interpretation of the capital spending data alone somewhat problematic. As large capital programs such as the construction of the interstate highway system are completed and the first generation of facilities built under the program matures, it is natural that the infrastructure spending mix should shift toward maintenance. Indeed, until legislative modifications in federal highway financing were made in 1982, one of the principal criticisms of federal highway aid was that it was inefficiently directed almost exclusively to new construction. Now, some 40 percent of federal highway funding goes for repairs and rehabilitation of existing roads and bridges.

More active maintenance throws into question some of the assumptions about depreciation that are built into estimates of the public capital stock. In principle, depreciation rates should be treated as endogenous. Better maintenance and repair can stretch the useful life of infrastructure facilities and even keep them in "good as new" condition for a significant period.

The level of capital spending for highways in 1968–71 was the product of a decade's climb in gross capital investment. From a longer perspective, the decline in gross investment may seem to be more a cyclical receding from the initial impetus of the highway program than a secular trend. As Tarr has pointed out, broad cyclical swings have long characterized infrastructure investment in the United States, as one wave of building programs subsides and another begins to rise.

In 1956 Congress passed the federal highway program. In 1982 it boosted the federal gas tax to augment the highway trust fund. Both measures triggered strong growth in highway investment; ironically, the two pieces of legislation were adopted, twenty-six years apart, at almost the same level of real state and local gross investment in roads and highways. Wastewater investment began its upward swing shortly after passage of the 1972 Water Pollution Control Act, which first incorporated grants for municipal treatment facilities.

International comparisons also extend the frame of reference for capital spending. A comparison of net public investment as a share of gross domestic product in the Group of Seven countries, for example, seems to show investment trends for several European countries comparable to those in the United States.

In fact, interpretation of these trends points to some important definitional issues that underlie current discussions. "Infrastructure" spending has been equated with public nonmilitary investment and, in the United States, with state and local investment. Many infrastructure functions, however, can be provided by either the public or the private sector. In fact, in response to budgetary pressures on government, a tendency has developed to shift previously public capital responsibilities into private hands. The most widely publicized privatization efforts are those that involve complete and sudden breaks with public supply—for example, the building of private toll roads or the United Kingdom's sale of regional water authorities to the private sector.

However, closer examination shows that total sectoral capital growth has been the product of two strikingly different trends. Telecommunications investment has been rising rapidly, while highway investment has been falling. The fact that in Sweden both are public responsibilities masks a shift in investment pattern that in other nations would reveal itself as a relative decline in the public capital stock. As privatization initiatives accelerate, it would seem important to begin measuring infrastructure capital in functional terms, summed across the public and private sectors, as well as according to ownership or source of financing. Government-produced infrastructure may be of special interest because of the way expenditure and financing decisions are made. If, largely for historical reasons, infrastructure networks serving fast-growing sectors of the economy have been assigned to the private sector while networks serving manufacturing and slower-growth sectors are in public hands, the shift toward lesser intensity of public capital in production may reflect not a failure of government supply but an orderly change in factor usage that would occur regardless of public or private provision.

Failure to Take Advantage of the Joint Products of Infrastructure

Business and consumer demands are not entirely separable, of course—households presumably value the same congestion savings in the journey to work as producers. Nonetheless, the areas of overlap are limited.

Unfortunately, the mechanisms normally used to express infrastructure demand at the local or state level are ill-suited for aggregating business and consumer preferences. Most referendum voting operates under the principle of one man, one vote. Unless the tax costs of a project can be allocated so that cost shares are matched with willingness to pay, voting results are likely to under represent efficient infrastructure provision levels, since each voter's opinion is counted equally rather than being weighted by willingness to pay. Some voting systems have attempted to weight votes in a way that approximates willingness to pay. For example, it has been common in Texas and some other states to weight votes in municipal utility districts by the number of individual lots the owner possesses. That is, the decision whether to install utility networks is decided on a one lot, one vote basis. A developer may control a thousand lots or more and therefore have his economic interest represented far more strongly in the referendums than an individual owner. This system has been shown to lead to much higher demand for infrastructure provision. As a result, business demand is likely to be under represented in traditional referenda. Business can be more effective in government through lobbying and logrolling arrangements, but this demand too has proved difficult to unite with the interests of final consumers. In states where ultimate voter approval is required for most infrastructure financing, business persuasion of the legislature in any event may be an insufficient condition for realizing greater infrastructure investment.

The jurisdictions that have achieved the most dramatic turnarounds in infrastructure investment are those that have managed to forge a business-taxpayer alliance to take the case for infrastructure spending to the public. Business typically has taken the lead in organizing and financing these alliances, and sometimes has accepted a mix of general taxes and fees that falls more heavily on the business community, in order to increase voter support. The recent campaign to increase California's gas tax and dedicate the proceeds to transportation investment was a joint business-citizen effort organized by business. The constitutional proposal, which increases state capital spending on highways by an estimated $15.5 billion over ten years, passed with 52 percent of the vote. If subject to the super-majority voting standard of an ordinarily local bond proposal, it would have failed.

Conclusions

In the end, the undersupply of public infrastructure is as much a problem of political economy as of pure economics. The view most commonly expressed by public officials is that they know more public investment is desirable, but their hands are tied by an electorate that does not share their opinion and makes the final determination about expenditure levels. The evidence reviewed here suggests that this explanation for undersupply of infrastructure is spurious. If anything, voters appear to be ahead of public officials in their willingness to support the costs of increasing public capital investment. Nevertheless, a great deal of political ingenuity during the past two decades has been devoted to circumventing the need for voter approval of infrastructure spending proposals. Over the long run, this effort is likely to be counterproductive. Proponents of stronger infrastructure investment seem to be better off taking their case directly to the public.

22. Anatomy of the Voluntary Nonprofit Sector

Burton A. Weisbrod

Excerpted and reprinted by permission of the publishers from *The Nonprofit Economy* by Burton A. Weisbrod, Cambridge, Mass.: Harvard University Press, copyright © 1988 by the president and fellows of Harvard College, pp. 59–74. Burton A. Weisbrod is professor of economics at the University of Wisconsin at Madison.

There are three general categories of nonprofit—one private and two public types. The private type consists of commercial, or proprietary, nonprofits. Although they do not operate to reap profit themselves, they are instruments for generating profits for their constituents—private firms or members. Proprietary nonprofits include trade associations as well as clubs and associations that do little but seek the betterment of their own members—country clubs, dog and garden clubs, farmer cooperations, mutual insurance companies, and chambers of commerce.

There are two forms of public-type nonprofits—collective and trust. A collective nonprofit provides services that generate sizable "external" benefits to persons who do not help to finance the organization's activities—for example, medical research, museums, wildlife sanctuaries, environmental protection, and aid to the poor. The activities of collective nonprofits are virtually indistinguishable from those of governmental agencies. Some nonprofits, for example, finance research on causes and cures for diseases, and various United Way organizations aid the poor and handicapped. The work of these nonprofits is essentially the same as that performed by the National Institutes of Health and the U.S. Department of Health and Human Services, as well as various state and local governmental agencies.

The second public-type nonprofit provides "trust goods"—combinations of a private good and consumer protection. Nursing homes, daycare centers, and blood banks are potential examples. They sell their services, just as proprietary firms do, but the services they sell are of the kind about which consumers are often poorly informed.

Although these three categories—proprietary, collective, and trust nonprofits—are useful, the nonprofit sector is more complex than they would suggest. There are borderline cases, such as organizations that ostensibly provide collective or trust goods but may actually take advantage of their privileged position to operate as a proprietary nonprofit would. This can happen because the high cost of regulating a nonprofit permits some organizations to take advantage of their opportunities and subsidies and reap private rewards for the organizers or managers. For example, two exporters of used clothing were charged in the federal district court of Philadelphia with paying kickbacks to Salvation Army officers to ensure a steady supply of clothes for shipment abroad; the case involved an alleged misuse of a public-type nonprofit for the attainment of private profit. Enforcement of the laws constraining the behavior of nonprofits poses the same problems as are found elsewhere in society.

In the United States, the tax laws determine which organizations are classified as nonprofit. The government "nonprofit" (or tax-exempt) classification is useful for two reasons. First, the determination of tax-exempt status through a democratic decision-making process gives a nonprofit organization some legitimacy. Second, the IRS makes available data it gathers on organizations so classified. Simply designating an organization nonprofit does not, of course, change its objectives or its behavior. The nondistribution constraint, however, applies to all organizations that receive tax-exempt status by the IRS.

There is, in short, an enormous diversity of organizations that the Internal Revenue Service can certify as tax exempt. To some people, the nonprofit sector is interesting because of its charitable or "philanthropic" activities, such as may be engaged in by organizations that qualify for tax deductibility of donations—largely the 501(c)(3) organizations—or, perhaps, by those organizations plus those that would qualify were it not that they engage in a "substantial" amount of legislative lobbying, the 501(c)(4) organizations.

The Size of the Nonprofit Sector

Organizations in the United States that are legally classified as nonprofit (that is, tax exempt) are far more common than most people would guess.

They engage in hundreds of distinct activities; they are growing at the rate of thousands per year; they employ millions of workers; and they have hundreds of billions of dollars of annual revenues and assets.

In 1967, 309,000 organizations were designated tax exempt by the IRS. In fewer than twenty years that number nearly tripled, approaching 900,000. The tax-deductible, "charitable" nonprofits have similarly leaped in number, from 138,000 in 1969 to 366,000 in 1985—an increase of over 160 percent; these are the nonprofits that have been granted special privileges, presumably because they are thought to provide substantial public benefits (collective or trust). Nonprofits are growing at a more rapid rate than for-profit corporations, which increased by 100 percent—although from a larger base—from about 1.5 million in 1967 to 3.0 million in 1983, the most recent year for which data are available. The total revenues of the charitable nonprofits have also increased markedly in recent years, from $115 billion in 1975 to $314 billion in 1983.

Even more striking is the recent tidal wave of applications for tax-exempt status. Through the late 1950s and early 1960s the IRS was receiving some 7,000 applications for tax-exempt status annually. In one year, however—1965—the number more than doubled, to over 14,000, probably as a consequence of the Great Society programs of the federal government; by 1984 it had more than quadrupled again, to over 64,000, although it dropped substantially in 1985, to some 59,000.

Throughout this period, the IRS continued to approve 70 to 80 percent of applications for nonprofit status. The result: The number of new nonprofits rose dramatically. The IRS approved about 5,000 new nonprofits per year through 1963; in 1964, the IRS approved nearly 40 percent more—7,000. This was only the beginning of a new era for the nonprofits. In 1965, the IRS approved nearly 12,000 applications; by 1977 the IRS was approving over 35,000 applications annually, and in 1984 and in 1985 more than 44,000 new nonprofits entered the economy.

The number of nonprofit organizations says nothing about their size, of course. Nonprofits are typically small, and, overall, they own only 1.8 percent of the nation's assets. It would be a mistake, though, to dismiss this share as inconsequential. Many nonprofits provide government-type services (collective and trust). If nonprofits are compared with government, a very different picture emerges. Assets in the nonprofit sector are substantial when compared with those of the federal government—3.9 percent of national assets—or with the assets of all state and local governments—8.5 percent. Thus, assets of the nonprofit sector equal nearly 50 percent of the assets of the federal government and some 15 percent of the assets owned by all levels of government in the United States. Moreover assets of the nonprofit sector have been growing, whereas those of government have declined.

The nonprofit sector's contribution to national income has also been growing, but cyclically. Since World War II, the relative importance of the nonprofit sector has shown an almost uninterrupted climb.

Because nonprofit organizations are typically labor intensive, they are far more important as employers of labor than as contributors to national output. As of 1977, when the U.S. Department of Commerce last comprehensively surveyed employment in the service sector, nonprofit organizations employed well over 5 percent of the entire labor force.

I have estimated employment in the nonprofit sector using another approach and find a considerably higher level. I assume that employment in the nonprofit sector bears the same relation to total revenue of the sector as it does in other parts of the economy. By this standard there are an estimated 9 million full time equivalent (FTE) employees in the nonprofit sector—80 percent more than the Census Bureau figure (which was clearly an underestimate) and fully 12 percent of the nation's FTE labor force of 74.4 million workers in 1976. In any case, the range of estimates shows that the nonprofit sector employs a substantial portion of the labor force.

Whatever the true number of paid workers in the nonprofit sector, the total amount of labor working in this part of the economy is considerably greater. The difference is unpaid volunteers, who supply billions of hours of time annually. The most recent estimate, based on a 1985 survey, put time volunteered to formal organizations at the equivalent of 5.7–6.7 million FTE workers (depending on whether a work year of 2,000 hours or 1,700 hours is assumed); this was some 6 percent of the employed labor force, 106 million, in that year. Since paid employment in the service sector is about 20 percent of the total labor force, volunteer labor is an even larger percentage in the charitable social services subsector, where nonprofits are concentrated.

The supply of volunteer labor (as well as revenue in monetary form) is influenced a great deal by public policies, but unsatisfactory record keeping is a major handicap to our understanding the full extent of this influence. Volunteer labor is unpriced, so it is not included in Department of Labor statistics on employment and unemployment.

What Does the Nonprofit Sector Do?

Nonprofit organizations, as defined by the International Revenue Code, engage in literally hundreds of activities: They operate schools, churches, hospitals, museums, advocacy and civil rights campaigns, and scientific research centers—most of which qualify as tax-deductible charities serving a "public purpose"—as well as trade unions, mutual insurance companies, and far more. These latter organizations—along with country

clubs, farm bureaus, chambers of commerce, and fraternities and sorori-
ties—pursue the private interests of their constituents or members and
have only modest or nonexistent external benefits to outsiders. These are
the private or commercial nonprofits; their effects can be judged, and
their behavior understood, in terms of their influence on the profit or
welfare of their members rather than in terms of their own revenue surplus or "profit."

The largest class of nonprofits—about 40 percent of the total—includes
the educational, health, welfare, scientific, and cultural organizations that
benefit from being tax exempt; donations to them are tax deductible.
These are most of the organizations whose requests for donations arrive
in our daily mail—to help the poor at home and abroad; to support
medical research; to foster a local theater, art, or music group; to aid
"public" radio and television; to facilitate a college's educational activities; and so on. They include such diverse groups as the American Statistical Association, the Fellowship of Christian Athletes, the American
Museum of Natural History, the National Wildlife Federation, and the
Grand Rapids (Michigan) Symphony Society. This is also the class of
nonprofits that has grown the most. Nearly 49 percent of the total growth
between 1969 and 1985 in the number of nonprofits was in this philanthropic class, which grew by nearly 170 percent.

Growth in the number of nonprofits has by no means been limited to
the tax-deductible organizations. There is another group of social welfare
nonprofits that is very similar to this class except that donations to it are
not tax deductible because the organizations engage in a "substantial"
amount of legislative lobbying; Sierra Club, an environmental protection
organization, is a prominent example, and Common Cause is another. So,
too, are the Veterans of World War I, the Conference of Presidents of
Major Jewish Organizations, and the National Hot Rod Association.

The revenues of both deductible and nondeductible social welfare
nonprofits are also rising dramatically. Between 1973 and 1982, gross
receipts of the tax-deductible, 501(c)(3) nonprofits quadrupled, rising
from $57 billion to $234 billion, while receipts of the 501(c)(4) organizations, although nondeductible, grew nearly as rapidly, from $15 billion to
over $58 billion. The combined receipts of these, the two most numerous
groups of nonprofits totaled 5.4 percent as much as the gross national
product in 1973 and rose to 9.5 percent as much by 1982.

We get a clearer picture of the activities of nonprofits from a 1977
survey by the Census Bureau of the service sector of the economy, where
nonprofits are overwhelmingly concentrated. Organizations that provide
health services are a major component of the nonprofit service sector.
They include only 7 percent of the 166,000 tax-exempt service organizations covered in the survey, but they accounted for nearly 50 percent—2.4

million—of the 4.95 million paid workers in the industries surveyed. Hospitals alone employed some 86 percent of the 2.4 million workers in health services. The number of employees of nursing homes has grown appreciably since 1977, both absolutely and relative to the number of hospital workers.

Education is the second-largest employer in the nonprofit service sector. The 9,160 educational organizations in the survey, including mostly schools but also some 1,400 nonprofit libraries, comprised another 19 percent of total employment in the nonprofit service sector. There are nearly twice as many social service nonprofits as there are for health and education combined, but they are typically small. Encompassing family social services, job training and vocational rehabilitation, child care, and so on, social service nonprofits constitute one-quarter of all nonprofit establishments. Despite their prevalence, they are responsible for only 14 percent of paid employment and 10 percent of the payroll of the nonprofits surveyed.

Among the private-type service nonprofits, membership organizations, including some 23,000 labor unions and 12,000 business associations, are extremely numerous. Although they constitute half of all the nonprofit service organizations, they are relatively small employers. They employ 600,000 people—only 12 percent of the total—but their impact on the economy is surely understated by either their share of employment or their share of expenditures, which is 14 percent of the entire service sector.

Another type of membership organization is the "civic, social, or fraternal" nonprofit, of which there are more than 34,000. The Census Bureau classified these quite dissimilar organizations together, but they ought to be distinguished. Many civic and fraternal organizations provide important public-type services for their communities even while they are in other respects providing proprietary, club-type services to their own members. Difficult as it is to differentiate organizations by their contributions to nonmembers, that is what must be addressed in any public policy debate; public subsidies ought to reflect public benefits.

About 4 percent of the nonprofit service organizations exist to promote "amusement and recreation," and most of them are proprietary-type nonprofits. More than 80 percent of them—5,910—are membership sports and recreation clubs, which presumably bring benefits to members alone; the balance are orchestras and other entertainment organizations, which typically charge admission fees. The social desirability of public subsidies to entertainment organizations has not been clearly resolved in this country, although such subsidies are commonplace in Europe.

23. A Monetary Perspective on Underground Economic Activity in the United States
Richard D. Porter and Amanda S. Bayer

Excerpted from the *Federal Reserve Bulletin*, March 1984, pp. 177–87. Richard D. Porter and Amanda S. Bayer are in the Division of Research and Statistics of the Federal Reserve Board.

A growing underground economy in the United States and in other countries has been widely reported in recent years. The underground economy is thought to reflect efforts to evade taxes and government regulation. Although no single definition of such activity has been universally accepted, the term generally refers to activity—whether legal or illegal—generating income that is either under reported or not reported at all. Some investigators narrow the definition to cover only income produced in legal activity that is not reported in the national income statistics.

Discussion of underground economic activity intensified in the late 1970s with the publication of two estimates, derived from aggregate monetary statistics, of the size of the underground economy in the United States, one by Peter Gutmann and the other by Edgar Feige. Since then, numerous estimates have been made of the scope of this sector in the United States and in other countries. The magnitude of some of these estimates has occasioned congressional hearings and various government studies. In 1979, the Internal Revenue Service estimated that for 1976, individuals failed to report between $75 billion and $100 billion in income from legal sources and another $25 billion to $35 billion from three types of illegal activity—drugs, gambling, and prostitution. In 1983, the estimates of unreported income from legal sources for 1976 were raised to $131.5 billion, while the estimates of income from illegal sources dropped to $13.4 billion.

In this more recent study, the IRS estimated that unreported income from legal sources grew at a 13 percent annual rate over roughly the last decade, from $93.9 billion in 1973 to $249.7 billion in 1981, while unreported income from the three selected illegal activities grew at a 17.7 percent annual rate, from $9.3 billion to $34.2 billion. To estimate unreported income from legal sources, the IRS drew mainly upon data on individual taxpayers from its Taxpayer Compliance Measurement Program, which audits a sample of income tax returns, and upon data from its Information Returns Program, which uses information from the payers of income tax. It developed estimates of unreported income from legal sources for individuals not filing returns by cross-checking information from two nationwide household surveys against its own records and those of the Social Security Administration. Finally, the IRS estimated unreported income obtained in the selected illegal activities from survey data and arrest records.

This approach to estimating the size of the underground economy has been subject to criticism. Some contend that the estimates derived from administrative records and surveys are likely to understate actual unreported income. They believe that estimates derived from monetary statistics offer a better gauge of underground activity and unreported income.

Aside from issues such as the underpayment of tax liabilities, the existence of an underground economy that may be growing relative to the recorded economy creates problems for analyses of public policy issues, including monetary policy. For example, policies developed from data on the recorded economy may not necessarily stabilize the total economy; or, movements in monetary aggregates that reflect changes in the underground economy may be interpreted as signaling change in the recorded economy. Thus, policy makers need to assess the scope of the underground economy to see whether these potential issues deserve more explicit consideration.

The analysis of underground activity has not progressed enough to permit a reliable estimate of the scope of such activity from an analysis of monetary data. Given current techniques, these data do not convincingly support the hypothesis that the share of the underground economy in the total U.S. economy has grown recently. Perhaps as more satisfactory data and techniques emerge, better estimates can be developed.

24. Managerial Decline: The Military Industrial Influence
John E. Ullmann

Excerpted from John E. Ullmann, *The Prospects of American Industrial Recovery* (Westport, Conn.: Quorum Books, 1985), pp. 12–20. Reprinted with permission of Greenwood Publishing Group, Inc., Westport, CT.

The military industrial firm (MIF), the chosen instrument of military production, has distinctive characteristics in its managerial organization, in the risks from which it is protected, and in the manner in which society has chosen to sustain and almost encourage its inefficiencies and dysfunctions. Furthermore, as the arms race accelerates, there is the likelihood that its mode of operation and organization will increasingly become something of a norm in the American economy. This would present a sharp departure from what are usually regarded as the characteristic activities of the private sector. Under these conditions, private enterprise will increasingly lose many of the qualities that now distinguish it from governmental operations, and thus diminish its claim as the essential driving force of industrial and general recovery.

Specifically, a combination of financial and technical profligacy, bloated payrolls, wasted motion, unwholesome relationships with government agencies, and technical concentration away from commercial products will increasingly lead to a condition where much of what is left of private industrial competence will have been thrown out of what Ronald Reagan's military experts called the "window of vulnerability." With it may well go a large chunk of the sociopolitical consensus that has nurtured the private sector in the past and given it legitimacy.

The military industrial firm is an organization engaged in the production of weapons or other specialized equipment for which the Department of Defense is the only customer, or unrelated research, development, testing, and evaluation. It may be an independent corporate entity or a division or other unit of a firm making other products as well. It may be a nonprofit organization or specialized unit of a university. This definition excludes firms supplying their usual product to the Department of Defense, e.g., food, fuel, or other standard supplies. For such firms, government business is not essentially different from what they normally do.

The double condition of specialization and monopsonistic dependency has led to a phenomenon which is fairly new in American life. Ostensibly, the military industrial firms are private. They have shareholders, they are organized in the hierarchical way typical of American firms, and their securities are traded on the exchanges or over the counter when they are publicly owned. Governmental ownership of such securities tends to be minimal and is typically undertaken only for purposes of bailing the enterprise out.

There is a profound difference between the military industrial firms and the rest of the business community. The essential point is that a central direction, unparalleled in American business experience, was put in place. In December 1967, Murray L. Weidenbaum, who was to serve President Reagan as chairman of the Council of Economic Advisers from January 1981 to August 1982, described the relationship as follows:

To a substantial degree the government is taking on the traditional role of the private entrepreneur while the companies are becoming less like other corporations and acquiring [many] of the characteristics of a government agency or arsenal. In a sense, the close, continuing relationship between the Department of Defense and its major suppliers is resulting in the convergence between the two which is blurring and reducing much of the distinction between public and private activities and is an important branch of the American economy.

Actually, the relationship was more accurately described by Seymour Melman as "state-management," and it functions more like a central office controlling a number of divisions. Each of the "divisions," meaning individual military industrial firms, may have a substantial degree of operational autonomy at the local level. The firms are certainly operated as individual profit centers. Nevertheless, the "central office" sets policy in a wide range of activities and maintains a substantial supervisory and controlling organization that sees to it that the central directives are obeyed. It could indeed be argued that the presence of local controllers and the rules under which military procurement takes place are a good deal more burdensome and detailed than those in many a decentralized nonmilitary corporation or conglomerate. The system of rules is essentially contained in the *Armed Services Procurement Regulations (ASPR)* and in the *Defense Procurement Handbook*, which serves in part as a training manual for those involved in the procurement and control process, both from the Pentagon side and at the receiving end in the military industrial firms.

In the United States, private business has traditionally resisted, to the maximum degree of its influence, any significant government controls that would encroach upon its decision power. Such restrictions are considered by business leaders as manifestations of socialist tendencies. To a degree, they occur in all capitalist countries, but central governmental direction of industrial structure, output, purpose, and policies would most certainly not sit well with American business. It is therefore surprising that American business has over the years strained at many a regulatory gnat but swallowed the camel of Pentagon state management.

What to Make

The Department of Defense (DOD) essentially decides what products it wants industry to make. There is, to be sure, a mechanism for feedback from the suppliers, and follow-up ideas from existing contracts certainly may make their way to the top of the procurement process. There is, however, no record of a major weapon having been the result of an unsolicited bid; a mechanism for submitting such bids does exist but is regarded in the industry as the longest of long shots. In practice, orders for specialized products are put out for bids or negotiated without bids (a very common practice) after having been specified in the greatest detail.

This detailed control is different from and much closer than what is exercised by the head office in a decentralized, multidivision firm. In such structures, each division typically has a product development department that works closely with divisional engineering, marketing, and production. It is charged with responsibility for keeping a constant watch on the product line, identifying opportunities, and giving direction to new product development. It is true that divisions in large firms are constrained by central office determinations of what business the company is supposed to be in; however, in these times of variegated conglomerates especially, such specifications of product are likely to be deliberately vague.

If bids are required, then, before any company is considered eligible, it must be included on the list of approved bidders. Inclusion depends upon a variety of prior experience, but one characteristic appears to be that certain firms are taken to "belong" to a particular unit of the armed services. In other words, for such a company, it might be considered real "diversification" to supply a different Air Force command or perhaps the navy rather than the army; meanwhile, it is very much a "division" of the Pentagon conglomerate or its parts.

A second item often noted has been that once a unit of a company is strongly dependent upon military orders, any efforts on its part to diversify into commercial areas are not viewed with approval by their military controllers; rather they cast the contractor in the role of the "undeserving poor." This too is part of the quasi-divisional structure characteristic of the Pentagon state management. This is not to say that the relationship is always formally hierarchical. To the contrary, it is often collegial and symbiotic to a fault. There is a well-worn career path between the armed services, contractors and back to the Pentagon management.

Decline in Products

Throughout the pcst–World War II period, the product flops in weaponry present a long, continuing, and weary procession. Among the first was the B–58 bomber, which, in those palmy days when gold cost $35 a troy ounce, wound up costing more than gold and proved so unsafe that it had to be abandoned after very short service. Since then, we have had troubled products such as the C–5A transport and the F–111. At present, the A–6, F–14, and especially F–18 aircraft continue that tradition; on land and sea there are, among others, the M–1 (main battle) tank, the Aegis cruiser, the Sergeant York anti-aircraft gun, and the Hummer vehicle. The latter, a replacement for the jeep, is especially noteworthy because its troubles occurred in the land where the jeep was created—a vehicle that has shown its mettle over decades and which, together with a whole group of foreign imitations, is indispensable to transportation in much of the world. Technical debility could hardly have a more painful illustration—and it is technical debility.

These projects, and many others like them, show a combination of poor design, poor manufacturing quality, and poor reliability and maintenance. In June 1983, Paul Thayer, deputy secretary of defense, asserted that poor work added from 10 to 30 percent to military costs. Neglect of maintenance, more than almost anything else, is an indicator of a profound decline in the total technical capability of society. In November 1983, Congress forced a reluctant Pentagon to demand warranties by which contractors would have to "bear the costs of all work promptly to repair or replace" defective items. Even though warranties may be waived for reasons of national defense or cost effectiveness (a rather broad exemption), barely three months later, the Pentagon added a total repeal provision to its fiscal 1984 supplementary budget request, with a parliamentary maneuver to place the measure before a sympathetic Senate subcommittee.

Meanwhile, the reports of gross overcharges and malpractice have continued unabated, whether it is of $400 paid for a claw hammer, $7,622 for a coffee maker for the C–5A transport plane, excluding its stainless-steel pot, improper disposal of still useful spare parts, standard work hours charged at over $6,000 each or that from 20 to 30 percent of navy air-to-air missiles and 80 percent of Marine anti-tank missiles being unusable because they cannot hit anything, cannot tell friend from foe, or return to destroy their dispatchers. The Pentagon has responded by noting that its own watchdogs have brought such misdeeds to light. Nevertheless, the worst ones have usually been revealed by whistle blowers who face great difficulties as a result and countered by various public relations exercises.

At the same time, it was becoming clear that the above kind of performance is the rule rather than the exception. This suggests that an extremely serious condition has beset the economy in that, over increasing areas, the managers of the industrial system are no longer capable of organizing production competently. In the conventional private sector of a capitalist system, such failure would speedily engender a decline of profits and insolvency. MIF management is immune from such retribution. However, as its way of doing things metastasizes in other parts of the economy, the survival of the entire system in its familiar form is called into question. It is not a matter of profit declining overall, which is part of the Marxist scenario for capitalist decline; rather, the decline comes from the catastrophic fall in the quality of organization, innovation, deployment of physical assets, managerial control, and degree of commitment to competence which the grotesque distortions described in the above sampling clearly demonstrate. It is no excuse that the Pentagon often loses sight of reality in setting its specifications. That too is part of MIF management. No halfway sane industrial purchase in the commercial sector would tolerate it.

The repeal of the warranty law was advocated in order to protect "innovation" from excessive risks, but innovation itself has been a prominent victim of military priorities. Its decline in the United States is shown by such objective measures as the so-called patent balance. After decades of American advantage, American patents taken out by foreigners have come to exceed substantially the number of patents taken out abroad by Americans. More evidence is provided by simple comparison between the periods 1945–60 and 1961–76. Since about 1960, there has been a hiatus in technical innovation that contrasts painfully with the enormously productive period between 1945 and 1960. In that time, the antibiotics, steroids, television (black and white and color), new plastics and fabrics, insecticides, computers, etc., all made their debut, as did more star-crossed developments like nuclear power. After 1960 this stream of innovation largely dried up. Promising leads such as those in solar and other energy, transportation, and sea water desalination were no longer followed up. When some of them were taken up again following the energy problems of the early 1970s, it was almost as if everyone had gone to sleep for a decade. Many of them lag badly even now.

The beginning of this fallow period coincided quite precisely with the sharp expansion of American military research and the concentration of effort in those areas, following President Kennedy's alleged missile gap, the escalation of the Vietnam War, and the moon shot.

There is a frequently expressed view that technology is something of an independent variable; it produces its innovations in an almost random manner, and somehow society then has to cope with the result. If this was ever true, however, it certainly is not now. Rather, a society gets the technology it chooses to support and pay for. Engineers and scientists only work when someone wishes to invest in their products and provides them with the requisite expensive and sophisticated equipment. This holds true of science in general. "Pure" science uses some of the most expensive equipment to be found anywhere; in fact, just the computer services may involve huge expenditures. In the absence of these tools and employment opportunities, engineering and scientific talent either lies fallow or is directed toward those areas to which a society wishes to accord priorities. This in the United States has overwhelmingly been in the military direction, in contrast with such major competitors as West

Germany and especially Japan, which, unencumbered by such distortions, were able to secure for themselves a leading role in the technically oriented industries.

25. Health Care: Dynamic Technology and Changing Demographics
Council of Economic Advisers

Excerpted from the *Economic Report of the President* (Washington, D.C.: U.S. Government Printing Office, 1991), pp. 135–42. The council members responsible for the report were Chairman Michael J. Boskin, John B. Taylor, and Richard L. Schmalensee.

Health care has been one of the fastest-growing and most innovative sectors of the U.S. economy during the last three decades. Although many factors have contributed to the rapid pace of change, the fundamental driving forces have been technological advances and shifts in the demographic makeup of the population. These forces, along with the lack of market incentives for cost-conscious behavior, have resulted in escalating costs and much concern about lack of access to health care for many Americans—particularly the 33 million people who lack health insurance coverage. While government programs finance care for many of the poor and elderly, increasing government involvement in the health care financing system has aggravated the problems of cost and access.

Recent Trends

The most dramatic illustration of the growing importance of the health sector is its rising share of GNP. In 1960, health care accounted for 5.3 percent of GNP; its share rose to 11.6 percent in 1989. To put those numbers in perspective, total health care spending in 1989 was twice as large as federal spending on defense and more than six times larger than the value of U.S. farm output.

The growing share of health care in the U.S. GNP can be traced to developments on both the supply and demand side of the health care market. On the supply side, technological advances have made possible a vast array of medical treatments unheard of even a decade ago. Developments in diagnostic equipment and pharmaceutical, for example, have promoted earlier and more successful treatment of many diseases. Much of this technology, however, is costly. Therefore, while technological advance has undoubtedly improved the quality of treatment received, it has simultaneously made the treatment more expensive.

In addition to technological advances and economic growth, health costs have increased because of the aging of the population. Older individuals incur more health expenditures, on average, than the young or middle-aged. The percentage of Americans aged sixty-five and older rose from 9.2 percent in 1960 to a projected 12.6 percent in 1990, representing an increase of 14.9 million older Americans. During that period, life expectancy rose by more than five years and infant mortality rates declined by 63 percent. *These statistics indicate that increases in the amount of resources devoted to health are not necessarily bad, since to a large extent they represent an investment in health, the changing preferences of a wealthier society, and the extra cost of a long lived population.*

Table 25.1 shows that the aging of the population will continue to exert a large influence on the health care system for several decades. Even without above-average increases in medical prices, the rise in the elderly population means that the United States will pay much more for health care in the coming decades unless dramatic developments occur that reduce costs.

Perceived Problems of the Existing System

Despite the beneficial effects of much spending on health care, there is a general perception that the U.S. health care system should perform better than it does. Costs are seen to be out of control, and millions of households do not have health insurance and are perceived to have inadequate access to care.

Rising Government Health Care Costs

Health care costs paid by federal, state, and local governments have exploded. The combined total spent by all levels of government on health care rose from $28.1 billion in 1960 (in 1989 dollars) to $253.3 billion in 1989 and is expected to continue to rise. These escalating costs place great stress on the ability of governments to fund current and future liabilities in health care.

Medicare, the principal program for providing medical care to the elderly and disabled, illustrates the changes in government spending on health. Medicare expenditures were $17.6 billion (in 1989 dollars) in 1967, the first full year of the program, and 19.5 million people were enrolled. By 1989 the federal government was spending $100 billion on Medicare,

Table 25.1

Aging of the U.S. Population, 1960–2040

Year	Population (millions)		Over 64 as percent of total
	Total	Over 64	
1960	180.7	16.7	9.2
1980	227.8	25.7	11.3
2000	268.3	34.9	13.0
2020	294.4	52.1	17.7
2040	301.8	68.1	22.6

Sources: Department of Commerce and Bureau of the Census.

and 33.6 million elderly and disabled Americans were enrolled. The enormous increase in outlays for Medicare can be traced to the increase in the number of people covered by the program, general increases in medical care expenses, and the increased share of program costs borne by the federal government. For example, the federal government originally shared equally with enrollers the cost of covered physician services, but in recent years beneficiaries have paid only 25 percent of the cost. Even when all benefits and patient payments are included, the federal government pays out $3 for every $1 spent by Medicare patients.

Medicaid, the program that funds health care for some of the poor, illustrates the effect of changing demographics on both the type of care received and increasing government costs. Started in 1965, Medicaid was initially designed as a joint federal/state program to provide health care of women and children receiving welfare payments and the disabled. Medicaid eligibility has expanded in recent years, but even today it is not designed to provide medical care for all poor Americans. Total Medicaid expenditures in 1967 were only $7.6 billion (in 1989 dollars). In 1989, the federal government financed 57 percent of a total Medicaid bill of $59.3 billion.

The most significant trend in recent years has been the increase in Medicaid spending on nursing-home care for the elderly. Spending on long-term care for the elderly accounted for about 25 percent of all Medicaid spending in 1989. As the number of elderly citizens continues to rise, the costs of long-term care will also increase.

Health Care Price Inflation

Rapid increases in the real price of health care have contributed to the overall rise in health care spending. From 1980 to 1989 the price index for medical care rose by 99 percent, twice as fast as the average for all goods and services, though difficulties in measuring the inflation rate in technologically dynamic sectors suggest that the real difference in inflation rates was probably somewhat less. Those rapid price increases, combined with growth in the volume of services demanded, raised total health care expenses.

The health care sector has responded to cost escalation in several innovative ways. One of the most significant changes is the growth in health maintenance organizations (HMOs) and preferred provider organizations (PPOs). HMOs charge a fixed annual fee for medical services rather than a separate fee for each service provided. In a PPO, a group of providers negotiates prices and patient volume with a large health care purchaser, such as an insurance company or employer. Through their greater potential for supplying cost-effective care, HMOs and PPOs provide competitive alternatives to traditional fee-for-service insurance policies. The rapid growth of HMOs and PPOs illustrates both the important role of competition and the ability of the health care sector to respond innovatively to the challenge of cost escalation.

The Medically Uninsured

One of the most critical deficiencies of the U.S. health care delivery system is the large number of people who lack health insurance. Although estimates vary, recent calculations place the number of uninsured Americans at around 33 million. Because the very poor are usually covered by government programs such as Medicaid, many of the uninsured are employed workers or children and spouses of workers. They may lack insurance coverage because their employers cannot afford to offer it, they cannot afford to purchase it on their own, and they do not qualify for government-subsidized programs.

Many of the uninsured are not poor; 39 percent of uninsured Americans have incomes more than twice the official poverty level. Many young, healthy workers prefer not to purchase insurance when given a choice, since the cost of a policy outweighs its perceived benefits. To a great extent, the lack of access to health care or affordable insurance is due to the increase in health care costs during the last few decades.

Two policies enacted in 1990 will help to protect families particularly at risk from lack of insurance. Low- and moderate-income families will receive a tax credit covering part of the cost of purchasing medical insurance covering the whole family rather than just obtaining single coverage for the worker. In addition, Medicaid coverage was extended to all pregnant women and children up to age six in families with incomes below 133 percent of the poverty line. The administration's new infant mortality initiative and its proposed expansion of the Special Supplemental Food Program for Women, Infants, and Children, along with a variety of initiatives emphasizing preventive care, will further enhance the health of low-income families.

CHAPTER IV

The Evolution of the Business Sector

26. The Company in the Postwar World
Mansel G. Blackford and K. Austin Kerr

Excerpted from Mansel G. Blackford and K. Austin Kerr, *Business Enterprise in American History*, pp. 345–80. Copyright © 1990 by Houghton Mifflin Company. Reprinted with permission. Mansel G. Blackford and K. Austin Kerr are professors of history at Ohio State University.

The years following World War II saw tremendous growth in the American business system. With the American government backing free-trade policies, American products invaded the world market, and increasing numbers of American business executives began thinking in global terms. The domestic market also broadened as the consumerism of the 1920s and 1930s continued apace in the postwar years. Just as they had created a new type of business firm—the multidivisional, decentralized company—to take advantage of new business opportunities in the 1920s, so business leaders forged additional types of business structures to take advantage of opportunities in the postwar period. As these new forms of big business developed, the division between center and peripheral firms in America's business system widened, continuing a trend that had begun with the rise of big business in the nineteenth century.

The Postwar Economy

Economic Growth

"Growth" is the word that best characterizes the economy of the United States for the two decades after World War II. Many Americans feared a recession, or even a depression, after the end of the war, but such worries proved unwarranted. The American economy experienced rapid expansion into the 1970s, its growth interrupted by only a few short and mild recessions. Between 1945 and 1960, America's real GNP rose by 52 percent, and its per capita GNP increased 19 percent. Over the next decade the nation's real GNP soared an additional 46 percent, and its per capita GNP rose by 29 percent. Price stability accompanied and contributed to this economic growth.

Structural Changes in the Economy

Major alterations accompanied the growth in America's business system, opening opportunities for entrepreneurs in a variety of fields. Within the United States, structural changes begun before World War II accelerated after the conflict, most notably the production of a vast array of consumer durables. Cars, television sets, and household appliances poured off assembly lines as America continued to develop a consumer society. Even more noticeable was the remarkable expansion in the nation's service industries.

The economic expansion that occurred in this period greatly enlarged the scope of the modern American consumer society, the outlines of which had become readily apparent in the 1920s. One indication was the continuing growth of the advertising industry. Spending on advertising had declined during the slump of the 1930s, and the decline had continued during World War II when mobilization commanded attention. In the five years after the end of the war, however, advertising expenditures soared from $2.9 billion in 1945 to $5.7 billion in 1950, or 2 percent of GNP. In 1986, firms spent $102.1 billion on advertisements directed at American consumers, or 2.4 percent of GNP. Although the proportion of advertising expenditures to the size of the economy did not grow very significantly, the total volume of advertising messages increased dramatically as expenditures kept pace with the nation's growth. This trend, combined with the ability in the decades after 1945 to exploit the new medium of television for commercial purposes, meant that advertising was more ubiquitous in Americans' lives.

The economy of the United States became increasingly linked to that of other nations after the war as a series of international trade and monetary agreements promoted free trade. American leaders believed that free trade stimulated both economic growth at home and global economic development, from which they expected international political stability to spring. American exports and imports, which together came to 10 percent of the nation's GNP in 1965, equaled 20 percent of the nation's GNP in 1985. World trade itself expanded by a factor of five between 1950 and 1970, and America participated in this expansion. As we shall see, American multinationals, in particular, greatly increased their involvement in the global economy during the 1950s and 1960s.

A major area of opportunity for American entrepreneurs in the postwar era lay in service industries, which have always been important in America's economic growth. In the nineteenth century, manufacturing and services developed together, reinforcing each other. Transportation improvements helped create the national market so necessary for large-scale industrialization, and investment banking houses marketed the securities of the nation's railroads. The pattern of complementary development continued in the early twentieth century. New advertising firms, for instance, allowed manufacturers to reach the growing market for consumer goods in the 1920s. The significance of service industries became increasingly pronounced after World War II.

The service sector, broadly defined to include trade, finance, transportation, and government, accounted for 68 percent of America's GNP by 1970, and the proportion remained about the same in the 1980s. By contrast, the contributions of the extractive industries (agriculture and mining) and manufacturing declined. Of the 36 million new jobs created in the United States between 1957 and 1987, 90 percent were in services, and of the 23 million women who found jobs in America during that period, 97 percent became employed in service industries. While some of the service jobs were in low-paying, dead-end positions, others were in well-paying industries with good prospects for advancement. Exports of services—business consulting, telecommunications, and computer services were the most common—also improved the foreign trade picture of the United States. In 1980, the United States was the single greatest exporter of services, accounting for 12 percent of the world's total exports.

IBM and the Data-Processing Industry

The data-processing industry—dominated by International Business Machines (IBM)—illustrates the increasing importance of service industries in American daily life. The data-processing industry first developed to serve the needs of the federal government and America's growing number of big businesses. The managers of government and business bureaucracies depended on more and more data supplied at an ever-faster pace as the basis for their decisions. It was the availability of such data, for instance, that allowed decentralization to proceed at Du Pont and General Motors in the 1920s. This requirement of business and government created a market for new office machines, such as tabulators and calculators, before World War II and for computers in the postwar period. In the early and mid-1980s, the market for computers broadened, as new types became available for small and medium-sized businesses and found their way into household use. By the 1980s, computers had become a ubiquitous feature of the American scene.

The origins of the computer industry and of IBM stretch back to the founding of the Computer-Tabulating-Recording Company (CTR) in 1910. CTR made time clocks, scales, and—most important for the future—tabulating machines. The federal government used those tabulators in processing census returns, and some railroads employed them in handling their statistics. In 1914, Thomas Watson, who had begun his business career selling cash registers, joined CTR, and a year later he became the company's president.

Watson remade CTR in the 1920s and 1930s by focusing its resources on tabulators and other office machines. Renamed IBM in 1924, the firm offered electrically powered office machines that were among the most advanced in the United States. IBM based its growth not on technological prowess, however, but on sales and service. Before joining CTR, Watson had worked at National Cash Register, and his experiences there—first as a salesman and later as a corporate officer in the company's Dayton, Ohio, headquarters—molded his approach to business. National Cash Register stressed sales and service, and Watson took this emphasis with him to IBM. One of his favorite sayings was "We sell and deliver service." This salesmanship, backed up by service, made IBM a leader in the business-machine industry. With earnings of $9 million on revenues of $40 million in 1939, IBM was more profitable than any of its competitors—Burroughs, National Cash Register, Remington Rand, and Underwood—and trailed only Underwood in size.

The demands of the military began reshaping the data-processing industry during World War II. Fed by federal funds, some companies moved beyond the production of tabulators and calculators to the making of the world's first computers (unlike tabulators, computers have electronic memories that can retain mathematic rules and apply them to new sets of data automatically). IBM, generally more interested in sales than in pioneering new technologies, initially lagged behind Remington Rand and some other companies in developing computers. However, when Thomas Watson, Jr., took over as president from his father in 1952, IBM entered the computer market, and by the mid-1950s it had a line of mainframe computers that competed directly with Remington Rand's

UNIVAC. This first generation of computers was based on vacuum-tube technologies, and the resulting machines were large, bulky, and difficult to cool.

By the 1950s and early 1960s, the first generation of computers was being replaced by a second generation that utilized transistors and diodes rather than vacuum tubes. Smaller, more reliable, and cooler in their operations than their predecessors, these machines represented a major advance in computer technology. Sperry Rand (the Sperry Corporation and Remington Rand merged in 1955) led the industry in making this switch. Characteristically, IBM allowed others to blaze the trail with transistorized computers, only to seize the lead through superior salesmanship and service. "It doesn't do much good to build a better mousetrap," noted Louis Rader of Sperry Rand's UNIVAC division, "if the other guy selling mousetraps has five times as many salesmen."

As it grew in importance within the United States, IBM also expanded overseas. With revenues of almost $1.1 billion in 1965, IBM World Trade had become one of America's major multinationals.

The computer industry entered a new stage of development in the mid-1980s with the invention of powerful microchips that allowed personal computers and minicomputers to handle many tasks once done only by mainframes. In 1984, revenues from the sale of microcomputers surpassed those from mainframes for the first time. This alteration in the nature of the computer industry brought realignments among the leading firms making computers. IBM continued to possess the lion's share of the world market for mainframes, 68 percent in 1986. In 1981, IBM successfully entered the personal-computer field, but in 1986 IBM possessed only 34 percent of the personal-computer market, and two years later a scant 23 percent. IBM's failure to exploit fully the nonmainframe computer fields opened the way for a host of new companies—Apple, Compaq, Zenith, Amstrad, and Digital Equipment, among others—and made the computer industry more competitive than at any time since the mid-1950s. In an unprecedented move, nine makers of personal computers announced in 1988 that they would no longer follow IBM's lead in the development of a new electronic circuitry but would employ an alternate design of their own. By this time some computer makers, most notably Digital, were also challenging IBM for much of the mainframe business.

The Conglomerate Commotion

Diversification and Decentralization

As the example of IBM demonstrates, the expansion of the American economy opened new opportunities for business firms. Influenced by the earlier pioneering efforts of Du Pont and General Motors, an increasing number chose diversification as their growth strategy. As they diversified their products and markets to take advantage of growing consumer desires, these companies often adopted decentralized, multidivisional management systems similar to the one developed at General Motors by Alfred P. Sloan, Jr., in the 1920s. By 1970, some 86 percent of the five hundred largest industrial companies in the United States were diversified to the extent that they possessed at least three different divisions. By that time, seventy-three of America's largest one hundred industrial companies had adopted some form of decentralized management.

As it diversified its product lines and regional coverage, for instance, IBM decentralized its management structure. World Trade was set up as a division separate from domestic operations in 1949. Decentralization occurred within IBM's domestic operations in 1956.

In the postwar years, business diversification took four routes in the United States. Some companies diversified through internal development, moving outward into new areas from a base in either a broad technology or a narrow specialty. Thus, internal research led Uniroyal, originally a maker of rubber products, into the related fields of chemicals, plastics, and fibers. Others diversified by purchasing companies to complement their existing technologies. White Consolidated Industries found itself in the mid-1950s in the unprofitable business of making sewing machines and moved into the general area of industrial equipment and consumer appliances as a defensive maneuver by acquiring other firms. By the same token, Continental Can, which started as a manufacturer of tin cans and crown caps, diversified after 1939 by purchasing companies making metal, glass, and paper containers, glass closures, bottle caps, and flexible packaging material. Still other businesses diversified by buying companies that sold products using the same or similar channels of distribution for similar markets. In 1966, for example, American Brands (formerly American Tobacco) entered the fields of prepackaged foods and alcoholic beverages. In each of these three types of diversification, fairly clear relationships existed between the old and the new goods a company made and sold. Such clear relationships did not exist in the fourth type of diversification, conglomerate diversification.

The Coming of Conglomerates

Conglomerates became the hot news of the American business world in the 1960s. "The word 'conglomerate' lands on the business pages with monotonous regularity these days," observed a financial writer in 1967. "Indeed, a case might be made that conglomerates are the most important current trend in the universe of big business." A new phenomenon in the late 1950s and the 1960s, conglomerates were (and are) companies with many different divisions—usually eight or more—making and selling totally or almost totally unrelated products.

Conglomerates became increasingly common in the 1960s as the United States experienced its third major merger movement of the century. Mergers of manufacturing and mining companies reached a peak in 1968 at 2,500, and 715 of those were conglomerate-type mergers. Even so, conglomerates did not become the dominant form of big business in the United States. Even in 1966, at the height of the conglomerate movement, only forty-six of the five hundred largest industrial companies in America were conglomerates.

There were many reasons for the formation of conglomerates, but several stand out. First, some firms doing business in one field diversified into additional areas as a defensive strategy. Companies of that type sought more profitable investment opportunities for their funds. Textron diversified for that reason, moving capital out of its declining textile plants. So did the Borden company. Worried about low profits in milk products, Borden's officers led their company into the production of chemicals, cosmetics, and fertilizers.

Second, some business executives formed conglomerates on the assumption that all businesses, no matter how diverse, could best be managed by a small group of executives in the head office. These executives, it was argued, could coordinate the accounting, planning, and financial services of the many divisions for the benefit of the entire company. And it was thought that expertise acquired in the one area of operations could be transferred to other areas—again for the benefit of the whole company. Those believing in this approach to business called it synergy, and they often expressed the idea in shorthand as $2 + 2 = 5$. Officers in those corporations tended to be ambitious empire builders who viewed diversification as a natural part of growth. Those at Litton Industries were a good example of this type of business practitioner. They began expanding and diversifying without any real notion of where they were headed.

The gains that could be made from "paper entrepreneurialism" also contributed to the rise of conglomerates. Business managers found that they could often boost the earnings of their companies by acquiring other firms, even though no new assets were created. By rearranging the ownership of companies (the stock certificates), they could show a dramatic rise in profits. One method worked in the following way: If the stock market price of a company was less than its book value (the market value of its assets), another firm could increase its earnings by buying the undervalued company and combining the books of the two companies. If the purchased company had losses, this situation was an additional benefit, for the acquiring company could use those losses to lower its taxes.

Finally, government actions spurred the development of conglomerates. Although the Justice Department sometimes brought antitrust actions against other forms of big business in the 1950s and 1960s—in 1957, for instance, it forced Du Pont to sell its stock holdings in General Motors—it took no action against conglomerates. In fact, conglomerates were initially viewed as increasing competition in the American business world, because their many newly established divisions entered fields dominated by well-established firms. In 1950, Congress passed the Celler-Kefauver Act, which placed new limitations on horizontal and vertical integration as growth strategies for expanding businesses. As a result, business executives trying to increase their operations often did so by forming conglomerates, which were not affected by the Celler-Kefauver Act.

The Management of Conglomerates

In the 1960s, the officers of conglomerates often asserted that a new type of business executive was evolving: a young, ambitious manager with generalized management talents, a person who was versatile, adaptable enough to solve any problem in any business. Trained especially in the techniques of financial management, this new breed could, it was claimed, run a company well without knowing much about its products or production methods.

How successful were the managers cast in this mold? They did put together large companies. Gulf & Western, for instance, expanded its sales from $10 million in 1958 to $1.3 billion just ten years later. But most of the expansion of conglomerates was done through buying other companies—seventy-two mergers in the case of Gulf & Western—not by internally generated growth. Earnings—that is, profits—provide a better measurement of the success of conglomerates. On the average, conglomerates performed no better than other types of big businesses in either the 1960s or the 1970s.

In fact, management problems limited the success of many conglomerates. Two major difficulties surfaced. Too often, executives in the head offices of conglomerates failed to supervise and coordinate the work of their company's many divisions. Conglomerates usually lacked the good information flow and statistical controls established at decentralized, multidivisional companies like Du Pont and General Motors. Sometimes, the head office did not know what the divisions were doing. In 1960 through 1962, General Dynamics lost $435 million because the corporate office located in New York failed adequately to supervise and place controls on sloppy work done by the Convair Division, which was making commercial jet airplanes in Los Angeles. Moreover, as time passed, it became apparent that more than generalized management talents, more than agility with numbers, was needed to run a corporation. Some knowledge of a corporation's production operation was also needed, but too often conglomerate managers did not possess that basic knowledge.

Conglomerates and American Business since 1969

Darlings of the stock market and the American public during the 1960s, conglomerates fell into disrepute in the early 1970s, only to rise again during the late 1970s and 1980s.

Merger activity slowed in the early 1970s, particularly among conglomerates. The number of conglomerate-type mergers dropped from 715 in 1968 to only 301 in 1974 and to 123 one year later. Most important in slowing merger activity was a recession that began in 1969 and lasted into the 1970s. Conglomerates had come of age with a boom in the stock market in the 1960s. In the early 1970s, the stock market collapsed, and so did many conglomerates. The earnings of conglomerates—often burdened by heavy debts incurred for financial expansion in the 1960s, as in the case of Ling-Temco-Vought (LTV)—plummeted. So did their stock prices. After reaching a high of $169 per share in 1967, the price of LTV's stock dropped to $7 per share in 1973. The price of a share of stock in Litton Industries dropped from $104 to $4 and that of a share of Textron from $58 to $15 in the same period. By exposing the financial weaknesses of the conglomerate structure, the recession made them less attractive investors.

In the late 1970s and the 1980s, merger activity once again increased; 1,530 mergers (of companies worth at least $1 million) whose values totaled over $34 billion took place in 1979, 2,391 worth almost $53 billion occurred in 1983, and 4,381 worth almost $205 billion took place in 1986. Despite the drop in number of mergers in 1987, there were thirty acquisitions of firms worth at least $1 billion by other companies; the most active fields for merger activity in that year were, in descending order, chemicals, retailing, banking, communications, machinery, mining, oil and gas, and petroleum refining. Although 1988's number of mergers fell further—to 3,487—they were valued at almost $227 billion.

There were several causes for this revival in merger activity. America's political system permitted it. The federal government took few actions to try to prevent the mergers. Key appointees of President Ronald Reagan were reluctant to take actions interfering with the mergers. In 1983, the new head of the Antitrust Division of the Department of Justice was an attorney who previously had defended large corporations against antitrust suits. At the same time, state laws that aimed at restricting takeovers by preventing out-of-state companies from buying in-state companies were declared unconstitutional. The U.S. Supreme Court, under the interpretation of the commerce clause of the Constitution first enunciated in the 1937 decision upholding the National Labor Relations Act, struck down such state laws as illegally giving individual states the power to regulate trade crossing state lines, thus impinging upon what was seen as one of the exclusive powers of the federal government. Moreover, until the mid-1980s, stock markets were depressed. The prices of many common stocks were low relative to the actual value and earnings potentials of the firms, and this situation encouraged takeovers. Finally, companies or individuals were able to secure the financing required for the purchases; brokerage houses and banks, which earned giant commissions, were active participants in the merger frenzy, eagerly arranging financing for takeovers.

Issues Raised by Conglomerates and Mergers

The conglomerate activity of the 1960s and the renewed merger movement of the late 1970s and the 1980s raised significant questions about the nature of the economy and society of the United States. Merger activity, its critics argued, was a misallocation of the nation's economic and financial resources. Companies spent too much time, effort, and money buying or trying to buy each other, without adding to the country's productive capacity. And in fact, by the late 1970s, acquiring companies typically had to pay 50 percent more than the market price of a target company's stock to purchase it through a stock tender offer. The acquiring companies often went deeply in debt, a situation that could later hurt them severely. The merger movement may have injured the economy as a whole, as well as individual companies, by siphoning off into the acquisition game funds desperately needed to modernize factories. Also, the time and energy business executives spent in preparing for or trying to avoid mergers distracted them from the other aspects of running their companies.

Those involved in the mergers argued that, to the contrary, the mergers strengthened the economy. Mergers they claimed, created more efficient, more competitive companies—corporations better able to sell American products in the international market.

Social and political as well as economic issues surfaced. The matter of the concentration of power, first raised in the antitrust campaign following the rise of big business in the 1870s and 1880s, reappeared. As a result of mergers, for example, oil companies came to control about 35 percent of the copper, 25 percent of the uranium, and 25 percent of the coal in the United States by 1978. While conceding that this situation might be efficient in technological and economic ways, critics complained that it placed too much power in the hands of a few large corporations.

Multinationals

Postwar Multinational Enterprise, 1945-70

Just as the growth in the American economy opened up opportunities for the further diversification of business at home, the expansion of the global economy after World War II encouraged worldwide business diversification. U.S. multinational corporations were among those companies benefiting from this situation. U.S. companies began overseas operations well before World War II, but the return of prosperity after the war brought increased foreign activity. By 1970, at least 3,500 U.S. companies had direct foreign investments in some 15,000 enterprises. The total amount of direct foreign investments came to $78.2 billion in 1970 (in current dollars), an increase that more than kept pace with the expansion of the American economy.

As it had since the 1920s, when it replaced mining in importance, manufacturing attracted the greatest share of the investment funds of U.S. multinationals. Also, as in times past, the types of manufacturers investing abroad remained the same: those with technological advantages or unique products (such as companies in the electrical, office equipment, and chemical industries) and those already well established overseas. As in earlier times, most of those businesses invested in foreign plants and factories to extend the markets for their products—something they discovered they could not do by simply increasing their exports from the United States. Language, cultural, and legal barriers often made it necessary for U.S. companies to set up manufacturing plants, not simply sales offices, overseas. Moreover, cheap foreign labor often made a move abroad very attractive.

As early as the 1920s, U.S. multinationals realized that they had to respect and adapt to the customs and regulations of the countries in which they did business. This concern took on a new urgency in the postwar world, as independence movements in Latin America, Africa, the Middle East, and Asia rearranged the social and political environments of those regions. Increasingly, U.S. companies had to enter into partnership agreements (often as the junior partner) with newly created nationalistic governments if they hoped to continue operating at all (the new governments sometimes confiscated foreign ventures). U.S. oil companies, which replaced British domination of the Middle East (and particularly Saudi Arabia) immediately after World War II, made such arrangements with many Middle Eastern governments in the late 1960s and the 1970s.

As they adapted to worldwide changes, U.S. multinationals altered their management structures. In the 1920s, some American corporations with investments in foreign manufacturing set up foreign companies that, in turn, evolved into international divisions within their parent corporations, and over the next three decades additional companies established international divisions. This arrangement, however, was not wholly satisfactory, for all too often these foreign divisions became isolated from the rest of the company. During the 1950s and 1960s, multinationals began moving away from structures with separate international divisions. Instead, they adopted "global," "worldwide," or "cosmopolitan" management structures. In some of these structures, the top operating management of the domestic products divisions took over the prime responsibility for the international business in their products (they were usually given advice by staff officers who were experts on specific countries or regions). In another type of new structure, multifunctional operating subsidiaries overseas (usually defined by region) were accorded equal status with operating divisions in the United States. In yet a third type of structure, divisions based on product and region were commingled. Most of these reorganizations, regardless of specific forms, had one common result: The top management of the companies became more involved in worldwide operations than before. The isolation of the international division from the rest of its company ended.

U.S. Multinationals in the 1970s

U.S. multinationals continued to grow, but at a slower rate than in the 1950s and 1960s. This slower growth rate resulted partly from an increasing number of restrictions placed on the multinationals' activities by assertive national governments eager to tax them, alterations in accounting policies that made acquisitions less desirable, the countervailing power of the beginnings of multinational labor unions, and the increasing difficulties multinationals encountered in the protection of their patents. In part, too, U.S. multinationals were, like other U.S. businesses, losing their competitive edge in the international marketplace. A major indication of the slowing of the expansion of multinationals was that they sold many of their foreign subsidiaries in the 1970s. Between 1971 and 1975, they divested themselves of 1,359 foreign subsidiaries, nearly 10 percent of the total. Most of these divestitures, one-third of which involved European subsidiaries, were made on a voluntary basis because of declining profits. They were not simply the result of pressures from the host country.

Issues Raised by Multinationals

Multinationals raised important questions about their effect on the American economy and their influence on the economies of foreign nations.

Domestic critics argued that the operations of the multinational companies injured the economy of the United States in a number of ways. The capital outflow for direct investment abroad, they claimed, hurt America's balance of payments. By constructing plants overseas rather than at home, multinationals also reduced U.S. exports while increasing imports. The building of overseas factories cost Americans their jobs as lower-priced imports entered the market. Then, too, technically trained personnel and advanced technology needed at home ended up overseas instead. Critics of multinationals also focused on the issue of control. The United States, they pointed out, could not tax most profits earned by multinationals until (and unless) those profits were sent home. Even more disturbing was the possibility that the interests of U.S. multinationals might, at times, run contrary to those of the United States and that the companies might therefore act against the foreign policy of the nation. (In 1982 and 1983, Dresser Industries was caught in just such a controversy. Its French subsidiary, with the strong support of the French government, sought to sell pumps to the Soviet Union for a major oil and gas pipeline. The U.S. government, however, ordered Dresser's head office in the United States to have the French subsidiary stop the sale.)

Defenders of multinationals replied that the companies contributed in a positive way to the economic growth of the United States. They helped, it was said, ease the balance-of-payments problem by creating overseas markets for American goods. Moreover, it was pointed out, American subsidiaries abroad were large purchasers of goods made in the United States. Then, too, their defenders argued, multinationals gave the United States access to advanced foreign technology, thus making the U.S. economy more competitive. As for the question of control, the proponents of multinationals observed that the companies could act as instruments of U.S. foreign policy (the possible cooperation between the International Telephone and Telegraph Corporation and the Central Intelligence Agency in trying to influence politics in Chile was an example of this) and that multinationals could serve United States foreign policy and defense needs by preventing others from securing monopolies over such key raw materials as oil, iron ore, copper, bauxite (aluminum ore), and uranium.

The expansion of direct investments abroad by multinationals also raised issues for foreign nations. Some recipient nations feared that U.S. investments would stunt their economic growth by taking large earnings out of the country, by destroying local business initiative, and by hurting their balance of payments. Yet, as defenders of multinationals observed, the corporations helped develop the economies of their host countries by providing capital, technology, and managerial skills that might otherwise not be available. Far from sapping local business initiative, they could stimulate it by showing people new ways of doing things.

The Modern Corporate Business System

The Spread of Big Business and the Revival of Small Business

Conglomerates and multinationals were two variants of big business, and their development continued a trend begun in the mid-nineteenth century when a relatively small handful of big businesses dominated key segments of the U.S. economy, especially manufacturing. In 1962, the five largest industrial corporations accounted for over 12 percent of all assets used in manufacturing, the fifty largest possessed over one-third of the nation's manufacturing assets, and the top five hundred had over two-thirds. Some companies grew especially large and important. In 1965, three industrial giants—General Motors, Standard Oil of New Jersey (now Exxon), and Ford—had more gross income than all the farms in the United States. In 1963, the revenues of General Motors were eight times those of New York State and nearly one-fifth those of the federal government.

However, the development of big business did not end the importance of small business to the American economy. Manufacturing, in which big businesses were especially important, became less significant in the economy of the United States in the postwar years. In 1982, small businesses accounted for 38 percent of the nation's GNP. Small businesses helped the U.S. economy in several ways. They generated new jobs, an especially important factor when big businesses were laying off workers. Small businesses, particularly service companies, were especially important as employers of women and minorities. Small businesses also helped the economy by commercializing technological innovations. Big businesses continued to account for most of the private spending for basic research and development, but small firms nonetheless played an important role in bringing innovations to the marketplace.

The position of small businesses varied considerably in the different segments of the nation's business system. In the late 1970s and the 1980s, as throughout the twentieth century, opportunities for small business ventures in farming continued to decline. In numbers, small businesses dominated the service industries, a fast-growing field with promising prospects for the future. (Big companies were, however, becoming increasingly significant in services as time passed. In 1984, for example, large banks such as Citicorp and Bank of America possessed assets twice as large as those of such leading industrial firms as Exxon and General Motors.) Most of the remaining small firms were in sales, a field in which profits differed tremendously. Relatively few small businesses were found in manufacturing, but their prospects seemed to be improving. Small businesses seemed to benefit especially from the growth of a competitive global market, which called for smaller, more flexible factories. Reversing their century-old reliance on vertical integration, more and more big businesses in manufacturing turned instead to small companies to supply components for their finished products. Small companies came increasingly into demand as subcontractors because the larger firms— again responding to the demands of the fast-paced world market— sought flexibility in their operations.

Agribusiness

A trend toward concentration took place in farming as large farms, "agribusinesses," came more and more to dominate agriculture in the United States. The earlier division of farming into two segments—small family farms, often operating in the red, and large corporate farms, usually more efficient and profitable—continued in the postwar years. Many family farmers found their economic positions untenable and left farming for other occupations. Between 1945 and 1974, 4.2 million more Americans left farming than entered the field. By 1988, only 2.2 percent of the nation's working population was engaged in agriculture, down from 27 percent in 1920, 14 percent in 1945, and 4.5 percent in 1973; and many of these "farmers" worked at farming only part-time. In just one decade, the 1960s, some 900,000 independent farms disappeared, many swallowed up by large corporate farms. By 1964 the largest 10 percent of America's farms were responsible for 48 percent of all farm output in the nation, up from 24 percent in 1948. By 1986, 10 percent of the farms, those with annual gross receipts of over $250,000, accounted for 75 percent of all farm income.

The main problem facing family farmers was the growing need for large amounts of capital. A scientific and technological revolution transformed farming in the postwar years: large tractors and other types of mechanized equipment, hybrid seeds for corn and other crops, and chemical fertilizers (whose use soared tenfold between 1940 and 1970) all cost money. By 1970, an Illinois farmer raising corn on four hundred acres required a minimum capital investment of $250,000. Successful farming became capital intensive, and the amounts of capital needed grew ever larger, as farm size (the average farm consisted of 200 acres in 1950, 450 acres by 1983) and equipment requirements rose.

Problems faced by Americans with small and medium-sized farms, already apparent by the 1960s and 1970s, deepened in the 1980s. Temporarily blessed by high prices for their crops, farmers purchased new farmland and equipment in the late 1970s, hoping that crop prices and land values would keep rising, and they did so by borrowed money; the debt of farmers increased from $54 billion in 1971 to $212 billion by 1985. However, the rosy future hoped for by farmers failed to materialize.

Foreign markets for U.S. farm products collapsed in the early 1980s because of the growing self-sufficiency in food production of many other nations, the rising value of the dollar (which raised the cost of farm exports), and an inept U.S. foreign policy regarding agricultural products. The loss of foreign markets proved catastrophic because, by the late 1970s, foreign sales had taken one-third of the production of U.S. farms: 47 percent of the total annual sales of the wheat crop, 38 percent of the soybean crop, and 20 percent of the corn crop. As a result of lost sales, crop prices and land values plummeted: farmland values fell from $844 billion in 1981 to just $690 billion four years later. In Iowa, the average price for an acre of farmland dropped from $2,000 in 1981 to $841 in 1986; in Minnesota, the decline was from $1,281 to $609, and in California, from $1,900 to $1,571.

Many Americans with medium-sized family farms were forced to sell out because they could not pay the loans that they had used to buy land and equipment. Those with small farms often suffered the same fate but were sometimes able to hang on to their marginal farming operations—which they continued to view as a way of life as much as a way to make a living—by taking other jobs and farming only part-time. Large corporate farmers did better in this economic crisis: They possessed varied sources of capital that they could draw on to get through the hard times. Increasingly, their farms were part of large, vertically integrated farm-products business empires, such as Holly Farms and Cargill, which made profits not from growing food but from processing and marketing it. In fact, corporate farms often bought the family farms that failed. While the number of farms in the United States declined, the amount of land in production remained about the same, and the trend to larger farms continued.

Franchising

Although the distinction between big business and smaller concerns became pronounced in most fields as the twentieth century progressed, some blurring occurred in the form of business franchising. In franchising, a would-be entrepreneur (the franchisee) purchases the right to do business in a certain line of work from a company in that field (the franchiser). In return for that sum, and also usually for additional yearly payments based on the amount of sales made, the franchiser usually provides national advertising (including a well-known trademark), advice and guidelines about conducting business (and often training in the business at its national headquarters), and the benefits of mass-purchasing discounts. Many Americans came to view franchising as an ideal combination of, or middle ground between, large and small businesses. Franchisees embraced franchising as a way to have the independence and entrepreneurial opportunities that they associated with small business without forsaking what they perceived to be the security of big business. For the franchiser, franchising offered the possibility of rapid business expansion at little cost, since the franchisee supplied most of the capital. And the various annual fees levied on the franchisees promised a prosperous future for any franchiser whose product caught on with the American public.

Franchising has had a long history in the United States. Cyrus McCormick used franchised dealers to sell his reapers in the nineteenth century. Building on McCormick's experience, automobile manufacturers and petroleum companies began selling cars and gasoline through franchised dealers in the opening decades of the twentieth century. Soft-drink makers, led by Coca Cola, sold their goods through franchised bottlers. Restaurant franchising began in the 1920s with A&W Root Beer and Howard Johnson establishments.

Franchising grew at a phenomenal rate after World War II. By the 1950s and 1960s, it seemed as if everything was being franchised: fast foods (McDonald's, Kentucky Fried Chicken), motels (Holiday Inn was one of many), coin-operated laundries, companies selling household pets, and businesses making security systems. By 1967, sales made by franchised businesses accounted for about 10 percent of America's GNP.

This franchise boom slowed temporarily in the early 1970s. The economic recession that opened the decade exposed weaknesses in the financing and management of many franchised businesses, just as it had with the conglomerates. In addition, government investigations revealed fraud, shoddy business practices, and other problems. Some franchised businesses, it became clear, were simply pyramid schemes in which the only way the franchisee could hope to make money was to sell additional franchises to others. Above all, it became apparent that the franchisees often could not obtain independence or even financial stability in the franchise system. The parent company often profited at the expense of the franchisees. Despite these revelations, the franchise movement recovered momentum during the late 1970s and early 1980s. Americans continued to view franchising as a way to fulfill their dreams of becoming independent entrepreneurs, and franchising spread from lawn care to daycare for children. In 1980, some 442,000 franchise outlets generated $336 billion in sales in the United States.

The Business Executive

The Socioeconomic Background of Business Leaders

As in times past, most business leaders continued to come from the upper-income ranks in the United States. Rags-to-riches stories remained exceptions, not the rule, in American business. In 1976, some 85 percent of the business leaders of the United States came from middle-class backgrounds. All but one were men, and none were from minority groups. Most were well educated. About 86 percent had graduated from college, where 33 percent had majored in business, 25 percent in engineering, 23 percent in economics, and 15 percent in the humanities. Another 24 percent had earned master's degrees, and 16 percent had earned doctorates. Of those who professed a religion, 71 percent were Protestant, 13 percent Roman Catholic, and 7 percent Jewish. An increasing number came from a background in finance. By 1979, one-third of the leaders of America's top one hundred companies had a background in finance, up from only 14 percent thirty years earlier.

Women in Business Management

With the exception only of Katherine Graham of the *Washington Post,* no woman had reached a top managerial position in big business as late as 1984, and women remained under represented in the management of American business in general. Even though they composed 40 percent of the labor force in 1976, women held only 19 percent of the jobs in management (and of those women managers, 20 percent were either self-employed or unpaid family workers). This situation, in part, reflected the generally low position of women workers in the American economy. In 1975, the median income of working women was only 57 percent of that of men, and the average female college graduate earned less than the average male high school dropout. In 1984, even though women composed 69 percent of the white-collar work force, only 10 percent of all managers were women.

By the late 1970s and 1980s, however, a growing number of women were obtaining entry-level and middle-management positions in big businesses, heralding their later arrival in the top ranks of business. During this time women also came to compose an ever larger proportion of the students in graduate business programs at colleges and universities. In the early 1970s, women typically made up about 5 percent of the MBA classes at most institutions, but a decade later—by which time the MBA was fast becoming the required degree for entry-level management positions—women composed 30 percent of such classes. Not all areas of American business were equally receptive to these women; they had more success in finance and the service industries than in basic manufacturing.

Women also advanced as entrepreneurs on their own. They started businesses at twice the rate of men in the late 1970s and early 1980s, so that between 1977 and 1985 the number of businesses owned by women doubled, reaching a total of 3.7 million. Companies owned by women nonetheless generated less than 10 percent of the sales made by U.S. businesses.

Blacks in Business

On the evening of January 14, 1983, William Brock committed suicide by shooting himself in the head. As personnel manager, Brock had been the highest-ranking black officer at Volkswagen of America's assembly plant in New Stanton, Pennsylvania. He found himself caught in the middle of a dispute between the firm and its black employees on the issue of job discrimination and, unable to resolve the conflict, killed himself. Brock's death highlighted a fundamental question for blacks beginning to move into management ranks in the postwar era: how to maintain a black identity while climbing the corporate ladder.

Advancement in America's predominantly white companies called for adjustments on the part of blacks. Fleming Golden, thirty-four-year-old black executive, recalled the changes he had to make at IBM. "I was always a flashy dresser, I had lots of orange and green suits," he observed. "Then one day an older white guy took me aside and said, 'Hey, don't get offended, but it's about those suits you wear. They just don't blend in at IBM.'" He switched to wearing pinstriped suits: "My boss mentioned that he liked the suit I was wearing. I got the message." Golden also gave up playing basketball with black friends after work in favor of golf with other IBM executives. For Golden these changes worked, and he got ahead. But, as the case of William Brock illustrates, the pressures of trying to remain black in the white corporate world were sometimes overwhelming.

Most blacks never enjoyed even the opportunity to try to succeed in white-owned businesses. In 1980, for instance, only 130 of McDonald's 5,554 domestic outlets were owned by blacks. While they made considerable gains during the 1970s, blacks nonetheless remained grossly under represented in U.S. management ranks at the close of that decade. In 1978, about 4 percent of the managers and officers of major corporations were black (blacks composed about 12 percent of the American work force). Moreover, of those few blacks in management, only a handful had made it into top management in big businesses.

Black capitalism—black ownership of businesses—offered some hope for blacks excluded from management in white businesses. Black-owned businesses have long existed in the United States, some serving primarily black communities. In recent years, black-owned businesses have grown in importance. Between 1972 and 1981, the total sales of the one hundred largest black-owned businesses in the United States rose from $473 million to $1.9 billion, an 81 percent increase when adjusted for inflation. Despite this progress, black enterprise remained small when compared with leading nonblack businesses. No black-owned business made *Fortune*'s list of the top five hundred industrials in 1983. Johnson Products, the largest black-owned business of any type, with assets of $30 million, trailed far behind Ametek, the five-hundredth-largest industrial company, which had assets of $292 million. In fact, the combined sales of the top one hundred black businesses were less than the sales of Uniroyal, number 177 on *Fortune*'s list.

The Social Responsibility of Business

Prodded by the federal government, which greatly increased its regulatory powers over businesses, and by the desires of business executives to win social acceptance of themselves and their companies, U.S. corporate leaders espoused the doctrine of the "social responsibility" of business in the years after 1945. By this doctrine they meant that their companies would act responsibly toward the American public on such matters as truth in advertising, the hiring of women and minorities, and cleaning up the environment. Like their predecessors in the 1920s, business leaders asserted that their companies existed to serve society, not simply to make a profit. As did the business professionals of earlier years, the corporate leaders of the 1950s, 1960s, and 1970s accomplished less than they claimed, but some changes did occur. Under pressure from the federal government, more women and minorities were hired, advertising became somewhat more honest, and steps were taken to avoid air and water pollution.

Measuring what was accomplished under the doctrine of the social responsibility of business is difficult; clearly, business deeds and business rhetoric did not coincide. For instance, at the same time that they were trying to project an image of corporate social responsibility, the officers of a number of leading oil companies acted in ways that hurt consumers and independent retailers of gasoline. In the 1960s, these officers conspired to prop up the retail price of gasoline in several states and cooperated to keep the price of the crude oil they purchased in California low. Another controversy involved the promotion of beer drinking on college campuses. Despite reports that implicated alcohol abuse as the cause for low grades, vandalism, and occasional student deaths, major brewers and distributors spent in the neighborhood of $20 million in 1984 to promote their beers on campuses across the nation.

Attracting the most public attention were scandals in 1986 and 1987 that besmirched the reputations of several of the nation's leading brokerage houses. Investigations by the Securities and Exchange Commission revealed that numerous members of brokerage firms had used knowledge gained from their work in arranging mergers to speculate in the stocks of the companies involved in the mergers. Called insider trading, this practice blatantly violated federal statutes and traditional ethical norms.

One item that can be measured is corporate giving to philanthropy. By 1980, corporations were donating $2.9 billion annually to philanthropic causes. In that year, Exxon gave $38 million, IBM $35 million, and Atlantic Richfield $34 million. Even companies reporting losses made contributions: General Motors $27 million, Ford $11 million, and Chrysler $2 million. Where did these funds go? About 40 percent went to education, including universities, 30 percent to health and welfare projects, 15 percent to parks and civic improvement projects, and 10 percent to art and culture. Generally speaking, while the largest corporations were the biggest donors in absolute terms, they did not give the highest proportions of their earnings to philanthropy. Medium-sized companies, especially those in retailing and wholesaling, gave a higher percentage—probably because they had stronger ties to their local communities than big businesses with offices across the United States and the world.

As in the past, corporate giving raised questions about business goals. Should a company exist to make a profit for its stockholders or to serve society somehow? If a corporation does want to serve society, how best can that goal be accomplished? By making contributions to philanthropic causes? Or by reinvesting its profits in more modern plants and equipment, thus strengthening the nation's economy? Agreement has still not been reached on answers to these questions.

The Modern Company

By the mid-1980s, big businesses in the United States had changed considerably from those of thirty or forty years earlier. Above all, they were more diversified. They produced and sold a broader range of products for a wider variety of consumer markets both at home and abroad. But big businesses did not squeeze smaller concerns out of the U.S. economy altogether. Small businesses remained significant, especially in sales and service. If the opportunities of the postwar world brought changes to the business firm, they also altered the nature of government-business relations in the United States. The growth of a consumer society, based on the outpouring of consumer products from U.S. factories, led the federal government into a much broader range of regulatory activities than ever before. And these activities, some critics argued, contributed to the economic decline of the United States to the extent that deregulation was necessary.

27. Recent Developments in Corporate Finance

*Leland E. Crabbe, Margaret H. Pickering,
and Stephen D. Prouse*

Excerpted from the *Federal Reserve Bulletin*, August 1990, pp. 593–603. Leland E. Crabbe, Margaret H. Pickering, and Stephen D. Prouse are with the Division of Research and Statistics of the Board of Governors of the Federal Reserve System. They note that Brian H. Levey provided research assistance.

Recent years have seen dramatic changes in the financial structure of U.S. nonfinancial corporations, in corporate securities markets, and in corporate financing techniques. Many of these changes have been associated with the wave of mergers, acquisitions, and other corporate restructurings during the last half of the 1980s. In particular, the outstanding debt of the nonfinancial corporate sector soared as corporations borrowed heavily to finance retirements of equity resulting from restructuring activity. Furthermore, a substantial portion of this step up in borrowing involved low-grade debt. At the same time, investors became more receptive to these bonds, responding to the promise of attractive yields and recognizing the opportunities for diversification of their portfolios. This shift not only provided funds for mergers and restructurings, but also enabled more firms that were less well known to tap public debt markets.

With the repayment of the debt from many mergers hinging on subsequent sales of assets, acquirers turned to new sources of temporary financing from commercial and investment banks and made innovative use of bonds with deferred interest payments and variable coupon rates. Because bondholders were dissatisfied with losses occasioned by downgrading in the wake of unanticipated restructurings, many corporations included protection against this special risk in their new bond issues to reduce borrowing costs.

With the rise in debt, many measures of corporate financial condition deteriorated: interest expenses claimed a significantly higher share of corporate cash flow; downgrading of debt accelerated; and bond default rates, while still relatively low, began to climb. In contrast, debt-equity ratios based on market values increased very little, as higher stock prices offset much of the growth in corporate indebtedness. Nonetheless, the nonfinancial corporate sector appears, on balance, to be more exposed to potential financial problems than it was in 1984. In this environment, banks and other investors have become more cautious in extending credit to finance highly leveraged mergers and acquisitions, a shift that has contributed to an increase in the use of equity financing and to a slowing in merger activity.

While the changes associated with the restructurings captured the public's attention, significant developments were occurring elsewhere during the last half of the decade. The differences between debt and equity as sources of funds to finance corporate activity narrowed significantly with the expansion in the use of financial instruments having features of both. Interest rate swaps and other methods for hedging interest rate risk also blurred the traditional distinction between short-term and long-term debt. Nonfinancial corporations relied more heavily on bonds, commercial paper, and loans from foreign banks for new funding and less on credit extended by domestic banks. For investment-grade nonfinancial corporations, medium-term notes became a growing source of funds. Issuance of privately placed debt was robust over the last half of the 1980s, despite growth in the public junk bond market (low-quality rated, unsecured, high-risk, corporate bonds), which many believed might supplant the private market. Moreover, in a recent ruling the Securities and Exchange Commission removed restrictions on secondary trading of private placements by larger institutional investors. The ruling likely will spur continued growth in the private market fed by increases in the participation by foreign issuers and, perhaps, by domestic issuers drawn from the public market.

Restructuring and Corporate Financial Developments

Merger and acquisition activity, which was instrumental in shaping corporate financial patterns, was strong throughout the decade. The number of transactions rose moderately through 1983 and then accelerated between 1984 and 1986. Although the number fell over the remainder of the decade, it remained high by past standards. More important, the dollar value of the transactions continued to climb rapidly until 1989, easing only briefly in 1987, after the October stock market break. Acquisitions of U.S. firms by foreign companies since 1987 have added significantly to the volume of merger activity. Divestitures rose at a strong pace throughout the 1980s, accounting in the last five years for nearly one-third of the dollar value of the mergers and acquisitions.

Many explanations have been offered for the dramatic expansion of mergers and acquisitions. One is the search for the fullest potential of the firm's assets through a transfer of corporate control to new management teams. Another focuses on the tax benefits of higher leverage, the capture of tax-loss carryovers, and an increase in the asset basis used for depreciation allowances and other purposes (although the Tax Reform Act of 1986 and subsequent legislation essentially eliminated the last two incentives). A third explanation views the restructuring as a vehicle for transferring wealth from bondholders, workers, and other corporate stakeholders to shareholders. A fourth ascribes the merger boom to highly sophisticated investors who doubted that the equity values of many firms fully reflected the appreciation in their assets during the inflation of the 1970s and early 1980s. These investors were aided by legal advisers and financial intermediaries who increased investors' awareness of the potential gains and developed financial instruments to facilitate the transactions. A final explanation points to a less restrictive antitrust enforcement policy that permitted most of the proposed mergers and acquisitions to go unchallenged. Although it is early to draw firm conclusions, preliminary research has suggested that several of these factors played a role in the restructuring boom.

Corporate Balance Sheets and Profitability

Whatever their cause, corporate restructurings have resulted in an unprecedented retirement of outstanding equity shares, which far outstripped the moderate level of new equity issuance. Overall, retirements of nonfinancial corporate stock have exceeded new issues by about $600 billion since 1983, in sharp contrast to the rest of the postwar period, when retirements of shares exceeded new issues in only a handful of years, and then by very small amounts. Even the stock market break in 1987 had little effect on retirements because a pickup in stock repurchases by many corporations largely offset the brief pause in merger activity.

Unlike the mergers of the 1960s, which were financed largely by an exchange of securities, acquisitions in the 1980s relied heavily on borrowed funds to pay cash to selling shareholders. Leveraged buyouts (LBOs), the most highly leveraged acquisitions, mushroomed from less than $5 billion in 1983 to more than $60 billion in 1989, the year that included the $25 billion RJR-Nabisco transaction. LBOs served to transfer assets from publicly held corporations to closely held partnerships and private corporations. Some were structured with as little as 10 percent equity, provided largely by buyout pools that takeover specialists assembled. To finance the remainder, the new firm effectively pledged the assets of the acquired company as collateral for new debt obligations. The LBO firms then sought to lower the debt burden through improved cash flow and sales of some operations. Many of these divestitures were themselves structured as LBOs.

In addition to financing LBOs and other mergers and acquisitions, debt commonly was used to finance defensive measures such as leveraged recapitalizations undertaken to discourage unsolicited or "hostile" takeovers. As a result of all these restructuring activities, the indebtedness of nonfinancial corporations grew rapidly, as illustrated by the sharp increase in the ratio of the market value of debt to the gross domestic product of nonfinancial corporations.

The rapid buildup of debt in the nonfinancial corporate sector was accompanied by rising net interest payments that absorbed a growing share of corporate gross product. The interest share expanded even though interest rates were lower, on balance, during the last half of the 1980s, and the expansion was one factor acting to depress corporate profitability. Before-tax profits slipped from roughly 9 percent of corporate output in 1987 to about 7.75 percent in 1989. Over the same period, net interest payments rose from about 4.25 percent to more than 5 percent of corporate gross product, accounting for more than half of the drop in the profits share.

The use of debt to retire equity boosted corporate borrowing beyond that required to finance capital outlays. The financing gap, the difference between capital expenditures and internal funds, represents the extent to which corporations must draw on external sources of funds—credit market borrowing, new equity issuance, or asset liquidations—to finance capital expenditures. Although credit market borrowing exceeded corporations' needs for external funds for most of the postwar period, changes in total borrowing generally reflected changes in the financing gap. However, this pattern changed dramatically after 1983. The financing gap showed little trend between 1982 and 1989, while borrowing increased sharply, reflecting the surge in merger activity.

Merger Financing and the Junk Bond Market

Although the merger and buyout activity of the past decade contributed significantly to the radical transformation of the junk bond market, part of the early growth of that market was related to developments in private placements. Before the 1980s, few new speculative-grade bonds (bonds rated below Baa3 by Moody's Investors Service or below BBB- by Standard and Poor's Corporation) were publicly offered because most investors shied away from their higher risk of default. Higher-risk borrowers, typically small and medium-sized companies, tended instead to rely on loans from commercial banks and on private placements, primarily with life insurance companies. When policy loans began to absorb the investible assets of life insurance companies in the late 1970s and early 1980s, these institutions turned from the private placement market toward more liquid investments. Consequently, many of these higher-risk companies were forced to seek new sources of credit. In response, securities firms, led by Drexel Burnham Lambert, began actively promoting public offerings of high-yield bonds in the early 1980s. At the same time, institutional investors in the public market became convinced that the bonds' higher yields more than compensated for their greater risks, especially when the bonds were held in a diversified portfolio. The economic expansion also provided a favorable environment by seeming to mitigate risk.

These developments interacted with the growth of financing needs arising from mergers and restructurings to spur a dramatic increase in the issuance of junk bonds. Between 1983 and 1989, nonfinancial corporations issued $160 billion of junk bonds to the public; that sum accounted for more than 35 percent of public bond offerings by the sector. About two-thirds of the high-yield bonds offered during this period were associated with restructurings—leveraged buyouts, other mergers and acquisitions, divestitures, stock repurchases, leveraged recapitalizations, or other restructuring activities. In most cases, junk bonds provided permanent financing for cash buyouts, which replaced part or all of the funds supplied initially by commercial or investment banks.

Recent Developments in Merger and Restructuring Activity

Early in 1989, the hectic pace of debt-financed restructuring began to subside. The amount of stock-for-stock exchanges in merger transactions rebounded in 1989 from the extremely low levels of 1987 and 1988. This rebound largely reflected the increase in emphasis on friendly strategic corporate acquisitions in which the new, combined company issued new common shares to stockholders of the two original companies. The deepening difficulties in the market for below-investment-grade bonds further encouraged combination offers of cash and securities, particularly preferred stock, to shareholders of the acquired company.

The acquisition market was jolted when a few companies involved in highly leveraged transactions failed to perform up to expectations, defaulted on bond issues, and sought bankruptcy protection. Others, seeking to prevent default, have reached agreement with bond-holders to reschedule debt or are attempting to do so. These "distressed" exchanges typically replace existing debt with securities carrying a longer maturity, lower interest rate, some substitution of equity, or a combination of these features; and they must be approved by a predetermined share of bond-holders specified in the original bond's covenant. Whereas such exchanges are still few, this unraveling of acquisitions and the general vulnerability of highly leveraged firms to adverse economic developments have heightened concerns in the financial markets; and thus they have made investors much more cautious in extending funds to highly leveraged borrowers.

Uneasiness about rising bond defaults contributed to chaotic conditions in the market for speculative-grade bonds as prices of restructuring-related issues dropped precipitously. The withdrawal of the savings and loan associations from the junk bond market and outflows from high-yield mutual funds further curtailed demand for these issues. The liquidation of Drexel Burnham Lambert was another negative factor for the market to absorb, even though Drexel's participation had already dwindled.

New merger proposals dropped off noticeably during the first part of 1990 as a consequence of the virtual unavailability of funds for new financing in the low-grade bond market; the more cautious attitude of commercial banks, both domestic and foreign; and the weakening in the market for asset sales. Nevertheless, although considerably less than it was in 1988 and 1989, restructuring activity remains substantial.

28. The State of Small Business: A Report of the President
U.S. Small Business Administration

This report was transmitted to the Congress by the president along with the *Annual Report of the Small Business Administration* (Washington, D.C.: U.S. Government Printing Office, 1989), pp. 17–41.

The Number of Small Businesses

For several reasons, there are numerous answers to the question of how many small businesses exist. First, there is no standard size definition of a small business. (In Europe, the generic term for small businesses is small and medium enterprises [SME]. This term has the virtue of highlighting that there is a continuum of business sizes from very small to very large.) The size of a business may be measured in terms of employment, assets, or receipts. For most statistical purposes, the Office of Advocacy of the Small Business Administration defines small businesses as those of under either five hundred or one hundred employees.

The definition used may depend on the policy issue or question being analyzed, or the industry being studied. An upper limit of one hundred employees may be most useful in a discussion of retail stores because most retail establishments have few employees, and most retail firms have few establishments. The average entity in the industry, whether establishment or enterprise, is small, and that smallness is captured within a lower size limit. In some industries, such as automobile manufacturing, the typical establishment may be much larger than one hundred employees, and the "less than five hundred employees" limit accurately captures the fact that a firm with three hundred or four hundred employees may be small relative to the industry average.

Once agreement is reached on an upper boundary for the size of small businesses, the question of a lower boundary becomes an issue. Many people implicitly define a business as an organization having one or more employees. But most businesses have no employees other than the owner (who may or may not be counted as an employee, depending on the federal agency that does the counting), and many business owners work only part-time at their business. The definitional issues concerning these business owners are even more confused when they are identified as self-employed, referring to their employment status rather than their business or legal status.

Statistics published by the Internal Revenue Service provide the broadest measure of nonfarm businesses in the United States. An estimated 19.0 million business tax returns were filed in 1988. Returns were filed by 4.0 million corporations, 1.8 million partnerships, and 13.2 million sole proprietorships. Fewer than seven thousand of these businesses would qualify as large businesses if an employment cutoff of five hundred employees was used to define small and medium-sized businesses.

Other agencies also produce counts of the number of businesses. Every five years the Bureau of the Census publishes *Enterprise Statistics*, based on information collected in years ending with a two or a seven.

The Small Business Administration's Small Business Data Base (SBDB) covers only businesses with employees and accounts for approximately 93 percent of private employment. There were 3.80 million businesses (enterprises) in the SBDB in 1986, of which over 3.79 million had fewer than five hundred employees. The SBDB identifies approximately 15,000 businesses with five hundred or more employees compared to between 6,000 and 7,000 in census reports. Total employment for these 15,000 businesses is approximately equal to the employment shown in census reports. The SBDB treats many large subsidiary firms, actually owned by a parent company, as if they were independent firms.

Small Business, GNP, and Gross Product Originating

How large a share of gross national product is contributed by small firms? As its name implies, GNP is a measure of the nation's final product or output. Unfortunately, output measures are not generally available for firm size; however, it is possible to measure small firms' contributions from the factor cost or supply side. This measure is known as net national

Table 28.1

Small Business Share of Private, Nonfarm Gross Product Originating (GPO)

Year	Percent
1982	50
1977	52
1972	54
1967	53
1963	54
1958	57

Source: Joel Popkin and Company, *Small Business Gross Product Originating: 1958–1982* (Washington, D.C.: U.S. Small Business Administration, Office of Advocacy, prepared under award No. SBA-1040-OA-86, April 1988).

Note: Years correspond to the availability of *Enterprise Statistics* by the Bureau of the Census, U.S. Department of Commerce.

income at factor cost and is equivalent to gross product originating, or GPO, which is a measure of output by sources located within the country's borders.

Small firms' contribution to private nonfarm domestic GPO was 50 percent in 1982, down from 52 percent in 1977, according to the most recent analysis of available census and IRS data. Small firms' share of GPO has been declining since it was first measured in 1958 (Table 28.1). To ascertain why, it is important to understand the major components of GPO, as well as some of the industrial trends that have shaped small firm growth in recent years.

The largest of the components of GPO as measured from the income side is labor, measured by employment compensation. Other income components—indirect measures of the productivity of capital, land, and profit—include indirect business taxes, capital consumption allowances, net interest (returns to capital), and profit-type income.

Employment compensation has been declining in small firms relative to large firms in recent years because benefits in large firms grew faster than benefits in small firms. However, small business employment has been rising, particularly in industries that have relatively few small firms, such as mining, transportation, and finance. Industry deregulation may be a major reason for the recent small firm employment increase in mining and transportation. The small firm share of payrolls increased in these industries between 1977 and 1982.

Much of the decline in small firm GPO share has been caused by

Table 28.2

Shares of Gross Product Originating in Small and Large Firms, 1958 and 1982

	Small Firms		Large Firms	
	1958	1982	1958	1982
Total	57	50	43	50
Mining	35	28	65	72
Manufacturing	30	21	70	79
Construction	90	80	10	20
Transportation, communication, utilities	27	20	73	80
Wholesale trade	94	86	6	14
Retail trade	76	55	24	45
Finance, insurance, real estate	25	60	25	40
Services	93	81	7	19

Source: Joel Popkin and Company, *Small Business Gross Product Originating: 1958–1982* (Washington, D.C.: U.S. Small Business Administration, Office of Advocacy, prepared under award no. SBA 1040-OA-86, April 1988).

declines in the nonwage components: profit-type income, net interest payments, indirect business taxes, and capital consumption allowances. In fact, while the overall small firm GPO share fell 2 percentage points from 1977 to 1982, the small firm share of nonwage factors fell further—by 5 percentage points.

Offsetting the decline in small business GPO—and helping to stabilize the small firm GNP share—has been the growing importance of the service sector in the economy. Services made up 18 percent of small business GPO in 1958 and 30 percent in 1982. The change in service GPO in the overall economy increased from 11 percent of nonfarm GPO in 1958 to 18 percent in 1982. The net effect of this shift has been to partially offset the small business decline.

Small firms remain an important contributor to the nation's output, particularly in the construction, trade, finance, and services sectors (Table 28.2). As small firm growth increases in other nontraditional sectors, it is possible that more recent data (from 1982 to 1988) will in fact show an end to the downward trend in small business GPO. Other recent research has demonstrated that the smallest and largest firms in the economy tend to be among the most productive, and that the smallest firms accounted for 38 percent of job growth from 1980 to 1986.

Self-Employment Rates

People who own their own business are a continuous source of new products, services, and jobs in the economy. Self-employment allows individuals to test and acquire entrepreneurial skills and by so doing provide the economy with the benefits of their successful (and unsuccessful) attempts in the marketplace.

Self-employment continues to grow in absolute numbers. The number of people who operate full-time businesses increased from 5.99 million in 1981 to 6.46 million in 1985. However, the rate of self-employment has declined: The fraction of workers who operate businesses increased from 9.3 percent in 1981 to 10.0 percent in 1983 and then fell to 9.1 percent in 1985.

The self-employed are a heterogenous group, encompassing highly skilled and highly paid professional workers, as well as small business owners, selling merchandise or offering specialized services, such as child care in homes. At the turn of the century, one-third of all nonfarm workers were self-employed, compared to one-tenth in recent years.

For both men and women, the rate of unincorporated self-employment declined until the mid-1970s, increased through the early 1980s, and decreased in the mid-1980s. The rate of self-employment for men fell from 8.0 percent in 1967 to 7.4 percent in 1975, rose to 8.3 percent in 1983, and then fell to 7.2 percent by 1985. For women, the rate fell from 3.4 percent in 1967 to 2.7 percent in 1975, rose to 3.9 percent in 1982, and declined to 3.3 percent in 1985. The rate of incorporated self-employment, for both genders, followed a similar pattern for 1975–85, although the increases were somewhat more pronounced.

The increase in the aggregate rate of self-employment over the 1970s resulted primarily from increases in the rate of self-employment among blacks. White women have experienced especially sharp increases in incorporated self-employment, which pulled up the total rate of self-employment for women over the last decade.

Determinants of Changes in Self-Employment

About 90 percent of the variation in self-employment can be statistically explained by the interplay of changes in four factors: the composition of demand in the economy, experience in the labor force, educational attainment, and economic policy variables.

Changes in the Composition of Demand

Self-employment is more common in such industries as services, retail trade, and construction than in mining and manufacturing because of large capital requirements to start a business in the latter industries. Recent shifts in employment favor industries in which self-employment is more common for a combination of reasons: Individuals are more likely to start businesses in industries in which they have work experience, and increased demand for the products of industries in which self-employment is prevalent has opened up business opportunities in those areas.

Experience in the Labor Force

The period of time over which individuals have been able to discover self-employment opportunities is clearly important. Older people have had a longer period of time to make the switch into self-employment; veterans are less likely to be self-employed because they have had fewer years during which they could have switched; people with more years of work experience are more likely to have acquired assets and work experience. Women who have had lower rates of labor force participation than men are less likely to be self-employed; women who have had fewer children, who belong to age groups for whom labor force participation is higher, and who are better educated are likely to have had more labor force experience and are more likely to be self-employed.

Educational Attainment

Education affects the relative returns to self-employment, compared to wage-and-salary work. People with a graduate education are more likely to be self-employed because self-employment is more common in many of the traditional professions such as medicine and law. Graduate education is a more important factor in explaining self-employment rates for females than for males.

Economic Policy Variables

Changes in taxes and interest rates and cyclical changes in the economy all affect the rate of self-employment. Taxes are an important consideration in choosing between self-employment and wage work. It is easier for self-employed individuals than for wage earners to avoid taxes by overstating business expenses or under reporting earnings. Higher average tax rates increase the gains from tax avoidance and therefore increase the returns to self-employment. On the other hand, FICA taxes are 50 percent higher for the unincorporated self-employed and 100 percent higher for the incorporated self-employed than for wage workers. Higher interest rates also increase the costs of financing the startup of a new business. Finally, cyclical changes in the economy affect the number of self-employment opportunities, as well as the relative returns to wage work and self-employment.

The fact that the ebb and flow of self-employment over time can be statistically explained almost entirely by structural and demographic changes in the economy means that there is no support for the notion that individual preferences to try entrepreneurship have shifted.

Self-employment in the economy depends on distribution of full-time workers across ages, educational levels, and industries, and on tax rates and business conditions. The entry of the baby-boom generation into the labor force beginning in the later 1960s led to a decrease in the average age of the full-time nonagricultural work force and tended to decrease the self-employment rate. The decline of manufacturing employment, the rise of service jobs, and the increase in educational levels have tended to increase self-employment. Fluctuations in business conditions and tax rates have also been factors: Increases in the effective federal income tax burden in the 1970s tended to increase self-employment, while decreases during the 1980s tended to decrease self-employment rates.

Will self-employment rise or fall in the coming decades? The aging of the baby-boom generation will by itself lead to sharply increasing rates as members of that age group, who began turning forty in 1986, pass through the peak ages of self-employment. This upward trend may be offset by a number of structural changes in the economy. For example, if the sharp decline of the dollar reinvigorates manufacturing at the expense of services, self-employment may decline. Increasing concentration in the retail and services sectors may reduce opportunities for self-employment. Female labor-force participation rates and educational levels among both men and women may have reached a plateau. It is likely that the absolute number of self-employed individuals will continue to rise, while their share of the work force decreases over the next several years.

CHAPTER V

The Labor Force and Labor Organization

29. Issues in Labor Supply
Janice Shack-Marquez

Excerpted from the *Federal Reserve Bulletin*, June 1991, pp. 375–84. Janice Shack-Marquez is with the Federal Reserve Board's Division of Research and Statistics.

The Determinants of Labor Supply

In an accounting sense, the supply of labor available for the production of goods and services depends on the size and the composition of the population, the proportion of the population working or looking for work (the rate of labor force participation), the number of hours worked each week, and the number of weeks worked each year. Over the past four decades, these determinants have affected the supply of labor in various ways.

Population

The size and composition of the population is the first major building block of the labor force. Over the past forty years, the working-age population of the United States (that is, noninstitutionalized civilians sixteen years of age and older) has grown significantly. At the end of 1990, it stood at 189 million, 84 million more than its level in 1950. Three sources of change determine the pattern of growth in the population: births, deaths, and net immigration.

During the 1960s and 1970s, the growth of the working-age population was influenced mainly by the sharp rise in birth rates from the end of World War II to the early 1960s—the period of the so-called baby boom. As the large baby-boom cohort reached working age between 1961 and 1979, the overall working-age population grew 1.9 percent per year, and the number of inexperienced workers seeking jobs bulged. For example, sixteen to twenty-four year olds, who had accounted for 18 percent of the working-age population in the 1950s, made up nearly 22 percent of the working-age population by 1970. In contrast, the baby bust, which began in the early 1960s, slowed the pace of growth of the working-age population to about 1 percent in the 1980s; and the proportion of sixteen to twenty-four year olds in the working-age population shrank back to 17 percent by 1990.

The average lifespan, the second determinant of population trends, has lengthened because of advances in health care. Average life expectancy has increased from seventy years in 1960 to seventy-five years in 1989. As a result, people sixty-five years of age and older are a growing proportion of the population.

The final factor that has influenced population growth in recent decades is the net flow of immigrants. Between 1980 and 1989, legal immigration to the United States averaged 580,000 persons per year—about one-quarter of 1 percent of the U.S. population. This pace was well above that of the 1970s, which was 450,000 per year. Although estimates are imprecise, illegal immigration, according to the Immigration and Naturalization Service, probably has added another 100,000 to 300,000 per year to the total of legal immigration.

Recently, new laws have resulted in large fluctuations in the flow of immigrants. Efforts to control illegal immigration led to the Immigration Reform and Control Act of 1986, which attempted to restrict the employment opportunities of illegal aliens by imposing penalties on employers who hired them. However, the Immigration Act of 1990 works in the opposite direction: It allows for an increase in total immigration, for an increase in the immigration of individuals with skills that are in short supply, and for the admission of immigrants from under represented countries. The Immigration and Naturalization Service estimates that this act could increase legal immigration from roughly 600,000 in 1989 to as much as 800,000 annually over the next several years.

Labor Force Participation

Besides sizable increases in the working-age population, the proportion of the working-age population that is either working or looking for work has been on an upward trend throughout the past four decades. In the early 1950s, the rate of labor force participation averaged roughly 59 percent; by 1990, the rate had risen to more than 66 percent.

Perhaps the most noteworthy change that has taken place in the labor market over the past forty years is the vast increase in the proportion of women in the civilian labor force. Increasing participation among women has more than accounted for the overall rise in the labor force participation rate. As late as 1950, only 34 percent of women were in the labor force. By 1980, women's participation rate had risen to 52 percent; and by 1990, it had moved up to 58 percent.

Rising participation among women has occurred in most age categories, with the greatest increases evident for women of childbearing age. The participation rate for women twenty to twenty-four years of age increased from 46 percent in 1960 to 69 percent in 1980 and now stands at nearly 72 percent. For women twenty-five to thirty-four years of age, the participation rate has more than doubled, from 36 percent in 1960 to 74 percent in 1990. Indeed, the jump in the labor force participation rate of married women with children under the age of six has been dramatic, tripling from 19 percent in 1960 to 59 percent in 1990.

In contrast, participation rates among men generally have declined over the past three decades. The most substantial decreases have been among men from fifty-five to sixty-four years of age, whose rate fell from 87 percent in 1970 to 68 percent in 1990; the participation rate for men over sixty-five years of age also has dropped significantly, from 33 percent in 1970 to 16 percent by 1990. These declines reflect a trend toward earlier retirement. In contrast, participation rates for men from twenty-five to fifty-four years of age have declined only slightly.

Labor Supply over the Longer Run

Broadly speaking, hourly wage rates tend to be relatively low when young people first enter the work force and are learning new skills. Wage rates rise until they peak, typically when workers are around forty-five to fifty-five years of age, and then they decline. The so-called life-cycle model of labor supply predicts that the labor supply of individual households will change as the members of the household age. In particular, workers are assumed to participate most heavily during the period of their life cycle when their expected wages are highest and to substitute leisure for work when expected wages are low.

The rates of men's participation in the labor force over the past three decades appear to be consistent with this view, as they rise from men's teenage years into middle age and then fall off in their later years. The rates of labor force participation for women in 1960 and 1970 were broadly consistent with the life-cycle model, although participation among women of childbearing age tended to drop off sharply. By 1990, however, the profile of labor force participation rates for women had essentially the same shape as that for men.

As previously discussed, over the past few decades movements in labor supply for men and women have diverged: The participation of women in the labor force has risen sharply, while the participation of men has trended down. The life-cycle model alone does not fully explain these long-term trends in labor force participation. Other economic forces that underlie these developments include demographic changes in the labor force as well as shifts in social customs and tastes that have influenced changes in relative income, fertility patterns, attachment to the labor force, and retirement decisions.

Relative Income Effects

One way that demographic changes can affect participation decisions is through their influence on the relative incomes of various age groups. Over the past three decades, relative income effects have been most pronounced for younger workers. The income of year-round, full-time workers aged fifteen to twenty-four years (the best available proxy for the wage rate), relative to that of men aged forty-five to fifty-four years, began to decline sharply in the mid-1960s and continued falling through the 1970s and into the 1980s. The decline coincided with the influx of young workers into the labor market. Relative income flattened out for young men and women in the second half of the 1980s, as the small current generation of youth (the baby-bust generation) replaced the baby-boom generation, although reduced demand for lower-skilled workers apparently prevented a reversal of the earlier decline.

The changes in the relative wage levels for young men and women affected the labor supply decisions of individual young people in two ways: first, through changes in their own relative wage, and, second, through changes in the relative wages of their spouses or other family members. For young women, econometric evidence suggests that the effect of the declines in their own relative wages, which ordinarily would have reduced labor supply, was more than offset by the positive influence on participation of the potential drop in family living standards associated with the decline in the relative wage of young men. In contrast, the econometric evidence suggests that these effects are about offsetting for the participation decisions of young men.

Fertility and Home Responsibilities

Women's decisions to participate in the labor force and to have children are not independent. For example, a woman's decision to increase the size of her family may be affected by the level of her family's income and by the wage she expects to receive by entering the labor market. At the same time, a woman's decision to participate in the labor force may be affected by whether she has young children. In the 1960s and the first half of the 1970s, the birth rate fell sharply. For the next ten years, birth rates flattened out, and then in the late 1980s they began to increase.

The lower birth rates probably were closely related to the sharp rise during the 1970s in the participation rate of women twenty-five to thirty-four years of age. Of course, the importance of the birth rate to levels of labor force participation is influenced by changes in the availability, cost, and quality of child care and the propensity of mothers of young children to work outside the home. Currently, the proportion of mothers of young children who are in the labor market is at a historic high. This finding suggests that childrearing and young women's participation in the labor force are more compatible than in the past.

Retirement

An important element of the slow decline in labor force participation rates for men is a trend, beginning as early as the 1930s, toward earlier retirement. Between 1960 and 1990, labor force participation rates for men fifty-five and over fell substantially; and despite an increase in participation among women twenty to fifty-four years of age, participation rates for women fifty-five and over dropped to rates similar to those for men. Data on nonparticipation also show the trend toward early retirement for men between the late 1970s and the 1980s.

Participation rates for older men reached historically low levels in the mid-1980s and since then have changed little. Factors contributing to the decline in participation include wider coverage of the labor force by social security, the extension of old age assistance to persons sixty-two to sixty-four years old, the greater availability of social security and disability payments, the greater prevalence of pension plans, the provision of early retirement benefits in many pension plans, and efforts by employers to cut back payrolls by inducing early retirement. These factors dramatically lowered the cost, in terms of foregone earnings, of retirement. In addition, as lifetime incomes rose, individuals substituted leisure for work in their later years. In recent years, the enactment of laws prohibiting mandatory retirement may have been a factor working to stem the decline in participation among older men.

The cause of increased retirement among women is somewhat different. From 1960 to 1990, among women in their preretirement years (forty-five to fifty-four years of age), labor force participation increased markedly. Consequently, in 1990 a larger proportion of women fifty-five years of age and older were eligible for retirement than had been eligible in earlier years. Nevertheless, the finding that the rate of labor force participation for these women has remained fairly steady since 1960 suggests that factors favoring retirement have influenced women as well as men.

Labor Force Attachment

The rise in participation rates among women is also due to a greater attachment to the labor force of women who are currently working. If all labor force participants stayed in the labor force for the entire year, the annual average labor force participation rate would be a direct measure of annual labor force experience. However, some individuals will be out of the labor force for part of the year. Consequently, to study the effect of changing patterns of work experience on labor force participation, annual participation rates are divided into two components: the proportion of the population that worked or looked for work at some time during the year and the mean number of weeks those individuals spent in the labor force.

The average number of weeks worked annually by men who were in the labor force at any time during the year had drifted up slightly over the thirty years to just under fifty weeks. This finding reflects the fact that most men with labor market experience work at full-time, year-round jobs or, if unemployed at some point in the year, remain active in searching for work. However, the proportion of men with labor force experience during the year has shrunk slowly over time because of the trend toward early retirement.

For women, the average number of weeks worked has steadily increased from thirty-nine weeks in 1958 to more than forty-seven weeks in 1989. This finding highlights the extent to which, over time, women have developed firmer attachments to the labor market. This trend has occurred as women's exits from jobs, or from a search for a job, to nonparticipation each year have become less frequent. Indeed, by the late 1970s, the average amount of time women spent in the labor force had moved to within three weeks of the average for men. At the same time, the proportion of women with some labor market activity during the year has trended higher, this trend further boosting the participation rate of females in the labor force.

Part-time employment has made up a growing share of all jobs over the past four decades. The fraction of employed workers who voluntarily work part-time rose from 13 percent in the late 1960s to 14 percent in the 1970s and accounted for the trend in total part-time work over this period (Table 29.1). The increase occurred partly because employers sought to

Table 29.1

Part-time Work as a Percentage of Total Employment, 1968–90

Age group and reason for part-time work	1968–69 (average)	1970–79 (average)	1980–89 (average)	1990
All workers	15.2	17.3	18.8	18.0
Voluntary	12.7	13.7	13.6	13.6
Involuntary	2.6	3.7	5.3	4.5
Workers 16–19	51.7	54.6	63.0	64.9
Voluntary	45.7	46.0	51.2	55.0
Involuntary	6.0	8.6	11.8	10.0
Men 20+	5.4	6.8	8.7	8.7
Voluntary	3.8	4.3	4.8	5.2
Involuntary	1.7	2.5	3.9	3.5
Women 20+	23.5	24.9	24.9	23.8
Voluntary	20.2	20.5	18.9	18.8
Involuntary	3.2	4.4	6.0	5.0

accommodate the preferences for short hours of students and house-wives, the fastest-growing groups in the labor force in the 1970s. However, voluntary part-time work has remained a fairly constant proportion of total employment since the 1970s. Instead, involuntary part-time employment has propelled the upward trend in total part-time work since the early 1970s, largely because employers view part-time work as a means to cut labor costs, not because workers want shorter schedules. With a sizable proportion of the work force holding part-time jobs, it would seem that the aggregate amount of labor supplied could be increased by lengthening the work week of those working part-time. However, many workers hold more than one part-time job and thus essentially work full-time schedules.

Indeed, a final way that employees can exercise choice over their hours of employment is to work at more than one job. Between 1970 and the middle of the 1980s, the percentage of workers holding two or more jobs showed no apparent trend, with the proportion fluctuating around 6 percent. Historically, most holders of multiple jobs were men working a second job to supplement income from a primary, full-time job. However, while the aggregate multiple-job-holding rate held fairly steady over this period, the rate for men moved down from 7 percent in 1970 to around 6 percent by the mid-1970s, where it stayed through the middle of the 1980s. At the same time, the rate for women moved up from 2.25 percent in 1970 to 4.75 percent in 1985.

Between mid-1985 and mid-1989, the number of people holding more than one job increased nearly 1.5 million, and the proportion of multiple-job holders climbed substantially from 5.5 percent in 1985 to 6.25 percent in 1989. Women accounted for nearly two-thirds of the increase in multiple-job holding over this period. Multiple-job holding for men continues to be a way of supplementing income from a full-time job with work after hours. In contrast, nearly one-third of the female multiple-job holders work at more than one part-time job; they work, on average, nearly fifty hours per week.

All told, more women are participating in the labor force than at any time in the past four decades, and those women who are participating work more hours per week and more weeks per year. In many ways, women's labor supply decisions are more and more resembling those of men.

30. The 1980s: A Decade of Job Growth and Industry Shifts
Lois M. Plunkert

Excerpted from the *Monthly Labor Review*, September 1990, pp. 3–15. Lois M. Plunkert is chief of the Branch of National Estimates, Division of Monthly Industry Employment Statistics, Bureau of Labor Statistics.

The 1980s began with two recessions in three years and then posted the longest peacetime expansion on record. Although growth did slow as the decade came to a close, the service sector still added large numbers of jobs month after month.

Not all industries experienced the prosperity of the 1980s. Many manufacturing and mining industries never recovered their production levels, or did so with fewer workers. Growth also was uneven within service-sector industries: one new job in four was in business or health services, while some service-sector industries lost jobs—notably, communications, railroads, and water transportation. Other industries, such as finance and special construction trades, that showed strong growth for most of the ten-year period were experiencing job losses or sluggish growth at the end of the decade. As a result of the interplay of job gains and losses among industries, the 1980s witnessed the shifting of another 6 percent of employment from the goods-producing to the service-producing sector. Just over three-fourths of all jobs are now in the service sector.

This continued shift of jobs into the service economy was not at the expense of manufacturing output, which remained at about 23 percent of GNP over the decade, while factory jobs dropped from 23 percent to 18 percent of employment. During the two recessions early in the decade, many marginal jobs were eliminated throughout the economy. Marginal plants were closed down, some permanently. With the start of the recovery in 1983, industry began to take on a leaner look. In an effort to compete in a worldwide market, many factories were modernized during the 1980s, with more and better machines enhancing workers' output. At the same time, the size of the labor force swelled: Not only did the working-age population grow by 21.5 million, but also a larger percentage of women entered the job market. As a result, women's participation in the labor force increased from 51 to 57 percent over the decade.

A Tale of Two Sectors

The underlying theme of industry employment shifts experienced in the 1980s has been playing for decades. At the middle of the century, 41 percent of all nonfarm jobs were in the goods-producing sector. Forty years later, that proportion had declined to 24 percent. Within the service sector, the number of private jobs grew faster than government jobs.

Although the goods-producing sector has experienced a decline in its share of jobs, the actual number of jobs has remained relatively stable over the years, falling during recessions and rising again during subsequent recoveries. The service sector, on the other hand, survived the recessionary years quite well and, in some cases, even continued to add jobs. This resilience during economic downturns was followed by rapid growth during expansionary periods. Thus, the shifting job distribution resulted from the combination of flat employment levels in the goods-producing sector with steady growth in the service sector.

Trends in Major Industries

Mining lost an astounding 25 percent of its employment over the decade, and manufacturing lost 7 percent. The only goods-producing industry division to gain jobs was construction, which grew by 19 percent. Government and transportation and public utilities, the slowest growing of the service-sector industry divisions, each increased their employment by 11 percent. The large service division—including business, health, and other general services—grew faster than any other division and accounted for half of the job growth over the decade.

Table 30.1

Percent Employed in Major SIC Industries, 1979 and 1989

Industry division	1979	1989
Total nonagricultural	100.0	100.0
Goods producing	29.5	23.6
Mining	1.1	0.7
Construction	5.0	4.9
Manufacturing	23.4	18.1
Service producing	70.5	76.4
Transportation and public utilities	5.7	5.3
Wholesale trade	5.8	5.7
Retail trade	16.7	18.0
Finance, insurance, and real estate	5.5	6.3
Services	19.1	24.8
Government	17.8	16.3

The impact of these varying rates of change on the distribution of jobs is seen in Table 30.1. Currently, one job in four is in the services division, up from less than one in five at the beginning of the decade. Manufacturing's share dropped by 5 percentage points to 18 percent. Government lost a 1.5 percentage point share, while retail trade gained about the same amount. Mining's loss of 0.4 percentage point brought it to well under 1 percent of employment. The remaining industry divisions just kept up with overall growth and ended the decade within a percentage point of the share of employment they held in 1979.

Services

The main reason for the impressive 1980s expansion was the performance of the services industries, which were responsible for half of all job growth during the decade. Of the twenty fastest-growing industries, eleven were services, as were seventeen of the thirty industries adding the most jobs.

The business service industry was both the most rapidly growing and the biggest employment gainer of the industry groups within the services division, doubling its employment and adding 2.9 million jobs. As business emerged from the 1981–82 recession, one approach taken by many to retain a lean posture was to contract for some of the services that they previously performed in house. Employment mushroomed in such services as advertising, mailing and production, to buildings, and management and public relations. Within the business services industry group were five of the most rapidly growing industries, including computer and data-processing services, which nearly tripled its employment by adding a half million jobs. Much of the strength in computer services was in specialized programming and software. Personnel supply services grew nearly as fast, adding 825,000 jobs. This industry is dominated by temporary-help supply firms, which grew very rapidly during the recovery period as organizations looked for ways to increase their staffing flexibility. Although categorized under miscellaneous services rather than business services, the accounting, auditing, and bookkeeping services industry profited from the same demand factors affecting business services in general and increased in employment by three-fourths, adding 220,000 jobs over the decade.

Health service employment grew at half the pace of business services, but this was still three times the rate for all industries. The large health services industry group added 2.6 million workers during the 1980s. Factors behind this growth include the growing elderly population; technological advances that make new treatments possible; and more requirements for paperwork, imposed by both government and private insurers. Employment growth was somewhat restrained by cost-cutting efforts aimed at reducing inpatient hospital stays when care could be provided on an outpatient basis and shortening the length of hospital stays when they were required. As a result, employment in outpatient care facilities nearly tripled over the decade, making this component the second fastest-growing industry, while the hospital industry, with a 34 percent growth rate, was one of the slower-growing health services. Nevertheless, considering the large number of people employed in hospitals, this moderate growth rate was sufficient to place the industry fourth on the list of job gainers. Office assistants of physicians also made this list, adding nearly half a million jobs and increasing employment by two-thirds over the decade.

Another rapidly growing health service industry was nursing and personal care facilities; the aging population was a factor behind a 46 percent employment increase in the industry, amounting to 435,000 new jobs. A related social service industry, residential care, benefited from the same demographics. Employment more than doubled in residential care institutions, which provide twenty-four-hour, year-round personal care with only incidental health care. The industry added 225,000 jobs over the decade, placing it on both the list of biggest gainers and the list of fastest growers. A similar performance was posted by another social service industry, individual and family services, which includes elderly daycare and senior citizens' centers, as well as private community social service agencies.

The legal services industry also is noteworthy because of both its high growth rate, 95 percent, and the large number of jobs added, 435,000, over the decade. Part of this strength can be attributed to the rising number of high-income families that need and can afford more sophisticated legal services.

Government

One of the two slowest-growing of the service-sector industry groups, government, added nearly 1.8 million jobs during the 1980s. Within this industry division, the number of state government jobs grew most rapidly, with a 17 percent increase, and local government added the most jobs, accounting for more than half of the total added.

The federal government demonstrated slow growth over the decade, with a 7.8 percent increase in jobs. The substrata within the federal government, however, showed divergent patterns. Civilian employment in the Department of Defense gained 80,000 jobs, reflecting the military buildup during the 1980s; civilian defense jobs had dropped by three times that amount in the prior decade as the country adjusted from war to peace. During the 1980s, the postal service added one worker for every four already employed, for a total of 170,000 new jobs. In sharp contrast, all other executive agencies lost a total of 40,000 employees, reflecting, among other things, a cutback in the number of federal grant programs and their funding. The relatively small legislative and judicial agencies also had divergent movements. Legislative agencies lost two thousand jobs, or one employee in twenty, while the judicial branch added three employees for every five employed at the beginning of the decade—a gain of eight thousand jobs and almost as rapid a growth rate as for private legal services.

State and local governments, affected by the recessions and by the California-led revolt against taxes (proposition 13), lost 430,000 jobs in the early 1980s. State and local governments later benefited from increased revenue attributable to growth in the economy, state and local tax increases, and increased income from user fees and state lotteries. Although growth in school enrollments decelerated markedly during the 1980s, new resources were geared toward initiatives to improve education following the release of a critical report by the National Commission on Excellence in Education.

Against this backdrop, state general administration added a half million jobs, or one new worker for every two employed in 1979. State education added another quarter million jobs, for an 18 percent increase, even though enrollment in public four-year colleges grew by only 4 percent. State hospitals, on the other hand, lost 90,000 workers, reflecting, at least in part, the trend to deinstitutionalize mental patients.

Like that of state education, employment growth in local education cannot be explained by enrollment trends. Schools added three-quarters of a million jobs, for a 15 percent growth rate, while enrollment in grades K–12 fell by 3 percent and the number of students in public two-year colleges increased by just 2 percent. Local general administration grew at a more modest rate than state administration, but accounted for more than a quarter million new jobs. Local government hospitals added nearly as many jobs as state hospitals lost, but transportation and public utilities owned by local governments suffered significant job losses over the decade.

31. The Changing Labor Force: Some Provocative Findings
William E. Cullison

Excerpted from *Economic Review* (Federal Reserve Bank of Richmond, September/October 1989), pp. 30–36.

Discouraged Workers

Some analysts argue that individuals will drop out of the labor force if they become too discouraged about their job prospects. Workers therefore would be expected to increase their labor force participation in periods of economic expansion and decrease it in times of economic contraction.

The data show, however, that since 1976 the only participation rates that were significantly related to changes in real GNP were those of males in the twenty-five to fifty-four age group, and that those participation rates were not related to GNP growth in the way predicted by the discouraged worker hypothesis. Thus, the analysis implies that a decline in the rate of growth in real GNP, other things equal, will induce a rise in the rate of labor force participation of males aged twenty-five to fifty-four, which is exactly opposite to the sort of behavior predicted by the discouraged worker effect.

This inverse relation between real GNP growth and male twenty-five to fifty-four participation rates is consistent with either (1) the backward-bending supply curve of labor, according to which workers opt for more leisure and therefore drop out of the labor market when their incomes rise and come back in when their incomes fall, or (2) a variant of the backward-bending supply curve, the additional worker effect.

Additional Workers

Underlying the additional worker effect is the concept that secondary workers (nonbreadwinners) enter the labor force in times of adversity to enable the family to maintain its standard of living. As noted above, the labor force participation rate behavior of age twenty-five to fifty-four males, who increase their participation as the economy expands and reduce it as the economy contracts, would be consistent with the additional worker hypothesis if those workers were indeed secondary workers. If male twenty-five to fifty-four participation rates were dominated by the additional worker effect, however, the regression of them on the misery index, the CPI, or the unemployment rate should also have been significant. It was not.

Evidence of the additional worker effect is found, however, in the regression of female twenty-five to fifty-four labor force participation on the trends and the misery index. The regression results showed a significant positive relation between the misery index and participation rates in the female twenty-five to fifty-four age group.

As mentioned earlier, if a significant negative correlation between the rate of growth of real GNP and the female participation rate had been found, that result would also have been consistent with the additional worker hypothesis. Intuitively, however, it seems most appropriate to identify the misery index more closely with the additional worker effect than with the change in real GNP, for inflation and unemployment have immediate and direct effects on family real incomes. Therefore, it seems likely that the female twenty-five to fifty-four participation rates were affected more strongly by the additional worker effect than were the participation rates of males twenty-five to fifty-four.

The labor force participation of age twenty-five to fifty-four males seems more likely to stem from behavior consistent with the classic backward-bending supply curve. The rationale for the backward-bending curve is that as individuals achieve certain levels of income, leisure becomes progressively more desirable. As a result, wage increases may sometimes induce workers to substitute leisure hours for work hours.

Speculations about Possible Effects of the Revolution in Female Labor Force Participation

The composition of the labor force in 1988 is radically different from that of 1950. If the 1950 participation rates had continued to prevail, the 1988 labor force would contain 22 million fewer female workers and 8 million more male workers. Moreover, the growth in the female labor force has drawn from the prime twenty-five to fifty-four age population, while the source of decline in the male labor force participation has been in the older, fifty-five and over, ages.

One of the early rallying cries of the feminist revolution in the 1950s was that females were not encouraged to enter the labor force but rather were expected to remain home and nurture their children. If that were true in the fifties, it has changed in the eighties. Over 55 percent of all women over sixteen participated in the labor force in 1988, far higher than the 35 percent female participation rate registered in 1950.

Whether the work situation for females has turned out to be consistent with the expectations of the feminist revolution, however, is open to question. First, a number of traditionally female jobs continue to pay lower wages than traditionally male jobs. Second, the correlation of participation rates of twenty-five to fifty-four year-old females with the misery index provides evidence that a proportion of female workers have jobs not because they desire to work, per se, but because they and their families need the income.

How have males fared since 1950? Apparently quite well. Almost 45 percent of the male population over sixty-five was in the labor force in 1950, but only 15 percent was in 1988. Such a change, of course, could indicate that prospective employers now tend to discriminate against older men, but that explanation seems unlikely. Rather, the reduction in labor force participation of sixty-five and over males most likely is beneficial to older men, as more of those who want to retire are now able to do so. The data also show declining participation rates for fifty-five to sixty-four men, especially since 1970. Again, the trend could be interpreted as hurtful to the welfare of the fifty-five to sixty-four men, but the accuracy of such an interpretation would be questionable. It seems much more likely that the declining rates for fifty-five to sixty-four men indicate an increase in welfare as more men are able to choose early retirement.

This decreasing male labor force participation has come in the face of stable (sixty-five and over) or rising (fifty-five to sixty-four) female labor force participation rates in the older age groups. Does this development mean that the older men are now living a life of leisure secured by their retirement benefits and the earnings of their breadwinning spouses? It could. Does it mean that older men and older women are now living lives of leisure, traveling around the country in their RVs, using up the inheritance that might otherwise have gone to children and grandchildren? It could, for although female labor force participation rates have risen, they still do not exceed male labor force participation rates. Does it mean that laid-off older males get discouraged about their job prospects and drop out of the labor force? It might, but participation rates of older men do not seem to vary in any consistent way with the rate of growth of real GNP, so if they get discouraged, it relates more to secular than to cyclical developments.

So who has benefited from the feminization of the work force? If benefit is based on freedom to follow one's preferences without worrying about breadwinning, the beneficiaries are not all female, nor have all females benefited. Rather, older men are now apparently able to choose to retire at earlier dates, while some prime-age females apparently work outside the home only because they and their families are facing hard times and they cannot afford not to work outside the home.

32. The Labor Movement

Mary C. King

Mary C. King, an assistant professor of economics at Portland State University, would like to thank Lee Badgett, Bill Dickens, Todd Easton, Alan King, Clifford Lehman, Vicky Lovell, Lisa Saunders, Dick Sasuly, Craig Wollner, and her editors for their careful, constructive criticisms. This paper is an original contribution to this volume.

The American labor movement is driven from the bottom by the hopes and efforts of its members. However, the fortunes of the American labor movement in the twentieth century have risen and fallen with its political and legal support. Union membership exploded in the late 1930s after Franklin D. Roosevelt's White House pushed through a substantial legislative package that legitimated labor unions. During the late 1930s and World War II, labor was supported by the legal institutions created to administer union elections, and American business lowered some of its characteristic resistance to unions.

The 1940s and 1950s witnessed a capital–labor accord, or an *entente cordiale*, between large unions and large firms. Since then, unions have lost political and institutional support, and private-sector union membership has slid steadily downward. Now the proportion of American workers organized in unions in the private sector is comparable to that during the late 1920s and early 1930s. By contrast, public-sector unions, sanctioned during President John F. Kennedy's administration in 1962, faced many fewer political and legal obstacles than confronted by unions in the private sector, and public-sector union membership has skyrocketed.

Historians now see that the decline of the labor movement in the private sector began at the end of World War II with the enactment of the Labor-Management Relations (Taft-Hartley) Act of 1947. However, the strength of the unions diminished slowly through the "golden age of collective bargaining," which lasted through what has been called the longest and most successful period of expansion in American history, ending around 1970.

The United States emerged from World War II as the only country with an intact major industrial plant. Organized labor, galvanized by the Great Depression and legitimized by the 1935 National Labor Relations (Wagner) Act, forged a wartime working relationship with business closely supervised by the War Labor Board. Unions then grew strongest in those industrial sectors that after the war enjoyed a market environment devoid of international competition. Wages and working conditions in the growing service sector also improved, although not as significantly as in manufacturing.

Since the early 1970s, union membership in the private sector has fallen precipitously, as have many measures of economic health. Profits and productivity growth rates have slumped. Real hourly earnings have not approached their 1973 peak in the twenty years since. Income inequality has grown nearly continuously since 1968. Between 1945 and 1975 the unemployment rate topped 6 percent only twice, but it has dipped under 6 percent in only four years since 1975. African-Americans and Latinos have made little further progress since the 1960s and 1970s. Only for women have economic gains been better through the 1970s and 1980s than previously, though part of what appeared to be advances for women were really losses for men on the lower rungs of the labor market.

During the 1970s, 1980s, and early 1990s, labor has been battered by anti-inflation policies, by automation and technological change, and by business cost-cutting in response to increased international competition and stagnating productivity growth. Labor has taken the brunt of the fight against the inflation of the late 1960s through the early 1980s, because anti-inflation policies cause unemployment and reduce real wage growth. Technological advances and capital investment have meant that many fewer people are required in fields, mines, and factories. Productivity gains were such that the absolute number of people employed producing tangible goods, including agriculture, construction, and manufacturing, increased by only 4 percent from 1948 to 1968, while the real value of our GDP grew by three and one-half times.

Still, American productivity growth rates have fallen behind those of

Europe, Australia, and Japan since the 1960s. The industrialized countries have recovered from World War II and have been joined by some third world countries that now produce not only shoes and clothing, but electronics, autos, and steel that rival American goods in price and quality. In response, American businesses have mounted increasingly determined campaigns to lower labor costs and to deflect union organizing, and have been aided in this effort by anti-labor public policies.

The Labor Movement before World War II

Despite a long history of efforts, labor unions made relatively little headway in the United States until passage of new labor legislation in the 1930s. The events of the thirties changed the labor movement so drastically that one scholar has called the post-1930s stage of labor history "the second American labor movement." The first labor movement was predominantly composed of craft unions, which represented skilled workers in a single trade, or in a few closely allied trades, such as printing, cigar making, or electrical work. Craft unions typically retained control over training and admission to their trade. These unions represented a small proportion of workers, who were restricted by most union charters to white men, and were called with some justice the aristocracy of the working class. Craft workers were relatively well paid in comparison with other workers, if not in relation to management, and enjoyed some leverage with employers as a result of their monopoly on particular skills and their small numbers in relation to the work force as a whole. The craft unions grew from city locals into national affiliations and then organized nationally into the American Federation of Labor (AFL) in 1886.

Samuel Gompers, founder of the AFL and its leader for thirty-seven years, defined the mission of the American labor movement as "business unionism," or the attainment of better wages and working conditions through collective bargaining by individual unions with individual firms. By contrast to American business unionism, European unions took on far larger roles in management and politics, supporting labor parties that enacted society-wide, rather than job-related, benefits for health, old age, parenting, and income maintenance. Many American unions considered themselves advocates of free enterprise and did not support social legislation until after World War II.

Though workers organized by craft unions were in many senses the elite among nonmanagement employees and a small proportion of the labor force, the fight for recognition of the craft unions was hard-fought and bloody. American employers were supported by the courts, police, and militia in their position that most aspects of labor organizing were an illegitimate conspiracy against property rights, and backed up their legal position with thugs, both paid and volunteer, including the infamous Pinkerton detectives.

Business in the United States has sustained a far more consistent media and political campaign against union organizing than has been true in Europe. The National Association of Manufacturers (NAM), formed in 1895 to increase trade opportunities, by 1903 found its fundamental and enduring purpose in the opposition to union organization. In the 1920s the National Association of Manufacturers popularized the open shop as the American Plan, which in effect was a strategy to keep unions out of the workplace. In an open shop, where employees have voted for union representation, all employees need not join the union, though the union must represent all employees and all employees earn union-bargained wages. The alternatives are a closed shop, now illegal in this country, in which only union members are hired; a union shop, in which employees must join the union within a certain amount of time; and an agency shop, in which employees who do not wish to join the union are required to pay fees to the union for its services as an agent bargaining on their behalf.

The second or post-1930s labor movement, built on industrial unions as well as craft unions, developed in response to the increased strength of corporations, which were growing in size and complexity, increasing their scope both geographically and in the number of functions they incorporated. Only industrial unions, which included most nonmanagement employees, skilled and unskilled, working in one industry could successfully confront the new corporate behemoths. Small locally based craft unions lost their ability to affect American business, grown strapping through the merger movement and vertical integration. Centralized, disciplined, bureaucratic organizations were required. Further, it was very difficult to organize the preponderance of workers, who were unskilled and semiskilled, along craft lines.

John L. Lewis, the powerful leader of the United Mine Workers, was unable to sway the 1935 AFL convention to support industrial unions including unskilled and semiskilled workers, as well as workers in one or more crafts. Later that year Lewis and others committed to industrial unionism formed the Committee for Industrial Organization, which began organizing unions of steel, auto, rubber, glass, and radio workers. Unable to reconcile with the AFL, the industrial unions reconstituted themselves as the Congress of Industrial Organizations (CIO) in 1938. These mass-production unions grew rapidly, feeding on the militancy resulting from the terrifying unemployment and abysmally low wages of the Great Depression and legal changes that gave unions leverage against the intransigent resistance of American employers to union organizing.

Depression-Era Changes in the Legal Environment for Organizing

Much of the legal framework that empowered the second American labor movement was part of the New Deal response to the Depression. Key legal developments included the pre-New Deal Norris-LaGuardia Anti-Injunction Act of 1932, as well as Section 7(a) of the National Industrial Recovery Act (NIRA) of 1933, superseded and expanded by the Wagner Act in 1935 and the Fair Labor Standards Act of 1938. The Norris-LaGuardia Act outlawed "yellow dog contracts," in which employees had to agree to abstain from all union activity as a condition of employment, and legitimated unions' use of pickets and strikes. Previously, courts had granted employers injunctions against strikes and pickets as illegal restraints of trade, effectively disarming the unions by forbidding their primary mechanism for pressuring employers.

The NIRA proclaimed the right to organize, which was included in the Wagner Act when the NIRA was struck down by the Supreme Court as unconstitutional. The Wagner Act put the weight of the law behind workers' right to organize and bargain collectively, developed the administrative infrastructure to oversee this process, and delimited several business tactics as "unfair labor practices." Specified unfair labor practices included interfering with employees in exercise of their rights; discriminating against employees associated with organizing activity; refusing to bargain in good faith; and dominating, supporting, or interfering with labor organizations. The latter prohibition effectively outlawed company unions, which are unions set up and funded by management.

The Wagner Act created the National Labor Relations Board (NLRB) as a labor court to determine appropriate bargaining units, hold union certification elections, and investigate alleged unfair labor practices. The powers of the NLRB are remedial rather than punitive. The Board can require reinstatement and back pay for workers illegally fired but has never had the authority to assess financial penalties on a scale that would economically deter an employer from engaging in unfair labor practices.

Militant strikes, including the new sit-down strike pioneered by the United Auto Workers in 1936, encountered continuing employer resistance and occasional violence, as both unions and management tested the new federal structure of labor relations. The National Labor Relations Board in general supported unions in their push to organize during the 1930s, and was backed by the Supreme Court. Later, during World War II, the War Labor Board was inclined to promote the organization process in order to avoid any slowdown in production, though to limit inflation the Board allowed little in the way of wage increases. In this new environment, unions organized over 80 percent of the production workers in the steel, auto, aircraft and agricultural equipment, rubber, electrical machinery, and meat-packing industries.

Other Depression-era legislation that altered the landscape for the American work force included the Davis-Bacon Act of 1931, promoted by the AFL. This act held the hours on public works projects to eight hours per day and required pay to meet prevailing local standards, which now tends to mean the local union wage for each occupation. The Fair Labor Standards Act, also known as the Wages and Hours Act, established the minimum wage in many industries, notably exempting agricultural, retail, and most service employment; set protective standards for children; and called for time-and-one-half pay for work in excess of eight hours a day.

The Social Security Act of 1935 was not supported by the labor movement, which still held to Gompers's philosophy that benefits stemming from collective bargaining were preferable to society-wide social insurance. The Social Security Act created a two-tiered and piecemeal system of income maintenance. Included in the act for workers were systems of unemployment and old-age insurance, and for the children of widows, Aid to Dependent Children (now AFDC). From the beginning these two tiers have differed significantly, not least in the level of benefits provided, the first being perceived as earned and the second as charity. Consequently, families that lose their husbands and fathers to industrial accidents or disease, and thus receive survivors' benefits under the social security program, are much better off than families who lose a man to desertion or divorce and are eligible only for AFDC.

These legal changes together are referred to as the Wagner Act framework, which supported a tremendous increase in union membership and income security for working Americans.

World War II and Its Immediate Aftermath

War production left the United States with a well-developed industrial plant, enhanced by public wartime investment, which converted to the production of consumer durables such as automobiles and appliances. The organization of the labor force in these industries had been consolidated under the then-receptive auspices of the National Labor Relations Board and the War Labor Board. By 1945, union agreements covered 69 percent of production employees in manufacturing and 36 percent of all employees not working in agriculture. This level of organization was unprecedented in American history.

Wartime institutions facilitated expansion of union membership rolls, while holding labor demands in check with a system of wage and price controls and no strike–no lockout agreements. The proportion of the

Table 32.1

Percent of Civilian Nonagricultural Labor Force in Unions
(by industry 1935–92)

Year	Mining	Const.	Manuf.	Transp.	Service	Govt.	Total
1935	54.4	71.5	16.4	25.8	2.6	9.0	13.5
1940	72.1	77.0	30.5	47.3	5.7	10.7	22.5
1947	83.1	87.1	40.5	67.0	9.0	12.0	32.1
1953	64.7	83.8	42.4	79.9	9.5	11.6	32.5
1966	35.7	41.4	37.4	50.3	n.a.	26.0	29.6
1973	37.6	38.1	38.8	49.3	12.9	37.0	28.5
1980	32.1	31.6	32.3	48.0	11.6	35.0	23.2
1984	17.7	23.5	26.0	38.7	7.3	36.7	19.4
1992	15.1	20.0	19.7	30.8	7.2	36.7	15.8

Sources: Leo Troy and Neil Sheflin, *U.S. Union Sourcebook: Membership, Finances, Structure, Directory, 1985.* U.S. Bureau of the Census. *Statistical Abstract of the United States*, 1993.

labor force in unions had reached or nearly reached its historic peak in mining, construction, manufacturing and transportation at the end of the war, as is suggested by the data in Table 32.1.

At the end of the war the Truman administration worried about both potential inflation if wage and price controls were completely lifted and the return of unemployment in the aftermath of demobilization. The White House convened a national labor-management conference and pressed for a continuation of no strike–no lockout agreements and over-sight of wage increases by the National Wage Stabilization Board, estab-lished in early 1946.

Prices rose faster than either the War Labor Board or the National Wage Stabilization Board allowed wages to rise, and workers were laid off as factories converted to civilian production. Labor leaders, remem-bering the 1920s rollbacks of labor's World War I gains, set off a one-and-a-half-year strike wave through 1945 and 1946. These strikes were different from earlier strikes in their number, breadth, and duration; in their focus on wage demands rather than union recognition; and in the relative lack of violent opposition.

Walter Reuther of the United Automobile Workers (UAW), then the largest union in the country, hoped to use the auto workers' 113-day walkout beginning in November 1945 to bargain for consumers as well as for auto workers. Reuther called for an arbitrator to examine General Motors' books to determine how large a wage increase GM could afford without raising prices. Despite GM's vehement opposition, the White

House appointed a fact-finding panel, which fixed upon 19.5 cents an hour as a wage increase that would not require higher prices for cars and trucks.

General Motors refused to agree either to the particular recommendation or to the ideas that a corporation's ability to pay should affect its wage offer or that a private company should open its books to anyone. The strike dragged on. Meanwhile, the Steelworkers, the second largest union in the country, called a strike in 1946. Reportedly, Philip Murray, president of the CIO and of the Steelworkers, wanted steelworkers, not auto workers, to set the postwar wage standard and disagreed with Reuther's concern with consumer prices. The steel companies settled, granting an 18.5-cent-an-hour raise, but only with the proviso that the White House would allow them to raise the price of steel by $5 a ton. In the context of the steel settlement, the UAW backed down from its attempt to prevent price increases to consumers, accepted the 18.5-cent raise, and watched GM win price increases from the government.

However, Reuther's idea was picked up and modified by Charles Wilson, GM's chief executive, who in 1948 proposed a formula for union wage increases he called progress sharing. The formula included an "annual improvement factor," intended to pass along to workers the benefits of increased productivity by raising hourly wages with GNP growth, and a cost of living adjustment (COLA), which maintained purchasing power by adjusting wages for inflation. This practice spread throughout the auto and steel industries, as well as to other large firms operating in oligopolistic markets. Progress sharing and the annual improvement factor became the basis of the "capital–labor accord," or *entente cordiale*, between the big unions and many large firms, wherein unions were accepted as part of the industrial environment, wages were high and standardized, and union-management relations became ritualized and more predictable.

Meanwhile, in 1946 Republicans gained majorities in both houses of Congress. Campaigning against "communism, chaos, and confusion," the Republicans melded business dissatisfaction with labor's legal and organizational strength, popular sentiment against unions resulting from the postwar strike wave, and the anti-communism of the emerging Cold War. Business efforts to amend the Wagner Act, relentless since its passage, bore fruit with the Labor-Management Relations (Taft-Hartley) Act, enacted in 1947 over Truman's veto. The long and complicated Taft-Hartley Act outlawed most forms of mass picketing and secondary boycotts, created legal rights for employers to sue unions for damages, increased the difficulty of the union certification process, allowed employers greater latitude in their anti-union campaigns, banned closed shops, required all union officials to sign affidavits stating that they were not members of the Communist party or any organization supporting it, allowed the federal government to enjoin a strike "against the national interest," and created the framework for states to pass a wave of "right to work" laws, which disallowed union shops. Although ostensibly a "bill of rights for workers," designed to prevent employees from being coerced into union membership, the bill was heavily promoted by employers organized through the National Association of Manufacturers. Senator Taft said, "The bill . . . covers about three-quarters of the matters pressed upon us very strenuously, by the employers."

Employers succeeded in labeling unions as Big Labor, in whose favor the legal pendulum had swung too far. However, the labor movement was not strong enough to stave off business's whittling away of its New Deal position, nor to pass its own amendments to the Wagner Act framework. The White House was ambivalent; while the Democrats relied on labor's support, Truman detested the big strikes and needed Republican backing for his foreign policies. The AFL disliked the Wagner Act framework, regarding it as aiding industrial unionism at the expense of the craft unions. Factional politics inside the CIO meant that some labor leaders stood to gain as others were forced out when unwilling to sign the non-Communist affidavits.

Though the labor press universally condemned the Taft-Hartley Act as a "slave-labor" act, Lewis was the only prominent unionist to oppose signing the affidavits. He advocated giving up the protection of the NLRB if it came at the price of an increased government role in the internal affairs of unions. Lewis had also vehemently opposed connecting wage increases to the cost of living, having negotiated gains for the miners while prices were falling. One of the first unionists to see the need for political support for the labor movement, as demonstrated by his support for Roosevelt in the 1930s, Lewis also saw the perils of relying on government support which might be fickle. He called for free-market unionism and resisted pressure by the CIO and the White House to abjure strikes "in the national interest" when he thought that the interest of the miners lay elsewhere.

A few prophetic observers saw that passage of the Taft-Hartley Act was the end of the growth period for U.S. labor unions and the beginning of a long holding action. In the context of a swelling labor force and employment shifting to industrial sectors outside labor's strongholds, a holding action in fact meant the decline of American unionism.

The Merger of the AFL and the CIO

After passage of the Taft-Hartley Act, the labor movement stepped up its political activity, moving ever further away from the position of the first labor movement that it owed allegiance to no party but merely rewarded its friends and punished its enemies individually at the polls. In practice, the labor movement had found most of its friends and potential for influence in the Democratic party, and it became increasingly allied with the Democrats, if decreasingly influential. Labor played an important role in the extension of social security, unemployment insurance, and the minimum wage. Repeatedly defeated in attempts to repeal or amend the Taft-Hartley Act and seeking to develop labor's political and organizational strength, Walter Reuther of the CIO and George Meany of the AFL worked toward reunification of the labor movement.

One substantive obstacle to unity had been the AFL's antipathy toward the Communist presence in the CIO. Communists had risen to leadership positions in several of the CIO unions, without internal dissension except on foreign policy issues. The Communist-led unions had opposed U.S. participation in World War II as inimical to the interest of international working-class solidarity until the Soviet Union joined the combatants, and later these unions opposed the Cold War. However, in the 1948 presidential election, several of the left-led unions of the CIO supported Henry Wallace and the Progressive party, rather than Truman and the Democrats. Other CIO leaders thought that breaking ranks imperiled the Democrats and labor's influence on Capitol Hill. Some union leaders felt that the labor movement needed to appeal to an increasingly anti-Communist public influenced by the witch-hunt atmosphere created by Congressman Martin Dies with his House Un-American Activities Committee and Senator Joseph McCarthy. Communists were barred from executive office at the CIO's annual convention in 1949, and a mechanism was established for expelling any union following the "Communist line." The following year eleven unions were expelled, amounting to one-fifth of the CIO membership, and the CIO established new affiliates to compete with its recently expelled members.

Since the "purges" of Communists, other leftists, and the unions in which they were strongest, the labor movement has consistently supported anti-Communist foreign policies. Truman looked to labor as a key ally in support of the Marshall Plan, designed to prevent the growth of communism in Europe and rehabilitate the Western European economies. American unions were the principal actors in the creation of a new, anti-Communist International Confederation of Free Trade Unions in 1949, were an important constituency in support of U.S. involvement in Vietnam, and have been a partner around the world in the U.S. campaign to promote market-based economies.

The principle behind the emergence of the CIO from the AFL in 1935 had been the difference in organizing philosophies of craft and industrial unionism, a distinction that came to mean less and less as unionists pragmatically accepted both organizing strategies. More important to the leaders of unions in both camps was that the other group be restrained from "raiding" its members, on which the AFL and the CIO reached agreement in 1953. Later negotiations by the Joint Unity Committee produced a merger agreement whereby the AFL delegates agreed to fight corruption and racial discrimination and the CIO organizers to eliminate the influence of Communists. The AFL and the CIO merged in 1955, under the presidency of George Meany.

The AFL did little to change its racist practices, but Meany was determined to end the corruption rampant in particular AFL unions and locals. U.S. Senator John McClellan held televised hearings that focused public attention on Jimmy Hoffa and the Teamsters in particular, providing ammunition to the ongoing business-led public relations campaign against unionism. At the second convention of the newly merged AFL-CIO in 1957, the Teamsters were expelled. Although the AFL-CIO had sacrificed its largest and strongest union in the fight against corruption, Congress passed the Landrum-Griffin Labor Management Reporting and Disclosure Act in 1959. This act did much more than counter corruption, bringing the federal government into monitoring union activities for democratic practices, barring Communists and ex-convicts from union office for five years after leaving the party or prison, tightening some of the Taft-Hartley prohibitions on union activities, and giving greater jurisdiction over the unions to individual states, many of which had recently passed open-shop laws.

After the merger, the AFL-CIO turned its focus to a potential campaign to organize the South. At the end of World War II, both the AFL and the CIO had expended considerable resources to increase the southern union presence, without much success. A new campaign fizzled in the face of an AFL-CIO commissioned study indicating little hope of improvement on the postwar Operation Dixie. Labor organization in the South faced considerable obstacles, including an economic elite concerned that unions would sabotage the South's chance to industrialize, entrenched social conservatism, difficult race relations, significant anti-labor legislation, a large supply of poorly paid agricultural employees, and the demoralizing legacy of a history of unsuccessful organizing efforts. In addition, organizers faced a nonunion employment base in industries such as textiles and oil, which were relatively concentrated in the rural South and but little organized elsewhere.

Politically, the labor movement continued to expand its purview, becoming what Meany described as "the people's lobby." The AFL-CIO lobbied hard for civil rights legislation enfranchising African-Americans. Indeed, Meany told the House Judiciary Committee that federal legislation was needed to end race discrimination by unions. The AFL-CIO also

Table 32.2

Weekly Earnings of Production or Nonsupervisory Workers on Private, Nonagricultural Payrolls by Industry, Selected Years 1950–88
(1982–84 dollars)

| Year | Mining | Const. | Manufacturing | | Retail | Service | All |
			Heavy	Light			
1950	279	289	259	222	165	n.a.	220
1960	355	381	328	271	195	n.a.	273
1970	424	504	369	310	213	249	309
1980	482	446	377	310	179	231	285
1988	456	417	378	320	155	246	272

Source: Bureau of Labor Statistics, Handbook of Labor Statistics, 1989. Adjusted by author using the CPI-U.

promoted the Equal Rights Amendment, which would have banned discrimination on the basis of sex; the Age Discrimination in Employment Act (1967), which prohibited discrimination against people between the ages of forty and sixty-nine; the Occupational Safety and Health Act of 1970, which requires all employers to meet safety standards set by the Secretary of Labor; and Medicaid and Medicare to provide medical care for the poor and elderly.

Who Organized Labor Represented at Its Peak

In terms of the proportion of the labor force organized in labor unions, the unions hit their historic peak in 1953, just prior to the merger of the AFL and the CIO. Union strength was concentrated in manufacturing, construction, and mining, where jobs were predominantly held by white men and the pay well exceeded that of laborers, clerical and service employees. As shown in Table 32.2, earnings in the United States have varied considerably and consistently by industry. To this day, wages for high-school-educated workers are much higher in the organized primary and secondary sectors than in the tertiary, or service sector, where women and ethnic minorities were and are disproportionately employed.

During World War II, women and ethnic minorities made inroads into manufacturing, moving up the occupational ladder from agricultural, service, and clerical work into war production. However, even with a wartime labor emergency, it took a threatened March on Washington to pressure President Roosevelt in 1941 to issue Executive Order 8802 urging employers to begin hiring African-Americans. A further executive order, issued in 1943, forbade labor unions from discriminating on the basis of race, sex, or creed, which had been the almost universal practice of American unions since their formation.

Black and Latin men were able to retain their beachhead, though not their relative numbers, in industrial positions after the war. Women, unsupported by their unions, lost ground in manufacturing after the war and were pushed back into unorganized clerical and service occupations.

Consequently, the labor movement at its peak primarily represented adult white men in manufacturing, mining, and construction jobs. There were exceptions. For example, the United Mine Workers (UMW) represented both black and white men. The International Ladies Garment Workers Union (ILGWU) represented women and men of many ethnicities in the needle trades. The Hotel and Restaurant Employees (HERE) included many strong female-only locals, as well as mixed-gender locals.

The Unorganized Sectors of the Labor Market

Two-thirds of the labor force remained outside the umbrella of organized labor as the labor movement lost momentum. In contrast to Europe, workers in the growing service, wholesale and retail trade, and clerical occupations were very lightly organized, as were managerial, professional, and technical personnel.

Researchers have debated the explanation for the American labor movement's confinement to construction, mining, and heavy manufacturing. Often the women employed in service, retail, and clerical positions were described as unorganizable, uninterested in unions, and uncommitted to work and the labor force. Other scholars claim that the attitudes and practices of the labor movement itself were the most important source of the low level of organization among women historically, citing examples of exclusion, lack of support, and the frequently voiced assertion that men should earn family wages and women should remain in the home.

Certainly, the AFL took the position that African-Americans and Asians were inassimilable and unorganizable. Samuel Gompers played a leadership role in the anti-Chinese campaigns of the 1870s and 1880s while president of the Cigar Makers' International. These campaigns not only forced the Chinese out of cigar making, but also resulted in considerable anti-Chinese violence and the Chinese Exclusion Act of 1882. Gompers and AFL organizers displayed similar attitudes toward the organizing of African-Americans, holding that, "Caucasians are not going to let their standard of living be destroyed by negroes, Chinamen, Japs, or any others."

However, the exclusion of women and ethnic minorities was by no means unusual at the time. All other American institutions were at least as racially segregated, including churches, schools, and the military. Further, exclusion is the logic of craft unions, which are stronger the smaller the group that holds a monopoly on a particular skill.

The inclusive logic of industrial unionism, that industrial unions are stronger the larger their membership, is part of the reason that the record of the CIO is more mixed. Some CIO locals were egalitarian in principle, though many created segregated locals or dead-end job ladders for their black and female members. Some scholars have pinpointed racial divisions as one source of the weakness of the U.S. labor movement as compared with those abroad, recounting the history of employers deliberately pitting different groups of workers against one another.

Most likely, however, unions were strongest in the industries where white men were concentrated because these industries were the most profitable and the highest paying. American unions took hold in the large plants, where organizing large numbers of employees was easiest, and where capital-intensive production and high profits allowed for relatively large union wage gains. Some analysts have characterized unionized industries as "core" industries, where oligopolistic product markets and regulation created high profits, which unions were able to force firms to share with their workers. In the industrial "periphery," where firms face stiffer competition, volatile demand, and smaller profit margins, unions remained relatively weak when they were able to get a toehold at all.

The Decline of the U.S. Labor Movement in the Private Sector

The proportion of employees in the private sector represented by labor unions has diminished steadily since 1953. At the peak, 36 percent of the nonagricultural, private-sector labor force was organized; by 1992 that proportion had fallen to 11 percent. That decline has attracted a lot of attention from scholars, who variously attribute it to:

• increasing business resistance to unions;
• growing legal and political obstacles to unionism;
• the growth of employment in regions where labor has been weak: in the West, which developed as a nonunion environment; in the South, where right-to-work laws have hampered union organizing; and overseas, beyond the reach of American unions;
• the shrinking proportion of the labor force employed in manufacturing industries, the base of union strength;
• the rise in all industries of the numbers of white-collar and female workers, who have traditionally been unorganized;

- decreasing employee interest in unions due to the shift of employment to "white-collar" industries; public perception of union leaders as corrupt and self-interested; or a shrinking need for unions due to the growing government role in promoting equity, safety, and fair pay;
- the idea that unions have priced themselves out of existence by raising wages too high;
- the inability of the labor movement to adapt to a new environment and agitate more vigorously on major relevant political policies and legislation.

Addressing these in reverse order, certainly the world in which the second U.S. labor movement took hold no longer exists. The kinds of work available, the characteristics of the workers employed, the profitability and competitiveness of American employers, the legal environment for organizing, and the political clout of the labor movement have all altered drastically. The AFL-CIO formed the Committee on the Evolution of Work, which met through the early 1980s in order to examine this question, resulting in the February 1985 report "The Changing Situation of Workers and Their Unions," which calls on the labor movement to adapt to new realities.

The notion that union wages are too high is taken on by labor economists who claim that unionized workplaces are often more productive than nonunion firms. If unions attain relatively high wages, it pays employers to invest in more training and capital equipment so that workers are worth their hire. Further, the job security and communication channels established by unions allow workers to "voice" criticisms and complaints, which, if acted on, increase productivity. However, these analysts caution that union productivity effects are found primarily in organizations with good labor relations and in firms in competitive product markets.

Other economists, however, have sometimes thought that high union wages caused inflation and unemployment. As inflation built in the late 1960s, union wage increases based on "progress sharing" were identified as a possible culprit. Wages and fringe benefits represent roughly 70 percent of GNP, for although labor costs may be only 20 to 40 percent of the costs of production of any given firm, the intermediate goods purchased by firms embody significant labor costs. Inflation, measured by the GDP deflator, tracks closely over the long run with unit labor costs, or the firm's cost of labor per unit of output. The question is whether unit labor costs were rising and pushing employers to raise prices, or prices were rising for other reasons and employees then bargained for higher wages to maintain their real purchasing power.

The consensus opinion among economists now is that wages were not the primary source of inflation during the 1960s and 1970s, but that

COLA-based wage increases played a role in sustaining inflation once started. Wage increases in new union contracts seem to lag the inflation rate by a year or two. Rising unemployment levels stem more fundamentally from structural change and macroeconomic policies.

Public opinion polls indicate that while unions remain popular, union leaders are not. Many people, including union members, subscribe to the idea that union leaders are corrupt and self-serving. Nonunion workers, however, are as interested in joining a union as they have been in previous periods.

As to whether white-collar workers are less interested in union membership than blue-collar workers are, one researcher has found that professional, technical, and clerical workers are less organized than manufacturing workers partly because they are less interested in unionization and partly because they are less able to find union jobs. Service workers are less organized primarily because they are less able to secure union work.

The idea that the slide in union membership is related to the increase in the number of women in the labor force is contradicted by surveys of workers' attitudes toward unions. Unorganized women appear to be more interested in joining a union than unorganized men but are less able to obtain a union job. In fact, the proportion of women who are union members has not declined, as it has among men, reflecting the large female presence in health, education, and clerical positions in the growing public-sector unions. Further, the most successful union campaigns now are in workplaces with a preponderance of women workers earning low wages in nonmanufacturing settings.

The shift of employment in the American economy to the tertiary sector—services, including government—continued through the 1970s and 1980s. Fifty percent of the labor force was employed in the service sector in 1948, rising to 62 percent in 1968 and to 75 percent in 1988. Manufacturing employment fell particularly rapidly through the 1960s and 1970s, prompting a debate over whether the economy was deindustrializing or evolving to a postindustrial phase.

Advocates of the position that we are becoming a postindustrial society liken the disappearance of manufacturing jobs to the historical shift of employment out of agriculture, which they characterize as a natural consequence of economic development. Other analysts believe the decline in manufacturing, or deindustrialization, is not completely natural. They claim that particular business and government policies are leading to the early, unnecessary, and destructive demise of manufacturing. One of the consequences of deindustrialization is that jobs that pay relatively well for people without college educations are vanishing, to be replaced by low-wage service employment or nothing at all.

Higher education is increasingly necessary for a job that will underwrite the middle-class lifestyle that the strongest of the unions won for their members. Not only are high-wage, unionized manufacturing jobs disappearing, but case studies indicate that job ladders that employees once climbed from entry-level positions into more responsible ones are shortening. Education is becoming the exclusive route to better positions, displacing seniority and experience as sources of upward mobility.

However, scholars of union decline find that the diminishing role of manufacturing in the U.S. economy is responsible for only a small part of the drop in the proportion of the private-sector labor force working in union jobs. Indeed, unionization is on the decline within manufacturing.

The shift of employment to the South and the West does seem to be responsible for another small part of the union losses, particularly as employers have moved to states with right-to-work laws. The Sunbelt has always been hostile to unions, and many of the newer industries, including electronics, were determined to remain union-free from the beginning. Right-to-work laws, on the books in twenty-one states located primarily in the South, the western Midwest and the more rural mountain states, ban union shops. Under right-to-work laws employees in a unionized firm need not join the union, nor pay any dues to support union efforts, but must be represented by the union regardless and earn union-bargained wages.

In addition, union efforts are undermined by employers' threats to relocate work abroad. This threat is made real by the development of very advanced industrial plants in the third world and the shift even of clerical work to the Caribbean, Asia, and Ireland. National unions emerged in the United States when private companies grew beyond the reach of city locals, but effective international unions are harder to imagine and to build.

Many observers of the labor movement assert that legal and political obstacles to union organizing have grown since the passage of the Taft-Hartley Act in 1947. They point to the relatively cumbersome American union election process, which has allowed longer and longer delays between the time that a majority of employees are convinced that they would be better off with a union and the time those workers can expect to be working under a union contract. By contrast, the process is much expedited in Canada, and the proportion of private-sector employees in unions there is much higher.

Further, officials on the National Labor Relations Board, which controls the union election process, are appointed and can be actively hostile to unions, as was particularly the case during the Reagan and Bush administrations. The chair of the NLRB during the Reagan administration was quoted in the *New York Times* as saying that "collective bargaining frequently means the destruction of individual freedom," and that "strikes are a concerted effort employing violence, intimidation and political intervention to prevent people who want to work from working."

Increasingly effective business opposition to unionization has played a large role in the decline of private-sector unionization. A 1979 study by the National Association of Manufacturers found that the top personnel priority of nonunion firms was to remain nonunion, and that one-third of firms whose work force was at least partly union found keeping as much as possible of the company nonunion more important than getting a favorable bargain with their union employees. Trade associations, including the National Association of Manufacturers, the American Hospital Association, the Associated Builders and Contractors, the Associated General Contractors, the National Retail Merchants Association, and the National Public Employees Relations Association, run union avoidance programs for their members.

Anti-union management consultant firms have become standard allies in the fight against labor unions. An AFL-CIO official testified before Congress in 1979 that such consultants were involved in two-thirds of organizing campaigns of ten workers or more. Charges of unfair labor practices, and instances of NLRB ordering reinstatement and back pay to employees illegally fired during organizing campaigns have increased geometrically since 1950, despite the fact that union organizing activity has declined. Labor economists found that the cost to employers of violating the Wagner Act, even if caught, is much smaller than payment of union wages.

The impact of the growing use of illegal practices to discourage union organizing, the increasing tendency of employers to permanently replace strikers, and the far lengthier organizing procedure required of unions in the United States, as compared with nations such as Canada, has led to persistent, but as yet ineffective, calls for labor law reform. The most successful effort to change legislation to facilitate union organizing was the relatively mild National Labor Reform Act of 1977, which was supported by President Jimmy Carter and killed by filibuster in the Senate after passing in the House. Most recently, Senators filibustered labor law reform supported by the Clinton administration in 1994.

To summarize, the most important reasons for the long slide in the proportion of union members among the private-sector labor force appear to be the loss of institutional and political support for the labor movement and greater business resistance to union organizing. Unions do reduce profit margins, and the increasing determination of American businesses to operate without unions may reflect the low profit rates of recent decades. The shift of employment out of the geographical regions and industrial sectors where unions have been strongest appears to be responsible for some smaller portion of the decline. The other possible explanations of shrinking unionism do not seem to account for decreases in union membership.

Despite the growing obstacles to union organizing, the labor movement has a notable few private-sector successes to its credit in the last twenty-five years, including that of the United Farm Workers. Many observers have described attempts to organize farmworkers, as well as sharecroppers and tenant farmers, in the United States as futile. However, the United Farm Workers, led by Cesar Chavez and Dolores Huerta, organized a five-year strike and consumer boycott of table grapes that ended in 1970 with union recognition and significant improvements for farmworkers, primarily in California. Advances for farmworkers have been hard to maintain or to build on, though; once consolidated under the California governorship of Jerry Brown, they were substantially undone by his successor, George Deukmejian, by changing the political makeup of the state Agricultural Labor Relations Board.

After a decades-long record of union resistance and labor law violations, textile giant J.P. Stevens signed contracts with the American Clothing and Textile Workers Union (ACTWU) in 1980. The struggle with J.P. Stevens yielded a new union tactic, the "corporate campaign," which reaches out into the community to organize consumer boycotts, favorable publicity for the union, and pressure from other businesses.

The Rise of Public-Sector Unionism

Recent growth in the labor movement has been concentrated in the public sector, where unions do not confront employer hostility. The number of government employees organized by labor unions has expanded tremendously since 1962, when President Kennedy issued Executive Order 10988 reiterating and expanding federal employees' right to organize though not to strike. About half of the states gradually followed suit, creating legislation allowing state and local workers to organize, as well as legislation that sought to constrain union powers in the public sector. By 1993, 44 percent of government workers were represented by unions and 38 percent were members of unions, higher proportions than in any other broad industrial sector, and 41 percent of all union members in 1992 were employed in government. Public-sector unions include not only those workers whose jobs are somewhat akin to the crafts, such as police and firefighters, but clerical workers, service workers, and teachers.

While public employees clearly gained the right to organize, their right to strike remained ambiguous, differently construed by different states, and generally prohibited. However, public-sector workers have increasingly struck over unmet demands. In a gesture widely interpreted as setting the tone toward organized labor during the 1980s, President Reagan fired 11,500 air traffic controllers, members of the Professional Air Traffic Controllers Organization (PATCO), who were staging a nationwide "sickness" stay-away for better wages and working conditions.

More than a decade later a small number of the air traffic controllers were reinstated by President Clinton, in response to pressure from the labor movement and the shortage of well-trained personnel.

Public-sector unions account for a substantial segment of the women in labor unions. This concentration of women has been reflected in the attention public-sector unions have given to issues of pay equity, child care, and parental leave, as well as to the more traditional union issues of compensation and working conditions. Public-sector unions have not been completely hospitable, however, to the aspirations of women, or to those of ethnic minorities. Union locals in the uniformed services have demonstrated widespread and entrenched resistance to the hiring and promotion of women and ethnic minorities.

Many students of the American labor movement assert that the success of unions in the public sector indicates that political and legal support are the keys to union success. They assert that a much higher proportion of private-sector employees would be union members if political and legal barriers to organizing were diminished.

Recent History

The 1980s were a hard decade for the labor movement. The tone set by the Reagan administration in the PATCO firings was carried through by a hostile NLRB. Hard fought by employers, and little supported by the NLRB, fewer than 25 percent of employee groups attempting to unionize obtained an initial contract, even with a significant majority of employees supporting the effort. The 1981–82 recession, engineered by the Federal Reserve to fight inflation induced primarily by oil price increases, created the highest unemployment rates since the Great Depression. As a result, labor lost its leverage with employers as the spectre of unemployment decreased workers' willingness to jeopardize their jobs by making demands. Also, business moved production to the right-to-work Sunbelt and expanded overseas. Automation continued to replace less-skilled workers in many industries.

In this environment, labor unions were forced into concessionary bargaining, giving back wages in hopes of saving jobs and constructing two-tier wage structures, which paid new employees far less than more senior workers. Unions lost long, painful strikes against Hormel, Greyhound, Eastern Airlines, and Phelps Dodge, at the cost of jobs, wages, and union representation.

Politically the AFL-CIO continued to work as "the people's lobby" under the leadership of Lane Kirkland, George Meany's liberal protégé and successor. That "hardly a sparrow falls here or abroad that we do not take within the jurisdiction of the trade union movement," as proclaimed by Kirkland at the AFL-CIO's 1983 Constitutional Convention, is well demonstrated by the breadth of the issues for which the AFL-CIO lobbied during the 1980s. In addition to a long list of employment concerns, the AFL-CIO worked on foreign trade, infrastructure planning, health care insurance reform, tax reform, housing issues, urban mass transit, interest rates, the third world debt, environmental issues, sanctions against South Africa, education, child care, and consumer protection. The unions continued to regularly support the Pentagon at budget time until the 1980s. Only when the Reagan administration built up the military at the direct expense of social welfare programs did the AFL-CIO protest.

However, the labor movement has not been able to achieve its own political agenda. The trouncing of Walter Mondale, the lackluster Democratic presidential candidate anointed by the AFL-CIO to challenge Ronald Reagan at the polls in 1984 helped to solidify the image of the labor movement as an ineffective "special interest group."

In recent years, little progress has been made toward the primary concerns of the labor movement: labor law reform, a prohibition against permanently replacing striking workers, health care reform, greater protection of American workers from the dislocation due to global competition and automation, a higher minimum wage, and full employment.

Labor Movement Accomplishments

Scholars have long debated whether unions truly raise wages for organized workers. Some argue that union wages are higher because unions can pressure employers into sharing profits with their labor forces. Others claim that unions were most able to organize those workplaces where profits are high and wages would be high even in the absence of unions. The balance of evidence now suggests that unions do raise wages, paid for by increasing productivity and lowering profits. Also, in union workplaces, women and members of ethnic minorities earn more relative to white men in union than they do in nonunion workplaces.

U.S. unions have bargained other improvements for workers, as well. Unions pushed for the provision of fringe benefits during World War II when real wages were kept from rising, and benefits (e.g., pensions, sick leave, medical insurance, vacations, holidays, company recreation, fitness and athletic facilities) now represent 28 percent of compensation on average. Union benefits are substantially better than are those of nonunion employees. Unions provided a crucial push toward the development of personnel systems, replacing the arbitrary power of foremen to hire, fire, and set individual wages with a system of internal rules incorporating new principles of equal pay for workers on the same job and a role for seniority in layoffs and promotions. Unions have provided a measure of job security, a voice for employees, and grievance procedures, which are a mechanism for pursuing worker complaints.

Assessments of the impact of unions on workers who are not organized are mixed. Many analysts see that higher union wages pull wages up in general, and push nonunion employers to improve wages and working conditions in hopes of deflecting union organizing. Further, since the 1960s, unions have been a political voice for all workers, lobbying heavily for civil rights, safety, health, parental leave, a higher minimum wage, and full employment. On the other hand, by raising wages in union industries, unions may have reduced employment in organized sectors and increased the supply of workers to the unorganized sectors. Greater numbers of nonunion workers would push wages down and increase unemployment among the unorganized.

The Future of the American Labor Movement

Many who see a future for organized labor in the private sector are calling for labor law reform and new structures for the labor movement. One of the most sought-after changes in labor law is the enactment of legislation prohibiting firms from hiring permanent replacements for employees on strike. Another is to hold elections immediately after a majority of employees have signed union cards; now companies can force lengthy delays by manipulating NLRB procedures. A third proposed reform is to increase penalties for firms committing unfair labor practices, such as firing employees who attempt to bring in a union.

Labor unions may need to move away from limiting membership to those working for a firm with a current union contract to include unemployed workers, employees of nonunion firms, and employees of American firms operating abroad. In their groundbreaking 1985 self-assessment, the AFL-CIO recommended providing memberships, services, and benefits to employees who do not have a union contract, moving toward what has been termed associational unionism.

Unions are also positioning themselves to work with new ideas of participation in the workplace, introduced in part in response to Japanese management styles. While unions are wary of employee participation as a cover for increasing workloads without compensation, they are also interested in gaining more skills for their members and more influence over the way work is organized. Labor unions are making the case that employee participation works best in unionized settings.

Whether or not American labor unions will continue to be effective at raising wages, improving working conditions, and providing a voice for American employees is an open question, particularly in the private sector. Many observers have said that the era of vigorous unionism in this country is over. However, the most enduring characteristic of U.S. labor history may be its unpredictability.

Conclusions

A survey of the recent history of the American labor movement suggests several conclusions. The strength of the union movement is legally and politically based. Until passage of the Wagner Act and associated legislation, unions made relatively little headway in the United States. Union membership expanded rapidly from that time until passage of the Taft-Hartley Act. Since then unions have lost ground in the private sector, hemmed in by increasingly restrictive legislation such as the Landrum-Griffin Act and right- to-work laws and the ever more creaky and sometimes hostile administration of the NLRB.

Unions have been an important force in raising wages and living standards for American workers. Compensation has been increased directly through collective bargaining, indirectly by inducing employers to offer more to their nonunion employees, hoping to avoid unionization, and politically by lobbying for an increasingly broad array of progressive legislation. While historically the labor movement as a whole was only slightly more open to the concerns of women and ethnic minorities than were other American institutions, currently race- and sex-based differences in compensation are smaller in union than in nonunion settings. In recent decades, labor has been an ally for the civil rights and women's movements.

The viability of the labor movement in the future, particularly in the private sector, depends critically on the prospects for labor law reform and the ability of the unions themselves to adapt to the twenty-first century.

CHAPTER VI

Changing Material Conditions and the Quality of Life

33. Social and Economic Change since the Great Depression: Studies of Census Data, 1940–80
Elizabeth Evanson

Excerpted and reprinted with permission of the publisher, University of Wisconsin–Madison, Institute for Research on Poverty, from *Focus*, Fall 1988, pp. 1–10. Elizabeth Evanson is senior editor at the Institute for Research on Poverty at the University of Wisconsin–Madison.

The 1940 census has been termed the first modern census. It was the first to ask about income and seek a wide range of other social and economic information, the first to be designed and planned by a full-time professional staff that included social scientists. Since then the decennial censuses have become increasingly detailed, taking advantage of advances in sampling techniques and, beginning in 1960, of computerization to permit the release of public use sample tapes providing data on a host of household and personal characteristics.

When the 1940 census entered the field, the United States was still struggling with the devastating effects of the Great Depression. Not until the country geared up for entry into World War II did economic conditions begin to improve. But the war effort did more than fuel economic growth: it set in motion a series of extraordinary social changes.

A special project designed and executed by demographers at the University of Wisconsin has permitted the construction of microdata computer tapes from the 1940 and 1950 censuses to provide information comparable to that for 1960 through 1980. The results have enabled institute researchers to conduct time-series analyses of trends in poverty and well-being over the 1940–80 period.

The Changing Profile of Poverty

Christine Ross, Sheldon Danziger, and Eugene Smolensky have constructed from the five decennial censuses for 1940 through 1980 a record of the course of poverty and its changing incidence across particular groups. The only measure of poverty that can be accurately extended back to 1940 is that based on earnings alone, here termed "earnings poverty," since the 1940 census restricted precise income information to wages and salaries. From 1950 onward, data on all sources of cash income are available, providing a time series of "income poverty." The authors took the set of official income-poverty thresholds that were developed in the 1960s and extended them back to 1940 and 1950 by means of the Consumer Price Index, the same means by which the thresholds have been updated yearly since their adoption.

Earnings poverty stood at almost 70 percent of all people in 1940 but dropped steadily thereafter, reaching its low point of 27 percent in 1970, then rose to 29 percent in 1980. Income poverty consistently decreased, from 40 percent in 1950 to 13 percent in 1980. Its strong and steady decline and the rise in unearned income evident in the census data point to the increasing antipoverty effectiveness of government transfers.

Examining the changing incidence of income poverty across groups as defined by age, sex, and race of the household head, the authors found that poverty declined more among the elderly—who form the subject of a set of studies described later—than the nonelderly, more among whites than nonwhites, and more among men than women, reflecting (1) increased social security benefits for the elderly; (2) higher amounts of property income among men and among whites; and (3) higher lifetime earnings of, and consequently greater social security benefits for, whites as compared to nonwhites and men as compared to women.

Demographic changes have contributed to poverty, because the groups more likely to be poor—notably those living in households headed by women—have proportionately increased, while those less likely to be poor—those headed by white men of working age—have proportionately decreased. To measure the effect of those changes, Ross, Danziger, and Smolensky first calculated the percentages of all people living in households categorized (by age of head of household, as young aged fifteen to twenty-four, prime aged twenty-five to sixty four, and elderly over sixty-four) during each of the five censuses. They found that over the forty-year period the proportion of all people living in households headed by white men aged twenty-five to sixty-four fell from 70 to 58 percent. All other age groups increased their relative shares, and the largest increases were registered among the young and households headed by nonwhite women.

To estimate the effect of these demographic shifts on the incidence of poverty, Ross and colleagues then applied the 1980 poverty rates for each group to the 1940 composition of the population. They calculated that, had no demographic changes occurred in the intervening years, earnings poverty would have been 13.5 percent lower than it actually was in 1980 (25 percent rather than 29 percent), and income poverty would have been 23 percent lower (10 percent rather than 13 percent). To this extent changes in household structure have contributed to increases in poverty.

The level of poverty has also been influenced by the movement of married women into, and of older men out of, the labor force. From 1940 to 1980, families in which both husband and wife worked rose rapidly, earnings poverty rates declined sharply among such households, and the earnings gap between white and nonwhite couples narrowed.

Thus, trends in the composition of households according to race or ethnicity and sex, on the one hand, and according to employment status of household head and spouse, on the other, have had offsetting effects: The proportions of households headed by nonwhites, Hispanics, and women have grown, and the greater likelihood of such households to be poor has raised poverty levels, but the increased tendency of married women to seek paid work has tended to reduce poverty.

Children and the Elderly

Policy discussion in recent years has centered on the worsening economic circumstances of children since the 1960s, in contrast with the rapid improvement in the economic status of the elderly after 1965. Eugene Smolensky, Sheldon Danziger, and Peter Gottschalk have placed this discussion in historical perspective by examining the comparative situations of young and old not just since the 1960s but since 1940. They challenge the interpretation that government policy may bear large responsibility for the plight of the young, finding instead that the erosion of earnings of parents is a prime cause of rising poverty among children. Also implicated is the fact that an increasing percentage of children live in families headed by single women.

Government policy is the primary cause of declining poverty among the elderly. Economic expansion yielded rapid earnings growth from

1940 to 1970 (real median earnings increased by more than 50 percent between 1940 and 1950 alone), but social security retirement benefits changed very little until the mid-1960s. Thus, poverty rates for both old and young declined over the immediate postwar period, and children enjoyed the lead. That situation reversed in the 1970s. Government transfers to the elderly rose rapidly while real earnings fell, and as a consequence poverty fell among the elderly but increased among children, a trend that continued into the 1980s. "For most of our history," the authors point out,

> there has been a dependent population of young and old whose standard of living was virtually determined by the income of the working population with whom they resided. This remains true today only for children in intact families. It is no longer true for the many children in single-parent families dependent on child support and Aid to Families with Dependent Children, and it is certainly past history for the elderly.

They emphasize that if we look behind the aggregate figures for the old and the young, we find that subgroups in both populations are extremely vulnerable. Using data from the March 1986 Current Population Survey to update the 1980 census, Smolensky, Danziger, and Gottschalk identify subgroups for whom poverty rates remain high. They include all elderly people who are minority-group members, all children who are minority-group members, and white children in single-parent families.

The authors therefore advocate that policies should not focus on the elderly population as a whole (e.g., cuts in social security, which would harm the poor among the elderly) or on children as a group (e.g., children's allowances, which would benefit many who are not in need). They instead recommend higher tax credits for the parents of poor children, enhancement of the Supplemental Security Income program to help the elderly poor, and reductions in the tax benefits enjoyed by the well-to-do elderly. In these recommendations need, not age, is the overriding criterion.

Families

Three of these census studies concentrate on marriage and the family, offering insight into the evolving condition of single-parent and married-couple households.

Families Divided: The Poor, the Middle Class, and the Affluent

James P. Smith divides all families into three income groups. The poor are defined by a measure that applies the official poverty thresholds for 1960 (the census year closest to the date the thresholds were first developed, 1963) and adjusts them in other years to rise fifty cents for every dollar increase in real per family income, thus incorporating elements of a relative poverty measure. The affluent are defined as those who in 1960 had incomes equivalent to the top 25 percent of white families; that standard is adjusted dollar-for-dollar to account for real income growth in the other years. The middle class contains the remainder of families.

The encouraging news is the considerable decline in poverty among two-parent families in all demographic groups. The aggregate poverty rate among them dropped precipitously. Compare the results for families headed by women: poverty declined only from 47 to 36 percent. And whereas the proportion of affluent two-parent families stood at almost the same level at the beginning as at the end of the period, the proportion of affluent female-headed families declined from 17 percent to 6 percent. There was a strong growth of black and Hispanic middle classes and a dramatic rise in affluence among married-couple black families after 1960.

Because the incomes of women heading families grew more slowly than the average among all families, particularly after 1960, Smith analyzed the changing characteristics of these women. Single mothers now tend to be young and unwed, of limited earning capacity, receiving little in child support from the fathers of their children. These trends are stronger among blacks than whites, which helps explain a paradox: while racial wage differences among employed women have narrowed (twenty-five years ago the typical black employed woman earned half the wage of a white woman; now there is very little difference in their wage), a wide racial gap in the income of families has remained virtually unchanged: in 1970 and in 1980, black family income was about 62 percent of white family income.

The Growth of Female-Headed Families

Whereas Smith documented the low economic status of women who head families, a paper by Roger Wojtkiewicz, Sara McLanahan, and Irwin Garfinkel examines the sources of their increase within the U.S. population.

In the 1940s, the years of the war and its aftermath, the fraction of female-headed families declined somewhat. In the next decade blacks and whites experienced small rises in female headship, followed by larger ones in the 1960s and 1970s. It is interesting that the *rate* of growth among whites and blacks in the last two decades was quite similar, even though much greater public attention has been given to black female headship. Because this type of family is much more common among blacks (almost 50 percent of all black families, versus about 15 percent for whites), similar growth rates have led to larger increases for blacks.

A variety of factors influence the formation of female-headed households with children, among them out-of-wedlock and marital birthrates; marriage, divorce, and remarriage rates; and the willingness of single mothers to establish their own households.

The major source of such growth among white families, the researchers found, was an increase in the numbers of single mothers who had previously been married. After 1960, marriage and fertility rates dropped, and the rise in white single-mother families resulted primarily from higher divorce rates and lower rates of remarriage. The propensity of single mothers to live independently rather than in the households of other people also contributed, but it was a much stronger influence in the 1950s than in the 1960s and 1970s.

Among blacks, however, growth in the population of never-married mothers after 1960 resulted primarily from declines in marriage rather than increases in out-of-wedlock birthrates. In fact the latter declined in the 1970s. The propensity to establish independent households was a significant factor in the 1950s and 1960s but had little influence in the 1970s.

In short, among both blacks and whites, changes in marital behavior account for the rise in female headship. Whites are more likely to divorce and not remarry; blacks are not as likely to marry.

The Economic Condition of Wives

A complement to the examination of single-mother families is a study by Sorensen and McLanahan of married couples over the same period of time. Sorensen and McLanahan summarize their results as follows:

> The situation in 1980 is greatly different from the situation in 1940, when the vast majority of married women were completely dependent on spouses for economic support. Today, completely dependent wives constitute a distinct minority. Minority women have been less dependent than white women throughout this period.

Nonwhite wives have consistently been less dependent than white wives. This greater equality of minority women partly reflects, however, the relatively disadvantaged position of minority men, who are more limited in their ability to be breadwinners.

Wives' dependency may be expected to vary with age, since familial responsibilities play a large role in their ability and willingness to work. The authors therefore were surprised to find only small differences in dependency among women under sixty years old and very few changes in life-course variations over time. Beyond that age, however, dependency declined substantially over the years, indicating reliance on social security and other unearned income, which is more evenly distributed among older spouses.

To identify sources of dependency, Sorensen and McLanahan analyzed the more detailed information on work effort and personal characteristics that is available in the censuses of 1960, 1970, and 1980. They found that the increase in wives' work effort was a major source of their growing independence and that married women must work longer hours than their husbands to contribute equally to family income.

The Elderly

Five studies concentrate on the changes in effects of such events associated with aging as retirement, widowhood, and alterations in living arrangements.

Demographic Changes

Population patterns are sketched in a paper by Gary Sandefur and Nancy Brandon Tuma, who included in their definition of the elderly all persons aged fifty-five and up, rather than the usual characterization of sixty-five or older, because important behavioral changes, notably retirement (scrutinized in detail below), are occurring with increasing frequency at younger ages.

The authors first examined the changing age composition of the U.S. population in the twentieth century. The proportion of people over fifty-four has increased steadily, rising from 10 to 21 percent between 1910 and 1980. As a result the ratio of those over fifty-four to those under twenty shifted from 1 : 4 in 1910 to 1 : 2 in 1940 and to about 2 : 3 in 1980. Since 1940 alone, the proportion of those over fifty-four has grown by 141 percent, and of those over eighty-four by 450 percent, while the U.S. population as a whole has increased by 71 percent.

Differential fertility and mortality rates across racial and ethnic groups have produced in the 1980s considerable variation in the proportions of the elderly within each group. Sandefur and Tuma cite the figures for those aged sixty-five or older as of 1982: 12 percent of whites as compared to 8 percent of blacks, 5 percent of Hispanics, and 5 percent of American Indians.

The life expectancy of both men and women has lengthened, but more so for women. As a consequence, the predominance of women in each age subgroup of the elderly has increased with each census, especially at older ages. Among the "old old," those eighty-five or more, the proportion of women rose from 55 percent in 1910 to 70 percent in 1980. This gender shift is becoming increasingly apparent at younger ages as well: 47 percent of those aged fifty-five to fifty-nine were women in 1910, 53 percent in 1980. The economic circumstances of the elderly are described below.

Economic Status

Ross, Danziger, and Smolensky, who analyzed the changing income positions of young and old described earlier in this article, have interpreted changes in the economic circumstances of the elderly since 1950. Their results confirmed the rise in well-being of older people. In 1980 the average person aged sixty-five or older had a much higher income in relation to needs and a much smaller chance of being in poverty than was true in 1950.

The researchers used cohort analysis (five-year age groups) to examine the factors that influence the well-being of the average individuals in particular cohorts across census years. They separated individuals not only by age but also by sex, labor force participation, and marital status. They found that retirement for men brings a large income decline, but that drop is then followed by income increases. For women, widowhood brings a large income decline followed by slow or no increases thereafter. Their analysis suggests that the typical individual experiences increases in income relative to needs during working years, a large one-time decline in his or her income-to-needs ratio with retirement, and increases thereafter. Married women share changes in income of their husbands but have an additional drop in income if they become widows. After that point, their income increases slowly.

Retirement

In recent years the proportion of the elderly who work has declined, and retirement is being chosen at earlier ages. The greatest declines in work occur at ages sixty to sixty-four and sixty-five to sixty-nine, but Sandefur and Tuma found that in 1980 a decline in male employment was apparent at ages fifty-five to fifty-nine as well, a trend that was even stronger in the 1985 Current Population Survey data.

In contrast, employment among women aged 55–64 has steadily risen since 1940. Because of these opposite trends by gender, the pattern of work among aged Americans has become increasingly similar for men and women. The authors also observed that people over sixty-five who have been out of work for at least a year are unlikely ever to enter the labor force again.

The falloff in work effort of men has often been attributed to the increased generosity of social security. Ross, Danziger, and Smolensky documented the decline in male labor force participation rates and the relationship between male earnings, retirement, and social security benefits. Benefits and retirement scarcely changed between 1940 and 1950, yet median earnings rose by more than half. In the next ten years, benefits jumped by about 40 percent, earnings by one-quarter. From 1960 to 1970, both benefits and earnings increased by about 20 percent. The relationship reversed after 1970, when benefits rose by 36 percent, but earnings declined by 7 percent. The result was that in 1980 the average benefit for a retired couple was equivalent to 134 percent of the poverty line and 55 percent of median earnings of male workers. It does not seem coincidental that by then the retirement rate among men over sixty-four had risen to 80 percent.

Yet Ross and colleagues caution that the decline in male work effort should not be attributed solely to the rise in social security benefits, for the labor force participation rates of older men have declined over the entire twentieth century—from 63 percent in 1900 to 42 percent in 1940 and 19 percent in 1980. The decision to retire is influenced, the authors point out, by the availability of income from *all* sources—savings, pensions, dividends, rents, in addition to earnings and social security—as well as health conditions, employment opportunities in the event of layoff or compulsory retirement, and a desire for leisure.

Ross, Danziger, and Smolensky reviewed five surveys of retirees conducted by the Social Security Administration between 1941 and 1982. Although the surveys are not strictly comparable because the populations sampled, the questions asked, and the survey formats were not identical, this information can serve as a gauge of changes in motivating forces.

Respondents in 1941–42 cited as the leading reasons for retirement loss of jobs (56 percent) and poor health (34 percent). Forty years later, few respondents (20 percent) in the same age group reported that they retired because they had lost their jobs, and fewer (17 percent) attributed retirement to poor health. Over half of the 1982 respondents had retired voluntarily. The authors sum up their finding: "The increased likelihood that an elderly person will retire in the years since social security benefits began to be paid continues a trend that dates back to at least 1900. Perhaps the most important contribution of social security to this trend is that to an increasing extent retirement could be chosen solely on economic grounds."

34. The Changing Fortunes of American Families in the 1980s
Katharine L. Bradbury

Excerpted from *New England Economic Review* (Federal Reserve Bank of Boston, July/August 1990), pp. 37–38. Katherine L. Bradbury is assistant vice president and economist at the Federal Reserve Bank of Boston.

Most families made significant income gains in the 1980s as the national economy expanded. Some families, however, did not participate fully in the general growth. In the early part of the decade, job-related earnings weakened for low-income families more than for those with higher incomes, and interest and dividend income expanded faster for high-income families than for those lower on the income scale. As the expansion progressed in the latter half of the decade, families at all income levels made gains, but the poor did not recover to their previous position. Average income of nonelderly families in the two lowest-income quintiles declined over the 1979–88 period, while higher-income families enjoyed income growth. As a result, the family income distribution became more unequal. Why did the bottom of the income distribution fail to keep pace?

Losing ground were young families, families with key workers unemployed, and those with poorly educated family heads. The biggest gainers were families with jobs, preferably full-time, the more the better, and especially in manufacturing. Also gaining were families with no children, husband-wife families, and highly educated families.

A critical thread in these lists is employment. As the economy expanded, families without workers were not carried along. Earnings comprise the bulk of family income, but the importance of employment does not simply reflect burgeoning earned income and a corresponding increase in family income for those with a high share of income from earnings. First, earnings grew faster than average for earners in high-income families. This was especially true of primary female earnings. Second, families with two earners made faster gains than families with one (or none), and high-income families had more earners than families with lower incomes. Third, increases in work effort during the decade seem to have been a key factor. Changes in labor force participation were not proportional to rates of labor force participation at the beginning of the period. Labor force participation rates of wives in low-income families were moderately higher in 1988 than in 1979, but wives' participation rates for high-income families in 1988 were much higher than in

1979. Similarly, female-headed families made more modest income gains than husband-wife families because the labor force participation rates of wives rose much faster than participation rates of female heads.

Increased family work effort, of course, clouds the translation of family income into family well-being. But if slow productivity growth continues to keep a lid on real wage growth and the wage distribution continues to become more unequal, a critical question for family income prospects may be how much more women's labor force participation rates can or will rise.

A notable exception to the importance of employment was the elderly, who are generally retired from the labor market, but who moved up the income ladder in striking fashion in the 1980s. They benefited from continuing federal policies aimed at maintaining their living standards and also from holding savings, the returns on which grew apace in the decade. By contrast, nonretirement transfer income declined over the period for low-income families.

The employment link sheds little light on why families without children would move ahead, except perhaps that they have more time available for market work, or why the young fared so poorly. The young, it turns out, experienced a sizable decline in labor force participation rates in the 1980s. Studies that have found early labor market experience to be a critical determinant of lifetime job prospects certainly heighten concern about the currently young cohort's future.

35. Wage Inequality Takes a Great U-Turn

Bennett Harrison, Chris Tilly, and Barry Bluestone

Excerpted and reprinted with permission of the publisher, M.E. Sharpe, Inc., from *Challenge*, March–April 1986, pp. 26–32. Bennett Harrison is professor of political economy and planning at MIT; Chris Tilly is a Ph.D. candidate in Economics and Planning at MIT; Barry Bluestone is professor of economics at Boston College.

Inequality among the annual wage and salary incomes of American workers declined steadily throughout the 1960s and well into the decade of the 1970s. Then, somewhere between 1975 and 1978, the distribution of wages and salaries took a sharp U-turn. This was before the election of Ronald Reagan, before the passage of the sharply regressive tax act of

1981, and even before the official commencement of the monetarist experiment in 1979. Inequality of wages and incomes has been increasing ever since.

What is causing increasing polarization of wage incomes among American workers? At this point, we do not know for certain. The factors most commonly suggested in recent years by Washington-based researchers, columnists, and politicians—the business cycle, the entrance of the baby-boom generation into the work force, and post-1973 fluctuations in the exchange value of the American dollar in international trade—explain at most a third of the growth in wage and salary inequality since the Great Society officially left town in January 1969. That such conventional wisdom explains so little suggests the need to probe much more deeply into the changes that have taken place in the structure of the American economy over the past fifteen years, and how corporations and governments have responded to those changes.

We hear much talk these days about the need for greater wage "flexibility" in order to achieve enhanced "competitiveness" with foreign business. All of the mechanisms now being proposed or already in place—the substitution of wage bonuses for fixed, contractual rates of pay, two-tiered company wage systems, and the creation of a subminimum wage for younger people—would almost certainly have the effect of exacerbating wage inequality among workers, quite apart from their particular skills and contributions to overall productivity.

The trend of wage inequality had already turned upward even before these new schemes were introduced into the workplace (and into official discourse in Washington). Making the situation even worse through deliberate public policy or through official sanction of private business policy could create a situation that would come back to haunt us in the future. If it turns out that we are indeed facing a long-term tendency toward increasingly unequal wage incomes, work incentives and conceivably even long-run economic growth could be threatened. Perhaps even more disturbing is the fear—expressed by a growing number of journalists and political analysts—that the frustrated expectations of significant numbers of younger workers unable to attain the living standards of their own parents could lead to potentially serious social unrest.

If market forces and public policies are indeed giving us an increasingly polarized distribution of income, it is only a matter of time before a large and probably increasingly diverse mass of citizens is going to begin pressing the federal government to correct these inequities. At a time when everyone in Washington is trying desperately to fashion ways to *reduce* the federal budget deficit, what the country surely does not need is yet another source of pressure on an already fragile public sector.

The Revival of Concern with Income Inequality

During 1985, we have seen an extraordinary revival of public interest in the problem of income inequality. So far, this interest has focused almost entirely on what is happening to the distribution of *family* incomes. There has been a flood of academic papers, reports written for congressional committees, and an important new book. Taken together with the earliest statements on this subject in the current period, all of this work indicates a rise in family-income inequality in the United States since at least the middle of the last decade (the Congressional Research Service dates the turnaround in family-income inequality to 1969).

Inequality in Wages and Salaries

There are any number of ways to characterize "inequality." We employ here the economist's standard indicator: the variance of the natural logarithm. By concentrating on annual labor income, we are including in our measure both fully employed workers and those who are able (or choose) to work for only a portion of the year. At this point in our research, we deliberately did not want to focus on year-round employees, or to study, say, hourly wage rates. We believe that variation in the hours and weeks of employment available to a job holder constitutes a criterion fully as important for evaluating the quality or adequacy of that person's work situation as does the hourly rate of pay.

During the long macroeconomic expansion of the mid-1960s, wage and salary inequality fell dramatically. The decline continued (albeit at a slower rate) until 1978. In that year, the pattern of inequality in annual labor income underwent an abrupt U-turn, rising rapidly thereafter. By 1983, what we will abbreviate as "wage inequality" was considerably above the level of the late 1960s. This is a robust finding. To at least some extent, the U-turn appears in every series we studied: year-round, full-time workers; men and women; youth and middle-aged people. Certainly *every* subgroup shows a sharp increase in inequality after the middle of the decade.

Accounting for the Business Cycle

The first of three pieces of conventional wisdom about wage inequality that we have been able to subject to rigorous scrutiny concerns the business cycle. It is widely held that wage differentials contract during periods of macroeconomic expansion and widen during recessions. The reason conventionally offered by labor economists is that high wages tend to be relatively "stickier," i.e., better protected by explicit or implicit contracts, than low wages (middle-level wages have their own forms of protection, such as unionization and civil-service status). Low-wage jobs are far less likely to be protected. In recessions, it is therefore the low wages that tend to be eroded vis-à-vis the rest, while during recoveries, employers are relatively freer to augment low wages if temporary shortages appear. The policy implication is that "sound" macroeconomic policy can smooth the path of aggregate economic growth and, in the process, promote a continued tendency toward income equality.

There is certainly no doubt that the seventies were a rocky decade for the U.S. economy, with three recessions between 1970 and 1980. Yet, in our statistical analysis when we control for the effect of year-to-year variations in the cycle—whether the cycle is measured by the aggregate rate of unemployment or by the Federal Reserve Board's index of capacity utilization—the U-shaped pattern of inequality in individual wage and salary incomes becomes, if anything, even more pronounced. The movements of the business cycle are simply not a statistically significant cause of the post-1969 variations in wage inequality in the United States.

The Baby Boom

Another explanation of aggregate income inequality is the entrance into the work force of the post–World War II baby-boom generation. Standard economic theory clearly leads to the inference that an excess supply of labor offered by younger workers will, holding other things constant, depress the wage of that cohort, thereby increasing intergenerational wage variations. The policy implication seems to be that we need do nothing about any apparent trend in growing inequality; it will disappear by itself as the baby boomers mature.

The baby boomers' entry into the world of work probably created conditions of excess supply. The share of the civilian labor force made up of workers under the age of thirty-five rose from 41 percent in 1969 to 51 percent only ten years later. And yet once again conventional wisdom turns out to be empirically difficult to support. After statistically removing the effect of both the business cycle and the baby boom, we see a pattern of wage inequality that is fundamentally unchanged. The great U-turn of the late 1970s is still apparent.

The Strong Dollar

Still another widely held view is that the 38 percent increase in the exchange value of the American dollar between 1980 and 1983, weighed against the currencies of our nine major trading partners, has so decimated American export industries as to dislocate factory workers who are predominantly "middle-level" wage earners. The implication seems to be that a policy of judiciously managed trade, combined with reduced federal deficits (to bring down interest rates and therefore foreign demand for dollars), can substantially eliminate this dollar-based source of trading disadvantage, thereby restoring the vitality of U.S. export industries and the concomitant expansion of "good" jobs.

Since the exchange rate did not begin to rise until 1980, we already know that this factor cannot possibly explain the timing of the U-turn in wage inequality, which occurred at least two years earlier. Certainly the rapid increase in exchange rates is correlated with the rise in inequality. To find out just how important this correlation is, we designed our formal analysis to remove the joint effects of all three explanatory variables. Only about a third of the year-to-year variation in wage inequality is explained by these often-cited variables. While the three predictors do have some impact on wage inequality, the underlying U-shaped time path of our indicator of wage inequality still vividly stands out in the data. The last finding is in no way inconsistent with Lester Thurow's argument that the recent sharp decline in U.S. manufactured exports has contributed to increasing wage inequality (with disproportionate impact on middle-level jobs). What our analysis implies is that this development is only weakly connected to exchange-rate movements per se.

Postscript

It now seems fairly clear that both family income and individual wages and salaries are being distributed more and more unequally among the working people of the United States. There is still much to learn about the causes, precise magnitudes, and possible political-economic consequences of this development. Nevertheless, even with what we already know, two striking ironies become apparent.

Since the 1960s, the very mention of the word "inequality" has tended to raise images of the black inner-city ghetto or of the desperately poor rural hollow. In both the popular media and political forums, inequality has for all practical purposes been the study of the poor. The new research on inequality suggests that this comfortable notion has become outmoded. The sense of relative deprivation, of frustrated expectations, of falling behind, of being badly paid—this is becoming the common experience of a growing number of Americans. They are white as well as persons of color. They are men as well as women. Having a full-time, year-round job is no longer a guarantee of being sheltered from this experience.

The second irony has even farther-reaching implications. It was in 1954 that Nobel laureate Simon Kuznets first proposed that income inequality tends to increase during the early stages of economic development, then levels off and diminishes as development proceeds. Economic historians and other social scientists have for a generation taken the Kuznets curve as an article of faith. The long gradual movement toward greater equality within the developed industrial countries has been held out to the workers and farmers of the third world as the eventual payoff to current sacrifices in the process of transcending "underdevelopment." Surely the perception that the long-run tendency toward greater equality in the United States may have been arrested can be expected to undermine the legitimacy of existing strategies of economic development throughout the developing world.

36. Trends in the Distribution of Wealth among American Families

Democratic Staff of the Joint Economic Committee, United States Congress

Excerpted from *The Concentration of Wealth in the United States* (Washington, D.C.: Joint Economic Committee of the United States Congress, July 1986), pp. 7–43.

Only twice has the federal government attempted comparable and comprehensive surveys that could provide a much greater, and firsthand, base of information about the concentration of wealth. The first Survey of Financial Characteristics of Consumers was conducted under the supervision of the Federal Reserve Board in 1963. In 1983, a second survey was sponsored by the Fed, the Department of Health and Human Services, the Comptroller of the Currency, and other government agencies. Both were conducted for the Fed by the Survey Research Center of the University of Michigan.

The forms of wealth held by most Americans are rather limited. They include homes, automobiles, furnishings, appliances, and a little money in checking and savings accounts. Only a small minority of families owns corporate stock or commercial real estate, and even fewer families will ever own a corporate or municipal bond or a Treasury bill.

In the aggregate, American families owned about $12 trillion in gross assets in the spring of 1983, when the Survey of Consumer Finances was

conducted. Their net worth totaled nearly $10.6 trillion in holdings rang-
ing from real estate through IRAs to business assets. In general, the
wealthier the family, the greater the holdings in stocks, bonds, businesses, and commercial real estate.

Hard work and saving out of income appear to account for about a
third of today's wealth. Part comes from inheritance and the inevitable
working of the axiom that money makes money. A considerable part of
the change in wealth between 1963 and 1983 resulted from market reval-
uations of accumulated wealth.

While households account for the vast majority of the nation's wealth,
they do not account for all of it. Governments hold significant wealth in
land, buildings, highways, weapons, and so forth, and it is virtually impossible to establish any meaningful market value for most government-
owned assets. Altogether, households account for almost nine-tenths of
all wealth not held by federal, state, or local governments.

Personal residences accounted for almost 30 percent of gross wealth
held by American families in 1983. Business holdings in nonincorporated
businesses (proprietorships, partnerships, etc.) accounted for another 27
percent. Nonresidential real estate accounted for 15 percent; stocks and
bonds 11 percent; checking and savings accounts, certificates of deposit,
money market funds, and call accounts 8 percent; and trusts 4 percent.
Another 6 percent was accounted for by IRAs, land contracts, cash sur-
render value of insurance, and other miscellaneous items. Of the $1.5
trillion in debts owed by American families, more than three-fourths was
related to either residential or commercial real estate holdings.

The most striking result from the survey data is the extraordinary
amount of national wealth held by the top half of 1 percent of families.
These super rich households accounted for more than 35 percent of gross
wealth. If the equity in personal residences is excluded from net wealth,
the top half of 1 percent of households owned more than 45 percent of
the privately held wealth of this country. These households appeared to
have a very strong grip on the nation's businesses. They owned 58 percent of unincorporated businesses and 46.5 percent of all personally
owned corporate stock. They also held 77 percent of the value of trusts
and 62 percent of state and local bonds.

The next richest 420,000 households, or the second half of the top 1
percent of wealth holders, were decidedly less well off than the top half
of the top 1 percent. These very rich families held net assets ranging from
$1.4 million to $2.5 million. They owned 7 percent of the nation's net
wealth, or about one-fifth as much as the 420,000 super rich families. When
their business holdings are combined with those of the super rich families,
66 percent of unincorporated businesses and 60 percent of personally held
corporate stock are in the hands of the top 1 percent of all households.

Table 36.1

Average Net Wealth per Household, 1963–83 (1983 dollars)

Wealth category	1963 average wealth per household	1983 average wealth per household	Dollar change per household	Percentage change
Super rich	$3,588,489	$8,851,736	$5,236,247	147
Very rich	1,037,543	1,702,376	664,833	64
Rich	253,187	419,616	166,429	66
Everyone else	27,390	39,584	12,193	45

Rich families, those between the 90th and 99th percentiles of wealth holding, had net assets that ranged from $206,000 to $1.4 million. This group is made up of a little more than 7.5 million households. When the assets of the rich were combined with those of the very rich and the super rich, 71.8 percent of the net wealth of American families was owned by this top 10 percent of families. This included almost 94 percent of unincorporated business assets and nearly 90 percent of all personally owned stock.

The remaining 90 percent of American families owned only about 28 percent of the nation's wealth held by families, and most of that was tied up in the equity of family homes. If home equities were subtracted from net assets, the bottom 90 percent of American families would hold only 16.7 percent of the remaining family-owned wealth of this country.

From 1929 to 1962 there was a significant downward trend in the portion of wealth held by the top one-half of 1 percent of individuals. In 1962, their portion of individually owned wealth was estimated at 22.2 percent.

The distribution of wealth among American families changed remarkably during the twenty years 1963–83. The wealthiest one-half of 1 percent increased its share of wealth holding from 25.4 percent to 35.1 percent, or by 38 percent. The bottom 90 percent of families dropped from an almost 35 percent share of the nation's wealth in 1963 to just over 28 percent in 1983.

The average wealth holding for the bottom 90 percent increased from $27,400 to $39,600. That increase was less than a quarter of the national average increase per household (see Table 36.1).

37. How Family Spending Has Changed in the United States
Eva Jacobs and Stephanie Shipp

Excerpted from *Monthly Labor Review*, March 1990, pp. 21–27. Eva Jacobs is chief of the Division of Expenditure Surveys, Bureau of Labor Statistics. Stephanie Shipp is chief of the Branch of Information and Analysis in the same division.

Expenditure Trends

Food as a percent of total expenditures has declined from 46 percent in 1901 to 19 percent of total current consumption. Within the food budget, however, spending for food away from home has increased. Homeownership has increased dramatically, as have outlays associated with owning a home. Data from the 1901 survey show that only 19 percent of workers' families owned a home, compared with 44 percent in 1950 and 56 percent in 1986–87. The invention of the automobile has contributed dramatically to changes in the lifestyle of the American family. Outlays for transportation now account for 26 percent of current consumption—a significant rise from 1901, when they were included in the "other purposes" (miscellaneous) category. Advances in health care also have had a revolutionary effect on households. Even as family size has declined over time, health care expenditures for workers' families have increased. Finally, the budget share allocated for entertainment and reading has increased as the workday and workweek became shorter and recreational activities became more accessible to more people.

Food Expenditures

The increasing command of purchasing power of the urban wage earners served a dual function that led to generally improved diets. People were able to buy more and better foods. Too, increased purchasing power supported the development of low-cost mass-production techniques and the marketing of new and better foods, many of them fully processed. As a result, the percent of expenditure allocated for food and beverages declined from 43 percent in 1901 to 19 percent in 1986–87. The shrinking share allocated for the food budget vividly confirms early studies, which found that the share of expenditures for food declines as income increases.

For the working man and his family in the early 1900s, diets were monotonous. Said one writer about the customary winter diet: "We never thought of having fresh fruit or green vegetables and could not have got them if we had." Today's diet includes more meat, poultry, fruits, vegetables, and milk. Improvements in the food distribution system have freed cities from depending on produce and meats from local farms. High-speed refrigerated transportation has increased the variety and reduced the cost of purchasing food. Another aspect of the increasing availability of foods since the early 1900s is the revolution in retailing. Chain grocery stores began to appear early in the century. The supermarket combined into one establishment the butcher, produce vendor, bakery, and other specialty stores. The supermarkets purchased directly from the food producers, thus reducing the costs of distribution through large-scale operations. The spread of ownership of refrigerators allowed families to reduce the number of food shopping trips. The availability of foods that are partially or fully prepared continues to increase to accommodate dual-earner families and the busier lifestyles of families today.

Another important trend has been the increasing share of the food budget allocated for food away from home. Data from a 1909 report (the earliest such information available) show that only 3 percent of the food budget went for food away from home. This share has grown steadily to 29 percent today. Even this increase probably understates the increase in the number of meals eaten away from home because of the changing nature of the eating-away-from-home activity. In 1909 or 1920 or even 1950, a meal away from home was taken in a restaurant, but the proliferation over the last three decades of fast-food establishments, with relatively low prices for a meal, has changed the eating-out habits of the population. More recently, the increase in the use of carry-out prepared foods is further altering food purchasing habits and obscuring the distinction between at-home and away-from-home food consumption.

Shelter

Rising incomes and technological change have also allowed for the improvement in housing conditions and the growth in homeownership. The 1901 expenditure survey found that only 19 percent of worker families owned a home.

By 1917–19, homeownership was enjoyed by 27 percent of all families, and the share of the family budget spent on housing had declined from 18 percent in 1901 to 14 percent in 1917–18—the only period under study for which such a decline occurred.

Legislation within the depression environment of the early 1930s dealt with the financing aspects of homeownership. The creation of the Federal Housing Administration "to encourage improvement in housing standards and conditions, and to provide a system of mutual mortgage insurance" resulted in changes in residential loan practices that stimulated the construction of medium-priced housing. By 1950, the incidence of homeownership had increased to 44 percent for urban worker families. Homeownership continued its rapid rise through the 1960s and 1970s—reaching 56 percent in 1960 and staying at about that level for worker families through 1986–87.

The rise in homeownership slowed during the late 1970s and early 1980s for the population as a whole because of changing demographics and soaring house prices and mortgage interest rates. Even so, the incidence of homeownership continued to grow among married couples, as favorable tax treatment and the advantages of having a fixed mortgage in time of inflation made buying a house a good investment. The estimated market value of homes rose faster than the Consumer Price Index during this time, adding to the incentive to invest in homeownership.

The share of expenditures allocated for shelter, which includes rent as well as payments on owned homes, has fluctuated, but the overall trend has been upward. Working families allocated 14.6 percent of their outlays for shelter in 1960, 16.4 percent in 1972–73, and 20.2 percent in 1986–87. Homes have continued to increase in size as well. According to the U.S. Bureau of the Census, the median owner-occupied home surveyed in 1985 had six rooms, compared with 5.6 rooms in 1970. Homes today also have many amenities unheard of in the earlier years. For example, in 1988, 79 percent of all new homes had a garage, up from 64 percent ten years earlier; three-fourths had central air conditioning, an almost 50 percent increase; and 42 percent had more than 2.5 bathrooms, almost double the number in 1978.

Transportation

Ownership of cars increased dramatically during the 1920s, 1930s, and 1940s, stimulated by lower auto prices, advertising, the introduction of consumer credit, and generally rising incomes. By 1950, auto installment credit was 26 percent of total consumer (nonmortgage) credit outstanding, and increased to nearly 40 percent by 1987. The 1934–36 expenditure survey found that 44 percent of working families owned a car and that 10 percent had purchased during the survey years. Working families during the mid-1930s allotted 8.5 percent of their expenditures to transportation.

The purchase of automobiles continued to increase, as did the percent of total expenditures allocated for transportation, which rose from 8.5 percent in 1950 to 25.7 percent in 1986–87. During the 1970s and 1980s, other vehicles were added to the family's driveway—vans, trucks, recreational vehicles, and motorcycles. Data from the 1986–87 expenditure survey show that 91 percent of all worker households owned a vehicle and that the average number of vehicles per household was 2.2, for an average family size of 2.9 people!

As vehicle ownership became widespread, related expenditures also increased dramatically. In 1986–87, an average household spent about as much to own and maintain a car—that is, to pay for gasoline, insurance, repairs, and licenses—as it did to feed that household at home. In 1950, auto-related costs were only about 20 percent of the food bill.

Health Care

During the 1920s and 1930s, changes in the health field began to occur. The number and quality of hospitals increased. Nonprofit organizations that provided services in free clinics were established. Private-sector firms began to offer in-house medical care and provide health insurance for employees. Other medical advances, such as improved control of drugs and scientific breakthroughs, also have contributed to the lengthening of the lifespan from about fifty years in the early 1900s to more than seventy years by the 1980s. Longer life expectancy and improved health have increased the earning power of the worker. In addition, the emphasis placed on sanitation, nutrition, and recreation in health education programs has stimulated the demand for a variety of consumer goods and services.

The 1901 detailed expenditure survey found that families spent 2.9 percent of their total outlays for products and services in the category "sickness and death," that is, medical care and funeral expenses. This share rose to 6.6 percent by 1960–61 as improved economic conditions, education, and the availability of insurance led households to purchase more health care, and declined to 4 percent by 1986–87, as practices of financing health care changed.

In the 1920s and 1930s, unions played a role in providing much of the insurance coverage. Significant changes began to occur during the 1940s with the expansion of the concept of fringe benefits. By the late 1960s and extending into the early 1980s, the practice of employer-provided health insurance had spread. In 1987, 64 percent of individuals had employment-related health insurance, some or all of which was paid for by employers. These programs reduced the out-of-pocket medical costs to households, and the share of the household budget going for health care cost declined. It is evident that an increasing share of the family medical budget is being spent on insurance and less on services and prescription drugs directly.

Recreation

The increase in leisure time that resulted from the shortening of the workday to eight hours and the workweek to five days is yet another improvement in the life of the American family. Unions began to argue for the eight-hour day late in the nineteenth century. However, it was rising productivity that ultimately made the eight-hour day possible. In addition, it was recognized that time had to be left for the worker and his family to consume and enjoy the resulting products and services. In 1926, when Henry Ford announced the five day week for his company, he said: "The industry of this country could not exist long if factories generally went back to the 10-hour day, because people would not have the time to consume the goods produced."

Increasing free time and incomes meant that families had more time for sports—once the exclusive province of the "idle rich"—travel, and entertainment. The introduction of the motion picture and the nickelodeons after the turn of the century gave rise to another form of entertainment. The nickelodeons permitted workers to stop on their way home to enjoy a fifteen-minute film for five cents. Radios were introduced in the 1920s and televisions in the late 1940s. Today there are videocassette recorders, compact disc players, and new mechanical toys every day. And the popularity of participatory sports and spectator sports continues to grow.

Although many leisure activities are free of cost, the expenditure surveys since 1901 do indicate that increasing amounts are being spent for recreation and for reading. The budget share spent for these items increased from 5.7 percent in 1917–19 to 8.3 percent in 1986–87.

38. American Living Standards

Excerpted from *The Economist*, November 10, 1990, pp. 19–22. Copyright 1990 The Economist Newspaper Group, Inc. Reprinted with permission. Further reproduction prohibited.

The Industrial Revolution and its promise of sustained economic growth came hard on the heels of American independence. That coincidence, as much as the ready availability of land beyond the frontier, explains the resilience of the American dream. In America, more than anywhere else, the notion has grown up that ever-rising prosperity will enable each generation to live better than its predecessor.

With a few blips, such as the Depression of the 1930s, the notion has become gratifyingly true for every generation in the past two hundred years. That has made the American middle-class way of life into something for other people and other countries to aspire to. It has fed the vision of generations of immigrants. It has demonstrated the triumph of capitalism and free enterprise over communism and state intervention.

Now, as communism crumbles, America's ability to deliver the dream also is in doubt. The latest Census Bureau numbers, for 1989, confirm that, for all the fanfare of the Reagan boom, median family income is in real terms barely above the level of 1973. Even more strikingly, the Bureau of Labor Statistics (BLS) records that average real earnings have fallen to the level of 1961.

With the economy teetering on the edge of another recession, there is every prospect that these numbers will decline further. A generation whose parents saw living standards rise faster than ever before is growing up with a new nagging fear: that, far from living better than its predecessor, it will live significantly worse.

How accurate is this gloomy picture? Does it rest on some statistical artifact? If not, what has gone wrong and what can be done about it?

Lies, Damned Lies, and Statistics

The statistics, for a start, are disputable—and disputed. About the only thing that everyone agrees on is that 1973 was a break year. After 1973, income growth slowed considerably. Democrats parade figures showing living standards for the middle class holding roughly steady in the Carter years and then tumbling in the 1980s, as the benefits of limited economic growth were funneled to the rich. Republicans say the Carter years, especially 1979–80, were terrible, and that income growth for everyone resumed the moment Mr. Reagan and his supply-siders took office.

Average real earnings rose from 1947 until 1973, then fell back. Median family income has gone rather differently. It too fell after 1973, but not so steeply, thanks to the growing number of working wives. It has fallen twice since 1973 and recovered twice to a little above where it started.

But the argument tends to focus less on the level of income than on its distribution. This has become more unequal since the late 1970s, a trend exacerbated by tax cuts that benefited the rich, while the tax burden on the poor rose. The distribution today is close to what it was in 1947.

Economists and politicians have several quibbles about the official statistics. The BLS earnings figures, for instance, show a more pronounced fall in real wages than do the Social Security Administration's wage-index numbers. Anyway, individual earnings figures do not say a great deal about standards of living, because they do not take into account the increase in two-earner households. The numbers for median family income, which do, are thus a better guide to living standards. But they too have problems:

(1)   Family size has shrunk. This explains how recorded family incomes have remained unchanged while national income per head has been rising. And since a smaller family costs less to support—even if not in direct proportion—figures showing stagnant family income give a misleading impression of what has happened to individual living standards.

(2)   The price index used to deflate the income numbers is misleading. Experts agree that, because of the way it treated housing costs, until the formula was changed in 1983, the official consumer price index overstated inflation in the late 1970s and so exaggerated the drop in real family incomes.

(3)   The census numbers ignore noncash income like health care benefits, which aid many families, or the food stamps that go to poor ones. Noncash income has been growing, so leaving it out understates the recent rise in family living standards.

(4)   The income numbers are all pretax. Despite Mr. Reagan's tax cuts, the tax burden has risen since 1973, thanks mainly to rising payroll taxes. So pretax numbers, in contrast, overstate the rise in living standards.

The Congressional Budget Office and the staff of the House Ways and Means Committee have adjusted the Census Bureau numbers for family income on the first two counts, but not the third and fourth (for which the numbers are not good enough and may possibly cancel out anyway). Their series for "adjusted family income" turns the picture of barely changed incomes from 1973–89 into one of an average real rise of around 15 percent. That is still only 1 percent a year—far below the 3–4 percent a year increases that families expected in the 1950s and 1960s.

It also ignores the fact that, while the spread of the two-earner household is sustaining family incomes, it also adds to family costs. The spread has been remarkable. In 1960, 30 percent of married women with a child under eighteen worked. By 1987 that figure had risen to 65 percent. Social and industrial trends were encouraging women to work. But two-earner couples have found that the result is far from pure gain.

Inevitably, their household expenses rise, too. Services like cleaning and cooking that were done, unpaid, at home, now have to be bought. Travel-to-work expenses are higher. Child care has to be paid for. A Democratic party study this year concluded that, for the average family, 20–30 percent of the money brought in by a second earner went straight out again in extra costs.

There is also a generation gap to consider. The traditional picture of poor old folks supported by their rich (because working) children has been blotted out in the past two decades. In 1970 the poverty rate among the old was 25 percent, twice the national rate of 12.5 percent. By 1989 the poverty rate among the old had fallen to 11.5 percent, while the national rate had crept up to 13 percent. Among children the poverty rate had risen from 15 percent to 19.5 percent over the same period.

Growing affluence among the old partly reflects their political power. Through the budgetary fights of the past decade, the "gray" lobby has zealously protected its pensions and health care programs—to such an extent that Congress now regards them as largely off limits. The share of the federal budget (excluding defense and interest) that goes to the old has risen from a third in 1970 to nearly a half today. Most of that is financed by payroll taxes levied on working people. But the statistics of household incomes, being pretax, do not reflect this growing burden.

Of Mortgages and Colleges

Flat middle-class incomes and the shift in favor of the old could on their own be enough to shatter the American dream. But they are not the only worry. Of even more concern is the inexorably growing cost of traditional middle-class goals like owning a house and sending the kids to university. Such burdens are captured by the consumer price index only in broad terms.

In the 1970s, just as real growth in family incomes had slowed to a crawl, house prices did the opposite. On average, they tripled from 1973 to 1988; in the Northeast they quadrupled, a rise of about a half in real terms. Higher interest rates added to the burden. In the 1950s a thirty-year-old middle-class man in an average family home typically spent 14 percent of his gross income on mortgage payments. By 1973 that had risen to 21 percent. Over the next ten years it shot up to 44 percent. When mortgage payments can absorb nearly half of a typical earner's income, it is not surprising that rates of home ownership, having risen steadily since 1918, have in the past few years dropped back, especially among the young.

The costs of college too have soared. After lagging behind prices for a time in the 1970s, they then more than made up lost ground. From 1977 to 1989, tuition fees in private colleges, on average, more than tripled, while prices generally doubled. Fees at the grandest universities rose the most. A Harvard graduate who in the 1960s chose one of the less glamorous professions whose pay has since lagged—a career in the State Department, say, or teaching—finds himself today hard-pressed, or unable, to send his children to his alma mater.

Housing and college costs are the staple grumbles of middle-class cocktail parties. A third trend that may be more insidious for living standards is less talked about, because it is less obvious. That is the growing number of services that middle-class people readily—though not always voluntarily—purchase, but that can often be seen as lowering rather than raising living standards.

If you can afford two cars instead of one, or a better car, clearly you are better off. Ditto, in most cases, if you can afford more or better services. But not always. Who really gains from hiring two lawyers?

Well, the lawyers do. As their fees and incomes have headed for the stratosphere, so have their numbers. In 1960 America had 260,000 lawyers. Ten years later the number had risen by a third, to 355,000. Then the real fun began. By 1980 541,000 lawyers were in practice; this year the number has swelled to 756,000—more, it is said, than in the rest of the world put together. In the thirty years from 1960, the number of lawyers per 100,000 Americans has gone up from 145 to 301. Much of the "demand" for the output of this swollen industry is created not by clients but by other members of the industry, as if doctors went round injecting diseases for other doctors to cure. Is this really a boost to living standards?

Lawyers are not alone. In 1960 the United States Senate had 365 paid lobbyists on its register. In July 1990 it had 33,704: 337 for each senator. Whether legislation is improved by their activity is dubious. What is certain is that their incomes are reflected in higher prices for the goods and services that their paymasters produce—and so lower living standards for consumers. There are countless other examples. In 1970 the National Association of Realtors, which reckons to cover four-fifths of the country's estate agents, had fewer than 100,000 members. Today it has nearly 800,000. Their incomes too do not come for free—property prices and the costs of moving are higher as a result. Sellers of financial services too have proliferated, maybe beyond the point at which they add to well-being.

Health care is another bottomless pit for middle-class spending that shows little return in higher welfare. True, most of it is paid for by employer-provided insurance, but in a competitive world that simply means lower wages. In 1960 medical care took about 5 percent of total personal consumption; by 1989 the figure was 13 percent. The number of practicing doctors in America has gone from 279,000 in 1970 to 554,000 in 1988—a rise from 137 to 225 per 100,000 inhabitants. In the decade to 1988, while other middle-class incomes were stagnating, those of doctors rose by a quarter, to an average of just under $150,000 a year. Judged by indicators like life expectancy or infant mortality, they have done little for health.

There is a pattern threading through these examples. It might be called the rising frictional costs of middle-class life. While family incomes stagnate, they have to support extra burdens: the activities, costs, and incomes of a swarm of highly paid professionals whose contribution to the nation's welfare is, at best, unclear.

Friction Not Fiction

For all these reasons, the stagnation or even decline in middle-class living standards since 1973 is a reality affecting most Americans, not a fiction of the statisticians. Yet it has taken some years to sink into the national psyche. And it has aroused surprisingly little political debate.

There are three reasons. One is that, thanks to the redistribution of income, stagnation has affected the upper quintile—the top 20 percent—of families least. The rich (and articulate) were able in the Reagan years to keep their living standards rising by taking a bigger share of the same pie. The House Ways and Means Committee reckons that "adjusted" family income for this top quintile rose by 25 percent in 1973–88, a full ten points more than for those in the middle. Tax changes too helped them. The average federal tax bite on the top quintile fell in 1980–90 by 5.5 percent (and on the top 1 percent of incomes by nearly 15 percent).

Meanwhile, adjusted family income of the bottom quintile fell by 9 percent in 1973–88, and their federal tax bite rose by 16 percent in 1980–90. These people were not just relatively poorer than before but absolutely so.

These last are typically the people who did badly at school. Median family income for those who dropped out of high school fell by a quarter in real terms between 1973 and 1989. Once there were well-paid unskilled jobs in the local steelworks, textile mill, or car factory. Now many of those jobs have gone to cheaper or better-managed workers abroad. The premium in higher earnings that rewards better education and greater skills has never been bigger.

A disproportionate number of those at the bottom are black. On top of poor school records, their family structure—or lack of it—tends to reduce living standards. Four out of every five black children spend at least part of their lives in a lone-mother household. While better-off and white Americans have grown richer, poor and black ones have grown poorer.

A second reason for the apparent lack of fuss over stagnating living standards is that the fuss has taken disguised forms. The recent budget rows over taxes and spending; rising racial tensions; generational conflict between the pampered elderly and the frazzled workers; political pressures for child care or against Japanese imports; the intractable budget and trade deficits: all have discernible roots in stagnant family incomes. The huge welcome given to Senator Pat Moynihan's mischievous proposal to roll back payroll taxes was another such sign. Had the economy and living standards grown after 1973 at the same pace as before, real incomes would today be 50 percent higher than they are. That would surely have made these social and political problems easier to face. Some might even have been solved.

The third reason is that there is little mileage in fussing about stagnant living standards because there is no obvious cure. The basic answer would be to restore labor productivity to its pre-1973 levels. The recipes for that sound obvious enough—higher savings and investment, better education—but no one knows how to put them into effect. Even so, it is a cop-out for policy makers to refuse to recognize what has happened, and not to devote more of their efforts to rectifying it.

39. Participation in Government Benefits Programs
Bureau of the Census

Excerpted from *Population Profiles* (Washington, D.C.: Bureau of the Census, 1989), pp. 32–33.

The Census Bureau recently released the first data from a new ongoing survey called the Survey of Income and Program Participation (SIPP). The survey focuses on various economic topics, such as participation in government benefits programs, for which no continuing survey data have been available. Based on the survey result, on a monthly average nearly one of every three nonfarm people (30 percent) received benefits from one or more government programs during the third quarter of 1983.

Social security, the nation's disability and old-age pension plan, benefited 31.7 million people—48 percent of those receiving benefits from government programs, or 14 percent of the total population. Medicare (hospital and physician insurance plans for the aged and disabled) was the second most often reported benefit program, utilized by 26.7 million Americans, or 40 percent of people receiving benefits of any type. These two benefits differ in that social security is a direct cash payment to individuals or families, while Medicare is a "noncash" benefit of medical care, and payments are not made directly to the patient.

People can qualify for social security or Medicare regardless of economic need; that is, neither program requires that the income and/or assets of the person or family be below specified levels in order to qualify for benefits. Programs that require the individual or family to meet a specified level of need are called "means tested."

About 19 percent of the total population (42.1 million people) received benefits from one or more means-tested programs. The two largest such programs were food stamps (a federally funded program that increases the food-purchasing power of low-income households) and Medicaid (a program furnishing medical assistance to needy families with dependent children and aged, blind, or disabled members). Food stamps benefited a 1983 third-quarter monthly average of 18.7 million people (8 percent of the total population and 28 percent of those receiving any program benefits), while Medicaid was provided to 17.5 million people.

There was a large difference by race in the proportion of households receiving means-tested program assistance: About 13 percent of white households received such benefits, compared with 42 percent of black households and 34 percent of Hispanic households.

The type of household most likely to receive means-tested benefits was a family with a female householder with children under eighteen years and no husband present. About 55 percent of those households received such assistance, compared with about 10 percent of married-couple families. One of three families receiving benefits was maintained by a woman with children under eighteen years old and no husband present.

Since many of these government programs were designed to complement each other, it is not surprising that nearly half of all households receiving means-tested noncash assistance received benefits from two or more different programs. The most common form of multiple recipiency for means-tested programs was food stamps and coverage under Medicaid. This combination of benefits was received by 4.3 million households.

40. Health Status of the American Population
Council of Economic Advisers

Excerpted from the *Economic Report of the President* (Washington, D.C.: U.S. Government Printing Office, February 1985), pp. 130–32. The members of the council responsible for the report were Chairman William Niskanen and William Poole.

The life expectancy of Americans has improved steadily since 1900, when the average American could expect to live for 47.3 years. At the turn of the century, females lived two years longer than males, on average, and blacks lived 33.0 years, substantially fewer than 47.6 years for whites. By 1982 the average life expectancy had increased to 74.5 years. The male-female gap had widened to 7.4 years, but the black-white gap had narrowed to fewer than 6 years.

The factors mainly responsible for increases in life expectancy during the first half of this century—improved sanitation, heating, and other amenities, along with significant breakthroughs in immunization against communicable diseases—contributed most significantly to the survival of infants and children. For adults over sixty-five, life expectancy statistics show only modest gains during this period, from 11.9 years in 1900 to 13.9 years in 1950. As of 1982, however, the life expectancy of older adults had increased 16.8 years.

Increased life expectancy at older ages, along with declining birth rates, has led to the well-known "graying" of America. The age distribution of the population has shifted markedly since 1950, when the over-sixty-five population represented 8.2 percent of the total population. In 1983 the elderly accounted for 11.7 percent of the total population. Because the elderly spend about 3.5 times as much per capita on medical care as do the nonelderly, population aging has profound implications for medical care spending. Greater demands are placed on Medicare and on that part of the Medicaid program that finances long-term care for the elderly poor.

Increasing life expectancy at older ages is evidence of the improving health status of the American population. Additional evidence is that infant mortality rates and fetal death rates have fallen since 1950. (Infant deaths occur within the first year of life; fetal deaths are the deaths of fetuses of twenty weeks or more gestation.) Large declines have occurred for both blacks and whites. However, in 1981 (the latest year for which data are available) the infant and fetal death rates for blacks remained substantially above those for whites.

Between infancy and age sixty-five, there are distinct differences in the causes of death by age, sex, and race. The leading cause of death for whites and blacks of both sexes below the age of fifteen is accidents. In fact, accidents are the leading cause of death below the age of forty-five. From ages fifteen to twenty-four, accidents are the leading cause of death for whites, whereas homicide is the leading cause of death for blacks. Cancer is the leading cause of death for black females between the ages of twenty-four and forty-four and for white females between the ages of twenty-five and sixty-four. After age sixty-five, heart disease is the major cause of death.

The dominant role of accidents and homicides makes clear that behavioral factors play an extremely important role in mortality. Moreover, because many of these deaths occur at early ages, accidents and homicides have a disproportionate effect on life expectancy at birth.

Other than through mortality statistics, there are problems in measuring the public's health status. For example, people's willingness to report certain nonfatal diseases may change over time. The health status indicators must also be adjusted for the age distribution of the population, because the population is aging and many diseases appear more frequently among the elderly.

Even with these qualifications in mind, it is useful to examine trends in the self-reported health status of the American population from nationwide surveys of households. One measure of health status is "restricted activity days," which are days that a person cuts down on his or her usual activities because of illness or injury that occurred during the two weeks prior to the survey. A day spent in bed at home or in the hospital (a "bed-disability day") is, of course, a restricted activity day.

Surveys indicate that the number of restricted activity days decreased among all age groups from 1957 until the middle or end of the 1960s, after which the trend has reversed. The number of bed-disability days per person fell during the late 1950s and early 1960s and has remained roughly constant since then. Some increase occurred within the forty-five-to-sixty-four age group.

Another health status indicator is limitations of activity caused by chronic conditions that began more than three months prior to the survey. A striking trend emerges: The proportion of males ages forty-five to sixty-four who were unable to perform their major activity increased from 7.2 percent of that age group in 1969 to 11.5 percent in 1981. Smaller but very noticeable increases are shown for this activity limitation among other males and females aged forty-five to sixty-four.

41. The Crisis in Health Insurance
Consumers Union

In the United States, the ticket to health care is insurance. If you are in good health and have a well-paying job with a large firm, chances are you have a ticket, and your employer pays for it. But if you work for yourself, have a low-paying job, or are sick, chances are you'll have to pay for the ticket yourself—if you can buy one at all.

Tickets are becoming harder to get. Between 31 million and 37 million people have no health insurance, either because they can't afford it or because insurance companies refuse to sell them a policy at any price.

Others lose their tickets. People who once had insurance may suddenly find themselves without it when employers discontinue health care coverage or go out of business, or when insurance companies cancel policies or become insolvent.

Millions more have no protection against catastrophic illness. They may have some insurance but lack coverage for the very conditions that will one day require unusually heavy expenditures.

"If the employed population knew how vulnerable they were, they'd be up in arms demanding national health insurance," says Bonnie Burns, a counselor with California's insurance counseling program. "Most of these people are three paychecks away from disaster."

The health insurance crisis is a fairly recent phenomenon. At the beginning of World War II, few Americans owned a health insurance policy. As recently as 1965, most had coverage only for hospital stays. The health insurance system as we know it today evolved in the 1960s and 1970s. Under that system, workers came to expect their employers to supply medical coverage, with employers and employees splitting the cost.

That worked well for a while. More workers had health insurance, and their coverage broadened to include doctors' visits, prescription drugs, and even treatment for mental illness. But now the system stitched together over the last fifty years is unraveling, and people are being deprived of needed health care.

Lack of prenatal care translates into babies who are too small when they are born and babies who die soon after birth. The United States trails twenty-three other nations in the percentage of babies born with an inadequate birth weight and ranks twenty-second in the rate of infant mortality, behind such countries as East Germany, Spain, and Singapore.

Shifting the Cost

When the uninsured are able to obtain health care, everyone pays. Each year thousands of people are dumped into emergency rooms of public hospitals because private hospitals don't want patients who can't pay.

In 1988, unpaid hospital bills totaled more than $8 billion, up 10 percent from the previous year. To recoup the costs of unpaid care, hospitals and doctors simply raise their fees to those who do pay—primarily the private insurance carriers and the federal government.

Such cost shifting drives up the price of insurance, resulting in even more people who can't afford coverage. In New Jersey, for example, every hospital bill now carries a 13 percent surcharge, reflecting the hospital revenue lost to unpaid bills. That, in turn, feeds into higher insurance premiums.

Cost shifting accounts for about one-third of the increase in insurance premiums, which are rising as much as 50 percent a year. The cost of medical care—which is increasing two to three times faster than the rate of inflation—is responsible for the rest.

Unaffordable Premiums

The higher the price tag for insurance, the more people who go without it. Firms with fewer than one hundred workers employ about one-third of the work force in the United States, but only about half of them offer health insurance to their employees. Small-business owners say they have enough trouble staying afloat without assuming the heavy burden of health insurance premiums.

Even when employers do offer coverage, not all their employees take it. The Service Employees International Union, whose members are hospital workers, janitors, and government employees, found that 48 percent of its low-wage members were offered insurance but turned it down because they could not afford the premiums. In 1987, 25 percent of the uninsured worked for very large employers, most of whom offered health insurance.

People who want coverage and must buy it on their own have little choice but to pay what the insurance company demands. In many instances, that can mean thousands of dollars each year. And premiums continue to rise dramatically.

Spiraling premiums also affect millions of people whose employers provide their health insurance.

One major employee-benefits survey found that employers now spend an average of $2,700 annually to cover each employee. In many cases, employers are shifting some of these ever-increasing costs to their workers by requiring them to pay a greater share of the premium and a larger portion of their medical expenses through higher deductibles and copayments. Other companies, such as American Airlines, try to reduce their insurance bill by refusing to cover preexisting health conditions for new employees.

In 1984, Hewitt Associates, a benefits consulting firm, found that 37 percent of large employers paid the full premium for their workers. By

1988, that figure was down to 24 percent. In 1984, 53 percent of large firms paid all hospital room-and-board charges for their workers; in 1988, the figure was 29 percent.

Losing Coverage

About half of all large- and medium-sized firms try to trim their insurance outlays by self-insuring. They invest the money they would otherwise spend on premiums and pay employees' claims directly when they arise.

The Employee Retirement Income Security Act (ERISA) exempts these self-insured plans from state insurance regulations meant to protect consumers. For example, employers may not have to offer certain coverages, such as care for newborn children, or provide for continuation of coverage when employees leave.

Employers hire a third-party administrator, or TPA, to handle the claims. Because the administrator may be the local Blue Cross plan, employees think that Blue Cross (or some other insurer) is actually underwriting their coverage. They don't always know that the loopholes created by ERISA can leave them without insurance if things go wrong. If the employer goes out of business or drops the coverage, employees could be out of luck.

The Woes at HMOs

When a health maintenance organization closes its doors, the people who received medical care there may also be left uninsured. Established as alternatives to traditional insurance policies, HMOs provide a variety of prepaid health services to their members. Unfortunately, a number of HMOs have fallen on hard times.

Several states don't require conversion policies or continuation of coverage for members whose HMO has gone out of business. Even in states that do, HMO members have no assurance that their new coverage will be anything like the old. They may well find themselves assuming a greater portion of their medical expenses.

Clinging to Coverage

Millions of Americans have yet to lose their insurance but could at any time fall victim to an insurance company's business practices. As health care providers continually raise their fees and pass on the higher cost of medical care to insurance companies, the companies respond by insuring fewer people. People who must buy coverage on their own and workers in small firms feel this pinch the hardest.

Insurance companies are not charities. Their goal is to make a profit, and they can increase their odds of success by insuring good risks who are unlikely to have health problems. Competition among carriers for the healthiest risks has become cutthroat.

In large businesses with many employees, it doesn't matter if some employees have serious medical conditions. The risk they pose can easily be spread among the healthy workers. But in a small group with few employees, insurance companies cannot collect enough in premiums to pay the claims of those who are sick. So the rules for insuring workers in small businesses are more rigorous.

Insurers use a controversial scheme to insulate themselves from risk. They offer to insure employees in a small firm (usually those with fewer than twenty-five workers) at a "lowball" premium for at least the first year. If members of the group experience costly health problems in the second and third years, the carrier tosses the firm into a pool with other groups whose health care costs are high and jacks up its premiums as much as 200 percent.

By placing firms into several "rate tiers," insurance companies can bid for the healthiest groups with rock-bottom premiums. But employers and their employees who have had serious health problems are stuck with their present insurance carrier; they can't move to another because no other company is likely to take them at any premium. Worse, the present carrier may decide not to renew the group's coverage, forcing employers and employees to find other insurance. And that may be impossible.

No Coverage for the Sick

Companies insuring small groups require employees and their dependents to meet tough health requirements, just as they do for individuals buying policies on their own. No carrier wants to insure employees and dependents who have had heart attacks or cancer. They will exclude them from the policy or decline to insure the group altogether. Sometimes a single employee with a serious disease is enough to earn a rejection slip for the whole group.

Increasingly, insurance companies are turning down people with far less serious health conditions than cancer or heart disease, excluding everyone except those in perfect or near perfect health. "We don't want to buy a claim," is how one company official puts it.

Many people who become ill while they are working may find themselves without insurance when they leave the security of their employer's policy. Indeed, many are held hostage to their current job just to keep their insurance.

42. We the Americans . . . Our Homes
Department of Commerce

Excerpted from *We the Americans . . . Our Homes* (Washington, D.C.: U.S. Department of Commerce, Economics and Statistics Administration, Bureau of the Census, September 1993), pp. 2–7.

Housing Population Up

In 1990, there were 102,263,678 housing units in the United States, up by 16 percent from the 1980 census, a net increase of nearly 14 million housing units. There has been an increase in the housing stock every decade since 1940. The 1970s had the largest percentage change, at 29 percent, while the 1980s had the smallest, at 16 percent. The 1970s had the largest numerical increase in housing units, almost 20 million, while the 1940s had the smallest increase, almost 9 million. The South (22.6 percent) and the West (22.3 percent) regions had the greatest increase in housing units, while the Northeast and Midwest regions had more modest gains of 9 percent and 7 percent, respectively.

Housing and Population Growth Almost Always Go Hand in Hand

Since 1890, the percentage increase between decades for the number of occupied housing units has always been greater than that for the number of people. This is related to a decline in household size and an increase in one-person households. The 1910 census showed the largest percentage increase between decades for occupied units, and 1990 had the smallest increase. The 1910 census also showed the largest increase for number of people, but the 1940 census had the smallest.

The 1980 census was the first in the twentieth century to show a divergence between the growth rates of population and occupied housing units. After years of moving almost in parallel, the growth rate for housing increased between 1970 and 1980, while the growth rate for population declined, so there was a greater supply of housing units in relation to the total population than before. In 1990, the pattern of growth rate for population and occupied units returned to the pattern exhibited before 1980, that is, both percentages moved in the same direction when compared to the previous decade.

Dream of Homeownership

Owner-occupied units increased by 14 percent during the 1980s, while renter-occupied units increased by 15 percent. As a result, the homeownership rate in the United States decreased slightly for the first time since the Great Depression.

The homeownership rate increased dramatically between 1940 and 1960, because of new legislation introducing mortgages that made it easier to afford a home. Since 1960, the homeownership rate has increased at a much slower rate. The Midwest had the highest homeownership rate at 68 percent, while the South was not far behind at 66 percent. The Northeast was below the average for the United States at 61 percent, and the West had the lowest, at 59 percent.

Single-Family Homes

In 1990, among all housing units, single-family homes increased the most in absolute terms, by almost 7.5 million units during the decade. Almost 30 percent of all housing units were in multi-unit structures, with almost 10 percent in buildings of two to four units and 18 percent in buildings of five or more units.

Mobile homes, the fastest-growing type of housing, increased nearly 60 percent but represented only 7 percent of all units. The South led the nation, with 11 percent of its units being mobile homes, while the Northeast had the smallest percentage, at only 3 percent. The South also had the highest number of mobile homes, almost 4 million, while the Northeast had the smallest number, with only 640,000.

A Room of Our Own

Since 1950, the median number of rooms for all units has increased steadily from 4.6 to 5.2, with the largest increase occurring between 1950 and 1960. The largest difference in median number of rooms (2 rooms) between owner-occupied units and renter-occupied units was in 1990. The smallest difference (1.5 rooms) occurred in 1940 and 1950. In 1990, owner-occupied households were the largest they have ever been, on average, with a median number of rooms of 6.0.

The number of rooms in renter-occupied units peaked in 1940 with a median of 4.1 rooms. The number of rooms in both owned and rented units was smallest in 1950, with medians of 5.3 rooms and 3.8 rooms, respectively.

Units with more than one person per room are often considered crowded. This proportion rose from 4.5 percent of occupied units in 1980 to 4.9 percent in 1990. This was the first increase since 1940 (the first census to include housing data), when the proportion was just over 20 percent.

The steady decline or minimal increase in the percentage of units with more than one person per room and the recent substantial increase of units with 0.5 persons or fewer per room resulted in an overall decline in persons per room, showing improved living conditions.

The decade of the 1970s showed the greatest increase in units with 0.5 persons or fewer per room, from 50 percent in 1970 to 61 percent in 1980. The 1940s showed the greatest decrease in units with more than one person per room, from 20 percent in 1940 to 16 percent in 1950.

When Our Homes Were Built

A large portion of the nation's housing units in 1990 were built before 1960. Despite the large proportion of older homes, about 21 percent of all housing units in the United States were built during the 1980s. The 1970s saw the most housing units constructed, just over 22 million, while the 1940s had the least, about 8.5 million, primarily because of the lack of homebuilding during World War II.

The South had 44 percent of all new units built in 1990. The Northeast had the lowest percentage of these units, at 14 percent, while the West had 25 percent and the Midwest had 17 percent.

Moving Trends

Over 45 million households, or about 49 percent of all households, changed residences between 1985 and 1990. Of these, over 19 million moved during the fifteen months preceding the 1990 census. Still, almost one-tenth of all households had lived at their 1990 residence since 1960.

Renter households were more than four times as likely to have moved between 1989 and 1990 as owner households, 42 percent versus 9 percent. Conversely, only 4 percent of renters lived in the same residence for more than twenty years, compared with 26 percent of owners.

43. Family-Related Benefits in the Workplace
William J. Wiatrowski

Excerpted from *Monthly Labor Review*, March 1990, pp. 28–32. William J. Wiatrowski is an economist in the Division of Occupational Pay and Benefit Levels, Bureau of Labor Statistics.

One of the more striking developments in personnel administration over the past seventy-five years has been the growing complexity of employee compensation. Limited at the outbreak of World War I largely to straight-time pay for hours worked, compensation now includes a variety of employer-financed benefits such as health and life insurance, retirement income, and paid time off. Although the details of each vary widely, these benefits are today standard components of the compensation package, and workers generally have come to expect them.

One function of employee benefits is to protect workers and their families from financial burdens. Health care plans help soften the impact of medical expenses and, perhaps, encourage workers and their dependents to seek care that might otherwise be forgone. Retirement income plans allow older employees to stop working and maintain certain living standards. Similarly, disability benefits provide income to those unable to work, and survivor benefits protect against loss of earnings resulting from the death of a spouse or other relative.

Employers provide benefits to their employees for a variety of reasons. One theory suggests that employers have a legitimate concern for the welfare of their employees beyond any economic motive, and this "paternalism" is expressed through the offer of protection against economic hardship. Employers may also offer protection that they feel employees are unable to provide for themselves. According to this theory, employers assume that employees will tend to favor current consumption over prudent savings and will therefore be unprepared for emergencies. Finally, employers may offer benefit plans to meet union demands in collective bargaining, to attract and keep good employees, or to remain competitive with other employers in the labor market.

Besides employers, another source of benefits is the government, which provides direct benefits such as social security and mandates employers to provide protection such as workers' compensation. Over the past seventy-five years, the government has increased its role in the area of employee benefits substantially. In 1915, workers' compensation laws were just being introduced in several states. Since then, nationwide programs such as social security and unemployment insurance have been developed, and discussions of mandatory employer-provided benefits such as health care and parental leave are periodically on the agenda of policy makers.

The growth of employer-provided and government-mandated benefits has changed the character of employee compensation: By 1989, benefits accounted for nearly 30 percent of the total cost of such compensation.

While the Depression years saw relatively few changes in benefit practices, the war years gave rise to a number of changes. Employment grew rapidly after America entered the war, and women entered the labor force in large numbers to support the war effort. To stabilize prices, the War Labor Board restricted wage increases but was more lenient in allowing improvements in benefits. Employers responded by offering a variety of benefits in lieu of increased wages.

1945–59: Return to Prosperity

Following World War II, the country reverted to a largely male-dominated labor force, as the return of servicemen led to a boom in marriages and children. These traditional families had needs that employers could address through benefit programs, such as time off with pay, payment of medical expenses, and protection against loss of income. The period saw the widespread adoption of these practices into the compensation package.

One of the most notable benefits to emerge from the change in family structure and legal environment of the era was health care. Previously, some lost-income benefits were available during an illness or accident, and perhaps an informal arrangement existed for employees to receive medical care at a company clinic or other local facility, but formal medical insurance was uncommon. Needs had changed by the late 1940s and 1950s, however. Hospital admission rates stood at 120 per 1,000 people in 1945, more than double the 1931 rate. And the amount spent on health services and supplies topped $10 billion in 1948. This amounted to $68 per capita, considerably more than twice the 1929 figure.

To meet this need, employers began providing formal health care plans to employees and their families, through either commercial insurers or Blue Cross/Blue Shield organizations. Typically, plans would pay for a limited number of hospital days and up to a specified maximum dollar amount for various medical services. Such plans offered only basic medical protection and looked very different from the extensive plans of the late 1980s. One Bureau of Labor Statistics study showed that by 1960 about 80 percent of plant and office workers in metropolitan areas received a health care plan through their employers.

1960–74: On the Verge of Change

While the years from 1960 to 1974 are considered turbulent in American history, in the history of benefits they were but a prelude to more dramatic changes. This era saw the U.S. Congress debate major pension reform for nearly fifteen years. The result—the Employee Retirement Income Security Act—was signed into law on Labor Day 1974. Also on the verge of major change was the demographic makeup of the labor force: Women of the baby-boom generation were going to college and preparing for future employment.

The era was not, however, one of stagnation in the area of employee benefits. Employers established and expanded on typical benefit plans such as paid leave, retirement income, health care, and survivor and disability insurance. More generous early retirement pension benefits and expanded survivor income payments were among the provisions added to benefit plans during this time. Benefit packages were primarily geared toward a typical family, with a working husband, a nonworking wife, and school-age children.

1975–89: Plans for the "New" Family

The period from 1975 to the present is an era dominated by two major trends: substantial changes in the demographics of the labor force and sweeping government regulation of benefits. During this period, women joined the labor force in large numbers, two-earner families became the norm, and employee needs changed from those of the traditional post–World War II family. As indicated earlier, the Employee Retirement Income Security Act of 1974 began a wave of benefits legislation that is still continuing. The new law sets standards for pension plan provisions and funding, and established reporting and disclosure requirements aimed at keeping employees and the government alert to the soundness of benefit plans.

The rising cost of providing benefits has led to changes in the character and scope of benefits in the past fifteen years. Benefits accounted for 17 percent of compensation costs in 1966 but rose to 22 percent by 1974 and 27 percent by 1989. To combat these rising expenditures, employers attempted to fix their benefit costs and shift some of the burden to employees.

In recognition of the changing demographics of the labor force during this period, employers have provided several new benefits and offered employees more opportunities to choose benefits suited to their family needs. Examples of newly emerging benefits include parental leave (time off for parents to care for newborn or adopted children), child care (employer-provided facilities or financial assistance), and flexible work schedules. Benefit choices, among a variety of medical plans or among plans in multiple benefit areas, also attracted considerable attention as the typical family of the 1950s and 1960s became less prevalent and the needs of the varied family arrangements of the 1980s could no longer be satisfied by a fixed set of benefits.

44. Children in Two-Worker Families and Real Family Income
Howard V. Hayghe

Excerpted from *Monthly Labor Review*, December 1989, pp. 48–51. Howard V. Hayghe is an economist in the Office of Employment and Unemployment Statistics, Bureau of Labor Statistics.

Family Trends

The primary change in the family situation of children has been the well-publicized increase in the proportion who are living in dual-worker families, that is, families with both parents employed (including fathers in the armed forces). Secondarily, the proportion living in single-parent families maintained by mothers has also increased. These developments, of course, were coupled with the decline in the number of children living in "traditional" families (two-parent families in which only the father was employed). At the same time, the total number of children under eighteen years was also declining.

Dual-Worker versus Traditional Families

In March 1988, 24.9 million children under the age of eighteen lived in dual-worker families. These children accounted for 43 percent of the total in families. Just thirteen years earlier, children in such families numbered 18.9 million and constituted barely 30 percent of the nation's children. Meanwhile, the number in traditional families fell from about 29 million (46 percent of all children) to fewer than 17 million (29 percent of children).

Children whose parents both work tend to be better off than other children. For instance, in 1987, median family income for children in dual-worker families ($41,000) was nearly 30 percent higher than for children in traditional families ($32,000) and more than four times that of children in single-parent families maintained by women.

Single-Parent versus Two-Parent Families

The growth in the proportion of children living in single-parent families has not been as dramatic as the shift from traditional to dual-worker families. In 1975, 16 percent of children under eighteen lived in single-parent families; by 1988, the proportion was 22 percent. The overwhelming majority of these children lived with their mothers, but a growing segment lived with their fathers.

Though small, this shift has some important implications for the well-being of children because of the employment situation of single parents, especially mothers. As a group, these women face many difficulties that inhibit labor market success. Consequently, 45 percent of the children in single-parent families maintained by a woman lived with a mother who was either unemployed (7 percent) or not in the labor force (38 percent). Of the children in families maintained by unmarried men, 21 percent lived with a father who was not employed. In contrast, only 4 percent of the children in two-parent families had no employed parent.

Thus, as might be expected, children in families maintained by women tend to have very low incomes. In 1987, median family income for children living with single mothers was only $9,000 ($15,400 if the mother worked); it was $20,800 for children living with single fathers. This compares to $35,600 for children in two-parent families.

Race and Hispanic Origin

Black children accounted for nearly 14 percent of all children in 1988, while the proportion who were Hispanic totaled almost 11 percent. Both proportions were somewhat higher than in 1975. Typically, white and Hispanic children live in two-parent families, whereas a little more than half of black children are in single-parent families (53 percent). For each group, the proportion living in two-parent families has declined. The decline was least for whites (6 percentage points) and greatest for blacks (about 10 percentage points). Among Hispanics, the decline was also substantial (from 80 percent in 1975 to 72 percent in 1988).

For the children in these families, part of the significance of these shifts lies in the employment problems of single parents, the effects of which were discussed above. The majority of black and Hispanic children in such families (54 and 59 percent, respectively) lived with a parent who was not employed, compared with 37 percent of white children in such families.

Income Trends: 1974–87

To the extent that income measures economic well-being, there has been little overall improvement in children's welfare over the period from 1974 to 1987. In fact, family income trends indicate that children's well-being declined, on average, in the early 1980s. However, as the economy recovered from the recession of the early 1980s, family income began rising, so that by 1987 some groups of children were in families with median incomes that were equal to, or slightly above, their 1974 levels (in constant 1987 dollars). However, other groups were in families in which the median was below its 1974 level.

In 1974, children's real median family income was about $29,600. From 1974 to 1979, the median edged upward. However, under the pressure of recession, the median fell to $26,800 between 1979 and 1983. Subsequently, as the nation entered a protracted growth period, the median rose, reaching $30,000 in 1987—only a little above the 1974 level.

45. Economic Status of the Elderly
Council of Economic Advisers

Excerpted from *Economic Report of the President* (Washington, D.C.: U.S. Government Printing Office, 1985). The members of the council responsible for the report were William A. Niskanen and William Poole.

Retirement as it is known today is a relatively recent phenomenon. In 1900 life expectancy at birth was forty-six years for males and forty-eight for females. While most women did not work outside the home once they married, two-thirds of all men over sixty-five were still in the work force. Many men retired only because of poor health or company rules, and retirement usually consisted of a few years of declining health. Often the elderly relied on their children for housing and financial support.

Since 1900 the fraction of elderly men with jobs has declined dramatically, while the life expectancy of the elderly (sixty-five and older) has improved substantially. Now a man who is approaching the end of his working career can expect to spend about fifteen years in retirement, a retirement that is often shared by a spouse who also makes a transition from worker to retiree. Because life expectancy has increased more for women than for men in the twentieth century, the retirement years have become especially important for women. These are years that women are likely to face alone; two-thirds of women over seventy-five are widows. Elderly widows rarely remarry, and on average they live sixteen years beyond their husbands. Higher divorce rates have added to the number of elderly women living alone, so that today only two-fifths of all elderly women live with their husbands.

Resources to support these new retirement patterns rarely come directly from the families of retirees. The elderly receive less than 1 percent of their income from their children, and the fraction of elderly people living with their children has declined sharply.

Current Financial Status of the Elderly

Thirty years ago the elderly were a relatively disadvantaged group in the population. That is no longer the case. The median real income of the elderly has more than doubled since 1950, and the income of the elderly has increased faster over the past two decades than the income of the nonelderly population. Today, elderly and nonelderly families have about equal levels of income per capita. Poverty rates among the elderly have declined so dramatically that in 1983 poverty rates for the elderly were lower than poverty rates for the rest of the population.

These encouraging statistics do not tell the whole story. The elderly are not a homogeneous group. Those with spouses have relatively high levels of family income, especially when leisure opportunities, lower tax rates for the elderly, noncash transfers, and assets are taken into account. A good deal of evidence supports the contention that the elderly with spouses are, on average, more financially secure than the nonelderly. But many of the elderly live alone, and these individuals, particularly women, often have very limited financial resources; they are often poor. Poverty rates for elderly blacks and the very old are also high.

The income of today's elderly can be compared with the income of the elderly in the past. Since 1950 the mean income of elderly families has gone up more than 80 percent in real terms, and the mean income of the unmarried elderly living in a household without relatives (unrelated individuals) has more than doubled. The income of the elderly can also be compared with the income of the same individuals when they were younger. On average, elderly families in 1980 had higher levels of income than they had closer to retirement. Elderly families have real incomes below levels they attained in middle age but similar to levels attained when the head was younger.

One common measure of relative financial well-being is the average income of the elderly, those currently sixty-five and over, compared with the average income of adults now aged 25 to 64. Since the 1950s the average age of the elderly has increased because the fraction of the very old among the elderly has increased. The average age of the nonelderly has also changed, reflecting low birth rates in the 1930s and the high birth rates that produced the post-World War II baby boom. Between 1970 and 1983 the relative status of the elderly improved dramatically. In 1983 before-tax per capita mean income was virtually the same for elderly and nonelderly families. Two-thirds of the elderly lived in family units. Per capita income ratios are higher than family income ratios because families with an elderly head tend to be smaller than younger families. In 1983 elderly families contained an average of 2.4 people compared with an average of 3.5 people for nonelderly families. The elderly to nonelderly income ratios are lower for unrelated individuals because the elderly in this class are frequently older widows, who tend to be the poorest of the elderly.

Income levels of the elderly have improved both absolutely and relatively in spite of several forces that worked in the opposite direction. The most dramatic of these forces was a decline in labor force participation of the elderly and a simultaneous increase among the nonelderly. Along with increasing income, the elderly have benefited from increasing amounts of leisure over the past few decades on both an absolute and a relative basis.

Demographic factors have also tended to depress the average income of the elderly. The age distribution of the elderly has shifted toward those over seventy-five. Because income typically declines with age and because older generations have lower levels of lifetime income, increases in longevity tend to lower average income levels for the elderly. In addition, the ratio of women to men among the elderly has increased from six women for every five men in 1960 to three women for every two men in 1980. In 1983 mean income for elderly females living alone was equal to 80 percent of mean income for elderly males living alone.

The elderly have lower average tax rates than the nonelderly and thus have more to spend out of a given income than the nonelderly. Approximately two-thirds of the elderly pay no income tax. The elderly benefit from several tax provisions. Individuals sixty-five and older with low incomes receive a 15 percent credit against their tax, and all individuals aged sixty-five and over are entitled to an additional $1,000 tax exemption. Those over fifty-five also receive preferential tax treatment on the capital gain from the sale of one principal residence. Social security benefits were not taxed at all before 1984. Now individuals with incomes well above average levels for the elderly must include a portion (up to one-half) of their benefits in taxable income.

Income levels of the elderly have improved despite offsetting demographic trends largely because of increases in social security benefit levels and coverage. Between 1950 and 1983 the fraction of the elderly receiving social security benefits rose from 16 to 94 percent. Furthermore, the average level of nominal benefits went up much faster than the price level during the same period. Real benefits went up by almost 150 percent. Income levels of the elderly have improved relative to the nonelderly since 1970 because social security benefits increased by 46 percent in real terms while earnings from wages and salaries, the major source of income for the nonelderly, decreased by 7 percent in real terms. Thus, younger families have had to work more to keep up with inflation since 1970; older families have not.

46. The Social and Economic Status of the Black Population
Bureau of the Census

Excerpted from *The Social and Economic Status of the Black Population in the United States: An Historical View, 1790–1978* (Washington, D.C.: U.S. Government Printing Office, Department of Commerce, Bureau of the Census, no date).

The 1940s marked the beginning of the predominantly one-way migration stream of blacks from the South to the North; this movement continued to the 1970s. (The South lost close to 1.5 million blacks in each of those decades.) One of the major factors contributing to this migration was that the wartime acceleration of the movement of blacks from the South to job opportunities in the industrialized areas of the North. As a further consequence, the geographical distribution of the black population changed; by 1970, only 53 percent of blacks lived in the South, and 81 percent lived in urban areas.

A large increase in average life expectancy at birth for blacks was recorded during the World War II period: seven years for black males and females. As the major diseases of the early 1900s—childhood and infectious diseases—were brought under control by an improved standard of living, expanded public health programs, etc., progress was made in reducing mortality levels among blacks. Fertility levels for black women began to increase in the late 1940s and reached an apex in the 1950s.

Progress in educational attainment was most impressive for the black population, especially for young black adults. Most of the change has occurred since 1960. For instance, in 1940 (the first census in which information on years of school completed was collected) one out of ten blacks twenty-five to thirty-four years old had completed high school; two decades later, in 1960, the proportion was three out of ten; and only one decade later, in 1970, about five out of every ten blacks twenty-five to thirty-four years old were high school graduates.

Information on the composition of black families, available only since 1940, indicates a trend of declining proportions of families with both a husband and a wife present and increasing proportions maintained by a woman. Specifically, in 1940, 77 percent of black families had a husband and wife present; by 1970, the figure was reduced to 68 percent. Concomitant to the trend of declining proportions of families with a husband and wife present has been a decline in the proportion of black children living with both parents.

In 1940, blacks were greatly concentrated in the lowest-paying, least-skilled jobs; few had white-collar or craft positions. By 1970, advances had been made, with the proportion of blacks in white-collar jobs quadrupling from 6 percent in 1940 to 24 percent in 1970.

The Census Bureau began collecting income information by race on a continuing basis in 1947. Since then, there has been overall moderate income growth for black families, interrupted by several recessions. From 1947 to 1969 (after accounting for inflation in terms of 1974 dollars), the most pronounced upgrading (36 percent increase) in the income levels for blacks occurred during the period 1964 to 1969. Increases were noted during the 1947–53 and 1959–64 periods; however, little or no progress was made during the period from 1953 to 1959 as a result of the 1953–54 and 1957–58 recessions.

Unemployment rates for blacks have fluctuated since 1948 (the first year these data were available by race from the Current Population Survey). The rates were lowest during the Korean War years (1951 to 1953). After the Korean War, rates began to rise and reached high levels between 1958 and 1963, reflecting the effects of the 1957–58 and 1960–61 recessions. Declines were recorded in the mid- and late 1960s, but by 1970, jobless rates had begun to creep upward again.

In examining the trends from 1940 to 1970, of particular note is the 1960s decade, especially the mid- and late 1960s, when blacks made major social and economic advances in income, employment, education, voter registration and participation, home ownership, and election to public office, and the number of blacks in poverty was reduced. It has been suggested that expanded government programs, the civil rights movement, and efforts to reduce segregation and discrimination are some of the factors that contributed to that progress.

Unlike the patterns noted for the 1960s decade, the 1970s portray a mixed picture for black Americans. They continued their progress in the areas of education, home ownership, and election to public office. Nevertheless, the prolonged dual impact of the recessions and inflation continued to adversely affect income and employment. For instance, the 1977 median income for black families ($9,560) showed no improvement over the 1974 level; the number of blacks in poverty in 1977 (7.7 million) rose by over one-half million from the 1974 level; and unemployment levels remained high despite slight improvement in mid-1978.

The 1970s decade has been further distinguished by changes in migration patterns, family composition, fertility levels, and the work experience patterns of family members. Undoubtedly, these factors and their interrelationships have had, and will have in the future, an imprint on the demographic, social, and economic characteristics of the black community.

In summary, significant advances have been made by black Americans since the first census was taken in 1790. However, in 1978, the 25.4 million blacks in this country remained far behind whites in almost every social and economic area.

47. In Black America, Life Grows Shorter
Carlyle C. Douglas

Reprinted with permission from Carlyle C. Douglas, "In Black America, Life Grows Shorter," New York Times, December 2, 1990, p. 7.

Not since such measurements began have black Americans had lifespans the equal of whites. Now, in a development that has alarmed health experts, the life expectancy gap has begun to grow, primarily because blacks began to die younger in the 1980s.

In a study released last week, the National Center for Health Statistics said the average black infant born in 1988, the latest year for which statistics are available, could expect to live 69.2 years, down from 69.4 in 1987. All told since 1984, black life expectancy has shrunk by half a year, while it has increased among whites, from 75.3 years to 75.6 years.

The gap is widest for black men, whose average life expectancy fell from 65.2 years in 1987 to 64.9, less than retirement age, in 1988. For black women, life expectancy dropped from 73.6 to 73.4. For white men, it rose slightly to 72.3, and for white women it remained level at 78.9.

Experts said the growing gap was "discouraging," "unconscionable," and, to some degree, could be affected by changes in health policy. There were sharp increases in deaths from AIDS and drug and alcohol abuse among blacks. There was also a decline in the percentage of black women getting early prenatal health care, from 62.7 percent in 1980 to 61.1 in 1988. Infant mortality, notably higher among blacks than whites, was also a factor in the widening life expectancy gap. An unrelated study, reported last week in the *International Journal of Epidemiology*, found that blacks, who account for about 13 percent of the population, account for nearly 80 percent of premature deaths—those occurring between the ages of fifteen and forty-four—from a dozen disorders, such as appendicitis, asthma, bladder infections, and pneumonia, that are normally not fatal if treated early.

The study noted that a disproportionate number of blacks are among the 37 million Americans who have no access to routine health care services and therefore tend to "postpone seeking primary care until their need for treatment becomes urgent."

Dr. Reed V. Tuckson, a vice president of the March of Dimes and a coauthor of the study, said that some premature deaths were related to behavior. But he said that such behavior was "often a function of hopelessness, a disenfranchisement from the community that are related to ethnicity and poverty."

"The nation has to decide whether or not citizen survival is of the highest priority," he said. "We have to decide as a nation to care."

48. We the American . . . Hispanics
Department of Commerce

Excerpted from *We the American . . . Hispanics* (Washington, D.C.: U.S. Department of Commerce, Bureau of the Census, November, 1993), pp. 1–7.

Introduction

We, the American Hispanics trace our origin or descent to Spain or to Mexico, Puerto Rico, Cuba, and many other Spanish-speaking countries of Latin America. Our ancestors were among the early explorers and settlers of the New World. In 1609, eleven years before the Pilgrims landed at Plymouth Rock, our Mestizo (Indian and Spanish) ancestors settled in what is now Santa Fe, New Mexico.

Several historical events also shaped our presence in America: the Louisiana Purchase, admission of Florida and Texas into the Union, the

Treaty of Guadalupe Hidalgo that ended the Mexican-American War, the Spanish-American War, the Mexican Revolution, labor shortages during World War I and World War II, the Cuban Revolution, and political instability in Central and South America in the recent past. Although our common ancestry and language bind us, we are quite diverse.

Hispanics have not always appeared in the census as a separate ethnic group. In 1930, "Mexicans" were counted; in 1940, "Persons of Spanish mother tongue" were reported; and in 1950 and 1960, "Persons of Spanish surname" were reported. The 1970 census asked people about their "origin," and respondents could choose among several Hispanic origins listed on the questionnaire. In 1980 and 1990, people of "Spanish/Hispanic" origin could report as Mexican, Puerto Rican, Cuban, or "Other Hispanic." The 1990 census tabulated information for about thirty additional Hispanic-origin groups.

We Are a Large, Fast Growing Segment of the Nation's Population.

Since 1930, some segments of the Hispanic population have been counted in the census. In 1930, 1.3 million "Mexicans" were reported; in 1950, 2.3 million "persons of Spanish surname" were reported; and in 1970, 9.1 million people of different Hispanic origins were reported.

In 1990, there were 22.4 million Hispanics in the United States, almost 9 percent of the nation's nearly 250 million people. The Hispanic population in 1990 was slightly less than the entire U.S. population in 1850. The Census Bureau's 1992 projections suggest rapid growth may continue into the twentieth century. The Hispanic population could rise from 24 million in 1992 to 31 million by the year 2000, 59 million by 2030, and 81 million by 2050.

Our Population Grew Over 7 Times as Fast as the Rest of the Nation between 1980 and 1990.

The Hispanic population grew by 53 percent between 1980 and 1990 and by 61 percent between 1970 and 1980. Several factors contributed to the tremendous increase since 1970. Among them are a higher birth rate than the rest of the population and substantial immigration from Mexico, Central America, the Caribbean, and South America.

The Mexican population in the United States nearly doubled between 1970 and 1980, and nearly doubled again by 1990. Both the Cuban and Puerto Rican populations grew at a rate of at least four times as fast as the rest of the nation. Other Hispanic populations grew dramatically between 1980 and 1990, as well.

We Made Great Strides in Educational Attainment Since 1970.

In 1990, about half of the Hispanic population had at least a high school diploma, and one in eleven had earned a bachelor's degree or higher. However, Hispanic adults were less likely than non-Hispanic adults to complete high school or college.

In 1980, about four of ten Hispanics completed four years or more of high school, and one of every thirteen completed four years or more of college. In 1970, only three of ten Hispanics twenty-five years old and over completed at least four years of high school. Less than one in twenty completed four years or more of college.

About Half of Us Who Were Foreign Born Came to the United States between 1980 and 1990.

Whether pulled by the need to be reunited with families or pushed by political events in the country of birth, many Hispanics moved to the United States between 1980 and 1990. Just over half of the Hispanic foreign born have arrived in America since 1980. About 28 percent arrived between 1970 and 1979, 15 percent between 1960 and 1969, and about 7 percent before 1960.

About 20 percent of the those Hispanics born in Central America arrived between 1970 and 1979, and about 70 percent arrived between 1980 and 1990. Central Americans represented the largest proportion of newly arrived Hispanic immigrants during the 1980s. About 46 percent of the Cuban foreign born arrived between 1960 and 1969. Many Cuban refugees arrived in the United States following the Cuban Missile Crisis in the early part of that decade.

Nearly 3 Million of Us Are Legal Immigrants Who Arrived between 1980 and 1990.

Prior to 1950, the vast majority of legal immigrants arrived from Europe, but from 1950 to 1990, a new wave (nearly 20 million) of legal immigrants arrived, many from Latin America. Between 1951 and 1960, over 2.5 million people entered the country legally. Of those, one in five came from Latin America. Between 1961 and 1970, 3.3 million immigrants entered the United States, with one in three coming from Latin America. During the 1970s, there were nearly 4.5 million immigrants, with about 40 percent coming from Latin America. By the 1980s, 47 percent of immigrants were from Latin America.

49. The Minimum Wage: Its Relation to Incomes and Poverty

Ralph E. Smith and Bruce Vavrichek

Excerpted from *Monthly Labor Review*, June 1987, pp. 24–29. Ralph E. Smith and Bruce Vavrichek are economists at the U.S. Congressional Budget Office.

Federal minimum wage legislation provides a floor on the hourly wage rate that employers are allowed to pay most workers. First enacted as part of the Fair Labor Standards Act of 1938, the minimum wage statute now requires a wage of at least $3.35 per hour for the almost 90 percent of nonsupervisory civilian workers to whom the act applies. Although the minimum wage has been increased numerous times since it was established, it has remained unchanged since January 1981. Because prices and wages have risen since that time, the real value of the minimum wage has fallen.

One issue relevant to debates on the minimum wage is the relation between that wage and poverty. Proponents of increasing the minimum wage argue that it should be at least high enough to provide above-poverty earnings to workers with families to support.

Background of the Minimum Wage

Historically, changes in the minimum wage provisions of the Fair Labor Standards Act have consisted primarily of increases in the wage rate and expansions in coverage. The minimum wage was originally set at $0.25 per hour in 1938, reached $1 per hour in 1956, $2 per hour in 1974, and the current level of $3.35 in 1981. Coverage originally was limited to workers directly engaged in interstate commerce, or in the production of goods for interstate commerce, but has been expanded considerably. In 1985, about 73 million nonsupervisory workers—or almost 90 percent of that work force—were covered by the minimum wage. Major groups currently not covered by the minimum wage include executive, administrative, and professional personnel; employees in some small firms; and, of course, the self-employed.

Prices, Wages, and the Minimum Wage

One perspective on the size of the minimum wage today can be obtained by analyzing the real purchasing power of the wage over time and by examining its relation to average wages.

The purchasing power of the minimum wage—that is, its value after taking account of inflation, here measured with the consumer price index—has fluctuated considerably over time, but today is less than at any time since the mid-1950s. In 1985 dollars, the minimum wage was worth just under $2 per hour when the legislation was enacted in 1938. By 1968, the real value of the wage had reached a high of nearly $5 per hour, but by 1985, it had declined to $3.35. In the five-year period between January 1981—when the minimum wage was set at $3.35—and January 1986, average prices increased by about 26 percent. To have the same purchasing power it had at the start of 1981, the minimum wage would have to have been about $4.22 per hour in January 1986.

In recent years, the minimum wage also has fallen as a share of average wages. After hovering around 50 percent of average hourly earnings in private nonagricultural industries during the 1950s and 1960s, the minimum averaged just over 45 percent in the 1970s. By 1985, it had declined to about 39 percent of average wages. Comparisons with the broad private nonfarm series are less useful in the early years, however, when minimum wage coverage was considerably more limited.

Relationship to Poverty Thresholds

During most of the 1960s and 1970s, a person working full-time, year round, at the minimum wage would have received an income roughly equal to the poverty threshold for a three-person family. Full-time, year-round earnings at the minimum wage have declined relative to poverty thresholds since then, however, because these thresholds are adjusted to account for changes in prices, while the minimum wage has not increased since 1981.

A person working forty hours per week for fifty-two weeks at the minimum wage would have earned about $7,000 in 1985. That income level was well above the poverty threshold for individuals living alone and about equal to the threshold for two-person families, but was well below the threshold for families of three or more people.

The Minimum Wage and Family Incomes

Examination of some of the characteristics of workers paid at or below the minimum wage—henceforth termed "minimum wage workers"—and the activities of their families in March 1985 suggests several reasons why being a minimum wage worker and being poor are not synonymous. About 70 percent (3.6 million) of the 5.2 million minimum wage workers were in families in which at least one other member held a job in the survey reference month. Seventy percent of the minimum wage employees worked only part time in March. Teenagers held almost one-third of all jobs paying at or below the minimum wage.

The likelihood of a minimum wage worker being poor in 1984 was also closely linked to the employment status of other family members. Minimum wage workers who were the only job holders in their families had a poverty rate of 44.5 percent, compared with 7.9 percent for those with other employed family members. This comparison was more dramatic for those in families of four or more people (who had a poverty threshold of $10,500 or more)—61.7 percent versus 7.0 percent.

Low Annual Earnings and Poverty

Examination of the poverty status of full-time workers with low annual earnings provides further information about the relationship between low wages and poverty and confirms the critical roles of family size and the presence of other workers in the family in determining whether a low-wage earner will be poor. For this part of the analysis, people who reported being employed full-time year round in 1984 were counted as low-wage workers if they earned less than $7,000. That amount corresponded to the earnings of someone who worked all year, forty hours each week, and was paid the minimum wage.

The Bureau of the Census reported that in 1984 there were 70.4 million people who worked at least fifty weeks primarily on full-time schedules (that is, thirty-five hours or more per week). Nearly 2.1 million of those workers were poor. Detailed examination of the data revealed, however, that 8 million of those people, including more than 800,000 poor workers, reported that their primary activity was self-employment, or that they had worked without pay. The incomes of those workers would not be directly affected by a change in the minimum wage.

50. The Changing Family in International Perspective
Constance Sorrentino

Excerpted from *Monthly Labor Review*, March 1990, pp. 41–55. Constance Sorrentino is an economist in the Division of Foreign Labor Statistics, Bureau of Labor Statistics.

Far-reaching changes are occurring in family structures and household living arrangements in the developed countries. The pace and timing of change differ from country to country, but the general direction is the same practically everywhere. Families are becoming smaller, and household composition patterns over the past several decades have been away from the traditional nuclear family—husband, wife, and children living in one household—and toward more single-parent households, more people living alone, and more couples living together out of wedlock. Indeed, the "consensual union" has become a more visible and accepted family type in several countries. The one-person household has become the fastest-growing household type.

In conjunction with the changes in living arrangements, family labor force patterns have also undergone profound changes. Most countries studied have experienced a rapid rise in participation rates of married women, particularly women who formerly would have stayed at home with their young children.

Scandinavian countries have been the pacesetters in the development of many of the nontraditional forms of family living, especially births outside of wedlock and cohabitation outside of legal marriage. Women in these societies also have the highest rates of labor force participation. However, in at least two aspects, the United States is setting the pace: Americans have, by far, the highest divorce rate of any industrial nation, as well as a higher incidence of single-parent households, one of the most economically vulnerable segments of the population. Japan is the most traditional society of those studied, with very low rates of divorce and births out of wedlock and the highest proportion of married-couple households. In fact, Japan is the only country studied in which the share of such households has increased since 1960. But even in Japan, family patterns are changing: sharp drops in fertility have led to much smaller families, and the three-generation household, once the mainstay of Japanese family life, is in decline.

Demographic Background

Major demographic and sociological changes directly influencing family composition have taken place in this century, with the pace of change accelerating in the past two decades. Almost all developed countries have seen changes of four principal types: a decline in fertility rates, the aging of the population, an erosion of the institution of marriage, and a rapid increase in childbirths out of wedlock. Each of these four trends has played a part in the transformation of the modern family.

Marriage and Divorce

Almost everyone in the United States gets married at some time in his or her life. The United States has long had one of the highest marriage rates in the world, and even in recent years it has maintained a relatively high rate. For the cohort born in 1945, for example, 95 percent of the men have married, compared with 75 percent in Sweden. The other countries studied ranked somewhere between these two extremes.

A trend toward fewer marriages is plain in all of the countries studied, although the timing of this decline differs from country to country. In Scandinavia and Germany, for example, the downward trend in the marriage rate was already evident in the 1960s; in the United States, Canada, Japan, France, the Netherlands, and the United Kingdom, the decline began in the 1970s. Swedish data that include all cohabiting couples indicate that family formation rates have remained stable since 1960, even though marriage rates have dropped.

Divorce rates have shown a long-term increase in most industrial nations since around the turn of the century. After accelerating during the 1970s, the rates reached in the 1980s are probably the highest in the modern history of these nations. While a very large proportion of Americans marry, their marital breakup rate is by far the highest among the developed countries. Based on recent divorce rates, the chances of a first American marriage ending in divorce are today about one in two; the corresponding ratio in Europe is about one in three to one in four.

Births out of Wedlock

Rates of births to unmarried women have increased in all developed countries except Japan. The phenomenon arises from the decline of marriage, the increase in divorce, and the rising rates of cohabitation. Close to half of all live births in Sweden are now outside of wedlock, up from only one in ten in 1960. Denmark is not far behind. In the United States, France, and the United Kingdom, unmarried women account for more than one out of five births, while the rates are far lower in the Netherlands, Italy, and Germany.

A relatively high proportion of births out of wedlock in the United States and the United Kingdom are to teenagers—more than 33 and 29 percent, respectively. In Sweden, teenagers account for only 6 percent, and in France and Japan about 10 percent. More than half of the births out of wedlock in Sweden are to women between the ages of twenty-five and thirty-four, while only one-quarter are to women in that age group in the United States and the United Kingdom.

Household Size Declines

One of the major ramifications of the demographic trends, especially the declining fertility rates and the aging of the population, is that households have diminished in size throughout this century. All of the countries studied have seen declines from an average of four or five members per household in the 1920s to an average of only two or three people living together in the mid- to late 1980s. Denmark, Germany, and Sweden currently have average household sizes in the range of 2.2 to 2.3 people. The United States, Canada, France, Italy, and the United Kingdom have households in the 2.6- to 2.8-person range. Japan maintains the highest average, at about three people per household. This is explained, in part, by the prevalence of three-generation households there. Married couples living with both their children and their parents made up 12 percent of all households in Japan in 1985.

Rise of the Consensual Union

As noted previously, there has been a rapid increase in the incidence of cohabitation outside of marriage in a number of countries. Such arrangements became much more widespread in the 1970s and, by the 1980s, received more general acceptance in public opinion. For some couples, particularly younger ones, consensual unions may be a temporary arrangement that eventually leads to marriage. For others, it is an alternative to the institution of marriage.

The high marriage rate in the United States means that, so far at least, the country has maintained a fairly low level of nonmarital cohabitation, a rate lower than in most European countries and in a different league entirely from Scandinavia. The Census Bureau reports the number of households comprising two unrelated adults of the opposite sex, with or without children. Although some may be roommate or landlord-tenant arrangements, most of these households can be viewed as consensual unions. According to the Census Bureau data, the incidence of such arrangements has risen from 1.2 percent of all couples living together in 1970 to 3.1 percent in 1980 and 4.7 percent in 1988. Moreover, these percentages are understated to the extent that people in common-law marriages report themselves as married couples and are, therefore, not included in these statistics. By definition, no more than two unrelated adults are present in an unmarried-couple household, but the household also may contain one or more children. About three out of every ten unmarried-couple households included a child under fifteen (not age eighteen, as in other U.S. statistics on children) in 1988, slightly higher than the proportion for 1980. Thus, a minority of consensual unions in the United States involve a parent-child family group.

Single-Parent Families Increase

All countries except Japan have experienced significant increases in single-parent households as a proportion of all family households with children.

Allowing for definitional differences, it is clear that the United States has the highest proportion of single-parent households. In 1988, more than one in five U.S. households with dependent children were single-parent households, up from fewer than one in ten in 1960. Only Denmark approaches the U.S. level in the 1980s, and the Danish data are overstated because they count single-parent families instead of households.

The paths to single parenthood are numerous: marriage and childbirth with subsequent widowhood; separation or divorce; and childbirth without marriage or consensual union. Combinations of events may lead to an exit from or reentry into single-parent status—for example, divorce and subsequent remarriage. The growth in the number of single-parent families has some common demographic elements in all the countries studied.

In Europe and North America, there is a growing proportion of those entering single parenthood through marital dissolution (separation and divorce) and childbirth outside marriage, and a diminishing share arising through the premature death of a spouse. Prior to the last three decades, single-parent families were usually formed as the result of the death of one of the parents.

A recent study indicates that, with the exception of the United States, the growth in the number of divorced and separated mothers was responsible for the vast majority of the net increase in one-parent families since 1970. In the United States, family dissolution also accounted for the majority of the net increase, but the growing number of never-married mothers contributed about 40 percent of the increase as well. Even in Japan, divorce or separation has become the predominant route to single parenthood.

More People Living Alone

Historically, virtually all household units have been families in some form. To live in a household was at the same time to live in a family. This is no longer the case. Many households in modern societies do not contain families, and the one-person household is the most common type of nonfamily household. Except in Japan, this type of household has shown the most rapid growth of all household types since 1960.

In the United States, one-person households increased their share from thirteen percent of all households in 1960 to virtually one-quarter of all households in 1988. France, the Netherlands, and the United Kingdom reached about the same level in the 1980s. Sweden and Germany have even higher proportions of single-person households.

The fastest-growing groups in the living-alone category tend to be young people in their late teens and twenties, the divorced and separated, and the elderly. In many cases, living alone is the choice of people who can afford separate housing coupled with the increased availability of such housing; higher personal incomes and pensions over the past three decades have allowed people who want to live alone to do so. From this point of view, living alone can be seen as a privilege of affluent people and an expression of individual autonomy.

Mothers at Work

The developed countries have witnessed notable increases in women's labor force participation since 1960, with an acceleration in the 1970s. More and more, these increases have involved mothers of dependent children, with profound effects on family life because of the problems of reconciling employment with family responsibilities. Consequently, the availability of child care facilities has become a significant issue for many families in these countries.

51. The Economic Effects of Immigration

Council of Economic Advisers

Excerpted from *Economic Report of the President* (Washington, D.C.: U.S. Government Printing Office, 1986), pp. 219–34. The members of the Council responsible for the report were Chairman Beryl W. Sprinkel and Thomas Gale Moore.

Characteristics of the Foreign Born

The foreign-born population enumerated in the decennial census includes naturalized U.S. citizens as well as aliens, some of whom live here illegally.

Census data show that newly arrived foreign-born residents are younger on average than native born Americans. The median age of those who entered the country between 1970 and 1980 was 26.8 in 1980, compared with 30.0 for the population as a whole. The newly arrived foreign born are predominantly of working age. Seventy-seven percent of those arriving in the United States between 1970 and 1980 were fifteen to sixty-four years of age in 1980, compared with 66 percent of the entire population. The Bureau of the Census estimates that illegal aliens are younger, on average, than legal immigrants.

The 1980 census shows that about half of the foreign born who entered the United States between 1970 and 1980 were female. The proportion of females among illegal aliens, however, is estimated to be lower.

The recently arrived foreign born have larger families than the native born. On the average, there were 3.8 people in families of those who came in the 1970s, compared with 3.3 people in native born families. In addition, the proportion of the foreign born of more than fifteen years of age who are married is higher than that of the native born, and the proportion who are divorced is lower.

The distribution of educational achievement is much broader for the recently arrived foreign born than for the native born. A significant fraction has little education. Among those twenty-five years of age and older who entered the United States between 1970 and 1980, 13 percent completed fewer than five years of school, as compared with 3 percent of the native born. In contrast, 22 percent of the recent arrivals completed four or more years of college, compared with 16 percent of the native born.

Although U.S. immigration policy is based primarily on the humanitarian principles of family reunification and refugee resettlement, most of the foreign born, including illegal aliens, enter the labor force. The employment-to-population ratio of recent arrivals is higher than that of the native born. A higher proportion of the foreign born work in blue-collar and service jobs: 39 percent of recent arrivals had blue-collar jobs compared with 32 percent for all U.S. employed persons; 18 percent held service jobs compared with 13 percent of the U.S. total. The incomes of those who entered the United States between 1970 and 1980 are lower on average than incomes of the native born, but incomes of those who arrived before 1970 are similar.

The recently arrived foreign born are concentrated in a few states. More than half live in California, New York, and Texas. Ten states accounted for 80 percent of total immigrants, and no other states had more than 2 percent of the total. The vast majority of the foreign born live in metropolitan areas; one in five of the recently arrived foreign born live in the Los Angeles area. Illegal alien residents tend to settle in the same areas as legal aliens, but they are even more geographically concentrated. According to estimates based on the 1980 census and INS (Immigration and Naturalization Service) data, 70 percent of illegal aliens were living in California, New York, and Texas, compared with 53 percent of legal alien residents.

Effects of Immigration on Output and Income

The economic benefits of immigration are spread throughout the economy. These include increased job opportunities and higher wages for some workers as well as the widely diffused benefits of lower product prices and higher profits. Many people share in the higher returns on capital because capital ownership is widespread through personal and pension holdings. One in four Americans holds stock directly in U.S. firms. In addition, wage and salary workers own a considerable portion of productive capital, mainly through assets in pension funds. In contrast, job losses or wage reductions that may occur as a result of immigration are likely to be more visible than the economic gains. Such losses are likely to be concentrated among groups who compete directly with immigrant labor.

Some have suggested that labor market displacement may be widespread: In 1980, 6.5 million foreign born residents held jobs, while a total of 7.6 million workers were unemployed. This view implicitly assumes that the number of jobs is fixed and that if immigrants find employment, fewer jobs will be available for the native born.

Arguments supporting the restriction of immigration to protect American jobs are similar to those favoring protectionism in international trade. Restrictions on immigration, however, like restrictions on trade, are costly. Limiting the entry of immigrant labor may increase the demand for some groups of native born workers, but it will impose costs on consumers, investors, and other workers.

Evidence on Labor Market Effects

Studies that take a broad view of the labor market have found no significant evidence of unemployment among native born workers attributable to immigration. Any direct effects of immigration on domestic employment either have been too small to measure or have been quickly dissipated with job mobility. Although existing studies may not be conclusive, the evidence currently available does not suggest that native-born American workers experience significant labor market difficulties in areas that have attracted immigrants. Several studies, moreover, have shown that the presence of immigrants in labor markets is associated with increased job opportunities overall, including job opportunities for native-born minority groups.

The experience of the Los Angeles labor market in adjusting to a growing concentration of unskilled immigrant labor is instructive. One study estimated that more than a million foreign born people settled in Los Angeles County between 1970 and 1983. During the early 1980s the foreign born in Los Angeles County represented close to a third of the total population. Job growth in the area was strong, and the new immigrants were quickly absorbed into the labor market. New immigrant workers accounted for some 70 percent of the net growth in employment in the

1970s. Job gains by native-born workers were predominantly in white-collar occupations, which expanded rapidly. Job growth among immigrants was concentrated mainly in unskilled jobs. Wage growth was lower than the national average for workers in manufacturing, particularly unskilled manufacturing jobs. In jobs outside manufacturing, however, including jobs in services and retail trade, wage growth was higher than the national average. This study also showed that the unemployment rate in Los Angeles, which had exceeded the national average in 1970, fell below the average by the early 1980s. These results were not, of course, the consequence of international migration alone, but they suggest a smooth labor market adjustment to the inflow of migrants.

Legal and Illegal Aliens

Although aliens who are eligible to hold jobs in the United States are clearly distinct from those who are not, researchers have not been able to isolate separate economic effects of illegal alien workers. Demographic differences between legal and illegal aliens may affect their patterns of labor market activity, but those differences appear to be small. Illegal aliens have a higher proportion of males than legal aliens, are younger, and are less likely to bring family members with them. Illegal migrants are likely to remain in the United States for shorter periods of time than legal migrants. Illegal migrants also tend to have lower levels of education and to work in jobs requiring lower skill levels. Illegal aliens may have less incentive to invest in schooling or other activities that are specifically useful in the U.S. labor market.

Legal and illegal aliens tend to settle in the same geographic areas, making it difficult to distinguish their separate labor market effects. Also, deportation risk notwithstanding, many illegal aliens have been living in the United States for a long time; it is estimated that a quarter have been U.S. residents for more than ten years. The economic distinction between legal and illegal aliens is further blurred by the fact that many legal resident aliens were undocumented when they initially entered the United States but later acquired legal status.

Labor Market Absorption of the Foreign Born

Migrants have initial disadvantages in the labor market because many do not speak English, lack familiarity with national customs and institutions, and are not educated and trained for jobs in the United States. As they invest in education and develop skills, their labor market experiences and earnings can be expected to resemble those of the native born.

Conclusion

For much of the nation's history, U.S. immigration policy has been based on the premise that immigrants have a favorable effect on the overall standard of living and on economic development. Analysis of the effects of recent migrant flows bears out this premise. Although an increasing number of migrants, including many illegal aliens, have entered the country in recent years, inflows are still low relative to population and relative to U.S. labor force growth.

International migrants have been readily absorbed into the labor market. Although some displacement may occur, it does not appear that migrants have displaced the native born from jobs or reduced wage levels on a broad scale. There is evidence that immigration has increased job opportunities and wage levels for other workers. Aliens may also provide a net fiscal benefit to the nation, often paying more in taxes than they use in public services. Immigrants come to this country seeking a better life, and their personal investments and hard work provide economic benefits to themselves and to the country as a whole.

The economic gains provided by international migration, however, do not justify the presence or employment of aliens in the United States on an illegal basis. Illegal aliens knowingly defy American laws while their presence establishes claims to economic opportunity and Constitutional protections. As a sovereign nation, the United States must responsibly decide not only who may cross its borders but also who may stay.

CHAPTER VII

Government Growth and Government as Manager

52. The Inevitability of Government Growth
Harold G. Vatter and John F. Walker

Excerpted from *The Inevitability of Government Growth* by Harold G. Vatter and John F. Walker. Copyright © 1985 Columbia University Press. Reprinted with permission of the publisher. Harold G. Vatter is professor emeritus and John F. Walker is professor of economics at Portland State University.

One hundred years ago a conservative German economist, Adolf Wagner, observed that the government had been growing faster than the private sector of the economy for much of the nineteenth century. He predicted that the pattern he observed for that century would continue in the industrial nations as long as they continued to grow. This prediction that the government will grow faster than the rest of the economy has been tested many times in many countries and has always proved correct. Economists now call it Wagner's Law. Since it has been proven correct for many countries for more than a century and has never been found incorrect, it is probably the most accurate economic prediction ever made.

The Era of Big Government

Americans have always thought of big government in peacetime as an ogre to be exorcised if at all possible. But in spite of ourselves the creature

Table 52.1

Government Civilian Employment, Selected Years, 1950–93
(thousands)

Year	Federal	State and local	Total	Civilian labor force	Government employment as percent of civilian labor force
1950	1,928	4,098	6,026	62,208	9.7
1960	2,270	6,083	8,353	69,628	11.0
1965	2,378	7,696	10,074	74,455	13.5
1970	2,731	9,823	12,554	82,771	15.2
1980	2,866	13,375	16,241	106,940	15.2
1987	2,943	14,120	17,063	119,865	14.2
1993	2,914	15,927	21,755	128,040	14.7

Sources: Economic Report of the President, 1988, pp. 284–97. *Economic Report of the President*, 1994, pp. 306–19.

seems to become ever more distended. The federal government, which is deemed out of touch with the grassroots, is particularly derided. Hence it is sporadically vowed with renewed vehemence that the government must be cut down to size at all costs.

A whole series of presidents have taken this vow. President Carter liked to discuss an era of governmental limits and asserted that government could not do everything. President Reagan unabashedly called for a reduction in the share of the economy going to the government. That is, these presidents have asserted that Wagner's Law must and can come to an end. But they have also advocated economic growth and a further expansion of the benefits of the modern industrial economy, which they mistakenly associate with an end to the growth of government.

After 1970 the growth rate of government employment slowed. For six years all government civilian employment hovered about its historic peak of some 16 million people. Federal employment, always much smaller than combined state and local employment, is only slightly higher today than it was in 1970. Only the state and local work force has continued its invincible upward creep, although it too has distinctly slowed. Thus on balance it begins to look, at least on the basis of the employment criterion, as though the first phase of a stoppage may have been completed. These changes may be seen in Table 52.1 for government employment.

The concomitant battle of the government cutters to call a halt on the expenditures front also seems to have been victorious—at least in the relative sense of government spending as a share of total economic activity. Government purchases of goods and services amounted to about 21.5 percent of GNP in 1970 and 20.4 percent in 1987. Voila!

Modern conservative economic advisers describe the government as an institution hampering growth and taking resources away from the "productive" private sector. Wagner also divides the economy into private and public sectors, but Wagner, an adviser to Otto von Bismarck, did not see government as unproductive.

There is more to the size of government than nominal public spending and employment, as every regulated person or group, every lobbyist, every tax accountant, every military contractor, every subsidized farmer knows full well. We have connected government and private employment in many ways. For example, when we decide to build a Star Wars defense system, we do not need more soldiers, we need more physicists, technicians, and assemblers in the laboratories and factories of the private sector. But surely government causes those nominally private jobs.

Budget and employment measures do not get at the true influence of the government on the economy. There is another criterion for measuring the size or influence of the government in the economy and society. The criterion is administrative involvement in the economic and social process. We find that the growth of administrative involvement is the basic change in the character of Wagner's Law that has developed in the twentieth century. Such involvement encompasses a wide range of government guidance programs, but they usually employ very few people and often do not cost very much money. However, they exert sufficient government influence over the way the so-called private sector behaves to eliminate the notion of truly "private" activities in many of our industries and in the economy and society at large.

The Keynesian perception of unemployment equilibrium that so mightily contributed to the establishment of the mixed economy in the United States and elsewhere in the 1930s is a phenomenon of the highest import for anticipating the government's future role. As crystallized in the Employment Act of 1946, a powerful new social consensus assigned to government permanent responsibility for overcoming the failure of the market to provide sustained high employment. Many of the heterogeneous social and political components from that consensus were quite unaware that anything had gone awry with the private investment growth mechanism. What was perceived was only the immediate malaise.

The experience since the end of World War II is that the U.S. economy grows at about 4 percent per year when government spending grows rapidly and at only a little more than 2 percent per year when government spending grows slowly. This is illustrated in Table 52.2.

Table 52.2

**Average Annual Compound Percentage Growth Rates, GNP and
Government Purchases** (1982 dollars)

Period	GNP/GDP	Government purchases
1947–53	5.3	15.1
1953–60	2.0	0.5
1961–68	4.5	5.0
1969–83	2.2	0.6
1983–87	3.9	4.5
1987–93	2.1	1.1

Source: Calculated from *Economic Report of the President*, 1988, pp. 250–51, using centered three-year averages; *Economic Report of the President*, 1994, pp. 270–71.

Although there have been many prophets forecasting extensive periods of rapid economic growth with little or no government growth, we have not had such a period since about 1910. We have every reason to believe that such a period is impossible in the contemporary U.S. economy. Presidents, presidential candidates, the U.S. Congress, and the aggregate of state and local government officials that push for significant reductions in public spending are advocating deliberate sabotage of the material betterment that Americans so dearly and proudly cherish.

The public decision to discard laissez-faire over a half century ago in the United States, and the subsequent rise of big government, was an irreversible change. That upheaval created in the form of the "mixed economy" a partial but growing fusion of the market system with a greatly enlarged government sector. Big government changed the composition of total demand. It cut private household consumption from laissez-faire's three-fourths to about two-thirds of total spending. Already by the end of the Great Depression government purchases had permanently superseded gross business investment in plant and equipment, making it the second largest of the four great spending streams.

Business investment developments reveal in microcosm much of the history of business-government manipulative involvement. Still erroneously considered an almost sacred source of economic growth and productivity rise, business succeeded in making "private" investment the spoiled child of public policy. Public mortgage risk underwriting, sympathetic interest rate policies, liberal depreciation tax privileges, investment tax credits, and corporate bailouts have been easily wrung from many a willing Congress and Federal Reserve Bank, allaying the earlier business fear of big government's "interference." The interference was so benign that, unlike household consumption of private market products, the share of strategic plant and equipment investment in GNP has persistently remained as high as it was in the laissez-faire 1920s.

President Reagan and Congressman Jack Kemp were associated with a relatively new group of semi-Keynesian conservatives called supply-side economists. This group has a hoary faith in the power of private investment spending on capital goods to lead an economic expansion—hence, all the public inducements and tax subsidies, especially to "private" investment in business plant and equipment.

But the history of such investment belies these alleged powers. Technological advance has made improved capital goods so productive that the growth of expenditures on them typically creates more capacity to supply additional products than demand for those additional products. So unless the net production of such investment goods is restrained to its customary proportions, 10 to 11 percent of total demand, depressing excess capacity results. Capital saving investment has killed itself off as a demand growth stimulus by its own capacity-raising successes.

It is distressing to the supply-siders but most instructive to the rest of us to realize, for example, that from 1968 to 1985 real gross business investment spending on producers' durable equipment rose at a vigorous 4.33 percent a year, yet GNP expanded at only a sickly 2.5 percent a year. High (publicly subsidized) investment has not, therefore, despite the conventional wisdom of the supply-siders and their followers, been necessarily connected with high growth rates of total product. Instead, we had in that distressingly long period under-utilized capacity and relatively slow growth.

It is essential to appreciate these limitations of the growth role of investment, not only to dispel supply-side illusions, but more important, to grasp the vital notion that autonomously rising government expenditures are in the long run the only escape from the contemporary economic stagnation malaise. Yet so overwhelming is the public denial of the usefulness of public spending that almost no one dares express the notion that we need it to maintain economic growth—even the minority who is conscious of it.

Application of the principle that the economy needs growing demand to buy the growing supply that investment creates yields the bottom line for the future growth of government spending: It must rise approximately as fast as GNP (as it did from 1983 to 1988 under the stimulus of large, unwanted federal government deficits). In the past it has grown faster. Between 1968 and the recession trough of 1982 government spending stopped growing approximately as fast as GNP, explaining the long-run slowdown in GNP growth. Whatever the future growth rate of government spending, it will be a policy decision.

But in the future we can add to government's spending growth the element of pervasive public involvement in much, if not most, of the economy's activities. This additional element of public participation will assure total government's continued relative growth.

Some of what we call public involvement in the economy is no doubt represented in the expenditure or employment totals. There is a certain overlap. But very substantial kinds of public intervention bear little connection with either the budget or the number of employees in the pertinent agencies. For example, the government performs a vast oversight and assistance role in the activities of our financial institutions and related financial markets. But its great influence on that sector is insufficiently expressed in the number of people working for the Securities and Exchange Commission, the Federal Deposit Insurance Corporation, the Federal Reserve Banks, the Farm Credit Administration, the Home Loan Bank Board, or the section of the Internal Revenue Service that indulges "financially troubled" banks.

53. Real Public-Sector Employment Growth, Wagner's Law, and Economic Growth in the United States
Harold G. Vatter and John F. Walker

Reprinted with permission of the original publishers, Foundation Journal Public Finance, The Hague, from *Public Finance/Finances Publiques* 41 (1986), pp. 116–38. Harold G. Vatter is professor emeritus and John F. Walker is professor of economics at Portland State University.

John Musgrave's estimates of the federal government's constant dollar gross stock of fixed capital (structures and equipment) show that the magnitude jumped from 2.4 percent of all fixed nonresidential gross capital stock in 1929 to 13.5 percent in 1949 but thereafter fell steadily to only 8.8 percent in 1979. This is hardly in accord with the constancy of federal employment relative to the total civilian labor force after 1949 or with the many pecuniary measures of federal government growth after 1949. Furthermore, the federal percentage jump from 1929 to 1949 reflects in large part the special circumstance that the private capital stock grew only 7 percent in that twenty years. If we turn to the state and local stock, the trend record is similar; the percentage is 25 in 1929, jumps to 41 in 1939, and rises only to 44 in the next four decades. This conflicts with everything we know about the rise in the relative importance of state and local government, on any measure, after World War II. Therefore, we conclude that the use of the public capital stock is an inappropriate criterion for appraising the relative growth of government.

This paper is concerned with the United States and apprises the growth of government therein, particularly since 1929, using employment mainly, but not exclusively, as the measure. It is thus concerned with the long-run record of real human resources engaged. The federal and the state and local (S&L) levels are also disaggregated. The appraisal furthermore treats the size and character of the government sector as it impinges upon economic growth.

Despite the commendable work of Morris Beck and others on real public-sector growth, an expenditure approach is seriously flawed in its capacity to show trends in absolute, and even relative, real resource absorption. This is readily acknowledged by Beck et al. All-government expenditure and purchase totals suffer from the distressing effort to form a single separate package out of the federal and S&L totals, and then to sum the two into one aggregate encompassing: (1) purchases, mostly of goods, from the private sector; (2) purchases of the services of government employees; and (3) transfer payments to persons, net grants-in-aid from the federal to the S&L governments (and net interest paid). What such a heroic summation process can show, and what it signifies regarding impact, is not easy to discern. The procedure is beset with much more precarious pitfalls than GNP calculation because there is only a handful of components. Furthermore, conversion from nominal to real expenditure aggregates requires selection of the appropriate deflator. A word of our own on this seems in order.

One difficulty would arise from the selection of a deflator for government purchase of goods. When the government contracts to purchase eight hundred fighters at $17 million apiece, no reasonable person believes this stipulates that the government will either buy eight hundred fighters or pay $17 million apiece for however many it eventually buys. To describe correctly the prices government pays and the quantities it receives, we need actual payments made. Unfortunately, for major military durable contacts and public works that means the public prices are incalculable for many years after the purchase decision is made. This may be readily appreciated with regard to the important element of military goods, for which no reasonable deflator can be constructed.

Again with respect to labor services, there is a 14-percentage point difference between two sources, the government services purchases deflator from the United States Department of Commerce and the annual government employee earnings deflator from the Tax Foundation. To deflate the heterogeneous all-government expenditures collection, to say nothing of disaggregated levels of government, is thus a heroic task much in need of alternative perspectives such as ours.

In summary, the development of our modern industrial nation has been accompanied by a proliferation of socially expressed demands for public solutions to broad human problems. These demands and their solutions, while typically shot through with economic content, have nonetheless played an exogenous role vis-à-vis the operation of the private market system. Hence, government has been able to act as balancing wheel in the intermediate time period and growth stimulator in the longer run.

Beck's ratio of real total government expenditure (including transfers and interest payments) to real GDP is about 29 percent for 1977. His expenditures include the military outlays. A calculation of the military plus civilian total public employment, inclusive of S&L education, yields 17,520,000 people for 1977. This figure, comparable to Beck, was 17.7 percent of the civilian labor force. Since the chief reason for the expansion of all civilian government, looked at from the pecuniary viewpoint, was the growth of transfers, it should be no surprise that public employment, which scarcely responds to transfer payment increase, reveals a much lesser rise in the relative importance of government.

Our aggregate ratio of government to total employment is still far below the figure for all-government involvement based on pecuniary criteria. On the other hand, if only *government purchases* are considered, Beck's ratio to real GDP plummets to only 13.4 percent, and the use of the employment criterion as a measure of level gives a notably larger importance to government in the economy; i.e., it suggests that the government sector is labor intensive.

Our measurements of the relative size of government using employment indicate that government excluding transfers is bigger than Beck's results, and including transfers is smaller than Beck's results. So intuitively our results on the relative size of government are reasonable and conform with the results of his more extensive study.

We now turn to disaggregation of the all-government employment totals, using the breakdown of federal compared with S&L.

The contrasting record of the two levels of government is most striking and informative. Both levels of government contribute to the long-run rise in the relative importance of public employment in the 1930s, but only the fast-growing federal government leads in the 1940s. Thereafter, the federal government's position in the total labor force remains fixed, without any discernible trend. But S&L employment, on a decadal basis, continues its trend of rising relative importance for the entire half century that begins in the Great Depression. In other words, the rise in all-government's comparative importance after World War II is entirely due to the growth of the state and local governments, and the importance of federal civilian employment in total public civilian employment declines from rather over half of S&L employment (excluding education) in 1949 to less than one-third in 1979. Including education in S&L employment involves a fall of the federal share of total civilian government employment from less than a third to only 15 percent over the same period. A "new federalism" directed toward transferring government activity from the federal to the state and local levels of operation (if not financing) would not be at all new but would only accentuate a decentralization trend that has long been taking place in terms of real labor resources committed. The administration of the contemporary mixed economy has thus long been overwhelmingly and increasingly in the hands of the "grassroots" employee echelons. This is consistent with what Wallace E. Oates found for expenditures in a number of advanced countries over the period 1950–70.

The process of decentralization after World War II is similarly reflected in pecuniary criteria. For example, with respect to civilian expenditures, in current dollars S&L purchases of goods and services increased from 150 percent of federal nondefense outlays in 1949 to 442 percent in 1979. Even if S&L purchases from their own revenue sources (i.e., excluding grants-in-aid from the federal government) are used for the comparison, the S&L expenditures rose sharply, from 119 percent of federal nonmilitary outlays for goods and services in 1949 to 299 percent in 1979. If all federal purchases, including national defense, are related to S&L purchases, decentralization is still the pattern: S&L/federal is 88 percent in 1949, 182 percent in 1979; and the rise is still true when the trend is calculated from S&L's own revenue sources.

In terms of civilian real expenditures for "collective consumption," or government purchases of goods and services, in 1979 the federal government total was about one-fifth the S&L purchases of goods and services. But federal civilian employment in that year (excluding DOD) was only about 15 percent of S&L employment (including education). This would seem to be a sensible comparison. It might suggest that the federal government was doing more (purchases) with less labor than the S&L governments. However, federal purchases of services were substantially enlarged compared to S&L purchases by the fact that the average annual nominal earnings per federal employee were 40 percent higher than S&L (including education) average earnings; and real earnings were 44 percent higher. More, "new federalism" would entail a sectoral shift to lower-wage public employment, a shift that would reduce real all-government collective consumption in pecuniary terms even if the number of government employees was not decreased.

54. The Midwest Response to the New Federalism
Peter K. Eisinger and William T. Gormley

Reprinted with permission of the publisher from Eisinger, Peter K., and Gormley, William T., Jr., eds., *The Midwest Response to the New Federalism*. LaFollette Public Policy Series. © 1988 (Madison: University of Wisconsin Press), pp. 3–6. Peter K. Eisinger is professor and chairman of the Department of Political Science at the University of Wisconsin–Madison. William T. Gormley is professor of political science at the University of Wisconsin–Madison and associate director of the Robert M. LaFollette Institute.

Federal involvement in the domestic policy concerns that so greatly fueled federal expansion in the 1960s and early 1970s began to contract in the eighties, leading to a transformation in the system of intergovernmental relations in the United States. This contraction involves several different developments. The most dramatic is the reduction of federal fiscal assistance to states and cities, ending an upward trend that began during the Depression. The high point for intergovernmental fiscal assistance was 1978: in that year Washington passed down $231 per capita in grants-in-aid (in constant 1972 dollars) to subnational governments, fully 3.7 percent of the gross national product. In the next year real spending for such aid declined by 2.6 percent, as Congress eliminated several antirecessionary programs. Then Ronald Reagan was elected on a platform to reduce the size of the federal government even more, and by 1985 per capita spending for grants-in-aid had fallen to $180. The aggregate total amounted only to 2.8 percent of GNP (see Table 54.1). Federal aid as a proportion of state and local budgets fell from 26 percent in 1978 to just over 20 percent by 1983. In constant dollars the real value of federal aid to state and local governments fell by 39 percent from 1980 to 1987.

A second development concerns the consolidation of nearly eighty categorical grants into several block grants and the elimination of several other programs, such as General Revenue Sharing. When President Reagan took office, there were by one count 539 different intergovernmental aid programs; by 1984 that figure had dropped to 404. The federal implications of block grant consolidation—since 1981 Congress has established ten of them—have been to devolve administration and policy-

Table 54.1

Federal Grants-in-Aid to State and Local Government

Fiscal year	Amount in current dollars (in billions)	Percent of state-local own-source receipts	Amount in constant (1972) dollars	Percent real Increase or decrease over previous year
1955	3.5	11.8	5.6	3.7
1960	7.0	16.8	10.8	8.0
1965	10.9	17.7	15.5	5.4
1970	24.0	22.9	27.3	11.6
1975	49.8	29.1	39.2	3.4
1980	91.5	31.7	48.2	0.2
1984	97.6	23.7	41.3	1.5
1987 est.	100.4	19.5	37.7	−6.0

Source: Significant Features of Fiscal Federalism. (Washington, D.C.: Advisory Commission on Intergovernmental Relations, 1985), p. 19.

making responsibilities to the states for programs once controlled more closely by Washington.

A third development has involved the federal effort to reduce Washington's regulatory role in the affairs of state and local governments. Part of this effort has been a concomitant of block grant consolidation. For example, regulations implementing seven health and social service block grants were reduced to the extent that the paperwork burden on subnational governments fell by an estimated 83 percent between 1981 and 1982, according to the Office of Management and Budget. There may be less to these figures than meets the eye because the benefits of deregulation do not seem to have "trickled down" to local governments. Thus, a common state response to relaxed federal mandates has been to impose tighter restrictions on local governments. Nevertheless, federal regulations and state regulations may differ in kind, if not in volume. Certainly there is no denying that a significant amount of regulatory responsibility has been turned over to the states in such fields as environmental protection, surface mining reclamation, and occupational safety.

The object of all these developments has been a self-conscious attempt, impelled both by ideological commitment to limited government and by the fiscal pressure generated by high federal deficits, to reduce the programmatic scope and capability of the national government in domestic affairs. The reduction of federal interest in domestic policy and the deliberate effort to devolve responsibilities to the states is commonly known as the "new federalism."

Scholars may argue that characterizing the current pattern in intergovernmental relations as new betrays a substantial ignorance of American history. During the nineteenth century the national government left much of domestic policy in the hands of the states, and the concept of intergovernmental fiscal assistance was rudimentary at best. In the early 1970s President Nixon sought to reduce federal involvement in domestic matters in the name of a new federalism by devolving power "back to the people" through the novel instrumentality of block grants. The Housing and Community Development block grant of 1974 and the Comprehensive Employment and Training Act of 1973 were products of that effort. Nixon was unable, however, to stem the rising level of intergovernmental aid. Indeed, federal aid increased sharply during the Nixon years.

It is also important to contrast Reagan's new federalism with the Supreme Court's old federalism during the same time period. In case after case, the Supreme Court upheld the authority of the federal government to preempt state and local governments (wholly or partially) in areas "in or affecting interstate commerce." In *Hodel v. Virginia Surface Mining and Reclamation Association* (1981), the Supreme Court upheld a federal statute making state regulation of strip mining conditional upon acceptance of minimum federal standards. In *FERC v. Mississippi* (1982), the Supreme Court supported a congressional requirement that state public utility commissions "consider and determine" the merits of rate structure reforms aimed at promoting energy conservation. In *United Transportation Union v. Long Island Railroad Company* (1982), the Supreme Court upheld the application of the federal Railroad Labor Act to state-owned railroads. In *Equal Employment Opportunity Commission v. Wyoming* (1983), the Supreme Court extended the federal government's ban on age discrimination to state and local governments. In *Garcia v. San Antonio Metropolitan Transit Authority* (1985), the Supreme Court extended federal minimum wage and overtime pay provisions to state and local governments, thus reversing the Supreme Court's own ruling in *National League of Cities v. Usery* (1976). Yet while the Supreme Court has been zigging, President Reagan has been zagging, and with greater effort. The Supreme Court's impact has been significant only in particular policy domains, such as labor relations. In contrast, the Reagan administration's new federalism has had a broader impact.

Reagan's New Federalism

What is unusual about federal developments in the 1980s is not simply the scope of change, but the conjunction of diminished federal fiscal aid and program initiatives with continuing high public expectations of an array of domestic programs solidly in place. State and local governments are expected, in short, to shoulder responsibilities dropped or passed back as options by the federal government, even though Washington has declined to offer the policy leadership to help them do so and has cut fiscal assistance. By 1985 the talk at the annual meeting of the nation's mayors was of the "new localism," a strategy based on building coalitions with the private sector "to fill the resource gap left by dismantling the Federal programs." At the annual meeting of the Council of State Governments, former governor of Mississippi William Winter noted that "we can no longer depend on Federal largesse. What we do now is based on our own devices and our own resources."

The irony of the new federalism is that decreased federal aid sometimes coincides with increased federal requirements: At any rate, this is true of transportation policy, welfare policy, and environmental policy. In some instances—for example, environmental policy—regulatory federalism is the result of congressional action unsuccessfully opposed by the Reagan administration. In transportation policy and welfare policy, however, regulatory federalism has been embraced by an administration supposedly committed to deregulation and states' rights. Thus, in evaluating the new federalism, we must distinguish between rhetoric and practice, which do not always coincide.

55. A Microeconomic Analysis of the Tax Reform Act of 1986
Council of Economic Advisers

Reprinted from the *Economic Report of the President* (Washington, D.C.: U.S. Government Printing Office, 1987), pp. 83–87. The members of the council responsible for the report were Chairman Beryl W. Sprinkel, Thomas Gale Moore, and Michael L. Mussa.

The Personal Income Tax

The Tax Reform Act (TRA) significantly lowers tax rates on personal income. When the law is fully effective in 1988, two tax brackets, set at 15 and 28 percent, will replace the fourteen that ranged from 11 to 50 percent. The 15 percent bracket and the personal exemption are phased out for high-income returns, which results in an implicit 33 percent tax rate for a broad income range. TRA reduces average tax rates to levels that are similar to those that prevailed in 1965.

These rate reductions are made possible, in part, by TRA's base-broadening measures. TRA broadens the personal tax base, or taxable personal income, to include the following: all long-term capital gains, state and local sales taxes, IRA contributions for high-income individuals with employer-provided pension plans, nonmortgage consumer interest payments, miscellaneous itemized deductions of less than 2 percent of adjusted gross income, net losses from passive investment, and net losses from active real estate investments for high-income taxpayers. These base-broadening measures are partially offset by substantial increases in the standard deduction and personal exemption. By 1988, the personal exemption is nearly doubled, and the standard deduction is increased 36 percent for joint returns and 21 percent for single returns.

TRA limits tax shelters directly and indirectly. The elimination of the capital gains preference, the deceleration of tax depreciation deductions, more stringent limitations on investment interest deductions, and the lowering of marginal tax rates all serve indirectly to make tax shelters less attractive. Moreover, any remaining tax avoidance opportunities are subjected to TRA's provisions concerning passive business losses and real estate losses. In particular, net losses from passive business investments and real estate investments for high-income taxpayers cannot be deducted from ordinary income; they must be carried forward and deducted from net income from like activities in later years.

These tax-shelter limitations not only make the personal income tax more equitable, but they should also result in more economically efficient investment decisions. Investments that previously provided opportunities for tax avoidance are put on a more equal footing with other investments. Investment funds, therefore, should have a greater tendency to flow to their most highly valued uses.

The elimination of the nonmortgage consumer interest deduction should also improve the current allocation of investment funds. Consumer durables yield a flow of services that, unlike alternative investments yielding monetary income, is untaxed. By disallowing nonmortgage consumer interest deductions, TRA partially eliminates the tax preference that is currently afforded to consumer durables. TRA, therefore, puts consumer durables on a more equal footing with alternative investments and should lead to more efficient investment decisions.

Allowing state and local taxes to be deducted from the federal income tax base is both inefficient and inequitable. It is inefficient because it reduces the perceived cost of state and local government services and, except possibly in cases where state spending generates appreciable spillover benefits, encourages excessive state and local spending. It is inequitable because it causes residents of low-tax localities, who enjoy relatively small amounts of state and local government services, to pay a disproportionate share of federal taxes. TRA ameliorates these problems in two ways: It disallows the state and local sales tax deduction, and, by lowering the marginal federal tax rate, it lowers the value of other state and local deductions.

TRA disallows IRA deductions for high-income individuals with employer-provided pension plans. However, it still allows most working individuals to deposit $2,000 (nondeductible) each year in IRAs and defer tax on accrued interest until the funds are withdrawn at retirement. This tax advantage is substantial, accounting for a large portion of the tax savings afforded by deductible IRAs.

Although TRA significantly limits itemized deductions, it substantially raises the standard deduction. As a result, it is estimated to reduce the number of itemized personal federal income tax returns in 1988 by 11.5 million, thereby yielding an approximate $1.3 billion reduction in compliance costs.

Equity

TRA will cut total personal income taxes by about 6.6 percent in 1988. Table 55.1 gives the percentage tax cut for eight income classes. The estimates are based on an expanded definition of income that equals adjustment gross income plus such items as excluded capital gains, passive business losses, and tax-exempt bond interest.

The percentage tax cut under TRA is largest for low-income returns. The number of poor families paying federal income tax is estimated to fall by 4.3 million in 1988 under TRA. With one small exception, the estimated percentage tax cut under TRA steadily falls for higher-income returns. Thus, these estimates indicate that TRA actually increases the effective progressivity of the personal federal income tax despite a less graduated rate structure. This result is shown in the last two columns of Table 55.1, which give the estimated average tax rate for each income class under TRA and the prereform tax law. TRA cuts the average tax rates much more for taxpayers with income less than $50,000 than it does for higher-income taxpayers.

Table 55.1 concerns only personal federal income taxes. Because all taxes are ultimately paid by individuals, a complete analysis of tax incidence would allocate undistributed corporate income and federal corporate taxes to the various income classes. Exactly how this should be done, however, is uncertain. Current evidence is not conclusive, but it suggests that part of the corporate tax burden is borne by workers and that the majority is borne by owners of capital. If this inference is correct, it would imply that high-income taxpayers, who earn a disproportionate share of

Table 55.1

Effects of the Tax Reform Act of 1986 on Federal Tax Liabilities and Average Federal, Personal Income Tax Rates, by Income Class, 1988

Income class (1986 dollars)[a]	Percent change in Income tax liability	Average tax rate (percent)	
		Prereform	TRA
0 to 10,000	−56.2	2.0	0.9
10,000 to 15,000	−27.8	5.4	3.9
15,000 to 20,000	−14.8	7.0	6.0
20,000 to 30,000	−8.5	8.9	8.1
30,000 to 50,000	−7.1	11.0	10.3
50,000 to 100,000	−0.9	13.9	13.7
100,000 to 200,000	−1.0	17.4	17.1
200,000 and over	−0.9	13.6	13.4
All income classes	−6.6	10.3	9.5

Source: Department of the Treasury, Office of Tax Analysis.

Note: Distributions reflect most but not all of the provisions of the individual income tax code.

[a]The income concept (modified expanded income) is one of many possible income classifiers and was used by the Joint Committee on Taxation to present the distributional effects of the Tax Reform Act of 1986. An alternative measure, "economic income," was used in the Treasury Department's *The President's Tax Proposals* in 1985.

capital income, bear a relatively large share of the corporate tax burden. Because TRA shifts 6.6 percent of the individual income tax burden to corporations, it would follow that a proper imputation of corporate taxes to the various income classes would probably reinforce the conclusion that TRA enhances the effective progressivity of the federal income tax.

TRA increases the long-run horizontal equity of the federal income tax. Horizontal equity concerns the degree to which taxpayers with equal amounts of economic income have equal tax liabilities. Because of TRA's limitations on tax preference, limitations on tax shelters, and a stricter minimum tax, it substantially reduces the variation in the amount of tax paid by taxpayers with the same real income.

As does any significant reform of the tax system, TRA will cause a one-time change in asset values that will redistribute wealth. Special transition rules make these changes in asset values less severe in some cases. The deductions for passive business losses and real estate losses attributable to assets acquired prior to tax reform, for example, are phased out gradually over four years. The same is true for deductions of interest payments on preexisting nonmortgage loans.

This phenomenon of changing asset values is one reason changes in the tax law should be infrequent and implemented only for compelling reasons. Investments tend to be inherently risky; further riskiness introduced by frequent changes in the tax law unnecessarily destabilizes the business environment.

Business Taxes

The proper measurement of economic income from investments in real assets requires that deductions be made for the decline in real asset values attributable to depreciation. Since 1954, tax law has allowed investors to deduct for more rapid depreciation on most assets than actually occurs. Accelerating depreciation in this manner lowers the cost of capital, which is defined as the minimum pretax investment return that is profitable. The cost of capital has also been reduced by the investment tax credit, which applied primarily to equipment assets and allowed investors to deduct a percentage of an asset's purchase price immediately from tax liabilities.

TRA repeals the investment tax credit, allows less accelerated depreciation, and lowers the corporate tax rate from 46 to 34 percent. These provisions taken together have two general effects: They tend to raise the cost of capital overall, and they tend to equalize the cost of capital for alternative capital investments. The latter effect is due primarily to more equal effective rates of tax on investments in corporate equipment and corporate structures.

TRA substantially increases the cost of debt-financed capital investments. This result follows largely because the value of interest deductions falls with the fall in corporate and personal tax rates.

56. Do Taxes Change Behavior?
Council of Economic Advisers

Reprinted from the *Economic Report of the President* (Washington, D.C.: U.S. Government Printing Office, 1994), pp. 88–89. The members of the council responsible for the report were Chairman Laura D'Andrea Tyson, Alan S. Blinder, and Joseph E. Stiglitz.

A central tenet of economics is that relative prices matter. Taxes on capital and wage income change the relationships among the various prices that people face when deciding how much to save, invest, and work, and thus have an effect on the way people choose to allocate their time (between supplying labor and taking leisure) and their income (between current consumption and saving). This observation serves as the basis of the supply-side dictum that a reduction in taxes, by inducing people to work harder and save more, can induce higher rates of investment and economic growth.

The extent to which changes in the marginal tax rate on income affect labor supply and saving has been a subject of extensive research for many years. The preponderance of evidence seems to indicate that the changes are small. Saving rates seem to be little affected by movements in after-tax interest rates, and hours worked and labor force participation rates for most demographic groups show only limited sensitivity to changes in after-tax wages.

It is undeniable that the sharp reduction in taxes in the early 1980s was a strong impetus to economic growth. But it is unlikely that the principal source of this growth was people reacting to reductions in marginal tax rates by working and saving more. The expansion that took place over the 1980s was tax-induced mainly insofar as lower taxes raised disposable income, which led to increased consumption. For example, between 1981 and 1986, the consumption share of GDP increased from 64.5 percent to 67.4 percent. In other words, the 1980s saw a classical Keynesian, demand-driven expansion—not the kind of expansion that supply-side theory predicted. Those who would point to the effects of the 1980s tax cuts as evidence of strong supply-side effects of taxation are grossly overstating the case.

The increases in the top marginal income tax rates enacted by the Congress in 1993 will affect directly only the top 1.2 percent of American families. Moreover, top marginal tax rates remain low by historical standards. While some individuals may alter their behavior because of the higher tax rates and, for example, cut back their hours worked, others may actually increase their work effort in order to meet saving or consumption objectives. Overall, it is unlikely that the administration's plan will induce large responses in labor force participation, hours worked, or savings in overall economy.

57. Do Higher Tax Rates Increase Tax Revenues?
Council of Economic Advisers

Reprinted from the *Economic Report of the President* (Washington, D.C.: U.S. Government Printing Office, 1994), p. 89. The members of the council responsible for the report were Chairman Laura D'Andrea Tyson, Alan S. Blinder, and Joseph E. Stiglitz.

Some argue that tax collections do not vary much when top marginal tax rates increase or decrease. In this view, an increase in income tax rates provides such a strong incentive for people to reduce their taxable income that the tax base shrinks and no additional revenue is generated. For example, a worker facing higher taxes on wages might choose to take some compensation in the form of nonwage benefits, such as more vacation time or larger future pensions. Similarly, individuals facing higher tax rates on unearned income might change the composition of their savings (while keeping the level constant) by investing in tax-exempt bonds rather than stocks or corporate debt.

History can serve as a guide to determining whether these offsetting effects of a change in tax rates are strong enough to have a significant impact on revenues. For the United States, contrary to the supply-siders' claims, income tax cuts have generally reduced income tax revenues, and tax increases have generally raised them.

(1)   The 1964 tax cut reduced the top marginal rate from 91 percent in 1963 to 77 percent in 1964 and then to 70 percent in 1965. Income tax revenues as a share of GDP dropped sharply.

(2)   The special Vietnam War surtax imposed additional charges equal to 7.5 percent of tax in 1968, 10 percent in 1969, and 2.5 percent in 1970. The result was a sharp increase in revenues in 1968 and 1969, followed by a decline as the surtax was phased out.

(3)   The 1981 tax cut reduced the top marginal rate from 70 percent to 50 percent in 1982 and cut tax rates for lower-income individuals over the 1982–84 period. Since then, personal income tax revenues as a share of GDP have never regained their 1981–82 levels.

(4)   Similarly, the 1986 tax reform reduced marginal rates in stages over 1987 and 1988, and revenues as a share of GDP in 1988 fell slightly below their 1986 level.

In short, evidence from postwar experience strongly suggests that personal income tax revenues rise when marginal rates are increased, and fall when marginal rates are reduced.

58. Activist Government: Key to Growth

Walter W. Heller

Reprinted with permission of the publishers M.E. Sharpe, Inc., from *Challenge*, March/April 1986, pp. 4–10. Walter W. Heller was regents' professor of economics at the University of Minnesota and chairman of the Council of Economic Advisers under Presidents Kennedy and Johnson.

In a period when government activism, especially in economic affairs, is under attack—indeed, when President Reagan, charming, disarming, and sometimes alarming, tells the country that government's impact on the economy is somewhere between baneful and baleful and that the greatest contribution he can make is to get government's clammy hands out of our pockets and government monkeys off our backs—against that background, the Joint Economic Committee's fortieth anniversary is an especially appropriate time to take stock of the role government has played and should play in the economy.

Let me begin with a broad-brush comparison of U.S. economic performance in the pre- and post-activist eras, with World War II being a convenient dividing line.

First, with respect to comparative economic stability: Excluding the Great Depression of the 1930s—for including it would make all comparisons a statistical cakewalk for postwar economic activism—we find that the prewar economy spent roughly a year in recession for every year of expansion. Postwar, it has been one year in recession for every four years of expansion. Pre-1930 recessions were not only much longer but much deeper than postwar recessions, with a standard deviation relative to trend growth that was twice as great prewar as postwar. The shape of the typical prewar cycle was a deep, symmetrical V, but postwar it was more of a shallow checkmark.

Second, as to comparative economic growth: updating some of Arthur Okun's numbers, I find that the era of economic activism wins again. Compared with an average real growth rate of 2.8 percent from 1909 to 1929 (and 2.3 percent from 1929 to 1948), the postwar pace was a hefty 3.8 percent before slowing down after 1973 and lagging even more in the eighties.

Third, as to the comparative use of our GNP potential: The postwar activist economy operated far closer to its potential than the prewar economy. Measuring the "net gap" under the trend lines connecting prosperity years, one finds that the gap averaged 5 percent of GNP, prewar, even leaving out the Great Depression, but less than 1 percent postwar (from 1948 to 1979).

The Impact of Public Policy

Now, where has that progress come from? You would not expect me to give the same answer that Richard Nixon gave an audience in Jackson, Mississippi, during the 1960 campaign, when he noted that the mayor told him that they had a doubling of population during his twelve years as mayor. Nixon went on to say: "Where has that progress come from? That progress has not come primarily from government, but it has come from the activities of hundreds of thousands of individual Mississippians, given an opportunity to develop their own lives."

Contrary to Mr. Nixon's answer, I would agree with Okun that the improved performance record, especially the greater economic stability, must be credited to public policy. As he put it, "It was made in Washington." The automatic stabilizing effect of a larger public sector—both on the tax and on the spending sides—undoubtedly played an important role. Coupled with it was an aggressive fiscal-monetary policy that, while not always on time and on target, assured private decision makers that recessions would be relatively short and shallow and depressions a thing of the past.

Paralleling the improved economic performance in the postwar era of economic activism was a dramatic decline in the incidence of poverty. From an estimated 33 percent of the population in 1947, poverty fell by one-third, to 22 percent, by 1960—a decline that must be attributed primarily to economic growth plus some increases in public assistance and transfer programs. Then came the uninterrupted growth of the 1960s, coupled with the War on Poverty and other Great Society programs, which cut the remaining poverty in half.

Contrary to Mr. Reagan's assertion that "in the early sixties we had fewer people living below the poverty line than we had in the later sixties after the Great War on Poverty got under way," the president's 1985 *Economic Report* (page 264) shows us that the percent of the population in poverty dropped steadily from 22 percent in 1960, to 19 percent in 1964, to 12 percent in 1969 and then bottomed out at 11 percent in 1973. From then until 1980, growing transfer payments just managed to offset sluggish economic performance, and poverty stayed in the 11–12 percent range until it shot upward in the 1980s.

Down Memory Lane

The early postwar years were really vintage years in our fiscal-policy annals. We ran appropriate surpluses (that alone shows I'm dealing in ancient history) in 1947 and 1948. Then, in mid-1950, the Joint Economic Committee, in one of its finest hours, recognized the inflationary potential of the Korean War and led the charge to reverse gears, i.e., to take a tax cut that was halfway through the congressional mill and help convert it to a tax increase. When Ike dismantled the Truman-era wage-price control in 1953, demand had been so successfully curbed that wages and prices hardly budged. In fact, 1952–56 were years of calm on the inflation front.

But the 1953–60 period, with three recessions in seven years, was hardly activist policy at its best, especially during the 1959–60 period of overly tight fiscal-monetary policy.

The Good Times

Then came the Golden Sixties, truly watershed years, with a revitalizing of the Employment Act of 1946. President Kennedy asked us to return to the letter and spirit of the act. He ended equivocation about the intent of the act by translating its rather mushy mandate into a concrete call for meeting the goals of full employment, price stability, faster growth, and external balance—all within the constraints of preserving economic freedom of choice and promoting greater equality of opportunity. He went on to foster a rather weak-kneed antirecession program in 1961 and a powerful growth-promoting tax-cut program in 1962–64. In that process, I counted six firsts for presidential economics:

• He was the first president to commit himself to numerical targets for full employment—namely, 4 percent unemployment—and growth—namely, 4.5 percent per year.
• He was the first to adopt an incomes policy in the form of wage-price guideposts developed by his Council of Economic Advisers. The guideposts, flanked by sensible supply-side tax measures to stimulate business investment, by training and retraining programs, and the like, helped maintain a remarkable record of price stability in 1961–65—only 1.2 percent inflation per year.
• He was the first president to shift the economic policy focus from moderating the swings of the business cycle to achieving the rising full-employment potential of the economy.
• In that process, he moved from the goal of balanced budget over the business cycle to a balanced budget at full employment.
• He was the first president to say, as he did in January 1963, that budget deficits could be a positive force to help move a slack or recession-ridden economy toward full employment.
• As a capstone, he was the first president to say that a tax cut was needed, not to cope with recession (there was none), but to make full use of the economy's full-employment potential.

Those were the halcyon days of economic policy. Aided and abetted by the Fed, the 1964 tax cut worked like a charm. In mid-1965, just before the July escalation in Vietnam, we saw the happy combination of an inflation rate of only 1.5 percent; unemployment coming down steadily, to 4.4 percent; defense expenditures continuing their four-year decline from 9 percent of GNP in 1960 to 7 percent of GNP in 1965; and the cash budget running $3 billion in the black.

The Downturn Begins

Then came the dark years of Vietnam, in economics as well as in foreign policy. Unlike 1950–51, we did not reverse gears in spite of the timely warnings of the Joint Economic Committee and of most of the economists, both inside and outside the government, who were advising President Johnson. He did not propose a tax increase until early 1967, and no tax action was completed until 1968, long after the inflation horse was out of the barn.

As I put it in testimony before the JEC in July 1970, "There are no magic formulas, no pat solutions, no easy ways to reconcile full employment and price stability. No modern, free economy has yet found the combination of policies that can deliver sustained high employment and high growth side by side with sustained price stability." That was all well and good, as far as it went, but in light of the experience of the 1970s it did not go nearly far enough.

The policy travails of the seventies are too well known to require lengthy review:

(1)   There was the Nixon fiasco of freezes and phases serving as a facade for pumping up the economy with tax cuts, spending increases, and a rapid run-up in the money supply, with sure-fire consequences of an overheated economy.

(2)   Superimposed on that were the supply shocks in 1973–74—oil prices quadrupling, food prices jumping 40 percent in two years, and other world raw-material prices doubling in about the same time—that served to consolidate stagflation.

The shocks, of course, were not just to the price level, but to the economics profession, led by Keynesians. We learned the sad lesson that as to wages and prices, what goes up, propelled by overstimulative monetary-fiscal policy and a series of external shocks, does not necessarily come down when the fiscal-monetary stimulus and supply shocks subside. We have since learned a lot about sticky wages and prices that stay in a high orbit even without visible means of fiscal-monetary support. At least, they stayed there until we administered a dose of sadomasochism, better known as the double-dip recession of the eighties, the deepest since the Great Depression.

One should not recite the economic sins of the seventies without acknowledging one bright fiscal episode, namely, the tax rebate and tax cut enacted in the second quarter of 1975. Granted, it was a bit late to blunt the recession, but it provided a welcome boost to an economy that had fallen into what, until topped by the recession of the early eighties, was the deepest postwar recession. The 1975 tax cut was a winner in both size and timing.

Though prices behaved very well in 1976, when inflation averaged 4.8 percent (with the help of good crops and no increase in the real price of oil), the combination of an overly strong expansion (partly resulting from economists' overestimates of GNP potential) and the second oil price shock soon pumped inflation back into the double digits. It was a time for economists to be mighty humble—though I suppose one should bear in mind Golda Meir's admonition: "Don't be so humble, you're not that great."

As one surveys the whole postwar period, activist economics and New Deal intrusions into the marketplace can surely take credit not only for building strong defenses against depression but also for twenty-five years (1948–73) of high-octane operation of the economy and sharply reduced instability. Within that framework, one can criticize antirecession fiscal policy as often too little and too late, monetary policy as sometimes too easy and other times overstaying tightness. The far-too-late and considerably-too-little tax increase to finance the war in Vietnam, coupled with excessive monetary ease in 1967–68, has to go down in the annals as one of the flat failures of postwar fiscal-monetary policy. And the stagflation experience of the 1970s still hangs like a pall over expansionary policy today.

Still, it is worth reminding ourselves that even in the face of high performance of the economy, inflation in the 1949–72 period rose above 6 percent only once (during the Korean War) and averaged only 2.3 percent. If inflation was the price of activism in public economics, it was a long time in coming.

The Haunted Prosperity of the 1980s

Now we pass through the economic portals into the eighties, the age of antigovernment. Some of this actually began with that social liberal but fiscal conservative, Jimmy Carter. I don't refer to deregulation of transportation, communication, and finance, where competition has a fair chance to do well what regulation did badly. Nor do I refer to the harnessing, where possible—that is, without sacrificing public purpose and values—of market incentives, the profit motive, and private self-interest to the accomplishment of the public purpose. Using taxes or auction rights to make depollution profitable and pollution costly is a case in point. I do refer to sloughing off functions and responsibilities on grounds that delivery of the services has been inefficient in the past or that there is an inevitably too-costly clash between efficiency and equity.

Exactly what is it that haunts our prosperity in this new era of belittled government? The answer is sobering, not to say alarming.

First, it is slow growth. After enjoying 4.2 percent annual real growth in the sixties and managing to average 3.1 percent even in the seventies, we have slipped to less than 2 percent in the first six years of the eighties. Even if we optimistically assume that there will be no recession in the next four years and an average 3 percent growth rate, the decade would come out with just a 2.4 percent real growth rate. [Ed. note: actual real GDP growth 1980–90 was 2.56 percent annually.] And even if we adjust these numbers for the slowdown in the growth of the labor force, the eighties as a whole seem destined to go into the economic annals as a period of pallid performance.

Second, we are haunted by resurgent poverty. The percentage of our population in poverty jumped by nearly a third, from 11.7 percent in 1979 to 15.3 percent in 1983. Recovery brought the poverty rate down to 14.4 percent in 1984, but leaving aside the Reagan years, this is still the highest rate since 1966.

59. Should Growth Be a Priority of National Policy?
Herbert Stein

Reprinted with permission of the publisher M.E. Sharpe, Inc., from *Challenge*, March/April 1986, pp. 11–17. Herbert Stein is A. Willis Robertson professor emeritus of economics at the University of Virginia and was a member and later chairman of the Council of Economic Advisers under President Nixon.

Growth As Policy

About ten years after the Employment Act of 1946, economic growth began to appear as a proper object of policy in the United States. This was partly because the prevention of mass unemployment, the real concern of 1946, no longer seemed a problem, and the policy makers, in office or aspiring, needed new worlds to conquer and new promises to make. Also, we were seeing that other countries, some enemies and some friends, were growing more rapidly than we, which worried and challenged us.

Much of what passed for progrowth policy in the 1960s was simply policy to speed up the growth of aggregate demand in the belief that the result would be a lower level of unemployment and consequently more output. It was essentially policy to implement more vigorously the mandate of the 1946 Act. But other kinds of proposals were also advanced, and some adopted, in the name of economic growth. Rather similar lists of measures could be found in a 1958 policy statement of the Committee for Economic Development, the section on economic growth of the Commission on National Goals set up by President Eisenhower in 1959, and various annual reports of the Council of Economic Advisers before and after 1960.

The Drive for Full Employment and Growth

Reference to economic growth as an object of national policy was submerged from about 1965 to 1975 by concern with the Vietnam War, inflation, price control, and the energy crisis. But in the middle 1970s the growth flag was raised again for two quite different purposes and from two quite different sources. One of these movements came from the more liberal wing of the Democratic party and culminated in the Full Employment and Growth Act of 1978. The motivation here was to complete the limited victory achieved by the Employment Act of 1946 by moving beyond the avoidance of mass, involuntary unemployment to "full employment"—the term specifically rejected in 1946. Full employment had a numerical definition—the adult unemployment rate should not exceed 3 percent. But the interesting thing is that by 1975 or so one could not put up the flag of full employment without attaching the word "growth" to it, even if that had to be qualified by the word "balanced" to show that it was not meant in a hard-hearted Darwinian sense but in some more compassionate sense. But even the addition of the goal "balanced growth" was not sufficient to launder the claim to full employment.

The Act specified a great many other goals to assure that no one could take offense—"a balanced federal budget, adequate productivity growth, proper attention to national priorities, achievement of an improved trade balance through increased exports and improvement in the international competitiveness of agriculture, business, and industry, and reasonable price stability." The proliferation of goals needed to get the Act adopted did not make it meaningful; it only showed that by saying everything, the Act said nothing. Its authors thought to repeat the success of the Employment Act of 1946. But the 1946 Act, although a symbol, was a symbol of a real thing—a new national priority and a new approach to serving it. The 1978 Act was only a symbol. After seven years that Act has had no consequence and is only worth mentioning as an example of the use of "growth" as a presumably acceptable symbol.

The Supply-Side Experiment

In the past five years there has been an experiment testing the connection between tax rates and economic growth. The experiment did not satisfy scientific experimental requirements, it is not over, and dispute about its lessons will surely continue for a long time. Nevertheless the experience is suggestive.

The 1981 tax cut was one of the largest, possibly the largest, in history. It emphasized reduction of marginal rates in all income tax brackets, acceleration of depreciation allowances, and enlargement of the tax credit for business investment. Since this happened, the following developments, or lack of developments, have been observed:

(1)   The rise of total output over the five-year period from 1980 to 1985 was not exceptionally large; in fact, it was less than in any five-year period between 1962 and 1981 except for the five years 1970–75. The rise of total output from 1982 to 1985 was from an unusually low point. There is no evidence of any increase in the rate of noncyclical growth.

(2)   Disentangling the trend of productivity growth from its cyclical behavior is difficult, but the best estimate is that the trend of productivity growth has not increased.

(3)   Revenue has not increased enough to prevent the emergence of the largest deficit, relative to GNP, in peacetime history.

(4)   The ratio of net private savings to GNP is about the same as its average in the 1960s and 1970s. There is no evidence that the tax changes designed to increase the after-tax return to savings have increased the propensity to save. The idea that the existence of a budget deficit, with the implication of higher future tax burdens, would by itself raise the private savings rate has not been borne out.

(5)   All of the foregoing confirmed the expectations of conventional economics. The only surprise was that, despite the increase in the deficit and the failure of the private savings rate to rise, the rate of net domestic private investment by 1984 was almost as high as in the 1970s. The explanation was the exceptionally large capital inflow

Table 59.1

Net Saving and Investment (percent of GNP)

	1960–69	1970–79	1984	1985[a]
Net saving available to finance private investment	7.0	6.3	6.6	5.7
Private saving	7.8	7.2	7.4	6.3
Federal surplus	−0.3	−1.8	−4.8	6.3
State and local surplus	0	0.8	1.4	1.3
Foreign capital inflow	−0.5	0.1	2.6	3.1
Net private investment	7.0	6.4	6.4	5.5
Statistical discrepancy	0	−0.1	0.2	0.2

[a]First three quarters.

from abroad, which financed the difference between the unchanged private investment rate and the reduced rate of domestic private savings available for private investment (see Table 59.1). Enthusiasts for tax reduction as the route to economic growth pointed to the example of Puerto Rico. Skeptics replied that there was a vast difference between a small island that could import large amounts of capital from the rest of the world, and a United States that was half of the world economy. But it turned out that the United States could be much more like Puerto Rico than anyone had expected.

Expenditures and Growth

The point is also often made that the 1981 tax cut would have yielded the promised benefits of more investment and growth if expenditures had also been cut, so that the deficit would not have risen so much. This may or may not tell us something about the growth effect of cutting expenditures. It does not tell us anything about the growth effect of cutting taxes.

For example, expenditures rose from 22.6 percent of GNP in 1980 to 23.5 percent in 1984. Suppose that expenditures had been held at 22.6 percent. The question is whether, given that expenditure level, investment would have been higher in 1984 if receipts had been kept at 20.3 percent of GNP rather than reduced to 18.6 percent. The deficit would have been smaller by 1.7 percent of GNP, and given the unresponsiveness of savings to the tax rate, as I see it, investment would have been higher with the higher tax rates.

Merely to say that private investment will be higher, the lower government expenditures are, given the tax rate, does not say that reduction of government expenditures will increase growth. Everything depends on what the government expenditures are for. Take defense: The common assumption that cutting defense expenditures would increase growth derives from a short-sighted view, because it ignores the possible effects on economic growth that would follow from failure to defend the country. Suppose, for example, that cutting the annual defense budget by $100 billion and getting all of that amount added to business investment would increase the annual growth rate, in peacetime, by 0.3 percentage points—say, from 3.0 to 3.3 percent. Suppose also that cutting the annual defense budget would reduce by 10 percent the probability of surviving any year after 2000 without a nuclear war. One would require an extraordinarily high rate of discount to conclude that cutting the defense budget would increase economic growth—and there is more to life, of course, than economic growth.

A point must be made about government expenditures more conventionally for education, research, roads, ports, and so on. Not every expenditure put in one of these categories in the budget necessarily promotes growth. But many of them do, and discrimination is required in equating expenditure cutting with growth stimulus.

Looking at American history is instructive at this point. In the thirty-seven years from 1948 to 1985, federal expenditures have averaged around 20 percent of GNP and federal revenues around 18.5 percent. In the thirty-seven years from 1892 to 1929, federal expenditures were around 4.5 percent of GNP and revenues around 3.5 percent. (Most of the difference was run up in World War I.) In the early, small-government period, real GNP rose at an annual rate of 3.4 percent. In the later, big-government period, real GNP also grew at an annual rate of 3.4 percent. In the small-government period, output per worker-hour rose by 1.5 percent per annum; in the big-government period, it rose by 2.3 percent per annum. These figures are not meant to demonstrate that big government is good for growth; and, of course, one must consider the consequences of big government for values other than growth. These simple facts do suggest, however, that the truth is much more complicated than it is often claimed to be.

Twenty years ago I would have said that affecting the rate of economic growth was part of the government's business—unlike the creation of conditions for high employment. The national rate of economic growth is simply the sum of the results of decisions of tens of millions of individuals about the use of their own resources. The government should stay out of that. I would not say the same thing today. I would find it hard to define what "staying out of it" means. The government must make a number of decisions that affect the growth rate, and some of those decisions, notably the size of the deficit or surplus, cannot be sensibly made without considering their growth effects. Moreover, if the society through its government decides that it has a strong preference for a higher growth rate than "uninfluenced" private efforts would yield, I can see no way to deny the legitimacy of any effort to achieve that, as long as basic freedoms are not impaired.

But when that has been said, the priority to be given to the goals of increasing growth remains a question. In my opinion that goal does not deserve high priority.

60. Stagnation and Government Purchases
Harold G. Vatter and John F. Walker

Reprinted with permission of the publisher, M.E. Sharpe, Inc., from *Challenge*, November/December 1992, pp. 55–57. Harold G. Vatter is professor emeritus of economics and John F. Walker is professor of economics at Portland State University.

Some economists like to refer to the period following the interminable Bush recession as a "weak recovery." The real (inflation-adjusted) gross domestic product reached an apparent trough in the first quarter of 1991. Usually, the first year after a trough produces a GDP growth rate of between 5 and 7 percent. But this time, real GDP grew at only 1.4 percent after 1991. Such a miserable performance should probably be thought of as an extraordinarily long trough (the low point or range of a business cycle).

Will it ever end? For more than a year now, the business press has been calling for a rise in consumption to lead the economy out of the doldrums. *Business Week* recently observed that worker incomes were not rising and worker spending could hardly rise without income increases. Now the press is pining for an investment increase to reinvigorate the engine of economic expansion. But why should business invest in new productive capacity when the capacity they now have is badly underutilized? Our problem has both short-run and long-run elements. The economy has been stagnating since about 1969. Stagnation means growth well below potential. Recessions are not necessarily the same as stagnation. But long recessions occurring regularly will produce long-run average growth well below potential unless the growth in the years between recessions is extraordinarily high. We have not had a period of extraordinarily high growth since the 1960s. That is the long-run problem.

Table 60.1

The Long-Run Problem: Annual Growth Rates of Real GNP/GDP, Government Purchases, and Private Fixed Investment
(in percent)

	GNP/GDP	Government purchases	Private business fixed investment
1900–29	3.53	4.19	2.70
1929–49	2.35	4.52	1.72
1949–69	4.12	5.23	3.54
1969–91	2.40	1.43	2.52

Source: Long-Term Economic Growth.

Throwing Money at Problems

Surprisingly, the cure for both the short-run and the long-run problems is the same. It is to increase significantly the rate of government purchases. For the years 1900–69 government purchases grew rapidly in every period shown in Table 60.1. The economy grew rapidly in every period except 1929–49. That period began with a collapse in investment and was followed by a major depression, World War II, and the postwar transition. Investment stayed down throughout the period. If government had hired and used the workers private enterprise was firing from 1929 to 1932—that is, if government spending had risen as private spending fell—the Great Depression would have been a mild recession.

The current stagnation is driven by the oft-repeated assertion of recent presidents, "Government cannot solve problems by throwing money at them." Yes it can. It always has. Within the previous stagnation of 1929–49 there was a great problem, World War II, which the government clearly solved by throwing money and everything else at it.

If we break down the years after 1969 (Table 60.2), we can see the evolution of the current stagnation and its cure.

Parallels in Stagnation

The years 1982–88 were boom years, with real GNP growth much like the best periods of the twentieth century. That boom was caused by a rise in government spending. Ronald Reagan was the last of the big spenders, and he presided over a rapidly growing federal government and economy. The periods of 1978–82, dominated by Jimmy Carter, and 1988–91, dominated by George Bush, represent seven years of almost no economic growth.

Table 60.2

The Short-Run Problem: Annual Growth of Real GNP/GDP, Government Purchases, and Private Fixed investment (in percent)

	GNP/GDP	Government pur-chases	Private business fixed investment
1969–78	2.85	–0.15	3.75
1978–82	0.38	1.68	1.25
1982–88	3.86	3.45	3.42
1988–91	0.91	1.85	–1.17

Source: Economic Report of the President.

There is a striking parallel between the two periods. But the parallel is grim. In the Carter period we had the worst four years of total output performance in the post-World War II era. Real GDP was $3,704 billion in 1978 and $3,760 four years later. The stagnation parallel recently is $4,719 billion in 1988 and $4,849 in 1991, amounting to an annual increase of less than 1 percent. And the prospect for 1992 is little better. We are not "recovering"; we are stagnating.

In the earlier stagnation period (1978–82), the capacity utilization rate fell from 85.5 percent to 75.0 percent at the period's end. In 1988–91, that rate dropped from 84.0 percent to 78.0 percent in the first quarter of 1992. There was a similar rise in the civilian unemployment rate in both periods.

It is significant that in both stagnation periods, total demand fell. At least equally significant is the fact that real government demand—the nation's second-largest spending stream—grew at less than 2 percent a year. It took Reagan's military spending spree and a spurt in state and local government outlays to pull the economy out of the 1978–82 stagnation. Real state and local government purchases, the biggest component of government spending, had been absolutely constant from 1979 to 1982! Currently, many states from New York to California are cutting their budgets, which will exacerbate the stagnation.

Government Spending and Investment

Many commentators worry about the government taking resources away from investment and thus slowing the long-run growth of the economy. This is theory without fact. In every period of rapid GNP/GDP growth in this century there has been rapid government growth and above-average investment growth. It is recessions and stagnation that hamper investment and make the future poorer as well as the present.

To solve our economic problems we need rapid economic growth. There have been no extended periods of rapid economic growth in this century without rapid growth in government purchases.

We hear political leaders say that government cannot afford to pay for the things we all know the society needs, such as better infrastructure, civilian research, education, child protection. By taking that position, those leaders are really proposing to keep us all feeling poor forever, so that we will not do what we should do for the good of society and the economy. Any increase in government spending will help. A useful increase will help doubly.

Strangely, our government is pressing the Japanese government to adopt a supplemental budget increasing Japanese government purchases by several trillion yen to raise the Japanese rate of GDP growth, so that they will then buy more American products. These simple Keynesian truths are accepted by our government as correct policy for the Japanese and the Germans but not for ourselves. The Germans have begun to expand their territory. The Japanese are voting to allow their army to go overseas. Both programs have been advocated by our government. Our current economic and foreign policies strengthen our rivals and weaken ourselves.

We will ignore this simple collection of output and demand data in the 1990s at our peril. Yet we appear to be on the threshold of doing precisely that. The outgoing national leadership has seemed determined to cut public purchases, which they assert is the fountainhead of all economic evil. All we have heard is a cry against too much government spending, taxing, and debt. It is a pretty sure bet that unless we and the new administration repudiate these allegedly greater evils, we will face continued stagnation and all the evils that entails. Perhaps a strong dose of civilian Reaganomics is in order.

61. Rethinking Regulation

Council of Economic Advisers

Reprinted from the *Economic Report of the President* (Washington, D.C.: U.S. Government Printing Office, 1989), pp. 187–221. The members of the council responsible for the report were Chairman Beryl W. Sprinkel and Thomas Gale Moore.

Much regulation is motivated by a perception that the marketplace does not adequately address a particular economic or social problem. For example, child labor laws help prevent the exploitation of children. Environmental legislation tries to improve the quality of the air people breathe and the water they drink. Safety legislation to protect coal miners was enacted to help reduce on-the-job injuries. In other cases, legislation was introduced to limit what was viewed as potentially "destructive competition," or to help save a cherished institution, such as the family farm. While many of these regulations had beneficial effects, they were not without their costs.

The success of regulatory programs can be measured by quantifying the costs and benefits of regulation. Regulatory costs imposed on the economy have been estimated to be in the neighborhood of $100 billion annually. The benefits of regulation are more difficult to measure but are real nonetheless, particularly for programs designed to promote environmental quality, health, and safety. Critics say that the costs are too high, arguing that regulation tends to favor special interests and is generally inefficient. Proponents of an increased government role in the marketplace point to the myriad of social, environmental, and economic problems that have not been adequately addressed.

There are signs that some important aspects of the regulatory process are undergoing a fundamental reexamination. Over the past two decades, numerous reforms have been aimed at deregulating or partially deregulating several industries. The transportation industries, most notably trucking, railroad, and air transport, have experienced tremendous gains as a result of deregulation. One study estimates that the benefits of trucking deregulation are between $39 billion and $63 billion annually, while another estimates the benefits of airline deregulation at $15 billion per year. A third study found that the partial deregulation of railroads has led to efficiency gains of between $9 billion and $15 billion annually. These gains, which have largely occurred in the 1980s and have helped produce the improved economic performance of the past six years, have translated into lower prices and a wider range of services for consumers. Where increased competition has been promoted in other sectors, a similar story emerges. The widespread introduction of money market accounts that followed reduced financial industry regulation has allowed consumers to obtain a higher return on their savings. The introduction of increased pricing flexibility for stock commissions has helped to promote a booming discount brokerage industry. The relaxation of the restrictions on overnight mail delivery has led to dramatic increases in the provision of next-day delivery services by private companies.

The movement toward deregulation represents one kind of regulatory innovation. More recently, other efficiency-enhancing innovations in the regulatory process, although not completely removing regulation, have been aimed at fostering greater innovation in the marketplace. For example, the U.S. Environmental Protection Agency (EPA) has pioneered the development of market-based approaches designed to achieve a given level of environmental quality at lower cost. These approaches have resulted in cost savings in the billions of dollars over the past decade.

Another area undergoing a great deal of change is the regulation of public utilities, such as phone companies, gas companies, and electric utilities. In many cases the fundamental rationale for public utility regulation has been called into question. The general thrust of these changes is to develop institutions that encourage firms to operate more efficiently. Thus, where new electric generating capacity is needed, for example, some state public utility commissions now encourage competitive bidding for constructing new generating capacity. Formerly, a single company that served the area was given a monopoly over the right to build new capacity. In some cases states are also allowing utilities to provide economic incentives for energy conservation as an alternative to building additional capacity.

Economists have identified two broad classes of regulation. The first, sometimes referred to as "economic regulation," usually covers the regulation of specific industries. This regulation takes three basic forms. The first places restrictions on the prices a firm can charge or on which firms can enter a particular industry. For example, prior to 1978 airlines needed approval from the Civil Aeronautics Board for specific routes and fares. Truckers and railroads still have to file rates with the Interstate Commerce Commission. These transport industries represent a more general category of industries that could operate more efficiently in the absence of price and entry restrictions. Fortunately, much of this regulation has been removed in recent years, resulting in lower prices and an expanded menu of services for consumers.

A second form of economic regulation concerns industries for which it is less costly to have a single large firm provide a product than to have several smaller firms provide the product—i.e., so-called natural monopolies. Industries thought to have elements of natural monopoly include local telephone networks and transmission and distribution systems for electricity and natural gas. For example, it is sometimes cheaper to build one large natural gas pipeline than several small ones. Some industries with natural monopoly elements, such as electric utilities, are regulated by federal and state agencies. The typical approach of these regulators is to provide limitations on the overall return on investment that firms are permitted to receive.

The second broad class of regulation, referred to as "social regulation," is aimed at tackling problems that are not always adequately addressed by the marketplace. Examples include health, safety, and environmental regulation. This class of regulation is not directly related to issues of prices and market structure but rather attempts to address problems where there is a perceived "market-failure." For example, a firm may generate too much pollution because it does not include in its costs the effect of its pollution on others. Unlike much economic regulation, social regulation is rarely targeted at specific industries.

Although the preceding taxonomy of regulatory activity covers a lot of ground, it is far from complete. For example, not all economic regulation is targeted at specific industries; minimum wage laws clearly represent a form of economic regulation that applies to almost all industries in one form or another. Similarly, antitrust policy, whose purpose is to promote competition by placing limitations on different kinds of business conduct and policies, is also an important form of economic regulation.

Several factors appear to have contributed to this dramatic change in the approach to regulation. First, an outpouring of research on economic regulation suggested that the costs of regulation were quite high. Second, some "natural" experiments provided further evidence that deregulation would result in large benefits. For example, in the case of airlines almost all intrastate markets were heavily regulated. A comparison of the fares between Los Angeles and San Francisco with those between New York and Washington, D.C., suggested that people in the latter market were paying much higher fares as a result of regulation. Third, technological changes in industries such as telecommunications and electric utilities led some firms to lobby for reduction in the entry barriers that protected existing firms. Finally, as the social costs of regulation grew, some politicians may have seen an opportunity to claim national credit by promoting policies that would result in significant gains for a large group of consumers. Although these factors help to motivate the movement toward deregulation, they do not explain why a wave of such activity began in the 1970s; nor do they explain what is likely to be in store for the future.

The scope of regulation has broadened considerably since the first federal administrative agency, the Interstate Commerce Commission (ICC), was established in 1887. The Sherman Antitrust Act became law in 1890. This was followed by the Federal Trade Commission Act and the Clayton Act in 1914, which were designed to protect consumers and to regulate competition. The New Deal period witnessed the creation of several financial regulatory agencies, including the Federal Deposit Insurance Corporation, the Securities and Exchange Commission, the Federal Home Loan Bank Board, and the Farm Credit Administration, as well as other regulatory agencies, such as the Civil Aeronautics Authority (later the GAB) and the Federal Communications Commission. Prior to 1960 federal regulation was primarily aimed at affecting the market structure of specific industries. For example, the Interstate Commerce Commission regulates the rates of truckers and railroads involved in interstate commerce. The now defunct Civil Aeronautics Board regulated prices and entry into various domestic airline markets. In short, the focus was on economic regulation.

Although economic regulation was predominant prior to 1960, some federal agencies were charged with addressing health and safety issues during that period. For example, the Food and Drug Act of 1906 required inspection and labeling of certain foods and drugs. The Federal Aviation Administration was created in 1958 to help ensure safe air travel. These agencies have played an important role in shaping the structure of the industries they regulate.

Since the mid-1960s the focus of new regulatory activity has changed. While traditional regulation of prices and entry still exists in some industries, there has been a virtual explosion of social regulation concerned with safety, health, and environmental quality. The Consumer Product Safety Commission sets safety standards for consumer products from carpets to cribs. The Environmental Protection Agency develops environmental standards and approves state pollution control plans. The Occupational Safety and Health Administration regulates hazards in the workplace. The growth in this type of social regulation has led to an increased federal presence not only in business activity, but also in the day-to-day activities of the general public.

One of the most surprising and noteworthy changes in the regulation of markets has been the movement toward deregulation over the past two decades. Table 61.1 chronicles the deregulatory initiatives that have occurred from 1971 through the present. Most of these initiatives have occurred in the area of economic regulation, although a handful have occurred in social regulation.

The Shift in Antitrust Policy

Antitrust policies limit the type of business agreements firms can use. For example, one aspect of antitrust policy places restrictions on price-fixing, because price-fixing is presumed to be anticompetitive. A second aspect of antitrust policy that has come under increasing scrutiny in recent years is the review of proposed mergers between different businesses. A marked shift in antitrust merger policy has occurred since 1980. While horizontal mergers involving similar companies are still monitored closely when entry barriers and concentration levels are high, the view of vertical mergers has evolved considerably. Vertical relationships, such as those in the petroleum industry, where some firms refine petroleum and also distribute petroleum products, are viewed with less suspicion. The principal reason for this change in perspective is that the efficiency-

Table 61.1

Deregulatory Initiatives, 1971–88

Year	Initiative
1971	Specialized common carrier decisions (FCC)
1972	Domestic satellite open-skies policy (FCC)
1975	Abolition of fixed brokerage fees (SEC)
1976	Railroad Revitalization and Reform Act
1977	Air Cargo Deregulation Act
1978	Airline Deregulation Act
	Natural Gas Policy Act
	Standards revocation (OSHA)
	Emissions trading policy (EPA)
1979	Deregulation of satellite earth stations (FCC)
	Urgent-mail exemption (Postal Service)
1980	Motor Carrier Reform Act
	Household Goods Transportation Act
	Staggers Rail Act
	Depository Institutions Deregulation and Monetary Control Act
	International Air Transportation Competition Act
	Deregulation of cable television (FCC)
	Deregulation of customer premises equipment and enhanced services (FCC)
1981	Decontrol of crude oil and refined petroleum products (executive order)
	Truth-in-lending simplification (FRB)
	Automobile industry regulation relief package (NHTSA)
	Deregulation of radio (FCC)
1982	Bus Regulatory Reform Act
	Garn–St. Germain Depository Institutions Act
	AT&T settlement
	Antitrust merger guidelines
1984	Space commercialization
	Cable Television Deregulation Act
	Shipping Act
1986	Trading of airport landing rights
1987	Sale of Conrail
	Elimination of fairness doctrine (FCC)
1988	Proposed rules on natural gas and electricity (FERC)
	Proposed rule on price caps (FCC)

Source: Adapted from R. Noll and B. Owens, *The Political Economy of Deregulation: Interest Groups in the Regulatory Process*, and updated by the Council of Economic Advisers.

enhancing aspects of vertical relationships are more widely appreciated. In addition to the change in thought on vertical restraints, there is also increasing recognition that many U.S. firms now compete in global markets, which means that the appropriate measure of market size must be enlarged.

Reflecting this change in perspective, the Department of Justice in 1982 adopted new guidelines for determining when it would challenge mergers or acquisitions as anticompetitive. The Federal Trade Commission at the same time adopted a comparable policy statement. These new guidelines provide a firm conceptual basis for evaluating horizontal and vertical mergers. They also provide more leeway for vertical mergers. In 1984 the Justice Department issued revised guidelines that placed even greater weight on competition in a global setting.

Another important change in policy, which should complement the recent merger guidelines, is the National Cooperative Research Act of 1984. This act was designed to promote greater collaboration on basic and applied research among private companies. The act should encourage domestic firms to engage in cooperative arrangements, such as research and development. Like the revised merger guidelines, the act is supposed to make it easier for U.S. firms to compete in a global setting.

Banking: The Need for Reform

Much of the concern over the health of the banking industry results from the marked increase in bank failures over the past decade. Failures remained high through the end of the Depression, stayed at relatively low levels from 1945 to 1979, and then rose dramatically. Net outlays for bank failures by the major federal deposit insurance agencies reveal a similar pattern after World War II but were inconsequential prior to that time.

The sharp rise in failures has placed a major burden on the deposit insurance systems. The Federal Savings and Loan Insurance Corporation (FSLIC), which provides deposit insurance for savings and loan associations, has been insolvent since 1986. The Federal Deposit Insurance Corporation (FDIC), which insures commercial banks and some savings banks, is still solvent but will run a loss for 1988. Estimates of the costs to the FSLIC of closing insolvent thrifts have risen steadily. The Federal Home Loan Bank Board, which regulates these institutions, now estimates this cost to be in the range of $50 billion. Other estimates range as high as $100 billion, but costs will vary depending on how soon the problem is addressed. Unless something is done promptly, these costs are expected to climb rapidly.

Two recent government studies provided careful examination of banking regulation. The 1984 President's Task Group on Regulation of Financial Services chaired by the vice president and the 1985 Cabinet Council on Economic Affairs both made suggestions for streamlining the oversight process and for providing more appropriate incentives for banking institutions. Some of the more salient recommendations included risk-related deposit insurance, higher capital requirements, stronger disclosure requirements, limitations on insurance to insured depositors, and increased monitoring and more vigilant enforcement by oversight agencies.

Rethinking the Limits of Natural Monopoly

There has been a long-standing debate about how best to regulate natural monopolies. The traditional approach to such problems has been to regulate selected firms in order to prevent excessive profits. This regulation usually assesses the value of the firm's capital stock and then allows the firm to obtain a "reasonable" return on its investment. In practice, federal and state regulatory commissions do not fix the rate of return per se, but rather agree on prices that the firm can charge. The prices result in a revenue stream for the firm that is not supposed to, but sometimes does, exceed the allowable rate of return.

Rate-of-return regulation has several problems. It tends to be time-consuming and expensive. Given the costs associated with the rate-making process and the attendant inefficiencies, there have been several suggestions for reforming the process. For example, one approach is to allow firms to bid on the right to offer a particular service, and give the contract to the highest bidder. Such franchise bidding schemes can present difficulties. Once the bidder wins the contract, it may be difficult to ensure adequate performance. Moreover, the contractor may be able to create conditions that make it difficult for new entrants to enter the market when the contract has expired. Such problems tend to limit the applicability of this approach.

A second approach to the issue of natural monopoly is to revise institutional mechanisms that permit competition to thrive even where the production of a commodity has certain characteristics of natural monopoly. An idea that appears to hold great promise for introducing competition is that of shared capacity rights. These rights allow private parties to use property jointly in a way that benefits them all. One example is the sharing of common space and facilities in a shopping mall. A second example is the joint ownership of a fiber-optic cable for transatlantic calls.

The impetus for change has come mainly from industries that stood to gain from changes in the regulatory environment. For example, new entrants in telecommunications saw an opportunity to gain by providing consumers with lower rates on long-distance calls than were being offered. Similarly, low-cost producers of electricity see an opportunity to increase their profits as markets are opened up. Indeed, in virtually all cases of regulatory reform, an outside stimulus was provided by an interest group that stood to gain from those changes in direct economic terms. Such interest group stimulus is not, however, sufficient to generate regulatory changes.

One of the more important pieces of recent legislation to promote the move toward a more competitive generating sector was the Public Utility Regulatory Policies Act of 1978 (PURPA). The primary purpose of this legislation was to encourage cogeneration and small power production, and it has done just that. Cogeneration involves the joint production of heat and electricity at a single facility. This process often facilitates the generation of electricity at a cost lower than is possible at a conventional power plant.

Cogeneration has increased dramatically since the implementation of PURPA. A report recently issued by the North American Electric Reliability Council projects that between now and 1997, some 20,000 megawatts, or 27 percent of all new capacity coming on line, will come from sources that are not owned exclusively by traditional electric utilities. While PURPA promoted the use of different generation technologies as well as small facilities, it also led to the purchase of some unneeded capacity. The principal problem was that the states sometimes provided price signals to builders of capacity that did not reflect the underlying economics of the particular power system receiving the electricity.

Although the implementation of PURPA has created inefficiencies, it has helped to create a group of entrepreneurs interested in having greater access to the market for producing electric power. The legislation also demonstrated that an electricity generation market with several participants was technically feasible. That is, it was possible to allow new entrants into the generating sector without compromising the reliability and stability of the entire power system. Having shown the technical feasibility, the principal challenge that remains is to design rules that promote efficiency in the generation sector.

Regulation of Oil and Natural Gas: Some New Developments

Energy regulation over the past two decades provides a textbook study of the effects on markets of price controls and government intervention. Fortunately, the wave of price controls introduced in the 1970s has for the most part been reversed. Price controls remain on some fuels, such as natural gas. However, controls on gasoline and crude oil prices were removed at the beginning of this administration.

Privatization

Privatization is a natural extension of deregulation. Eliminating government provision of services fosters competition by increasing the role of the market. Government provides a large array of goods and services that the private sector could also provide. Examples include the air traffic control system, the enrichment of uranium, and the postal service. From an efficiency point of view, the critical question is whether firms could provide a similar or improved menu of services at lower cost. The answer depends on the nature of the service; however, there is widespread agreement that the government now performs several tasks that the private sector could more effectively and efficiently handle. The motivation for keeping these functions within the sphere of government is usually to achieve objectives other than economic efficiency.

However, recent history suggests that even privatization measures that clearly promise efficiency gains are likely to encounter substantial political resistance. As with other regulatory reforms, the key to the success of privatization lies in designing institutions that will allow the beneficiaries of such change to compensate adequately those who stand to lose.

There are essentially three techniques for the privatization of goods and services now supplied by the government sector. One involves selling government assets to persons who will manage them privately. The sale of Conrail in 1987 is an example of federal government divestiture of an enterprise as a functioning unit.

A second privatization technique is contracting out, whereby government contracts with private firms to provide goods and services that it would otherwise supply directly. The federal government now contracts to purchase approximately $200 billion of goods and services annually. Contracting out usually results in cost savings because of the competition for contracts among vendors.

Contracting out is most likely to succeed when the terms and measurement of service delivery are clear and easily defined, when at least several firms have the capacity to perform the contract, when the contractor does not have to make large new capital expenditures, and when the contract can be subject to regular renegotiation and renewal. Examples of areas particularly well suited for contracting out include data processing, laboratory testing, and payroll services.

A third technique for privatization is the use of vouchers, through which the government, rather than directly providing goods or services, distributes chits, such as food stamps, that allow eligible consumers to purchase those goods and services from private suppliers. For example, the government now provides housing vouchers usable for rental payments to more than 140,000 low-income households as a substitute for public housing. A comparable proposal often discussed is the provision of education vouchers as a partial substitute for public schools.

Rethinking Social Regulation

Just as the nature and scope of economic regulation may be changing significantly, there are signs that new approaches to social regulation are emerging. Whereas economic regulation appears to be receding, there is no sign that social regulation is on the wane. A large portion of the public believes that the federal government should take a strong leadership role in protecting the public from environmental, health, and safety risks. Elected officials frequently accommodate these concerns by passing legislation aimed at "fixing" the problem. Unfortunately, much of this legislation has fallen far short of its goals. In some cases, this was because the goals were highly symbolic. For example, 1972 amendments to the Clean Water Act called for the elimination of all discharges into navigable waterways by 1985—a solution that, even if possible, would have been prohibitively expensive. In other cases the legislation itself led to decisions that inadvertently increased both the risks and the costs to society. For example, the Consumer Product Safety Commission requirement for child-proof caps on products such as aspirin appears to have led initially to an increase in the number of poisoning accidents. Evidently, parents became more lax about leaving hazardous products within the reach of children.

Agencies involved in social regulation tend to specialize in one of two areas. "Standard-setting" agencies focus on defining acceptable levels of risk and setting standards accordingly. These agencies seek to lower the current amount of risk society faces from activities such as breathing polluted air, working in hazardous areas, being exposed to excessive airport noise, and driving automobiles. Each agency faces the burden of proof, both legally and politically, in setting standards. By and large the standard-setting agencies seek to reduce the levels of risk that are already commonplace in society.

A second type of regulatory agency focuses on screening new risks by requiring manufacturers to prove that their product is not harmful. Absent such "proof," the agency may prohibit the product from being sold to the general public. While statutes for standard-setting agencies sometimes require a recognition of the costs imposed on the regulated, statutes for screening agencies rarely contain such provisions. Consequently, agencies are not permitted to weigh the safety of a new product against the safety of a product it would replace. Moreover, screening agencies often need not justify, either to the courts or to the Congress, the costs, or forgone benefits, of prohibiting the sale of potentially valuable products.

The Impact of Social Regulation on Innovation

While regulatory screening can protect the public from certain risks, it can also have undesirable side effects. Screening can, and sometimes does, lead to the banning of products whose expected benefits outweigh their costs because the screening procedure frequently focuses almost exclusively on a narrow definition of risk. Since 1958 the Delaney Clause has required the Food and Drug Administration (FDA) to prohibit any food additive found to cause cancer in either man or animals. Such zero-risk strategies do not permit explicit comparison of the costs and benefits of various chemicals. Thus, screening of new risks can serve as an entry barrier that limits the introduction of new products, even in cases where the new item is less harmful than the one it would replace.

Screening agencies can dramatically affect the rate of innovation. A case in point is the Food and Drug Administration. Following the 1962 amendments to the Food, Drug, and Cosmetic Act, FDA required pharmaceutical companies to prove not only that their proposed new drugs were not harmful, but also that they were "effective" (i.e., do what the manufacturer claims they do). Several studies have documented the impact of the requirements on slowing the approval of "new chemical entities." One study showed that on average fifty-four new chemical entities were approved annually in the thirteen years preceding 1962; for a similar period after the amendments, the average number fell to just over sixteen, a 70 percent decline. The decline in new drug innovations restricts the public's choice of remedies, a choice often made under a physician's guidance.

In response to criticism about the FDA's slow approval process, which took on average ten years to complete, the agency has attempted to streamline its screening procedures, in both the research and the market approval stages. Administrative measures have reduced the average drug processing time by two years. In addition, the number of pending new drug applications fell from 343 at the end of 1983 to 204 just three years later. Moreover, the average annual number of new drug applications approved by FDA jumped from 86 between 1976 and 1979 to 109 between 1980 and 1986. More recently, FDA has agreed to help companies design drug studies that will produce data as early in the process as possible, and in certain cases to hasten the approval process for drugs where serious illness or death threatens, as in the case of acquired immune deficiency syndrome (AIDS) or hairy cell leukemia. The reforms in the FDA approval process could result in a significant increase in the number of new drugs, provided that they actually reduce the costs to firms of getting drugs approved.

One of the biggest challenges for screening regulation will be in the emerging field of biotechnology. The United States has the potential to be a commercial giant in this field while still protecting the public from unnecessary harm. The development of new technologies in this field can lead to important applications in agriculture (such as pest and climate resistance), medicine (such as the FDA-approved recombinant DNA-derived human insulin), containing oil spills, and cleaning up hazardous waste sites. Worldwide demand for biotechnology products has been estimated to be as high as $100 billion annually by the turn of the century. The proper federal role in biotechnology is to ensure that new processes and products do not, on balance, pose an unreasonable risk to the public.

Although these new developments in screening procedures are encouraging, there is a fundamental design problem inherent in the current approach to screening: Regulators are not given enough credit for allowing new products to reach the marketplace sooner. At the same time, they often have to shoulder a major share of the blame if something goes wrong after a new product or chemical is approved.

62. Taking the Measure of Environmental Regulation
Paul R. Portney

Reprinted with permission of the publisher, Resources for the Future, from *Resources*, Spring 1990, pp. 2–4. Paul R. Portney is vice president and senior fellow at Resources for the Future.

There are many ways to measure the success of public policies. These include public opinion polls and ballot box results; by either of these measures the environmental laws and regulations enacted since Earth Day 1970 have been successful. Several students of public opinion polling have recently pointed to the record-high support now being given to environmental regulatory measures. This is made all the more impressive by the fact that questions asked in these polls explicitly require respondents to balance environmental protection against economic growth. Similarly, when environmental initiatives are put to a popular vote, they are generally strongly supported no matter how uncompromisingly worded.

Another way to measure the success of environmental initiatives is benefit-cost analysis. This approach involves ascertaining the improvements that have resulted from environmental regulations and translating those improvements into physical effects such as the reduced incidence of human disease, curtailment of damage to materials and crops, and so on. Dollar values are then assigned to these favorable effects and compared with the costs of the regulations. Such comparisons are very difficult—sometimes impossible—to make, but those that exist suggest a more sober assessment of the last two decades of environmental regulation.

In spite of the considerable progress environmental economists have made in estimating benefits, there exists no estimate of the cumulative benefits associated with the environmental regulatory programs implemented since 1970. Notwithstanding this unfortunate fact, there exists a fair bit of scattered evidence worth reviewing.

While some serious problems remain, the substantial improvements in urban air quality made between 1970 and 1990 have been the most impressive success story in federal environmental regulation. To be sure, other factors have played a role in these improvements—not the least of which are the closings or relocations of some major industrial facilities— but the 1970 amendments to the Clean Air Act have played a major role. Among the most notable improvements in air quality is a decline in the average ambient concentration of lead of more than 90 percent since 1980. Since 1978 the average ambient concentrations of sulfur dioxide and particulate matter have decreased 35 and 21 percent, respectively. These are truly significant accomplishments since lead and fine particles, particularly sulfate aerosols, are among the most harmful pollutants from the standpoint of human health. Averaged nationally, ambient concentrations of carbon monoxide, nitrogen oxides, and even ozone—the most stubborn air pollution problem facing the nation—have declined over this same period.

But what is the dollar valuation of the health improvements, reduced damage to exposed materials, increased agricultural output, improved visibility, and other physical changes that have accompanied reduced air pollution concentration? More than a decade ago, A. Myrick Freeman III, a senior fellow at Resources for the Future, attempted to make such an estimate for the year 1978. In 1984 dollars, his best estimate of air pollution control benefits for that year was about $37 billion, although he said the true number could fall anywhere in a range of $9 billion to $90 billion. At the time of his analysis, Freeman's estimate was limited by some gaps in information and by unavoidable assumptions that he readily acknowledged; recent developments in epidemiology and economics have further eroded the confidence we can place in the estimate. Nevertheless, Freeman's attempt stands as the only one thus far to comprehensively estimate annual air quality control benefits.

When it comes to estimating water pollution control benefits, the situation is more discouraging. Because of the inadequacy of the national water quality monitoring network, there are fewer data concerning the overall improvements in water quality since the 1972 amendments to the Clean Water Act. Dramatic improvements in water quality in a number of major metropolitan areas are, unfortunately, an insufficient basis for comprehensive benefit estimates. What is needed are better and broader data on changes in water quality, coupled with credible estimates of the increase in water-based recreation such changes would effect, along with estimates of any health and other improvements that would follow. Once again making use of any and all existing information on changes in water quality and individual valuation thereof, Freeman pegged the most likely national benefits associated with the Clean Water Act at $14 billion for the year 1978. His uncertainty range was between nearly $6 billion and $28 billion.

No such comprehensive estimate of national water quality benefits has been made since that time. This is unfortunate because now-available data on physical changes in water quality and an improved understanding of the way individuals value fishing, boating, swimming, and other types of water recreation benefits would allow an up-to-date estimate to be more accurate.

The Clean Air and Clean Water acts are only two of more than twenty major federal environmental laws. Statutes exist for regulating pesticides and herbicides, drinking water contaminants, solid and hazardous wastes, and new chemicals, but there are virtually no estimates of the annual benefits of these laws.

Although information is lacking, it is likely that the corpus of environmental laws and regulations passed since 1970 has produced substantial economic benefits—surely in the tens of billions of dollars annually. Considering the substantial costs of implementing and enforcing this legislation, one should hope so.

Measuring environmental costs is not straightforward. As RFF researchers Raymond J. Kopp and Michael Hazilla have pointed out, the costs associated with a particular regulation should be measured by the amount of money required to compensate those harmed by the regulation (through higher prices, job losses, and the like) so that they are just as well off after the regulation as before. This is analogous to, and no simpler than, measuring benefits by willingness to pay, the widely accepted metric. Nevertheless, the appropriate measure of costs bears some resemblance to out-of-pocket expenditures for pollution control equipment, cleaner fuels, sewage treatment, and other environmental ends. About such expenditures better data exist.

A survey of a wide variety of estimates suggests that total annual expenditures necessitated by federal environmental regulation are now in the order of $85 billion. Approximately $30 to $35 billion of this is a result of regulations written pursuant to the Clean Air Act. Another $30 billion can be attributed to the Clean Water Act requirements. The remainder arises from regulations to protect drinking water, ensure the safe disposal of solid and hazardous wastes, control pesticides and toxic substances, and further other environmental goals.

It is important to realize that this $85 billion is just an estimate: There is no very precise way to tally just what industries, governments, and individuals are required to spend for environmental protection. The true total may be somewhat higher or lower than $85 billion, but it is probably close (within 10 percent or so)—something that cannot be said about estimates of aggregate national benefits. As evidence of the accuracy of the $85 billion total, the Environmental Protection Agency independently estimates, in a draft report, that the annual cost associated with all federal environmental regulations is $93 billion.

For the purpose of comparison it is worth noting that the federal government spends about $40 billion annually on health care for the indigent under the Medicaid program and another $10 billion for the food stamp program.

There is always interest in knowing what the macroeconomic effects of these environmental compliance expenditures may be. That is, what effect does this spending have on the inflation and unemployment rates, the rate of growth of GNP, the trade balance, and so forth? The most recent study came to about the same conclusions as previous ones: Environmental regulation adds slightly to the inflation rate, has a negligible effect on the unemployment rate, and somewhat reduces the rate of productivity growth.

What about expenditures for environmental purposes over the whole twenty-year period since Earth Day 1970? Based on the annual reports of the Environmental Quality Commission from 1971 through 1981, studies performed by or for the EPA since that time, and other sources, it would appear that total expenditures necessitated by federal environmental regulation have been on the order of $600–700 billion. (In the early 1970s, few regulations had been written under the Clean Air and Clean Water acts; as a result, compliance expenditures began to grow in earnest only toward the middle of the decade.) The draft EPA report alluded to above puts cumulative spending from 1970 to 1990 at closer to $1 trillion; however, the report may count spending for solid waste disposal that is more correctly attributed to local ordinances. Either way, the total is eye-catching.

63. The Road We've Traveled

Phyllis Myers

Reprinted from *EPA Journal*, September/October 1990, pp. 57–60. Phyllis Myers is president of State Resource Strategies.

The creation of the Environmental Protection Agency on December 2, 1970, was not a major press event. Only brief articles inside the *Washington Post* and the *New York Times* mentioned the new agency and Congress' unanimous confirmation of William Ruckelshaus as its first administrator. To the *Wall Street Journal*, the occasion merited seven lines at the end of its domestic news summary.

With words still surprisingly fresh, President Nixon called for the creation of "a strong independent agency ... to make a coordinated attack on the pollutants which debase the air we breathe, the water we drink, and the land that grows our food."

There was little quibbling in Congress over Nixon's reorganization plan, which transferred air, solid waste, radiological monitoring, water hygiene, and pesticide-tolerance functions from the Department of Health, Education and Welfare; water quality and pesticide-label review from the Department of the Interior; radiation-protection standards from the Atomic Energy Commission and the Federal Radiation Council; and pesticide registration from the Department of Agriculture. Transfers included fifty-six research laboratories located all over the country. Many of the "charter" employees at their desks on December 2 in the new agency remain with the EPA today—about 300 at headquarters and 1,200 throughout the regions and field stations.

EPA's authority was strengthened within weeks by the reauthorization of the Clean Air Act. The new amendments called for national standards for ambient air quality and state plans describing how the standards would be attained. After EPA approval, the plans were to be enforceable by state and federal law.

EPA's Early Years

Each of the responsibilities transferred to EPA would receive stronger authority within the decade; and new programs would be added. Congress addressed each issue separately, in part because its own responsibilities for the environment were fragmented.

Ruckelshaus let his staff know early on that he wanted to "hit the ground running." Soon after, he announced that EPA was filing violation notices on three cities—Atlanta, Cleveland, and Detroit— for lagging performance in building wastewater treatment plants. He followed with action against Jones and Laughlin Steel Company and other industrial giants.

His commitment to stronger enforcement was evident in the number and quality of attorneys brought on board. The first two months saw five times as many enforcement actions as all the programs united under EPA had initiated during any similar period.

DDT was already under a limited ban when Ruckelshaus took office; the issue he faced was whether to suspend its use entirely. Testimony from blue-ribbon scientific panels about its effects on mammals, manufacturers' arguments that direct effects on humans had not been proven, agronomists' warnings about its importance to the economy, and a lawsuit filed by the Environmental Defense Fund crossed his desk. He made the long-awaited announcement to phase out domestic use of the pesticide in June 1971 at the United Nations Conference on the Human Environment in Stockholm. He said he was convinced by "evidence in the record" that the storage of DDT in human tissue and its persistence in the food chain posed "a warning to the prudent" that people "may be exposing [themselves] to a substance that may ultimately have serious effects on . . . health."

Reauthorization of the Clean Water Act in 1972 completely revised the nation's approach to water pollution. After contentious debate about "zero discharge," Congress set an interim goal of "fishable" and "swimmable" waters be attained within a few years. It mandated national effluent limits for industrial and municipal discharges and a permit system based on those guidelines. The measure was approved over White House objections to the "budget wrecking" $18 billion grants program to build wastewater treatment plants.

Confidence that environmental protection was a finite job soon began to erode. Dr. Robert Fri, who was Ruckelshaus's deputy, remembers: "It seemed so straightforward at first. But even in the two years I was there, one could easily see how difficult it would become." The statutes reflected Congress' conviction that technological breakthroughs would follow only if industry were forced to spend enough money. "At this stage the agency was able to argue that cost was not an issue. Pollution was egregious. It would have been difficult to spend dollars unwisely." Ruckelshaus refused to grant extensions requested by automobile manufacturers to meet hydrocarbon and carbon-monoxide standards, in effect forcing adoption of the catalytic converter.

As Watergate clouds darkened over the nation's capital in 1973, the White House asked Ruckelshaus to take over the troubled FBI. His successor at EPA was Russell Train. The climate had changed perceptibly,

Train recalls. His confirmation by Congress took three months, in contrast to one day for Ruckelshaus. A *Who's Who* description of Train as a "conservationist" and his earlier work on a surface mining bill disquieted some industry critics. "There was a nice passing of the flame, though," says Train. "I was sworn in by Attorney General Elliot Richardson, with Deputy Attorney General Ruckelshaus looking on. They both were soon gone, after Richardson was fired and Ruckelshaus resigned."

The DDT decision was put to the test when a plague of tussock moths hit the northwest forests. The only known control was DDT. "All the region's governors, including Tom McCall, a strong environmentalist, its powerhouse Senators—Jackson and Magnuson—and the entire House delegation supported using DDT," Train recalls. "We were told that the normal cycle would lead to the collapse of the tussock moth at some point. But when? If it went beyond one year, the economic impact would be enormous. I announced my decision to approve the use of DDT under carefully controlled conditions in a Seattle press conference. I remember today environmentalists sobbing in the room."

Despite his strong conservation credentials, says Train, "my relations with environmental groups were about as hairy as that of most administrators. One evening [Supreme Court Justice] Byron White said to me, 'You're the most litigious son of a bitch. Your name is on a thousand lawsuits.' "

Nevertheless, by January 1975, writing in the *EPA Journal's* inaugural issue, Train could point to "real headway. . . . Our investments in municipal and industrial point-source controls are beginning to pay off in pollution reduction—in lower counts of bacteria and biodegradable oxygen demand, and in less phenols. In air, total suspended particulates and sulfur-dioxide concentrations have significantly declined." In 1976, the Toxic Substances Control Act (TSCA) was finally passed. The Kepone tragedy at Hopewell, Virginia, PCB contamination of the Hudson River, and the accidental poisoning of cows by PBBs in Michigan had kept the toxic issue simmering. Al Alm and Terry Davies, who worked under Train at the Council on Environmental Quality (CEQ), had written an influential report on toxic substances that led to the law.

"We began to think about ways to deal with risk," says Alm, who became an assistant administrator under Train at EPA. "Train asked me to develop a policy on cancer. The Carcinogens Assessment Group was the beginning of risk assessment machinery. We issued effluent guidelines and set up the organization for TSCA. The Safe Water Drinking Act was passed, and then the Resource Conservation and Recovery Act (RCRA). We set up the beginnings of the Science Advisory Board (SAB). We did a lot. There weren't so many encumbrances then."

The Late Seventies

"We didn't realize how complex the job would be," says Doug Costle, President Carter's choice for EPA administrator. Costle directed the study that led to EPA's creation.

Costle faced not only a growing backlog of regulations and lengthening deadlines, but also widening recognition of the costs and time it would take to meet the ambitious goals mandated by Congress—if they could be met at all. In the beginning, "Most of us thought we would take care of the big problems in short order, and then it would be a matter of maintenance," says Elkins. "We began to see this wasn't the case in the late 1970s when we were missing all the deadlines in new programs. We thought then that the deadlines were tough, but now we see they were laughable."

"The laws were written so that we would need a policeman at every corner," worried Costle. Court suits, filed by environmentalists on one side and industry on the other, became a fact of agency life. "The Clean Water Act . . . assumed zero emissions were achievable," says Costle special assistant Mary Ann Massey. "The Natural Resource Defense Council sued, and the court directed EPA to comply with the law. 'How can we do it?' we asked. 'You figure it out,' said the court."

"But," says Massey, "we also began to think about the bubble policy. This was Bill Drayton's idea, putting an imaginary dome over a region and allowing industry to trade emissions within the region, providing they didn't exceed the limits for the overall bubble." Drayton, who directed the Planning and Management Office, observes: "First government writes the rules. Then it creates the situation where the regulatees can make a counterproposal and find cheaper ways of accomplishing the same things. Innovation in pollution control technology is unquestionably the most important need. . . . If you're stuck with static technology, then the environment is in big trouble, since pollution is increasing."

Meanwhile, Three Mile Island, Valley of the Drums, and Love Canal catapulted to headlines and TV screens. Grassroots heroes and heroines aired fears about "ticking time bombs." As a result, EPA was positioned more firmly as a health protection agency.

Hazardous waste had been addressed in the Resource Conservation and Recovery Act (RCRA), the "cradle to grave" legislation enacted in 1976 to regulate its generation, storage, transportation, and disposal. Today one of EPA's largest programs, the Solid Waste Office then had eleven people watching over an inventory of municipal landfills.

The crisis also led to the creation of a groundwater office in 1984. Marian Mlay, today the office's director, said, "Costle asked us, 'What are we doing about groundwater?' I didn't know what groundwater was. Yet it supplies half our drinking water."

In 1980, in one of his last presidential acts, Jimmy Carter signed the Comprehensive Environmental Response, Compensation and Liability Act (CERLA), authorizing a "shovels first, lawyers later" approach whereby EPA would respond immediately to emergencies caused by abandoned waste dumps. A five-year, $1.6 billion trust fund—Superfund—was established, financed primarily by a tax on industrial chemicals. The federal government could sue for recovery of costs if the liable parties could be found.

Defederalization

In 1981, the Reagan agenda of defederalization, severe budget cuts, and regulatory reform swept through the nation's capital. EPA was widely seen as a special target. In the words of Anne Gorsuch, EPA's new administrator, "When President Reagan asked me to head the Environmental Protection Agency, I understood that he wanted me . . . to get out better environmental results with fewer people and less money. . . . Excessive regulations, burdensome paperwork for industry and government, federal-state friction, and huge costs at a time of increasing economic stringency . . . were clear signs that change was needed in the 1980s."

Personnel was reduced by 22.6 percent and the budget pared from $701 million to $515 million, in constant dollars, excluding Superfund. The federal share of construction grants was reduced to 55 percent and the long-term federal commitment from $90 billion to $36 billion. Nevertheless, widening public perception that serious environmental hazards were being mismanaged or worse was brought to a head by dioxin contamination at Times Beach, Missouri, the firing of Rita Lavelle, who administered EPA's Superfund and RCRA programs, and the refusal of Gorsuch to comply with Congress' demand that she turn over internal agency documents dealing with Superfund enforcement. She resigned in 1983 because, she said, she "had become an issue in the intense congressional controversy about administration policies."

Back on Track

President Reagan asked Ruckelshaus to serve again as administrator. The caption on the *EPA Journal*'s cover called his return the dawn of a new era. Al Alm returned as deputy.

"I thought it was important to move quickly," Alm points out. " We needed to deliver, after years of slower pace, to get the agency back in a positive mode." Alm set up ten task forces to deal with such issues as groundwater, dioxin, acid rain, and risk assessment. Enforcement was reinvigorated. Civil penalties increased in number and size. And, he says, "We brought great new people in."

The role of the Science Advisory Board was strengthened. "When EPA was created, we had a large base of information about air and water built up over many years," says Erich Bretthauer, current head of Research and Development. "In the mid-1980s different problems surfaced—acid rain, climate change, sedimentation—that were much more complex and for which we lacked a research base."

Lee Thomas, who was named administrator following Ruckelshaus's resignation at the end of Reagan's first term, was the first career government official and first non-lawyer to serve in the post.

First among his accomplishments Thomas unhesitatingly singled out the 1987 Montreal Protocol, an unprecedented international agreement. The agency had banned CFCs, or chlorofluorocarbons, in aerosol cans in 1978 in response to reports about ozone depletion. The Protocol froze the level of CFC consumption and required steady reduction by 1998. "The involvement of industry in the final agreement was a model for other environmental actions," says Thomas.

Thomas asked an EPA task force to compare the agency's budget priorities with experts' assessments of risks to public health, welfare, and natural systems posed by an array of environmental hazards. Their report, *Unfinished Business: A Comparative Assessment of Environmental Problems*, concluded that EPA's priorities appeared to be more closely aligned with public opinion, often expressed through congressional mandates, than with estimated risk.

The continuing role of crisis and emergency response at EPA was amply demonstrated to William Reilly, who succeeded Thomas in 1989. A popular TV program aired charges by the National Resources Defense Council that the pesticide Alar was a carcinogen; wholesale apple prices dropped 50 percent.

One of Reilly's first actions was to ask the Science Advisory Board to review *Unfinished Business* and to suggest ways to improve the comparative risk process. In releasing the board's report at the National Press Club this past September, he said, "We have to find a better way of setting environmental priorities. . . . Risk is a common metric that lets us distinguish the environmental heart attacks and broken ankles from indigestion or bruises."

64. Consumer Protection: Problems and Prospects
Laurence P. Feldman, ed.

Reprinted with permission from Laurence P. Feldman, ed., *Consumer Protection: Problems and Prospects* (St. Paul: West Publishing Company, 1980), pp. 9–19. Laurence P. Feldman is a professor at the University of Illinois at Chicago.

The Contemporary Era of Consumer Protection

Although several consumer protection measures were enacted previously, the contemporary period of heightened consumer protection activity did not begin until the decade of the 1960s. It is a commentary on the effectiveness of earlier phases of consumer protection that the first major issue to emerge during the decade again related to the policing of the drug industry.

Senator Estes Kefauver had been concerned for some time with the drug testing and marketing practices of the pharmaceutical manufacturers. In the course of Senate hearings over which he presided, it was brought out that companies were selling drugs that had not been demonstrated as effective for the use for which they were prescribed, and that were of questionable safety. Events dramatized this point when an American pharmaceutical manufacturer sought to market a German-developed tranquilizer drug in the United States. The drug, thalidomide, was found to produce deformities in children of European women who had taken it during pregnancy. It was only through the persistence of a single FDA doctor, Frances Kelsey, that the formality of FDA permission to market the drug in the United States had been denied.

The resulting publicity overcame the strenuous opposition of the pharmaceutical manufacturers to the legislation, and the result was the Kefauver-Harris Amendment (1962) to the federal Food, Drug and Cosmetic Act. This amendment established new procedures for testing the safety and effectiveness of all new drugs prior to marketing, and it applied retroactively to all drugs that had been marketed since 1938. Subsequently, the amendment was to play a major role in consumer protection measures relating to drug products.

At the time of the passage of this legislation, however, there was still little to indicate a heightened level of interest in consumer protection on the part of the typical American consumer. Several other consumer-oriented legislative proposals were defeated, including a "truth in lending" bill, with little visible indignation on the part of consumer interests.

There were other rumblings in the background, however. Concern had been growing about the high level of accidents and deaths on the nation's highways. In 1964, in a move to spur the development of safer automobiles, the General Services Administration was authorized to establish safety standards for automobiles purchased by the federal government. In 1965, a landmark year in consumer protection, Senator Abraham Ribicoff convened a Senate committee to hold hearings on automobile safety. In the process, he uncovered what appeared to be an amazing lack of concern on the part of auto industry executives about safety-related design defects.

To some extent this may have been a reflection of a lack of information on the part of industry executives. For example, questioning of General Motors executives in which they admitted to having insufficient information on highway safety revealed that only $1.25 million was being spent by GM in all areas of safety-related research, including support of the National Safety Council. Another example of industry ignorance was the confession by a Chrysler vice president that he didn't know whether dealers who had been informed about a serious defect in the steering gear of some of their cars had taken the trouble to inform the buyers about the problem.

An important spokesman for the consumer at these hearings was an obscure lawyer named Ralph Nader, who, in the public interest, had taken upon himself the task of holding automobile manufacturers accountable for defects in their products. His book, *Unsafe at Any Speed*, was a catalogue of these defects and the accidents they had caused; and it effectively disseminated knowledge of the problem of auto safety to the general public. The passage of the National Traffic and Motor Vehicle Safety Act the following year was in large part attributable to Nader's efforts.

Within the next few years, Ralph Nader was to figure prominently in many congressional hearings on a wide variety of subjects relating to consumer protection. He was the central figure in publicizing U.S. Department of Agriculture data on the unwholesome conditions prevailing in some meat processing plants that shipped meat intrastate only and were therefore not subject to the 1906 federal Meat Inspection Act. These plants, which accounted for about 25 percent of all meat sold, had been subject only to the far less rigorous standards of state meat inspection. The effect of Nader's disclosures was the passage of the Wholesome Meat Act of 1967. Since then, Ralph Nader has become an institution in the struggle to safeguard the public interest, including consumer protection, with his sponsorship of the Center for Study of Responsive Law in 1968 and later the Public Interest Research Group.

The consumer protection pot was bubbling on other burners besides those of auto safety and meat inspection. In late 1965, voluminous hearings were held on the subjects of fair packaging and labeling, reflecting alleged consumer frustration with deceptive and confusing packaging practices, particularly in food products. The culmination of these hearings was the passage of the Fair Packaging and Labeling Act of 1966, a relatively weak bill that established some standards for the packaging and labeling of consumer goods and provided for the establishment of voluntary uniform packaging standards by industry.

Since the middle of the 1960s, these consumer protection measures have been followed by many others. However, a review of much of this legislation, as well as bills passed in the preceding periods of consumer protection activity, reveals a general similarity in the circumstances of their passage. First there is public disclosure of the existence of circumstances considered to be adverse to the consumer interest, followed by a proposed legislative remedy. Almost invariably, this generates opposition by business interests, and occasionally regulatory agencies, who feel themselves threatened. If the proposal becomes law, it frequently reflects the play of opposing forces and often contains little of its initial thrust.

There are some who believe that the current phase of consumer protection is a short-lived phenomenon that will fade away in much the same manner as its predecessors. Frequently, those who hold this belief are reductionists who tend to relate the occurrence of complex phenomena to single causes. This viewpoint is particularly likely to be held by people who find it difficult to adapt to changing circumstances.

Although their number has diminished over the last decade or so, there are still businessmen who think that if it weren't for Ralph Nader the present consumer movement would not have occurred. Other ascribe the current interest in consumer protection to a desire for publicity and self-aggrandizement on the part of the politicians and others. This point of view was typified by Edward Thiele, president of a large advertising agency, who described what he called "consumeritis" as "a contagious inflammation of the consumer-interest portion of the brain often resulting from political ambition or desire to derive favor from groups of consumers through personal publicity. Symptoms include a strong tendency to invent issues where no issues exist. If not treated, severe cases may lead to demagoguery." There is an element of unconscious irony in the last part of that statement.

Marketing Practices

A central factor in the upsurge of consumer unrest was the pervasiveness of an array of questionable marketing practices. Many of them are attributable to competitive pressures as much as any deliberate intent to deceive or shortchange consumers. They are the result of the application of two key marketing ideas: the "marketing concept" and "market segmentation."

A firm's application of the marketing concept leads to a concentration on marketing rather than production. It begins with the identification of an unfilled consumer need. The seller then develops a product and a marketing program designed to meet that need rather than first developing a product and then seeking to determine the need it will satisfy.

The evolution of the marketing concept in the late 1950s was a reflection of marketing's prior success in satisfying basic needs. Sellers in a society in which those needs are not satisfied face a situation where consumers are relatively undiscriminating. It is largely a matter of producing goods that will be bought uncritically as long as they provide a reasonable approximation of need satisfaction. Under these circumstances, a Henry Ford can ignore the factor of car color preferences and give buyers "any color as long as it's black."

But when basic needs were satisfied, as appears to have occurred in the mid-1950s, it is difficult to make one product that will satisfy a wide spectrum of consumer needs. Instead, it becomes necessary to differentiate the needs that exist in a given market. This is the process of market segmentation. Following a policy of market segmentation, a toothpaste manufacturer, for example, looks beyond the basic need satisfied by his product (and those of his competitors) for clean and healthy teeth. He attempts to identify large groups of consumers—market segments—that have other needs that toothpaste might satisfy, such as the desire for "fresh breath" or "sex appeal."

Theoretically, the application of the marketing concept and market segmentation should lead to more perfect consumer satisfaction. Ultimately, however, under competitive pressure, continual refinements of segmentation tended to lead to an emphasis on the satisfaction of needs that some critics consider to be either trivial or irrelevant, as in the toothpaste with sex appeal.

In addition, as part of their efforts to differentiate their products, many marketers relied on contrived rather than objectively real product differences. This led to situations where TV commercials asked one to believe that the most relevant aspect of an automobile was the physical dimensions of the pretty girl selling it; where several makers of analgesics were claiming that their respective products dissolved faster, although this bore little relation to their pain-killing qualities; and where uncommon characteristics were imparted to common, yet mysteriously named, ingredients such as Shell gasoline's "platformate." Other problems arose from advertising's use of phrases such as "the better mouthwash" and "gets clothes 25 percent cleaner," without specifying the basis of comparison.

Advertising was not the only problem. Other promotional practices designed to capture market share included the use of "cents off" on items where it was impossible to determine the original selling price. Contests and games of chance designed to increase patronage were often rigged and had minuscule and secret (to the consumer) odds of winning.

Packaging, too, came in for its share of criticism. A relatively few packages were nakedly deceptive, but there were other packaging problems. Some had their source in the belief that consumers were responsive to a greater array of package sizes, or that more in-store exposure would result. Others stemmed from a desire to conceal a price increase or maintain a customary price by making small reductions in package contents. The result was what many consumer advocates claimed to be a bewildering array of packages that made rational buyer choice difficult if not impossible. This problem was compounded by the use of fanciful names for the package sizes such as "jumbo half quart" to describe a pint bottle.

These marketing practices, none of which led to extreme consequences for the consumer, were nonetheless widespread and covered the type of items most frequently purchased. For less frequently purchased durable goods, such as appliances or automobiles, a favorite sales stimulation device was the annual model change. While in the long run this policy might lead to substantial product improvements, in the short run the model changes were often superficial. They added to consumer expense through complications of inventory and repair without providing commensurate benefit.

Technological Change

An additional factor in consumer unrest was an accelerating rate of technological change, which manifested itself in various ways. First, and most obviously, it generated a stream of new products that both delighted and bewildered many consumers. They were delighted to the extent that the new products provided an opportunity to satisfy longstanding needs but were bewildered by the demands these products made on their knowledge as consumers.

One major application of technology was in the substitution of synthetic for natural products. In recent years, for example, it became possible to synthesize food products with respect to both flavor and nutrition. This gave us meatless "meat" products, synthetic coffee creamers, so-called "filled" milk products, and eggless eggnog. In addition to these synthetic foods, developments in food technology permitted the introduction or modification of food ingredients. Numerous chemical preservatives and additives, the long-term effects of which were unknown, were added to foods; and the opportunities for food adulteration were increased. For example, the development of a fat-encapsulation process permitted raising the fat content of frankfurters to 50 percent in a manner undetectable to the consumer. Facing these complexities, as well as many others, made it difficult for the consumer to identify the best and most healthy food buy.

The substitution of synthetic for natural fibers affected the consumer's ability to make judgments about textile products in terms of basic characteristics like durability, porosity, and absorbency, and also with respect to laundering or dry cleaning. The housewife who was once faced with the relatively simple choice among cotton, linen, rayon, wool, and silk was now confronted with a wide array of synthetics. Even though the various labeling acts helped her to identify the basic fiber composition of an item, it strained her expertise to differentiate between the performance characteristics of such synthetic fibers as nylon and polyester.

The aspect of the problems faced by consumers in coming to grips with the products of modern technology was succinctly summed up by Betty Furness, White House special assistant for consumer affairs, when she said:

> You gave us nylon but didn't tell us it melts. You gave us insect spray, but you didn't say it would kill the cat. You gave us plastic bags, but didn't warn us that it could, and has, killed babies. You gave us detergents, but didn't tell us they were polluting our rivers and streams. And you gave us the pill, but didn't tell us we were guinea pigs.

Technology, of course, also played a role in increasing the technical complexity of products. The modern American automobile with its 1,400 parts is vastly more complex than was the Model T Ford. With addition of such items as air conditioning, automatic transmission, and other power options, complexity increased greatly, and with it came a geometric progression in the probability and cost of breakdown. The same can be said for many other items introduced on a wide scale into the American home within the last two decades, ranging from automatic dishwashers to self-cleaning ovens.

Technological complexity tended to increase production and repair problems, both of which fostered consumer frustration. The consumer was not the only one to be frustrated, however. In 1968, an appliance retailer, commenting on the low quality of the appliances he was getting from the manufacturer, said: "It's a horror story. I'm being overwhelmed by inferior, poorly manufactured merchandise. When people ask me what business I'm in, I tell them 'the garbage business.' " Presumably, the customers who ultimately received the merchandise were inclined to agree.

Part of the repair problem was attributable to poor design. This was particularly true in the automobile industry, where styling, rather than repair considerations, seemed to predominate. In the same year that the appliance dealer was voicing his complaints, an automobile insurance executive was citing examples of poor automotive design: the car that required removal of a bumper to gain access to a burned-out taillight, and the replacement bumper-grille assembly that required three men to align it and fifty-seven bolts to attach it to the car.

Another aspect of the repair problem was attributable to the fact that marketing had been too successful in stimulating and satisfying the consumer's demand for convenience. Consumers were buying everything from "space command" remote tuning on TV sets to automatic ice-cube makers on refrigerators. It was not until these broke down that they were faced with the full cost of such conveniences. Some of that cost involved the difficulty of finding a competent repairman, partly because repairmen themselves had difficulty keeping up with the latest product developments. In addition, some sellers abdicated their responsibility for ensuring adequate after-sale service.

Technology had a post-purchase impact on consumers, apart from repair problems. In the 1960s the computer became common in retailer inventory, credit, and billing operations. Frequently, consumers benefited indirectly through this application of computer technology as the lower costs and better inventory control that resulted increased retailer efficiency. The realities of this benefit were usually unknown to consumers, however, and were sometimes overshadowed by the impact of various deficiencies in the computer system that impinged on them more directly.

Often, consumers who had been used to personal contact in their dealings with retailers found that they were communicating their problems about billing errors, etc., to a machine programmed only to handle relatively routine occurrences and incapable of exercising judgment. "The normal result," as Martin L. Ernst of the consulting firm of Arthur D. Little pointed out, "is that the customer writes letter after letter in a non-answering void, his resentment growing at each cycle—[no company] has . . . provided an indicator mechanism for customers to register disagreement with the billing data reported to them. This depersonalization and resentment undoubtedly played some role in fostering the general mood for consumer discontent."

Social Developments

Social developments were also conducive to the growth of the consumer movement. As a whole, consumers were becoming more educated and more affluent. At the same time, expectations were rising. This was reflected in the growth of popular activism, which appeared to have its roots in the civil rights movement. By the beginning of the 1960s a widespread activist civil rights movement had developed that culminated in the 1963 civil rights march on Washington. The civil rights protests demonstrated that it was possible for popular activism to change unjust and outmoded institutional forms. The discovery of this popular power helped to shape other protest movements like the ones that mounted demonstrations against the Vietnam War, then at its peak, and against other policies and institutions. It was the era of picketing, "civil disobedience," and "nonnegotiable demands." Although many of these efforts were undoubtedly counterproductive, they were successful to some extent.

The spirit of protest demonstrated by these movements helped to infuse the energies of consumer protesters, who, while they were less militant, occupied a broader popular base. Protest groups representing consumers and armed with various consumer grievances quickly learned the arts of buttonholing legislators, mounting store boycotts, and picketing to express their discontent. An example is the successful picketing and publicity campaign mounted in 1970 by a group of suburban Chicago housewives protesting local supermarkets' use of food freshness codes that were incomprehensible to shoppers. Such activities were much more visible than the isolated consumer's letter of complaint dashed off to a company executive. Unlike the consumer acting in isolation, popular protest activities with a consumer orientation were considered to be newsworthy by the popular press and received widespread coverage.

If any movement as diffuse and all-encompassing as consumerism could be said to have a leader at the national level, that leader was Ralph Nader. He had come into the public limelight in connection with his book on auto safety and other consumer protection activities. But the event that established him as the principal consumer spokesman occurred at a 1968 Senate hearing on auto safety, when the president of General Motors was forced to admit that GM had subjected Nader to an intensive investigation of his personal background in an attempt to discredit him. With this disclosure of a corporate Goliath picking on a consumer David, Ralph Nader became an instant hero to millions of American consumers. It is ironic that the large damage settlement subsequently awarded to Ralph Nader by the courts because of this incident helped to finance an intensification of his involvement in consumer-protection activities.

The protest movements and the riots of the late 1960s also served to focus public attention on the needs of special groups of consumers. Particular attention was paid to the consumer problems of minority groups and the poor, with the appearance of several books about the victimization of the poor such as David Caplovitz's *The Poor Pay More*. The War on Poverty declared by President Johnson provided the impetus for a Federal Trade Commission examination of unsavory selling practices in Washington, D.C., and the findings led to an upgrading of intelligence activities on deception practiced on the poor. As Esther Peterson, then the President's adviser on consumer affairs, put it: "If we are overcharged, we can absorb the loss. When a poor person overpays, he sinks that much deeper in poverty."

In addition, attention was given to the consumer problems of the elderly; and the role of children as targets of marketing efforts was considered. An activist group, Action on Children's Television, was formed that was concerned, among other things, with the amount of television commercials directed at children.

Reinforcing and interacting with the current of consumer protest were a number of books that addressed themselves to various topics relating to consumer protection. These ranged from John Kenneth Galbraith's relatively intellectual *The Affluent Society*, a central theme of which was the misallocation of society's resources, to Jessica Mitford's more popularly oriented *American Way of Death*. There were many others, including several published by Ralph Nader and investigative groups operating under his aegis, and one by a U.S. Senator.

One book whose significance was largely unrecognized in 1962, when it was published, was Rachel Carson's *Silent Spring*—the muted opening gun in the environmental pollution battle. Although that issue is related only peripherally to consumerism, two aspects of the book were more directly relevant. First, the revelations in *Silent Spring* with respect to pesticide chemical contamination served to sensitize the American public to their unwelcome ingestion of chemicals in what they had formerly believed to be completely wholesome food. This was to surface later in consumerism's concern with both direct and indirect (through animal consumption of harmful chemicals) chemical food additives. Second, the public concern about pollution that emerged subsequently provided a focal point for latent antibusiness attitudes that would later play a role in consumer protection.

The popular press, too, played a role in sensitizing the general public to consumer protection issues. Major newspapers and mass circulation magazines began to run regular columns on the subject, as well as devoting more space to everyday reporting of current developments.

As might be expected, an issue that was gaining visibility and that had such broad public appeal attracted the attention of politicians. President John F. Kennedy gave the initial impetus to political recognition of consumer problems in 1962 with his "consumer bill of rights" embracing "the right to safety," "the right to be informed," "the right to choose," and "the right to be heard." Subsequent years saw additional messages on the subject by Presidents Johnson and Nixon. These presidential messages helped to legitimize the consumer protection movement, but of greater immediate importance was President Johnson's creation, in 1965, of the White House post of special assistant to consumer affairs. Its position in the executive branch sometimes caused it to be overshadowed by political considerations, but it was quite effective in providing an official consumer spokesman.

Political action on the consumer front was not confined to the presidency, however. As the number of bills mentioned earlier suggest, many legislators became involved in the passage of new laws intended to give the consumer more power in the marketplace. In the process, extensive hearings were held, of which many received widespread press coverage. One outgrowth of these hearings was the exposure of major shortcomings in the government agencies charged with administering existing consumer protection legislation.

Often, there seemed to be a greater concern with the rights of those being regulated than with consumers, who were supposed to be protected. For example, referring to a legislatively imposed deadline for reducing the fat content of hot dogs, an internal memorandum of the Consumer Marketing Service of the U.S. Department of Agriculture said: "One point we must emphasize is that we will not take hasty action in enforcing regulation. There will be no set deadline for enforcement of the regulations." As Senator Ribicoff pointed out, the public was being misled if after the great amount of publicity the fat limitation had received, it was not enforced as of its implementation date. He called the memorandum the "Department's plan to subvert its own regulations."

Although the interest of politicians in consumer protection was propitious, from the consumer's viewpoint there were factors other than considerations of consumer welfare that played a role in the legislative process. One of these was that consumer protection was relatively inexpensive. At a time when the federal budget was strained by the costs of the Vietnam War, consumer protection measures promised to be a palliative with low cost and wide popular support. Second, it was a time when the political initiative was increasingly being taken by the White House. Consumer protection legislation offered an opportunity for legislative initiative in an area that was relatively free from White House influence. Finally, in a period when war-caused inflation was eroding consumer purchasing power, it was consistent with a common legislative strategy of dealing with symptoms rather than causes. It was legislatively easier to attempt to enhance the value of consumer goods themselves than to deal with a more basic problem—a progressive reduction in the value of the dollars used to buy the goods.

The Maturation of the Consumer Movement

By the end of the 1970s there was considerable evidence of change in the consumer movement. One manifestation of this change was a marked slowdown in the rate of passage of new consumer legislation at the federal level. Between 1966—a year when the movement for consumer protection legislation was getting into high gear—and 1975, fourteen pieces of consumer legislation were enacted. This decade of consumer protection activity saw the enactment of approximately the same quantity of consumer legislation as had appeared in the six decades that preceded it.

The passage of the Magnuson–Moss Warranty / Federal Trade Commission Improvement Act in 1975 was probably the legislative high-water mark of the current era of consumer protection. The years since its passage have seen little in terms of the enactment of significant consumer legislation. Since the passage of the Magnuson–Moss Act, the most significant legislative development was the defeat, in 1978, of a bill to establish an agency for consumer protection to plead the consumers' cause before various federal agencies. The defeat of that proposal, which had been around in one form or another for almost ten years, may ultimately be seen as the turning point in the current era of consumer protection.

Several factors contributed to a reduction in the momentum of the consumer movement. First, it was inevitable that the frenetic pace of consumer legislation that marked the preceding decade could not be maintained if other areas of legislative activity were to receive adequate attention. Second, experience with newly passed consumer protection laws was revealing problems ranging from a lack of resources for their efficient implementation, to administrative inadequacies on the part of regulatory agencies concerned in implementation. Added to this was a general change in the political climate. Offsetting the public's desire for legislative protection against unfair or misleading seller practices was a growing awareness, distrust, and resentment of the role of government in everyday life. There was a greater tendency to question government action and the resulting benefits, if any, in terms of costs. Finally, there was evidence that leadership of the consumer movement at the national level was faltering, partly as a consequence of its success. During the administration of President Carter, several associates of Ralph Nader were placed in regulatory positions where they found that the task of implementing legislation was considerably harder than helping to formulate and lobby for it. Related to this was the fact that as time passed, Ralph Nader, who had been at the legislative heart of numerous consumer protection measures, appeared to suffer a diminution of political effectiveness. However, his public popularity as spokesman for the consumer movement was still strong.

Some might say that in combination these facts mark the end of the current era of consumer protection. It is probably more valid to conclude that what we are witnessing is an institutionalized acceptance of the idea of consumer protection, with a change in emphasis from rapid expansion into new areas to the perfecting of existing consumer protection laws and the improvement of their administration by federal regulators.

65. An Overview of Agricultural Policy . . . Past, Present, and Future
Raymond E. Owens

Reprinted from *Economic Review* (Federal Reserve Bank of Richmond, May/June 1987), pp. 39–50.

Recent Agricultural Experience

The most recent agricultural "boom and bust" cycle began in the early 1970s. The boom was caused by the combination of small world stocks of grains, strong economic growth, and relatively abundant credit worldwide. The price of grain was bid up globally as nations sought to improve their dietary standards. The United States, which held a large portion of world grain stocks, liquidated those stocks on the world market. The strong demand and decreasing stock levels raised prices an caused agricultural producers, especially in the United States, to invest in more efficient production techniques. Increased capital investment in farming was often funded by long-term debt.

As agricultural prices moved up, federal support prices followed. A price support is a guaranteed minimum, or floor price: At that price the federal government will buy whatever the market will not absorb. Because prices could fall only as far as the support price, farmers were willing to take on long-term debt to finance land and equipment that expanded production.

The expansion of demand enjoyed by farmers during the 1970s vanished by the early 1980s. The boom ended in a manner similar to that following World War I. With world prices high in the 1970s, many nations began producing more of their own food and feed. Adding to their decision to do that in the early 1980s were their lower income prospects and lessened access to credit. With lower export earnings and the need to service debt, many countries found themselves with less foreign exchange to purchase agricultural goods abroad. As a result, world demand for agricultural exports declined. The United States, which had benefited in the 1970s when world trade expanded, shouldered a large part of the decrease when world trade declined.

The poor prospect for agricultural prices in the 1980s was not recognized by those who formulated farm policy in 1981. The 1981 Farm Bill, structured in a manner similar to all agricultural legislation since the Agricultural Adjustment Act of 1933, increased price supports for a variety of crops from 1981 to 1985. As a result, the gap between domestic price supports and world prices widened, providing additional incentives for American farmers to produce surpluses, and domestic stocks of grain to accumulate rapidly.

At the same time, a number of producers who had taken on long-term debt in the 1970s found that the price levels of the early 1980s provided them with insufficient income to service their debt. Such farmers, especially those who encountered drought or unforeseen problems, experienced financial stress and in some cases left agriculture through bankruptcy, foreclosure, or other means.

Striking parallels exist between the situation facing American agriculture in the 1930s and the 1980s. Today, as then, the farm sector is experiencing a period of depressed farm prices resulting from stock buildups. In both instances these stock buildups occurred after a slump in foreign demand. And finally, in both cases, the basic farm policy approach is similar. In fact, many farm analysts believe that current farm policy may have hampered adjustment by the agricultural sector to the latest episode of weak demand, and thus, may have contributed to the current problems facing agriculture.

The 1985 Farm Bill

The architects of farm legislation in 1985 faced large and increasing government holdings of commodity stocks, widespread financial stress among farmers, and the overfarming of land and the resulting depletion of land resources. Of course, there were other influences. Tighter money and higher interest rates often made the rollover or expansion of loans more difficult. Also exports were affected adversely by the increased foreign exchange value of the dollar and trade barriers and restrictions imposed on United States agricultural products by foreign countries.

The drafters of the 1985 Farm Bill had two primary goals: the support of farm income and the reduction of domestic government-held grain stocks. Their secondary goal was to modify farm credit mechanisms, which were facing financial problems. Initially, these goals were to be met through programs that placed greater reliance on market signals to make agricultural policies effective for the long term.

The policy tools chosen by Congress, however, turned out to be little different from those employed almost continuously over the past fifty years. The Food Security Act of 1985 was hardly a revolutionary departure from previous farm policy, although it was billed as such during its formulation. Although the Bill eliminated the yearly increases in support prices in effect since 1977, it retained the traditional two-tiered price support system and otherwise merely extended production limits, trade incentives, and farm credit programs.

Commodity Programs

The commodity programs that are the backbone of the 1985 Farm Bill attempt to limit commodity production by inducing farmers to voluntarily constrain their production in a manner prescribed by the government. Farmers who comply with the constraints are eligible to receive price supports or other financial incentives from the federal government. Such programs are usually administered through the United States Department of Agriculture (USDA).

Export Incentives

In addition to commodity programs, the 1985 Farm Bill establishes incentives for foreign nations to purchase American farm commodities. These programs are intended to reduce surplus stocks by encouraging additional foreign demand.

A primary incentive included in the export programs is providing credit assistance for foreign purchases of American farm products. Additionally, stocks of government-held grain and dairy products are to be made available to exporters and others to counter "unfair" trade practices, to offset high domestic price supports and unfavorable movements in the exchange value of the dollar, and to expand markets. Promotional programs, designed to provide information to foreign nations, are also provided for under the bill.

Public Law 480 is another conduit for exports. This law allows a qualifying nation to receive United States food grain stocks and dairy products free or at favorable long-term financing if the recipient qualifies under the law.

Food Stamps

As a corollary to the export subsidies, the food stamp program is aimed at subsidizing domestic consumption of agricultural products. This program, along with programs such as the school lunch program, however, has a relatively small effect on total domestic demand for agricultural products.

Credit Programs

Agricultural credit policy is channeled through two programs: the Farmers Home Administration (FmHA), a government agency, and the Farm Credit System (FCS), a government-sponsored agency. The programs are similar in that they originated in the 1930s and both are charged with making loanable funds available to the agricultural sector. Their specific areas of responsibility and methods used to achieve their objectives differ in many respects, however.

FmHA initially provided credit to small farmers to help them adjust to economic changes; those receiving credit were normally poor credit risks. In recent years, FmHA credit has been made increasingly available to larger farmers. Still, many borrowers remain poor credit risks, and FmHA loans usually carry more favorable terms than commercial alternatives.

FCS is a member-owned cooperative system consisting of twelve regional banks with numerous branches. The FCS seeks credit worthy farm borrowers for a variety of loan terms. The system has three lending arms. The federal land banks make the long-term loans usually collateralized by real estate. The Federal Intermediate Credit Banks and Production Credit Association provide short- and intermediate-term credit. The Central Bank for Cooperatives provides loans to farmer cooperatives. FCS raises funds through the issuance of bonds and lends the proceeds to the agricultural sector.

The economic difficulties of agriculture over the past few years have contributed to weak earnings for the FCS. In 1985 Congress put in place a federal line of credit that may be used to cover temporary liquidity problems of the FCS should the need arise.

The Cost of Farm Policy

Farm policy affects domestic farmers, consumers, foreign policy makers, and others. When policy changes, these groups benefit and lose to different extents. As a result it is difficult to fully measure the net welfare effects of farm policy.

A relatively simple method by which part of the cost of farm policy may be measured is to examine the annual budget USDA devotes to direct agricultural programs for price supports and product promotions. In the early 1980s, the direct budget costs (those borne directly by the taxpayer) totaled $3 billion to $5 billion per year. In 1987, the cost is projected to reach about $3 billion, or about $700 for every nonfarm family in the United States.

The cost of farm policy is thus of great concern to Congress, taxpaying households, and farmers. The high cost impedes congressional efforts to reduce the federal budget deficits. Households, who bear the cost of farm policy, are questioning this wealth transfer with a more critical eye. Farmers themselves are divided over the effectiveness of the farm policies. Certain farmers have come to believe that the policies allow inefficient producers to remain in agriculture, and they argue that too many farmers contribute to the problem of mounting agricultural surpluses. Many farmers also express concern that their incomes depend increasingly on federal dollars. With 25 percent of farm net cash income coming from direct government payments in 1986, recipients fear that shifts in agricultural policy could result in sharp reductions in farm income.

The Effectiveness of Farm Policy

As noted earlier, the primary goals of agricultural policy are to reduce the accumulation of surplus stocks of farm commodities and to support farm income. The success of policy in accomplishing these objectives is open to question.

Commodity Stocks

Carryover stocks have been rising in recent years despite acreage-reduction programs. The increases have occurred because agricultural production levels have been maintained while exports have fallen sharply.

Domestic grain production has remained at relatively high levels because set-aside acreage has often been offset by increased yields. For example, 13 million acres of corn were set aside in 1986, but total production was 8.2 billion bushels, the second highest harvest ever. Weak corn exports compounded the problem of large production, leaving ending stocks at 5.7 billion bushels, far above the previous record of 4 billion bushels set in 1985. Other major crops show a similar, though often not as dramatic, pattern.

Income Supports

A second major goal of the 1985 Farm Bill was the support of farm income. Farm cash receipts from marketings declined sharply in 1986 and are expected to decrease further this year. The decrease comes entirely out of crop cash receipts, as livestock cash receipts are actually increasing over the period.

This pattern is influenced by the price support mechanisms. Crop cash receipts are based on sales at the prevailing market price or government loan price. Since market prices and loan prices fell sharply, it is not surprising that crop cash receipts also fell.

Farm income has been supported, however, despite the decline in cash receipts. As noted earlier, farmers' total price support compensation includes deficiency payments and the loan price. It was also pointed out that deficiency payments grow when loan prices drop and target prices remain relatively unchanged.

The effect of higher direct government payments and lower costs of production has meant higher income levels to farmers. It appears, therefore, that income is being maintained by higher government payments and not by a greater reliance on market forces as early architects of the 1985 Farm Bill had hoped.

66. Investment in Natural Resources

Council of Economic Advisers

Reprinted from the *Economic Report of the President* (Washington, D.C.: U.S. Government Printing Office, 1962), pp. 133–37. The council members responsible for the report were Chairman Walter W. Heller, Gardner Ackley, and Kermit Gordon.

Economic growth is not simply a matter of growth in the size and skills of the labor force, in the quantity and quality of capital goods, and in the productivity of the processes by which these inputs are combined. It is equally a matter of turning more and more of the earth's endowment of natural wealth—soil, sunlight, air, water, minerals, plant and animal life—to the purpose of man. America's position has generally been one of natural plenty, but we cannot complacently assume that the abundance of the past will characterize the future.

But neither is there any reason to suppose that resource limitations will in the foreseeable future place serious limits on the growth of the economy. Technological change, substitution of abundant and cheap raw materials for scarce and expensive ones, investment in improved resource management and conservation, and increased reliance on imports all provide important offsets to the effects of increasing scarcity on the real cost of obtaining resource inputs. Taken together, these factors tend to keep the economy growing along the path of least resistance so far as its resource requirements are concerned. If the various offsets to increasing scarcity are not fully effective, resources can be obtained by digging and drilling deeper, utilizing lower-grade deposits, constructing dams and better waste treatment facilities, and other measures involving higher costs. But the necessity to devote more labor and capital to these tasks would constitute a drag on the economy, tending to cancel some of the efforts we make to stimulate growth. Indeed, taking the economy as a whole, it is equivalent to a decline in productivity.

The Historical Record

A rough judgment as to the probable consequences of continued depletion of resources in the future can be derived by examining the record of the past. The long-term trend of raw materials prices relative to the prices of finished products is a useful, though by no means ideal, indicator of the effectiveness of the offsets to natural scarcity.

The outstanding example of a strong upward price trend is forest products. Even in forestry, however, there are preliminary indications that productivity gains are beginning to offset the effects of scarcity on prices. The index for all minerals has risen slightly less than that for all raw materials, and the subgroups of the minerals index would undoubtedly have occurred if the opportunities of international trade had not been available. This is particularly true of the metals subgroup, where net imports accounted for 44.8 percent of apparent consumption of metallic ores in 1957.

The index for agricultural products shows the effects of the Great Depression, World War II and its aftermath, and the accelerated improvement of agricultural productivity in the 1950s. The last is largely responsible for the decline of the overall index from its 1950–54 peak. It is reasonable to expect that improvements in agricultural productivity will continue to exert a substantial downward pressure on the overall index in the future.

Implications for Public Policy

The lessons to be drawn from this review of past trends are these: First, it is likely that increasing resource scarcity has had only a negligible retarding effect on economic growth during the present century. Rising real costs of obtaining some resources have been largely compensated by declining costs of obtaining others. Second, the historical record does not indicate that more rapid economic growth will simply result in our "running out of resources" more quickly. On the contrary, past investments have permitted resources to be extracted more efficiently and used more efficiently.

Public policy has contributed to this success by limitation of economic waste, the development and adoption of improved methods in agriculture, forestry, and other fields, the unified development of river valleys, and a variety of other measures. Finally, the opportunity to obtain raw materials from abroad has been important in the past and will be increasingly important in the future.

Preventing resource scarcity from being a drag on economic growth is by no means the only objective of policy in this field. Particularly for water, forest, and scenic resources, an important objective is the provision of aesthetic and recreational benefits which are not reflected in aggregate measures of economic activity because they do not pass through the marketplace. The difficulty of determining objective standards by which such benefits can be weighed is obviously not a valid reason for neglecting them.

Water Resources

There is wide agreement that one of the most serious resource problems facing the United States at present and in the immediate future is the development of water resources. The use of water has been increasing rapidly as a result of population growth, higher living standards, increasing urbanization, rapid growth of industries that are heavy users of water, increases in the amount of land under irrigation, and other factors. In the eastern United States and the Pacific Northwest, the problems presented by these trends can be met for the next few decades by an adequate and appropriately timed program of investment in: (1) multiple purpose water resource development, which, in addition to other benefits, permits the collection and storage of water for use as needed; and (2) facilities for treatment of industrial and municipal wastes. In some of the dry regions of the West, however, the opportunities for further development of water resources will be exhausted within the next two decades. Barring major scientific breakthroughs, the continued economic development of these regions will soon come to depend on how effectively an almost fixed supply of water is used to satisfy the most important of the various industrial, agricultural, and municipal needs for water.

It is certain that additional investment to increase the quantity and improve the quality of the supplies of water will be a major part of any solution to the problem. Pollution control, in particular, will require major investment expenditures in the coming decades. The enactment last year of the administration's proposal for an expanded program of grants under the Federal Water Pollution Control Act and extension of federal authority to seek abatement of pollution of navigable waters were important steps forward. But the fact that water resources in some regions of the country will soon be close to fully developed calls attention to a consideration that is relevant to water resources policy for the country as a whole: Investment in development of existing water supplies is not a complete solution to the problem of water scarcity, nor is it necessarily the economically desirable solution under every particular set of circumstances. A variety of offsets to increasing scarcity are available, and each has a role to play. In particular, additional research and development in methods of conserving and augmenting water supplies, including desalinization, weather modification, reduction of evaporation losses, cheaper and more effective waste treatment, and more efficient use of water in industry and agriculture may produce high returns.

Since expensive investments must be undertaken to increase the quantity and quality of water supplies, it is appropriate that the costs be reflected in prices charged industrial and agricultural users. To treat a costly commodity as if it were free only encourages excessive use. There is evidence that significant reductions in water withdrawals could be achieved in many important water using activities and that they can be expected to occur if proper deterrents are provided. The burdens of scarcity on the economy cannot be entirely eliminated by using scarce capital to augment the supply of scarce water. But the burden can be minimized by a proper balance between investments in increased supply on the one hand, and price increases to eliminate efficient use on the other.

Agricultural Land

The problem of agricultural land stands in sharp contrast to the problem of water resources. Whereas in the latter the problems requiring attention are those posed by increasing scarcity, in the former they are problems of adjusting to abundance.

Agriculture is the major source of downward pressure on the price index for all raw materials, and land is in ample supply. There are approximately 640 million acres of land suitable for cultivation in the United States at present, but only about 450 million are actually used for crops or pasture. Present indications are that only slightly more than 400 million acres of cropland (including cropland pastured and idle) will be in use by 1980 to produce agricultural products.

The major land resource investments required during the next several decades will, therefore, involve the conservation and protection of remaining farmland and the transfer of land to nonagricultural use rather than bringing more land into agricultural production. There are currently close to 70 million acres of land used for cropland that are subject to severe erosion hazard or otherwise not suitable for cultivation over the long run. Much of this land could be transferred to provide products or services, such as forestry and recreation, for which the demand is rising. At the same time, about 17 million of the 240 million acres of good land now in pasture or forest could be converted to cropland.

The Department of Agriculture currently has plans for a long-range land-use adjustment program. This program has three major facets: transfer of cropland to grass; transfer of cropland to forest; and greater emphasis on wildlife and recreational development in the small watershed programs. As the program develops, it will be possible for supply management to place less emphasis on temporary diversion of acreage from the production of specific crops.

The present problems of U.S. agriculture, which reflect in part the fact that the pace of technological progress in agriculture exceeds the rate of growth in demand for farm products, should not blind us to the important lessons to be drawn from the record. When strong policy measures are taken well in advance, technological progress affords an escape from increasing scarcity. Indeed, it is technology that largely determines which portions of the environment are regarded as resources and which are not. Research not only makes possible the more effective use of existing resources, as in the case of agriculture, but may create important new ones. The record of agriculture also illustrates, however, the long lag between the decision to act and the appearance of the benefits. Careful and continuing analysis of present and future resource needs, coupled with readiness to act when the indications of potential difficulties become persuasive, is the best hope for success in meeting the resource requirements of rapid economic growth.

67. Two Decades of Energy Policy

Hans H. Landsberg

Reprinted with permission of the publisher, Resources for the Future, from *Resources*, March 1990, pp. 5–8. Hans H. Landsberg is senior fellow emeritus in energy and natural resources at Resources for the Future.

There is a perennial debate over whether the country has ever had an energy policy or has merely had a collection of policies, each applying to a specific segment of the industries that comprise the U.S. energy sector. Whatever the answer, it is arguable that the early seventies constitute a dividing line between an era for which the second characterization holds true and an era that saw a closer approach to an energy policy with broadly defined goals applicable across the board. In the latter era energy policy appears to have been driven initially by concern for supply security and stability, including diversification of source; by efforts to use energy more efficiently; and increasingly, by the need to reconcile energy production and consumption with the maintenance of environmental integrity. It is fair to say that few realized on Earth Day 1970 how difficult it would be to understand the underlying complexities of that last-named goal; agree on specific targets; make the required measurements; and shape appropriate, effective, efficient, and equitable policies.

To appreciate the change in the focus of energy policy that began in the early seventies, it is useful to review the 1960s, during which the United States was on an energy binge. In that decade energy consumption averaged 5.2 percent per year, as compared to 1.4 percent per year between 1970 and 1980. Oil consumption soared 4.8 percent per year in the sixties but slowed down to an average annual rate of 1.5 percent between 1970 and 1980. Electricity generation rose an average of 10.3 percent per year in the sixties and decreased to a rate of 4.9 percent annually between 1970 and 1988.

Obviously, the rate of growth in demand that prevailed in the 1960s could not long be sustained. A number of factors suggested that in the future energy would no longer be in abundant supply and at low cost from domestic sources. These factors included a turnaround in the decline of the Btu:GNP ratio, which indicated a worsening in the efficiency of energy use; the failure of oil and gas reserves to grow commensurate with increases in consumption; the declining efficiency of power plants; environmental deterioration requiring remedies that would entail higher energy costs; and doubts about the availability of nuclear energy supplies at the low costs previously predicted. Many expressed concern about the future cost and reliability of oil imports.

Pre-OPEC Energy Policy

It has become conventional wisdom that late 1973 constitutes the great divide between pre-OPEC and post-OPEC energy. It is convenient to think in these terms as long as one realizes that the 1973 OPEC oil price shock merely accelerated the consequences of worsening supply and demand trends and aggravated the impact of rising environmental concerns.

On the whole, energy policy in the pre-OPEC era addressed separately the issues of each energy system, without any attempt to produce an integrated policy system. Moreover, policies were heavily directed at controlling the fiscal environment in which the energy industry operated, and employed regulatory measures to do so. For instance, oil policies addressed matters such as the industry's tax situation and the extent and nature of state regulation of the industry's output. Beginning in the late fifties, these policies were supplemented by attempts to curb oil imports that were perceived as threatening to domestic producers because they cost less than domestic oil supplies. Ironically, the control system collapsed just months before the OPEC oil price shock. Among other things, it had encouraged the depletion of domestic energy resources and disturbed oil exploration and development decisions.

Regarding coal, pre-OPEC policies addressed principally three areas: the conditions under which federal land was to be leased for mining purposes, the health and safety of miners, and the fate of surface-mined land. All three affected coal prices, the location of mining activity, and the financial condition of coal companies—none of which were the policies' objectives. No attempt was made to link policies concerning coal to those affecting oil. As for natural gas, the third fossil fuel, policies primarily addressed the price that gas producers could charge.

Hydro and nuclear energy were relatively small contributors to the nation's total energy supply in the pre-OPEC era. With hydro energy, the issue had long been the power of the federal government to fix the conditions, including rates, under which a given hydro project could be built and operated. With nuclear energy, the main issues were, in the early years, safety, health, proliferation, and management of nuclear waste, all within the purview of the federal government.

The above sampling suggests that policies for each of the energy systems were separate lots, related to the others at best inadvertently. At times the policies conflicted. Nonetheless, they reflected a common goal—the supply of abundant, cheap, and reliable energy to support a growing economy and allow a reasonable profit to producers. A secondary goal was to retain, or where necessary establish, a role for the federal government, initially as steward of the nation's resources, and later as provider of acceptable conditions of life for those involved in the production process. The government's role as steward of the nation's resources had wide ramifications, as indicated by the establishment of a prorationing system for oil production, the regulation of shipping rates for coal transported by rail, and the regulation of natural gas prices, to name only three. The government's regulation of the electric power industry affected everything from the siting of plants to allowable returns on investment to rates charged to different classes of customers.

The government's role was strong throughout the energy system. Yet there was no mechanism to assess whether energy policies, either singly or jointly, in fact favored cheap, abundant, and reliable energy supplies, or whether low cost, abundance, and reliability were indeed consistent objectives. For example, the prorationing of oil coupled with the setting of output targets only served to make oil more, not less, costly, though not necessarily so for the long run. Land reclamation policies no doubt raised the price of coal. Certainly the restrictive leasing of federal land containing oil made energy supplies less abundant.

Post-OPEC Energy Policy

By the 1970s it was obvious that the goal of abundant and cheap energy was becoming obsolete. The OPEC embargo of 1973 undermined the goal of reliability. As a result, the post-OPEC era generated energy policies that directly addressed both the supply of and the demand for energy within the context of the performance of the overall economy. These policies have been driven by the search for supply security and a concern for environmental protection. In particular, security acquired a priority status. Legislation now aimed at both reducing the consumption of energy and increasing the supply of energy sources that could replace oil. There was a good deal of ambiguity regarding these policies, for the idea of suppressing demand and letting prices rise was indeed alien to a country richly endowed with energy resources. The government's gut reaction to OPEC's price-boosting enterprise was to control prices. However, the cure was worse than the disease. By holding down the price of domestic oil and thus confronting the consumer with an average domestic/import price that was lower than the OPEC price, the government masked the high OPEC price and prevented demand from responding adequately. Moreover, keeping prices low slowed oil exploration and development. This counterproductive policy was not abandoned until 1981. Freeing the price of natural gas took even longer and was accomplished by a highly complex regulatory regime.

Attempts to reduce demand took various forms, all of them laid down in elaborate statutes. Indeed, the 1970s were the most intensive years of energy legislation. Starting in 1974, Congress passed a series of laws aimed at imposing efficiency in the use of energy, reducing the consumption of oil and gas, establishing tax and fiscal incentives for the use and research and development of renewable energy sources, strengthening supply security by building a strategic petroleum reserve, and so on. Some laws were short-lived and others proved ineffective, but increasingly the goal of energy policies shifted from the attainment of abundant and cheap energy to that of secure and clean energy with prices shaped by market forces.

Congress first attempted to address the need for energy security in 1974, when, ignoring coal's adverse impact on the environment, it ordered oil- and gas-burning power plants to convert to coal—provided that they were equipped with coal-handling and transportation facilities. The effort accomplished little, as few plants made the switch.

In 1975 Congress tried to promote conservation by setting automobile efficiency standards and mandating a ten-year reduction in energy consumption in federal buildings, as well as setting efficiency standards for household appliances. Unhappily, this measure also greatly broadened the oil price control policy that began in 1971 under President Nixon, thus frustrating conservation. Appliance standards never became law, and improving energy efficiency in federal installations remained a minor effort.

Congress made still another stab at conservation in 1976 by requiring the establishment of energy-efficient building standards and by authorizing so-called weatherization grants for low-income households. The first of these measures was stillborn. The second had minimal results.

One of the early actions of the Carter administration was to develop the National Energy Plan, which called for conservation and fuel efficiency, rational pricing and production policies, reasonable certainty and stability in government policies, substitution of abundant energy resources for those in short supply, and development of nonconventional technologies for the future. Its targets for 1985 were to reduce gasoline consumption by 10 percent, establish a petroleum reserve of one billion barrels, increase coal consumption to more than one billion tons per year, bring 90 percent of the existing U.S. homes and all new buildings up to minimum efficiency standards, and use solar energy in more than two million homes. Monetary incentives and disincentives associated with specific standards were to bring about these changes. While the plan reflected a lack of realism in such areas as buildings and solar energy and overestimated industry's willingness to switch to coal, it correctly diagnosed price controls as counterproductive and called for their demise.

Congress responded by establishing the gas-guzzler tax to penalize grossly inefficient automobiles and by authorizing subsidies for alcohol fuel. It also authorized residential energy audits by utilities, ordered the Department of Energy to set appliance standards, and set rules for phasing out price controls. In addition, Congress required utilities to purchase independently generated electricity and encouraged them to institute rate reform. It extended the existing restriction on oil and gas burning in power plants and large industrial facilities and authorized federal loans for investment in pollution control equipment, as well as assistance to areas with increased coal and uranium mining.

Collectively, this legislation aimed at the promotion of energy efficiency and security through diversification of sources; environmental considerations were a minor feature. Indeed, by stressing coal use, it was apt to aggravate environmental stress.

One unhappy legislative initiative rounded out the major energy actions of the post-OPEC era. The Energy Security Act of 1980 is notable because it established the ill-fated Synfuels Corporation, though it also provided additional assistance to alcohol fuel plants and established a

Solar Energy Bank. None of these provisions bore much fruit, especially as this kind of federal activity was anathema to the incoming Reagan administration. The rise and fall of Synfuels Corporation is important not so much for failing to lead to a viable alternative fuel as for leaving a bad taste for federal enterprises that get involved in "picking winners and losers"—a cliché that figures in the ongoing tug of war between interventionists and free marketeers.

What has survived since the legislative frenzy of the 1970s? There is the strategic petroleum reserve, not at the legislated 1-billion-barrel level but approaching a respectable size of 600 million barrels. Lengthened daylight savings time and a reduced speed limit have also proved sturdy survivors. Price controls are gone. Automobile efficiency standards continue to be in force but are not being tightened. Federal aid to nascent technologies has continued, though the fitful nature of annual appropriations has tended to slow research efforts.

There are other encouraging developments. Recently President Bush requested a $19 million congressional appropriation to construct a new laboratory to advance the work of the Solar Energy Research Institute. Photovoltaics may be on the threshold of commercial viability in special utility applications.

Successes are matched by the failures noted earlier. Looking at this ledger, one is tempted to say that consumer- or demand-oriented legislation has fared poorest. Conservation is hard to foster by government fiat. Trying to motivate millions of consumers is a daunting task. But then, some would argue, so is commercializing new technologies.

No Easy Solutions

What will the 1990s bring? Most likely a return to more regulation, and that for several reasons. Perhaps the most important is the ever increasing significance of environmental issues associated with energy. Acid rain, greenhouse gases, and urban smog are three examples. Though there are attempts to manage acid rain through the use of market forces, regulation appears unavoidable. Urban air pollution will require tighter tailpipe emissions standards, possibly modification of cars, and lifestyle changes—none of which will be "demanded," in the market sense, by fuel users. Use of market forces appears even less promising in the management of greenhouse gases.

Connected with these issues is the need to deemphasize coal; yet coal is the most abundant, most widely distributed, and cheapest source of heat and electricity. Nothing short of government intervention will make its users abandon it in favor of oil and gas, which are more costly, less abundant, and, in the case of oil, subject to supply perturbations outside the nation's control. Nor does nuclear energy offer a way out unless or until nuclear reaction designs meet with public approval and waste disposal problems are satisfactorily resolved. Despite continuing advances in technology, the diffusion of renewable energy sources will be years in coming. Nor will the ongoing restructuring of the electric power industry proceed without major government participation.

Looking back on the seventies and early eighties, one finds a broadly spread technological optimism. Nuclear fission, the breeder reactor, fusion, coal liquefaction, oil from shale, gas from unconventional sources, and other technological advances were widely believed to bring relief in the foreseeable future. They have so far failed to do so. At the same time, we have run out of easy solutions. Above all, environmental considerations no longer allow us to regard coal as the universal alternative fuel.

The big question remains: How can we tell when government intervention is indicated? During the Reagan years the federal government sanctioned intercession when the task in question had a high risk, an extended time horizon, and, if successful, a high payoff. It now seems that this triple test holds true for more and more initiatives—and therefore becomes increasingly useless. Thus, more than ever, technological enterprises will, like it or not, call for greater government intervention. So will attempts to motivate consumers, as well as increased international collaboration concerning energy matters. The tendency in the 1980s to rely on the market to bring about desirable results is likely to be reversed in the 1990s—no matter one's ideological inclination.

68. Welfare Dependency: Fact or Myth?
Richard D. Coe

Excerpted and reprinted with permission of the publisher, M.E. Sharpe, Inc., from *Challenge*, September/October 1982, pp. 43–49. Richard D. Coe is an assistant professor of economics at the University of Notre Dame.

The decade of the eighties has been ushered in by a rising conservative attack on the liberal social welfare policies of the 1970s and the late 1960s. The attack has been focused most sharply on those public welfare programs that grew rapidly in the last decade, most notably Aid to Families with Dependent Children (AFDC) and the food stamp program. The most damaging criticism is the argument that these programs actually hurt the poor rather than help them. The central tenet of this argument is

that the growth in the public welfare program has resulted in the concomitant growth of a "welfare class"—a group of people who go through
life subsisting on government welfare checks, trapped in a system that
perpetuates their poverty and dependence.

Does the evidence support such a contention? Until now the data have
not been available for a thorough examination of the long-term dynamics
of welfare use and dependency. With the advent of large-scale panel
studies, we are now in a position to determine the pattern of welfare use
over an extended period of time. Utilizing data from the Panel Study of
Income Dynamics (PSID) initiated at the University of Michigan, this
paper examines the welfare experience of a representative sample of the
U.S. population over the ten-year period 1969–78, inclusive. The PSID
originated in 1968. Since that time it has followed approximately five
thousand families, interviewing them (and any offshoots from the original sample families) each year. Detailed questions are asked concerning
the sources of income of the household, including public welfare income.

Conclusions

Over a ten-year period a surprisingly large percentage of the population had
some experience with the welfare system. In the aggregate, a relatively stable percent of the population (approximately 10 percent) received welfare
income each year. However, over the decade fully one-quarter of the population was in a household that received welfare income at some time.

While the receipt of welfare income was surprisingly widespread, it was
also usually of relatively short duration. Of the 25 percent of the population
that received welfare in the decade, one-half received it in only one or two of
the ten years between 1969 and 1978 (inclusive). Less than one in five (17.5
percent) received welfare in eight or more of the ten years.

Receiving welfare income was clearly not synonymous with being dependent on welfare income as the primary source of a person's means of support. Of all persons who were ever in a household that received welfare,
only one-third were ever in a household that was dependent on welfare
income.

Long-term welfare dependency was the exception rather than the rule
in the decade of the seventies, both for welfare recipients and, perhaps
more important, for that subset of welfare recipients who were at some
time dependent on welfare income. Of all welfare recipients, less than
one-tenth (7.7 percent) were dependent on welfare income in eight or
more of the ten years between 1969 and 1978. Of all welfare recipients
who were ever dependent on welfare income, only one in five (22.3 percent) were long-term dependent. Preliminary results from a more sophisticated econometric analysis by David Boomsma of the effect of entering

the welfare system indicate that previous welfare receipt is not a powerful causal factor in determining current welfare use.

It is difficult on the basis of these results to conclude that there is something inherently pernicious about the welfare system—that it poisons those who touch it with a debilitating dose of dependency. Quite the contrary. The welfare system would seem to be more accurately portrayed as a temporary fallback position for those individuals who suffer unexpected shocks to their more normal style of life. For nonelderly men, those shocks would most likely be an involuntary job loss; for married women, a divorce or separation; for an unmarried woman, the birth of a child. For the vast majority of those people, the welfare system serves as a stepping-stone back to a more normal standard of living. In essence, the welfare system, despite its numerous flaws, by and large fulfills the role that most people probably believe it should fulfill—that of an insurance system against unforeseen (and largely uncontrollable) adverse circumstances. If this characterization of the welfare system is correct, then the idea that the welfare system promotes and perpetuates long-term dependency must be rejected as myth with little grounding in reality. Unfortunately, like all good myths, there is a germ of truth underlying it. A small subset of all welfare recipients—a subset consisting mainly of individuals (and their dependents) who face extremely unfavorable labor market prospects—are indeed dependent on the welfare system for an extended period of time. The question that the reader, and our society, must answer is whether the existence of such a group justifies the wholesale condemnation of the liberal welfare state.

69. The Case for a National Welfare Standard

Paul E. Peterson and Mark C. Rom

Excerpted and reprinted with permission of the publisher, The Brookings Institution, from *The Brookings Review*, Winter 1988, pp. 24–32. Paul E. Peterson is director of the Center for the Study of American Politics at Johns Hopkins University. Mark C. Rom is a graduate student in the Government Studies program at the University of Wisconsin.

Origins of Federal Welfare Assistance

The federal government's major cash assistance program, Aid to Dependent Children (ADC), was originally established in 1935 as a short-term program. It was designed to supplement state and local general assistance programs that had been a meager source of support to impoverished families prior to the New Deal. The program was expected to assist dependent children under the age of sixteen who had lost their father's support as the result of death or disability. It was anticipated that the program would gradually disappear as worker contributions to the social security program made them eligible for death and disability insurance.

Because ADC was a short-term program intended to supplement state general assistance programs, its exact design and implementation were left to each state. Benefits were very low, eligibility was restricted, and the federal government funded one-third of the total cost. In 1938 fewer than 1 million children received aid, and the death of a father was the primary reason given for establishing a child's eligibility. The prewar cost of ADC in 1985 dollars was little more than $1 billion. (All costs in this article are calculated in constant 1985 dollars.)

Expansion of the Welfare Program

The program was destined to expand in the ensuing decades, albeit without much premeditation on the part of policy makers. By 1960 more than 3 million children were receiving assistance, and the program cost more than $3.5 billion dollars. Sixty-seven percent of the recipients needed assistance because a parent was absent due to divorce, separation, or imprisonment or because the parents had not ever been married. Death of a parent now accounted for only 8 percent of the recipients. The average state's monthly payment had increased from $231 in 1940 and $314 in 1950 to $413 in 1960. The federal share of the cost had increased from 33 percent to 60 percent.

By this time welfare recipients were no longer regarded as temporarily poor for accidental reasons but as a more or less permanent social group mired in poverty. Even though liberals and conservatives argued over the causes of poverty, they agreed that the ADC system could no longer be considered as purely transitory. Only changes in public policy that addressed the causes of poverty, not just its symptoms, could reduce the welfare assistance loads.

Presidents Kennedy and Johnson called for modifications in the welfare system that conformed to the more liberal understanding of the causes of poverty and welfare dependence. In addition to changing the name of the program to Aid to Families with Dependent Children (AFDC), in recognition of a substantive change that permitted assistance to two-parent families, Congress encouraged an increase in the number and range of social services states offered by raising from 50 percent to 75 percent the portion of the cost that the federal government would pay. Congress also established the Med-

icaid program, which provided free medical services to the poverty population, and inaugurated the food stamp program.

Efforts to Standardize Policies

Congress also began to limit to some extent the choices available to states.
For example, it required some AFDC recipients to make themselves available for work or training. To further facilitate the transition from welfare
to work, Congress enacted a law in 1967 that required states to disregard
the initial $30 a month and one-third of the remaining income a recipient
earned in calculating the amount that an eligible family should receive. It
was argued that since a recipient lost one dollar in welfare for every
dollar earned, recipients chose not to work in order to keep their welfare
benefits. This policy change was supposed to allow recipients to escape
from the poverty "trap" that welfare created.

The most ambitious effort to standardize welfare benefits was proposed by President Nixon on the recommendation of his domestic policy
adviser Daniel Patrick Moynihan. Proclaiming in 1969, "America's welfare system is a failure that grows worse every day," Nixon proposed a
guaranteed national minimum payment that would raise benefit levels in
ten states and for approximately 20 percent of the recipients. This family
assistance plan was defeated in the Senate, however, by a coalition of
conservatives, who opposed raising benefits in states where they were
low, and liberals, who were concerned that a national minimum would
induce high-benefit states to let their benefits fall.

President Carter also proposed a minimum welfare standard that
would have increased benefits to 65 percent of the poverty level and
would have raised the federal fiscal contribution to the program. His
proposals were approved in amended form in the House, but, once again,
movement toward a national standard was defeated in the Senate.

Welfare policy became decidedly more conservative after Ronald
Reagan assumed office. In 1981 Congress tightened eligibility requirements by curtailing the amount that a worker could earn and still receive
welfare benefits. All income earned after the first four months on welfare
(except an amount set aside for child care and transportation expenses)
had to be counted in determining the size of the welfare benefit. In 1984
Congress allowed a disregard of an additional $30 a month of earnings
but only for the first year the recipient was on welfare.

Interstate Variation

Even though more federal regulation has accompanied the awareness
that welfare assistance is now a permanent program, the states still exer-

cise wide discretion over the way in which the funds are spent. States decide whether to give aid only to one-parent or also to two-parent families. Half of the states have decided to adopt the two-parent policy, while the other half have kept the traditional one-parent restriction. States also determine the answers to questions such as the amount of assets a recipient can retain and still remain eligible for benefits, the number of days that can elapse between the time an application for aid is made and the time a decision is reached, and the age at which a child is no longer eligible for benefits. By 1985 there were at least thirty-two significant regulations affecting welfare eligibility that varied from state to state. In general, it was easier to gain access to the welfare rolls of the states with more generous benefit levels.

Each state currently determines benefit levels by first calculating the standard amount the state believes a family needs to meet reasonable food, clothing, and shelter requirements. Any family whose income is below the needs standards and is otherwise eligible can receive assistance. The state then decides the maximum amount it will give eligible families by determining what percentage of the needs standard it will supply. The actual grant is the difference between this maximum amount and the amount of income the family earns, disregarding a certain amount for child care costs, transportation costs, and, for a limited period of time, a portion of the income the recipient has earned.

Because states have established widely varying needs standards and because they provide different percentages of the needs standards, welfare benefits differ substantially from one state to the next. Indeed, the variation is quite extraordinary. California, the most generous state (outside of Alaska, whose distinctive, high-cost economy makes it an inappropriate point of comparison), provided welfare recipients in 1985 with as much as five times as large a welfare stipend as did Mississippi, the least generous state. The maximum welfare benefit paid to a California family of four was $698 a month, compared with $144 paid to a similar family in Mississippi.

These policy differences among the states are not just the peculiarities of one or two states, nor are they gradually disappearing as state governments gain in professional responsibility and fiscal capacity. Instead, benefit levels varied by as much in 1985 as they did in 1940. In 1985 the five most generous states paid an average of about $350 more each month for a family of four than the five least generous states.

Significantly, this variability in benefit levels has continued even though the value of welfare benefits in real dollars has been declining since 1970. After rising steadily throughout the early postwar period, both maximum and average benefit levels in constant dollars have fallen steadily, so that benefit levels in the typical states are today only two-thirds of what they were in 1970 and are, in fact, below the level they reached in 1950.

The food stamp program, which is funded entirely by the federal government, has eased both the decline in welfare benefits and the degree of interstate variation. If a dollar in food stamp coupons is considered to be worth as much to a welfare recipient as a dollar in cash benefits, then total welfare benefits today are at about the same level they were in 1960 before the food stamp program was established. In fact, it might be argued that food stamps, originally thought to be an addition to cash benefits, have become a substitute instead. As federal contributions in food stamps have increased, cash benefit levels set by states have fallen by a corresponding amount.

The establishment of the food stamp program has also reduced the interstate variation in total cash and food benefits by roughly one-half, compared with the variation in cash benefits alone. This leveling occurs because the federally funded and regulated food stamp program gives higher food stamp benefits to recipients in states where cash benefits are lower. However, combined food stamp and cash benefits in the most generous state remain more than double the benefits in the least generous state; the highest combined benefits for a family of four are $757 a month, the lowest, $369.

70. Social Security Programs in the United States

Excerpted from *Social Security Bulletin*, July 1989, pp. 2–43.

The term "social security" is popularly used in the United States to refer to the basic national social insurance program—Old-Age, Survivors, Disability, and Health Insurance. The term is used here in a broader sense to describe all types of social insurance, social assistance, and related programs.

Thus, this report provides a description of the history and current program provisions of this country's social insurance system: Old-Age, Survivors, and Disability Insurance; Medicare; unemployment insurance; workers' compensation; and temporary disability insurance. It describes the major income-support programs—Supplemental Security Income, Aid to Families with Dependent Children, Medicaid, and food stamps—as well as the smaller programs, such as Low-Income Home Energy Assistance, public housing, the school lunch program, and general assistance.

The development of social welfare programs in the United States has been strongly pragmatic and incremental. Proposals for change generally are formulated in response to specific problems rather than to a broad national agenda. Actual program experience and evidence of unmet needs or unintended effects subsequently lead to adjustment, extensions, or alternative approaches.

The original Social Security Act did not include the full range of programs that had developed in some European countries; it was anticipated that additional programs of social insurance and income support would be instituted later. The provision of benefits to dependents and survivors, legislated in 1939, and the enactment of assistance programs and insurance for the disabled during the 1950s are two examples of such anticipated extensions. Program developments in other areas followed more of a "problem solving" and incremental pattern. Thus, the Medicare and Medicaid programs were enacted in 1965 in response to the specific medical care needs of the elderly and the widely perceived inadequacy of "welfare medical care" under public assistance. Similarly, the introduction, in 1964, and subsequent extensive growth of the food stamp program was a response to evidence of the persistence of hunger and malnutrition among some population subgroups despite general affluence. And the Supplemental Security Income (SSI) program introduced a national minimum income guarantee for the needy aged, blind, and disabled, effective in 1974, to counteract wide differences in benefit levels and eligibility standards applicable to those groups under the federal state assistance programs. The Low-Income Home Energy Assistance Program (LIHEAP) incorporates another pragmatic response to demonstrated need caused by the rapid rise of home energy costs during the 1970s.

Both the food stamp and Low-Income Home Energy Assistance programs are available to individuals and families who are eligible for payments under the SSI or Aid to Families with Dependent Children programs and to those needy individuals and families who are not eligible for either program. In this way, a pragmatic compromise led to limited aid for certain groups without complete deviation from a major feature of federal and federally assisted income support: categorical eligibility.

A second characteristic of social policy development in the United States is its considerable degree of decentralization. One mechanism for this decentralization is the federal system of government with its division of responsibility among the federal, state, and local governments. Some programs are almost entirely federal with respect to administration, financing, or both; others involve only the states (with or without the participation of local governments); still others involve all three levels of government. The federal structure "has exercised three important political functions in public welfare policy: diffusion of power, mediation of conflicting claims, and facilitation of the flexibility that gives potential for institutional and social change. . . . Public welfare is much too expansive and too complex to be the program of a single government."

Another aspect of decentralization in the development of American social welfare policy is the important role played by the private sector in the administration of government programs. Thus, reimbursement activities under Medicare, and to a lesser degree under Medicaid, are handled by private organizations, and insurance protection for workers' compensation and temporary disability insurance benefits is underwritten in the private sector.

A further reflection of the decentralization of policy making is the fact that the various social welfare programs are not necessarily integrated with each other. For example, the food stamp and Low-Income Home Energy Assistance programs continue to be administered separately from other income support programs, such as SSI, AFDC, and general assistance.

A third salient characteristic of the nation's social welfare structure is the private sector's sharing of responsibility for social welfare expenditures. The private sector has a large role in the provision of health, medical care, and income-maintenance benefits in the form of employment-related pensions, group life insurance, and sickness payments. Private provisions are also significant in the areas of education and social services.

The dimensions of the nation's social welfare structure may be delineated by three measures: The number of beneficiaries under the major programs, total benefit payments, and expenditures in various social welfare categories in relation to the gross national product.

In December 1988, 38.6 million people—73 percent of them aged sixty-five or older—were receiving benefits under the largest single program—Old-Age, Survivors, and Disability Insurance (OASDI). As of July 1, 1987, the Medicare program covered 29.4 million people aged sixty-five or older and 3.0 million disabled people under age sixty-five. Medicaid benefits were paid on behalf of 23.2 million people in fiscal year 1987, and the food stamp program had 18.7 million participants in fiscal year 1988. Finally, AFDC payments were received by 10.9 million children and adults in 3.7 million families in December 1988, and federally administered SSI payments in December 1988 were made to 4.5 million people, of whom 2.0 million were aged sixty-five or older. Total benefit payments under these programs were disbursed as follows:

Total public welfare expenditures of $770.5 billion represented 18.4 percent of the gross national product in 1986. They included federal ex-

Program	Total Payments
OASDI	$217.2 billion in 1988
Medicare	$80.3 billion in 1987
Medicaid	$45.1 billion in fiscal year 1987
Food stamps	$11.2 billion in fiscal year 1988
AFDC	$16.6 billion in fiscal year 1988
SSI	$13.4 billion in 1988

penditures amounting to 11.3 percent of GNP and state and local government expenditures that were 7.1 percent of GNP. Social insurance benefit payments, excluding Medicare, totaled $314 billion; total spending for health and medical care, including Medicare and Medicaid, accounted for $186 billion; and income-support programs, excluding expenditures for health and medical care, came to $55.1 billion.

Estimated private expenditures for social welfare in 1986 were $474 billion, representing 11.2 percent GNP. This total includes expenditures of $268.5 billion for health and medical care; $37.7 billion for welfare and other services; $45.9 billion for education; and $122.5 billion for income maintenance programs (employee benefits), including employment-related pension benefits, group life insurance, and sickness benefits.

Social Insurance Programs

The introduction of identical legislation in the House and Senate was followed by passage of the Social Security Act, which was signed into law on August 14, 1935.

The 1935 law established two social insurance programs on a national scale to help meet the risks of old age and unemployment: a federal system of old-age benefits for retired workers who had been employed in commerce or industry, and a federal-state system of unemployment insurance. The choice of old age and unemployment as the risks to be covered by social insurance was a natural development of the Great Depression that had wiped out much of the lifetime savings of the aged and reduced opportunities for gainful employment.

Title II of the Social Security Act created an Old-Age Reserve Account and authorized payments of old-age benefits from this account to eligible individuals upon attainment of age sixty-five on January 1, 1942, whichever was later. The monthly benefit was to be determined by the total amount of wages earned in covered employment after 1936 and before age sixty-five. The initial benefit formula was designed to give greater weight to the earnings of lower-paid workers and people already middle-aged or older. The minimum monthly benefit was $10 and the maximum was $85.

Benefits were to be financed by payroll taxes imposed on covered employers and employees in equal shares under Title VIII of the act. The first $3,000 of annual salary from one employer was taxable and considered as counting toward the total of annual wages on which benefits would be computed. This amount covered the total earnings of 97 percent of those in the labor force. Although all wage and salary workers in commerce and industry were covered by the new program, many individuals were not covered—such as self-employed persons, agricultural and domestic service workers, casual laborers, and employees of nonprofit organizations. Railroad workers were excluded from Title II coverage by the Railroad Retirement Act of 1935.

Old-Age, Survivors, and Disability Insurance

The national Old-Age, Survivors, and Disability Insurance (OASDI) program, popularly referred to as social security, is the largest income-maintenance program in the United States. Based on social insurance principles, the program provides monthly cash benefits designed to replace, in part, the income that is lost to a worker and his or her family when the worker retires in old age, becomes severely disabled, or dies. Coverage is nearly universal: About 95 percent of the jobs in this country are covered. Workers in covered jobs and self-employed workers pay social security taxes on their earnings that, along with matching taxes paid by employers, constitute the primary source of revenue to finance benefits and pay for administrative expenses.

In 1988, about 130 million people were engaged in work covered by the social security program. At the end of 1988, about 38.6 million people were receiving cash benefits totaling about $18.7 billion per month. These beneficiaries included 27.4 million retired workers and their dependent family members, 7.2 million survivors of deceased workers, and 4.1 million disabled workers and their family members. Social security is an important source of retirement income for almost everyone; in 1986, nearly three in five beneficiaries aged sixty-five or older relied on social security benefits for at least half of their income. Social security is also an important source of continuing income for young survivors of deceased workers: 95 percent of young children and their surviving parents are eligible for benefits should the family breadwinner die. Finally, four in five persons aged twenty-one to sixty-four have protection in the event of the worker's long-term severe disability.

Health Care Programs

Health and medical care expenditures in the United States, including expenditures for medical research and medical facilities construction, were estimated at $500.3 billion for 1987. This amount constituted 11.1 percent of the gross national product. Fifty-nine percent of these expenditures originated in the private sector, and 41 percent represented expenditures by federal, state, and local governments.

Two-thirds of the public expenditures for health and medical care were for the Medicare and Medicaid programs—41 percent and 26 percent, respectively. Hospital and medical care costs for the Department of Defense and for veterans account for 10 percent; workers' compensation payments for 4 percent; and various public health expenditures, medical research, and construction of medical facilities for most of the remainder.

Through the Medicare and Medicaid programs, public health and medical care expenditures in the United States target two broad population groups. The Medicare program covers people aged sixty-five or older who are insured under the social security program and also people who have been receiving social security disability benefits for two years or more. The Medicaid program covers people with limited income and resources—for the most part, those receiving assistance under the Aid to Families with Dependent Children (AFDC) or Supplemental Security Income programs and those who would be eligible for such assistance if their income or resources were somewhat lower.

The first coordinated efforts to obtain government health insurance in the United States were mounted at the state level between 1915 and 1920. State health insurance programs were envisioned as a complement to the workers' compensation laws that had recently been enacted in the majority of states. However, those efforts came to naught, in part as a result of changed national priorities and public attitudes in the years following World War I.

In 1965, following a lengthy national debate, Congress passed legislation establishing the Medicare program as Title XVIII of the Social Security Act. As enacted, Medicare included not only Hospital Insurance (HI) benefits for the aged (Part A) but also Supplementary Medical Insurance (SMI) benefits for the aged (Part B). The HI program pays for part of the costs of in-patient hospital care and health care provided by skilled-nursing facilities and home health agencies. The program is financed by payroll taxes on employers, employees, and the self-employed. The SMI program covered services and supplies furnished by physicians, out-patient hospital services, and other specified expenses. Participation in the SMI program was voluntary for persons entitled under the HI program and was funded through premiums from participating people and a matching federal contribution from general revenues.

The 1965 legislation also created Medicaid (the Grants to States for Medical Assistance Program) as Title XIX of the Social Security Act. The Medicaid program replaced both medical vendor payments to public assistance recipients and the Medical Assistance to the Aged program for medically needy persons aged sixty-five or older. The new, unified program was designed to provide more effective medical care for needy people through improved standards of care, increased federal matching under a formula with no maximum, and liberalized eligibility rules.

Under Medicaid, the states were required to extend coverage to recipients of income-support payments—Aid to Families with Dependent Children, Old-Age Assistance, Aid to the Blind, and Aid to the Permanently and Totally Disabled. The three adult assistance programs were subsequently replaced by the Supplemental Security Income program. The states also were given the option of providing coverage to the medically needy—those who would have been eligible except that their income or resources were too high—under income-support programs. In addition, federal participation under the Medicaid legislation required states to liberalize certain eligibility rules besides those regarding income and resources.

71. Military Expansion Economic Decline
Robert W. DeGrasse, Jr.

Excerpted and reprinted with permission of the publisher from Robert W. DeGrasse, Jr., *Military Expansion Economic Decline* (Armonk, N.Y.: M.E. Sharpe, Inc., 1983), p. 53.

While numerous factors influence economic performance, America's heavier military burden seems to have stifled investment and reduced our economic and productivity growth over the last few decades. During the 1950s and 1960s, higher arms expenditures in the United States probably allowed other industrial nations to close the economic gap separating America from the rest of the world more quickly than if we had spent less on the military. While more industrialized nations tend to grow more slowly, our economy probably would have performed significantly better if the United States had reallocated a portion of the resources used by the military. For example, if the government had more heavily subsidized the development and repair of mass-transit systems in major metropolitan areas throughout the United States, we could have sustained and expanded the now-failing American mass-transit vehicle industry, reducing the need to import subway cars from Europe, Canada, and Japan to fill the needs of New York, Boston and Philadelphia. If the government had not spent so much on high-technology military products, the engineers doing military work might have developed commercial electronics products to compete more effectively with the Japanese. Our highly skilled people might also have worked on developing renewable energy resources. Moreover, we could have used part of the "peace dividend" to assist sound economic progress in some of the world's poorest nations, thereby helping open up new markets for our goods and services. Surely, given the wide array of possible alternatives, we would have found productive jobs for the thousands of engineers, scientists, and skilled workers who were building weapons for the "electronic battlefield."

Military spending also slowed economic performance during the 1970s. While the rising cost of energy clearly damaged performance across the board in the industrial world, military spending continued to draw away resources that could have been used to develop energy self-sufficiency. Moreover, if more engineers and greater investment had been available to the private sector after 1973, American business might have been able to offset part of the higher cost of energy by expanding exports of U.S. manufactured goods.

Increased arms expenditures during the Reagan administration could have the opposite effect on the economy that they had during World War II. As the "arsenal of democracy" during that war, America built its industrial base while other nations saw their industrial power consumed by the fires of war. Yet during the next decade, if we increase arms expenditures in the United States while most other advanced nations concentrate on expanding their industrial strength, we could be left watching our economic health continue to slip away.

72. The End of the Cold War
Council of Economic Advisers

Excerpted from the *Economic Report of the President* (Washington, D.C.: U.S. Government Printing Office, 1994), pp. 56–57. The council members who contributed to this report were Chairman Laura D'Andrea Tyson, Alan S. Blinder, and Joseph E. Stiglitz.

The end of the Cold War was a major geopolitical event for the United States, and the ensuing defense builddown has had profound economic effects. In 1986 defense spending accounted for 6.5 percent of United States GDP. By 1993 its share had fallen to about 4.8 percent, and by 1997 it is predicted to drop to about 3.2 percent. This massive shift of national resources away from defense has meant numerous base closings, cancellations of major weapons programs, scaled-back procurement plans, and attendant layoffs in the whole defense sector. For example, total defense-related jobs are projected to number 4.5 million by 1997, down from 7.2 million jobs in 1987. In a purely arithmetical sense, reduced defense spending subtracted roughly 0.5 percentage points off the real GDP growth rate in 1993. Moreover, the defense cutbacks have had a further adverse impact on aggregate demand through the expenditure multiplier. Moving resources out of the defense sector frees them for use in the production of consumption and investment goods and services, improving living standards. But this is a longer term effect. The conversion process takes time, and although the defense scaledown is not as large relative to the size of the economy as it was at the end of several wars, reconversion will cause painful dislocations in the short run.

73. A Decent Home

President's Committee on Urban Housing

Reprinted from the *Report of the Committee* submitted to the president December 11, 1968, pp. 55–59.

One effective measure to support the mortgage market was the establishment in 1933 of the Home Owners Loan Corporation (HOLC), which had the power to buy mortgages threatened with foreclosure. The corporation was able to rescue families for whom loss of home was imminent and also to provide an opportunity for mortgage lenders to convert "frozen" assets to cash, thereby shoring up the banking system and protecting depositors from the loss of their savings. Although established amid dire predictions of its financial future, the Home Owners Loan Corporation at its peak held over 15 percent of the mortgage debt of the entire country and proved extremely effective in its role. By the time of its end some years after World War II, it had fully repaid the Treasury, and its books showed a small profit.

Mortgage Insurance

A second major effort, this time in the area of mortgage instruments, was also highly successful. This was the National Housing Act of 1934, which established a system of mortgage insurance to be administered by the newly created Federal Housing Administration (FHA). The motivation was primarily that of creating jobs by improving the flow of mortgage credit, but FHA eventually brought about major changes in the practices used in financing housing.

Prior to the creation of HOLC and FHA, most mortgages had short terms with a large lump-sum payment due at the end of the term, when the homebuyer had to refinance. In addition, mortgages rarely covered more than 50 percent of the value of the structure, so that down payments were usually more than one-half of the purchase price. Second and third mortgages were common, adding to both interest costs and legal and recording costs.

The FHA mortgage insurance programs begun in 1934 were designed to reduce the risks of mortgage lenders in order to induce them to make credit available on more liberal terms. In return for a premium paid by the borrower, FHA insures the lender against the risk that the borrower will default. Thus, by making mortgage financing more readily available, the FHA programs brought the possibility of homeownership within the reach of millions of additional American families, all at no cost to the taxpayer.

Another development that helped primarily the middle-class market was the creation of secondary market facilities in which government insured mortgages could be bought and sold. The Federal National Mortgage Association (FNMA), commonly known as Fannie Mae, originally incorporated in 1938, is chartered to perform this function.

The War and After

With the revival of the economy that preceded U.S. entry into World War II, the home building industry experienced a brief spurt of activity. World War II also brought with it the creation of the National Housing Agency. For the first time many of the numerous activities of the federal government having a direct concern with housing were pulled together under one roof. A second major development of the war years was the creation in 1944 of the veterans' mortgage guarantee program administered by the Veterans Administration (VA). This was part of the package of veterans' benefits known as the GI Bill of Rights. The GI loan, as it became known, is in effect an extension of the FHA system. Instead of insuring mortgages, the Veterans Administration guarantees the top portion of a mortgage loan without fee, enabling qualifying veterans to borrow 100 percent of the cost of the house.

By the end of World War II residential construction had been at a relatively low level for fifteen years. The collapse of the housing credit system during the Depression and the restrictions of the war period contributed to a tremendous pent-up demand for housing that exploded after the war. Housing production leaped from 140,000 units in 1944 to 1 million in 1946 and close to 2 million in 1950.

The period immediately following World War II was a time of heated controversy over the policies of the federal government toward housing. Was public housing to be the only vehicle for slum clearance? Or was the need for federal support to local governments in the latter's efforts to eliminate slum conditions to be met in another way? This issue was settled in the landmark Housing Act of 1949. Although it authorized a public housing program of 135,000 units annually for six years, the act established a separate slum clearance and urban redevelopment program, which has since evolved into Urban Renewal. It was to be the responsibility of this program to clear slums and blighted areas and (later in its growth) to provide sites for private enterprise to build new moderate-cost housing as well as for such residential, commercial, industrial, and public facilities as were most appropriate for the sites.

The best-known provision of the act was its statement of a National Housing Policy. The most frequently quoted extract of this policy statement establishes the goal of "a decent home and suitable living environment for every American family." Other portions of this declaration of national policy are equally important but less well known. They include the statement that "private enterprise shall be encouraged to serve as large a part of the total market as it can," and that "governmental assistance shall be utilized where feasible to enable private enterprise to serve more of the total need."

The 1950s

The major housing legislation of the fifties was the Housing Act of 1954. It represented the first opportunity since the early 1930s for a Republican administration to have a major impact on national housing policy. Because the act of 1954 made few major changes in the programs that had been established in the two preceding decades, it was looked upon as a confirmation of the bipartisan nature of housing policy. In addition to the Charter Act, which created the framework of FNMA as it operated until 1968, the bill added conservation and rehabilitation programs to broaden the 1949 slum clearance and urban redevelopment program into a more comprehensive tool.

The Housing Act of 1954 also initiated the requirement that a local government develop a "workable program" for community improvement before it could be eligible for assistance under the Public Housing, Urban Renewal, and, later, the 221(d)(3) programs. To be certified as having a workable program, a locality was required to develop a master plan, to adopt or to update various codes governing building, zoning, and fire standards, and to muster relocation and financial resources. Although those requirements did not have to be in effect at once, a community had to show significant progress toward enacting the necessary local legislation and carrying it out.

The 1954 act modified Urban Renewal to enable production of housing at reduced cost. The more liberal multifamily and single-family terms offered under the new Section 220 FHA mortgage insurance program for Urban Renewal areas were designed, in combination with provision for a land cost write-down, to attract the private sector into building middle-income housing in Urban Renewal areas. FNMA special assistance was made available for these insured loans. Later in the fifties it was found that even with urban renewal write-downs and more liberal mortgage terms, housing cost levels within the reach of moderate-income families could not be achieved.

Evolution of Subsidies in Privately Owned Buildings

The 221(d)(3) Below Market Interest Rate (BMIR) program, established by the Housing Act of 1961, expanded opportunities for private development of subsidized housing. The program authorized FNMA to purchase mortgage loans made to limited dividend and cooperative, as well as nonprofit, entities at low interest rates based on the average interest paid on the outstanding federal debt. For the first time in the history of American housing, profit-motivated private organizations could develop subsidized housing. The subsidy was rather modest and indirect, being in effect a tender of the federal borrowing power through FNMA's special assistance functions.

More important steps toward the use of subsidies in privately owned buildings were taken in the Housing Act of 1965. By the spring of 1965 the average interest on the federal debt had risen above 4 percent. The 1965 act acknowledged the decreasing utility of the borrowing power technique used in the 221(d)(3) program and pegged the below-market interest rate at no higher than 3 percent. The program now enjoyed direct subsidies, since FNMA and ultimately the Treasury would have to make up the difference between the federal borrowing rate and 3 percent.

The year 1965 also saw the creation of the Cabinet-level Department of Housing and Urban Development (HUD) to succeed the Housing and Home Finance Agency.

The Housing Act of 1968 culminated the strong movement toward use of housing subsidies in private dwellings. Its most important new feature was the Homeownership program in Section 235. This program provided modest subsidies to enable lower-income families to purchase new and, in some cases, existing homes. The act also initiated a new rental program, Section 236, for families above the public housing income levels. Both of these new programs rely almost exclusively on private developers—profit-motivated, nonprofit, and cooperative. Both programs also rely totally on private mortgage financing supported by subsidies payable directly to the mortgage lender in contrast to the government's purchase of the mortgage in addition to the interest subsidy.

The act of 1968 contained many other important innovations. It made FHA mortgage insurance more easily available in declining urban areas and for families with imperfect (but defensible) credit histories. FNMA's secondary market operations were transferred to a new privately owned corporation, and the new Government National Mortgage Association (Ginnie Mae) was established within HUD to handle the special assistance management and liquidating functions. The National Housing Partnership proposal, which was developed by this committee, was enacted. Urban Renewal was given a new slant by the introduction of the "neighborhood development program," which provides greater program flexibility and encourages and rewards steady annual performance.

Most important of all, the act of 1968 authorized large appropriations for the new homeownership and rental programs, as well as rent supplements and public housing, thereby making possible the president's goal of the construction and rehabilitation of 6 million housing units over a ten-year period for low- and moderate-income families. In addition, the act extended and expanded the funding of the Model Cities, Urban Renewal, Code Enforcement, and Community Facilities programs to permit a comprehensive attack on central city programs.

74. A New Housing Policy for America
David C. Schwartz, Richard C. Ferlauto, and Daniel N. Hoffman

Reprinted with the permission of the publisher from *A New Housing Policy for America*, by David C. Schwartz, Richard C. Ferlauto, and Daniel N. Hoffman (Philadelphia: Temple University Press, 1988), pp. 60–62. David C. Schwartz is professor of political science at Rutgers University. Richard C. Ferlauto is on the staff of the New Jersey State Assembly. Daniel N. Hoffman is a consultant on housing and urban economic development with the Atlantic Group.

The Impact of Federal Policies on America's Housing

Bringing decent housing within reach of the people has been a basic priority of American government—one with deep historic roots. From the Homestead Act in the nineteenth century to the creation of the Federal Housing Administration, the Farmers Home and Veterans Administrations' home mortgage programs, and on through the creation of a smoothly functioning federal secondary mortgage credit market, the national government again and again has provided essential tools to make home ownership an attainable goal for a majority of Americans. From 1959 to 1977, five presidents—Republicans and Democrats alike—signed into law ten separate housing acts strengthening the home mortgage financing system and creating a network of programs to increase the supply and affordability of rental housing.

Since 1980, however, the basic thrust of national housing policy has been to withdraw the federal government from housing activity. It has been a policy of cuts in direct housing assistance, cuts in indirect (tax) incentives for housing supply, cuts and proposed cuts in federal support for housing credit. Let us examine the impact of these policies.

In the 1980s, America experienced a downturn in homeownership rates, especially among young families. Downpayment requirements, interest rates, and home prices increased faster than real incomes and savings. Homeownership became more concentrated among the wealthiest 20 percent of Americans amid a rising tide of mortgage default and delinquency.

National housing policies have exacerbated some of these problems and been irrelevant to others. Some federal credit agencies acted to increase downpayment requirements in the 1980s. Federal credit policy obviously failed to smooth out the interest-rate rollercoaster ride that has inhibited homeownership. Federal housing policies included no tax incentive for downpayment savings plans; no direct, cost-effective downpayment assistance program; no emergency mortgage default assistance plan. If, today, many Americans are finding that the door to homeownership is closed to them, U.S. housing policy has varied between ignoring their knocking and hiding the keys.

In the 1980s, too, we observed that a majority of America's tenants live in cost-burdened, overcrowded, or dilapidated dwelling units. Increasing the supply of rental housing might have helped reduce both crowding and cost burdens, but national housing policy was to cut, to all but abandon, both direct assistance and tax incentives for new construction. To the decline in the quality of rental stock, national policy responded by providing less rehabilitation funding. To the crisis in rental housing for the poor, the national government answered by cutting rental assistance and making it harder to get.

The 1980s witnessed a scandalous explosion in homelessness. Federal cutbacks in housing supply and rental assistance of the poor tended to increase this tragic phenomenon. Surely the president's announced view that most homeless people are on the streets by choice bespoke not even the kind of recognition of the facts from which decent policy might flow. National housing policy in the 1980s, a policy of knowing neglect of our public housing inventory and manifest unconcern about the stagnation and decline in the quality of our housing stock is more apt to produce homelessness than homeownership.

In the 1990s America will require more housing, better targeted to the life needs of an increasingly diverse population. We will require more housing: to provide shelter for a still-growing population; to accommodate the pent-up demand of people who delayed household formation in the 1980s; and to meet the homeownership goals of an increasing number of young families. We will need better targeting of our housing production, rehabilitation, and conversion in order to shelter the record number of frail elderly, single-parent families, and lower-income Americans we expect in the population of the 1990s.

It is hard to envision how any of this country's future housing needs will be met by continuing our current and recent policies. We are likely to need more housing, but recent and current housing policy has been to withdraw both direct assistance and indirect incentives for housing production. We will probably need to substantially rehabilitate a million or more existing units for use by the frail elderly, but funding that could be used for this purpose has already been cut. We may want to facilitate the conversion of older, larger homes for use by the smaller families of the future or to increase affordability to single-parent families or to accommodate the all-time high number of single people we expect; again, recent and current policy withdraws assistance and incentives for these purposes.

Recent and current national housing policies, if pursued into the future, give little promise that the government will help with the supply of decent affordable shelter in the 1990s. These policies simply do not adequately address the coming gaps and mismatches between America's people and America's housing stock. Continuation of our present policies will not expand homeownership or expand shelter in the America of the 1990s. The failed housing policies of the 1980s are unlikely to prove more appropriate or more successful in the decade ahead.

75. A Study of Public Works Investment

CONSAD Research Corporation for the Department of Commerce

Excerpted from a report submitted to the U.S. Department of Commerce, April 1980, pp. 3–16.

Historical Trends in Public Works Investment (PWI), 1790–1970

A long historical view suggests that almost any type of governmental expenditure has at one time or another been classified as a "public work." Certain activities have alternated between the private and public domains, and between federal and state or local levels of government. Both urban and regional development have received primary emphasis in different historical periods. During World War II, industrial construction was widely undertaken as a public work with government spending. After World War II, public works returned to the conventional categories of the years before 1932. But governments have not adopted tax and subsidy methods for encouraging an enormous range of private construction with public controls.

A View of PWI in 1977

In 1977, the terminal year of this study, current dollar PWI spending was $44.1 billion, or about 2.3 percent of GNP. Of this amount, about $6.5 billion of investment was undertaken as direct investment by the federal government, and the rest by state and local governments. However, about 40 percent of the investment by state and local governments was financed through federal grants-in-aid (roughly $15 billion). This, along with direct federal investment, provides the federal government with an important role in PWI decision making, since it funds close to 50 percent of total PWI expenditures.

Trends in Aggregate PWI, 1957–77

Focusing first on trends in aggregate, current-dollar PWI and then on trends after adjusting for inflation, the principal findings are:

(1) Current-dollar gross PWI (federal, state, and local combined but not adjusted for depreciation) was at an aggregate level of $44 billion in

1977 compared to $15 billion in 1957, an increase of 5.5 percent a year on the average. The pattern, however, was not one of steady rise. Current-dollar PWI peaked at $46 billion in 1975.

(2) From 1957 to 1968 gross PWI in constant dollars increased at an average annual rate of 5.3 percent, rising from $23 billion in 1957 to $41 billion in 1968. Between 1968 and 1977, however, gross PWI, in constant dollars, declined at an average annual rate of 3.7 percent and by 1977 had dropped to approximately $29 billion (again, in 1972 dollars).

The effect of inflation has been significant. The price of PWI projects has increased at a faster rate than prices in the economy as a whole. Over the study period, the GNP price deflator increased by 118 percent, but the price index of PWI projects increased by 133 percent. The greatest increase has occurred since 1972. A project costing $100 million in 1972 would cost $150 million in 1977.

Trends in PWI by Functional Category

The principal findings related to trends in PWI by functional category are:

(1) Two major functional categories, highways and educational facilities, dominate the decline in constant-dollar new investment that occurred between 1968 and 1977. If these two categories of expenditure are subtracted from the totals, the constant dollar value of gross PWI flattens out after 1967.

- The decline in new investment in highways is a consequence of the approaching completion of the Interstate Highway System; this nationwide project was also a significant contributor to the rise in PWI from the late 1950s to the mid-1960s.
- The rise and decline in construction of educational facilities over the twenty-one-year period is a consequence of the rise and fall of the school-age population.
- Despite the drop in spending, highways and educational facilities continue to be major components of total PWI, accounting for 24 percent and 19 percent, respectively, of constant-dollar PWI (across all levels of government) in 1977.

(2) Capital expenditures on utilities (in particular, sewer systems) showed the greatest net increase between 1957 and 1977. Other functional categories that showed major increases in constant-dollar PWI expenditure were health facilities and natural resource projects.

(3)   The general trend has been toward a more even distribution of spending over all functions.

(4)   All three levels of government had lower real (i.e., constant-dollar) spending in 1977 relative to their peak spending in the study period. For the federal government, the peak was reached in 1966; for the state governments, the peak occurred in 1967; the peak for the local governments occurred in 1968.

Trends in Public Capital Stock

An additional dimension in the assessment of PWI trends is the total value of the nation's public stock and its relation to gross PWI. The stock of highways, schools, and other functional types depreciates over time in accounting terms and gradually wears out or becomes obsolete in physical terms. The accounting value of capital stock will increase from one year to another if the amount of gross PWI is greater than the amount of depreciation allowances; in that case, net investment, which is an accounting concept, is positive. On this score, the record is one of the growth since 1957: The total value of public capital stock increased throughout the period, from about $348 billion in 1957 to $674 billion in 1977 (both in 1972 dollars).

However, the increasing stock, together with declining levels of gross PWI since 1968, has meant that an increasing share of gross PWI is being offset by depreciation allowances. As the stock of capital grows, the accounting value of depreciation also grows:

(1)   For the federal share of capital stock, depreciation exceeded gross investment in twelve of the twenty-one years. Nevertheless, federally owned capital stock grew 15 percent over the period.

(2)   For the state and local shares of capital stock, gross investment continually exceeded depreciation allowances; however, an increasing portion of the gross investment is accounted for by depreciation. From a high of $23.3 billion (1972 dollars) in 1968, state and local government net investment (gross investment minus depreciation allowances) fell to $6.8 billion in 1977. State and local governmental capital stock grew by 125 percent between 1957 and 1977.

(3)   The ratio of total PWI to GNP reached a twenty-one-year peak of 4.1 percent (based on 1972 dollars) in 1965. The low for the period was 2.3 percent in 1977.

(4)   Direct federal PWI in real terms increased at a faster rate than total federal government purchases since 1959, reaching 4.2 percent of government purchases of goods and services (GPGS) by 1977. State and local PWI relative to state and local GPGS has declined from 28 percent in 1959 to 15 percent in 1977 (based on 1972 dollars).

(5)   Gross private domestic investment (GPDI) grew at a faster rate than PWI over the twenty-one-year period.

• As a percent of total public and private investment, PWI dropped from 19 percent in 1957 to 13 percent in 1977, although it did reach a peak of 21 percent in 1967.
• If public and private investments are compared on a net basis (that is, after adjusting for depreciation), then net PWI as a percent of total net investment declined from 21 percent in 1957 to 10 percent in 1977.

76. How Federal Spending for Infrastructure and Other Public Investments Affects the Economy
Congressional Budget Office

Excerpted from a Congressional Budget Office study submitted to the Congress of the United States, July 1991, pp. 13–23.

Trends in Federal Spending on Infrastructure

Federal investment in infrastructure grew rapidly between 1955 and 1980 and has followed a slight downward trend since then. Adjusted for inflation, federal infrastructure investments rose from $6 billion (in 1990 dollars) in 1956 to $17.3 billion by 1960, and then rose fairly steadily to $29.4 billion by 1980. Since then, real infrastructure investments have fluctuated between roughly $29 billion and $24 billion annually. These investments totaled $26.2 billion in 1990, nearly the same in real terms as in 1978. As a percentage of total federal outlays, capital infrastructure spending rose from 2.0 percent in 1956 to a high of 5.5 percent in 1965 and then fell more or less steadily to 2.5 percent in 1990.

Rationales for Federal Investments in Infrastructure

Each of the nation's infrastructure programs was created to serve many purposes, but three motivations for federal involvement were paramount. First, federal cost-sharing was designed in part to increase state and local investment in infrastructure by compensating states and localities for the spillover effects of infrastructure investments. Many kinds of infrastructure—interstate highways, the national system of airports and air traffic control, inland waterways, and others—benefit residents outside the jurisdiction providing the facility. When the community that pays for a facility can recover the cost of providing services to nonresidents (through user fees, for example), no federal intervention may be necessary. But when the community receives only a fraction of the benefits from a facility yet must pay all of the associated costs, it has no incentive to provide the level of services most beneficial for the nation as a whole. By paying the portion of state and local expenditures that corresponds to the spillover benefits, the federal government can encourage states and localities to make appropriate investments.

Second, most federal transportation programs were set up to minimize the costs of providing integrated regional or national transportation networks. The programs in highways, airports, air traffic control, and inland waterways were undertaken at the federal level in part because no other jurisdiction could plan a system of such facilities from a national perspective. Through its role as financier, the federal government was able to coordinate and centralize the provision of some public works, reducing duplication and unnecessary investment.

Third, federal infrastructure programs have been designed not simply to provide the public works needed for national economic growth, but also to further a variety of social goals. The mass transit, aviation, and highway programs, for example, were all conceived in part as ways to increase the mobility of the population and to connect the various regions of the country. Similarly, federal subsidies for the construction of local wastewater treatment plants were designed to help achieve national standards for water quality. Finally, many infrastructure projects—such as the Interstate Highway System and the system of inland waterways—were designed in part to further national defense. In this sense, infrastructure programs have actively pursued the added benefits of meeting social needs while enabling economic expansion.

77. A Nation at Risk: The Imperative for Educational Reform

National Commission on Excellence in Education

Excerpted from a report submitted to the nation and the Secretary of Education, April 26, 1983, pp. 18–23.

Declines in educational performance are in large part the result of disturbing inadequacies in the way the educational process itself is often conducted. The findings that follow, culled from a much more extensive list, reflect four important aspects of the educational process: content, expectations, time, and teaching.

Findings Regarding Content

By content we mean the very stuff of education, the curriculum. Because of our concern about the curriculum, the commission examined patterns of courses high school students took in 1964–69 compared with course patterns in 1976–81. On the basis of these analyses we conclude that:

(1)   Secondary school curricula have been homogenized, diluted, and diffused to the point that they no longer have a central purpose. In effect, we have a cafeteria-style curriculum in which the appetizers and desserts can easily be mistaken for the main courses. Students have migrated from vocational and college preparatory programs to "general track" courses in large numbers. The proportion of students taking a general program of study has increased from 12 percent in 1964 to 42 percent in 1979.

(2)   This curricular smorgasbord, combined with extensive student choice, explains a great deal about where we find ourselves today. We offer intermediate algebra, but only 31 percent of our recent high school graduates complete it; we offer French I, but only 13 percent complete it; and we offer geography, but only 16 percent complete it. Calculus is available in schools enrolling about 60 percent of all students, but only 6 percent of all students complete it.

(3)   Twenty-five percent of the credits earned by general track high school students are in physical and health education, work experience outside the school, remedial English and mathematics, and personal service and development courses such as training for adulthood and marriage.

Findings Regarding Expectations

We define expectations in terms of the level of knowledge, abilities, and skills school and college graduates should possess. They also refer to the time, hard work, behavior, self discipline, and motivation that are essential for high student achievement. Such expectations are expressed to students in several different ways:

(1)   by grades, which reflect the degree to which students demonstrate their mastery of subject matter;

(2)   through high school and college graduation requirements, which tell students which subjects are most important;

(3)   by the presence or absence of rigorous examinations requiring stu-

dents to demonstrate their mastery of content and skill before receiving a diploma or a degree;

(4) by college admissions requirements, which reinforce high school standards; and

(5) by the difficulty of the subject matter students confront in their texts and assigned readings.

Our analyses in each of these areas indicate notable deficiencies:

(1) The amount of homework for high school seniors has decreased (two-thirds report less than one hour a night) and grades have risen as average student achievement has been declining.

(2) In many other industrialized nations, courses in mathematics (other than arithmetic or general mathematics), biology, chemistry, physics, and geography start in grade six and are required of all students. The time spent on these subjects, based on class hours, is about three times that spent by even the most science-oriented U.S. student, i.e., those who select four years of science and mathematics in secondary school.

(3) A 1980 state-by-state survey of high school diploma requirements reveals that only eight states require high schools to offer foreign language instruction, and none require students to take the courses. Thirty-five states require only one year of mathematics, and thirty-six require only one year of science for a diploma.

(4) In thirteen states, 50 percent or more of the units required for high school graduation may be electives chosen by the student. Given this freedom to choose the substance of half or more of their education, many students opt for less demanding personal service courses, such as bachelor living.

(5) "Minimum competency" examinations (now required in thirty-seven states) fall short of what is needed, as the minimum tends to become the maximum, thus lowering educational standards for all.

(6) One-fifth of all four-year public colleges in the United States must accept every high school graduate within the state regardless of program followed or grades, thereby serving notice to high school students that they can expect to attend college even if they do not follow a demanding course of study or perform well in high school.

(7) About 23 percent of our more selective colleges and universities reported that their general level of selectivity declined during the 1970s, and 29 percent reported reducing the number of specific high school courses required for admission (usually by dropping foreign language requirements, which are now specified as a condition for admission by only one-fifth of our institutions of higher education).

(8) Too few experienced teachers and scholars are involved in writing

textbooks. During the past decade or so a large number of texts have been "written down" by their publishers to ever lower reading levels in response to perceived market demands.

(9)   A recent study by Education Products Information Exchange revealed that a majority of students were able to master 80 percent of the material in some of their subject-matter texts before they had even opened the books. Many books do not challenge the students to whom they are assigned.

(10)   Expenditures for textbooks and other instructional materials have declined by 50 percent over the past seventeen years. While some recommend a level of spending on texts of between 5 and 10 percent of the operating costs of schools, the budgets for basal texts and related materials have been dropping during the past decade and a half to only 0.7 percent today.

Findings Regarding Time

Evidence presented to the commission demonstrates three disturbing facts about the use that American schools and students make of time: (1) compared to other nations, American students spend much less time on school work; (2) time spent in the classroom and on homework is often used ineffectively; and (3) schools are not doing enough to help students develop either the study skills required to use time well or the willingness to spend more time on school work.

In England and other industrialized countries, it is not unusual for academic high school students to spend eight hours a day at school, 220 days per year. In the United States, by contrast, the typical school day lasts six hours and the school year is 180 days.

In many schools, the time spent learning how to cook and drive counts as much toward a high school diploma as the time spent studying mathematics, English, chemistry, U.S. history, or biology.

A study of the school week in the United States found that some schools provided students only seventeen hours of academic instruction during the week; the average school provided about twenty-two.

A California study of individual classrooms found that because of poor management of classroom time, some elementary students received only one-fifth of the instruction others received in reading comprehension.

In most schools, the teaching of study skills is haphazard and unplanned. Consequently, many students complete high school and enter college without disciplined and systematic study habits.

Findings Regarding Teaching

The commission found that not enough of the academically able students are being attracted to teaching, that teacher preparation programs need substantial improvement, that the professional working life of teachers is on the whole unacceptable, and that a serious shortage of teachers exists in key fields.

(1) Too many teachers are being drawn from the bottom quarter of graduating high school and college students.

(2) The teacher preparation curriculum is weighted heavily with courses in "educational methods" at the expense of courses in subjects to be taught. A survey of 1,350 institutions training teachers indicated that 41 percent of the time of elementary school teacher candidates is spent in education courses, which reduces the amount of time available for subject matter courses.

(3) The average salary after twelve years of teaching is only $17,000 per year, and many teachers are required to supplement their income with part-time and summer employment. In addition, individual teachers have little influence in such critical professional decisions as, for example, textbook selection.

(4) Despite widespread publicity about an overpopulation of teachers, severe shortages of certain kinds of teachers exist: in the fields of mathematics, science, and foreign languages; and among specialists in education for gifted and talented, language minority, and handicapped students.

(5) The shortage of teachers in mathematics and science is particularly severe. A 1981 survey of forty-five states revealed shortages of mathematics teachers in forty-three states, critical shortages of earth science teachers in thirty-three states, and of physics teachers everywhere.

(6) Half of the newly employed mathematics, science, and English teachers are not qualified to teach those subjects; fewer than one-third of U.S. high schools offer physics taught by qualified teachers.

78. A Limited War on Crime That We Can Win
John DiIulio

Excerpted and reprinted with permission of the publisher, The Brookings Institution, from *The Brookings Review*, Fall 1992, pp. 7–8. John J. DiIulio is a professor of politics at Princeton University.

Since 1967 the federal government has waged two all-out wars on crime—and, in the view of most observers, lost both. The evidence is most irrefutable in the nation's inner cities. A quarter century of shattered hopes does not breed easy optimism about launching yet another war on crime. But there is no good practical reason to concede the future to the bleak past. Existing limits—political, administrative, budgetary, intellectual—on federal crime policy may preclude an all-out new offensive. But Washington can push boldly ahead on two fronts. First, the federal government can expand its drug treatment programs for offenders and extend them to the states. Second, it can help big cities develop community policing programs. By increasing its role in these two areas, the federal government can make city streets safer, repair drug-ravaged lives, invigorate local law enforcement efforts, maybe even save money.

The First War on Crime

Before Barry Goldwater made his run for the presidency in 1964, crime was not a big issue in American national politics. But once Goldwater had put it at the top of the national agenda, it stayed there. Lyndon Johnson embraced the issue, appointing, in 1965, a Commission on Law Enforcement and Administration of Justice chaired by Attorney General Nicholas de B. Katzenbach. The commission recommended dramatically expanding the federal role in crime control and attacking the socioeconomic maladies that breed crime, especially in urban areas. "Warring on poverty, inadequate housing, and unemployment," the commission urged in its final report, "is warring on crime."

In 1968 Johnson appointed a second commission, this one on the causes and prevention of violence, chaired by Milton S. Eisenhower. The commission's report focused on urban crime. Warning that "increasingly powerful social forces are generating rising levels of violent crime which, unless checked, threaten to turn our cities into defensive, fearful societies," the report proposed to increase federal spending on urban social welfare programs by $209 billion a year (in 1968 dollars) and to double federal spending on criminal justice.

Behind a thick fog of conservative political rhetoric, the Nixon administration adopted virtually every major crime policy of the Johnson administration. More quietly, the Ford administration, too, continued to manage the crime policies it inherited.

By 1976, however, crime rates, as measured by the FBI, were far higher than they had been in 1968. During the late 1970s a political and intellectual consensus emerged that the war on crime had failed. Liberals believed that the war had never really been fought, that too much money had gone to low-crime rural areas and to police departments, rather than to addressing the underlying socioeconomic causes of crime in urban areas. Conservatives were convinced that the federal money spent on social programs had been wasted. They believed that crime policy should ensure that penalties for crime were swift, certain, and severe. If crime did not pay, or at least paid less well, then fewer crimes would be committed.

The War on Criminals

In 1981, with the conservative view of crime in the ascendant, the Reagan administration launched a second war on crime. This time the federal government would sound the charge, but the states and localities would have to do most of the fighting—and spending. The Comprehensive Crime Control Act of 1984 was the most important anticrime package since the Johnson era. It required federal judges to follow new sentencing guidelines, permitted pretrial detention of dangerous defendants, restricted the use of the insanity defense, and increased penalties for drug trafficking.

During the 1988 presidential contest, supporters of George Bush ran the now famous Willie Horton television ad. (Ed. note: This ad described the criminal behavior of Willie Horton, who was paroled while Bush's opponent Michael Dukakis was governor of Massachusetts, implying Dukakis enabled Horton's subsequent crime spree.) Although there is no empirical evidence that the ad made any real difference in the election results, it did have some nontrivial political consequences. As John Biskupic noted in the *Congressional Quarterly*, it made democrats "determined to project a tough-on-crime stance."

During the second half of Bush's term, the political pressures surrounding the federal anticrime policy debate grew more intense, reflecting a widespread unease about the effects of the second war on crime. A national political and intellectual consensus began to emerge that the get-tough strategy of the 1980s was failing, especially in the area of urban drugs and crime.

Again there are two schools of thought about the second federal war on crime. At the heart of the debate are hard-to-reconcile interpretations of the statistics on post-1980 trends in imprisonment, criminal victimization, and antidrug law enforcement. On one side are those, usually liberals, who maintain that, together with mandatory sentencing laws, drug-law enforcement has resulted in inhumane, crowded conditions behind bars, unwarranted increases in corrections spending, and no reductions in crime. On the other side are those, usually conservatives, who deny that prison conditions have gotten worse, argue that more prisons have spelled less crime, and reason that the social spending on prisons has been worthwhile.

Few deny, however, that in the 1980s the drug-and-crime problem became the urban nightmare about which the Eisenhower Commission had warned. The decent, aspiring, law-abiding residents of the nation's inner cities were being mugged, murdered, extorted. They were afraid to send their children to school or let them go out to play for fear that drug dealers and gang members would prey on them. For these citizens the second war on crime was lost, and the first was irrelevant history.

79. Crime and Drugs
Harold G. Vatter and John F. Walker

Excerpted from *The Inevitability of Government Growth*, by Harold G. Vatter and John F. Walker. Copyright © 1985 Columbia University Press, pp. 261–65. Harold G. Vatter is professor emeritus of economics and John F. Walker is professor of economics at Portland State University.

There has been an explosion of the criminal population in the United States. Aside from the victims, the costs of this terrible development are mostly borne by state and local governments. The last row in Table 79.1 shows the totals that would obtain if the rates of increase are sustained to the year 2000. These numbers are too large. The growth must slow down.

A federal study of the urine of people arrested in twelve large cities finds that over 60 percent of them used illegal drugs. This proves the obvious to most police. Drug dealers are increasingly violent and well armed. Among the preferred weapons are assault rifles. The *New York Times* reports that most victims of assault rifle attacks are "drug dealers and other violent criminals." It quotes a study in the *Journal of the American Medical Association* as saying, "The annual cost of treating gunshot wounds nationwide was $1 billion, with 85 percent of it borne by the taxpayer." When President Bush defends the right of private citizens to bear antipersonnel rapid-fire guns, he increases the police, hospital, rehabilitation, and welfare expenditures of government.

We cannot let drugs continue to do so much damage to us all. The regulation of drugs is regulation of interstate and international trade, a responsibility unequivocally assigned to the federal government by the Constitution.

Strangely, the federal commitment to end the illegal drug trade does

Table 79.1

Adults Under Correctional Supervision (in thousands)

Year	Jail	Federal prison	State prison	Parole	Probation	Total
1980	191.0	20.6	295.4	220.4	1,118.1	1,845.5
1984	221.8	27.6	417.8	268.5	1,711.2	2,665.4
Annual percentage increases						
	3.8	7.6	9.1	5.1	11.2	9.6
Projected annual percentage increases 1980–84						
2000	403.3	88.9	1,671.9	591.4	9,388.2	11,597.3
Actual results						
1992	444.5	65.7	781.6	531.4[a]	2,670.2[a]	4,493.4
Annual percentage increases 1984–92 or 1984–90						
	9.1	11.5	8.1	12.1	7.0	6.7

Sources: *1987 Statistical Abstract of the United States*, pp.172–73; *1994 Statistical Abstract of the United States*, pp. 215–17.
[a]1990.

not show up strongly in the federal court reports on disposition of criminal cases. Table 79.2 shows a substantial increase in the percentage of federal imprisonments assigned to drug offenders. It also shows very little increase in the total number of imprisonments. The 9,907 narcotic imprisonments in 1987 is slightly more than one for every three high schools in the country.

The Reagan administration has argued that it is hard on the illicit drug industry. Indeed convictions and imprisonments for violations of the federal Drug Abuse Prevention and Control Act have increased. The average sentence has increased from 55.6 to 64.6 months. But the average time served is only 19.4 months and has increased only two months since 1976. If we kept the drug violators for their full sentences, there would have been 26,433 of them in federal prisons by 1985, making up 80 percent of all federal prisoners. As long as the total federal prison population is so small and drug imprisonments are so small, we cannot honestly say we have a serious antidrug program in the Department of Justice.

Serious, extensively imposed sanctions against illegal drug manufacturing, distribution, sale, and use would involve untold millions in prisons and vast armies monitoring or counseling them. Repression requires the leviathan.

Table 79.2

U.S. District Court Criminal Defendants Imprisoned

Year	Total	Narcotics	Percent
1972	16,832	3,050	18
1976	18,478	5,039	27
1977	19,613	5,223	27
1982	15,857	4,586	29
1984	17,710	5,756	33
1985	18,679	6,786	36
1986	20,621	8,152	40
1987	23,344	9,907	42

Source: Statistical Abstract of the United States, various years, table entitled, "U.S. District Courts—Criminal Cases Commenced and Defendants Disposed Of."

The U.S. government has been actively restricting the private market in the sale of drugs since the passage of the first Pure Food and Drug Act in 1908. For many of the products of the pharmaceutical industry this has presented no significant problems. Unfortunately, some of the opiates, marijuana and its derivatives, several forms of cocaine, and amphetamines are now illegally produced or imported and marketed throughout the nation. These black markets are pervasive and very profitable, and as part of a vast underground economy, they evade taxation while greatly increasing government law enforcement expenditures.

Much of drug law enforcement consists of attempts to interdict smugglers and discover and destroy the domestic and foreign farms and factories where the dope is produced. New York City has financed a special high-cost antidrug policy. The *New York Times* reports, "Despite the more than $500 million spent by the city in the last fiscal year on drug-related enforcement alone—more than twice the amount spent in 1986—the presence of crack is more pervasive, more violent and more insidious in its effects on New Yorkers, particularly the poor." It is reminiscent of the hopeless attempts to enforce alcohol prohibition in the 1920s. We cannot incarcerate the drug consumers, for their numbers are legion.

In a speech as far back as August 1986, President Reagan proposed that it was time to repress demand. He suggested that critical service workers and public employees be subjected to mandatory urine or blood tests. Those not giving up their "bad habits" could then be fired from their jobs. For the rest of the society such sanctions would be voluntary but encouraged. This is illustrative of the present misguided policy. If drug consumption is as pervasive as the government claims, such a policy would literally destroy the economy by depriving it of its principal input, labor. If only 5.5 percent of the employed are users, firing them would double the unemployment rate and massively increase unemployment compensation and welfare spending.

For almost eighty years the government has been telling people to neither want nor consume "recreational" (mind-destroying) drugs. The effect, we believe, has been to stimulate consumption. (Since its activities are illegal, there are no good data on the industry.) For that same period the government has been jailing, confiscating property from, and calling dirty names the suppliers of these substances. Yet their numbers have surely grown.

So far the government has tried two approaches. The first was to discourage demand through education, media campaigns, and criminal penalties for users. The second was to discourage supply by increasing the risk of doing business in the dope industry through loosely enforced criminal penalties and property confiscations, spraying paraquat on the fields, sending the U.S. Army to Bolivia, and hassling customers and suppliers. Neither approach is new. Both were used in the attempt to reduce alcohol consumption in the 1920s. That experiment was a notorious failure. We should not continue to imitate our failures.

A number of commentators have recently noted the similarity between the problems we had with alcohol prohibition and the problems we are having with the prohibitions on the production, sale, and consumption of recreational drugs. David Boaz, vice president of the conservative Cato Institute, argued on the Op-Ed page of the *New York Times* (March 17, 1988) that we should legalize drugs and thus eliminate the illicit drug trade. We concur, but with some very special exceptions.

There is no benefit to society in eliminating the Mafia and the Medellín drug merchants if we replace them with the American Marijuana Company, General Cocaine, Inc., and the United Poppy Growers Association. Such a policy simply trades in low-life drug pushers for corporate sales forces, media specialists, and advertising agents. Anyone with an ounce of faith in American business knows we can sell dope faster than they can. But the goal is to get rid of the broad use of mind-hampering drugs by people generally unaware or unconcerned with their personal or social damages.

We must both legalize these drugs and completely eliminate the potential for profit in their production and sale. The federal government should open shops all over the country and give away abused drugs to anyone who wants them. Making the drugs free destroys the profit potential for all possible suppliers. It also takes the thrill out of forbidden contraband. These shops should be easily accessible to most of the population all hours of the day. They should be staffed by pleasant clerks willing to help any person get numb. Without courteous staffing some people will prefer to do business with bootleggers even though the prices are higher. If private merchants find a new dope and try to develop a market for it, we should add it to the free list as soon as people start buying and using it.

With drugs available everywhere, very few people will try to make a living retailing drugs. The government with its enormous resources can hire the peasants of Latin America or the Golden Triangle to produce the raw materials for us. Since these are among the poorest people on earth, the costs will be minimal. Since most of the chemistry is so simple that ill-trained people working in motel rooms can at present produce many of the popular junks, the processing costs also should be low.

We should not try to cover the costs of the drug program by selling the drugs at low prices. The price of dope must be zero. The revenue potential of a sales program is enormous and the government might be tempted to make itself into a drug salesman to avert some fiscal crisis. The goal is to reduce consumption, not increase it. We should not use American farmers to grow the marijuana, coca, opium poppies, etc. They have a long history of successfully getting Congress to increase their incomes. No one should make any money from dope in America. The legalization route opens profit potential and lobbying to raise prices and income. Only with the total elimination of the possibility of profit from drugs will the private supply be dried up.

The savings from reduced law enforcement, drug-connected crime, jail spaces, border patrols, etc., should more than cover the cost of the program. The people generally would benefit from lowered crime, possibly lower taxes, and less pressure to invade poor neighboring countries.

A similar approach was taken by the Catholic church in the eleventh century, when it founded a chain of pawnshops throughout Italy. The purpose of the pawnshops was to make consumption loans to the poor at a "low" 10 percent rate of interest to deprive the moneylenders of their 24 to 36 percent usury. It worked.

This action entailed a price for the church, for it had long maintained that receiving interest was immoral. It did so to reduce the exorbitant exactions that the moneylenders were imposing on the poor people of the time. Similarly, if we give junk away to citizens, we will be enabling them to freely choose to maintain their bad habits.

CHAPTER VIII

The Financial
Superstructure, Prices, and
Monetary Policy

80. Financial Markets: Innovation and Stability
Organization for Economic Cooperation and Development

Excerpted from *OECD Economic Surveys*, 1987–88 Series: United States (Paris: OECD, 1988), pp. 75–114.

Introduction

The changes in macroeconomic conditions that have occurred in the last two decades have had an important impact on the functioning of U.S. financial markets. The increased volatility of inflation, interest, and exchange rates has caused lenders and borrowers to search for new ways to protect themselves against unexpected losses. High nominal and real interest costs have prompted borrowers to search for new sources and types of credit. The growth in world trade and income, movements in the value of the dollar, and associated changes in the net external investment position of the United States have boosted international linkages between financial markets and the role of foreign investors in the domestic economy.

Furthermore, a technological revolution has greatly reduced information and other financial transaction costs, and as a result has increased the ability of borrowers and lenders to meet directly in capital markets. Advances in computer technology and telecommunications, combined with the changes in the macroeconomic environment, have spurred a widespread process of innovation that can be loosely summarized under three headings:

• Homogenization. Broadly speaking, the 1970s and 1980s have seen many long-standing distinctions between institutions become blurred and in some cases disappear altogether. Insurance companies have bought securities firms, retailers and manufacturers have become major suppliers of credit through finance subsidiaries, commercial banks have increased their investment banking activities, and thrift institutions now make commercial and industrial loans.
• Securitization. The nature of credit granting has changed in important ways and has shifted away from traditional bank loans. Increasingly, corporations raise short-term credit directly on securities markets and not through intermediated deposits. Thrift institutions make home mortgages but then sell them to other institutions, which convert them into bondlike securities to be sold to other investors. New types of bonds and a variety of risk-hedging devices are used to increase the appeal of securities to investors.
• Internationalization. National capital and banking markets have become much more integrated; U.S. firms are important participants in markets abroad, as are foreign institutions in the intermediation of domestic funds. Disturbances in one market are rapidly transmitted across international borders.

These innovations have increased the options available to borrowers and lenders and have improved the quality and efficiency of financial intermediation.

In addition to promoting innovations, changes in the economic climate have placed strains on different sectors of the economy. Disinflation, high real interest rates, and swings in many commodity prices undercut the economic rationale of many ongoing investment projects in the first half of the 1980s. As a result, export earnings of many less developed countries (LDCs) have been squeezed, agricultural land values have fallen, many energy firms have gone bankrupt, and real estate development projects in certain parts of the country have failed. These and other troubles have caused a deterioration in the financial position of many businesses. Associated loan losses have reduced the profitability of the banking sector and have created capital problems for some institutions. The stability of banks, and the financial system in general, may also have been affected by the ongoing process of innovation to the extent that the adequacy of the existing institutional and regulatory structure has been called into question, leading to various proposals for its reform. On top of these developments there has been a marked increase in the general indebtedness of all nonfinancial sectors. All these factors together have increased the potential vulnerability of the financial system and the economy as a whole to further shocks.

Overview of the Financial System

In its broad features, the U.S. financial system is similar to that of other OECD member economies. Households are the primary savers and ultimate source (along with foreigners in the 1980s) of credit to other domestic sectors. Roughly 25 percent of household financial assets are held as bank deposits, and about 30 percent take the form of direct holdings of market securities, a large percentage in comparison to other countries. Households also have indirect stock and bond holdings in the form of pension fund and life insurance company reserves. Household liabilities are mostly made up of long-term mortgage debt. Unlike households, nonfinancial businesses are net financial borrowers despite being large gross savers. (This arises from high capital expenditures.) Outside of trade credit, their net holdings of financial assets are relatively small, and important liabilities include loans from banks and finance companies, mortgages, bonds, and trade debt. The government dissaves in the aggregate, although this masks approximate balance (net of contributions to pension funds) at the state and local level. Governments at all levels issue substantial amounts of debt, though only the federal government has a large outstanding volume of obligations with a maturity under one year. On the asset side, state and local governments are important participants in short-term wholesale money markets, and both federal and state governments lend to individuals, farmers, and business.

The flow of funds between and within these nonfinancial sectors follows many channels and involves a number of different types of financial intermediaries. The most important of these are commercial banks, which control one-third of all private intermediated assets. These institutions raise funds primarily through retail depository liabilities (household and small business accounts), but they also rely heavily on large-denomination certificates of deposit and other wholesale money market instruments. Their liabilities are in turn invested in loans to consumers and business, in mortgages, and in government securities. Aside from commercial banks, the banking system includes thrift institutions (savings and loan associations, mutual saving banks, and credit unions), which are also insured depository institutions. These differ from banks by mainly holding portfolios of home mortgages and mortgage-backed securities. Outside the banking system are a number of other financial institutions, which together control about half of all intermediated assets. The liabilities of these firms are not insured by the government and for the most part are long-term, e.g., pension fund and life insurance company reserves and shares in open-end mutual funds. This characteristic enables them to hold long-maturity assets such as corporate equities, bonds, and nonresidential mortgages. Money market mutual funds (MMMFs), by contrast, issue demand deposit-like instruments and invest in short-term securities. Other nonbank intermediaries include finance companies (which make loans to consumers and business funded in part by commercial paper issuance) and security dealers (which trade stocks, bonds, and other financial instruments on behalf of individuals and firms as well as on their own account). Alongside these private intermediaries are the government financial agencies. Aside from the Federal Reserve System, these include federal and state regulatory and deposit insurance agencies and federally sponsored corporations that are important in housing finance.

The broad similarity of this institutional structure with that existing in other countries masks some important differences. Foremost among these is the size and depth of U.S. financial markets, which are rivaled only by those in the United Kingdom and Japan. Total credit market debt outstanding, excluding corporate stock, stands at almost $10 trillion, and the market value of corporate equity adds an additional $3 trillion. Treasury obligations alone constitute the largest single market in the world, worth about $2 trillion. This tremendous volume of paper has given rise to large secondary markets in many different securities, allowing trading across a wide range of maturities and borrowers. Another difference from other financial systems is the relatively small share of total intermediation that takes place through the banking system. The percentage of financial intermediation occurring via monetary institutions (commercial banks, thrifts, and money market mutual funds) has averaged only about 35 percent since the mid-1970s; comparable figures for Germany, Canada, and the United Kingdom were around 90 percent, 50 percent, and 50 percent, respectively. This low percentage exists for many reasons but partly reflects another characteristic of the U.S. financial system: the existence of markets for the trading of a large number of nontraditional instruments, such as loan-backed securities and financial futures and options. The creation of these markets—along with economies of scale in financial operations—has increased the options available to borrowers and lenders alike and has helped to draw business away from the banking sector. Finally, direct lending by government plays only a minor role in total finance. Outstanding government loans and mortgages are equal only to about 5.5 percent of the total liabilities of households and nonfinancial business, although for certain groups, such as farmers and students, government credit is important. Instead, the chief credit role of government has been in the guarantee and securitization of home mortgage credit.

Like that of every country, the U.S. financial system has evolved subject to its own particular set of economic, political, and social forces. Via inherited legal and institutional structures, these forces continue to affect the economy long after they have disappeared. For example, a widespread fear of financial concentration led to the rejection of a centralized banking system in the early 1800s and the adoption of a state-centered structure. The federal nature of government, the power of local interests, and southern and western mistrust of eastern banks all combined to produce a system in which interstate bank activity was effectively prohibited. As a result, the United States today has over 13,000 commercial banks, with the largest ten controlling only 20 percent of total commercial bank assets, as compared to much higher percentages in other countries (Table 80.1). Another event that had major long-term institutional effects was the Great Depression. The stock market crash of 1929 and the widespread bank failures of the early 1930s prompted an overhaul of the federal regulations governing finance. Public disclosure rules for trading in corporate securities were strengthened, and the Securities and Exchange Commission was created to regulate bond and equity markets. The federal deposit insurance programs were started to restore faith in the safety of the banking system. Investment banking was largely separated from commercial banking by the 1933 Glass-Steagall Act, on the grounds that the soundness of the banking system had been compromised by imprudent security dealings.

Henceforth, direct access to the safety net of deposit insurance and central bank credit would be denied to almost all institutions engaged in corporate securities underwriting, real estate development, or insurance. Commercial banks and thrift institutions also were made subject to stricter prudential supervision, and the payment of interest-on-demand accounts was prohibited. Thrift institutions specializing in housing finance were retained alongside the commercial banks, and interstate banking continued to be effectively prohibited. After extensions and modifications provided by subsequent legislation, this structure was more or less the one in place in the start of the 1980s.

Strains in the Banking System

The past few years have been difficult for depository institutions. The net income after taxes of commercial banks fell to 0.64 percent of average net assets in 1986, down from much higher levels in the 1970s. Incomplete

Table 80.1

International Comparisons of Bank Concentration

United States	Out of 13,739 commercial banks, the largest 5 control 12.8 percent of total assets, the largest 10 control 20.3 percent, and the largest 2,100 control 57.5 percent. Adding the assets of thrift institutions to those of the commercial banks reduces these percentages to 7.5 percent, 11.8 percent, and 33.5 percent, respectively.
Japan	Out of 87 commercial banks, 13 city banks control 56.7 percent of total assets.
Germany	Out of 316 commercial banks, the largest 6 control 37.9 percent of total assets. Adding the assets of 4,232 other banking institutions reduces this percentage to 8.8 percent, but an additional 17 percent of assets are controlled by the postal and regional Giros.
France	Out of 367 banks, 3 control 41.7 percent of all assets. If one excludes foreign-affiliated banks, this percentage increases to 62.2 percent. Adding the assets of mutual and savings banks to those of banks reduces these percentages to 29.5 and 44.0, respectively.
United Kingdom	The 5 largest banks control 45.6 percent of the total assets of the monetary sector.
Canada	The 4 largest banks control 51.2 percent of all deposits, and seven banks account for over 80 percent of all deposits.

Source: "Interstate Banking Developments," *Federal Reserve Bulletin*, February 1987; Federation of Bankers Associations of Japan, *Analysis of Financial Statements of All Banks* (April 1, 1986 to March 31, 1987); Deutsche Bundesbank, *Monthly Report*, vol. 39, no. 8, August 1987; Commission Bancaire, *Rapport 1985*, France; Committee of London and Scottish Bankers, Abstract of Banking Statistics, vol. 3, May 1986; and Economic Council of Canada, *Competition and Solvency* (1986).

data for 1987 suggest a further worsening, and it is likely that average profitability approached zero last year. A decline in loan quality has been a primary factor in these difficulties, as loss provisions have more than tripled from the beginning of the decade. These asset quality problems have afflicted both small and large banks, although losses at the largest banks were especially great in 1987, due to ongoing problems with LDC loans. The falloff in earnings has affected investors' perception of the worth of commercial banks: bank stocks, especially money-center ones, have underperformed the general market by a significant amount. Nevertheless, most commercial banks have been able to improve their capitalization, and the ratio of primary capital (which includes reserves for loan losses) to assets has risen from below 6 percent in 1980 to 7.6 percent in 1986. Large money-center banks have been particularly successful in their efforts to increase primary capital, but these banks face large potential losses on loans to some Latin American countries.

Thrift institutions have fared even more poorly than commercial banks in the 1980s. Net after-tax earnings at savings and loan associations (S&Ls) fell from 0.77 percent of assets in 1977 to −0.73 percent in 1981. This precipitous decline occurred because S&Ls and mutual savings banks (MSBs) had portfolios dominated by fixed-rate long-term mortgages: as the Federal Funds rate jumped from 5.5 percent to 16.4 percent over this period, thrifts found it impossible to offset the resultant increase in their cost of funds. Since 1982, earnings have recovered somewhat—largely due to a decline in interest rates and turnover of the mortgage portfolio—but average profitability remains low because of loan losses on real estate development projects. This continued poor performance has threatened the viability of many of these institutions. Currently, 20 percent of all S&Ls have negative earnings, and almost 10 percent are insolvent.

Many of these problems have stemmed from changes in macroeconomic conditions, such as the rise and then rapid decline in inflation in the 1970–83 period, the 1980s increase in real interest rates and the value of the dollar, and the drop in commodity prices. These developments undercut the economic value of many ongoing investment projects. As a result, loans made to many developing countries, farmers, energy producers, and real estate developers became uncollectible or were renegotiated in a way that left the banks with large capital losses. Although large losses were unavoidable in the face of such shocks, other factors exacerbated the situation. For example:

• Insufficient prudential supervision, combined with legislation granting thrift institutions expanded investment powers, allowed many S&Ls to pursue imprudent strategies in the mid-1980s. Using large-scale wholesale money market borrowings and aggressively priced insured retail deposits, a significant minority of the industry expanded rapidly and invested in high-risk projects, such as commercial real estate. Default rates proved higher than expected, leading to large capital losses and insolvency in many cases. Limitations on interstate branching created commercial banks and thrifts that were insufficiently diversified across regions and tied too closely to the fortunes of the energy or agriculture sectors. Also, in view of branching restrictions, some banks expanded by relying heavily on money markets for raising funds. Such dependence can complicate bank portfolio management because wholesale deposit rates are more volatile than retail ones. Moreover, since wholesale deposits are only partially covered by federal insurance, large deposits tend to be especially responsive to changes in institutional investors' assessment of the financial health of individual banks.

• Other financial institutions continued to make inroads into the traditional markets of commercial banks, aided by restrictions on bank activities and a general freedom from regulatory requirements. This increased competition actually began well before the 1980s: from 1975 through the early 1980s bank assets grew significantly more slowly than those of other financial institutions. Adding to these competitive pressures was an increase in the issuance of securities, which reduced the relative importance of traditional bank intermediation. Moreover, restrictions on the securities activities of banks limited their ability to profit from these expanding markets.

Commercial banks have responded to those pressures by improving operations in traditional fields and finding new sources of income. Continuing a process begun in the inflationary 1970s, banks have increased the attractiveness of holding deposits through improvements in cash-management services provided to customers. Overseas operations have been expanded (by money-center and large regional banks) in order to take advantage of both the growth in international trade and foreign income and the absence of Glass-Steagall restrictions in many foreign markets. Earnings have also been augmented through fee income derived from a variety of sources, including the provision of back-up credit for commercial paper and tax-exempt industrial revenue bonds, arranging currency and interest rate swaps, and trading in interest rate futures and forward rate agreements. Because many of these new activities are off balance sheet, they have been attractive to banks trying to improve both earnings and capitalization. Their importance to bank profitability has grown substantially, and the ratio of noninterest income to assets stood at 1.40 in 1986, up from 0.78 in 1979.

Unlike commercial banks, thrift institutions have by and large concentrated on improvements in their traditional field of home finance, the most important being the use of adjustable-rate mortgages (ARMs). Like traditional mortgages these are typically thirty-year loans, but their interest rate is pegged to a shorter-term market rate, such as the yield on one-year treasury securities. By transferring price risk to households and decreasing the sluggishness of the mortgage portfolio yield, these instruments partially insulate thrifts from swings in income caused by fluctuations in market interest rates. Over half of all new mortgage loans made now carry such terms, and ARMs accounted for 43 percent of all outstanding mortgage debt in 1986. Thrifts have also increased the liquidity of their portfolios by substituting mortgage-backed securities for individual mortgage loans. These instruments, extensively traded in secondary markets, enhance the ability of institutions to adjust to deposit flows and to participate in wholesale money markets via repurchase agreement. The share of mortgage-backed securities in S&L portfolios has risen from 4.4 percent in 1980 to over 13 percent today. In addition to increased liquidity, this form of securitization has boosted portfolio diversification—by replacing local mortgages with securities backed by nationwide mortgage pools—and has enabled thrifts to earn off-balance-sheet income by originating and servicing mortgages held by other investors. Thrifts have also begun to diversify away from housing finance, and nonmortgage loans at S&Ls rose from around 2 percent of assets in 1978 to 6.5 percent in 1987. Increases at MSBs have been even more pronounced, and consumer and business loans now account for 14.5 percent of their portfolios, up from 4.5 percent ten years earlier.

Government regulation of the banking sector has also undergone important changes in the 1980s. Legislation passed in 1982 started a gradual process of deposit rate decontrol, which by 1986 left commercial banks and thrifts free to set their own rates on essentially all categories of deposits. These changes have improved the ability of the regulated banking sector to compete for funds. (For example, the 1983 decontrol bank rates on close substitutes for money market mutual fund shares led to a large flow of funds from MMMFs to banking in the succeeding months.) The permitted investment activities of S&Ls have been expanded to include consumer, commercial, and industrial lending. As noted above, many institutions have used these new powers to diversify somewhat out of housing financing, but others have entered unfamiliar fields and suffered large losses. The barriers separating commercial and investment banking have been weakened. For example, bank holding companies are now allowed to control discount brokerage firms (low-fee brokers that do not dispense investment advice or research) and separate investment advisory services. Beyond this, the major bank regulatory agencies have issued independent reports proposing various modifications to the Glass-Steagall Act, and legislation that would repeal the act's restrictions on bank securities activities has recently been introduced in Congress. There have also been major moves in the direction of interstate banking, initiated by the individual states. Forty states and the District of Columbia currently allow out-of-state holding companies to own in-state banks, although most do not allow equal entry to firms from all states. This movement has given rise to large regional banks, which should prove to be formidable competitors to the large money-center banks.

Securitization and Capital Markets

As noted above, traditional bank credit has increasingly been replaced by the issuance of securities, either directly by borrowers or indirectly through loan-backed instruments. The commercial paper market is one of the earliest examples of this phenomenon: the outstanding paper of nonfinancial corporations in the early 1960s was equal to only 1.5 percent of their bank and finance company loans combined, but it jumped to 6 percent in 1970 and to almost 11 percent in 1985. At the same time, a rising percentage of business and consumer loans has represented intermediated commercial paper (in the sense that lending institutions have raised funds through paper issuance), and outstanding commercial paper liabilities of bank holding companies and finance companies doubled as a percent of loan assets between the early 1970s and 1986. This circumvention of deposit intermediation arose from many factors. For example, technological advances reduced information and transaction costs, making it easier for ultimate lenders and borrowers to meet directly in capital markets. The institutionalization of savings via pension and mutual funds also decreased the relative value of bank expertise in investing—since institutional managers have a similar knowledge of financial markets—and boosted the demand for securities. Rising inflation and interest rates increased the incentives to minimize borrowing costs and led to a search for alternatives to bank loans. More generally, the strong growth of finance companies and other nonbank competitors increased the relative size of the commercial paper market, as it is a traditional source of funds for those institutions. However, banks themselves began to issue substantial amounts of paper (via their holding companies), at first to avoid reserve requirements, but later as a standard rounding tool. Overall, these factors underlying the growth of the commercial paper market probably gave rise to a further increase in its competitive position vis-à-vis deposit-intermediate lending, because the efficiency and flexibility of securities markets may have grown as the volume of issues and trading increased.

Securitization has also occurred in such areas as new car loans, life insurance policy loans, and credit card and lease receivables. (In all these cases, individual payment streams from the underlying assets are pooled and sold on the open market. The original owner usually continues to service the individual loans for a fee.) The cumulative gross issuance of car-loan–backed securities, first offered in 1985, now stands at $15.5 billion, or about 6 percent of all outstanding car loans. However, the largest growth in securitization has come in the area of housing finance through home mortgages that have been bundled into bondlike instruments. Such mortgage-backed securities begin by the issuance of conventional mortgages and are then resold to another institution that finances the purchase by selling conventional bonds, or by pooling the mortgages and selling the rights to the pool's income stream.

The creation of these instruments allows loan origination to be efficiently separated from the holding of mortgages. Although secondary trading in individual mortgages is possible, it is limited in scope because of risk diversification and divisibility problems. In contrast to individual loans, mortgage-backed securities can be sold in smaller denominations, and buyers do not need to worry about the characteristics of a particular individual but only about the risk characteristics of homeowners in general. Moreover, these instruments are relatively riskless, because most of the mortgage-related debt has been issued by the three government-sponsored agencies (the Federal National Mortgage Association, the Federal Home Loan Mortgage Corporation, and the Government National Mortgage Association), and it is widely believed that the credit of the United States government implicitly stands behind it, despite no explicit guarantees on non-GNMA securities. These advantages partly explain why the outstanding volume of these securities has risen from $20 billion in 1970 to about $700 billion today (over one-third of all residential mortgage debt). Thrift institutions and commercial banks hold just over 40 percent of this debt, as compared to around 50 percent of whole mortgage loans; the creation of these instruments has boosted the flow of housing credit that bypasses the banking system.

Innovation and Monetary Control

The conduct of monetary policy has also been influenced by a change in the behavior of the monetary aggregates. M1 velocity in the 1980s has deviated sharply from its trend growth path of the 1960s and 1970s, although M2 velocity appears more stable. While part of this shift can be explained by conventional demand-for-money equations, much of the increased demand for M1 is due to the decontrol of deposit rates and a resultant change in the character of M1 transaction accounts. Now that a major portion of M1 pays an explicit rate of return that is not much below that available on many nontransaction accounts, households use M1 deposits as both checking accounts and as vehicles for savings. Similarly, because some non-M1 components of M2 have limited check-writing privileges, consumers can use savings balances to pay bills. With the functional difference between M1 and M2 blurred by decontrol, the demand for M1 balances has on average been stronger in the 1980s than would have been expected on the basis of historical behavior. More important, the growth in M1 has been erratic in recent years, due in part to large shifts between M1 and the non-M1 components of M2 that have been caused by changes in the spread between various bank deposit rates. Because these fluctuations in M1 growth are difficult to interpret and have few implications for the growth in nominal GNP, the Federal Reserve has deemphasized M1; there are no longer any announced target ranges for M1. The behavior of M2 has also presented problems for the Federal Open Market Committee (FOMC), in that there have been substantial fluctuations around its trend that arise from a sluggish pricing policy on the part of banks. For reasons that are not entirely clear, banks do not adjust deposit rates quickly to changes in money market rates. This pricing behavior increases the short-run interest elasticity of money demand and weakens the relationship between reserves growth and nominal income. For example, money growth was extremely rapid in 1986 as market rates fell but then slowed abruptly in 1987 when rates began to go back up.

Another difficulty facing the monetary authorities in recent years has been the health of the financial system. Monetary policy works through the banking system and at times imposes substantial costs on banks and thrift institutions. A rise in interest rates caused by a decreased supply of reserves could hurt bank profits through an increased opportunity cost of holding required reserves (which earn no interest), capital losses on securities, decreased loan demand, and a rising cost of funds. Pronounced monetary contractions can also reduce the profitability of financial institutions by pushing up default rates on loans. If banks and other financial firms have weak capitalization and low earnings, the central bank may be somewhat constrained in its operations. Attempts to slow economic activity and fight inflation could be compromised in such a situation, since an important responsibility of the monetary authorities is to maintain the integrity of the payments system and the general functioning of credit markets. For example, the difficulties created by the Latin American debt situation, combined with the weakness of some banks in agricultural and energy-producing regions, probably have influenced the conduct of monetary policy. More recently, the stance of monetary policy was adjusted in the face of the stock market crash.

Debt, Savings, and Investment

Growth of Debt

An important feature of financial markets in the 1980s has been a sharp increase in borrowing by households, firms, and the government. Although the ratio of total nonfinancial sector debt to GNP remained remarkably stable at about 1.4 during the 1960s and 1970s, in the past few years it has climbed rapidly to above 1.8. All nonfinancial sectors have contributed to this rise, but the bulk of it is attributable to the federal government, households, and nonfinancial corporations. Since 1980, large budget deficits have boosted the outstanding credit market debt of the federal government by well over $1 trillion. Household debt has risen by about the same amount, as consumers have borrowed heavily to purchase homes, cars, and other durable goods. Corporate nonequity liabilities jumped about $800 billion over the same period, fueled by large outlays for capital goods during the recovery and by a wave of corporate buyouts in which debt-finance played a prominent role. Partly due to this increase in merger activity, rising gross corporate indebtedness has led to a decline in net worth relative to GNP, and the aggregate debt-to-equity ratio (par basis) for nonfinancial corporations rose from .35 in 1980 to .53 in 1986. (On a market-value basis the rise is smaller, even after allowance for the recent fall in stock prices.) Noncorporate businesses also experienced a deterioration in their balance sheets, partly due to a 40 percent decline in the value of farmland, and partly due to a boom in office and other commercial construction that was financed by mortgage lenders. (The recent end of this boom, combined with an excess supply of office space in many cities, has worsened the situation further.) In contrast, increased borrowing by consumers has not been matched by a decline in household net worth. Sustained in part by capital gains on holdings of corporate equities and land, personal net wealth in the mid-1980s was little changed (as a percentage of GNP or income) from the late 1970s. By and large, growth in household debt has not outpaced the accumulation of financial assets. The stock market crash of 1987 worsened the financial position of the households, but it came after a very large run-up in prices over the first eight months of 1987; as a result, household net worth at the end of 1987 was still greater than it had been one year before.

Debt and Stability

An important question raised by this increase in general indebtedness is the effect, if any, on the stability of the economy. In this regard, it is noteworthy that higher borrowing has been accompanied by a fall in the quality of debt, which is of particular concern because it has occurred during a period of strong economic growth. For example, loan loss provisions at commercial banks have more than doubled as a percent of assets since the late 1970s, reflecting rising default and delinquency rates in all categories. Although the vast majority of losses have been taken on business and foreign loans, the decline in quality also includes home mortgages and consumer installment loans, which have historically been among the safest of investments. The deterioration (albeit limited) in the quality of consumer debt is due to many factors, but they probably include a rising debt service burden; reduced homeowners' equity in economically depressed regions; and an increase in the number of heavily indebted families. The quality of corporate securities has also fallen. Reductions and omissions in dividend payments by corporations have been trending upwards, and 176 major firms had investment ratings on their corporate bonds downgraded in 1987, as opposed to only 69 upgradings. In general, annual net downgradings are up substantially from the average pace of the late 1970s. A portion of these downgradings has been due to industry-specified factors, such as difficulties associated with the construction and operation of nuclear power plants. Others are the result of broader-based trends, such as increases in corporate indebtedness associated with merger and takeover activities, or a squeeze on earnings caused by high interest rates and strong foreign competition. These problems have partly manifested themselves in a decline in the average investment grade of new bond issues. Until the late 1970s the percentage of issues below investment grade (Baa by Moody's or BBB by Standard and Poor's) never rose above 10 percent, but in the last few years it has consistently been above 20 percent and reached 29 percent in 1986.

Financial Innovation, Savings, and Investment

Financial innovation helps to explain some of the growth of debt in the 1980s, in that changes in financial markets have partially shielded firms and individuals from the effects of a historically high level of real interest rates. Improved access to foreign markets through Eurodollar borrowings, along with the development of new forms of corporate debt, have lowered interest expenses for large firms and reduced the extent to which business investment has been crowded out by the federal deficit and the low personal saving rate. Risk management techniques have possibly increased capital expenditures by reducing the uncertainty surrounding the finance costs of long-term investment projects. Households have benefited from mortgage securitization, which has made lending to homeowners more attractive to traditional lenders and has brought new sources of credit into the housing market. The use of ARMs has also boosted housing investment, in that the supply of mortgage credit would certainly fall if lenders could not transfer price risk to borrowers. Liberalized terms in certain areas of consumer finance have also been important in boosting consumption expenditures. For example, the spread between the yield on bonds and the rate charged on auto loans has fallen by over 4 percentage points since the early 1970s. The average maturity of car loans has also lengthened considerably; combined with the relative decline in auto rates, these innovations have decreased monthly car payments by about 40 percent. The use of credit cards has expanded, facilitating spending, and the development of home equity loans—lines of credit advanced by banks and thrift institutions based on the market value of a house net of outstanding mortgage debt—has enabled homeowners to tap existing resources more easily. This latter innovation has certain tax advantages (interest on such loans is tax deductible under the new tax law, unlike consumer lending) and so has become popular as a source of general purpose credit for homeowners.

81. Report of Special Study of Securities Markets
Securities and Exchange Commission

Excerpted from *Report of Special Study of the Securities Markets* (Washington, D.C.: U.S. Government Printing Office, 1963), pp. 21–26.

Growth of the Securities Industry

In one form or another, securities have been traded in the United States since its founding, but it was not until the sale of Liberty bonds throughout the country during World War I that securities became an accepted investment medium for the American public. Before that time, there were only approximately 250 securities dealers in the United States. Branch offices appear to have been few in number; indeed, it was not until 1881 that the New York Stock Exchange (NYSE) authorized the establishment of "branch houses."

While the growth of the securities business to its present size started in the 1920s, from 1929 until after World War II there was no sustained rise in employment in the securities industry. Since that period, however, there has been a large expansion in the market for securities and an elaborate extension of sales offices and selling efforts.

The Expansion of Markets

During World War II, the market for new securities in the United States virtually disappeared as corporations bent their efforts toward war production and the federal government assumed much of the responsibility for financing. With the war drawing to a close a shift occurred; corporations began to look to their civilian outlets once more and found it necessary to raise new money through the securities markets in order to convert their facilities to meet a rising private demand for goods. Reflecting this transformation, the volume of corporate securities that issuers offered for cash sale (excluding private placements and offerings exempt from registration), which had declined to an annual level below $700 million in 1942 and 1943, increased swiftly in each of the next three years to reach $4,113 million in 1946. From 1947 to 1950, a period that covered the sharp business decline between late 1948 and 1949, the volume of such securities offered for cash receded somewhat to an average level of slightly over $3,200 million a year. Thereafter, the figure has remained high, with the peak of $8,171 million attained in 1957.

The growth of the industry may also be seen in the trading markets. During the past ten years, the number of individuals owning shares in public corporations has almost tripled, from an estimated 6.5 million people in 1952, when the New York Stock Exchange undertook its first census of shareowners, to an estimated 17 million in 1962. This growth is reflected in the increasing number of publicly owned listed companies and the greater number of shares available for trading on exchanges. Between 1940 and 1962, with hardly a break, the number of companies with stocks listed on the NYSE has risen from 862 to 1,186, and the average number of shares listed from 1,445 million to 7,374 million. Changes in annual stock volume, which reflect many economic and psychological factors, have been more jagged but in general have traced a rising line and reached a record of 1,021 million shares in 1961, a figure that was previously exceeded only in 1929.

It should be noted, however, that volume has not increased in proportion to the growing number of shares listed each year. In 1929, when only an average of 942 million shares were listed, 1,125 million shares were traded, with an annual turnover of 119 percent. Even in 1945 and 1950, when volume was considerably below its present level, more than 20 percent of the shares were traded each year. In the past several years, the turnover rate has fluctuated between 12 and 15 percent.

The volume of over-the-counter sales also has grown. The study estimates that in 1949 this volume was $4.9 billion, compared with $38.9 billion in 1961, a gain of almost eight times. Another basis for gauging the growth of the over-the-counter markets is by the number of different stocks appearing in the daily sheets published by the National Quotation Bureau. This number, which includes various foreign, investment company, and exchange-listed issues, has expanded quite steadily from approximately 3,700 on January 15, 1939, to 8,200 on January 15, 1963.

The Growth of Broker-Dealer Firms

The expansion of the broker-dealer community has been characterized less by an increase in the number of firms than by a sharp rise in the size of those firms, as is shown by the number of their sales employees and branch offices. Thus, while the number of member organizations of the New York Stock Exchange has increased only slightly, the number of salespeople employed by those firms has risen from 7,989 at the end of 1945 to over 32,000 on December 31, 1962; the NYSE member firms' branch offices have increased from 841 to 2,737 over the same period. The National Association of Securities Dealers (NASD), whose membership has increased over 100 percent in the years since 1945, can boast a similar rapid growth: from about 25,000 to 95,000 registered representatives and from 790 to 4,713 branch offices over the same period.

A segment of the securities business that experienced particularly striking growth in the postwar period is that of the open-end investment companies, or mutual funds. Total net assets held by all mutual funds that were members of the Investment Company Institute were calculated at $1,284 million in 1945; by December 31, 1962, that figure had grown to $21,271 million and was as high as $22,789 million on December 31, 1961. The number of stockholder accounts in member mutual funds grew from approximately 500,000 in 1945 to almost 6 million in 1962.

The Growth of the Industry Relative to the Rest of the Economy

Employment in the securities industry contracted swiftly from 1929 to 1943, when employment in all industries reached what was virtually a wartime peak. Immediately thereafter, securities employment began to rise, while that of other industries was diminishing, as industry began to reduce war-inflated staffs. Since 1949, employment in the securities industry has risen at a particularly rapid pace, reflecting to a large extent the considerable augmentation of sales staffs that has been taking place. By 1961, there were about 160 percent more employees in the securities industry than in 1945. Employment in all industries, on the other hand, has shown less than a 10 percent increase in that period.

Summary

Out of this overall picture of the securities industry emerge several preliminary conclusions. On the one hand, the industry contains a small group of large broker-dealer organizations, dominant in their amount of public business and possessing large numbers of salespeople, supervisors, and branch offices. This group, in turn, consists principally of large firms doing a general business; some are members of the NASD and usually one or more exchanges, and some are not even members of the NASD. On the other hand, there are many small firms, with a much smaller but still significant share of public business, including a large number of mutual fund specialists and also a large group of firms doing a high proportion of their business in over-the-counter securities. Most of the smaller firms are NASD members, and the incidence of exchange membership among them is considerably lower than among the large general firms.

82. Why Deposit Insurance Was Established and How It Is Supposed to Work
Congressional Budget Office

Excerpted from *The Economic Effects of the Savings & Loan Crisis* (Washington, D.C.: U.S. Congress, January 1992), pp. 1–13.

Federal deposit insurance was established during the Depression of the 1930s to deal with bank and thrift closings on a massive scale. Depositors lost large portions of their savings in a plague of bank failures that threw into chaos farms, businesses, and local communities. Understandably, people were so frightened that a mere rumor that a bank or thrift would be closed could set off a run on deposits, which many times itself guaranteed that the failure would occur. To deal with these several problems, the Federal Deposit Insurance Corporation (FDIC) was established to insure bank deposits, and the Federal Savings and Loan Insurance Corporation (FSLIC) was created to insure deposits at thrift institutions. Many analysts consider these measures to be among the most important and enduring reforms of the Depression era.

A major weakness of deposit insurance is that it creates "moral hazard," a term used to describe actions by some individuals who further their own interest at the expense of another party to a contract. The terms of the contract do not prescribe penalties for all such actions. In the case of deposit insurance, financial institutions have an incentive to undertake riskier investments with depositors' funds because those funds are insured. Indeed, with insurance, depository institutions can engage in risky practices without much concern that depositors will withdraw their funds or that their cost of funds will sharply increase.

Exacerbating the problem of moral hazard for deposit insurance is the inappropriate pricing of risk. Because insurance premiums have traditionally been the same regardless of the riskiness of the institution's investments, the system has tended to subsidize risk taking. Firms that follow prudent practices in effect subsidize those that engage in bolder behavior. Problems of moral hazard become increasingly serious when the capital of a depository institution is lost. At that point, the institution has absolutely no incentive to avoid risk. It no longer shares in possible losses, and yet it still has much to gain if even its most dubious investment succeeds. In such cases, a little derring-do can pay off quite handsomely.

So What Went Wrong in the 1980s?

During the 1970s and 1980s, financial deregulation and financial innovation, such as the development of the money market funds, buffeted the S&L industry and the government's deposit insurance program. The result was to alter the competitive environment at a time when economic conditions were deteriorating, which brought about an unprecedented string of failures among insured S&Ls and massive federal obligations to their depositors.

In the early 1980s, while the deposit insurance fund appeared robust, some experts had warned that such events could have a catastrophic effect on the deposit insurance program. Nevertheless, the deposit insurance system continued to help minimize the contagiousness of financial shocks: hundreds of S&Ls failed, but surprisingly no panics took place. Regulation and supervision of the insured institutions ultimately proved woefully inadequate to the crisis, however, and these mistakes contributed substantially to the size of the S&L problem and its ultimate cost to taxpayers.

Regulatory Decisions and Moral Hazard Are Magnified

The troubles of the S&L industry prompted regulators and policy makers to seek solutions that would ease those woes. But their solutions only created more problems for the industry, ending with extremely large accrued liabilities to the government for deposit insurance. In particular, reductions in capital requirements for the S&L industry and the policy of regulatory forbearance contributed in a major way to the ultimate cost of the S&L crisis.

Regulators and policy makers took measures to lower capital requirements and ease oversight, partly in the mistaken belief that the industry's problems were transitory. In early 1980, the S&L industry had capital requirements of approximately 5 percent of assets; by 1982, capital requirements were reduced to 3 percent of assets—in part to avoid triggering regulatory actions against depository institutions with low capitalization. Moreover, a number of other changes were introduced that further weakened the reduced capital requirements.

The S&L industry and its regulators departed from generally accepted accounting practices in ways that expanded the measure of the capital of S&Ls, thus permitting more S&Ls to remain open. Under regulatory accounting principles, S&Ls were allowed to follow a more liberal set of rules for determining capital than under generally accepted accounting principles.

Constraints on resources for regulating and resolving insolvent S&Ls further compounded the crisis. Although the regulatory situation was becoming much more complex and the deposit insurance system subjected to much greater risks, the resources devoted to overseeing the S&Ls were not increased correspondingly. Indeed, the number of supervisors was actually reduced during some years in the first half of the 1980s. Later in the 1980s, constraints on resources caused the government's losses to mount extravagantly simply because regulators did not have enough cash to close the sharply escalating number of insolvent S&Ls.

Many analysts believe that this regulatory forbearance was an especially key cause of the escalating public liabilities in the S&L crisis. According to one recent study, for example, many of the most costly institutions to resolve had been reporting their insolvency five years or even longer. Obviously, the cost of resolution would have been much lower if it had been carried out properly. From the time these institutions became insolvent until they were resolved, their liabilities grew rapidly as they paid higher and higher rates to attract deposits and accumulated relatively high-risk assets. Correspondingly, the government's accrued liabilities for resolving insolvent thrifts increased dramatically.

Fraud Played a Role

Fraudulent practices—though especially difficult to quantify and assess—were probably not a major cause of the S&Ls' woes. Although some analysts believe that fraud could account for as much as 20 percent to 25 percent of the government's losses, more experts assign a much smaller weight to this factor—on the order of 3 percent to 10 percent. Economic forces, regulatory forbearance, and the incentives for S&Ls to take excessive risks were much more important fundamental causes.

How Great Are the Government's Losses?

Outlays for deposit insurance loom large and significantly affect the current size of the federal budget deficit and the outlook for deficits in the future. Federal outlays to insure deposits in savings and loan institutions and commercial banks, including the need for working capital, are projected to rise from $58 billion in 1990 to a high of $115 billion in 1992. Beginning in 1993, however, outlays for deposit insurance drop sharply, and by 1996 they are minus $44 billion.

The reason that outlays become negative is that the Resolution Trust Corporation will be selling more S&L assets than it will be buying, and these net proceeds count as an offset to program outlays. From 1990 to 1996, annual outlays for deposit insurance are projected to decline by $102 billion. As a result, the deficit is projected to fall by $64 billion over the 1990–96 period if deposit insurance is included but will rise by $38 billion without it.

The Financial Institutions Reform, Recovery, and Enforcement Act of 1989 (FIRREA) created the Resolution Trust Corporation (RTC) to handle resolving failed thrift institutions that the Federal Saving and Loan Insurance Corporation insured. The FSLIC Resolution Fund inherited the FSLIC's caseload (that is, institutions already closed before the RTC was created). In addition, FIRREA set up a new fund to insure thrifts, the Savings Association Insurance Fund (SAIF).

Some of the costs of resolving the S&L crisis have been obscured because of the way they have been financed. The Resolution Funding Corporation (REFCORP) was set up for the sole purpose of borrowing funds to finance savings and loan resolutions. The funds borrowed by REFCORP are treated as offsetting collections in the budget. Thus some $30 billion in spending ($18 billion in 1990 and $12 billion in 1991) is effectively excluded from the budget totals. The government and taxpayers have paid dearly for this arrangement, since an enterprise such as REFCORP has to pay a higher interest rate when it borrows in credit markets than the Treasury would have to pay. The REFCORP bonds have carried interest rates approximately one-third of a percentage point higher than comparable Treasury securities—adding about $2 billion in present-value costs for interest, according to estimates of the Congressional Budget Office.

For purposes of summarizing the costs of the S&L crisis, the single most useful figure is the present value of future costs. Present value reflects payments and receipts that will occur over many years and expresses those future flows in today's dollars. Present value discounts future cash flows. It takes into account that, because of interest, a dollar today is worth more than a dollar next year. Recent estimates by the Congressional Budget Office indicate that the present value of the government's costs to resolve the savings and loan crisis will be approximately $215 billion in 1990 dollars. This total includes the cost of dealing with the cleanup efforts of the original FSLIC, the FSLIC Resolution Fund, and the Resolution Trust Corporation.

83. Eroding Market Imperfection: Implications for Financial Intermediaries, the Payments System, and Regulatory Reform

Robert A. Eisenbeis

Excerpted from *Restructuring the Financial System* (Federal Reserve Bank of Kansas City, August 1987), pp. 28–30. Robert A. Eisenbeis is Wachovia professor of banking at the University of North Carolina at Chapel Hill.

Recent Developments in Financial Markets

A number of forces have contributed to the internationalization of U.S. markets. Freer trade flows have opened up opportunities for companies generally. The reduction in regulatory barriers has opened up foreign markets to international banking organizations. Foreign banks, for example, have expanded significantly in the United States and have widened the scale of their dealings with U.S. domestic customers. As of 1986, there were more than 250 foreign banking organizations that had a presence in U.S. financial markets, and these firms had aggregate resources of $500 billion. These institutions know many more U.S. borrowers than previously, and by virtue of their parent companies' positions in their home country markets, they are able to assist in flotation of the securities of U.S. firms abroad. Moreover, many are able to offer a wider array of securities and other financial services precluded to U.S. banks by regulation. These advantages are probably significant in explaining why foreign banks now account for about 20 percent of the commercial and industrial loans to companies with U.S. addresses. Similarly, U.S. banking organizations help foreign companies issue securities in U.S. and foreign markets. This latter activity has been facilitated by the recent opening of foreign securities markets to U.S. banking organizations. The 1986 Financial Services Bill, called Big Bang in the United Kingdom, for example, opened the London market more to U.S. banking organizations and provided for an integration of securities underwriting, distribution, and investment within banking conglomerates. As already suggested, the availability, access, and free flow of information has made it easier for lenders to assess the risks of dealing with offshore borrowers.

Internationalization has made it increasingly difficult for individual countries to maintain regulatory structures or regulations different from those in the rest of the world. There are two reasons for this. The first is the ease with which financial institutions, through financial innovation, can avoid the regulatory restrictions of individual countries. The second is that regulatory avoidance is encouraged by regulatory bodies in individual countries that seek, by providing accommodating regulatory climates, to attract and expand the institutions doing business in their country. It has now become extremely difficult, if not impossible, to pursue domestic regulatory policies without the cooperation of foreign regulators. For example, the U.S. regulatory agencies recently published for comment capital adequacy standards to be applicable to banks in the United Kingdom and the United States. Peter Cooke, associate director of the Bank of England, recently indicated that he had begun work to bring the Japanese into the arrangement as well to ensure competitive equality among the major competitors in financial markets.

84. Solvency Problems in the Insurance Industry
Congressional Budget Office

Excerpted from *The Economic Impact of a Solvency Crisis in the Insurance Industry* (Washington, D.C.: U.S. Congress, April 1994), pp. 1–10.

Like those in the banking and savings and loan industries, the number of insolvencies in the insurance industry has grown during the past decade. Between 1976 and 1980, a total of 77 insurance companies failed. Between 1981 and 1985, the overall number more than doubled, to 165; and the number doubled again, to 333, between 1986 and 1990. In 1991, a record number of insolvencies (110) occurred, but the number fell to 91 in 1992. About 30 insolvencies in those two years combined resulted from stricter regulatory oversight in Louisiana and catastrophic claims on damages caused by Hurricanes Andrew and Iniki.

Not only has the number of insolvencies increased during the past decade, but different types of insurance companies are now running into trouble. Before the 1980s, insolvencies were concentrated among small companies operating in a single state or on a limited regional basis; most of the insolvent property and casualty insurers were automobile insurers. More recently, however, insolvencies have involved larger companies operating over a much wider, multistate area and selling different kinds of insurance policies. Between 1976 and 1991, more than 40 percent of the insolvencies in the life and health insurance industry occurred among health insurers.

As the number and size of insolvencies have grown, so has the cost of resolving them. When an insurer becomes insolvent and the value of its assets is less than the value of its obligations to its policyholders, the remaining solvent insurers are assessed a percentage of their premium receipts to cover the claims of the insolvent firm's policyholders up to prescribed limits. The mechanisms for collecting and disbursing these assessments are the state guaranty funds—associations of licensed insurers in each state. During the 1980s, assessment for the insolvencies of both life and health insurers and property and casualty insurers grew rapidly.

Although the solvency problems of the insurance industry have grown to worrisome levels during the past decade, they have been considerably smaller than those of the savings and loan industry. The failure rates in the insurance industry have been similar to those of the banking industry, but the dollar amount and the percentage of the industry's assets held by insolvent firms have been much smaller. The costs of failure have also been much lower in the insurance industry than in the banking and savings and loan industries.

During the early 1990s, however, the solvency problems of the life insurance industry increased, climaxing in the failure in 1991 of several large insurers—Executive Life Insurance Company, First Capital Life Insurance Company, Fidelity Bankers Life Insurance Company, Monarch Life Insurance Company, and Mutual Benefit Life Insurance Company. Assessments for Executive Life are expected to total $2.1 billion over five years, with the bulk yet to be paid. Solvency problems among life and health insurers appear to have fallen considerably in 1993.

Of course, even though solvency problems of the insurance industry have been relatively small, they may not stay that way. Indeed, the life and health insurance industry arguably came close to a solvency crisis in 1991. Unknown factors may also act to raise the chances of a solvency crisis over the next few years. For example, book-value accounting and other inadequacies in the solvency regulation of insurers may be hiding losses on commercial mortgages and real estate that threaten a solvency crisis.

How the Insurance Industry Affects Economic Activity

The insurance industry affects economic activity by selling financial assets that people want to buy and by buying other financial assets that people want to sell. To put it another way, the insurance industry affects economic activity through its financial intermediation. The assets it sells—its liabilities—are insurance policies against a wide assortment of risks of economic loss and a variety of investment products such as annuities and guaranteed investment contracts (GICs) that life insurers sell. The assets it buys are mainly corporate stocks and bonds and commercial mortgages. This intermediation reduces the cost of avoiding risks and makes credit markets more liquid and efficient.

The insurance industry's financial intermediation is sizable according to a variety of measures. At the end of 1992, for example, the insurance industry ranked as the second-largest financial intermediary in the United States, holding about $2,200 billion in assets, after U.S.-chartered commercial banks (about $2,800 billion) and tied with private pension funds. The life and health insurance industry holds almost three-quarters of the insurance industry's assets, the size of which now surpasses the thrift industry, the fourth-largest intermediary (about $1,347 billion). In 1992, the amount of life insurance in force in the United States totaled about $10,400 billion, and the payments to policyholders and beneficiaries of life insurance policies totaled about $57 billion. Payments by U.S. property and casualty insurers on claims for losses totaled about $199 billion in 1992. Moreover, the insurance industry has channeled more than $120 billion annually to credit markets in the United States in recent years. That amount averages about 22 percent of all funds supplied by private financial intermediaries. Life insurers accounted for the lion's share—about 75 percent—of that total.

Credit Markets Most Affected by the Insurance Industry

The insurance industry has tended to have its greatest impact in the markets for corporate bonds, commercial mortgages, and tax-exempt securities. Its share of these markets has been significant and relatively stable since at least the early 1970s. Its share of residential mortgages has fallen over time, but its share of U.S. Treasury and government agency securities has risen.

The insurance industry—particularly the life and health segment—dominates the market for corporate bonds. Corporations rely quite heavily on bonds to finance investments in plant and equipment and for other purposes. For example, nonfinancial corporations obtained an average of about 57 percent of their credit-market funds from sales of bonds over the 1983–89 period. The insurance industry accounted for an average of about 45 percent of the purchases by U.S. residents of net issues of corporate and foreign bonds between 1982 and 1992. And at the end of 1992, the insurance industry held about 38 percent of the $1,966 billion of outstanding corporate and foreign bonds; private pension plans were the next largest holder with about 15 percent.

Most of the corporate bonds held by the insurance industry are public, investment-grade issues of large companies, and a significant fraction held by the life insurance industry are private placements, which are issues of mostly small and medium-sized businesses. These smaller companies depend on the life insurance industry for financing their longer-term needs because they have limited access to or cannot afford the public bond market, which is dominated by large companies.

The market for commercial mortgages also relies heavily on the insurance industry for funds. The insurance industry, particularly the life and health sector, has traditionally provided long-term financing for commercial properties such as office buildings, shopping centers, warehouses, and factories. At the end of 1992, the insurance industry was the second-largest holder of commercial mortgages, accounting for about 29 percent of the $710 billion outstanding in the commercial mortgage market. Commercial banks were the largest holder, with $328 billion, or 46 percent.

Typically, the industry's mortgage loans are for completed projects, replacing the short-term financing used for construction and start-up costs. These loans generally carry lower risk than other commercial mortgage loans because insurers require that the cash flow from the project cover a multiple of the property's debt service before the loan is made.

In recent years, however, some life insurers have made large amounts of risky, short-term loans on commercial real estate. These loans have the potential to create financial problems for those insurers that invested heavily in them.

The market for tax-exempt securities relies on the property and casualty industry for a large amount of financing. This financing takes the form of obligations that state and local governments, nonprofit organizations, and nonfinancial corporations issue in the form of industrial revenue bonds; the interest income from these obligations is exempt from federal income taxes. Households are the primary source of funds for this market, both directly and indirectly through mutual funds and money market mutual funds, but the property and casualty industry is also an important participant. The market for tax-exempt securities had $1,197 billion outstanding at the end of 1992, and the property and casualty industry was the third-largest holder, with about $134 billion, or 12 percent of the total.

Some issuers of tax-exempt securities also rely on the insurance industry to provide insurance, or guarantees, on their tax-exempt securities. The use of insurance coverage has been available since the early 1970s. By purchasing insurance, the issuers are probably able to reduce their interest costs because they can offer an extra layer of protection to investors against potential delays in interest payments or against defaults on interest and principal. An example of insured securities is those issued by state and local housing authorities to finance the construction of affordable housing projects.

Other mortgage markets directly receive relatively few of their funds from the insurance industry. The industry has reduced its share of home mortgages substantially, virtually abandoning the market for mortgages on one- to four-family structures. However, the industry indirectly supplies funds to this market by its purchases of mortgage-backed securities issued by government-sponsored enterprises. The industry has also reduced its share of the market for multifamily mortgages from about 20 percent in the 1980s to about 10 percent in 1992.

85. Dow Jones Industrial Average Is a Nonsense Number
John F. Walker

Reprinted with permission from *Willamette Week* (Portland, Oregon), September 6, 1976, p. 10. John F. Walker is professor of economics at Portland State University; this article was a part of his "Political Economy" column.

Nobel Prize-winning economist Paul A. Samuelson explains the connection between the economy and the stock market this way: "The stock market has predicted eleven of the last three recessions." Yet thousands of times every day radio and television reporters tell us the latest changes in the Dow Jones Industrial Average. Every metropolitan daily newspaper carries it, several national magazines and investors' news services specialize in analyzing it and comedians and politicians cite it. But what is the Dow Jones Industrial Average? I doubt that one person in 100,000 could explain it.

It is supposedly a simple average of the prices of thirty high-grade industrial stocks adjusted to account for splits in the number of shares outstanding. It is widely believed to reflect conditions in the stock market, and the stock market is widely believed to reflect conditions of the economy.

In reality it is a nonsense number that doesn't measure the stock market very well, and the stock market doesn't measure the economy at all. People cite it because it is simple and helps them avoid thought about the economy, which is hard and often unpleasant work.

In Table 85.1 I have listed the members of the stocks in various Dow Jones Industrial Averages (DJI) that have existed since Dow Jones started keeping a thirty industrial average in 1928. It has had industrial averages since 1896. Those stocks that make up the average have changed over time. So while this year's average is measuring apples and nuts, the

Table 85.1

The Dow Jones 30 Industrials on Various Dates

Dow Jones 30 1976	Dow Jones 30 1945	Dow Jones 30 1928
Alcoa	National Steel	Wright Aeronautical
Allied Chemical	Allied Chemical	Allied Chemical
American Brands	American Brands	American Brands
American Can	American Can	American Can
American Tel. & Tel.	American Tel. & Tel.	Victor Talking Machine
Bethlehem Steel	Bethlehem Steel	Bethlehem Steel
Chrysler	Chrysler	Chrysler
DuPont	DuPont	American Sugar
Eastman Kodak	Eastman Kodak	General Railway Signal
Esmark	Corn Products	Mack Trucks
Exxon	Exxon	Exxon
General Electric	General Electric	General Electric
General Foods	General Foods	General Foods
General Motors	General Motors	General Motors
Goodyear	Goodyear	Atlantic Refining
International Harvester	International Harvester	International Harvester
International Nickel	International Nickel	International Nickel
International Paper	Loew's	Paramount Publix
Johns Manville	Johns Manville	North American
Minnesota Mining & Mfg.	American Smelting	American Smelting
Owens Illinois Glass	National Distillers	Texas Gulf Sulfur
Proctor and Gamble	Proctor and Gamble	Nash Motors
Sears Roebuck	Sears Roebuck	Sears Roebuck
Standard Oil of Calif.	Standard Oil of Calif.	B.F. Goodrich
Texaco	Texaco	Texaco
Union Carbide	Union Carbide	Union Carbide
United Aircraft	United Aircraft	Radio Corporation
U.S. Steel	U.S. Steel	U.S. Steel
Westinghouse	Westinghouse	Westinghouse
Woolworth	Woolworth	Woolworth

average thirty years ago measured chick peas and barley. Is the market up or down as against thirty years ago? We don't know. The downs were thrown out of the average and potential uppers have replaced them.

Just last month Anaconda was replaced in the list by Minnesota Mining and Manufacturing—a clear case of throwing out a company that has been doing badly and replacing it with a company doing well. It has been argued that Anaconda was thrown off the list because it was absorbed by Atlantic Richfield. But the only two companies that have been on the list continually since its inception are General Electric and American Brands (formerly known as American Tobacco). Each has merged with literally dozens of companies and is a quite different business than it was in 1896.

Before 1928 the industrial list included only twenty stocks, and before 1916 only twelve stocks. Many stocks on the larger list are not replacing old stocks but are net additions. But when expanding the list, the Dow Jones Company grabbed the opportunity to drop some stocks from the old list. As a result, it is impossible to tell which new names are replacements and which are additions.

Since 1928 the list has been thirty stocks long, so all changes are replacements. I have tried to list replacements in the space previously held by the companies they replaced. Even that has not been completely accurate since some companies have dropped from the list and then later returned, replacing a different stock than the one that originally displaced them.

Some places in the list seem more "unlucky" than others. For example, the slot now held by Owens Illinois Glass was previously held by National Distillers, United Aircraft, International Shoe, and Texas Gulf Sulphur. Seventeen companies have been continuously on the list since 1928.

There are other averages compiled to reflect how the stock market is doing. The Dow Jones Company compiles the industrial, rail, utility, and composite indexes. Standard and Poor's and Value Line compile the averages of much larger numbers of stocks. The New York Stock Exchange compiles an average of all stocks. Most of the broader averages are weighted to reflect the relative importance of the stocks. The DJI is not weighted. That means a $1 change in the price of Johns Manville is treated as if it were as important as a $1 change in General Motors.

None of this is a criticism of the Dow Jones Company. It publishes the *Wall Street Journal*, which provides more high-quality economic and financial commentary than the rest of the working press combined. Through its Richard D. Irwin publishing company, it provides a large percentage of the best business and economics textbooks for colleges and universities. So it is a company that supplies large amounts of very good analysis and thought to the community. It also supplies nonsense to the financial community, with Barron's editorials, the DJI, and the "Abreast of the Market" column in the *Wall Street Journal*.

In "Abreast of the Market," brokers are asked to explain the daily price changes observed on the stock market. Their answers invariably reflect the headlines. So the Republican convention explains the stock price changes one week; the Democratic convention explains the changes another week. It matters not which way the prices change.

The tragedy is, most of the financial press imitates "Abreast of the Market" instead of the rest of the *Wall Street Journal*. Such is the state of financial journalism generally—a hodgepodge of myth, rumor and reactionary politics.

Formal analysis of stock prices has been done in universities for decades. The consensus among scholars is that security prices follow a random walk, or the best explanation of a stock price tomorrow is the price today plus a random number. Many financial experts fear this conclusion because it simply says better forecasts of stock prices will come from the ignorant (and therefore random) than can come from the informed (and therefore biased and nonrandom). This point was first proved mathematically by Bachelier in a doctoral dissertation presented to the University of Paris in 1901.

How it works is simple. Everyone who either buys or sells stock acts on some information or theory. The information or theory may or may not be correct. Still the person buys or sells. Each buy increases demand and price, each sell increases supply and lowers price. All facts and theories operated on are then registered in the changes in prices over time. The market reflects all information and theories, right and wrong; experts can never know that much.

An average of a set of random numbers is a random number. So a good way to predict the value of the DJI is to ask someone completely ignorant of America what he thinks it will be (any four year old is a better predictor than his parent).

While the business and finance pages of most newspapers are nothing but press releases and petty gossip, the home economics sections are generally accurate and excellent. When they say Mary Jane wore organdy to her wedding, it is true. When Zerpha Borunda tells you how to bake a cake, you learn how to bake a very good cake. When the business pages tell you how to get rich, beware. You are about to be impoverished.

So another myth goes down the drain. The reader of the financial press is probably a thoughtless gossip, but the reader of a cookbook is dealing with meaningful production theory that will vitally affect the health of us all.

86. A Review of *Predictability of Stock Market Prices*

G. H. Lawson

Book review of C. W. J. Grainger and O. Morgenstern, *Predictability of Stock Market Prices* (Lexington Mass.: Heath Lexington, 1970), reprinted with permission from the *Economic Journal*, September 1971, pp. 641–43. G. H. Lawson was on the faculty of the Manchester Business School.

This book is the offspring of the authors' long-standing interest in the predictability of stock market prices. It is an outgrowth of their well-known earlier studies, beginning in 1961, which were associated with the development of spectral analysis of economic time-series data.

In summarizing the authors' main conclusions, it must be emphasized that in this volume, as might be expected, important findings abound; a quick count shows over seventy. In a short review it is therefore difficult to do anything like justice to such extensive coverage, combined as it is with both scholarship and highly powerful technical skills. The reviewer's problem nevertheless has to be faced and a start can be made by focusing on those aspects of the work that are of special interest to this Journal's readership.

Until about a decade ago, economists had shown a surprising lack of interest in the actual behavior of the stock market. This absence of empiricism did not, however, preclude the formation of certain beliefs of an economic character and the emergence of important assertions about that market in economic theory; like all fallible human beings economists can also show that they are prone to confuse facts, evidence, theories and beliefs. Readers of this Journal will be especially interested to learn that, according to authors Grainger and Morgenstern, four widely held economic "principles" concerning the stock market are either untrue, or in need of very careful specification before they can be accorded scientific value status. These are the hitherto rather comforting and plausible opinions that:

(1) the market allocates investible funds optimally;
(2) aggregate stock market price movements predict fluctuations in the economy as a whole;
(3) a company's share price is a function of past earnings, assumed future earning power, expected dividends, and other characteristics peculiar to the company itself;
(4) share prices are predictable individually, and in aggregate, from their previous, mainly cyclical, movements.

Apart from striking these four heavy blows at economic theory, Professors Grainger and Morgenstern also present lethal challenges to a number of its related parts that have passed into the folklore (or conventional wisdom) which, even if it does not motivate in its entirety, tends to be associated with the professions and individuals who operate in stock markets. Thus their analysis of the evidence also suggests inter alia:

(1) there are no cyclical and noncyclical stocks;
(2) there are no seasonal variations in stock prices;
(3) there are no stock price movements that lead other stock price movements;

(4)   as there are no cycles in stock market prices, general economic development cannot be led by any such cycles;

(5)   currently used linear techniques for predicting share prices from price charts have no predictive value;

(6)   it is true only on average that a high volume of transactions is needed to move price;

(7)   stock markets in different countries are virtually unrelated to each other;

(8)   company earnings are unpredictable from past records;

(9)   dividend changes are difficult to predict from past records;

(10)   past earnings and dividends are not useful predictors of the future price of a stock;

(11)   there is a trend in present American data that is approximately exponential; in other countries there are other trends, and, especially in the latter data, there are no trends for long intervals.

Stated positively, the main inferences to be drawn from Grainger and Morgenstern's findings of the kind represented above are, first, that stock market prices vary according to random walk superimposed on possible long-term not readily detectable trends. Second, no method other than reliance on inside information will guarantee profits on the stock market.

The random walk hypothesis has already dominated the subject of share price prediction for about a decade or more and, although simple, exists in a number of alternative forms that have resulted in much confusion and a variety of misunderstandings. In some extremely interesting sections the authors not only clear away the misunderstandings, they also propose modifications that increase the usefulness of random walk.

An early chapter of the book describes the statistical techniques utilized, and unusually, but usefully, the description starts from a concrete data analysis standpoint rather than with the abstract underlying theory. This said, it now ought to be emphasized that while the not-so-numerate will probably experience a notable increase in rate of heartbeat on a first glance of this book, they can be assured that the amount to be gained from the prose alone is substantial indeed. Indeed, it ought to be strongly recommended to anybody who claims any sort of academic, professional, amateur, or merely superficial interest in the stock market.

Throughout the whole of this work the authors have adopted a rigorous scientific point of view and are at great pains to utilize and extend the work of others in this area. The result is that the reader is provided with excellent surveys and statements on the present position of the subject.

Having repeatedly demonstrated the randomness that characterizes the stock market with the analysis of data, the authors conclude their work with a descriptive (nonmathematical) model. This model not only makes it abundantly clear that price formation in the stock market is an extremely complicated mechanism, it also confirms its random nature.

In conclusion, one might speculate that this book, challengeable though it may appear to some, will add further stimulus to the great interest and work on the stock market, especially on relative price movements, that began in the early sixties. There can be small doubt that Professors Grainger and Morgenstern have, with this volume, especially some of its wider aspects, presented many problems for economists, accountants, stock market "experts," and possibly also the state.

87. A Half-Year Pause in Inflation: Its Antecedents and Structure

John F. Early, Walter Lane, and Philip Sturm

Excerpted from the *Monthly Labor Review*, October 1986, pp. 3–6. John F. Early is assistant commissioner for consumer prices and price indexes, Bureau of Labor Statistics. Walter Lane and Philip Sturm are economists in that office.

Background, 1960–81

The early 1960s were characterized by rapid economic expansion, with prices increasing at an annual rate of 1.3 percent for the five-year period that ended in December 1965. Price pressures developed in the late 1960s, however, as expenditures for the Vietnam War stimulated an economy already at nearly full employment. The rate of inflation in consumer prices rose from less than 2 percent in 1965 to more than 6 percent in 1969.

One can identify the general composition of price change in each of these periods. This seasonally adjusted overall inflation rate can be constructed as the sum of the individual contributions of four major classes of consumer expenditures: energy, food, shelter, and all other.

The acceleration in prices from the first half to the second half of the 1960s was widespread, except that energy prices had little impact.

The recession that began late in 1969 caused the rate of price increase to subside only partially, and much of that reduction was due to the effect of declining mortgage interest rates on the shelter component of the CPI. In reaction to the failure of inflation to abate swiftly and fully, President Nixon announced a wage and price freeze on August 15, 1971. The initial price freeze and subsequent Phase II economic controls were accompanied by a lower rate of inflation during the final months of 1971 and throughout 1972. Prices, however, started to rise more quickly in 1973, and further inflation followed with the relaxation of controls in August and the oil embargo in October. Although the direct effects of the oil embargo on inflation were substantial, they were far from unique. Sharply higher mortgage interest rates and house prices drove up shelter costs; food prices, influenced in part by worldwide commodity inflation, rose rapidly; and prices for most other goods and services began to accelerate.

Inflation climbed to double-digit rates during 1974 and registered what was then the largest calendar-year change in the history of the CPI, except for the inflationary periods directly associated with the two world wars. With the steep recession of 1973–75, inflation moderated substantially so that, by the end of 1976, consumer prices were rising at an annual rate of less than 5 percent. With the economic expansion of 1977, prices began to accelerate. Then sharp increases in energy prices were fueled by events associated with the Iranian crisis, and rapid price rises for food and shelter costs followed, pushing consumer price rises to unprecedented peacetime rates during 1979, 1980, and, indeed, for most of 1981.

Deceleration since 1981

Two back-to-back recessions (1980 and 1981–82), a tight monetary policy, and lessened control by OPEC of world petroleum supplies all contributed to a rapid reduction in the rate of inflation beginning in the fourth quarter of 1981. This moderation in prices brought an end to the "ratchet phenomenon" that had characterized inflation since 1960. Before 1981, each succeeding low point in inflation was higher than the preceding low, and each high point was also higher than the preceding high. The 3.09 percent price increase for 1982 was the smallest annual increase in ten years.

The price deceleration that occurred in the fifty-seven months through June 1986 was particularly apparent in the energy, shelter, and food components of the CPI. Advances in these items had, of course, been responsible for much of the increase in the CPI in the past decade. Unlike earlier episodes, however, the index excluding the energy, shelter, and food components also moderated substantially, rising at a 4.8 percent seasonally adjusted annual rate during the fifty-seven months through June 1986, compared with a 9.6 percent increase for the twelve months ended in September 1981.

The slowdown in food prices preceded the deceleration in the overall CPI. For the twelve-month period ended in September 1981, grocery store food prices had increased 5.5 percent, a rate half that of the overall index. Increases in each of the following four years were also less than those for the overall index. For the September 1981 to June 1986 period, grocery store food prices advanced at an average annual rate of 2.1 percent, and the overall food component at a 2.8 percent rate.

The shelter component registered steep advances throughout most of the period from 1978 through September 1981. The rate of increase fell off sharply beginning in the fourth quarter of 1981, principally due to the behavior of house prices and mortgage interest rates, and advanced at an annual rate of 2.2 percent from September 1981 through December 1982. Until January 1983, the CPI used an asset approach to measure shelter costs of homeowners. The asset treatment covered house prices, mortgage interest rates, property insurance, property taxes, and maintenance and repair costs. In January 1983, BLS introduced an improved measure of shelter costs for homeowners in the consumer price index for city wage earners and urban clerical workers (CPI-U), using a rental equivalence approach. During the first three and one-half years of the new measure, shelter costs rose at an annual rate of 5.3 percent.

Energy costs declined at an annual rate of 2.1 percent for the fifty-seven-month period through June 1986, compared with an increase at a 22.9 percent rate in the thirty-three-month period from December 1978 to September 1981. Although charges for gas and electricity continued to increase at double-digit rates through 1982, they slowed considerably beginning in 1983, rising at an annual rate of 2.6 percent in the forty-two months ended in June 1986. Prices for petroleum products peaked in early 1981 and then generally declined, with the exception of temporary spurts associated with short-term shortages and a five-cent-a-gallon gasoline tax increase in April 1983. The sharpest drop occurred during the first six months of 1986. As of June 1986, fuel oil prices were 35.2 percent lower and gasoline prices 31.2 percent below their 1981 peak levels.

The index for items other than food, shelter, and energy slowed more gradually than the excluded components. The price moderation in this group has been steady since 1981, when these prices rose, on average, by 9.4 percent. They increased less each year than in the preceding one, and by the end of 1985 the annual change was 3.7 percent. Within the groups, however, price movements for commodities and services have diverged. Initially, both groups slowed from their peak rates; further deceleration has occurred primarily in the goods sector, however, with service prices continuing to advance at a rate of more than 5 percent.

88. The Federal Reserve Response

Sherman J. Maisel

Excerpted and reprinted from *Managing the Dollar*, pp. 7–10, by Sherman J. Maisel, by permission of the author and W.W. Norton & Company, Inc. Copyright 1973 by Sherman J. Maisel. Maisel is professor of economics at the University of California–Berkeley and a former governor of the Federal Reserve.

Crisis threatened on Sunday, June 21, 1970, when the officers of the Penn Central Railroad filed for a reorganization. The Federal Reserve was greatly concerned because this failure jeopardized a major credit market—that for commercial paper. Commercial paper is securities sold by borrowers to lenders with very short terms, from 1 to 270 days. Borrowers generally hold commitments from their bank for funds to pay off loans coming due if the lender decides not to renew, or roll over, the loan through commercial paper. The firms issuing commercial paper (the borrowers) have prime financial ratings, and much of the paper is sold through reputable underwriters. Although most of the nation has never heard of the commercial paper market, from 1965 to May 1970 the amount being borrowed in this market at any given time rose from $9 billion to $40 billion.

Thousands of firms, individuals, trusts, foundations, and other lenders had purchased commercial paper on the assumption that it was a completely secure repository, with a rate of return from 1 to 1.5 percent above the yield on ultrasafe Treasury bills. However, the rapid growth of the market and its high rates had attracted inexperienced lenders, and even some experienced lenders had become careless of the criteria they used.

The Penn Central failure threatened the entire structure because it cast doubt on the basic assumption that the commercial paper of large, well-known companies was good security. Penn Central had $80 million in commercial paper outstanding when it went into receivership. Lenders on Penn Central's commercial paper suffered major losses. People who had lent money on the commercial paper of other companies suddenly, with the spectre of the supposedly secure Penn Central before them, realized that they had agreed to unforeseen and unwanted risks. Lenders asked themselves whether they should not withdraw their money and put it into safer securities as soon as possible.

The problem that faced the Fed was to make certain that there would be sufficient money available to permit all those who held maturing commercial paper to be paid off if they did not wish to renew. Banks had made such commitments to borrowers on commercial paper, but would they and could they meet them? Although banks were fully loaned up, they might not have to lend several billion dollars a week to those corporations that would need to pay off their commercial paper. Before making such loans, banks would have to decide whether their previous commitments were still valid, given their own liquidity position, the altered condition of the economy, and doubts about the solvency of borrowers. Banks could back out of these commitments by invoking responsibility to their depositors not to take undue risks, but that would cause failure for the rejected borrower.

The shock waves from the Penn Central failure could spread rapidly if reinforced by failures of additional firms. As working capital disappeared and customers were lost, corporations unable to borrow would shut down. Massive unemployment could ensue. At this point the Federal Reserve informed the major banks of the country that its discount window—where it makes short-term loans to member banks—was wide open. If they needed funds to make loans to their customers who were having difficulty in rolling over their commercial paper in the market, they were invited to borrow from the Fed. Further, to enable the banks to attract more money, the board raised interest rates permitted to be paid on certificates of deposit (CDs), which are funds that banks receive from large customers. Of course, if they preferred, they could find other sources than the Fed's discount window for their increased needs for funds.

The commercial paper market remained precarious for several weeks. Banks had to make numerous loans to companies having trouble rolling over their paper. Almost all banks met their commitments, using Federal Reserve discounts and new deposits attracted with the higher CD rates the Fed permitted. All told, they borrowed an additional $1 billion from the Fed over the following month. In the next three months, their certificates of deposit virtually doubled, a rise of nearly $11 billion. During the same period, the volume of commercial paper outstanding fell by $6 billion. In that quarter reserves furnished by the Fed grew at a 25 percent annual rate. The money supply increased at slightly over a 5 percent rate. All interest rates retreated from their record highs.

89. Volcker's Revolution at the Fed
Andrew H. Bartels

Excerpted and reprinted with permission of the publisher, M.E. Sharpe, Inc., from *Challenge*, September/October 1985, pp. 35–39. Andrew H. Bartels is a former staff member of the Subcommittee on Domestic Policy, Committee on Banking, Finance, and Urban Affairs of the United States House of Representatives.

Halting Steps toward Independence

A dominant Fed is a new phenomenon. Over most of its history, the Federal Reserve and its monetary policy have played second fiddle to the president, the Congress, and fiscal policy. While the Fed has been independent in principle since its creation in 1913, during its first two decades it was also fragmented and relatively ineffectual. Fed independence became more of a reality after the Banking Act of 1935 reaffirmed its distinct status and made it a potentially powerful central bank. However, for many years afterward, the Fed deferred to the president and acted like an agency of the current administration. Indeed, from the 1930s to 1951, the Federal Reserve was virtually a handmaiden of the Treasury, its monetary policy subordinated to the Treasury Department's desires to finance the U.S. government's debt at low and stable interest rates. Marriner Eccles, chairman of the Fed from 1935 to 1948, increasingly chafed at this constraint, but not until 1951 did the Fed gain operational as well as formal independence.

Even after the Treasury–Federal Reserve Accord of 1951 released the Fed from the task of maintaining set rates for Treasury securities, the Fed remained deferential to the president. During the 1950s and 1960s, Fed chairman William McChesney Martin was a forceful and articulate advocate of disciplined monetary and fiscal policies to Presidents Eisenhower, Kennedy, and Johnson. But when the president decided on an overall economic policy, the Fed went along. Contributing significantly to the Fed's acquiescence was the Keynesian orthodoxy that fiscal policy mattered most, and that monetary policy had only a modest and limited impact on the economy.

The first signs of a more assertive Fed emerged in the mid-1960s. A major reason was the difficulty encountered in implementing appropriate—especially anti-inflationary—fiscal policies. The excessive stimulus the Johnson program of Vietnam "guns" and Great Society "butter" gave the economy in 1964 and 1965 began to create inflationary pressures. Johnson's economists urged him to raise taxes, but the president ignored the advice. To counter worsening inflation in the absence of effective fiscal restraints, Martin and the Fed in late 1965 raised the discount rate, only to retreat when Johnson complained. In 1966, with Johnson still resisting taxes, the Fed again tightened monetary policy without his prior approval. When the economy began slowing in 1967, the Fed eased and growth resumed. Finally, Johnson proposed an income-tax surcharge in 1968, which the Congress adopted late in the year. With fiscal restraints now theoretically in place, Fed ease continued.

Monetary policy gained importance after Richard Nixon's election in 1968, but the Fed's relationship with the president remained ambiguous. The Nixon economic team accepted the economic theory of monetarism and encouraged the Fed to follow an explicit policy of sustained monetary restraint to bring down inflation. Both Fed chairman Martin's (until 1970) and Nixon's choice as chairman in 1970, Arthur Burns, supported the policy in principle. Burns also was a frequent and active participant in the administration's economic-policy decisions, and the Fed under him was a team player. However, like Martin, Burns saw the Fed's role as an independent and supplementary one, and he resisted committing the Fed to the steady money-growth rate that the monetarists wanted.

The more active use of monetary policy during Nixon's terms produced mixed economic results and increasing political controversy. Tight monetary policies in 1969–70 led to the recession of 1970, but inflation declined only modestly through 1971. The 1970–71 phenomenon of stagflation—relatively high inflation and relatively high unemployment—led both the administration and the Congress to criticize the Fed for keeping money too tight. Impatient with the failure of tight monetary policies to produce more rapid progress against inflation, the Nixon administration in the fall of 1971 launched an ill-fated experiment with wage and price controls. Under the cover of controls and pressured by the president, the Fed shifted to a highly stimulative monetary policy in 1972. Easy money along with deficit spending fueled a strong economic recovery, which helped re-elect Nixon.

As the administration became increasingly preoccupied with Watergate investigations in 1973 and 1974, Burns asserted a more prominent role for the Fed. When inflation accelerated in 1973, Burns slowed money growth. An economic downturn ensued as a result at the end of the year. At the same time, the first oil embargo occurred, sending inflation sharply higher. Despite the deterioration in business activity and employment, Burns tightened monetary policy even more in 1974 in an effort to halt rising prices. A longer and more virulent stagflation characterized the economy for that year and the next.

As Fed activism increased and economic performance deteriorated in 1973–75, Congress became more concerned with monetary policy. Long-term critics of the Fed such as Congressman Wright Patman and monetarist economists like Milton Friedman formed tacit alliances in support of bills to restrict the independence of the Fed and require it to achieve fixed money-growth targets. Congressional anger boiled over in 1975, after monetary policy became very restrictive in the last half of 1974 and unemployment rose to nearly 9 percent in the early months of 1975. Bills to require the Fed to achieve specified interest rates and/or money-growth rates were pushed in the House and Senate. The Fed with the support of the Ford administration strongly resisted these directives. Eventually, a compromise resolution—H. Cong. Res. 133—emerged from the Congress in March, directing the Fed to report to the Congress periodically on its objectives for growth in the monetary aggregates. These requirements were made part of the Federal Reserve Act in 1977 and linked to the president's economic projections in the Humphrey-Hawkins Act of 1978. While the Fed escaped with its independence largely intact, it was henceforth required to provide the Congress with its monetary policy objectives ahead of time.

The next three years were years of an acquiescent Fed. The threat of even greater congressional restrictions was a check on the Fed's assertion of its independence, and the Carter administration after 1977 expected Fed cooperation with its economic plan. Carter's appointment of G. William Miller as Fed chairman in 1978 symbolized the Fed's reversion to a subsidiary role in economic policy, for Miller lacked the public stature of either Martin or Burns. Not surprisingly, the money supply was allowed to grow at the rapid rate of about 8 percent from the end of 1976 until the end of 1979, as the Fed sought to accommodate political desires for low interest rates and strong growth, despite worsening inflation.

Volcker and the Assertion of Fed Autonomy

Although the period from 1975 to 1979 was a low point for Fed independence and assertiveness, there was one development that helped set the stage for the Fed's current renaissance. While individual senators and representatives continued to complain about monetary policy and the Fed, Congress as a whole displayed a great reluctance to go beyond the provisions of H. Cong. Res. 133. Legislation introduced in 1976 by the chairman of the House Banking Committee to restructure the Fed's policy-making Open Market Committee lost decisively in the committee. Similarly, the 1977 amendments to the Federal Reserve Act and the Humphrey-Hawkins Act in 1978 basically incorporated the provisions of H. Cong. Res. 133 with only technical changes, instead of further restricting the Fed. Members of Congress apparently decided that the requirement of periodic Fed reports to them on monetary policy offered enough influence over policy without the onus of actually having to make decisions on monetary tightening or easing.

The second development in the Fed's revival was the appointment of Paul Volcker as Fed chairman in August 1979. Volcker's many years of experience with the Treasury Department and the Federal Reserve Bank of New York made him acutely conscious of the political pressures that had impinged on the Fed. He believed that monetary policy had a major role to play and that a truly independent and conscientious Fed was needed.

Volcker's determination to make the Fed a more assertive force in economic policy was demonstrated in October 1979. With inflation worsening and the American dollar collapsing, the Volcker Fed initiated a major change in Fed procedures, focusing on controlling the growth of monetary aggregates and letting interest rates fluctuate. The decision was made without the investigation or prior approval of the Carter administration. The Fed under Volcker still deferred to the president when asked. For example, at the direction of the administration the Fed developed a program of credit controls in early 1980. However, when the program backfired, producing a steep (though brief) recession followed by resurgent inflation, Volcker and the Fed were even more determined to follow their own course. Accordingly, in the fall of 1980 the Fed tightened monetary policy and raised interest rates to check inflation, despite protests from the White House about the damage to Carter's re-election chances.

The third factor in the Fed's renaissance was the election of Ronald Reagan to the presidency. The Reagan administration assumed office in 1981 with a strong philosophical bias against government management of the economy. Its objectives were largely political: reduce the size of government, cut taxes, and eliminate regulation. It assumed that these actions would have beneficial economic results, but it never developed a consistent and credible program for making that happen. The attitude seemed to be that the economy would take care of itself if the government got out of the way. Indeed, the administration's plans for fiscal and monetary policies were inherently in conflict, for it adopted massive tax cuts to stimulate growth while endorsing a restrictive monetary policy that could not finance such growth given normal money demand. Moreover, the administration displayed a singular obtuseness about the macroeconomic effects of its spending, tax, and monetary policies.

The Reagan administration's abdication of the management of the economy created a vacuum, which Volcker and the Fed promptly filled. Their concern was the still-high rate of inflation in 1981. To slow down double-digit wage and price increases, the Fed embarked on a course of severe monetary restraint. The Fed took this step on its own, without explicit direction from the administration, although the president's support for a gradual reduction in the rate of money growth implied approval in principle.

Despite the onset of a severe recession in the fall of 1981, the Fed succeeded in its gambit. Although Volcker and the Fed were subject to intense criticism from many groups and many members of Congress in 1982, what is remarkable is how little the Fed was actually challenged.

There were several reasons the Fed got through the 1981–82 recession with its authority enhanced instead of diminished. First, the downturn was the result of factors besides the Fed's actions, including cutbacks in federal social spending in 1981 and the high interest rates fostered by the rising deficits from Reagan's fiscal policy. The Fed could and did deflect criticism of its policies by pointing to the administration's deficits as the cause of economic dislocations. Second, while many in the administration were clearly unhappy with the Fed's tight money policies and focus on budget deficits, they could hardly criticize an anti-inflationary monetary policy they had in effect endorsed. Consequently, administration officials could only carp about the Fed being tighter than desired or allowing too much variation in money-growth rates. Third, Democratic members of Congress were constrained in their criticisms of the Fed by their desire to attack the Reagan program. Given the distance between the Fed and the administration, they realized that focusing on the Fed would allow the president to escape blame. Fourth, Volcker, by constantly stressing the deficit issue, skillfully pitted the administration and congressional Democrats against each other instead of the Fed. Republicans were forced to concentrate on defending their fiscal policies, on which Democrats had been encouraged by Volcker to concentrate their fire.

The final element in the Fed's prominence was the economic record of declining inflation and strong economic growth after 1982. Unlike the stagflation that plagued prior Fed attempts to reduce inflation in 1968–69 and 1973–75, the rate of price increase slowed rapidly in 1981 and 1982. Factors beyond the Fed's control, such as declines in energy and commodity prices and a strengthening U.S. dollar, largely accounted for the difference. Nonetheless, the Fed could point to dramatic declines in inflation as positive results to offset the bad news of rising unemployment. Then, in mid-1982, when the recession was showing clear signs of worsening, the Fed shifted gears. Abandoning its monetary targets, it greatly relaxed monetary policy in order to stimulate economic growth. The sustained ease in Fed policy along with the highly expansionary fiscal policy produced a booming recovery and steep declines in unemployment in 1983–84. Yet inflation remained subdued, thanks in part to Fed tightening in late 1983 and the last half of 1984.

The achievement under the Fed's economic management of both low inflation and strong growth placed Volcker and the Fed in an unusually strong position politically. The Fed's effective handling of such crises as third world debts and the near failure of Continental Illinois further enhanced its authority. The many remaining problems in the economy—the strong dollar; the enormous trade deficit; the difficulties of heavy industry, agriculture, and natural resources; the persistence of relatively high unemployment—are widely, and probably accurately, blamed on the budget deficits. Volcker and the Fed have strong views on how these problems should be addressed, and, as the congressional budget targets show, those views are extremely influential.

90. How Monetarism Failed

Nicholas Kaldor

Excerpted and reprinted by permission of the publisher, M.E. Sharpe, Inc., from *Challenge*, May/June 1985, pp. 4–13. Nicholas Lord Kaldor is professor emeritus of economics at the University of Cambridge and is a fellow of King's College.

The great revival of "monetarism" in the 1970s, culminating in the adoption of the strict prescriptions of the monetarist creed by a number of Western governments at the turn of the decade—particularly by President Reagan's administration in the United States and Mrs. Thatcher's in Great Britain—will, I am sure, go down as one of the most curious episodes in history, comparable only to the periodic outbreaks of mass hysteria (such as the witch hunts) of the Middle Ages. Indeed, I know of no other instance where an utterly false doctrine concerning the causation of economic events had such a sweeping success in a matter of a few years without any attempt to place it in the framework of accepted theory concerning the manner of operation of economic forces in a market economy.

The central assertions of monetarism—assiduously propagated for a number of years by a single American economist, Professor Milton Friedman of Chicago—is that an excessive increase in the supply of money, caused by the decisions of the note-issuing authority, the central bank, is the main, if not the sole, cause of inflation, and that the cyclical fluctuations of the economy reflect the irregularities and aberrations with which the money supply is increased by the monetary authority, which is responsible also for distortions in the structure of production caused by imperfect anticipation of the delayed effects of increases in the money supply on prices. Since on account of unstable and highly variable "time lags" it is hopeless to expect that the monetary authorities can prevent such instabilities by well-timed measures (or compensate for them by well-timed countermeasures), the only safe rule to follow is to secure a modest and stable rate of increase in the rate of growth of the money stock, which by itself will serve to stabilize the value of money and gradually eliminate cyclical instabilities.

In the United States, the Federal Reserve traditionally followed much the same kind of policies as European central banks, operating mainly through short-term interest rates and engaging in open-market operations so as to ensure that actual rates conformed to the official rediscount rate. In addition, the Federal Reserve maintained tighter controls on its member banks through the institution of variable minimum reserve requirements. But there was no attempt to regulate the quantity of money other than through the instrument of interest rates and changes in minimum reserve requirements.

However, in the monetarists' view all this was the wrong policy for securing stability of prices. To stabilize the economy and to avoid inflation, they believe, what is needed first of all is to secure a steady growth in the money supply, not a steady rate of interest. Hence the "new" policy of the Federal Reserve, formally announced by Mr. Volcker on October 6, 1979, was to secure a slow and steady growth of the monetary aggregates M1 and M2 by varying the reserves available to the banking system through open-market operations, irrespective of the accompanying movements in the rates of interest. From that day on, dramatic changes started to happen that were quite different from those expected. The money supply failed to grow at a smooth and steady rate; its behavior exhibited a series of wriggles. The rate of interest and the rate of inflation, though both were very high at the start, soared to unprecedented heights in a very short time. By March 1980 the rate of interest rose to 18.6 percent and the rate of inflation to 15.2 percent (in annual terms), and a little later both were over 20 percent—something that had not occurred in the United States since the Civil War, whether in peacetime or in wartime. And there was a mushroomlike growth in new forms of making payments and new instruments for circumventing the Fed's policy—through the invention of money substitutes of all kinds, like NOW accounts and money market funds, the transfer of business to nonmember banks or to branches of foreign banks, and so on. The Fed's reply to all this was that the failures in its declared policies were all due to "loopholes" in the existing system, which must be closed. Congress obliged its friends in the Fed very quickly, passing the Monetary Control Act of 1980, supplemented by invoking the International Banking Act and the Credit Control Act. These extended minimum reserve requirements to all deposit-taking institutions, whether or not they were member banks of the Fed, as well as to U.S. branches of foreign banks. But none of this helped, as the British Radcliffe Committee had foretold twenty-two years earlier when it said that the extension and multiplication of controls through a wider spread of regulated institutions would only lead to the appearance of new forms of financial intermediaries and of transactions, causing the situation continually "to slip from under the grip" of the authorities.

The American monetarist experiment was a terrible failure, as was publicly admitted by Friedman and Meltzer in 1982—though they insisted that it was the fault of the authorities in not being able to run a monetarist policy properly, not of basic theory. Short of the old Chicago plan for 100 percent reserves, there was certainly no way in which the authorities could have stopped the banks. After a year and a half of continued failures and a chaotic volatility of everything—interest rates, exchange rates, inflation rates—the experiment was abandoned and the system returned, in effect, to the traditional policy of regulating interest rates, but with a more deflationary stance—partly, I presume, to offset the inflationary force of excessive federal deficits, and thereby causing the rest of the world to suffer (or benefit, as the case may be) from the consequences of an overvalued dollar.

In retrospect, none of this would have happened if the Fed had studied and understood the analysis and prescription of the Radcliffe Committee in 1958, according to which central banks should not really be concerned with the money supply as such. It is the regulation of interest rates, and not of the quantity of money, that, in the words of the committee's report, "is the centerpiece of monetary action."

The Turn Away from Monetarism

The U.S. and UK experiments in monetarism have thus left Friedman and the monetarists in an intellectually highly embarrassing position. Friedman has admitted that as far as the United Kingdom is concerned, the money supply is not exogenously determined by the monetary authorities, but he attributed this to the "gross incompetence" of the Bank of England. Later, he implied the same about his own country. However, this puts an entirely new complexion on monetarism. It was nowhere stated in the writings of Friedman or any of his followers that the quantity theory of money only holds in countries where the monetary authorities are sufficiently "competent" to regulate the money supply. If the Bank of England is so incompetent that it cannot do so, how can we be sure that the Bank of Chile or of Argentina or Mexico—to take only the highly inflationary countries—is so competent, or rather so competently incompetent, as to make it possible to assert that the inflation of these countries was the consequence of their central banks' deliberate action in flooding them with money? How, indeed, can we be sure that any of the central banks—not excluding even the German Bundesbank or the Swiss National Bank—are sufficiently competent to be able to treat their money supplies as exogenously determined? And what happens if they are not? Surely we need a general theory of money and prices that is capable of embracing the causes of countries with "incompetent" central banks, such as Britain and the United States.

91. Eurodollars
Marvin Goodfriend

Excerpted from *Monetary Policy in Practice* (Federal Reserve Bank of Richmond, 1987), pp. 85–90. Marvin Goodfriend is a vice president and senior staff economist at the Federal Reserve Bank of Richmond.

The Nature of the Eurodollar

Eurodollars are bank deposit liabilities, denominated in United States dollars, not subject to United States banking regulation. For the most part, banks offering Eurodollar deposits are located outside the United States. However, since late 1981 non–United States residents have been able to conduct business free of United States banking regulations at international banking facilities (IBFs) in the United States. Eurodollar deposits may be owned by individuals, corporations, or governments from anywhere in the world, with the exception that only non-United States residents can hold deposits at United States IBFs.

The term Eurodollar dates from an earlier period when the market was located primarily in Europe. Although the bulk of Eurodollar deposits are still held in Europe, today they are also held in such places as the Bahamas, Bahrain, Canada, the Cayman Islands, Hong Kong, Japan, the Netherlands Antilles, Panama, Singapore, and United States IBFs. Nevertheless, dollar-denominated deposits located in United States IBFs and anywhere in the world outside the United States are still referred to as Eurodollars.

Banks in the Eurodollar market, including United States IBFs, compete with United States banks to attract dollar-denominated funds. Since the

Eurodollar market is relatively free of regulation, banks in the Eurodollar market can operate on narrower margins or spreads between dollar borrowing and lending rates than can banks in the United States. This gives Eurodollar deposits an advantage relative to deposits issued by banks operating under United States regulations. In short, the Eurodollar market has grown up as a means of separating the United States dollar from the country of jurisdiction or responsibility for that currency, the United States. It has done so largely to reduce the regulatory costs involved in dollar-denominated financial intermediation.

The Size of the Eurodollar Market

The most readily accessible estimates of the size of the Eurodollar market are compiled by Morgan Guaranty Trust Company of New York and reported in its monthly bank letter *World Financial Markets*.

As of December 1985 Morgan estimated the gross size of the Eurocurrency market at $2,796 billion. The net size was put at $1,668 billion. Morgan also reports that Eurodollars made up 75 percent of gross Eurocurrency liabilities, putting the gross size of the Eurodollar market at $2,097 billion. No net Eurodollar market size is given. However, 75 percent of the net size of the Eurocurrency market yields $1,251 billion as an approximate measure of the net size of the Eurodollar market.

M2 is the narrowest United States monetary aggregate that includes Eurodollar deposits. M2 includes overnight Eurodollar deposits held by United States nonbank–non-money-market-fund residents at branches of Federal Reserve member banks worldwide. As of December 1985, M2 measured $2,567 billion; its Eurodollar component was $17 billion. Eurodollar deposits owned by United States nonbank–non-money-market-fund residents continue to grow, but this comparison shows clearly that such Eurodollar deposits still account for a relatively small portion of United States nonbank–non-money-market-fund resident holdings of monetary assets.

Incentives for Development of the Eurodollar Market

By accepting deposits and making loans denominated in United States dollars outside the United States and in United States IBFs, banks can avoid United States banking regulations. In particular, banks located outside the United States and in United States IBFs have no non-interest-bearing reserve requirements against their dollar-denominated deposits. These banks hold balances with United States banks for clearing purposes only. Moreover, there is no required Federal Deposit Insurance Corporation insurance assessment associated with Eurodollar deposits. Virtually no restrictions exist for interest rates payable on Eurodollar deposits or charged on Eurodollar loans, and there are few restrictions on the types of assets allowed in portfolio.

In most Eurodollar financial centers, entry into Eurodollar banking is virtually free of regulatory impediments. In addition, banks intending to do Eurodollar business can set up in locations where tax rates are low. For example, Eurodollar deposits and loans negotiated in London or elsewhere are often booked in locations such as Nassau and the Cayman Islands to obtain more favorable tax treatment. In fact, various states in the United States have amended their tax codes to grant IBFs relief from local taxes.

Foreign monetary authorities are generally reluctant to regulate Eurodollar business because to do so would drive the business away, denying the host country income, tax revenue, and jobs. Even if the United States monetary authorities could induce a group of foreign countries to participate in a plan to regulate their Euromarkets, such a plan would be ineffective unless every country agreed not to host unregulated Eurodollar business. In practice, competition for this business has been fierce, so even if a consensus should develop in the United States to regulate Eurodollar business, it would be extremely difficult to impose regulations on the entire Eurodollar market.

Arbitrage keeps interest rates closely aligned between Eurodollar deposits and deposits with roughly comparable characteristics at banks located in the United States.

92. Central Banking and Systemic Risks in Capital Markets

Andrew Brimmer

Excerpted and reprinted with permission of the author and copyright holder, the American Economic Association, from *The Journal of Economic Perspectives*, Spring 1989, pp. 11–15. Andrew Brimmer is president of Brimmer & Company, Inc., in Washington, D.C., and a former governor of the Federal Reserve System.

Federal Reserve Intervention Following the Stock Market Crash of 1987

The stock market crash on October 19, 1987, wiped out almost $1 trillion of financial wealth in the United States. While this dramatic decline captured the headlines, a far more serious threat to the financial system was occurring because of the near-failure of the clearing and settlement system that underpins stock and commodity markets.

In the United States, the market value of common stocks reached a peak on August 25, 1987. On that day, the Dow Jones Industrial Average of thirty common stock prices (the most widely followed measure of market values) closed at 2722.42. Between August 25 and October 14, 1987, the DJIA declined to 2412.70, a decrease of 11.4 percent. Over the next two days, a further decline of 6.9 percent brought the index to 2246.73 on October 16. Thus, a net erosion of 17.5 percent in the DJIA had already taken place prior to the market crash.

On Monday, October 19, a record of 604.3 million shares were traded on NYSE. The DJIA fell by 508 points and closed out at 1728.42. If the declines of October 16 and 19 are taken together, the two-day drop exceeded the two-day decline registered on October 28 and 29, 1929.

Many factors contributed to the original erosion and eventual collapse of stock prices in the fall of 1987; growing expectations of renewed inflation, the depreciation of the U.S. dollar, rising interest rates that made bond yields more competitive with common stocks, a fading of foreign investors' confidence, growing pessimism about near-term profitability for U.S. corporations, the unwillingness of Japan and Germany to stimulate their economies, concern over federal budget deficits, and a number of other developments. The result was a major attempt to sell stocks and take profits before prices fell further. Moreover, reinforced by a variety of computer-linked stock-trading strategies, decisions to sell led to an avalanche of more selling.

The most serious risk to the overall financial system posed by the stock market crash arose not from the sharp decline in prices but from the strains that were put on the system for clearing and settling securities and commodity futures transactions. Under ordinary circumstances, the clearing and settlement systems (CSS) operated by stock and commodity exchanges are hidden away in back offices. They normally facilitate the exchange of financial instruments for cash between sellers and buyers according to predetermined time schedules. The CSS relied on by each stock or commodity exchange evolved over many years to handle the requirements of each specific marketplace. However, because of innovations that have produced new types of financial instruments, the stock and commodities markets have come to overlap, and respective CSSs now impinge upon each other.

On the morning of October 20, 1987, when stock and commodity markets opened, dozens of brokerage firms and their banks had extended credit on behalf of customers to meet margin calls, and they had not received balancing payments through the clearing and settlement systems. Moreover, the clearing and settlement process was running several hours behind schedule. The magnitude of the risks faced by those market participants dependent on the system is illustrated by the situation of two brokerage firms: Goldman, Sachs and Kidder, Peabody. By noon on October 20, in combination, they faced a cash deficit of $1.5 billion. This was the amount of their own funds that they had advanced in response to margin calls on their customers. But because of failures in the clearing and settlement systems, these firms' accounts were not credited with funds until midafternoon. The exact amount of capital held by these firms as a cushion against loss is not known. However, if they had suffered actual losses on the scale of the recorded exposure, the adverse impact undoubtedly would have been quite severe. Many other brokerage firms faced comparable exposure.

It was in this environment that the Federal Reserve's second-stage intervention occurred. As margin calls mounted, money-center banks (especially those in New York, Chicago, and San Francisco) were faced with greatly increased demand for loans by securities firms. With an eye on their own capital ratios and given their diminished taste for risk, a number of these banks became increasingly reluctant to lend, even to clearly creditworthy individual investors and brokerage firms. As a result of this slowdown in lending, the response to margin calls also slowed down, and uncovered positions became larger and were outstanding for longer periods of time. To forestall a freeze in the clearing and settlement systems, Federal Reserve officials (particularly from the board and the Federal Reserve Bank of New York) urged key money-center banks to maintain and to expand loans to their creditworthy brokerage firm customers.

The banks responded, and the evidence stands out clearly in the statistics. For example, the weekly reporting banks in New York City expanded their loans to brokers and to individuals to purchase or carry securities from $16.7 billion in the week ending October 7 to $24.4 billion in the week ending October 21: a gain of $7.7 billion, or 46.1 percent. At one bank alone (Citicorp), loans to securities firms climbed to $1.4 billion on October 20, from a normal range of $200 million to $400 million.

Over the course of the next few days, the clearing and settlement system resumed its normal functioning. But on October 20, 1987, it staggered on the brink of collapse. If it had collapsed, it would have pulled down several other major financial sectors. The timely intervention by the Federal Reserve was aimed at diminishing the systemic risks faced by capital markets generally.

The analysis presented here leads to a clear conclusion: The Federal Reserve System, as the nation's central bank, has a major responsibility in the containment of those types of risks that threaten to disrupt the fabric of the financial system so vital to the economy at large. That responsibility extends well beyond the more narrowly defined tasks of controlling the growth rates of the monetary aggregates and influencing the level and structure of interest rates.

CHAPTER IX

The Foreign Balance and Foreign Economic Policy

93. World Trade and Economic Growth
Council of Economic Advisers

Excerpted from the *Economic Report of the President* (Washington, D.C.: U. S. Government Printing Office, 1989), pp. 148–67. The members of the council responsible for the report were Chairman Beryl W. Sprinkel and Thomas Gale Moore.

Economic Growth and Trade in the Postwar World

The end of World War II left a changed political and economic map. While the United States emerged from the war greatly strengthened, the economic output and industrial capacity of many of the combatants had been sharply reduced. Economic output in 1946 was well below its prewar (1939) level in France, Italy, West Germany, and Japan. As late as 1950, output in West Germany and Japan had not returned to prewar levels. By contrast, U.S. output in 1950 was two-thirds larger than the prewar level, having grown on average nearly 4.8 percent per year.

From this inauspicious beginning, the rest of the industrial world soon joined the United States in experiencing rapid economic growth. Average world output over the period 1950–86 grew at an average rate of more than 4.2 percent, nearly doubling the 2.2 percent growth rate over the period 1870–1950. Even during the economic expansion from 1870–1913, output had grown at an average rate of only 2.5 percent.

While Japan, West Germany, Italy, and France offer the most dramatic examples of this phenomenon, every major industrial country, with the sole exception of the United States, experienced faster growth in the postwar period than in the period 1870–1913. When viewed in terms of output per labor-hour—a measure of productivity—the superior postwar performance is even more striking. Average productivity in the major industrial countries grew at almost 3.8 percent during the postwar period, as compared with 1.7 percent from 1870 to 1913. Not only was productivity growth generally higher in the postwar period than earlier, but also in many countries the growth rate more than doubled, and in Japan and Italy it more than tripled the rate in the 1870–1913 period.

Accompanying this rapid economic growth was an even more rapid increase in trade flows between countries. Exports grew quickly during the periods 1870–1913 and 1950–87, while they were relatively stagnant from the onset of World War I to 1950. Furthermore, trade was expanded more rapidly in the postwar period than in the earlier period of economic growth. The growth in world trade is attributable to a number of factors, including dramatic declines in tariff barriers and the reduction of internal barriers throughout the industrial world, the reduction of internal barriers in Europe, and the formation of the European Community (EC)—a development promoted by the United States. The expansion in trade is most notable for those countries that grew most rapidly—Japan, West Germany, Italy, and France.

The postwar expansion was not confined to industrialized countries. Some countries that were impoverished at the start of this period made remarkable strides toward joining the ranks of the industrialized world. Between 1965 and 1985 developing economies as a whole grew at an average rate of more than 5 percent. Among the most successful economic performers were Singapore, Hong Kong, and South Korea. Singapore and South Korea grew at annual rates of more than 9 percent, while Hong Kong's annual growth rate was nearly 8 percent.

As in Europe, rapid expansion of exports accompanied fast overall growth in developing countries. Studies show that for the period 1963–85 real gross national product per capita grew at more than 6 percent, and manufactured exports at more than 14 percent, for developing economies with a strong outward, trade-promoting orientation, while for the same period countries characterized as strongly inward-oriented and favoring self-sufficiency had real GNP per capita growth rates averaging 1 percent and manufactured export growth rates under 5 percent. Successful export-led growth in many developing countries could not have occurred without the liberalization of industrial country markets in the postwar period. Yet the greater successes have occurred in developing countries that have also opened their own markets to imports.

Tariff Liberalization in the Postwar Period

Today, U.S. tariffs are the lowest in history, with average tariff rates on all imports under 4 percent. The passage of the Reciprocal Trade Agreement Act of 1934 marked the beginning of the U.S. tariff reduction policy that has endured to the present. Using the authority to negotiate reciprocal tariff reductions on nonagricultural goods by up to 50 percent of their Smoot-Hawley levels, the United States had entered into more than 20 bilateral agreements by the beginning of World War II. This approach brought average tariff rates back down to 35 percent of dutiable imports (and 12.5 percent of all imports) by 1940. The turnaround in trade flows, aided by the economic recovery, was dramatic: from 1934 to 1939 U.S. imports and exports increased by 40 to 50 percent.

Although the trade negotiations conducted at this time were on a bilateral basis, they already embodied a principle of nondiscrimination central to the multilateral approach the United States would promote after the war. Tariff reductions were applied not only to negotiating parties but to other trading partners as well, on a most-favored-nation basis.

U.S. Postwar Objectives

The United States emerged from World War II as the world's dominant military and economic power. Yet Soviet expansionism in Eastern Europe, and civil war in China, threatened global stability. Recognizing that political stability required economic prosperity, the United States adopted a policy of promoting rapid economic growth abroad. The three pillars of that policy were: a stable international monetary system to finance international transactions; an open trading system to foster global economic growth and cooperation; and economic aid to help speed postwar reconstruction.

Embracing a policy of free trade does not imply that governments have no role in regulating international commerce. As with domestic commerce, government policy must ensure a stable economic environment, open competition, free trade, enforcement of contractual rights, and protection of intangible and tangible private capital. Governments that make unpredictable or frequent changes in tariffs or other restrictions on trade are likely to disrupt economic activity. Countries' failures to protect foreign investment or intellectual property rights reduce the return to investment or innovation, decrease investment, and restrict the international flow of capital and ideas. Trade liberalization in one country generally benefits its trading partners as well as the country undertaking liberalization. International coordination raises the possibilities for additional liberalization efforts and the consequent gains from expanding trade. Thus, creation of a proper international trading environment requires active cooperation among nations to make and enforce the rules of the game. Recognizing the economic and political benefits of broad international participation in trade liberalization, the United States made a multilateral approach the cornerstone of its postwar trade policy.

Tariff Reductions in a Multilateral Framework: GATT

As the war drew to a close in 1945, the Congress authorized the executive branch to seek tariff reduction of up to 50 percent of rates prevailing at the beginning of that year. The United States worked to establish a multilateral framework for negotiations. Under U.S. leadership, an international conference was convened in 1947 to establish the International Trade Organization (ITO) that would ratify the principles of free trade and create rules for enforcing those principles. American calls for talks to reduce tariffs immediately led twenty-three countries to participate in tariff-reduction negotiations in Geneva later that year.

The talks in Geneva resulted in important achievements, both in the reduction of tariffs and in the establishment of general trading guidelines, which were drawn up as the General Agreement on Tariffs and Trade. Although the International Trade Organization was to have superseded GATT, the Congress failed to approve it, and it never came into being. Thus, GATT emerged as the major forum for conducting international trade negotiations and supervising the implementation of their results.

GATT Principles

The principles on which GATT was founded are the essential features of an open trading system. The GATT's aim of trade liberalization was to be achieved on a nondiscriminatory basis (that is, following the most-favored-nation, or MFN, principle); trade policy was to be transparent (hence favoring tariffs over quantitative restrictions whose effects on prices are less clear); tariff reductions negotiated under GATT, or "concessions" in GATT parlance, were "bound" so as not to increase above specified levels and were not to be replaced by other trade barriers ("integrity of concessions"); GATT members were to provide "national treatment" to each other's imports in matters of internal taxation and regulation; and nations were to follow an orderly process of dispute settlement, abiding by the internationally agreed upon rules and procedures, rather than emerging in unilateral retaliatory measures that might lead to escalating trade wars.

Tariff Reduction under GATT

In retrospect, GATT has had remarkable success in reducing, and in many cases virtually eliminating, tariffs. Three of the seven completed negotiating rounds stand out for their achievements in this area.

Inaugural Round in Geneva, 1947

This first round of GATT achieved substantial multilateral tariff cuts, as reductions negotiated in some 123 bilateral agreements were extended on a most-favored-nation basis to all participants. The United States made weighted-average tariff cuts of about 20 percent on dutiable imports. Participating European countries made less substantial cuts, from generally lower tariff levels, because the Smoot-Hawley tariffs had put U.S. rates in a higher range. But the effects of European concessions were not felt until the European nations made their currencies convertible, and abandoned most quantitative restrictions, at the end of the 1950s. The favorable economic climate in the United States allowed it to confer these asymmetric reductions. With most major U.S. industries enjoying trade surpluses, the spectre of U.S. protectionism—although not absent—was not dominant.

Tariff concessions in each of the four rounds held over the next fifteen years were comparatively minor, in part due to limited negotiating authority from the Congress, which demonstrated an increasing penchant to protect U.S. industry from competition. The combined effect of these talks was still notable, however, reducing U.S. tariffs by about 10 percent.

The Kennedy Round, 1963–67

The momentum for the Kennedy round came from the United States, which wanted to ensure continued trading access to the newly formed European Community. The Kennedy administration paved the way for more rapid progress on tariffs by obtaining enhanced negotiating authority in the Trade Expansion Act of 1962. Not only did this act allow for high tariff cuts (up to 50 percent), but it also eliminated some restrictions that the Congress had earlier put in place to prevent reductions in specific industries. The Kennedy round of GATT that ensued was even more successful than the Geneva round had been. In addition to reducing average tariffs on dutiable imports by more than one-third, it included much broader country coverage, as important trading countries such as Japan and West Germany had since acceded to GATT. Because the negotiating principle changed from an item-by-item focus ("request-offer" in GATT parlance) to a formula approach of automatic 50 percent cuts on all nonagricultural products with exceptions to be negotiated, the product coverage was also more comprehensive than any prior GATT round.

The Tokyo Round, 1973-79

Again using a formula approach, major industrial nations agreed to cut average tariffs by about one-third in the Tokyo round of GATT. The phased-in reductions from this round were completed in 1987. With weighted-average tariffs of major industrial nations brought down to levels below 5 percent (and in most cases these tariffs are bound not to increase under GATT), a case can be made that the goal of multilateral tariff liberalization is largely accomplished.

Yet the average figures mask considerable discrepancies on individual products, as countries have retained high "tariff peaks" on items for which there is strong domestic protectionist pressure. Nominal tariffs on raw materials and semimanufactures are lower than tariffs on manufactures. This escalated tariff structure, by reducing input costs for manufacturers, results in higher "effective protection" for processed goods than is reflected in the nominal tariff rate on these manufacturers. Finally, although country and product coverage has increased considerably since the inception of GATT tariff negotiations, large areas still remain less than fully incorporated. Because of previous "special and differential" treatment, developing countries, including those newly industrializing economies that have made rapid strides over the past twenty years, have participated little in either the reduction or the binding of tariffs. Although tariffs have been cut on agricultural products, those cuts have been less even across countries. Furthermore, agricultural tariffs are bound less frequently than are tariffs on manufactures.

Weaknesses of the GATT Framework

The exceptions in product and country coverage for GATT-sponsored tariff reductions conflict with the basic GATT aim of achieving broad-based trade liberalization. Yet these and numerous other exceptions to GATT's main principles to foster open and fair trade have been accepted as necessary compromises in an agreement whose only teeth are those lent willingly by member countries. Because those principles ultimately embodied in GATT had been honored more often in the breach than in the word prior to the formation of GATT in 1947, it is hardly surprising that the initial exceptions list was relatively long. More telling is the fact that, rather than shrinking, this list has grown longer. Safeguard clauses allow countries to take steps backward on the overall goal of liberalization by imposing quantitative restrictions (which also violate transparency) or by ignoring tariff bindings in the event of balance-of-payments concerns, injury to domestic producers (the "escape clause"), or a perceived threat to national security.

Although GATT's membership list continues to expand, effective country coverage remains elusive. Under what is known as "special and differential treatment," wide-ranging exemptions to GATT concessions and disciplines have been granted to developing countries since the Kennedy round. As another component of special and differential treatment, industrial countries have created a generalized system of preferences (GSP), which allows developing countries certain tariff concessions superior to the most-favored-nation rates of GATT. At the same time, special treatment in GATT has reduced the negotiating leverage of developing countries, preventing them from gaining GATT concessions of most value to them, including reduced tariffs on manufactures and progress on nontariff measures, safeguards, and the treatment of tropical products and agricultural commodities.

The Tradeoffs in U.S. Trade Legislation—Tariff Reductions versus Creeping Protectionism

Protectionist sentiment was not strong in the immediate postwar period, but some elements opposed liberalized trade. Those sentiments have been on the rise. As tariff barriers have steadily fallen, other barriers to trade have arisen. Because the Congress has granted authority to negotiate tariff reductions, while at the same time channeling protectionist sentiment into legislation, a curious pattern has emerged in the trade laws of the postwar period. Trade bills needed by the executive branch for negotiating authority to reduce protection often include provisions that make it easier for firms to qualify for protection and restrict presidential discretion to limit protectionist measures.

Protectionist sentiment grew in the 1970s and 1980s as some U.S. trading partners were perceived not to be offering equal opportunities for trade. Once again, enhanced textile protection, in the context of the Multi-Fiber Arrangement of 1974, was the price paid to gain congressional authorization for negotiating tariff reductions in the Tokyo round and for fast-track congressional approval of any agreement on nontariff measures negotiated through GATT. The Trade Act of 1974 also reduced presidential discretion in implementing International Trade Commission recommendations for protection, and introduced Section 301, a provision for countering foreign practices that "unreasonably" restrict U.S. exports.

The record of the 1980s has largely paralleled that of the 1970s. The 1988 *Economic Report of the President* documented the sharp increase in unfairness findings during the 1980s (against "dumping" at below fair prices and government subsidization of exports), cases for which no presidential discretion exists. Nontariff barriers, for products such as steel, autos, machine tools, and textiles, have been entered into or extended.

The Spread of Trade-Distorting Measures

Because most nations' tariffs are "bound" by GATT, the signs of increased protectionism in the 1970s and 1980s are found not in higher tariffs but in other, often more hidden, forms of protection. Using a potentially limitless array of measures, governments distort trade flows and production decisions by subsidizing exports and domestic production, and by constricting the flow of imports. Import barriers include assessed duties on unfairly traded products; "hard-core" nontariff barriers, such as quotas and voluntary export restraints or voluntary restraint agreements, which are poorly disguised quantitative restrictions; and "softer" nontariff measures, such as technical and health standards, which tend to distort trade if imposed for nonscientific reasons or applied in a discriminatory fashion. Many of these measures are difficult to quantify; no precise estimates of their tariff-equivalents, or their trade-distorting impacts, exist.

Yet convincing qualitative evidence of this rising interventionist and protectionist trend is available. One example of such evidence is the amount of domestic subsidies that governments supply to private industries and public corporations. Because these subsidies alter domestic production, they may distort trade flows and comparative advantage. As shown in Table 93.1, their amount has increased as a percent of GDP from 1960 to 1986 for most countries, the important exception being the United Kingdom, whose subsidy rate peaked in the mid-1970s. Two additional factors in the table qualify this observation. First, it would appear that the trend toward greater subsidization was reversed for many countries in the 1980s. Second, although the U.S. subsidization rate has grown, it is still significantly below that of other countries, reflecting the more market-oriented approach, and the sparsity of public corporations, in this country.

Countries also distort trade and compete unfairly for exports by providing export subsidies. In agricultural trade, many countries, including those in the EC and the United States, provide subsidies or rebates for exports of agricultural goods. For manufactured goods, the more common means is through "export financing," which provides subsidized credit to importers of the products.

While the United States is the dominant user of countervailing duty laws, other nations use antidumping provisions more aggressively. Of 460 countervailing duty cases reported to GATT between 1980 and 1986,

Table 93.1

Growth of Subsidies in Selected OECD Countries, 1960–86
(percent of GDP)

Country	1960	1970	1975	1980	1986
United States	0.2	0.5	0.3	0.4	0.6
Japan	(1)	1.1	1.5	1.5	1.1
West Germany	0.8	1.7	2.0	2.1	2.1
France	1.6	1.9	2.0	1.9	2.2[a]
United Kingdom	1.9	1.7	3.5	2.4	1.7
Italy	1.2	1.3	1.9	2.0	2.3[a]
Canada	0.8	0.9	2.5	2.7	2.0

Source: Organization for Economic Cooperation and Development.
Note: Based on national income accounts.
(1) Not Available.
[a]Data are for 1985.

more than 60 percent were initiated in the United States. But, of the 1,272 antidumping cases reported during the same time period, 27 percent originated in the United States, whereas 33 percent came from Australia, 22 percent from the EC, and 18 percent from Canada.

These actions significantly increased in the United States and abroad during the 1980s. In the United States, for example, the number of countervailing duty cases increased from an annual average of 21 during the period 1975–79 to an annual average exceeding 40 during the period 1980–86. In the EC, the number of antidumping cases reported increased from 71 for 1971–79 to 280 for 1980–86.

In contrast to antidumping and countervailing duty provisions, the protection offered through the "hard-core" nontariff measures falls largely outside of GATT jurisdiction.

The notion that imports cost American jobs is probably the most common argument for protection. While it is certainly true in a narrow sense that employment in an import-competing sector might decline if import protection were reduced or eliminated, this fact does not imply that total U.S. employment would fall. Rather, protection in that sector reduces the resources available for expanding output, and employment, in more efficient export sectors. Most studies of the consumer cost per "job saved" through protection put this cost at more than $100,000 per year, far exceeding the typical earnings in the affected industry. Moreover, protective policies that reduce foreign exports to the United States invite retaliation, which reduces the demand for U.S. exports, causing further inefficiencies in the allocation of resources or imposing extra costs on consumers.

Certainly, unexpected increases in imports can cause temporary unemployment as workers retrain for new jobs. But the appropriate response is to facilitate labor adjustment, not to discourage it through permanent protectionist policies. Trade Adjustment Assistance, first introduced as part of the Trade Expansion Act of 1962 and significantly liberalized by the Trade Act of 1974, may be viewed as one attempt to ease this adjustment and to mollify domestic opposition to trade liberalization. The program, which is designed for firms and workers hurt by import competition, provides financial, technical, and retraining assistance to make firms more competitive and to assist relocation of workers. If adjustment through normal market forces is allowed, the displaced workers will find employment in other industries. Currently, the average period of unemployment is a brief thirteen weeks. If permanent protection is offered, adjustment never occurs, and the cost of the policy remains forever. The rules governing explicit protection under the escape clauses in U.S. trade law (Section 201) and in GATT (Article XIX) recognize this danger and require relief to be temporary.

The recent economic record demonstrates that imports do not destroy domestic jobs. From 1982 to 1987 the volume of U.S. imports increased by more than 65 percent, while U.S. real GNP expanded by more than 21 percent and employment by 13 percent. Meanwhile, West German imports increased by over 27 percent, its GNP grew by nearly 12 percent, and employment stagnated. During this period the U.S. merchandise trade balance fell sharply, while the West German trade balance rose by more than $45 billion.

94. Multilateral Initiatives: The Uruguay Round
Council of Economic Advisers

Excerpted from the *Economic Report of the President* (Washington, D.C.: U.S. Government Printing Office, 1994), pp. 233–36. The members of the council responsible for the report were Chairman Laura D'Andrea Tyson, Alan S. Blinder, and Joseph E. Stiglitz.

The most far-reaching of the administration's market-opening efforts has been on a global scale: the Uruguay round negotiations of GATT, whose 116 participating countries account for approximately 85 percent of world trade.

In the Uruguay round negotiations effectively completed on December 15, 1993, the United States and other GATT members agreed not only to lower tariffs on merchandise trade, but also to integrate into GATT certain areas of trade and investment that had not been subject to effective GATT discipline, including agriculture, textiles, trade in services, investment, and intellectual property rights. The Uruguay round also made progress in reforming multilateral dispute settlement procedures and other multilateral trade rules, including those dealing with nontariff measures. The Congress is expected to ratify this agreement this year.

The stakes in the Uruguay round negotiations were enormous. In the short run, failure to complete the round would have significantly undermined business confidence around the globe and might have contributed to the erosion of the open trading system. In the long run, the successful completion of the round will mean a major boost to the world economy. Preliminary studies suggest that the likely gains to the U.S. economy alone are more than $100 billion but less than $200 billion annually by 2005. These efficiency gains will manifest themselves in the form of more and better jobs for American workers.

The round achieved major reductions in trade barriers facing industrial products. Key provisions of the market access agreement include the following:

(1)   Tariffs imposed by major industrial countries are to be eliminated, and those of many developing countries either eliminated or sharply reduced, in the following areas: construction equipment, agricultural equipment, medical equipment, steel, beer, distilled spirits, pharmaceuticals, paper, toys, and furniture.

(2)   Major U.S. trading partners agreed to deep tariff cuts, ranging from 50 to 100 percent, on important electronics items, including semiconductors, computer parts, and semiconductor manufacturing equipment.

(3)   Tariffs of industrial and major developing countries on chemical products are to be harmonized at very low rates (zero, 5.5, or 6.5 percent, according to product).

(4)   The agreement significantly increased access to markets representing approximately 85 percent of world trade by reducing tariffs on certain items of key interest to U.S. exporters. Progress in textiles and apparel was particularly significant. For decades, international trade in textiles and apparel products has effectively been exempted from GATT rules. Instead, the Multi-Fiber Arrangement establishes a procedure for limiting textile and apparel exports from developing to industrial countries. Under the final Uruguay round agreement, products covered by the Multi-Fiber Arrangement will be free of quotas after ten years, and textiles will be integrated into general GATT rules. Tariffs will be reduced as well.

Throughout the Uruguay round negotiations, one of the most contentious issues was agricultural trade liberalization. The final agreement on agriculture strengthens the long-term rules for agricultural trade and sharply limits national policies that distort that trade. U.S. agricultural exports will benefit significantly from reductions in foreign export subsidies and from market opening by our trading partners.

The United States was successful in its effort to obtain meaningful rules and explicit commitments to reduce export subsidies, cut domestic subsidies, and increase market access. Agricultural export subsidies and trade-distorting domestic farm subsidies are not only to be reduced, but for the first time will be subject to explicit multilateral disciplines. The United States also prevailed in establishing the principle of comprehensive tariffication, which will lead to the eventual removal of all import quota and other nontariff import barriers. Nontariff barriers will first be replaced by tariffs, ensuring minimum or current access, and then those tariffs will gradually be reduced.

Progress in creating a more hospitable trading system for high-technology products was achieved on two fronts. First, the United States was able to win greater protection for intellectual property rights, such as patents, copyrights, and trademarks. This is very important for a diverse set of U.S. industries, including the electronics industry (where semiconductor masks will be protected), the pharmaceutical industry (patents), and the communications industry (protection of copyrights).

Second, the Uruguay round agreement sets forth multilateral rules governing subsidies. Because of the beneficial social spillovers associated with research and development activities, government support cannot and should not be ruled out altogether. The challenge for the multilateral trading system is to find rules that permit governments to support innovations that benefit all nations while precluding rent-shifting subsidies designed to benefit one nation at the expense of others. The Uruguay round agreement makes progress in this respect by establishing clearer rules and stronger disciplines in the subsidies area. It also makes nonactionable certain subsidies relating to basic research, regional development, and environmental cleanup, provided they are subject to conditions designed to limit their distorting effects.

Negotiators were able to agree on comprehensive GATT rules governing trade and investment in services (the so-called General Agreement on Trade in Services, or GATS) such as telecommunications, professional, and financial services. The agreement contains a strong national-treatment provision: Member countries must accord to service suppliers of other countries treatment no less favorable than that accorded their own suppliers. GATS also includes a market access provision that incorporates disciplines on discriminatory measures that governments frequently impose to limit competition. These measures include restrictions on the number of firms allowed into the market, "economic need" tests, and mandatory local incorporation rules. Because of the breadth and complexity of these issues, not as much progress was made as was desirable. To realize additional progress, GATS established a procedural framework for further negotiation.

The Uruguay round negotiations also yielded systematic prohibitions on trade-related investment measures. For example, the agreement prohibits so-called local content requirements which force foreign firms to use a set amount of locally produced inputs as a condition for investment. It also prohibits "trade balancing" requirements, under which a foreign affiliate must export as much of its production as it imports for use as inputs. These requirements have bedeviled U.S. firms operating abroad in the past.

Last, the Uruguay round agreement prohibits so-called voluntary export restraints and other, similar measures that are often used as safeguards outside GATT rules. It also provides specific time limits for the formation and operation of dispute settlement panels and requires the automatic adoption of panel reports (except in the case of a unanimous veto). Previously, any country, including the country against which the complaint was lodged, could effectively block the implementation of a panel's decision. The new procedures will greatly expedite the resolution of international trade disputes. The members of GATT agreed to establish a new multilateral organization, to be called the World Trade Organization (WTO) to enforce these new agreements.

95. Changing U.S. Trade Patterns
Jack L. Hervey

Excerpted from *Economic Perspectives* (Federal Reserve Bank of Chicago, March/April 1990), pp. 2–10. Jack L. Hervey is a senior economist at the Federal Reserve Bank of Chicago.

The last year in which the U.S. merchandise trade balance recorded a back-to-back annual surplus was twenty years ago, in 1970. That surplus was $2.6 billion on the balance-of-payments basis. In 1987, the merchandise trade deficit bottomed out at $160 billion. By 1989, the deficit had been reduced to around $110 billion. Much has been made of the persistent U.S. trade deficit, why it became so large, why it has improved in recent years, and why, finally, it has not improved more.

Recent political and economic developments in Europe make likely major new developments in trade structures and patterns in the near term. World trade relationships are once again on the threshold of significant change.

The economic and political rebirth of Eastern Europe, the movement toward the economic and political integration of Western Europe in 1992 and beyond, and the interaction of those two developments will leave the European canvas with quite a different appearance than would have been thought possible as little as a year ago. Those developments also will have a profound impact on world economic and trading relationships.

Setting the Stage

During the decade of the 1960s, the international economic environment changed as it never had before. Western European countries were drawn more closely together economically in the form of the European Economic Community (EEC) and the European Free Trade Association (EFTA). The extent of this economic integration would have been hard to imagine a few years earlier as the region struggled to recover from World War II.

Japan, also recovering from the war, was not yet a major force in the world economy. Nonetheless, it was on its way to becoming an economic power as it regularly recorded annual real economic growth rates in the 10–15 percent range.

The Kennedy round trade negotiations were initiated and completed during the decade. Large reductions in tariffs on manufactured goods were begun. World trade growth accelerated. Manufactured-goods exports worldwide tripled in value from $64 billion in 1960 to $190 billion by 1970. The physical volume of manufactured-goods trade expanded 2.7 times between 1960 and 1970.

U.S. investment abroad, especially direct investment, increased at a rapid pace. The dollar dominated international exchange, although it was widely considered to be overvalued under the existing fixed exchange rate system. The high foreign exchange value of the dollar made the dollar price of foreign acquisitions attractive. Indeed, it was common to read critical foreign commentary on the undesirable aspects of U.S. companies "buying up" the economic base of Western European countries.

By the late 1960s evidence was plentiful that times and the world were changing, and rapidly. But how rapidly no one would have dared guess.

U.S. Dominance Dwindles

In 1968 and 1969 the U.S. merchandise trade surplus dropped from the $5–$7 billion range that had held during much of the decade to near balance. Concern in official circles intensified about the high value of the dollar and its increasingly detrimental impact on the ability of the United States to compete effectively in world markets.

Early in the 1970s the environment began to change quickly. The U.S. merchandise trade moved into deficit in 1971, by $2.3 billion. The gold window was closed; foreign holders of dollars could no longer claim U.S. gold reserves in return for dollars (August 1971). The dollar was twice officially devalued (effectively in August 1971 but formally at the beginning of 1972, then again in early 1973 prior to the general "floating" of exchange rates in March of 1973). The dollar depreciated further over the course of the decade. Meantime, OPEC gained effective control of sufficient crude oil supplies to enforce a quadrupling of world petroleum prices in late 1973. Large quantities of dollars acquired by the oil-exporting countries, especially the Arab oil exporters, were subsequently recycled to the developing countries of Latin America and Southeast Asia.

U.S. merchandise exports increased more than five times between 1970 and 1980. But during the same period imports increased more than sixfold and the trade balance slipped into constant deficit—averaging $26 billion annually during the last half of the decade.

Exports peaked in 1981, bottomed out in 1985, and not until 1987 did they exceed the 1981 level. Exports in 1989 are thought to have exceeded the 1981 peak by about 50 percent. All of that gain has occurred during the last three years.

Unlike exports, imports grew steadily throughout the 1980s and are estimated to have exceeded the 1981 level by about 80 percent during 1989. The divergence between export and import growth increased rapidly in 1983 and continued through 1987. During the period 1983 through 1989 the deficit averaged more than $120 billion annually.

Changes in trade flows of this magnitude over a period of two decades should reasonably be expected to include compositional changes— changes in both geographic patterns and commodity patterns of trade. To these we now turn.

Geographical Changes in U.S. Trade

Historically, the United States' primary international trade relationships have been with other Western Hemisphere countries and Western Europe. As recently as 1970, two-thirds of U.S. exports went to those regions and seven-tenths of imports came from those regions.

Canada long held the position of primary trading partner, accepting 21 percent of U.S. exports in 1970 and sending 30 percent of U.S. imports. In terms of total trade, that is, exports plus imports, Canada remains the largest single trading partner for the United States. But, the dominant magnitude of the U.S.–Canada trade relationship, as far as the overall U.S. trade picture is concerned, is not as secure as it once was. The United States actually exported a slightly larger proportion of its total to Canada in 1989, nearly 22 percent, than in 1970, when Canada received nearly 21 percent of U.S. exports. Canada's contribution to U.S. imports, on the other hand, dropped sharply, from nearly 30 percent in 1970 to just under 19 percent in 1989.

The pattern of U.S. international trade in the late 1980s indicates that Western Europe has also become a less prominent trading partner. In 1970, one-third of U.S. merchandise exports went to Western Europe, but by 1989 the proportion had dropped to 27 percent. Likewise, with imports. In 1970, 28 percent of U.S. imports came from Western Europe, but by 1989 the proportion had dropped by a quarter, to 21 percent.

U.S.–Latin American trade as a proportion of the U.S. total hovered in the low to mid teens throughout the two decades, diminishing only slightly in recent years.

If these traditional markets are accounting for a lesser share of the total than was formerly the case, it is clear that the excess has been picked up elsewhere. Imports from Japan increased sixteenfold between 1970 and 1989. The import value of $94 billion in 1989 was the largest from any single country and was equal to 93 percent of the total from all of Western Europe. In 1970, imports from Japan were just shy of 15 percent of total U.S. imports and less than half the total from Canada. By 1989, imports from Japan had risen to 20 percent of the total and were slightly greater than imports from Canada.

The Growth Area in Trade

The dollar value of U.S. international trade increased tenfold between 1970 and 1989—8.5 times for exports and 11.8 times for imports. But the shares accounted for by traditional markets in Western Europe and the Western Hemisphere had a net downward shift. Some increase in trade share has taken place with Japan, but it was not sufficient to offset a decline in shares of the magnitude recorded in trade with Western Europe.

That leaves us with one of the more interesting trade developments of the past two decades, the emergence of the newly industrializing countries of Southeast Asia (NICs) as a major trading bloc. These four countries—Hong Kong, the Republic of Korea, Singapore, and Taiwan—have become a formidable trade bloc and are the focal point of the Southeast Asia (excluding Japan) market. In combination they exceed in importance the United Kingdom and West Germany, together, as a market for U.S. exports and as a source of U.S. imports.

In 1970, the NICs accounted for 4 percent of U.S. exports and 5 percent of imports. By 1989, the proportions had increased to 11 percent and 13 percent, respectively. By comparison, the rest of Southeast Asia (primarily Malaysia, Thailand, Indonesia, and the Philippines) has maintained a steady 2 or 4 percent share of U.S. exports and imports throughout the two decades.

Finally, one additional regional bloc requires mention. Eastern Europe and mainland China are not particularly significant in the overall U.S. trade picture currently (although with respect to U.S. exports of agricultural commodities and imports of clothing they are of some importance). As a market for U.S. goods these two areas have increased their aggregate share of the U.S. total from less than 1 percent in 1970 to 3 percent in 1989, with the current shares equally divided between Eastern Europe (including the Soviet Union) and China. However, imports from Eastern Europe have held at one-half percent of the total throughout the period. Imports from China, on the other hand, which were nil in 1970, increased to a 2.5 percent share of U.S. imports in 1989; most of that increase in share occurred after 1980.

The Composition of Trade Has Also Changed

Even though the value of U.S. exports increased from nearly $43 billion in 1970 to more than $360 billion in 1989, the composition mix for major categories of exports appears to have changed surprisingly little. The aggregate figure may be somewhat misleading because of possible undercounting in the early part of the period, however.

Using an *adjusted* total as a base for calculating the export shares of various commodities indicates that the relative importance of agricultural exports has deteriorated, dropping from a 19 percent share in 1970 to 14 percent in 1988. Similar, but more modest, declines hold for exports of foods and live animals and intermediate manufactured materials, such as metals, building materials, and textile products.

Picking up the slack is the increased relative importance of chemicals, up from 10 percent to 12 percent of the export bundle, and machinery, up from 29 percent to 33 percent. In the latter category, the export share for business machinery and data processing equipment more than doubled to nearly 9 percent between 1970 and 1988. Electrical machinery, power generating machinery, and telecommunications equipment all recorded increases in relative share.

Commodity Imports

A twelvefold increase in the value of U.S. imports between 1970 and 1989 (from $40 billion to more than $470 billion) contained within it a substantial change in composition mix, in the aggregate as well as from the individual source countries of those imports.

The most dramatic compositional shift was that imposed by the oil price shocks in 1973–74 and again in 1979–80. These shocks greatly disrupted and distorted trade patterns during the period. While petroleum imports accounted for only 7 percent of imports in 1970 and a 10 percent share in 1989, they accounted for a 26 percent share in 1975, a 31 percent share in 1980, and a 14 percent share as recently as 1985.

Apart from these distortions, there were also trend changes occurring in the relative import composition of other major commodity groups. Not unlike the patterns noted above in U.S. exports to other industrial countries, the relative importance of U.S. imports of food and agricultural products dropped substantially during the period—from 14 percent of total imports in 1970 to 5 percent in 1988. Crude materials' share also declined, as did the share for intermediate manufactured goods (basically, industrial supplies)— down from a 21 percent share to a 14 percent share.

Offsetting those share declines were large share increases in finished-product manufactured goods of all sorts, including electrical and non-electrical machinery, transportation equipment, other finished manufactured goods such as professional and scientific equipment, and consumer goods. Machinery as a proportion of total imports increased from 13 percent in 1970 to nearly 27 percent in 1988. This increase was dominated by business equipment and computers, telecommunications equipment, and electrical machinery. Transportation equipment, especially automotive, also increased, from 15 percent to 18 percent. Miscellaneous manufactured-goods imports increased in share from 12 percent to 16 percent.

96. The North American Free Trade Agreement
Council of Economic Advisers

Excerpted from the *Economic Report of the President* (Washington, D.C.: U.S. Government Printing Office, 1993), pp. 310–15. The members of the council responsible for the report were Chairman Michael J. Boskin, David F. Bradford, and Paul Wonnacott.

The United States, Canada, and Mexico reached an agreement on NAFTA in August 1992. NAFTA will create a free-trade area with more than 360 million consumers and over $6 trillion in annual output, linking the United States to its first- and third-largest trading partners. NAFTA will stimulate growth, promote investment in North America, enhance the ability of North American producers to compete, and raise the standard of living of all three countries. NAFTA will also speed up technological progress and provide innovating companies with a larger market. Many economic studies show that NAFTA will lead to higher wages, lower prices, and higher economic growth rates.

NAFTA will also reinforce the market reforms already under way in Mexico. In recent years, Mexico has opened its markets and implemented sweeping economic reforms. In 1986 Mexico joined GATT and began unilaterally to lower its tariffs and other trade barriers. In mid-1985, for example, the production-weighted tariff in Mexico was 23.5 percent, but by 1988 it was only 11 percent. Mexico's reforms have raised its economic growth rate, making it an important export market for the United States. As economic opportunities in Mexico improve, Mexican workers have fewer incentives to migrate to the United States.

A stable and prosperous Mexico is important to the United States, from both an economic and a geopolitical standpoint. The United States shares a border roughly two thousand miles long with Mexico. In addition, the United States and Mexico are linked by centuries-old ties of family and culture. NAFTA will help the two countries forge a lasting relationship based on open trade and cooperation.

Existing duties on most goods will be either eliminated when the agreement enters into effect or phased out in five or ten years (for certain sensitive items, up to fifteen years). Approximately 60 percent of U.S. industrial and agricultural exports to Mexico will be eligible for duty-free treatment within five years. NAFTA will also eliminate quotas along with import licenses unless they are essential for such purposes as protecting human health.

Trade in Services and Investment

Under NAFTA the three countries extend both national treatment and most-favored-nation treatment in services to each other. Each NAFTA country must treat service providers from other NAFTA countries no less favorably than it treats its own service providers and no less favorably than it treats service providers from non-NAFTA countries. In addition, a NAFTA country may not require that a service provider of another NAFTA country establish or maintain a residence as a condition for providing service.

In financial services, Mexico's closed markets will be opened, allowing U.S. and Canadian banks and securities firms to establish wholly owned subsidiaries. In insurance, firms with existing joint ventures will be permitted to obtain 100 percent ownership by 1996, and new entrants can obtain a majority stake in Mexican firms by 1998. By the year 2000, most equity and market-share restrictions will be eliminated.

Intellectual Property Rights

NAFTA protects inventions by requiring each country to provide product and process patents for virtually all types of inventions, including pharmaceuticals and agricultural chemicals. Copyrights of computer programs and databases, as well as rental rights for computer programs and sound recordings, are also protected—sound recordings for at least fifty years. Service marks and trade secrets are also covered, along with integrated circuits both directly and as components of other products.

Agricultural Trade

Over a period of fifteen years, NAFTA will virtually eliminate barriers to trade in agricultural commodities between the United States and Mexico. About 50 percent of the agricultural trade between the two countries will be free of all trade barriers as· soon as the agreement takes effect. For remaining products, the phaseout will take between five and fifteen years. For most tariffs imposed by the United States, the phaseout will simply involve an annual reduction in the tariff rate.

Liberalization of agricultural trade between the United States and Canada continues as agreed to in the United States–Canada Free-Trade Agreement, under which existing tariffs on all agricultural commodities will be eliminated by 1998, while nontariff barriers for dairy products, poultry, eggs, and sugar will remain. In a separate agreement under NAFTA, Canada and Mexico agree to eliminate tariffs on bilateral agricultural trade between the two countries, exempting dairy products, poultry, eggs, and sugar. The three NAFTA countries also agree to move toward domestic agricultural policies that are more conducive to free international trade and to work toward eliminating export subsidies for agricultural products.

NAFTA is expected to lead to substantial increases in agricultural trade between the United States and Mexico.

Safeguards and Other Trade Rules

During the transition period, if increases in imports from a partner country cause or threaten to cause serious injury to a domestic industry, a NAFTA country may take safeguard action that either temporarily suspends the agreed duty elimination or reestablishes the pre-NAFTA duty. If a NAFTA country undertakes a global or multilateral safeguard action, each NAFTA partner must be excluded unless its exports account for a substantial share of the total imports and they contribute importantly to the serious injury.

The Environment and Labor

The three countries are committed to implementing the agreement in a manner consistent with environmental protection. The agreement requires that international environmental agreements regarding endangered species, ozone-depleting substances, and hazardous wastes take precedence over NAFTA provisions. NAFTA countries recognize that it is inappropriate to encourage investment by relaxing domestic health, safety, or environmental measures.

In the area of labor adjustment assistance, the administration announced in August 1992 a new comprehensive worker adjustment program, Advancing Skills through Education and Training Services. This program will nearly triple the resources now available for all worker adjustment by providing $2 billion annually, of which at least $355 million is specifically reserved for workers affected by NAFTA.

The U.S. and Mexican labor ministries have been implementing a 1991 memorandum of understanding that addressed issues ranging from worker rights to child labor. In September 1992 the United States and Mexico signed a new agreement establishing a consultative commission chaired by the U.S. and Mexican secretaries of labor that will provide a permanent forum for promoting the rights and interests of workers in both countries.

97. Multinational Corporations and the Trade-Investment Linkage
Council of Economic Advisers

Excerpted from the *Economic Report of the President* (Washington, D.C.: U.S. Government Printing Office, 1991), pp. 256–61. The members of the council responsible for the Report were Chairman Michael J. Boskin, John B. Taylor, and Richard Schmalensee.

The 1990s are likely to be marked by the increased globalization of companies, a trend that began in the early post-World War II years and continued throughout the 1980s. The greater global integration of the operations of multinational corporations is the result of increasing foreign direct investment—defined as the development of a new business or acquisition of an established business in a foreign market. It complements the globalization of markets engendered by the expansion of trade.

Indeed, the globalization of companies results in a close connection between trade and investment. This connection can be seen quite clearly in the remarkable extent to which border-spanning companies are involved in trade. About 25 percent of all U.S. exports and 15 percent of all U.S. imports, for example, are actually transfers between parents of multinational corporations and their affiliates abroad; that is, the goods are transferred within the same company, even though they cross international boundaries. The internationalization of operations underlying such "intrafirm" trade often means that a new product marketed globally is the fruit of research and development performed in one country, engineering carried out in a second, and production performed in a third.

The globalization of companies is a two-way street; many countries in which U.S. multinationals are most active are also the ones that are the most active investors in the United States. The global nature of companies has so progressed that sometimes it is difficult to decide which firms are foreign. Honda, for example, sells more cars in the United States than it does in Japan. In fact, some Hondas sold in Japan are actually made in Ohio. Whirlpool, while headquartered in Michigan, employs about 39,000 people, most of whom are non-American, in forty-five different countries.

Statistics on foreign direct investment reflect historical purchase prices, not current market values. Thus, comparisons of stocks of foreign direct investment can be quite misleading. For instance, the reported stock of foreign direct investment in the United States reached $400.8 billion at the end of 1989 and exceeded the reported stock of U.S. direct investment abroad by $27.4 billion. But much of U.S. direct investment abroad was made in the 1950s and 1960s, while the bulk of foreign direct investment in the United States was made more recently. Because prices have risen considerably since the 1960s, it is likely that the current value of U.S. holdings abroad exceeds the current value of foreign direct investment in the United States.

The Benefits of Foreign Direct Investment

Foreign direct investment in the United States is a sign of strength in the economy, not weakness. It is also a sign of the increasing internationalization of the economy, through which U.S. firms will be strengthened and made more competitive. This investment and the global orientation

Table 97.1

Parents of U.S. Multinational Corporations vs. U.S. Affiliates of Foreign Multinational Corporations: U.S. Operations in 1988 (dollars)

	Parents of U.S. multinationals	U.S. Affiliates of foreign multinationals
Average compensation per employee	35,154	30,517
Gross product per employee[a]	54,229	47,117
U.S. intrafirm exports per employee	4,491	6,637
U.S. intrafirm imports per employee	3,777	31,045

Sources: Department of Commerce and Council of Economic Advisers.
[a]Data are for 1987.

of companies benefit the United States. The unhindered flow of foreign direct investment leads to additional productive resources in the United States and facilitates the realization of cost-efficient scales of business by consolidating under one corporate roof separate, but related, operations. These boost the productivity and international competitiveness of the United States, create jobs, and promote innovation and productivity. The inflow of foreign capital helps to sustain U.S. investment, despite the current low U.S. national saving rate, and thus contributes to economic growth.

When U.S. multinationals first set up in Europe during the 1950s and 1960s, many Europeans feared that Europe was being bought out by Americans and that their economies were being Americanized. In retrospect, those concerns were unfounded. U.S. direct investment has benefited the European economies. The recent increase in foreign direct investment in the United States will similarly benefit the U.S. economy.

Foreign multinationals operating in the United States act in ways that are similar to U.S. multinationals in America. Table 97.1 shows that in terms of paying their employees and the value added per employee, these two types of multinationals are roughly the same.

In the area of intrafirm trade, however, there are pronounced differences. U.S. affiliates of foreign multinationals export and import more per employee than U.S. multinationals operating in America. While the difference in export behavior is appreciable—exports per employee are 48 percent higher for U.S. affiliates of foreign multinationals than for parents of U.S. multinationals—the more than eightfold difference in import behavior is particularly striking. The difference in import behavior is explained in part by the fact that a significant number of the U.S. affiliates of foreign multinationals act primarily as wholesale marketing offices for their parent companies. The higher import propensity is also a natural outcome of the newness of foreign multinationals in the United States.

When U.S. multinationals first set up in Europe during the 1950s and 1960s, they also tended to import more than local companies.

Judging from history, it seems likely that foreign multinationals operating in America will tend to become more "local" with time. The importance of imports in the input purchases of U.S. affiliates of foreign multinationals has been decreasing. Correspondingly, foreign multinationals are increasing the extent of vertical integration in their American operations, producing in the United States more of the inputs they use. Moreover, the local content of products made in the United States by foreign multinationals is quite high and has been rising.

Although foreign direct investment in the United States has increased greatly in recent years, the involvement of foreign firms in America is low by international standards. Indeed, foreign multinationals account for only about 4 percent of U.S. jobs and business output. Moreover, the recent rise in foreign direct investment is not unique to the United States but part of the worldwide trend toward the international integration of markets and companies. Another visible manifestation of this trend is the rise in joint ventures, technology and production-sharing arrangements, and other forms of international alliances. Such partnerships are found in many industries, such as medical equipment and computer chips.

98. The Changing Role of the International Monetary Fund
Council of Economic Advisers

Excerpted from the *Economic Report of the President* (Washington, D.C.: U.S. Government Printing Office, 1993), pp. 308–10. The members of the council responsible for the report were Chairman Michael J. Boskin, David F. Bradford, and Paul Wonnacott.

The International Monetary Fund (IMF) was envisaged by its creators at Bretton Woods as the institutional linchpin of the international monetary system. In recent decades, however, its role in lending to industrialized countries has diminished substantially, while its relationship with many developing countries has evolved considerably beyond temporary balance-of-payments financing. This evolution reflects important changes in the international financial system itself.

The IMF in the Bretton Woods Era and Afterwards

The IMF initially was intended to serve three functions in the Bretton Woods system: overseeing the system of pegged exchange rates, providing temporary financial assistance to countries with balance-of-payments problems (conditional on their adjusting domestic policies appropriately), and working to eliminate restrictions on transactions in foreign exchange that could limit the growth of international trade. It soon became apparent, however, that the IMF would not be as powerful as might initially have been intended. The resources provided by the United States under the Marshall Plan immediately after World War II largely dwarfed those available from the IMF, reducing the new institution's leverage over national policies. Subsequently, U.S. payments deficits continued to increase global liquidity and reduce dependence on the IMF for funding.

The move to floating exchange rates in the 1970s further reduced the need to draw on IMF resources, since governments no longer had to defend pegged exchange rates. The floating-rate system also transformed what initially had been envisaged as one of the IMF's key functions, the oversight of currency parities, although the IMF Articles of Agreement were amended in 1978 to authorize the institution to "exercise firm surveillance over the exchange-rate policies of members." Finally, the growing international integration of capital markets provided the industrialized countries with alternatives to the IMF. In particular, after the oil price increases of the 1970s, additional funds became available in the Eurodollar markets as the oil-exporting countries invested their surplus dollars. The last IMF loans to major industrial countries in support of adjustment programs were made to Italy and the United Kingdom in 1976.

Conversely, the oil shocks increased the financing needs of the oil-importing developing countries. While some of those countries were able to obtain commercial bank loans, that source of funding evaporated with the debt crisis of the early 1980s, when excessive accumulations of debt and rising global interest rates made it difficult for developing countries to repay their existing loans. In the 1970s and 1980s, the developing countries came to depend increasingly on the IMF for financing. The proportion of IMF credit outstanding extended to developing countries rose from an average of 58 percent in the 1950s to 65 percent in the 1970s and 100 percent in the 1980s.

Long-Term Financing, the IMF, and the World Bank

With the shift in focus from developed to developing countries have come other changes in the role of the IMF. First, the IMF has evolved from a type of credit union whose members took turns as temporary borrowers and lenders to a financial intermediary between developed and developing countries. A second and related development is that the current recipients of IMF loans typically suffer not from purely transitory payments imbalances but from longer-term payments difficulties associated with sustained structural imbalances and poor macroeconomic policies. As a result, some countries have undergone prolonged sequences of IMF programs, many of them never fully implemented. Increasingly, observers have recognized that solving the payments problems of some countries may require long-term programs of structural adjustment such as those supported by the IMF's Extended Fund Facility, which was created in 1974.

The Extended Fund Facility, and particularly the structural adjustment facilities developed for low-income countries in the 1980s, is similar in time frame and objectives to the structural adjustment loan program initiated by the World Bank in 1980. The World Bank, created along with the IMF at the 1944 Bretton Woods Conference, is an investment bank that traditionally has sustained much longer financing relationships with its members than has the IMF. The World Bank initially focused on financing specific projects such as roads, dams, power stations, agriculture, and education, but its activities subsequently evolved to include support for broader programs of structural reform such as the Structural Adjustment Loan program. As a result, the activities of the World Bank and the IMF increasingly have begun to parallel each other.

The ongoing efforts to assist the former Communist economies provide a good example of the convergence of roles between the IMF and the World Bank. While many of these economies certainly require financial assistance to meet their balance-of-payments deficits, their major problems are long term and linked to the need to develop strong market-oriented economies and credible macroeconomic policies. The IMF is an important conduit of technical assistance in the areas of macroeconomic analysis and exchange-rate policy, although its advice at times has been quite controversial. At the same time, the World Bank has been active in assisting these countries to privatize state-owned enterprises, restructure their financial sectors, and liberalize prices.

Despite the increasing similarity of their activities, the institutions clearly differ in the areas of focus: The IMF has a comparative advantage in macroeconomic policy analysis, and the World Bank is better qualified to provide assistance in the design of specific projects and sectoral reform programs. Because progress toward macroeconomic stabilization and microeconomic reforms are mutually dependent, close coordination between the IMF and the World Bank is essential. Discussions on the division of responsibility between the IMF and the World Bank led in

1989 to an agreement reaffirming the IMF's focus on macroeconomic and balance-of-payment issues and the World Bank's primary role in micro-economic and structural issues. It also strengthened the process of collaboration and coordination between the two institutions. However, the evolution of the roles of the IMF and the World Bank will continue to be important to the world economy in the coming years.

99. The Marshall Plan and Early Bilateral Aid

Stephen Browne

Excerpted and reprinted with permission of the publisher from *Foreign Aid in Practice* by Stephen Browne (New York: New York University Press, 1990), pp. 11–15. All rights reserved.

U.S. Secretary of State General George Marshall delivered his well-known speech at Harvard University in June 1947:

> The truth of the matter is that Europe's requirements for the next three to four years of foreign food and other essential products—principally from America—are so much greater than her present ability to pay that she must have substantial additional help or face economic, social and political deterioration of a very grave character. Our policy is not directed against any country or doctrine but against hunger, poverty, desperation and chaos. Its purpose should be the revival of a working economy in the world so as to permit the emergence of political and social conditions in which free institutions can exist.

The American offer was both magnanimous and far-sighted. Substantial funds would be lent on concessional terms to European countries to assist in the process of postwar reconstruction. The offer was extended to all of Europe, including Germany, and the program was to be prepared by the European countries themselves.

Marshall carefully placed the onus on the Soviet Union and the Eastern bloc countries to either accept assistance or decline to participate. With the world as it was, dividing on either side of Churchill's iron curtain, the Soviet bloc was unlikely to agree to participate, and duly declined. The Marshall Plan then inevitably became identified with American foreign policy in supporting the "free world" as a buffer against the spread of communism.

The Marshall Plan met with considerable success for two particular reasons. In the first place, Marshall aid was generous and concerted. Beginning in 1948 for a four-year period, the United States made available a total of over $12 billion, more than 90 percent of which was in grant form. During the period of disbursement, every person in Western Europe would have received an average annual amount of American aid of some $12, the equivalent of $50 at today's prices, comparing very favorably with the highest contemporary levels of per capita aid in developing countries. It was a classical example of Keynesian-style economic priming, and the turn-around in European fortunes was palpable. By 1950, the level of industrial production in the recipient countries was 25 percent higher than in 1938. The agricultural production level had grown by one-third since 1947, and, in the same three-year period, Europe's trade deficit had shrunk from $8.5 billion to $1 billion.

Second, the aid was timely and appropriate. Western Europe had the human resources and skills, but it was chronically short of capital. As Marshall had ordained, the Europeans formulated their own detailed plans for the assistance and created the Organization for European Economic Cooperation (OEEC) to coordinate disbursements and monitor the economic performance of the recipient countries. The success of the plan was also a lasting one. By 1952, the restored Western European economies were embarking on a period of unprecedented expansion that was to last over twenty years. Marshall aid contributed to the spirit and the reality of European unity by firmly planting the seeds of intergovernmental cooperation and witnessing a vigorous germination. The OEEC had already grown from a committee into an organization and subsequently was to gain additional non-European members. Also from the time of Marshall, there emerged the Franco-German agreements to coordinate coal and steel production; these were the wellspring of European cooperation, leading to the six-member European Economic Community and the European Atomic Energy Community, both created by treaty in 1947.

The Marshall Plan is, with good reasons, recorded as a landmark in the aid annals. It was not aid in the contemporary sense, but it was a forerunner of development assistance. It proved the efficacy of substantial transfers of capital for a sustained period from stronger to weaker economies to the mutual benefit of both. The domestic investment forgone by the American assistance was much more than compensated for by the demand for American exports generated by the revitalized European economies. There were lessons also in the carefully ordered process of absorption of aid into Europe. The aid had been determined by both donor and recipients as destined for certain broad purposes, for the disbursement of which the recipients bore the primary responsibility. Finally, the aid was provided in an atmosphere of mutual trust; it was known from the outset that the Americans would provide assistance in sufficient quantities to help stimulate economic recovery in Europe.

Marshall aid was an exemplary program in several important respects. All of the above conditions, of size and terms, mutual benefit, receptivity, and trust, have remained relevant to the success of subsequent aid programs. But the common failure to meet one, and usually more, of these conditions has compromised their effectiveness.

Marshall aid was unquestionably the inspiration, if not the model, for the first programs of American bilateral assistance to the developing countries. It seemed a relatively short step from the concept of European reconstruction to a more widely angled approach to the problems of the poorer countries. The often quoted Point Four of President Truman's inaugural speech of January 1949 might have been seen as an early declaration of American intentions:

> Fourth, we must embark on a bold new program for making the benefits of our scientific advance and technical progress available for the improvement and growth of under-developed areas. I believe we should make available to peace-loving peoples the benefits of our store of technical knowledge in order to help them realize their aspirations for a better life. And in cooperation with other nations, we should foster capital investment in areas needing development.

It was a worthy and altruistic statement, and it helped to fix in American minds—and the minds of some of the leaders of the developing countries—the notion of development assistance as a Western response to the needs of the world's poor. But the immediate practical significance of Point Four was more questionable. Whatever plans Truman might have had in mind at the time of his speech did not prove to be the basis of subsequent American policy.

In matters of aid policy, the major statesmen of this period were persuaded by their advisers to defer to more parochial instincts. In the United States, overseas assistance needed special justification in terms of American interests. The Mutual Security Act specified that assistance could be supplied only if it "strengthened the security of the United States," a general philosophy from which the United States has never departed. U.S. assistance could also be justified—as in the case of the Marshall Plan—to assist in economic rebuilding. Korean assistance was an important instance, and the distinctions between reconstruction and development (both types of assistance espoused by Bretton Woods when creating the International Bank for Reconstruction and Development) remained blurred. Reconstruction normally implied high returns on capital, which also helped to support the case for the diversion of public capital abroad, usually on commercial or quasi-commercial terms.

By 1955, official flows from the United States and the Soviet Union of what would most appropriately be termed economic assistance were heavily concentrated on the neighboring countries of the Soviet Union, but some geographical diversification was beginning. Military security considerations were still paramount but were becoming modulated by the concern of each superpower to extend its sphere of influence into the developing world as a growing number of previous colonies acceded to independence.

100. The Foreign Aid Programs and the United States Economy

Senate Special Committee to Study the Foreign Aid Program

Excerpted from *Foreign Aid Program: Compilation of Studies and Surveys* (Washington, D.C.: U.S. Government Printing Office, 1957), pp. 775–77.

During the period 1948–55, the United States provided approximately $43 billion of economic and military aid to numerous countries throughout the world. In recent years, approximately one-half of foreign aid has been for military assistance, one-third for defense support assistance, 7 percent for development assistance, 5 percent for technical cooperation, and the remaining 4–5 percent for various other uses, including the president's contingency fund.

The beneficial and adverse impacts of foreign aid programs on the United States economy should be viewed in the light of their effectiveness in helping to attain the objectives of the United States foreign economic policy. The objectives of the foreign aid programs have been the restoration and reconstruction of war ravaged areas, helping underdeveloped areas to help themselves, and strengthening the defenses of the free world.

The cost of the foreign aid programs seen in the perspective of the economy as a whole have been relatively small. Since 1948, the average share of our gross national product that has gone for foreign aid has been 1.7 percent. In 1956, this share has dropped to around 1.1 percent. During this latter year, the United States per capita cost of foreign aid programs, after deducting repayments from foreign countries, has been $23.07. Foreign aid, in 1956, accounted for about 6.4 percent of total United States government expenditures. The average for the period 1948–55 has been 9.4 percent of total United States government expenditures.

Foreign aid has taken about 1.5 percent of this country's total industrial, agricultural, and mining production during the last nine years. In the absence of foreign aid, production in those sectors of the economy would not necessarily have diminished by that amount. Tax reductions in the amount needed to support the foreign aid programs, or other government programs that might have been increased, especially in defense, could well have offset any drop in the demand for United States commodities resulting from abandonment of foreign aid. It is fair to say, however, that during a period of inflation, such as mid-1950 to mid-1951, the increase in foreign aid programs tended to aggravate, though very slightly, the inflationary situation. In contrast, during periods of recession, such as 1948 and 1954, the maintenance of foreign aid purchases tended to act as a stabilizing force. Once again, however, the importance of foreign aid as a factor of stability should not be exaggerated.

In the early years of the foreign aid program, agricultural commodities were quite important, in that more than 5 percent of total United States production of certain types of farm goods were shipped as foreign aid. Such commodities include bread grains, coarse grains, rice, cotton, and tobacco. In recent years of the foreign aid program, agricultural commodities tended to diminish in relative importance, and manufactured items came to the fore. Some of these manufactured items were also of importance during the earlier years of the program. The foreign aid items that account for a relatively important share of their industry's total production are tractors; conveying, mining, and construction equipment; machine tools; and engines and turbines. Since 1952, the foreign aid shipments of aircraft engines and parts have been of great importance, quite probably as a result of increasing military aid shipments.

Since on the average about 1.5 percent of United States production has been involved in foreign aid, it is difficult to claim that domestic employment, prices, or consumption as a whole could have been seriously affected, for better or worse, by foreign aid expenditures. The impact on employment varies from one region to another, depending on the commodity, and the effects differ during periods of inflation and recession. On the whole, however, the inflationary or stabilizing effects have been very slight.

Foreign aid programs have not been used generally to aid distressed industries. Indeed, in some instances foreign aid expenditures for certain commodities have decreased during periods of recession or of distress for those industries.

As to agricultural products, the inclusion of these items served the dual purpose of providing foreign aid and helping to support domestic industries.

In addition to the direct effects of foreign aid, there are also indirect effects, which enter into an analysis of the costs and benefits of these programs to the United States. Some industries that produce items for foreign aid utilize the products and services of other industries in order to make their finished goods. Moving the aid from this country to its destination utilizes the services and products of still other industries. It is estimated that approximately 600,000 workers have been employed each year in the United States directly and indirectly as a result of foreign aid expenditures.

Foreign aid, both in terms of goods and services, has helped to increase the flow of necessary commodities and raw materials to the United States. Some of these items are critical to our stockpile and defense needs. Others tend to raise standards of living and cut costs of consumer goods. At the same time, foreign aid has in some cases aided in the reconstruction or modernization of industries abroad that compete with similar industries in the United States. However, foreign aid has also brought about the development of industries and of stabilized economies abroad. Thereby, it has created an increasing demand for goods and services produced in the United States, which these countries were better able to purchase with their own foreign exchange earnings.

101. Overview of Foreign Assistance

House Task Force on Foreign Assistance

Excerpted from *Report of the Task Force on Foreign Assistance to the Committee on Foreign Affairs, U.S. House of Representatives* (Washington, D.C.: U.S. Government Printing Office, 1989), pp. 1–26.

The Current Program

For fiscal year 1989, total U.S. economic and military aid is about $15 billion. The major components are:

• Development assistance (DA), accounting for 15.9 percent of the total. The aim of DA is to promote long-term economic development through programs that help a host country use its resources more effectively. Currently, the Agency for International Development (AID) administers over two thousand projects in the fields of agriculture, rural development and nutrition, population, health, child survival, AIDS prevention and control, education and human resources development, and private sector environment and energy.

• Economic Support Fund (ESF), accounting for 23.9 percent of foreign assistance. It is allocated according to special economic, political, and security needs. It is programmed in three ways: as cash transfers to provide balance-of-payments and budget support to countries facing urgent foreign exchange requirements; as commodity import programs to fund imports from the United States; and as project assistance, supporting development projects. The ESF program is currently focused on the promotion of economic stability and political security in the Middle East and Central America.

• Food aid, accounting for 9.9 percent of foreign assistance. Under Public Law 480, surplus American agricultural goods are transferred to needy countries through low-interest loans and direct donations. The bulk of food aid is provided under Title I, as concessional sales in exchange for special self-help development activities. Under Title II, food is donated for humanitarian purposes, including child nutrition and emergency disaster relief. Since 1954, the Food for Peace program has delivered 303 million metric tons of food for more than 1.8 billion people in over one hundred countries.

• Military Aid, accounting for 35.8 percent of total assistance. It comprises grants and some concessional rate loans for equipment, and military training, provided to friendly nations.

• Multilateral assistance, accounting for 9.9 percent of all assistance. It includes contributions to multilateral development banks, such as the World Bank and the Inter-American Development bank, and contributions to economic and development programs of international organizations, such as specialized U.N. agencies working in health, food, agriculture, and the environment.

• Other aid flows include International Disaster Assistance, funding for the Peace Corps, the Trade and Development Program, Migration and Refugee Assistance, the Inter-American Foundation, the African Development Foundation, and the American Schools and Hospitals Abroad program.

The real dollar amounts for these programs during the most recent three years are shown in Table 101.1.

Table 101.1

U.S. Foreign Assistance, 1987–89, by Major Program
(in billions of constant 1989 dollars)

	Fiscal years			
	1987	1988	1989	1990[a]
Development assistance	2.4	2.5	2.4	2.3
Economic support fund	4.2	3.2	3.6	3.2
Food aid	1.6	1.5	1.5	1.4
Military aid	5.5	5.5	5.4	5.7
Multilateral assistance	1.6	1.5	1.5	1.8
Other economic aid	0.7	0.6	0.7	0.9
Total	16.0	14.8	15.1	15.3

[a]Requested by president in his 1990 budget.

Organization

The Agency for International Development is the principal U.S. bilateral economic aid agency. It is responsible for the implementation of most development assistance and Economic Support Fund programs. The geographical allocation of ESF is decided by the State Department in conjunction with AID. The geographic allocation of development assistance is proposed by AID, with State Department concurrence.

AID was established in 1961 as a relatively autonomous agency under the State Department. The AID administrator has the rank of deputy secretary of state. Currently ninety countries hold AID economic assistance programs of over $1 million. There are AID missions in forty-six countries, representational offices in twenty-three, and thirteen regional development offices abroad. In 1988 AID had 4,700 employees, down from 6,000 in 1980 and 17,500 in 1968 at the height of AID activity in Southeast Asia. About 52 percent of AID employees are stationed overseas, of which slightly less than half are foreign nationals. In carrying out its projects, AID also employs about 7,700 contractor personnel and details from other federal agencies.

The Department of Defense is responsible for most military assistance. Within DOD, the Defense Security Assistance Agency administers Foreign Military Sales and Credit programs and the Military Assistance Program. Other branches of DOD participate in planning and oversight of military aid, and in training and peacekeeping activities. The State Department approves military sales proposals to friendly countries and is in charge of assistance for antiterrorism and peacekeeping operations, which come under military aid.

Responsibility for food aid is shared by AID, the Department of Agriculture, the Department of State, and the Department of the Treasury. USDA has principal responsibility for determining quantities, selection, procurement, and shipping. AID is responsible for administering the program in the field, including negotiating food aid agreements and allocating grants. The Department of State plays a major role in country allocation. The Treasury Department oversees credit arrangements. Food aid is coordinated through an interagency committee, the Development Coordinating Committee subcommittee on food aid, which operates on a consensus basis.

Responsibility for multilateral assistance is shared. The Treasury Department shapes U.S. policy toward multilateral development banks (MDBs), including nominating and supervising the U.S. executive directors. The State Department leads in policy making and budget determination concerning the United Nations and other international organizations. AID coordinates country programs with the MDBs and provides advice to U.S. representatives on proposed MDB projects. In addition, AID is involved in the development and technical assistance activities of the U.N. specialized agencies. Other U.S. agencies are involved in the work of appropriate multilateral agencies. For example, USDA participates in the work of the Food and Agriculture Organization, and the Environmental Protection Agency in the activities of the U.N. Environmental Program.

Many of the programs counted under "other aid," such as the Inter-American Foundation, the Peace Corps, and the Trade and Development Program are autonomous or semiautonomous. International narcotics programs are the responsibility of the Department of State and the Drug Enforcement Agency. Refugee assistance programs are handled by the Department of State.

Table 101.2 shows the number of countries receiving U.S. assistance in 1987 and 1988.

There are sharp fluctuations in military aid, and, more recently, in ESF, compared to fairly steady levels of other programs. Military aid rose from just over $4 billion in FY 1977 to a high of $7.7 billion in FY 1984—a real increase of 85 percent. Amounts have fallen since to about $5.4 billion for FY 1989, leaving military aid with a real increase of 36 percent over the entire period from 1977.

ESF money is now only slightly higher than in FY 1977, but this follows a rapid increase of 78 percent between 1977 and 1985.

Funding for bilateral development assistance has remained fairly

Table 101.2

Number of Countries Receiving U.S. Assistance in Fiscal Years 1987 and 1988

| Fiscal year | Economic assistance | | | | | |
	DA and ESF	PL 480 (food aid)	Peace Corps and narcotics	Net total economic	Military assistance	Total all programs
1987	77	71	58	99	97	116
1988	77	69	57	97	100	117

Note: In columns including two types of assistance, each county only counts as one even if it receives both types of assistance.

steady over this period. But as in other programs, funding has been reduced since FY 1985.

Two programs—food assistance and contributions to multilateral institutions—have declined in real terms since 1977. Food aid has declined steadily each year, except for a brief period in the mid-1980s when the United States responded to the African famine with large quantities of emergency agricultural supplies. Funding for 1989 will be one-third below the 1977 level.

Trends in multilateral assistance are more difficult to assess because funds are allocated irregularly, depending on the schedule and outcome of international bank replenishment negotiations. In general, however, funds obligated for multilateral contribution have fallen from an earlier annual average of around $2.2 billion to about $1.5 billion during the past four years.

Program Shares

The share of the total foreign assistance budget going to development-related programs (development, food, and multilateral development bank support) has decreased from nearly 50 percent in the late 1970s to less than 40 percent today. Military assistance, which previously took 25 percent to 30 percent of the budget, increased to over 40 percent in the mid-1980s and has been running at 36 percent of the budget during the past three years. ESF obligations have ranged between 20 percent and 25 percent of the budget.

Military aid has been the largest aid category during much of the postwar period. Peaks appear in the early 1950s because of Greece, Taiwan, and Korea, and in the early 1970s because of Vietnam; the most recent peak occurred in 1985.

Grants versus Loans

In the 1970s, approximately one-half of the total U.S. assistance program was grants and the other half loans. Today, over 90 percent of the program is grants, largely in recognition of the growing world debt crisis. In particular, military aid has switched from being mostly loans in the 1970s to nearly all grants today.

Regional Composition

The Middle East has dominated U.S. regional allocations during the past thirteen years. U.S. assistance to the region ranged between $5 billion and $6.5 billion annually, excluding the Camp David–related support in 1979 and a special supplemental appropriation in 1985–86. In most years, the Middle East received over half of all U.S. bilateral aid.

Asia and Europe have received the next two largest shares of U.S. aid during this period. Aid to Asia was a little over $2 billion a year up to 1987. With the graduation of South Korea as an aid recipient, along with the general decline in budget levels, the region will receive only about $1.6 billion in fiscal year 1989.

Aid to Europe, where most U.S. assistance supports military base agreements, grew from about $1.2 billion in FY 1977 to a peak in the mid-1980s of $2.3 billion. Since then, it has declined to just over $1 billion, largely due to the graduation of Spain as an aid recipient.

Sub-Saharan Africa has received between $800 million and $1.4 billion in U.S. assistance annually since 1977. Famine relief in 1985 pushed the total up to nearly $2 billion for that year, but it fell to about $900 million in FY 1989.

The Role of the U.S. Aid Program Has Changed

The theory behind the program has evolved. The program began with an emphasis on large resource transfers during the Marshall Plan, shifted toward technical assistance during Point Four, to infrastructure during the 1960s, to basic human needs during the 1970s, and finally to the role of markets and policy reform during the 1980s. Clearly, there is no one path to development. U.S. assistance should focus on those types of assistance that the United States can provide most effectively and that meet the existing development needs of a country.

U.S. foreign assistance is highly concentrated on a few strategically important countries. The major strategic recipients—Israel, Egypt, Pakistan, Turkey, the Philippines, El Salvador, and Greece—received 72 percent of the $11 billion provided to countries for ESF, military, food, and development assistance. Israel and Egypt alone receive 50 percent of the total.

The focus of foreign assistance has changed. Over the past decade, the balance has shifted toward the Middle East, to military assistance, to grants rather than loans, and to bilateral rather than multilateral assistance. ESF is increasingly favored by the executive branch because of its greater flexibility and faster disbursement.

The Domestic Context of the Aid Program Has Changed

Budget constraints conflict with increasing demands on the aid program. Increasing demands on the foreign assistance program include the prospect of major new commitments in Afghanistan, Namibia, the Philippines, the Middle East, and to U.N. peacekeeping forces, as well as payment of arrears to the U.N. and MDBs. As the pie shrinks, members of Congress, interest groups, departments, and agencies will fight to protect their particular interests. In sum, the United States will have to do more with available resources.

The program does not enjoy broad public support. U.S. public support for helping poor people remains strong, but the public does not view the aid program as doing this effectively. The public has little concept of the aid program as an instrument of foreign policy, used to advance U.S. interests. There is evidence that the public would support development programs focused on key problems affecting the well-being of the United States.

102. U.S. Exchange Rate Policy: Bretton Woods to Present
B. Dianne Pauls

Excerpted from the *Federal Reserve Bulletin*, November 1990, pp. 891–908. B. Dianne Pauls is with the Federal Reserve Board's Division of International Finance.

Since 1973, the frequency and size of U.S. foreign exchange operations have varied. Intervention was substantial in 1977–79, when the dollar was deemed unacceptably low. U.S. operations were minimal during the first Reagan administration, in line with its policy of limiting government interference in markets generally; they were directed mainly at countering short-run market disruptions. Intervention was substantial again in the autumn of 1985, when the dollar was regarded as unacceptably high. By far the most extensive U.S. intervention operations, however, have taken place since the Louvre Accord of February 1987; since then U.S. operations have been guided largely by informal understandings with the other G7 countries about the limit of tolerance for exchange rate fluctuations. Throughout the floating-rate period, other countries' intervention policies have been mixed, with some countries adopting a consistently more active policy than the United States.

Although episodes of U.S. intervention have been relatively infrequent since 1973, the amounts involved sometimes have been sizeable. Accordingly, the United States at times has taken steps to increase foreign currency resources for intervention, particularly when the dollar was under sustained downward pressure.

During times when the dollar's exchange value raised particular concern—in 1977–79, 1984–85, and 1987—it became a significant factor in Federal Reserve decisions regarding monetary policy. Furthermore, consultation and cooperation on macroeconomic policies by the major industrial countries have increased over the floating-rate era amid a growing perception that the existing international monetary arrangements have not exerted as much equilibrating influence on payments imbalances, or provided as much independence for monetary policies, as had been hoped. Wide swings in exchange rates have occurred, contributing to large trade imbalances and resource reallocations, and pointing up the need for more compatible policies among the major countries.

During late 1989 and early 1990, the dollar's movements against the major currencies diverged. The opening of the Berlin Wall and subsequent steps toward unification of the two Germanys bolstered the mark, while political uncertainty and concern in exchange markets that monetary policy in Japan was too lax depressed the yen. Consistent with G7 understandings, U.S. authorities intervened in support of the yen in early 1990, buying more than $2 billion equivalent of yen. The Bank of Japan also bought yen against dollars. As the yen continued to weaken nonetheless, G7 officials—meeting in early April—issued a communiqué stating that they had discussed "developments in global financial markets, especially the decline of the yen against other currencies and its undesirable consequences for the global adjustment process and . . . reaffirmed their commitment to economic policy coordination, including cooperation in the exchange markets." In fact, there was little U.S. intervention in support of the yen after the communique was released. Concerns about Japanese monetary policy dissipated, and the yen recovered somewhat.

Between May and July of 1990, in order to adjust balances of foreign currencies and to facilitate the retirement of a portion of the amounts of foreign currencies held by the Federal Reserve under its warehousing arrangements with the ESF, the Treasury liquidated $2 billion equivalent of DM balances in ways that would not significantly influence prevailing exchange rates.

103. The Evolution of the Export-Import Bank
Export-Import Bank

Excerpted from U.S. Export-Import Bank, *Annual Reports*, 1984, 1987, and 1990.

The Export-Import Bank of the United States (Eximbank) is an independent corporate agency of the United States, which was first organized as a District of Columbia banking corporation in 1934. The primary legislation governing its operations consists of the Export-Import Bank Act of 1945, as amended through October 15, 1986, and the Government Corporation Control Act.

Eximbank's mission is to facilitate export financing of U.S. goods and services by neutralizing the effect of export credit subsidies from other governments and by absorbing credit risks that the private sector will not accept. Eximbank provides export financing through loans to foreign buyers, and through guarantees and insurance that provides repayment protection against political and commercial risks.

The commitment authority of Eximbank under the Export-Import Bank Act to lend, guarantee, and insure is limited to $40 billion outstanding at any one time. Loans are charged against the $40 billion limitation at 100 percent of their authorized amount. Guarantees and insurance are charged against the $40 billion limitation at not less than 25 percent of Eximbank's contractual liability, with the proviso that the aggregate amount of guarantees and insurance so charged may not exceed $25 billion outstanding at any one time. Thus, Eximbank's contractual commitments outstanding at any one time could reach $58.75 billion, consisting of $25 billion of guarantees and insurance outstanding, resulting in a $6.25 billion charge against the $40 billion limitation, and $33.75 billion (additional commitments) charged at 100 percent against the limitation.

The committed and uncommitted authority to lend, guarantee, and

Table 103.1

	$ in Millions	
	Commitments and contingent liabilities	Statutory authority charges
Outstanding loans	11,213.3	11,213.3
Undisbursed loans	2,378.5	2,378.5
Estimated recoveries on disbursed claims	1,591.0	1,591.0
Guarantees	6,948.6	1,737.1
Insurance	8,339.4	2,084.9
Committed balance		19,004.2
Uncommitted balance		20,995.0
Total	30,470.8	40,000.0

insure and the bank's commitments and contingent liabilities are shown in Table 103.1 as of September 30, 1987.

From the beginning, Eximbank viewed its role as one of supporting U.S. trade only where private banks were unable to provide financing. According to Eximbank's 1936 *Annual Report*, the bank's programs were designed to "supplement the facilities afforded by the rest of the financial community and by so doing to make available to U.S. exporters and importers the type of facilities supplied in other countries by the private capital market."

The president signed the Export-Import Bank Act of 1945 on the same day as the Bretton Woods Agreement Act, symbolizing the U.S. commitment to international trade. The Bank Act made four major changes in Eximbank's enabling legislation. It raised the limit on outstanding loans and guarantees from $700 million to $3.5 billion; removed the prohibition on loans to governments in default on obligations to the U.S. government; vested management of the bank in a board of directors consisting of the administrator of the Foreign Economic Administration, the secretary of state, and three full-time members appointed by the president with the advice and consent of the Senate; and made the bank an independent agency.

The Bretton Woods Act established the International Monetary Fund to maintain exchange rate stability among national currencies. The act also established the International Bank for Reconstruction and Development (the World Bank) to make long-term development loans. Because of a delay in the ratification of the Articles of Agreement for these new international organizations, Eximbank remained the principal source of development financing for several years.

In the aftermath of World War II, a "cold war" developed between the United States and the Soviet Union, and world peace was threatened in trouble spots spread through Europe, Asia, and the Middle East. The United States increased expenditures for national defense and for defense of its allies. Eximbank was given new authority to assist in this effort. As the World Bank became operational, Eximbank's role in development projects was reexamined. Through an extensive review of Eximbank financing, Congress determined that Eximbank was an effective and necessary institution. Its role in fostering the long-term commercial interests of the United States was reaffirmed, and its character was strengthened.

In the 1960s the scope of the bank's activities was modified through legislation addressing the increased foreign competition facing U.S. exporters and the U.S. involvement in the Vietnam War. At the same time, airlines around the world sought to modernize their fleets with new American jet aircraft. Because of the high cost and extended repayment terms needed to finance these purchases, commercial banks alone could not provide the necessary financing during the decade. Eximbank financed sales of U.S. commercial jets to airlines in forty countries. It also financed U.S. goods and services for a number of major projects and assisted a growing number of U.S. exporters through new medium-term commercial bank guarantees, discount loans, and insurance programs.

In March 1968, the bank's name was changed from the Export-Import Bank of Washington to the Export-Import Bank of the United States. Congress increased the limit on outstanding authorizations from $9 billion to $13.5 billion and increased the limit on guarantees and insurance issued against a fractional reserve from $2 billion to $3.5 billion.

Eximbank's authorizations continued to grow during the 1970s. In 1973 and 1974 détente thawed East-West relations. Eximbank extended financing for U.S. exports to the Soviet Union. As the energy crisis affected countries around the world, Eximbank assisted U.S. exports for major projects to develop new sources of hydrocarbons, such as the North Sea oil and gas fields, and for alternative power sources, such as nuclear energy. During the decade, Eximbank authorized $4.2 billion in direct credits and $2 billion in financial guarantees for nuclear power exports. Faced with the threat of an international trade war, Eximbank participated in successful international negotiations to establish ground rules for official export credits.

Eximbank's authorizations approved during the 1970s again more than doubled the total for all preceding years. Of the $75 billion authorized during the decade, 45 percent was in loans, 55 percent in guarantees and insurance.

U.S. exporters faced an increasingly competitive environment during the early 1980s. Newly industrialized countries such as Taiwan, Mexico, and Brazil captured a growing share of world trade. The industrialized countries increased their use of aggressive, officially supported export credits. In addition, U.S. exporters had to contend with inflation, a strong dollar, and record-high interest rates.

Eximbank supported many high-technology exports, including computers, CAT scanners, communications satellites, and space-shuttle launch services.

Many U.S. exporters turned to Eximbank for financial assistance to counter foreign governments' offers of export credit aid. Demand for Eximbank loans exceeded the bank's 1980 budget limitations. In fiscal 1981 a new record level of authorizations was set at $12.9 billion.

In the fiscal 1980–84 period, Eximbank authorized $52.8 billion in loans, guarantees and insurance, bringing total authorizations since inception to $158.8 billion. In its first fifty years of operations, the bank has been instrumental in supporting $167 billion in U.S. exports.

104. Immigration Policy: Political or Economic?

Vernon M. Briggs, Jr.

Excerpted and reprinted with permission of the publisher, M.E. Sharpe, Inc., from *Challenge*, September/October 1991, pp. 12–18. Vernon M. Briggs is professor of industrial and labor relations at Cornell University.

As the United States enters the last decade of the twentieth century, its labor market is in transformation. New forces that are restructuring the nation's employment patterns are altering the demand for labor. At the same time, the labor supply is in a period of rapid growth in size and unprecedented changes in composition. Assessing the evolving situation, Secretary of Labor Elizabeth Dole proclaimed in late 1989 that the nation's labor force was "woefully inadequate to meet the changes that lie ahead." Many other knowledgeable observers have expressed similar concerns. The nature of the work force is emerging as the number one economic issue confronting the nation. The implications extend not only to the competitiveness of the economy and the preparedness of the labor force but, given the multiracial and multicultural makeup of the population, to the prospects for maintaining domestic tranquility.

The forces altering the nature of labor demand in the United States are the same confronting all industrialized nations. They are associated with the pace of technological change, the expansion of international trade, and shifts in consumer spending preferences. Conceivably, the effects of reduced military spending may soon be added to the list. The consequences of these influences are reshaping the nation's occupational, industrial, and geographic employment patterns. Employment in most goods-producing industries and in many blue-collar occupations is declining, while it is increasing in most service industries and many white-collar occupations. Regional employment trends are extremely unbalanced, with growth generally more pronounced in urban than in rural areas and particularly strong in the Southwest and weak in the Midwest and Prairie regions.

The concurrent forces being exerted on the supply of labor, however, constitute a uniquely American experience. Over the twelve-year period ending in 1988, the U.S. labor force increased by about one-third more than the combined growth of the other nine major industrial nations of the free world. Moreover, much of the labor force growth in the other industrialized nations was in the form of increases in unemployment rather than in employment. In all cases, the growth in employment in these nations, compared with the United States, ranged from minimal to modest.

Historic Role of Immigration Policy

For present purposes, however, concern is about the one element that impinges on the size and diversity of the U.S. labor force and that is virtually unknown in other nations: the role of immigration. Since the mid-1960s, mass immigration has again surfaced as a distinguishing feature of life in the United States. Indeed, a recent study of contemporary American society stated that the single feature that continues to distinguish the United States from other industrialized nations is that "immigration continues to flow at a rate unknown elsewhere in the world."

With immigration currently accounting for 30–35 percent (depending on what estimate of illegal immigration is applied) of the annual growth of the U.S. labor force, it is essential to know how immigrants—regardless of their mode of entry—fit into the labor market transformation process. After all, our immigration policy is a purely discretionary act of the federal government. The flow of immigrants is one aspect of labor force size and character that public policy should be able to control and shape to serve the national interest.

When the industrialization process began in earnest during the later decades of the nineteenth century, the newly introduced technology of mechanization required mainly unskilled workers to fill manufacturing jobs in the nation's expanding urban labor markets. The same can be said of the other employment growth sectors of mining, construction, and transportation. Pools of citizen workers existed who could have been incorporated to meet those needs—most notably the recently freed blacks of the former slave economies of the rural South. But mass immigration from Asia and Europe became the chosen alternative. Before long, however, immigration from China and Japan was banned in response to negative social reactions, so various ethnic groups from eastern and southern Europe became the primary source of new workers during this era.

From purely an efficiency standpoint, the mass immigration of the late nineteenth century and the first two decades of the twentieth century was also consistent with the labor market needs of the nation. Jobs created during this expansive era typically required little in the way of skill, education, literacy, or fluency in English from the work force. The enormous supply of immigrants who came during this time generally lacked these human capital attributes but nonetheless reasonably matched the prevailing demand for labor. The technology of that period asked little in the way of human resource preparation. Available jobs required mainly blood, sweat, and tears, and most immigrants, as well as most native-born workers, amply provided all three.

Beginning with the outbreak of World War I, however, the nation experienced a sharp contraction in immigration. After the war, the United States imposed its first quantitative screening on the number of immigrants to be admitted. Moreover, the pervasive negative social reactions to many of the new ethnic groups also led to the adoption of overtly discriminatory qualitative restrictions. These restrictive actions were embodied in the Immigration Act of 1924 (often called the National Origins Act). Qualitative screening standards were enacted that favored immigrants from western and northern Europe, disfavored all other Europeans, banned virtually all Asians, and ignored most Africans. Immigration from the Western Hemisphere, however, was not included in the ceiling or the national origin quotas. It has only been since 1968 that Western Hemisphere immigration has been subject to prevailing immigration ceilings and their admission provisions.

In the 1920s, the expanding domestic economy was characterized by the widespread introduction of the assembly-line method of production. The adoption of capital-intensive mass production techniques no longer required an unlimited number of workers. Assembly-line technology, however, did require largely unskilled workers. To meet that need, employers turned to domestic labor surpluses. They found these pools of under utilized workers in the nation's massive rural economy. During the

1920s, the rural population declined for the first time. Among the new supply of workers to respond to these urban job opportunities were the native-born blacks of the rural South, who began their exodus to the large cities of the North, the South, and the West Coast.

The depression decade of the 1930s, with its general surplus of unemployed job seekers, was followed by the war years of the 1940s, when tight labor markets caused previously existing artificial barriers to the employment of women and minority groups to weaken, providing access to a wide array of jobs that were hitherto unavailable. These inclusive developments occurred when even the low entry quotas of prevailing immigration laws were not being met.

The pent-up demand for products and the forced saving of the World War II era led to economic prosperity in the 1950s. During this period of general affluence, the United States was finally forced to confront the legacy of racial inequality that had plagued it since its inception. The civil rights movement was launched in earnest and soon spread throughout the South and elsewhere, culminating in passage of the Civil Rights Act of 1964. This legislation sustained the principle that overt racism would no longer be tolerated. It was only logical that the next step would be to purge racist practices from the nation's relations with the external world.

Noneconomic Focus of New Policy

Enactment of the Immigration Act of 1965 ended the era of using immigration for racial and ethnic discrimination. It also ushered in the era of mass immigration that has continued to this day. Virtually dormant for more than forty years, this sleeping giant from America's past was aroused. Instead of seizing the opportunity to craft a new immigration policy to meet some positive definition of the public interest, however, Congress created a policy aimed primarily at fulfilling the private interests of the legal residents. It sharply increased immigration levels and adopted a politically popular new admission system based on the concept of family reunification; 80 percent of total visas available each year were reserved for various categories of adult relatives and extended family members of American citizens. In addition, immediate family members (spouses, minor children, and parents) of each adult visa holder were made exempt from all quotas and were usually admitted automatically. In other words, noneconomic considerations held sway as the guiding principles of designing the nation's revised immigration policy.

In response to mounting humanitarian pressures and difficulties in accommodating refugees under the legal immigration system, Congress passed the Refugee Act of 1980. This bill separated refugee admissions from the legal immigration system and, in the process, created a new entry route with no annual ceiling. The number of refugees admitted each year varies depending on the amount of political pressure exerted by special interest groups on the president, who has the authority to set the number of refugees to be admitted each year after a largely pro forma consultation with Congress. Subsequent annual figures have ranged from a low of 67,000 refugees in 1986 to a high of 217,000 refugees in 1981. The admission figure for 1991 was 131,000. Obviously, no labor market test is applied to refugee admissions. The preponderance of refugees since 1980 have been from third world nations in Asia, the Caribbean areas, and Central America. Most have been deficient in their levels of skill, education, and English language proficiency. Many have clustered together in a handful of urban enclaves.

The complex admission systems for both legal immigrants and refugees have proved easy to circumvent, however. Illegal immigration has flourished, and because of its nature, the exact number of illegal immigrants can never be known. Official estimates in the 1980s were about 200,000 a year, but that figure is suspected of being far too low. Apprehensions—admittedly a poor indicator—have soared from 110,000 in 1965 to a high of 1.7 million in 1986. The figure for 1990 was 1,087,786. Despite four generous amnesty programs in 1986, in which a combined total of more than 3.2 million illegal immigrants were allowed to legalize their status, it is believed that there are still close to 4 million illegal immigrants in the United States; and their ranks mount by the day. Of course, illegal immigrants enter without regard to their preparation for available jobs or to the effect they might have on citizen workers with comparable skills or education. Likewise, no labor qualifications were imposed on the amnesty recipients whose entry into the labor force has now been legitimized. As with refugees, most illegal immigrants and amnesty recipients have been from less economically developed nations and suffer deficiencies in their skills training, education, and ability to speak English. They, too, have tended to cluster in enclaves—mainly in urban areas but also in some rural communities where labor-intensive agricultural methods prevail.

Finally, the immigration system permits certain foreign workers to be employed in the United States under specified labor market circumstances. These workers are known as nonimmigrant workers; their numbers have been growing steadily and are now in excess of 300,000 a year. There are no annual ceilings on the total number of nonimmigrant workers who can be admitted. They are employed in a variety of occupations, ranging from agricultural workers to nurses, engineers, professors, and scientists. Most nonimmigrant workers can be admitted only if qualified citizen workers cannot be found. But typically, merely perfunctory checks are made to test for citizen availability. Supposedly the nonimmigrant workers are admitted only for temporary periods, but their visas can be extended in some cases for up to five years. The increasing dependence of U.S. employers on nonimmigrant workers is a symptom of something seriously wrong with the current system. It implies that the legal immigration system lacks the direction and the flexibility to respond to legitimate shortages of qualified workers to fill real job vacancies.

Policy Contrary to National Welfare

In altering admission standards and enlarging the scale of immigration flows after 1965, no one foresaw that the U.S. economy was entering a new phase of fundamental change. Even after the new employment trends became evident, the congressional committees responsible for designing immigration policy essentially ignored them. Therefore, it can be said unequivocally that, for the first time in the nation's history, immigration policy not only is inconsistent with labor force needs but also may be counterproductive to the country's welfare.

By definition, immigration policy can influence the quantitative size of the labor force as well as the qualitative characteristics of those it admits. Currently, there is little synchronization of immigrant flows with demonstrated needs of the labor market. With widespread uncertainty as to the number of illegal immigrants, refugees, and nonimmigrant workers who will enter in any given year, it is impossible to know in advance how many foreign-born people will annually join the U.S. labor force. Moreover, whatever skills, education, linguistic abilities, talents, or locational settlement preferences most immigrants and refugees possess are largely incidental to why they are admitted or enter.

The labor market effects of the politically driven immigration system are twofold. Some immigrant and nonimmigrant workers have human resource endowments that are quite congruent with labor market conditions currently dictated by the economy's needs, and some are desperately needed because of the appalling lack of attention paid by policy makers to the adequate preparation of citizens for that labor market. But many do not. The majority must seek employment in declining sectors of goods-producing industries (such as agriculture and light manufacturing) or low-wage sectors of the expanding service sector (like restaurants, lodgings, and retail enterprises). Such immigrants—especially those who have entered illegally—are a major reason for the revival of "sweat shop" enterprises and the upsurge in the child labor violations reported in the nation's urban centers. The revival of such third world working conditions in many cities is nothing for America to be proud of, regardless of whether these immigrants actually displace citizen workers in exploitive work situations.

Unfortunately, many citizen workers who are among the urban working poor or underclass are to be found in many of the same declining occupations and industries. A disproportionately high number of these citizen are minorities—especially young people and women. As these citizen groups grow in both absolute and percentage terms, the logic of fair play would say that they should have the first claim on available jobs and opportunities for employment preparation. The last thing these citizen groups need is more competition from immigrants for the declining number of low-skill jobs that provide a livable income or for the limited opportunities for training and education that are available to low-income workers.

A Legislated Retreat from Reality

On the last day of its legislative session, the 101st Congress passed the Immigration Act of 1990. President Bush signed it into law on November 29, 1990. Although its terms indicate more awareness of potential labor market effects than does extant immigration law, its primary focus is on increasing the quantity of immigrants. When the new law takes effect on October 1, 1991, legal immigration will increase by more than 35 percent over present levels, to 700,000 people a year. Like the law it replaces, the new law gives short shrift to the specific human capital endowments of those to be admitted or to the general labor market conditions of the U.S. economy that may prevail at any given time. Thus, the new legislation largely perpetuates the notion that immigration policy—despite its magnitude—has little responsibility for its economic consequences.

In the context of a continuation of significant labor force growth, and with persistent unemployment rates already in the high 6 percent range, it is inconceivable that the United States will have a shortage of potential workers in the 1990s. What the nation faces is a shortage of qualified labor. In this case, the appropriate remedy is to address the evolving problem of a mismatch between the skills of the citizen work force and the emerging skill and education requirements of the workplace. In other words, the real need is for an expanded national human resource development policy for citizen workers, not for a continuing increase in immigrants who are admitted mainly without regard to their human capital attributes.

CHAPTER   X

The Long Stagnation

105. Why Has the United States Operated Below Potential Since World War II?
John F. Walker and Harold G. Vatter

Excerpted and reprinted with permission of the copyright holder, M.E. Sharpe, Inc., from the *Journal of Post Keynesian Economics*, Spring 1989, pp. 327–45. John F. Walker is professor of economics and Harold G. Vatter is professor emeritus of economics at Portland State University.

> The truth, the central stupendous truth about developed economies today is that they can have—in anything but the shortest run—the kind and scale of resources they decide to have.... It is no longer resources that limit decisions. It is the decision that makes the resources. This is the fundamental, revolutionary change—perhaps the most revolutionary mankind has ever known.
>
> U Thant, 1962

If a trend line of real GNP were drawn through the higher years surrounding the peaks of cycles in the laissez-faire era from 1869 to 1929, the values for those years might be interpreted to show the economy's potential long-run performance. Such a graph would reveal that most of the time the system operated below its potential thus defined. That cyclical shortfall was traditionally viewed as the inevitable and uncontrollable price of progress.

From the Keynesian revolution we learned that we do not have to pay that price. Yet under the post-1929 mixed economy the price is still exacted, because we have permitted and even encouraged it.

In the present era of government intervention, the market has continued to exhibit its inherent cyclical impulses. So the problem of the cyclical shortfall abides. However, the existence of a large and stable public sector, together with new built-in stabilizers, has substantially reduced cyclical amplitudes since World War II. Therefore, from a policy standpoint what is more important today is the achievement of a robust trend potential. This we have not enjoyed for most of the time, and its lack is the focus of our analysis.

Keynes in the *General Theory* unfortunately addressed only the cyclical shortfall. In that static formal model we find no explicit theory of economic growth. On the policy level Keynes was a pump primer with implicit, classical faith in the efficacy of both the cyclical expansion and the growth role of private investment.

Alvin Hansen, however, projected a theory that emphasized the euthanasia of the role of private investment as an engine of economic growth. For him the trend rate of potential GNP itself was therefore threatened by a factor that was inherent in an advanced market economy. By showing that in a capital-rich economy, business fixed investment was reduced to a demand-dependent variable that was also killing itself in part by its own productivity enhancement, Hansen's long-run model completed the dismantling of Say's Law ("production creates its own demand"). Demand for physical capital creates its own total supply and sectoral composition, short run and long run, in that model. Both the output growth trend and the cyclical shortfall below it after Hansen could be seen as dependent on (expected) spending.

Subperiods of the Postwar Era

We speak of performance chronically below potential. Only a few oddballs question the empirical correctness of this for the 1973–86 period. But 1948–73 is more complicated to interpret. Angus Maddison refers to it as "the postwar golden age." It may have been for Japan and certain European countries. We do not think it was for the United States.

Before the "golden sixties" the performance of the economy was mediocre. Between 1949 and 1961 the annual net national product (NNP) rise was a modest 3.45 percent. The average capacity utilization rate in manufacturing was a little over a lowly 82 percent, and the average civilian unemployment rate was about 5 percent. The average of the gross/net fixed capital stock grew at only 3 percent a year, reflecting a lackadaisical fixed investment response.

There is more to it than the whole period 1949–61 reveals, however; closer scrutiny shows that 1949–54 was quite robust, whereas 1954–62 was quite stagnant. In the former period, NNP rose at the unusually high rate of about 5 percent a year, whereas in the latter span it increased at only 2.7 percent annually. The chief reason for the high NNP rate during 1949–53 was, of course, the federal Korean War expenditures and post-war rebuilding. For the whole period 1949–54, real total government spending increased at an annual rate of almost 11 percent. Of course, with unemployment in 1952 and 1953 below 3 percent, real NNP could not respond to increased spending because supply constrained the economy for the only time in the thirty-seven years reviewed, 1949–86.

During what Paul Samuelson has called the Eisenhower stagnation, 1954–62, total real government expenditures growth dropped to 2.17 percent a year, and the average gross/net fixed capital stock rose annually by only 2.8 percent. Neither the investment nor the stock record suggests any continuation of "postwar rebuilding." The average civilian unemployment rate was 5.4 percent and trending upward through 1961. Performance was therefore substantially below any reasonable definition of potential. Those eight years showed how poorly the contemporary economy operates under restricted government spending growth.

What creates the appearance of golden years for the entire period 1949–73 is the Korean War impact and the truly golden sixties, 1962–69. After 1968, expansion of the economy's autonomous leading sector—government—collapsed. As a result, chronic stagnation began to reappear. For example, the rate of NNP expansion from 1969 to 1973 was only 3 percent yearly.

The Strategic Role of Demand

A long list of first-class macroeconomic theorists have argued for over 150 years that demand, as shaped by autonomous government, and not supply constraint, is the principal determinant of economic growth in market economies. Malthus argued that the government should maintain the Corn Laws to shift the resulting surplus to the landlords who would spend it and lead the economy to investment in industries producing the goods demanded. The supply-sider Ricardo argued that the repeal of the Corn Laws would transfer funds to the capitalists, who would then spend them on investment goods. Both believed that government would choose the policies that led to the investment outlays that produced growth.

In a similar debate today many economists are arguing that the government has arrogated to itself the Malthusian landlords' role, through its large budget. They argue that to increase economic growth we must rearrange our institutions to take resources away from the government and give them to the capitalists who will then invest and make the economy grow. We have called them "investment engineers."

The investment engineers ignore the major work done on the declining role of investment in the economy by Keynes, Hansen, Harrod, Domar, Eisner, Denison, Solow, and many others. The investment dilemma is perhaps most clearly stated by Domar. He fully analyzed the model we call Harrod-Domar, which was anticipated by Keynes and appears in his Galton lecture delivered to the Eugenics Society in 1937. In that model all net investment raises the capacity to supply but only increases in net investment raise the capacity to demand.

Real net fixed nonresidential investment has been positive every year from 1948 through 1986. But only once has the rate of change of net fixed investment been positive for as many as five consecutive years. In fourteen of those years the level of net investment was below the previous year. In many years gross investment increases were small and consequent demand increases were small, even though total capacity increases were large. The reverse case, where the change in demand from the change in investment times the multiplier exceeded the change in supply potential brought about by the new level of investment, did not in all likelihood occur.

If the marginal propensity to save and the incremental output/capital ratio shifted in remarkably fortuitous ways, it would be possible for investment-stimulated demand to grow at the various annual rates necessary to equal the annual increase in supply capacity. But, of course, they did not.

With a higher output/capital ratio, any increment to the stock of capital increases the capacity to supply by a greater amount than the older investments did when it was lower. Increased rates of growth of potential supply from shifts to higher output/capital ratios can be balanced by increased investment additions or higher multipliers. We have not in fact had higher rates of investment increase, yet the investment engineers keep calling for higher savings rates, which imply a higher marginal propensity to save, which in turn implies a lower multiplier. The investment engineers cannot have it both ways.

Hansen used capital-saving innovation (a rising output/capital ratio) as one of his explanations for the laissez-faire secular stagnation he saw in the 1930s and fought against after the war. We are again in a period of stagnation. His student, Evsey Domar, clearly and completely eliminated with superb logic the simple-minded Ricardianism of the investment engineers. Small amounts of investment produce large amounts of productive capacity, and the change in investment may not exist at all. In such a case there is no new demand for the enlarged capacity. Or the addition may be small and thus produce a new demand capacity smaller than the new supply capacity. Hence depressing excess capacity is produced. The more excess capacity we produce, the less likely we are to get the large percentage increases in investment that we need to produce the demand to buy the output of the past investments and any new ones we undertake.

In 1947 Domar observed, "Indeed, it is difficult enough to keep investment at some reasonably high level year after year, but the requirement that it always be rising is not likely to be met for any considerable time."

Domar's student Robert Eisner, studying the question of what determines investment, found that it was demand. "Once increases in demand and the consequent pressure of demand on capacity are recognized as a major and decisive determinant of business investment, the way is clear to achieving a rate of investment and a general level of prosperity in the latter half of this decade (the 1960s) far exceeding anything we have known and most of what we have imagined in the past." Few forecasts have been more accurate.

Unfortunately, since the end of the 1960s the government and its economic advisers have been obsessed with the notion of making the economy grow rapidly by cutting business taxes to free resources for investment and cutting government spending to further free resources, which they assume investors will then take up. We have surveyed every *Economic Report of the President* from 1970 to 1987. Almost all of them call for federal action to expand the economy through tax cuts with almost no increase in government spending. Since passage of the Humphrey-Hawkins Act the president has been required to forecast the increase in government spending as a percentage of the economy each year. These forecasts almost always predict an increase in government spending that is less than the increase in the GNP. Such forecasts assert the opposite of Wagner's Law, which up to the present is one of the strongest relationships in all modern economies.

From 1979 to date, in compliance with a directive of the Humphrey-Hawkins Act, the *Annual Report of the Council of Economic Advisers* has included estimates of the growth of real GNP and several of its components for the year following the issuance of the report. It is issued in January of the year and forecasts the growth from the fourth quarter of the preceding year to the fourth quarter of the year of the report.

For the reports from 1979 to date the data have been presented in virtually identical form, so we can see the shape of the expectations of the president and his economic advisers. Part of these data are summarized in Table 105.1.

The average prediction in this period is for a slow growth in government spending, a rapid growth in investment, and a well-below historical average growth in GNP. This could be called expected stagnation. The expected stagnation was chronically overachieved. We grew even more slowly than the grim predictions. The advisers obviously expected fixed nonresidential investment to be a leading sector. It wasn't. Such growth

Table 105.1

Predicted and Actual Annual Percentage Changes in Real GNP, Federal Purchases, and Nonresidential Fixed Investment from the Council of Economic Advisers

Year	GNP		Federal purchases		Fixed nonresidential investment	
	Predicted	Actual	Predicted	Actual	Predicted	Actual
1979[a]	2.25	0.8	1.0	1.1	4.25	1.7
1980[a]	-1.0	-0.3	3.25	4.7	-0.25	-6.0
1981[a]	1.75	0.7	3.25	6.6	1.25	1.4
1982[a]	3.0	-1.2	-1.5	6.6	7.0	-8.4
1983	3.1	6.1	1.2	-6.0	-0.3	11.5
1984	4.5	5.6	3.7	14.2	9.5	16.6
1985	4.0	2.5	2.2	11.8	6.8	6.0
1986	4.0	2.2	-4.0	1.8	5.0	-5.4
Average	2.7	2.0	1.1	5.1	4.2	2.2

Source: Economic Report of the President, 1979–86.
[a]Average of range.

as we got was led by the unexpected growth in federal government purchases. On average in this period both the Carter and Reagan administrations were big spenders!

Since there was historically high unemployment of labor and low utilization of capital in this period, crowding out of investment by government could not occur. Hence, if the large increases in federal purchases had not occurred, the GNP growth would have been even less by the amount of the lost federal purchases plus the lost investment induced by the lost federal purchases and the lost consumption of the employees whose incomes those federal purchases represented. The council predicted government spending growth of 1.1 percent a year; the government achieved 5.1 percent. Without the big increase in government purchases, shown in Table 105.1, actual stagnation would have been even worse than it was.

In Table 105.2 we show the average annual growth rate of the GNP and of government purchases, together with net fixed nonresidential investment for 1948–85, and for five subperiods. The subperiods are chosen by the behavior of government spending.

Table 105.2 contains much of the empirical evidence pertinent to the analysis in this article. The periodization is of course based on the analysis. Thus, the periods are delineated by the rate of change of government purchases of goods and services and the relatively high or low level of G in every year of the period. The chosen periods are all periods in which the average annual growth of government purchases is either greater than 3.5 percent or less than 3.5 percent, and the period is at least three years long (except 1984–86).

We find that when the rate of government purchases is vigorously expanding, GNP growth is relatively robust. When the government purchases rate is sluggish, so is the GNP rate. This connection fits well our central thesis.

We find that rates of taxation (relative to GNP) move very slowly. This is not consistent with the startling differences in the growth of GNP. When the relative growth of the rates is negative, GNP grows more slowly.

The tax and spending relatives suggest that when the government taxes and spends, the society gets richer. When tax rates and spending slows, society gains less.

We are aware that many will at once accuse us of neglecting the role of business investment. Table 105.2 reveals conclusively why we do indeed denigrate its widely alleged impact. Investment in fixed nonresidential structures for the whole postwar era grew notably less rapidly than either government purchases or GNP. But in the first long-run subperiod of rapidly expanding G and GNP, 1948–68, it similarly exhibited a relatively

Table 105.2.

Annual Percentage Changes in Government Purchases, GNP, Gross Investment, Civilian Labor Force, Capital Stock and Output-Input Ratios, 1948–85 and Selected Subperiods

Period	Government purchase of goods and service G	Total government receipts (NIPA)/GNP Tx/GNP	Gross national product GNP	Gross private investment structure Ist	Gross private investment equipment Ipde	Average gross and net capital stock	
						Structures Kst	Equipment Kpde
1948–85	3.48	−0.14	3.25	2.92	3.96	2.67	4.56
Shorter subperiods							
1948–53	14.42	0.12	5.20	4.61	0.66	1.67	6.21
1953–60	0.49	0.13	2.42	2.91	1.32	2.57	3.55
1960–68	4.63	0.26	4.39	4.72	7.66	3.18	4.48
1968–83	0.72	−0.81	2.30	1.56	3.47	2.76	4.58
1983–86	4.31	n.a.	3.63	−0.37	8.55		
Longer subperiods							
1948–68	5.50	0.18	3.90	4.06	3.64	2.59	4.58
1983–85	1.15	−0.50	2.50	1.61	4.33	2.77	4.52
Weighted average of high G periods 1948–53 and 1960–68	8.40	0.21	4.70	4.68	4.97	2.60	5.15
Weighted average of low G periods 1953–60 and 1968–83	0.65	−0.51	2.34	1.99	2.79	2.70	4.25

Period	Civilian Labor Force CLF	Government Civilian Employees LFg	Output of Business Sector Q	Measures of Productivity of Private Inputs			Equipment Labor Ratio K/(CLF-LFg)
				Structures Q/K_{st}	Equipment Q/K_{pde}	Labor Q/(CLF-LFg)	
1948–85	1.77	2.90	3.23	0.54	-1.27	1.57	2.44
Shorter subperiods							
1948–53	0.81	3.28	4.46	2.75	-1.64	3.91	2.27
1953–60	1.44	3.11	2.56	0.00	-1.13	1.31	2.25
1960–68	1.60	4.50	4.45	1.23	-0.02	3.26	3.29
1968–83	2.35	2.01	2.36	-0.38	-2.12	-0.05	2.14
1983–86							
Longer subperiods							
1948–68	1.34	3.71	3.79	1.17	-0.76	2.74	2.67
1968–85	2.27	1.96	2.57	-0.19	-1.86	0.24	2.16
Weighted Average of High G Periods 1948–53 and 1960–68	1.30	4.03	4.45	1.81	-0.64	3.51	2.90
Weighted Average of Low G Periods 1953–60 and 1968–83	2.06	2.36	2.42	-0.26	-1.81	0.38	2.18

Sources: *Economic Report of the President,* 1987; *Statistical Abstract of the United States;* August 1987 *Survey of Current Business;* "Fixed Reproducible Tangible Wealth in the United States: Rev. Est.", and article with same title in *Survey of Current Business,* January, 1986.

Note: All calculations from three-year annual averages of the beginning and ending dates except capital.

high rate of growth. It is not hypothesized here that the good performance for structures is overwhelmingly a demand-induced phenomenon, for there was no doubt much postwar rebuilding; the value of the
stock of structures, for example, did not reach its 1930 secular high until
1955–56. The secularly desired output-structures ratio was apparently
reached around the mid-sixties, and the sluggish GNP rate after the sixties set the pace for the structures investment pace.

Gross investment in producers durable equipment (PDE) outpaced
both the GNP and structures investment rates for the whole postwar
period and in both of our long subperiods. The same is true of stock
growth record. The PDE investment and stock series advanced like a
juggernaut, quite independently of what was happening to GNP. Indeed,
neither the high flow nor the stock rates exhibit any response to the GNP
growth slowdown during 1968–85. Nor, compared to that sluggish GNP
period, do they show greater performance during the faster-growth
years, 1948–68.

From this we draw the significant conclusion that GNP growth in the
postwar era was not in any significant sense determined by the robust
performance of PDE investment spending. It is likely that the PDE performance was determined overwhelmingly by supply-side factors such as
major innovations and demand-side factors such as public policy stimuli.

When the PDE record is related to total private production, a remarkable fall in the partial productivity ratio emerges. The fall is particularly
dramatic in the excessively stagnant years of economic growth, 1968–
83. We do not attempt here to explain this economically "irrational" behavior. We do emphasize again that it shows the incapacity of a high rate
of PDE investment to control output behavior. Indeed, the relationship
must be considered quite perverse by an investment engineer.

The table shows that, with the possible exception of the Korean War
period, 1948–53, the growth rates of G and PDE investment rise and fall
together. Hence, there was no "crowding out." Rather, it is demanded in
Eisner's term is "crowd in." Even in 1948–53, crowding out seems unlikely, since that period had the second-highest rate of investment in
structures of the whole thirty-seven years studied.

Some of the more significant supply-side aspects of our demand-side
emphasis are also revealed in Table 105.2. For example, in the slower-
growing long period, 1968–85, the resources available to produce output,
i.e., K_{st}, K_{pde}, and CLF, grow either at the same or at a faster rate than
they do in the period of more rapid advance, 1948–68. Hence we see that
the expansion of output was not constrained by available inputs during
1968–85. Augmented supply factors did not produce augmented output
growth. Supply did not create enough demand.

Measures such as Q/K_{st}, Q/K_{pde}, and $Q/(CLF-LFg)$ in Table 105.2 are often used as expressions for the partial productivity functions of the various inputs. Unfortunately, Q is properly so connected with inputs only when the economy (or sector) is operating at or near full employment. A decline in capital and labor partial productivities of the sort seen in the sluggish 1968–83 period in the table makes no microeconomic statement. The failure of Q to grow sufficiently is not caused by inadequate or ill-designed capital, or by an excessively teenage and female work force. It is caused by a failure in the management of aggregate demand. When Q/K_{st}, Q/K_{pde}, and $Q/(CLF-LFg)$ all decline together, the government has failed.

We recognize that the available resources plus technology set limits to output rise. But we cannot discover the effect of technological advance, together with output/capital or output/labor potential, unless we enable society to purchase the potential output represented by the growth of those supply factors.

The last two rows of Table 105.2 touch further on the matter of potential. They average the good growth years together and the poor growth years together. They show that GNP growth in the years of relatively high government spending rates is double that for the years of low government spending growth. These measures may be thought of as crude approximations of potential output with active government and without active government. GNP, investment, and capital will grow in either case, but in the postwar period the chief cause of the robust advance of the nation's wealth appears to have been government spending.

Summary

All prevailing growth theories pertaining to advanced market economies are predominantly supply-side theories. While there are, of course, crucial contributions by factor inputs in the development process, the prevailing models neglect one blade of the scissors. Our theory calls for correction of this glaring defect by the incorporation of long-run demand into all models of potential growth.

The supply-side explanations of both actual and potential growth presume the empirical validity of Say's Law for the long run. Such presumption would possibly be proper for the United States in the nineteenth century. Today it is incorrect because economic evolution itself has negated and reversed the law. Now, within a wide relevant range of economic performance, demand is the initiator and creates its own supply.

In the second place, the supply-side theories give an excessive and obsolete weight to the growth impact of fixed capital investment, ignoring the impressive work of Denison and others. These theories also continue to rely heavily on investment demand stimulus to buttress their dependence on Say's Law for the long run. Their reiteration of Say's mechanical connection between capital supply and the demand for its output capacity is the only sense in which these theories concede that demand has something to do with fueling the growth engine.

The mistaken emphasis on physical capital accumulation reveals a third defect in the ruling growth models to which we have called attention: They are essentially laissez-faire constructs. Acknowledgment of the long-established presence of big government is considered ancillary to long-run growth analysis. Government is allowed to intrude mainly and merely into such matters as subsidization of sectors, regulation, research, and education of the labor force. Big government as the decisive, dynamic, autonomous source of demand growth, historically coming to replace private fixed investment, is, like the demand side in general, omitted from the usual model.

A fourth defect resides in the neglect of the fact that public spending growth, unlike private investment, generates income and spending without directly adding much to our chronically capacity-bloated market economy. This constitutes a colossal oversight in a theory that purports to address itself to the growth process in an advanced mixed market system. The oversight is shockingly congenial to the habit of burying Domar's insightful recognition of the dual character of private investment as both spending and capacity creating.

Finally, the supply-side method for construction of potential growth estimates ignores the considerable demand elasticity of inputs, particularly labor input. It is the failure to heed this demand factor that creates what Angus Maddison calls "the mystery concerning acceleration and slowdown" of growth in the advanced economies in recent times. This is but one example of the fact that endlessly debatable insolvables will plague our theory of potential growth until full consideration is given to the decisive influence of autonomous, robust, public demand growth.

I N D E X

ABOUT THE EDITORS

Harold G. Vatter, Professor of Economics Emeritus at Portland State University, is a specialist in the history of the American economy since the Civil War. He has written books on U.S. economic history covering the Civil War to World War I era (*The Drive to Industrial Maturity*), World War II (*The U.S. Economy in World War II*), and the 1950s (*The U.S. Economy in the 1950s*), as well as many other books and articles on economic topics.

John F. Walker was raised and educated in Utah, where his non-Mormon family migrated in the 1880s. Professor Walker has taught at the University of Utah, Idaho State, and since 1966 at Portland State University. He is the author with Harold G. Vatter of *The Inevitability of Economic Growth*, and many articles which have appeared in such journals as *Challenge, The National Tax Journal, The Journal of Post Keynesian Economics, Public Finance/Finances Publique,* and *Journal of Economic Issues.*

70 12|2 1ff 2b44

adam , hannam , rc
7hh   9:10:65 .   65

faskgruuv